Life, Liberty, and
the Pursuit of Happiness

Life, Liberty, and the Pursuit of Happiness

Ten Years of the *Claremont Review of Books*

Charles R. Kesler and John B. Kienker, Editors

ROWMAN & LITTLEFIELD PUBLISHERS, INC.
Lanham • Boulder • New York • Toronto • Plymouth, UK

Published by Rowman & Littlefield Publishers, Inc.

A wholly owned subsidiary of The Rowman & Littlefield Publishing Group, Inc.
4501 Forbes Boulevard, Suite 200, Lanham, Maryland 20706
http://www.rowmanlittlefield.com

10 Thornbury, Plymouth PL6 7PP, United Kingdom

British Library Cataloguing in Publication Information Available

Library of Congress Cataloging-in-Publication Data

Life, liberty, and the pursuit of happiness : ten years of the Claremont Review of Books / Charles R. Kesler and John B. Kienker, Editors.
   p. cm.
  Includes index.
  ISBN 978-1-4422-1333-3 (cloth : alk. paper) — ISBN 978-1-4422-1335-7 (ebook)
  1. Claremont review of books. 2. Political science—Book reviews—Periodicals. 3. Conservatism—United States—Periodicals. I. Kesler, Charles R. II. Kienker, John B.
  JA1.C5853 2012
  320—dc23
                                                                     2011032958

∞™ The paper used in this publication meets the minimum requirements of American National Standard for Information Sciences—Permanence of Paper for Printed Library Materials, ANSI/NISO Z39.48-1992.

Printed in the United States of America

Contents

Introduction

A Decade of *CRB*

Charles R. Kesler

Ten years ago the Claremont Institute decided to publish a book review. What could we have been thinking? It isn't unheard of for a think tank to publish a magazine, of course, though it is rare for a think tank to publish a good one. For the *Claremont Review of Books* to prosper it would have to be *very* good, and it would have to meet a need that the conservative intellectual movement, despite its fecundity, had not satisfied.

In the inaugural issue, I posed the threshold question: why a book review? Because, I wrote,

> it is a format that conservatives have not exploited, and we think that conservatives need, persistently and farsightedly, to wage the battle of ideas at the level of ideas rather than merely at the level of particular policies, important as they are. The galaxy of conservative journals and think tanks will continue to shine brightly . . . illuminating ideas as well as issues. But every month important conservative books and arguments languish, liberal tomes escape censure, and intelligent works of biography, history, politics, and literature remain unexamined.

The *CRB* set out to change that for the better, and we have succeeded remarkably, despite remaining a David compared to the Goliaths of the Left. Take our most conspicuous competitor (please!): the *New York Review of Books* has scores of staffers, publishes 20 times a year, and is read by tens of thousands of academics and liberal activists, always assuming one can distinguish between an academic and a liberal activist. The *Claremont Review of Books* operates with a handful of staff (we have never had more than four full-time employees), publishes quarterly, and is read by mere thousands of people—but *what* people. Our readers love their country not despite but *because* of its founding principles. They believe in the liberty of the individual not merely on account of its material benefits, though these are undeniable, but because human liberty reflects the divine image stamped on every human soul. They cherish the civilization of which America is such a distinguished part, the civilization which Americans are once again called upon to defend against new forms of barbarism and tyranny, at home and abroad.

1

Despite his size and shiny helmet, and his coat of mail and the greaves of brass upon his legs, Goliath had a weakness, which David exploited. He smote the Philistine in the forehead. The Biblical account adds the Tarantinoesque detail that the stone "sunk into" the giant, and "Goliath fell upon his face to the earth." When we at the *CRB* take up our little sling, we too aim our stones at liberalism's head—its most vulnerable point. Modern liberalism has never lacked academic credentials or intellectual pretensions, of course. Two generations ago, men as cultivated as Lionel Trilling and Louis Hartz could take it for granted that conservatism in America was either liberalism in disguise or a European affectation, at once aristocratic and ridiculous. Over here, conservatism was thought inarticulate—"bookless," John Kenneth Galbraith once sniffed—because it was presumed to have nothing valuable to say about, or to, America. With his usual acuity, Galbraith's pronouncement came in the midst of the century's greatest outpouring of conservative books—by such different thinkers and writers as Milton Friedman, Leo Strauss, Whittaker Chambers, and William F. Buckley, Jr. And the flow of important books and essays has continued—as a glance at the present volume will confirm.

So who's bookless now? Six years ago the publisher of the *New Republic* confessed, "It is liberalism that is now bookless and dying. Who is a truly influential liberal mind in our culture? Whose ideas challenge and whose ideals inspire? . . . There's no one, really." Perhaps Marty Peretz missed Barack Obama's autobiography, which inspired a lot of readers, or at least purchasers, once he entered the presidential lists. But in truth, it wasn't the book but Obama in the flesh, more precisely at the podium, that caused such devotees as Chris Matthews to go all tingly. In any event, the underlying problem is worse than Peretz realizes. As an intellectual movement, liberalism peaked a hundred years ago, shortly after it first emerged on the American scene bearing the calling card of Progressivism. The line of descent is straightforward. For example, today Paul Krugman recycles the arguments of Galbraith, who was recycling Simon Patten, who was recycling *his* friend Richard Ely—who was one of Woodrow Wilson's mentors at Johns Hopkins. Ely got his from his teachers in graduate school in Germany. Liberals believe in recycling, I know, but this is downright unimaginative. And, to switch metaphors, after so many generations of intermarriage, it's no wonder their ideas are getting a bit thin. Backhandedly, liberals have come around to admitting both their paternity and their problem. From Secretary of State Hillary Clinton to President Obama, leading liberals now prefer to be called small-p "progressives," hoping that everything old really is new again.

In some respects, to be sure, liberalism has changed over the years. Mostly, these shifts have been adaptations of its original concepts to new conditions: figuring out how to overcome the moral truths and constitutional limitations of the American political tradition, in favor of a new freedom, a new deal, a fair deal, a new frontier, a great society, etc. In that fatal *et cetera* one confronts the weariness, the growing exhaustion of the liberal idea. How many times can one loudly demand "change" of a fundamentally "transformative" sort? Bill Clinton wanted to call his formula for revolution "the new covenant," but as a notorious covenant-breaker had to retire the idea. Obama trotted out "the new foundation" but gave up when the jokes about ladies' undergarments got too thick. The ennui is not merely rhetorical, however. It is philosophical.

The original liberals believed in progress as a scientific inevitability, and they had the sciences to prove it. The new social sciences that sprang up with the American research universities in the late 19th century paved the way for Progressivism, teaching the critical views of capitalism and the Constitution that would become liberal staples, and inculcating the reform spirit that would gin up a government program for every social problem. From the beginning, the academy served as the unofficial "fourth department of the state, along with the judicial, executive, and legislative branches," as Frederic Howe (another Ely student) described the scene in Wisconsin, that laboratory of social democracy. The new economics, ethics, political science, sociology, and psychology all predicted, indeed guaranteed, the better world to come, very soon to come. For today's liberals, however, progress is more of a hope than a certainty. In fact, that may be too optimistic. The leftist professors are moving, sometimes reluctantly, from Hegel to Heidegger, from John Dewey to Richard Rorty, from a faith in progress to the cult of relativism that calls itself postmodernism. Progress is becoming "progress," in scare quotes; for who can say what it *is*, much less that it is inevitable or beneficial? President Clinton was on to something when he said it all depended on what the meaning of "is," is!

At the *CRB* we pay special attention to the evolution and devolution of liberalism, and we keep an eye on stirrings in the academy, the boot camp and parade ground of the contemporary Left. But we do so for reasons that go beyond Know Thy Enemy. We're eager to know our fellow citizens, for that is who liberals are, after all; to understand where this blessed but very confused country of ours is heading; and to help point it back to the paths of political and fiscal health, not to mention sanity.

* * * *

The Claremont Institute for the Study of Statesmanship and Political Philosophy, as its mouthful of a name suggests, is itself a by-product of the academy. Founded by a handful of graduate students at Claremont Graduate School (now Claremont Graduate University) in 1979, it set out to lead a counterrevolution against the ideologized university and to smash the idols by which it had mystified and misled the American public. The idea was to unravel Progressivism, to do what Wilson and Co. had done but in reverse. Other conservatives were thinking along the same track, but none had quite the steady, clear-sighted intention to rescue the country by plighting the conservative movement to the principles of the Founding Fathers and Abraham Lincoln (not a beloved figure, then or now, among many right-wingers). Among the Institute's early projects, under its founding president, Peter Schramm, was a newsprint tabloid called the *Claremont Review of Books*, which published 19 issues from 1981 to 1988. The late George Forsyth alongside Jack Barlow and William Flannery edited the first five, Doug Jeffrey the last two, and Ken Masugi the 12 in between. Published on a shoestring and by graduate students (or very recent Ph.D.s) who made very green (and I don't mean ecologically correct) journalists, the whole thing was remarkably good. It ran some classic articles and interviews (most of the issues are available on-line at http://www.claremont.org/publications/pageid.2087/ default.asp). But eventually it ceased publication, a casualty of strained resources and changing personnel.

The new birth of the *CRB* occurred in 2000, when Larry P. Arnn, the Institute's departing president, and Thomas B. Silver, its incoming one, decided to relaunch the journal as the Institute's flagship. They recruited me as editor, and soon the redoubtable John B. Kienker as managing editor (Ben Boychuk served as managing editor for the first two years). From the beginning, we sought to make it a national publication (the 1980s' version had circulated quite narrowly) that would command the attention of intelligent conservatives, liberals, and book lovers alike. The inaugural issue appeared in fall 2000, with Tom Silver as publisher. After Tom's death, Brian Kennedy succeeded him as our brave publisher and Institute president, and more than a decade later we sail on, "in spite of rock and tempest's roar, in spite of false lights on the shore."

We were a year into the enterprise (four issues) when the awful attacks of 9/11 occurred. Recently we commemorated their tenth anniversary. In the intervening years, the *CRB* published bracing commentaries on the war, arguing that America's goal should be the destruction of the regimes that abetted and encouraged the attack, but not the occupation and wholesale democratic reconstruction of the unfortunate countries misruled by these regimes. Shortly after 9/11 I phoned Angelo Codevilla, the well-known strategist and political analyst who was then teaching international relations at Boston University, and commissioned a series of essays that we called "Victory Watch." The nature of the attacks had raised the specter of an endless "war" against shadowy terrorist groups, which could have no definable end point, no victory. Our anxiety deepened when President Bush brought to the fore democratization of Iraq, the Middle East, and indeed the world as the putative goal of American strategy. The success of that strategy can perhaps be gleaned from the fact that the war continues ten years on, as does the series of essays, the first and the most recent of which are here reprinted. The brilliant novelist Mark Helprin, in his gimlet-eyed essays, amplified the critique and proffered an ingenious strategic alternative. I added my own criticisms of the rhetorical and strategic muddle so characteristic of the Bush Administration much of the time.

It was enough to get us in hot water with the administration's spokesmen, our fellow conservatives, and especially with many neoconservative backers of the Bush Doctrine. Codevilla, Helprin, and I had the exotic pleasure of being branded "Superhawks" by our friend Norman Podhoretz. But at least the measures we advocated would plausibly have spared us a protracted, indecisive conflict. It is now for the reader to judge, and the key writings are here. Concerning democratization, our point was not that it was impossible or always inadvisable, but that it was hardly possible in the Middle East under existing conditions, that it was imprudent particularly in countries that were not that strategically valuable to us, and that it was disastrous from many points of view to teach our citizens that American security rested decisively on events and personalities in far-away countries beyond our control. Although we yield to no one in our belief in the truth of the majestic propositions of the Declaration of Independence, we cautioned from the start that the right to self-government is one thing, the habits of mind and heart essential to self-government, quite another. In the current "Arab spring," which is far from the first (or the last) such season, we recommend a similar prudence.

These honorable disagreements over foreign policy were far different, however, from the reaction to 9/11 among the America-haters here and abroad. You may recall, for example, Ward Churchill, the faux American Indian professor in Colorado who compared the Americans slaughtered on 9/11 to "little [Adolf] Eichmanns" who got exactly what they deserved. Ward Churchill is now that rarest of rare beings: a tenured professor who has been fired. (Though this being America, he is suing for wrongful dismissal.) In the end, he was fired not for his slanders against those murdered in the Twin Towers and the Pentagon, but because his so-called scholarship was a tissue of lies. He made up events, invented sources, and spun everything in the most tendentiously anti-American way possible. And his colleagues, including those who had vetted him and recommended him for promotion and tenure at every turn—didn't notice. Or rather, didn't care to notice, until that is, Churchill's remarks about 9/11 drew public attention, for the first time, to the man and his mendacities.

I mention this sordid episode not because it is typical of the American academy. It is not, though precisely as an extreme case it sheds interesting light on the way his defenders thought to handle the matter. He had many such defenders, the late Howard Zinn among the most prominent. After many obfuscations and evasions, his diehard supporters admitted . . . he made stuff up. Nevertheless, they insisted, the ideological line he followed was the correct one: America was and is an unjust country dedicated to the suppression of blacks, Indians, women, and other minorities, and thus his falsehoods were *truer* than any of the so-called truths of his critics.

It is against perversions of truth such as these, and the smug cultural and intellectual superiority asserted in their name, that the *Claremont Review of Books* sets its face. A few years ago, for instance, Steven Hayward replied to two Australian environmentalists whose book he had reviewed, unfavorably, in the previous *CRB*. (The original review is reprinted herein.) Long ago Harvey Mansfield quipped that environmentalism is school prayer for liberals. In this case, however, the authors of *The Climate Change Challenge and the Failure of Democracy* seemed eager for downright authoritarian measures to force people to be green.

How did they respond to our reviewer's skepticism? Well, they did not deny that in their book "we make some favorable comments about China's authoritarian capacity to deal with environmental problems *potentially* better than liberal democracies can." Without quite admitting it, they proceeded to suggest why "saving the planet is a value that overrides democracy and freedom." "Is Hayward really implying," they asked incredulously, " . . . that freedom is more important than life itself? Is this a modern day version of 'better dead than red'? If so it is absurd. No life, no freedom. Why should freedom be the ultimate value?"

Why indeed? Why should freedom be worth dying for, when it is possible to live comfortably, and with a miniscule carbon footprint, as a slave? On the radical Left, and even among mainstream liberals, one senses a growing alienation from the republic's precepts and precedents that bodes ill not merely for comity between our political parties but also for our whole experiment in self-government.

* * * *

Yet we should not delude ourselves into thinking that conservatism is in robust good health, either. It is surely better off than liberalism, but the Right has its own problems, perhaps best signified by the gap between the political possibilities suddenly raised by the Tea Party's emergence and the electoral repudiation in 2010 of President Obama's agenda, on the one hand, and the confusion over what, exactly, a return to constitutional government could possibly mean, on the other.

Which is why the *CRB* seeks to reinvigorate the public mind by returning to the first principles of a distinctively American conservatism. Here we follow the lead of the Claremont Institute in seeking to restore the precepts of the American Founding to their rightful authority in our national life. As Harry V. Jaffa has argued wisely and often, a return to the principles of the Constitution and the Gettysburg Address requires something like a revolution not only against modern liberalism but also within modern conservatism.

Some conservatives start, as it were, from Edmund Burke; others from Friedrich Hayek. While we respect both thinkers and their schools of thought, we begin instead from America, the American political tradition in all its genius and profundity, and the relation of our tradition to revealed wisdom and to what the elderly Jefferson once called, rather insouciantly, "the elementary books of public right, as Aristotle, Cicero, Locke, Sidney, etc." We think conservatism should take its bearings from the founders' statesmanship, our citizens' loyalty to the Declaration and Constitution, and the scenes, both tender and proud, of our national history. This kind of approach clears the air. It concentrates the mind. It engages and informs the ordinary citizen's patriotism. It makes room for the heroes of our political tradition, and rightly bids us study and emulate them. And it introduces a new, sharper, less abstract view of American liberalism as descended not from the Enlightenment, the Industrial Revolution, nor (goodness gracious) Abraham Lincoln, but from that movement which, a century ago, criticized George Washington's and Lincoln's Constitution as outmoded and, as we'd say today, racist, sexist, and antidemocratic. The Progressives broke with the old Constitution and its postulates, and set out to make a new, living constitution and a new, unlimited state, and the Obama Administration's programs are merely the latest, though perhaps the worst, installment of that purported advance.

Even so, we don't regard this view of conservatism and liberalism as a dogma to which our writers must subscribe. And besides, man doesn't live by politics alone. Happily, we devote attention in our pages to Shakespeare, Edith Wharton, *Deadwood*, and other cultural blooms. Indeed, we aspire to comment on the whole panoply of the arts, sciences, and civilized delights that Cicero celebrates in his marvelous phrase *otium cum dignitate*—leisure with dignity.

In that connection, the reader may wonder about the magazine's distinctive look. Editors of magazines face a problem when they deal with questions of typography and illustration. Very few have the courage of Joseph Epstein, who insisted that his lively journal (the *American Scholar*, which he edits no longer) look as much as possible like a pharmaceutical manual. Sometimes the editor yields to the mode of the day and allows his magazine to be styled by a recent graduate of a fashionable art academy. In other instances, a serious publication adopts a deliberately vulgar format as a way of proving its populist bona fides. Uniquely, I think, for our time, the *CRB* has chosen the classical mold. A magazine that endorses *otium cum dignitate* could do no less.

The instrument of this classical approach is our art director, Elliott Banfield, who began in 2002 to design the magazine and has created illustrations for every issue since. At the rate of about 70 drawings per year, the accumulated work is considerable. A sampling is given in the portfolio section of this book. (Note, please, that the illustrations are integral to the *CRB* in a way that cannot be reproduced here.) Given the amount of illustration required, he developed a characteristic workflow. He receives a stack of 20 or so manuscripts, emailed to his office in New York City at the start of the production cycle. He has three months to develop ideas and create designs appropriate to each piece. The long lead time is a luxury rare in the illustration business (he tells me), which lets him transcend some of the familiar weaknesses of work produced on deadline. The cover art is scrutinized by the editors, but the smaller, inside works are usually accepted without alteration. In spite of his classical sensibility, Elliott relies on the latest advances in computer and internet wizardry. Indeed, he developed a novel and powerful use of Adobe Photoshop that allows him to "paint" his illustrations with black and white patterns, in a way that recalls the great tradition of 19th-century wood engraving. In the age of the internet, information is cheap, but beauty, like wisdom, is rare, and we are delighted to have Elliott's lovely designs grace our pages and help elevate us above the digital drabness.

Not for nothing was conservatism once defined as "enjoyment." Conservatives can appreciate the world as it is, with all its imperfections and disappointments, because these are the conditions of freedom, of striving for excellence, and for self-knowledge—and because with all life's limitations there is so much to be grateful for. In *Life, Liberty, and the Pursuit of Happiness* we present a representative selection of the *CRB*'s finest book reviews and essays, crystallized around seven broad themes of our engagement with the world over the past decade: the problem of liberalism, the nature of conservatism, the "war on terror," the possibilities of statesmanship, current political and social controversies, American citizenship and culture, and artistic grandeur and decadence. Among our contributors are Hadley Arkes, Martha Bayles, the late William F. Buckley, Jr., Paul Cantor, James Ceaser, Joseph Epstein, Christopher Flannery, Harvey Mansfield, Wilfred McClay, Cheryl Miller, the late Jaroslav Pelikan, Joseph Tartakovsky, Michael Uhlmann, Algis Valiunas, William Voegeli, and James Q. Wilson. We are proud of them all. And we're certain you will find plenty to instruct and delight you.

Ten years necessarily ring up many debts of gratitude, especially to our devoted staff, our expert contributors, and above all our readers. With your support, the *Claremont Review of Books* will continue to explore and express the common sense, and uncommon wisdom, of the American mind.

I

PROGRESSIVISM AND THE LIBERAL CENTURY

Taming Big Government

Michael M. Uhlmann

(Summer 2007)

Sir Lewis Namier, the noted British historian of an earlier generation, once wrote that "when discoursing or writing about history, [people] imagine it in terms of their own experience, and when trying to gauge the future they cite supposed analogies from the past: till, by double process of repetition, they imagine the past and remember the future." Great controversies, which often feature adversaries citing the same historical materials to opposite effect, confirm the truth of Namier's cautionary observation. In the United States, where great controversies tend to be constitutional controversies, disagreement about our charter's origins and meaning has been a defining feature of American political discourse from the republic's earliest days.

After nearly 220 years, one could say that Americans have more constitutional speculation than they know what to do with—a fact readily confirmed by almost any volume of any law review, not to mention the proliferating gaggle of legal experts who fill the airwaves on cable news shows. A cynic might infer from differing scholarly opinions that debate about constitutional meaning is so much rhetorical gamesmanship. But if that is so, if politics may indeed be reduced to sophistry, why bother to have a written constitution at all?

Most Americans would reply that a written constitution is the only kind worth having. They bear a decent respect for their nation's origins and founding documents, which they have no trouble believing were inspired by divine providence. They come by the millions every year from all over the country to the National Archives in Washington, or to the National Constitution Center in Philadelphia, to gaze upon the original parchments of the Declaration of Independence and the Constitution. They take pride in knowing that the Constitution, which was up and running before Napoleon came to power, has survived innumerable crises, including a dreadful civil war, yet emerged largely intact.

Liberals are wary of pious attachment to the past, considering it an expression of foolish sentimentality or a mask for some contemporary venal interest, but in either event as an impediment to progress. They are particularly suspicious about the framers' motives, which they tend to explain in terms of narrow self-interest, and are dogmatically skeptical about our founding documents' natural rights principles, dismissing them as so much wrong-headed and outmoded philosophical speculation. The resultant Constitution fares no better. It, too, is suspect for many reasons—failing to abolish slavery for one—but most of all because it sought to instantiate a regime of limited government. But, in the end, liberals care little about what the framers may have meant, for times have changed. They may object to the crudity of Henry Ford's assertion that "history is more or less bunk," but they do not essentially disagree with his sentiment. Liberals esteem not history, but History, which to them confirms the law of ceaseless change.

They are stuck, nevertheless, with a people reared under the aegis of a written Constitution whose authors affirmed the permanence of certain political truths. Most Americans remain stubbornly convinced that the framers got things mostly right on government's basic principles. From the Progressive movement's early days until the present hour, the liberals' medicine for this notable lack of popular enlightenment has consisted in one long effort to deconstruct the founding. The permanence of the Declaration's truths is denied; the framers' inability or refusal to resolve the issue of slavery is attributed to moral hypocrisy; the architecture of the Constitution is read as a series of mischievous devices to frustrate majority rule or to protect the ruling class's interests. These and similar critiques, which by gradual degrees have worked their way into standard textbooks and school curricula, have taken their toll on patriotic sentiment.

Old habits, however, die hard, which helps to explain the intellectual chaos of contemporary constitutional debate. Respect for the founding principles, though wounded, refuses to die; the new dispensation, though powerful, has yet to triumph. Whatever else may have accrued from the effort to deconstruct the founding, this much seems clear: the once common ground of constitutional discourse has fallen away. Witness the current debate between originalists and proponents of the "living constitution": they disagree about the meaning of constitutional wording, to be sure; but their deepest disagreement has to do with whether and why 18th-century words and concepts should now matter at all.

WHAT WILSON WROUGHT

The outcome of this debate has yet to be determined, but it has produced a number of notable anomalies, particularly with respect to the separation of powers. Ever since Woodrow Wilson set pen to paper, liberals have expressed frustration with, if not outright scorn for, the separation of powers. They read it almost exclusively in terms of its checking-and-balancing function, i.e., as a barrier that for many decades prevented the national government from enacting progressive social and economic policies. The other half of James Madison's elegant argument for separating powers—energizing government through the clash of rival and opposite ambitions—seems to have escaped their attention altogether, as has the framers' understanding that government powers differ not only in degree, but in kind. Transfixed by their own deconstruction of the founding as an effort to frustrate popular majorities, liberals find it hard to believe that the framers could have imagined the need for powerful government or a powerful chief executive. Indeed, a dominant theme of early Progressive thought—one still widely shared today—advanced the notion that the Constitution meant to enshrine legislative primacy. Accordingly, energetic presidents prior to the modern era are seen as exceptions that prove the rule, their boldness being variously attributed to the peculiarities of personality, short-term aberrational events, or national emergencies such as the Civil War—to everything, in short, except the intended purpose of Article II of the Constitution. It was only after decades of struggle, so the argument continues, that a new constitutional order, with the president as its driving force, came to ultimate fruition in the New Deal.

This reading of the founding and of American political history has a surface plausibility, fed in no small part by the republican Whig rhetoric that was so fashionable in much early American discourse. Upon closer examination, however, it turns out that congressional dominance is not the only story that emerges from 19th-century political history. As a large and growing body of thoughtful revisionist inquiry has demonstrated, that history is no less the story of effective presidential leadership that drew upon Article II's deliberately capacious language. Notwithstanding, contemporary liberal doctrine remains deeply indebted to the original Progressive indictment of the founding, and especially to Woodrow Wilson's thought, which remains the philosophical wellspring of almost every constitutional prescription in the liberal pharmacopoeia.

After flirting with the idea of grafting a parliamentary system onto the American constitutional structure, Wilson made a virtue of necessity by reconceiving the Office of the President. The nation's chief executive would defeat the original Constitution's structural obstacles by, so to speak, rising above them. Wilson's chosen instrument for this purpose was party government, which would breach the parchment barriers dividing president and Congress and unite both through a common policy agenda initiated by the president. The president would make the case for policy innovation directly to the people. Once armed with plebiscitary legitimacy, he might more easily prod an otherwise parochial Congress to address national needs. Madisonian fears about the mischiefs of faction would be overcome by separating politics and administration: Congress and the president would jointly settle upon the desired policy agenda, but its details, both in design and execution, would rely on non-partisan expert administrators' special insight and technical skill, operating under the president's general direction and control.

The presidency, thus reconceived, would by turns become a voice for and dominant instrument of a reconceived Constitution, which would at last detach itself from a foolish preoccupation with limited government. The old Constitution's formal structure would be retained, insofar as that might be politically necessary; but it would be essentially emptied of its prior substantive content. In Wilson's view, the growth of executive power would parallel the growth of government in general. The president would no longer be seen as, at best, Congress's co-equal or, at worst, the legislature's frustrated servant. Henceforth, he would be seen as proactive government's innovator-in-chief, one who was best positioned to understand historical tendencies and to unite them with popular yearnings. In an almost mystical sense, the president would embody the will of the people, becoming both a prophet and steward of a new kind of egalitarian Manifest Destiny at home and, in the fullness of time, perhaps throughout the world.

UNINTENDED CONSEQUENCES

The result of Wilson's vision is the administrative state we know today. Although it has retained the original Constitution's structural appearances, the new order has profoundly altered its substance—though not precisely in the way that Wilson intended, as we shall see. The arguments that once supported the ideas of federalism and limited government have fallen into desuetude: state power today is exercised largely at the national government's sufferance, and if there is a subject or activity now beyond federal reach, one would be hard-pressed to say what it might be. As for the separation of powers, while the branches remain institutionally separate, the lines between legislative, executive, and judicial power have become increasingly blurred. The idea that government power ought to be differentiated according to function has given way to the concept that power is more or less fungible. The dominant understanding of separated powers today—see the late Richard Neustadt's widely accepted argument in *Presidential Power* (1960)—is that the branches of government compete with one another for market share.

While most liberals continue to celebrate the old order's decline, the more thoughtful among them have expressed reservations of late about certain consequences of the Wilsonian revolution. It is widely remarked in the scholarly literature on the presidency, for example, that we have come to expect almost impossible things of modern presidents, and that presidents in turn come to office with almost impossible agendas to match heightened public expectations. After many decades of living with the modern presidency, it can be argued that the effort to rise above the separation of powers has only exposed presidents the more to the unmediated whimsies of public opinion. Far from being masters of all they survey, modern presidents are pulled this way and that by factional demands generated by an administrative state over which they exercise nominal but very little actual control.

The presidency's transformation has radically altered our system of government, but it poses a particular problem for liberals. The difficulty begins in their appetite for big government. Indeed, liberals can identify enough unmet needs, unfulfilled hopes, and frustrated dreams to satisfy the federal government's redistributionist and regulatory ambitions as far into the future as the eye can see. An already large and unwieldy federal establishment, expanding to meet the rising expectations of an ever more demanding and dependent public, threatens to become yet larger, more powerful, and harder to control. But, despite what bureaucrats might wish to believe about the beneficial effects of their expertise, the administrative state is not a machine that can run itself. It requires coherent policy direction; it needs to be managed with reasonable efficiency; and it has to be held politically accountable. As a practical matter, only a president can do these things, but with rare exceptions, presidents are prevented, mainly by Congress but also by the judiciary, from performing any of these tasks well.

It is here that a bastardized version of the separation of powers remains alive and well. The short history of the administrative state since at least the New Deal is a tale of protracted conflict between Congress and the president for control of its ever-expanding machinery. After initial resistance, which remained formidable until roughly 40 years ago, Congress has finally learned to love big government as much as, if not more than, presidents do. As political scientist Morris Fiorina has shown,

Congress loves it because it pays handsome political returns. The returns come from greasing the wheels of the federal establishment to deliver an increasing array of goods and services to constituents and interest groups, who reward congressional intervention with campaign contributions and other forms of electoral support. Such political benefit as may accrue from enacting carefully crafted legislation is much less, which is why legislators devote far more time to pleasing constituents and lobbyists than they do to deliberating about the details of laws they enact. Congress is generally content to delegate these details, which often carry great policy significance, to departments and agencies, whose actions and policy judgments can forever after be second-guessed by means of legislative "oversight."

THE NEW SPOILS SYSTEM

Indeed, congressmen have become extraordinarily adept at badgering this agency or that program administrator for special favors—or for failing to carry out "the will of Congress." In most cases this means the will of a particular representative who sits on the agency's authorization or appropriations committee, and who has been importuned by a politically relevant interest group to complain about some bureaucratic excess or failure. Modern congressional oversight has become an elaborate and sophisticated version of the old spoils system adapted to the machinery of the administrative state. When it comes to currying favors, congressmen know how to home in on programs under their committee's jurisdiction to extract what they want in terms of policy direction or special treatment, and there is enough boodle in a nearly $3 trillion federal budget to satisfy even the most rapacious pork-barreler. Likewise, when it comes to bashing bureaucrats, congressmen have little trouble identifying vulnerable targets of opportunity. The federal government is so large, and its administrators so busy trying to execute often conflicting or ambiguous congressional instructions, that Congress can, like Little Jack Horner, stick in its thumb and pull out a plum almost at random. The modern oversight investigation, which has less to do with substance than with conducting a dog-and-pony show for the benefit of a scandal-hungry media, has become a staple of the contemporary administrative state. And it almost always redounds to Congress's political benefit, for the simple reason that the exercise carries little if any downside risk. But political theater of this sort, however profitable it may be to particular representatives, is a far cry from the deliberative function that the framers hoped would be the defining characteristic of the legislative process.

It is an open question, to be sure, whether anything so large as the current federal establishment can be reasonably managed, and it is something of a miracle that it works at all. Even so, Congress would do itself and the nation an enormous favor if it devoted more time to perfecting the legislative art, which includes paying serious attention to the policy coherence and consequences of its delegated legislative authority. In general, however, Congress has little political motive or (given its internal dispersal of power to committees and sub-committees) institutional capacity for substantive evaluation of the many programs it enacts and ostensibly oversees. It complains endlessly about the administrative state's inefficiency and arbitrariness, but compounds the problem by creating new agencies and programs in response to political urgencies. As it does so, it takes care to protect its own prerogatives even as it denies to the executive the requisite authority to control the administrative system.

This reluctance to vest the president with control has sometimes expressed itself in the form of independent agencies (independent, that is, of the president), which mock the idea of separated powers by vesting legislative, executive, and judicial functions in the same institution. Consider Boston University law professor Gary Lawson's provocatively compelling description of the Federal Trade Commission, which typifies the workings of the system as a whole:

> The Commission promulgates substantive rules of conduct. The Commission then considers whether to authorize investigations into whether the Commission's rules have been violated. If the Commission authorizes an investigation, the investigation is conducted by the Commission, which reports its findings to the Commission. If the Commission thinks that the Commission's findings warrant an enforcement action, the Commission issues a complaint. The Commission's complaint that a Commission rule has been violated is then prosecuted by the Commission and adjudicated by the Commission. This Commission adjudication can either take place before the full Commission or before a semi-autonomous Commission administrative law judge. If the Commission chooses to adjudicate before an administrative law judge rather than before the Commission and the decision is adverse to the Commission, the Commission can appeal to the Commission. If the Commission ultimately finds a violation, then, and only then, the affected private party can appeal to an Article III court. But the agency decision, even before the bona fide Article III tribunal, possesses a very strong presumption of correctness on matters both of fact and of law.

This pattern has become an accepted feature of the modern administrative state, so much so that, as Lawson notes, it scarcely raises eyebrows. Presidents and Congress long ago accommodated themselves to its political exigencies, as has the Supreme Court, which since the 1930s has never come close to questioning independent agencies' constitutional propriety.

RAIDING EXECUTIVE AUTHORITY

When dealing with the executive branch as such, Congress frequently delegates and retains legislative authority at the same time. It does so, *inter alia*, through burdensome or unconstitutional restrictions on the exercise of presidential discretion, which it inserts in authorizing legislation, appropriations bills, or, sometimes, even in committee report language. It has also contrived a host of other devices to hamper executive control. For many decades, for example, it indulged broad delegations (e.g., "The Secretary shall have authority to issue such regulations as may be necessary to carry out the purposes of this Act"), but as the number of agencies expanded and as delegated regulatory authority began to bite influential constituencies, Congress responded by imposing (variously) two-House, one-House, or in some cases even committee vetoes over agency action. Although the Supreme Court declared most legislative vetoes to be unconstitutional in *INS v. Chadha* (1983), Congress has improvised additional measures to second-guess the operations of the executive branch.

Confirmation hearings in the Senate, for example, are increasingly used to extract important policy concessions from prospective executive appointees, who learn very quickly that while the president is their nominal boss, Congress expects to be placated and, failing that, knows how to make their lives miserable. To underscore this point, in addition to the omnipresent threat of oversight hearings, Congress has enacted extensive "whistle-blower" legislation and created inspector-general offices for every department and agency, which operate as semi-demi-hemi-quasi-independent congressional envoys within the executive branch. For a time (until Bill Clinton got caught in the web), Congress was also enamored of special counsels, empowering them by legislation to investigate and prosecute alleged executive malfeasance, and at the same time ensuring that their activities were not only beyond the president's authority to control, but beyond the Congress's and the courts' as well. (Demonstrating that the separation of powers in our time is more honored in the breach than the observance, the Supreme Court sustained the legislation with only one dissent.)

One may say by way of summary that Congress has, without fully realizing it, succumbed to Wilson's plan to eviscerate the separation of powers. It has failed to realize it in part because the administrative state's growth has occurred gradually; in part because it has learned how to profit politically by the change; and in part because it has convinced itself that conducting guerilla raids against executive authority is the most beneficial expression of the legislative function.

TAMING THE ADMINISTRATIVE STATE

Presidents have chafed under congressional controls, rightly complaining that they interfere both with their constitutional powers and their ability to make the administrative state reasonably efficient and politically accountable. They have responded with various bureaucratic and legal weapons of their own. These include a greatly expanded Executive Office of the President (in effect, a bureaucracy that seeks to impose policy direction and managerial control over other executive bureaucracies), a massive surge in the use of executive orders, and increasing reliance on signing statements reserving the president's right not to enforce legislation he considers to be unconstitutional. Ever since the New Deal, and growing proportionately with the size of the federal establishment, a good deal of White House energy has been devoted to trying to manage and direct the administrative state—and to reminding Congress in diverse ways that the Constitution provides for only one chief executive. But modern presidents, like the modern Congress, have also succumbed to the lure of Wilson's theory concerning the separation of powers. They clearly enjoy the prospect of becoming the principal focal point for national policy, but once in office soon discover that the mantle of plebiscitary leadership can be assumed only at great cost. Unlike Congress, presidents remain politically and legally accountable for the administrative state's behavior. In order to execute their office as their constitutional oath demands, they must pay serious attention to the separation of powers in ways that Congress does not.

Presidents sometimes win and sometimes lose in their struggles with Congress, but each new contest only serves to compound the constitutional muddle that now surrounds the separation of powers, a muddle made all the more confusing by the Supreme Court's Janus-faced rulings in major cases, which also bear the mark of the political revolution launched by Wilson's indictment of the structural Constitution. On a practical level, presidents have only modest gains to show for their continuing efforts to manage big government. Overall, when it comes to controlling the administrative state, the operative slogan might well be "Congress Won't and the President Can't." So much for Wilson's vision of the rational ordering of public policy through neutral expertise under the benign guidance of inspired presidents working in cooperation with Congress. Wilson dealt the separation of powers a mortal blow without understanding the full implications of what he had wrought. Without a vigorously enforced, reasonably bright-line distinction between the kinds of powers exercised by the different branches, the very presidency he hoped to create has been frustrated in its ability to execute coherent policy, or to manage those charged with fleshing out its details. For its part, Congress as a whole is even less interested today in deliberating about the coherence of national policy than it was when Wilson inveighed against its parochialism and committee structure in the late 19th century. And, it may be added, with each passing year the administrative state whose birth Wilson midwifed becomes increasingly harder for any of the branches, jointly or severally, to control.

HAVING IT BOTH WAYS

Liberals are not particularly happy with the present state of affairs, but their enthusiasm for big government leaves them little choice but to support expansive presidential authority; it is the only available instrument capable of seeing to it that their desired social reforms are carried out. They encourage Congress to create or expand progressive programs, and generally applaud congressional bashing of bureaucrats (especially when the targets come from the opposite end of the political spectrum); but they do not otherwise wish to see Congress heavily involved in the business of directing public administration, for they rightly suspect that when Congress does so, the likely beneficiary will be some private interest rather than the public good. As for presidential direction and control of policy, liberals tend to favor executive discretion when Democrats occupy the Oval Office, but are generally dubious about it when exercised by Republican incumbents. Like Al Gore, they're in favor of reinventing government so long as it doesn't disestablish or interfere with favored agencies or programs.

Liberals, in short, will complain about the administrative state's inefficiency and unwieldiness, and while they would no doubt like it to work better they haven't a clue about how to reform it—other than by tinkering with its machinery at the margins. In truth, liberals have no desire for systemic change. They do not wish to reduce government's scope; and they certainly do not wish to revive the old Constitution's structural distinctions that separate the branches of government by function, for that, too, might diminish or eliminate many of the cherished programs they spent so many decades creating. The era of big government may be over, but only in Bill Clinton's rhetoric; big government itself is here to stay, as is the constitutional confusion that surrounds the separation of powers and threatens to extinguish its purposes altogether.

Although liberals generally applaud the demise of 18th-century constitutional strictures when it comes to domestic policy, they are not above extolling the old Constitution's virtues in foreign and national security affairs. The late Arthur Schlesinger, Jr., surely the model of 20th-century high-toned liberal sentiment if ever there was one, raised the execution of this intellectual two-step to a fine art form. He began his scholarly career by discovering in Andrew Jackson's administration a pre-incarnation of Franklin Roosevelt's plebiscitary presidency. Later, in his multi-volume hagiography of the New Deal, he defended the expansion of unfettered executive discretion in domestic affairs as a necessary concomitant of the burgeoning administrative state. In foreign affairs as well, Schlesinger praised FDR's aggressive use of executive power, not only during World War II (which is understandable enough), but also in the pre-war years (which is more debatable). Schlesinger took a similar tack in his praise of John F. Kennedy, who in Schlesinger's eyes was a kind of reincarnation of FDR. Then came Vietnam, Watergate, and the assorted excesses of Lyndon Johnson and Richard Nixon, as a result of which the presidential powers Schlesinger had previously celebrated suddenly became harbingers of imperial pretension. The imperial presidency motif disappeared once Jimmy Carter came into office, only to resurface periodically and vociferously during the Reagan years. It disappeared yet again while Bill Clinton held the office, and reappeared like clockwork in criticism of George W. Bush's anti-terrorism policies.

Schlesinger's personal tergiversations to the side, his ambivalence about executive power is a perfect measure of the modern liberals' dilemma: they want a chief executive capaciously adorned with constitutional discretion when it comes to pushing government to carry out their social and economic agenda, but sound constitutional alarms when their own theory of presidential power gets applied to the execution of foreign and national security policies they do not like. That constitutional theory is sometimes bent to short-term policy preferences is hardly novel or shocking. But there is a deeper constitutional problem here as well, arising from liberals' embrace of Wilsonian theory. One simply can't have it both ways when it comes to the Constitution's grant of executive power—a small presidency for foreign affairs, but a large one for domestic affairs. If anything, a stronger case can be made the other way around: the Vesting Clause, the Take Care Clause, and the oath of office are common to both cases, but in war-related matters the president has an additional claim of authority stemming from his powers as commander-in-chief.

CONSERVATISM AND EXECUTIVE POWER

Not so long ago, conservatives might have been accused of harboring a similar inconsistency. For a long time, they were deeply suspicious of the executive branch, correctly seeing in its growth the dangers that flowed inexorably from the Wilsonian revolution in political thought—a notable increase in presidential caprice and demagogy, and a notable increase as well in the government's size, driven by the engine of the plebiscitary presidency. The memory of FDR's arguable abuses of executive power remained deeply etched in the conservative memory for the better part of three decades. Well into the 1960s conservatives remained congressional partisans, having bought into the academic consensus—ironically, a consensus Wilson also helped to create—that the Constitution meant to establish legislative dominance. There was a second, more immediate, ideological reason: Congress, precisely because it represented a federated nation in all its diversity and complexity, was less likely to embrace utopian liberal schemes or an expansive federal establishment. Willmoore Kendall, the resident political theorist at *National Review* in its early days, was justly famous for his 1960 essay on "The Two Majorities," the central argument of which was (a) that a regime of presidential supremacy was not the government America's framers fought for; and (b) that Congress, in its geographically and culturally distributed collectivity, was a better and more legitimate expression of democratic sentiment than could be found in the modern plebiscitary presidency. (Kendall was at least half-right. His essay is in any event a remarkable exercise in good old-fashioned political science, published before the behaviorists took hold of the profession. Warts and all, it remains an engrossing and rewarding read.)

In the year before Kendall's essay appeared, James Burnham, another important *National Review* editor with impressive academic credentials, published *Congress and the American Tradition*, an extended paean to the framers' wisdom in elevating congressional power to preeminence. Burnham's argument, like Kendall's, was designed in part to encourage Congress to become more aggressive in checking what Burnham saw as a dangerous trend toward executive self-aggrandizement and arbitrariness. The book, however, was as much a lament as a prescription for reform, for even as he wrote Burnham feared that Congress had already lost its edge as a countervailing force against the exponential growth of government in general and executive power in particular.

Nowadays, of course, *National Review* and most conservatives have become strong supporters of unitary executive powers, particularly in foreign and national security policy. The change appears to have begun during the late 1960s, when the execution of the Cold War took a bad turn in Vietnam. Conservatives certainly had no love for Lyndon Johnson or anything resembling his Great Society, but they realized that a vigorous executive, armed with as much discretion as could decently be allowed, was essential to keeping the Communists at bay. Congress, hitherto the collective repository of conservative wisdom (including quasi-isolationist tendencies), could no longer be counted on to defend the West. The Kendall-Burnham argument lost favor.

Such reservations as conservatives once had about presidential power on the domestic front became decidedly secondary to the overarching goal of deflating the Communist threat. For the most part, those reservations have not been reasserted, but not because conservatives came to embrace Wilson's general theory of history or of the state; rather, conservatives reluctantly resigned themselves to the fact that the administrative state is more or less here to stay. They would prefer, of course, smaller government, but as long as big government remains the order of the day, conservatives argue that the only way to make it reasonably efficient and politically accountable is to vest the president with sufficient authority to run it. On the conservative side, then, there is a rough symmetry between their position regarding presidential power at home and abroad.

WAR MEASURES

Not everyone on the Right shares this disposition, and President Bush's mismanagement of the Global War on Terror (if that's what the administration still calls it) has prompted some conservative thinkers to revisit the arguments advanced by Kendall and Burnham and to reassert the case for congressional authority over war-making. In this, they have plenty of company from liberals, who are dusting off their copies of Anti-Federalist tracts, Max Farrand's *Records of the Federal Convention of 1787*, and other primary source material on the framers' and ratifiers' intent.

But letting go of Kendall and Burnham is a lot easier for most conservatives than letting go of Wilson is for liberals. Much of the activity of the political science profession, as well as of the history profession, rests on the philosophical and political premises that made Woodrow Wilson famous and to which he devoted so much of his academic life. One takes a certain perverse pleasure these days in watching liberals wrap themselves in the arguments of James Madison (or at least the Madison who, in 1793, argued for the executive's limited role in foreign policy). One suspects they will not go much further into Madison's political thought than is necessary to bash George W. Bush or anyone else who supports expanded executive power in the war on terrorism—especially the "surge" in Iraq, military trials for the enemy combatants housed in Guantanamo, and the use of NSA intercepts. The Madison of 1793, and others from the republic's early days who were suspicious of executive authority, have their uses to Bush's opponents at the present hour, but liberals will not wish to carry their arguments so far as to undercut Wilson's justification for the modern presidency or his general indictment of the old Constitution's principles and structure: the entire liberal enterprise depends on holding on to that sacred Wilsonian bastion.

A Nicer Form of Tyranny

Ronald J. Pestritto

(Spring 2008)

When she was asked in one of last fall's presidential debates whether she still considered herself a liberal, Hillary Clinton sidestepped the question. She called herself, instead, a "proud, modern, American progressive," and boasted that her "progressive vision" for the country had roots going all the way back to "the Progressive Era, at the beginning of the twentieth century."

Modern, big-government liberalism has come home. The Progressives were the first generation of Americans to criticize the United States Constitution, especially for its limits on government's scope and ambition. They rejected the American Founders' classical or natural rights liberalism, offering instead a vision of the modern state as a kind of god with almost limitless power to achieve "social justice." When modern liberals like Senator Clinton call themselves progressives, therefore, they are telling the truth, even if their audiences don't fully understand the implications.

How gratifying it is then to have Jonah Goldberg's new book, *Liberal Fascism: The Secret History of the Left, from Mussolini to the Politics of Meaning*, to pursue these half-forgotten, if not exactly secret, implications. Although liberals throw around the term "fascist" to abuse conservatives (just as they do "racist"), Goldberg, the editor-at-large for *National Review Online*, persuasively shows that today's progressives are fascism's true descendents, embracing the statism at the heart of the 20th-century's most notorious outlaw regimes. What's more, for all the past century's liberal hand-wringing over the supposedly impending right-wing takeover of America, Goldberg maintains that the country has already suffered a quasi-dictator or two, but historians have looked the other way because these strongmen—Woodrow Wilson and Franklin Roosevelt—are certified heroes of the Left.

No wonder that liberals often have such a blinkered interest in their own intellectual heritage. Reviewing this book, for example, Michael Mann in the *Washington Post*, Michael Tomasky in the *New Republic*, and David Neiwert in the *American Prospect* so badly confuse classical liberalism and modern liberalism (by equating them!) that they can make little sense of Goldberg's account, dismissing it as "Bizarro history," "ignorant nonsense," and an attempt to shock readers and sell books. Neiwert even writes, missing the irony, that it is, "the consensus of historical understanding that *anti-intellectualism* is an essential trait of fascism."

But Goldberg's charge is no mere exercise in name-calling. He takes his title from H.G. Wells, the eminent liberal essayist and science fiction writer who coined the term "liberal fascism," or as he also called it, "enlightened Nazism." It was common at the time for progressive intellectuals on both sides of the Atlantic to see Benito Mussolini and Adolf Hitler as kindred reforming spirits, struggling to find a third way forward between the extremes of capitalist individualism and Communist collectivism. Mann believes this connection merely proves that "fascism contained elements that were in the mainstream of 20th-century politics," as much for Democrats and Republicans at home as for fascists and social democrats abroad. But Goldberg is getting at something deeper: he is trying to trace the quiet revolution that took place throughout modern thought when politicians of all stripes, led by the Progressives, were wooed by the power of a limitless State. To his credit, he stresses right from the start that he is not accusing American progressives, past or present, of being the kind of moral monsters associated with European fascism. Still, at some level the family resemblance asserts itself. As Goldberg aptly puts it, Progressivism "may have replaced the fist with the hug, but an unwanted embrace from which you cannot escape is just a nicer form of tyranny." (Hence the book's stark cover featuring a smiley face with the Hitler mustache.)

In his account of fascism, Goldberg even shows how some fairly prominent American liberals expressed real admiration for Mussolini, whom they saw in the 1920s as a kind of hero sticking up for "the little guy." Indeed, the Italian fascist movement, far from being a mere appendage to German Nazism, actually predated it and had a serious course of development all its own. Goldberg does well to set the record straight on this score, contending that fascism grew out of *il Duce's* left-wing statism. The First World War seems to have been decisive in this respect, teaching him that his radical socialist inclinations could profitably tap into both populism and nationalism as a means of becoming a major force in Italy. Goldberg moves from his account of European fascism to the origins of modern liberalism in America, and suggests that the two movements, for a time at least, tracked one another in their development.

In America, the origins of modern liberalism lie at the end of the 19th century, when Wilson, Theodore Roosevelt, John Dewey, Herbert Croly, and a host of others argued that the Constitution was outdated, that it was incompetent to deal with contemporary economic and social ills, and that, if applied at all, it ought to be applied as a "living" document. This notion of a "living constitution"—a pillar of modern liberalism—comes out of the doctrine of progress and, as the more honest Progressives admitted, the historicism of German political philosophy. Almost all of the leading Progressive intellectuals had been educated in Germany or had teachers who were. A sea change had taken place in American higher education in the second half of the 19th century. Most Americans at that time who wanted an advanced degree went to Europe for it, and by 1900 the faculties of America's colleges and universities were teeming with European Ph.D.s. Johns Hopkins University, founded in 1876, was established for the express purpose of bringing German education to the United States, and produced several prominent Progressives, including Wilson, Dewey, and Frederick Jackson Turner.

Like their European counterparts, American Progressives championed *der Staat* over the individual, seeking to redistribute wealth and use the national government to superintend the economy and society. This agenda was at odds with the founders' natural rights principles and the Constitution's limited government, but as Teddy Roosevelt is said to have quipped when challenged about his intrusion on private property rights during the 1902 coal strike: "To hell with the Constitution when the people want coal!" Even if the remark is apocryphal, it captures Roosevelt's animus.

The best example may be his 1910 speech on the New Nationalism, which subsequently became the foundation for his insurgent run for the presidency. Private property rights, which had been serving as a brake on the more aggressive Progressive policy proposals, were to be respected, T.R. argued, only insofar as the government approved of the property's social utility:

> We grudge no man a fortune in civil life if it is honorably obtained and well used. It is not even enough that it should have been gained without doing damage to the community. We should permit it to be gained only so long as the gaining represents benefit to the community. This, I know, implies a policy of a far more active governmental interference with social and economic conditions in this country than we have yet had, but I think we have got to face the fact that such an increase in governmental control is now necessary.

Although the Progressives differed among themselves on the means of achieving reform, there was little disagreement on the fundamental questions of state power and the place of individual liberty. As Frank Goodnow, the American Political Science Association's founding president and one of the modern administrative state's chief architects, put it, natural rights simply could not be allowed to stand in the way of the state's attempt to remedy any perceived social ill:

> The rights which he possesses are . . . conferred upon [the individual], not by his Creator, but rather by the society to which he belongs. What they are is to be determined by the legislative authority in view of the needs of that society. Social expediency, rather than natural right, is thus to determine the sphere of individual freedom of action.

The young Woodrow Wilson, writing in 1889, put this view of state power even more concisely: "Government does now whatever experience permits or the times demand."

It is good to see Goldberg single out Wilson for a special dose of blame in *Liberal Facism*, lamenting that "[i]n America we've chosen not to discuss the madness our Republic endured at Wilson's hands." Goldberg also appreciates the important role religion played for many (although not all) Progressives, who saw in history's supposed advance the will of God at work. For the Social Gospel movement, "the state was the right arm of God and was the means by which the whole nation and world would be redeemed." In fact, "Onward, Christian Soldiers" was the unofficial anthem of the Progressive Party convention in 1912, sung until the rafters shook.

European-style statism took greater hold over the country through FDR's New Deal. Roosevelt was no intellectual but he relied on his progressive and fascist predecessors for the model of state power that animated his programs. And Goldberg observes that although today's liberals may be in love with Jack Kennedy, they govern like Lyndon Johnson, whose Great Society further expanded progressive liberalism's influence. "[I]t's telling," writes Goldberg, "that Democrats wish to preserve the substance of the Great Society while maintaining the mythology of Camelot." The Great Society provides the framework for programmatic liberalism right down to the present day.

Goldberg is certainly right when he says that most academics have willfully ignored modern liberalism's progressive-fascist roots, although scholars such as James Ceaser, John Marini, and others (including me) have in fact been calling attention to the progressive origins of modern liberalism for the past 20 years. *Liberal Fascism* clearly draws from these works but makes surprisingly little reference to them, even in a few instances when the book's observations sound awfully familiar. Yet if Goldberg proceeds, in some respects, down a path blazed by others, he does so with the kind of terrific writing and energy that is certain to make the connection between modern liberalism and its statist ancestors a more prominent factor in America's political battles and debates.

In making his case, Goldberg does tend to conflate fascism and socialism. He wants to show that fascism, far from having been a "right-wing" ideology, actually was a movement of the Left (he calls Hitler a "man of the Left") and that its main characteristics were socialist. This point—perfectly valid—helps make the case that today's liberals are fascism's true inheritors. Goldberg has a deep, thoughtful chapter on Mussolini and another on Hitler to bolster this argument. And he is right that both fascism and socialism are statist—they rest on what he calls "statolatry" or "state worship," the principle that, in Wilson's words, "all idea of a limitation of public authority by individual rights [should] be put out of view," and "that no line can be drawn between private and public affairs which the State may not cross at will."

But at least two distinct forms of statism came out of the 19th century. Nazism in particular owed much to Friedrich Nietzsche's disdain for egalitarian, mass-based movements (e.g., Progressivism) that celebrated human fraternity and dignity. Although he was a great advocate of state power and thought individual rights a joke, Nietzsche's passion was for the rule of the strong over the weak—a love of inequality, enforced by the will to power. From Nietzsche's point of view, both the Soviet and the Anglo-American versions of egalitarianism were abhorrent. Nietzsche's disciple, Martin Heidegger, described the Soviets and the Americans as metaphysically the same, and Heidegger himself was sympathetic to the Nazi cause. Goldberg tries to show that Nazism was a mass-based movement of the Left, and he is persuasive that it attracted the lower classes in Germany more than it did the middle class. But he underplays the extent to which Nazism fed off a desire to reassert the perceived greatness and power of a particular people or race, as over against everyone else, in a manner that, say, American liberalism never did.

Goldberg's argument might have been clearer if he focused less on specific fascist regimes from the 1930s, and more on the roots of fascism itself (and Progressivism, and modern liberalism) in 19th-century German state theory. This is the common thread that would help Goldberg tie together fascism and socialism: both come from the historicism of philosophers like Hegel, both are antithetical to the natural rights-based liberalism of the American Founding, and both show why true constitutionalists ought to resist modern liberalism. By the 1930s, this 19th-century statism has evolved in many different directions—e.g., fascism, Nazism, several flavors of democratic socialism, the Communist International, and America's own welfare state liberalism. Tying these together becomes a tough and unnecessarily complicated chore. Instead of highlighting liberal "fascism," Goldberg's case might have been stronger, or at least sharper, if he had concentrated on liberal "statism."

After all, if fascism and modern liberalism are joined together by all-powerful government as the potential solution to every human problem, aren't there many self-styled conservatives who might fall under the same indictment? Far from thinking "fascism is strictly a Democratic disease," as David Oshinsky charged in his review for the *New York Times*, Goldberg tackles this question head-on in a superb Afterword in which he criticizes right-wing American statism as "me-too conservatism," identifying it squarely with the Progressive movement. For example, he describes George W. Bush as "strongly sympathetic to progressive-style intrusions into civil society" and spies the "ghost of the Social Gospel" in his big-government conservatism. Goldberg bolsters his case with some choice quotations from former Bush advisor Michael Gerson, an architect of "compassionate conservatism" and as his own recent book, *Heroic Conservatism* (2007) makes plain, no fan of limited, constitutional government. Goldberg's Afterword is so good, in fact, that one hopes for a book on the problem of conservative statism from this excellent writer. In order to defeat liberal fascism, American conservatives will need to awaken their own ranks from the progressive spell. With his new book, Jonah Goldberg has renewed for them, and for all friends of constitutional government, a vital argument for the political battles ahead.

Why the Election
of 1912 Changed America

Sidney M. Milkis

(Winter 2002/03)

The 1912 presidential election showcased four impressive candidates who engaged in a remarkable debate about the future of American politics. Besides William Howard Taft, the incumbent Republican president, the campaign was joined by Eugene Debs, the labor leader from Indiana, who ran on the Socialist Party ticket; the irrepressible Theodore Roosevelt, who bolted from the GOP and ran as the champion of the Progressive Party; and Woodrow Wilson, the Democratic governor of New Jersey, who was elected president. All four candidates acknowledged that fundamental changes were occurring in the American political landscape, and each attempted to define the Progressive Era's answer to the questions raised by the new industrial order that had grown up within the American constitutional system.

That the 1912 election registered, and inspired, fundamental changes in American politics suggests the historical significance of the Progressive Party. Not only was it the driving force of this election, but it remains the most important third party to appear on the American political landscape in the 20th century. With the celebrated former President Roosevelt as its candidate, the most prominent figure of his age, the Bull Moose party won 27.4% of the popular vote and 88 electoral votes from six states. This was extraordinary for a third party. In fact, no third-party candidate for the presidency—before or after 1912—has received so large a percentage of the popular vote or as many electoral votes. More importantly, as a party that embraced and helped legitimize new social movements and candidate-centered campaigns, it pioneered a plebiscitary form of governance that has evolved over the course of the 20th century and appears to have come into its own in recent elections. All these features of the Progressive Party campaign made the election of 1912 look more like that of 2000 than that of 1896.

T.R. AND THE BULL MOOSERS

"More than any single leader," the Progressive thinker and editor Herbert Croly wrote, "Theodore Roosevelt contributed decisively to the combination of political

27

and social reform and to the building up a body of national public opinion behind the combination. Under his leadership as president [from 1901 to 1908], reform began to assume the characteristics, if not the name, of progressivism." By bestowing national prominence on progressive objectives, T.R.'s presidency ushered in a new form of statesmanship—one that transformed the chief executive into "the steward of the public welfare," giving expression and effect to the American people's aspirations for social improvement. Roosevelt's concept of leadership and his great talent for taking the American people into his confidence made him virtually irresistible to reformers. "Roosevelt bit me and I went mad," the journalist William Allen White wrote about his participation in the Bull Moose campaign. He was not alone. Jane Addams, the renowned social worker who seconded Roosevelt's Progressive Party nomination for president (the first woman to nominate a major candidate for the presidency), declared that reformers supported T.R.'s candidacy because they viewed him as "one of the few men in public life who has responded to the social appeal, who has caught the significance of the modern movement." He was a leader, she added, "of invincible courage, of open mind, of democratic sympathies, one endowed with power to interpret the common man and to identify himself with the common lot."

Yet as Robert La Follette, one of T.R.'s critics, objected, "No party successfully organized around a man. Principles and issues must constitute the basis of this great movement." Thus the Progressive Party's political program was especially important in defining its collective mission; these proposals unified the movement and ensured its lasting legacy. Above all, the party stood for "pure democracy," that is, democracy purged of the impure influence of the special interests. The party platform's endorsement of "pure democracy" was sanctified as a "covenant with the people," a deep and abiding pledge to make the people the "masters of their constitution." Like the Populist Party of the late 19th century, the Progressives invoked the Constitution's preamble ("We the People") in proclaiming their purpose to strengthen the federal government's regulatory authority over the society and economy. Unlike the Populists, however, Progressives sought to hitch the will of the people to a strengthened national administrative power. Animated by the radical agrarianism that had accompanied the Jeffersonian and Jacksonian assaults on monopolistic power, the Populists had sought to mobilize the states and the Congress for an assault on the centralizing, plutocratic alliance between the national parties and the large corporations or "trusts." By contrast, the Progressives, with their "gospel of efficiency" drawn from the latest discoveries of political and social science, could not abide the Populists' localized, backward-looking democratic faith.

Today, scholars puzzle over the apparent contradiction between the Progressives' celebration of direct democracy and their hope to achieve more disinterested government, which seemed to demand a powerful and expert national bureaucracy. But Progressives came to see that the expansion of social welfare and "pure democracy," as they understood it, were inextricably linked. Reforms such as the direct primary, as well as the initiative and referendum, were designed to overthrow the localized two-party system in the United States, which for generations had restrained the growth of the national government. By the same token, the triumph of "progressive" over "pioneer" democracy, as Croly framed it, would put the American people directly in touch with the councils of power, thus strengthening their demands for government support and requiring the federal government to expand and transform itself in order to realize the goals of Progressive social welfare policy.

NEW NATIONALISM VS. NEW FREEDOM

Still, the profound shift in regime norms and practices represented by Progressivism did not entail a straightforward evolution from localized to "Big Government." Indeed, the Progressive Party was badly crippled by fundamental disagreements among its supporters over issues that betrayed an acute sensitivity, if not attachment, to the country's commitment to local self-government. The party was deeply divided over civil rights, leading to bitter struggles at the Progressive Party convention over delegate selection rules and the platform that turned on whether the party should confront the shame of Jim Crow. In the end, it did not, accepting the right of the states and localities to resolve the matter of race relations. Moreover, Progressive delegates waged an enervating struggle at the convention over whether an interstate trade commission with considerable administrative discretion or militant antitrust policy was the appropriate method to tame the trusts. New Nationalists, led by Roosevelt, prevailed, pledging the party to regulate, rather than attempt to dismantle, corporate power; however, this disagreement carried over to the general election. The Democratic Party, under the tutelage of their candidate, Woodrow Wilson, and his advisor, Louis Brandeis, embraced a "New Freedom" version of Progressivism, which prescribed antitrust measures and state regulations as an alternative to the expansion of national administrative power.

The split between New Nationalism and New Freedom Progressives cut to the very core of the modern state that, ostensibly, the programmatic initiatives touted by Progressives anticipated. As Croly acknowledged, the Progressive program presupposed national standards and regulatory powers that "foreshadowed administrative aggrandizement." And yet Progressives could not agree on how administrative power should be used. Indeed, the conflict between New Nationalism and New Freedom Progressives revealed that many reformers shared the profound uneasiness of their Populist forbears about the very prospect of expanding national administrative power. This anxiety was not merely a hastily contrived reaction to the administrative ambitions of New Nationalism; it was allied to a celebration of local self-government that was deeply rooted in American political culture.

Nonetheless, this reluctance to embrace centralized administration did not represent a commitment to local self-government as traditionally understood and practiced. The "compound republic," as James Madison called it, was shaped in the 19th century by party organizations and legal doctrines that formed a wall of separation between government and society. Progressives of all stripes were committed to breaching that wall. New Freedom Progressives wanted to expand the responsibilities of the national government, but hoped to find non-bureaucratic and non-centralized ways to treat the nation's economic ills. They advocated measures like the Sherman Act, enacted in 1890, that would rely on competition and law, rather than administrative tribunals, to curb the abuses of big business. Just as significant, New Freedom Progressives hoped to cultivate local forums of public discussion and debate that would "buttress the foundations of democracy." For example, Wilson and Brandeis were active in the "social centers" movement that sought to make use of school buildings for neighborhood forums on the leading issues of the day.

Still, the Progressive hope of strengthening self-government in the United States depended ultimately on somehow transmuting local self-government into direct rule of the people, who would not have to suffer the interference of decentralizing associations and institutions. Only then could individuals participate in a national movement of public opinion that might cultivate a "more perfect union." "Truly, the voice of the people is the voice of God," wrote a Progressive journalist, echoing Andrew Jackson, "but that means the voice of the *whole* people."

Although they disagreed about how to reform the economy, Progressives tended to agree on the need for direct democracy. No less than the Wilsonians, New Nationalist reformers championed institutions and practices that would nurture a direct system of popular rule on a national scale. Thus T.R. joined Wilson in calling for the use of school houses as neighborhood headquarters for political discussion. Indeed, T.R.'s bolt from the Republican Party freed him to make a bolder, more consistent defense of "pure democracy" than Wilson, who, as the nominee of the Democrats, was necessarily more constrained by the structure and organizational practices of the traditional two-party system. In disdaining party politics, and the local self-government it embodied, T.R. gave voice to Progressive faith in the American people's aspiration for social justice, and to the responsibility of leaders to give effect to these aspirations. As he stated this creed in his campaign address at Carnegie Hall:

> In order to succeed we need leaders of inspired idealism, leaders to whom are granted great visions, who dream greatly and strive to make their dreams come true; who can kindle the people with the fire from their own burning souls. The leader for the time being, whoever he may be, is but an instrument, to be used until broken and then to be cast aside; and if he is worth his salt he will care no more when he is broken than a soldier cares when he is sent where his life is forfeit in order that victory may be won. In the long fight for righteousness the watchword for all of us is, spend and be spent. It is of little matter whether any one man fails or succeeds; but the cause shall not fail, for it is the cause of mankind.

Ostensibly, the "cause" of Progressivism—the platform's commitment to direct democracy and social and industrial justice—gave reform leadership its dignity, indeed its heroic quality. But the celebration of public opinion left leaders at the beck and call of the people. As the influential Wisconsin reformer, Charles McCarthy, warned Roosevelt, the American people were "jealous of losing control" over their political destiny, and four years of Taft had only served to intensify their desire to "have greater control over the presidency." T.R.'s 1912 campaign exalted this desire into a creed. Sensing that "pure democracy" was the glue that held together the movement he sought to lead, Roosevelt made the cause of popular rule the centerpiece of his frantic run for the White House. As Roosevelt said in his "Confession of Faith," delivered at the Progressive Party convention, "the first essential of the Progressive programme is the right of the people to rule." This right demanded more than writing into law measures such as the direct primary, recall, and referendum. It also required rooting firmly in custom the unwritten law that the representatives derived their authority "directly" from the people.

Roosevelt's very appearance at the Progressive Party's convention symbolized a new relationship between leaders and the led. In the past, party nominees had stayed away from the convention, waiting to be notified officially of their nomination. A presidential candidate was expected to demur as a sign of respect for the party's collective purpose. T.R.'s personal appearance at the Progressive convention gave dramatic testimony to his dominance of the proceedings. More significant, it gave evidence of an important historical change, of presidential campaigns being conducted less by parties than by individual candidates who appealed directly for the support of the electorate.

Roosevelt's presence in Chicago, the record of the proceedings tells us, roused the delegates to such an emotional state that they could only be subdued by a reverential singing of the "Battle Hymn of the Republic." The delegate's reverence went beyond devotion for their candidate, however; it expressed their collective identity. T.R.'s dominant role in the Progressive Party campaign was not simply a matter of his personal popularity; it followed directly from the Progressive animus against mediating institutions, such as political parties, that discouraged direct contact between reform leaders and the people. Indeed, the reform-minded delegates who came to Chicago championed the direct rule of the people with a fresh enthusiasm that surprised and impressed the journalists who witnessed the proceedings. After observing an evening of reformist speeches, punctuated by the singing of hymns, "which burst forth at the first flash of every demonstration," a reporter for the *San Francisco Examiner* marveled that the convention "was more like a religious revival than a political gathering."

PROGRESSIVE DEMOCRACY AND THE AMERICAN CONSTITUTION

As important and controversial as T.R.'s defense of the direct primary was in 1912, it was not the most debated issue of the campaign. Even more controversial was T.R.'s call for the people's right to recall judicial decisions. Aroused by the judiciary's militant defense of property rights, Roosevelt undertook a wholesale attack on its authority. He first announced his support for popular referenda on court rulings in his February 1912 speech in Columbus, Ohio, the same day he finally, in his words, "threw his hat in the ring" as a candidate for president. Specifically, he called for popular referenda to apply only to state courts; but he more than hinted that they should apply to the federal judiciary as well. In fact, the Progressives championed a form of constitutionalism that would be more immediately responsive to the rule of the people. Roosevelt authored the party plank titled "Amendment to the Constitution," espousing the party's belief "that a free people should have the power from time to time to amend their fundamental law so as to adapt it progressively to the changing needs of the people." How this was to be done was left open, but the party pledged itself "to provide a more easy and expeditious method of amending the federal constitution."

The Progressive program seemed to challenge the very foundation of republican democracy: the idea, underlying the U.S. Constitution, that space created by institutional devices such as the separation of powers and federalism allowed representatives to govern competently and fairly. Likewise, the Progressive idea of democracy rejected traditional party politics. Forged on the anvil of Jeffersonian democracy, political parties in the United States were welded to constitutional principles that impeded the expansion of national administrative power. The origins and organizing principles of the American party system established it as a force against the creation of the "modern state." The Progressive reformers commitment to building such a state—that is, to the creation of a national political power with expansive programmatic responsibilities—meant that the party system either had to be weakened or reconstructed.

In the face of T.R.'s challenge to the prevailing doctrine and practices of representation in the United States, the burden of defending constitutional sobriety fell most heavily on William Howard Taft. In truth, the most important exchange in the constitutional debate of 1912 was the one between T.R. and Taft. In 1908, of course, Taft had been T.R.'s heir apparent. President Taft had supported and extended the pragmatic progressive program that was the legacy of T.R.'s presidency, working for specific policies such as the Hepburn Act with the cooperation of Republican Party regulars. And yet, Taft now found his own efforts to carry on that pragmatic tradition of reform the object of scorn and derision, the victim of T.R.'s celebration of "pure democracy." "The initiative, the referendum, and the recall, together with a complete adoption of the direct primary as a means of selecting nominees and an entire destruction of the convention system are now all made the *sine qua non* of a real reformer," Taft lamented. "Everyone who hesitates to follow all of these or any of them is regarded with suspicion and is denounced as an enemy of popular government and of the people." Yet his very "hesitation" allowed Taft to find honor in the charge of conservatism leveled against him. Even as T.R.'s defense of direct democracy found great favor throughout the country, Taft resisted this attempt "to tear down all the checks and balances of a well-adjusted, democratic, constitutional, representative government."

To be sure, he agreed that some reform of the national convention system was necessary. And while acknowledging that no political system could avoid the effects of corruption, he urged his fellow Republicans to rise above the patronage politics that had so long dominated party government. In fact, in order to fortify the polity against petty and virulent interest-group politics, Taft emphasized that political parties had the responsibility to endorse and defend fundamental constitutional principles. Accordingly, the Progressive Party's attack on representative institutions called for a new understanding of Republican conservatism, which, Taft argued, should be rooted less in a militant defense of property rights and business than in a Whiggish defense of ordered liberty. "The real usefulness of the Republican Party," he insisted, "consists in its conservative tendencies to preserve our constitutional government and prevent its serious injury."

Taft would thus "stand pat" in defense of the Constitution, which the Progressive idea of democracy threatened to destroy. He warned his fellow Republicans at a 1912 Lincoln Day dinner:

> With the effort to make the selection of candidates, the enactment of legislation, and the decision of the courts to depend on the momentary passions of the people necessarily indifferently informed as to the issues presented, and without the opportunity to them for time and study and that deliberation that gives security and common sense to

the government of the people, such extremists would hurry us into a condition which would find no parallel except in the French revolution, or in that bubbling anarchy that once characterized the South American Republics. Such extremists are not progressives—they are political emotionalists or neurotics—who have lost the sense of proportion, that clear and candid consideration of their own weakness as a whole, and that clear perception of the necessity for checks upon hasty popular action which made our people who fought the Revolution and who drafted the Federal Constitution, the greatest self-governing people the world ever knew.

Support for "pure democracy," Taft charged, found its "mainspring" in the very same "factional spirit" that Madison had warned against in his famous discussion of republican government in *Federalist* 10, an unruly majority that would "sacrifice to its ruling passion or interest both the public good and the rights of other citizens." In resisting this temptation to flatter the whims and passions of the majority, the most sacred duty of true conservatives was to uphold the courts. As Taft told an audience in Boston, T.R.'s defense of direct democracy "sent a thrill of alarm through all the members of the community who understood our constitutional principles and who feared the effect of the proposed changes upon the permanence of government." It was unthinkable to the great majority of leaders in Congress and the states, and to the great mass of people as well, Taft argued, that Roosevelt should seriously propose to have a plebiscite upon questions involving the construction of the Constitution. T.R.'s audacity drew most clearly the fundamental issue that divided Republicans and Progressives:

> The Republican Party . . . respecting as it does the Constitution . . . [and] the care with which the judicial clauses of that fundamental instrument were drawn to secure the independence of the judiciary, will never consent to an abatement of that independence to the slightest degree, and will stand with its face like flint against any constitutional changes in it.

Somewhat uncharacteristically, Roosevelt never flinched in the face of this controversy. Sensing that popular rule was the glue that held together the movement he sought to lead, his defense of it became bolder throughout 1912. Indeed, Roosevelt announced toward the end of September, in a speech at Phoenix, Arizona, that he "would go even further than the Progressive Platform," applying "the recall to everybody, including the president." As the *Nation* warned, "T.R. [now stood] upon the bald doctrine of unrestricted majority rule." Even William Jennings Bryan blushed and admonished T.R. for defending the nationalization of direct democracy. Such measures, the old populist insisted, must be confined to the states.

Despite Taft's charge that the Progressives threatened to destroy the Constitution, despite the hope of T.R.'s political enemies that such a bold campaign would kill him politically, the Progressive Party campaign of 1912 had an enduring influence on American politics and government. It was not Roosevelt but Taft who suffered a humiliating defeat, winning only two states—Utah and Vermont—and 23% of the popular vote. In contrast, T.R.'s strong showing and his dominant presence in that campaign signaled the beginning of an important change in American democracy.

From its own perspective, the Progressive Party did not seek to destroy the Constitution but to revitalize and democratize it—to renew the debate over issues that had divided the Federalists and Anti-Federalists, as well as the Jeffersonians and Hamiltonians. Indeed, the New Nationalists consciously and deliberately saw themselves as involved in a "neo-Hamiltonian" project. Of course, Progressives defended national public opinion with an enthusiasm that Hamilton would have found very dangerous. But in their celebration of national democracy, Progressives claimed, they were merely following Lincoln, whose legacy was abandoned by the latter-day Republican Party.

Most importantly, the Progressive faith in public opinion—this popular version of Hamiltonianism—was viewed as a compromise with, and an attempt to calm, the American people's fear of a centralized state. If national administrative power were to be strengthened and expanded, Progressives acknowledged, the people would have to be in command of it. Support for measures such as the primary, recall, and referendum displayed a willingness on the part of reformers to accommodate those fears, even as they sought to strengthen national administrative power. Jane Addams, who was no less essential than T.R. to Progressive reform objectives, explained this concession to public opinion clearly in a Lincoln Day address. A welfare state could not be created in the United States, she insisted, through the sort of corporatist arrangements that were being formed in Europe and Great Britain; it could not be formed with a centralized Social Democratic party as its agent, dedicated to building a national state that would link government and society. A welfare state could not gain popular support in the United States, Addams concluded, "unless the power of direct legislation is placed in the hands of the people, in order that these changes may come, not as the centralized government [has] given them, from above down, but may come from the people up; that the people shall be the directing and controlling factors in this legislation."

To the extent that Progressive democracy was radical, it represented a American form of radicalism—one conceived to rescue American individualism from a blind attachment to the Constitution, especially from fealty to the "high priests" of the Constitution. "[I]t is difficult for Englishmen to understand the extreme conservatism of my proposition as to the referendum to the people of certain judicial questions," T.R. wrote to a friend abroad; "and this difficulty arises from the fact that in England no human being dreams of permitting the court to decide such questions! In England no court can declare any legislative act unconstitutional." In fact, T.R. claimed, he sought to avoid the delegation of policy to an unchecked legislature that might truly embody the sort of factionalism that plagued France and England and had worried the architects of the Constitution. Recognizing that factionalism was abetted by militant partisanship in government, he wrote: "I do not propose to make the legislature supreme over the court; I propose *merely* to allow the people . . . to decide whether to follow the legislature or the court."

BACK TO THE FUTURE

The Progressive Party's "compromise" with public opinion in the United States points to its legacy for American politics and government. Arguably, the failure of the 1912 experiment and the Progressive Party's demise underscore the incoherence of the Progressive movement. Nevertheless, it was neither the Democrats, nor the

Republicans, nor the Socialists who set the tone of the 1912 campaign. It was the Progressives. Beyond the 1912 election, their program of political and social reform has been an enduring feature of American political discourse and electoral struggle. The Progressive Party forged a path of reform that left both social democracy and conservatism—Taft's constitutional sobriety—behind. Similarly, T.R.'s celebrity, and the popularity of the Progressive doctrine of the people's right to rule, tended to subordinate the more populist to the more plebiscitary schemes in the platform, such as the initiative, the referendum, and the direct primary, which exalted not the "grassroots" but mass opinion. Indeed, in the wake of the excitement aroused by the Progressive Party, Wilson, whose New Freedom campaign was far more sympathetic to the decentralized state of courts and parties than T.R.'s, felt compelled, as president, to govern as a New Nationalist Progressive.

Of course, the Progressive Party campaign of 1912 is only the beginning of the story—the *birth* of modern American politics. It fell to Franklin Delano Roosevelt, who was inspired by T.R.'s 1912 campaign, to consolidate developments begun by the Progressive Party. Like the Progressive Party, the Democratic Party of the New Deal was formed to advance the personal and nonpartisan responsibility of the executive at the expense of collective and partisan responsibility. Understood within the context of the Progressive tradition, the New Deal is appropriately viewed as the completion of a realignment that would make future partisan realignments unnecessary. It was to be but a way station on the road to Progressive democracy, where, to quote the important Brownlow Committee report: "Our national will must be expressed not merely in a brief exultant moment of electoral decision, but in persistent, determined, competent day-by-day administration of what the nation has decided to do."

The expansion of national administrative power that followed the New Deal realignment, however, did not result in the kind of state that Progressive reformers had longed for—one enshrining regulation and social welfare policy as expressions of national unity and popular commitment. In truth, the history of the Progressive Party sheds light on the love-hate relationship Americans forged with the state in the 20th century. The 1996 and 2000 presidential elections revealed that middle class entitlements like Social Security and Medicare are still popular. Yet the rejection of national health care reform and the devolution to the states of responsibility for welfare (Aid to Families with Dependent Children) show that Americans continue to abhor, even as they embrace in many important particulars, national administrative power. Meanwhile, "pure democracy" has evolved, or degenerated, into a plebiscitary form of politics that mocks the Progressive concept of "enlightened administration," and exposes citizens to the sort of public figures who will exploit their impatience with the difficult tasks involved in sustaining a healthy democracy. Those who blame television or campaign finance practices for this development would be well served by a careful study of the deep roots of the Progressive tradition.

For better or worse, the Progressive democracy championed by T.R. in 1912, and the love-hate relationship with the state it has led to, now seem enduring parts of our political life. In this sense, the Progressive Party campaign of 1912 might very well provide useful—and troubling—insights into the future of American politics.

FDR as Statesman

Robert Eden

(Fall 2004)

> *One of the few substantive political differences I had with my father was over his view that Franklin D. Roosevelt was a socialist, if not a communist. He has always been, next to Abraham Lincoln, the American leader I most admired, not only because he triumphed over a cruel infirmity, over national economic and psychological depression, over "the apostles of war and of racial arrogances" . . . but because he completely suborned, outwitted, and co-opted the American left and delivered the nation from the horrors those forces inflicted on most other advanced countries. Roosevelt the shaman was one of the great talents of American political history. This was the true Roosevelt whom I commended to my skeptical father. When he thought I was playing his speeches too loudly, he would appear and demand the volume be reduced. I did, but he continued to hear Roosevelt's apostolic cadences in his house occasionally.*
>
> —Conrad Black,
> *A Life in Progress (1993)*

Conrad Black has admired Franklin Delano Roosevelt for a long time—not least because, like Roosevelt, he thrives on controversy. And Lord Black is as spirited today, in his comprehensive defense of Roosevelt's statesmanship, as he was in the 1950s, celebrating "Roosevelt the shaman" to the horror of his conservative Canadian father. In the intervening decades, Black has mastered every pertinent document and book he could lay hands on; but his political biography of FDR is more than the culmination of these long and exacting studies. Like much of the best political science and history, *Franklin Delano Roosevelt: Champion of Freedom* is a deeply political work by a public-spirited and prudent observer. Black means to widen the historical horizon of current debate on urgent public questions, by showing that FDR is at the origin of our most important political controversies. Indeed, for Black, FDR is still at their center, because he was the chief architect of the free world in our time, and of the American regime which is the free world's center of gravity.

As a young man, Black no doubt cultivated his admiration for FDR pugnaciously. By contrast, in writing *Champion of Freedom* he has deployed it deliberately: first, to awaken students of Roosevelt's politics to the real challenge of their subject and to the rather merciless standards it imposes; and then, to recruit young readers to public life and to the study of statesmanship. His book is meant to inflame high ambition by FDR's example, as well as to give it form and direction. Will readers seize upon Franklin Roosevelt's statesmanship to form themselves into serious citizens, as Black did, and as his book invites his readers to do? Or will FDR go the way of Andrew Jackson—another fabulously popular president who swept all before him, inspired fierce loyalty in an immense following, but was practically forgotten six decades later? Black has labored as though the answer to these questions depended on his own accomplishment in framing them—for Americans, for the English-speaking public at large, and for defenders of freedom everywhere.

One might object that unlike Andrew Jackson, FDR is unforgettable; that he will forever be paired with the finest statesmen; above all, with Winston Churchill and Charles de Gaulle, who made him a central figure in their war memoirs. Since these are indelible classics in the literature of great statesmanship, one might suppose that Roosevelt's place in historical memory would be impregnable, so long as these great memoirs are studied. Black responds to this objection indirectly but with extraordinary care. He clearly gives pride of place to these most influential and widely read memoirs. He sees Churchill and de Gaulle as the most intelligent and capable statesmen who wrote from first-hand experience of Roosevelt. But Black knows that he cannot invoke their judgment of FDR's greatness without also facing their criticism of his dire mistakes.

For in their respective memoirs, Churchill and de Gaulle are sharply critical of FDR's wartime policies. Although in *The Second World War* he celebrated his warm friendship with Roosevelt, Churchill still managed to convey his reasoned condemnation of U.S. diplomacy from the Tehran Conference on: FDR's failure to present a united Allied front to Stalin and thus his surrender of the moral high ground, his willingness to side with Stalin on the elimination of Germany as a European state, his slowness to confront Communist subversion in Greece and Eastern Europe, and above all his failure to prepare Harry Truman to take over the presidency. De Gaulle's criticisms in his war memoirs took a different but equally damning tack. Among other things, he objected to Roosevelt's diplomatic dalliances with Vichy France; to his cunning policy of setting de Gaulle and Churchill at loggerheads, the better to reorganize Europe as FDR saw fit; and to Roosevelt's overweening desire to dismantle the French and British colonial empires and erect some sort of international New Deal in their place.

Black has tried to write a defense that weighs de Gaulle's and Churchill's assessments fairly and deals fully with their principal criticisms of Roosevelt. Moreover, *Champion of Freedom* aspires to be a sequel to Churchill's effort to persuade the European peoples that their dignity as well as security and freedom lie in friendship with the United States. Indeed, Black sees himself as improving upon Churchill's effort, chiefly in two ways.

First, the Canadian impasse over Quebec proved to Black the vital importance of meeting de Gaulle's critique of FDR candidly and defending the United States before the French-speaking peoples in the light of that critique. Black chairs the editorial board of the *National Interest*; he is a keen analyst of world politics. I believe he is convinced that serious citizens everywhere will be shaped by de Gaulle's impressive argument, unless it is met more forthrightly than Churchill did. For de

Gaulle wrote after Churchill; and he deliberately exploited his advantage as the last of the great wartime statesmen to write his memoirs. Black apprehends that de Gaulle could have the last word in much of the world—and this despite France's descent from the rank of a great power, or even because of it. *Champion of Freedom* is a sustained engagement with de Gaulle's claim that proud nations must choose against Roosevelt, and against the United States, to preserve their political dignity and pride—or to create it. Accordingly, one fulcrum of Black's defense is the striking claim that "Roosevelt's greatest foreign policy error wasn't his handling of Stalin, which was not particularly unsuccessful. It was his reflexive hostility to de Gaulle and his lateness in getting over it." Black defends Roosevelt on Stalin and Yalta, against Churchill's critique. And he condemns outright Roosevelt's handling of Free France (again in contrast to Churchill), while rebutting de Gaulle's argument about Roosevelt's baleful role in the great "debate over man," *la querelle de l'homme*. From his Canadian experience, Black knows that if its challenge goes unanswered, de Gaulle's argument can be deadly and demoralizing to the free world. Although his book was in press before the Iraq War, our experience with France over Iraq confirms Black's judgment that de Gaulle's argument remains a contentious force well beyond the Francophone boundary. "[T]he United States paid a price through most of the balance of the twentieth century for Roosevelt's reflexive and indiscreet early animosity to de Gaulle."

Secondly, Churchill took for granted the vivid memory of Roosevelt as an intelligent, resourceful figure acting with authority on the world stage. In Black's judgment this awareness can no longer be presupposed; it must now be reconstituted for the reader. Much of Black's art is designed to conjure up Roosevelt's authoritative presence, to crystallize it in writing and thus make it a possession for all time.

To accomplish this, however, Black finds it necessary to challenge Churchill's critique on key points of disagreement between the prime minister and the American president. Hence *Champion of Freedom* will awaken the suspicions of many stalwarts who otherwise share his judgments on world affairs. He knows that many of the serious citizens who successfully met the Cold War crisis found Churchill's critique indispensable in freeing their minds from Roosevelt's influence. For many, this was a wrenching experience. Such readers will initially be appalled by the critical dimension of Black's reply to Churchill, and especially by his defense of FDR's conduct at Yalta. They are justifiably determined that no American president ever be suckered by the likes of Stalin. So is Black. And (for reasons I shall discuss), he probably knows his book cannot persuade Cold War Churchilleans that FDR played his cards well.

Even if he cannot, however, Black might reply that Churchill's defense of his own realism, in *The Second World War*, will become inscrutable in the long run without a book like *Champion of Freedom*—and that Churchill's case for friendship with Roosevelt and the United States will be gravely weakened if readers can no longer credit what Churchill took for granted: Roosevelt's commanding presence as an intelligent statesman, and his reputation as a very hard trader. In this respect, *The Second World War* is greatly strengthened by having *Champion of Freedom* as its sequel or companion; and so Black's challenge to Churchill's influence can be called an improvement.

In replying to Churchill's critique and making its sustained case for Roosevelt's statesmanship, *Champion of Freedom* is hardly breaking fresh ground. Roosevelt's case is the case for American wartime policy. It has been made continuously and across a wide front since 1945 by American historians. The case is now firmly ensconced in the most widely used primary sources; for example, in Warren Kimball's annotations to his edition of the Churchill-Roosevelt correspondence. A relentless rebuttal of Churchill on the American conduct of the war has long been a leading feature of World War II scholarship. Yet while Black builds on and reinforces this American historiography, *Champion of Freedom* stands out because Black also responds to it. Moreover, he does so critically, bringing to the task a more acute sympathy with the concerns of Churchill and De Gaulle, and a deeper understanding of their writings, than most historians can muster.

Furthermore, British and American historians writing after the war had a much less vivid memory of Roosevelt's abilities than either Churchill or de Gaulle. What Churchill took for granted was based on first-hand knowledge of Roosevelt's performance that was never available to most diplomatic and military historians, who had to rely on Roosevelt's biographers in forming their estimates, much as laymen do today. While defending American policy, they have not been sufficiently confident in speaking of Roosevelt's capacities. Black does more than improve on the historical scholarship defending American conduct of the war under FDR, by incorporating the critiques advanced by Churchill and de Gaulle. He also restores their high estimates of Roosevelt's capability. This may come as a shock to many readers, because a much lower estimate of Roosevelt's ability is currently fashionable, while Churchill's and de Gaulle's have been progressively forgotten over the last five decades. Readers who suppose that Black's estimate is a product of youthful enthusiasm, or a bizarre idiosyncrasy, should ponder the evidence that his estimate was shared, in all essentials, by both Churchill and de Gaulle.

Because Black reasserts their higher estimate of FDR's faculties, *Champion of Freedom* is a decisive improvement upon all previous biographies as a companion to Churchill's *The Second World War* and de Gaulle's *Mémoires de Guerre*. For Black, statecraft is primarily the work of intellect, not of temperament. To judge Roosevelt's stature is therefore chiefly a matter of understanding his prudence and his practical reasoning. Posing the question of Roosevelt's stature in this way leads us to the heart of Black's study, and to his indispensable clarification of the fundamental problems that Roosevelt's statecraft poses for serious citizens, political scientists, historians, and even for students of political philosophy. These are problems, in the first instance, of knowledge.

Suppose one grants that Black has succeeded in recovering Roosevelt's masterful presence. What good is the presence of a sphinx, if we cannot get him to speak his mind? In formulating *that* difficulty, and in responding to it intelligently, *Champion of Freedom* excels not only the previous biographies of Roosevelt, but everything I have read on the subject, save for Churchill's and de Gaulle's memoirs. Black judges Roosevelt to have been a greater statesman than his two greatest peers because he was a more complete and subtler Machiavellian. He argues that Roosevelt exemplified a distinctively American political realism or pragmatism that came closer to the Machiavellian *verità effetuale* of politics than did Churchill or de Gaulle. And he does not hesitate to draw the conclusion that Roosevelt was a lesser man, while accomplishing more through his statecraft.

The primary myth that *Champion of Freedom* seeks to explode is that FDR was not a serious Machiavellian; the second is that he was relatively weak-minded. The two myths obviously reinforce one another. Both have been built up, according to Black, chiefly by Roosevelt's admirers, who soft-pedalled his Machiavellianism, accentuated his muddleheadedness, and then came to believe their own caricature:

> [E]ven perceptive historians have tended to believe that Roosevelt was a largely guileless man and that he became distressed when his puckish love of mischief led him to tactical excess . . . . His most fervent admirers have made him seem an amiable and capable man carried along to four terms in the White House on a tide of events over which he had little influence.

To the extent that Roosevelt devoted his intellectual powers to Machiavellian misdirection, strategy, and ruse, this way of touching up Roosevelt's public image would effectively dumb down his statesmanship again, though in a different way. Black combats this implication by making his volume an ascent from the cave of such misleading legends. The myth that most discourages inquiry, preventing any searching critique of Roosevelt's failures and accomplishments, is the notion that he could not know what he was doing because he was incapable of reasoning through the great problems with which he dealt during his presidency.

To explain how this prevailing low estimate of FDR's abilities took hold in the republic of letters, Black addresses himself first to the most widely credited authority for it. How, he asks, did we learn that Justice Oliver Wendell Holmes, Jr., judged FDR, at the time of his inauguration in 1933, to be "a second-rate intellect, but a first-class temperament"?

> [Tommy "the Cork"] Corcoran is the chief source for this last quote, which was corroborated by Donald Hiss, but it is not clear which President Roosevelt Holmes was talking about. This may even have been the first meeting between Holmes and Franklin Roosevelt, and Holmes had often referred to Theodore Roosevelt in similar terms in his correspondence. Whether Holmes said it or not, Franklin Roosevelt has been arraigned on this patronizing charge by historians for some time.

Black meets this condescension forthrightly and seeks to dismantle it: "If allowance is made for the supernatural acuity of his intuition and his almost infallible memory, which Holmes would have had little opportunity to appreciate, Roosevelt's intellect was first-class."

When a statesman deploys a superior intellect along Machiavellian lines, keeping his counsel to himself by following Machiavelli's precept "put nothing in writing," scholars and citizens face formidable difficulties in finding the evidence they require for judgment. At the dedication of the Hyde Park library, FDR is said to have chuckled all day at the prospect that historians would come there to find answers to their questions: he knew they would find nothing. Black is fully aware of the difficulty. He contends that the only avenue it leaves open is to reconstruct an account of *what Roosevelt must have thought and known* by inference backward from the record of *what he did.*

The historian is thus placed in precisely the position in which Roosevelt's opponents and associates were placed, *vis-à-vis* the sphinx: one has to make hypothetical estimates and test them against the pattern of FDR's behavior in order to deduce what Roosevelt was thinking, and by what plan or strategy he was acting. In certain respects, the historian's position is more problematic than that of Roosevelt's associates or opponents. For despite the superior information a scholar can deploy in retrospect, he cannot elicit *action* from FDR, by taking a provocative initiative of his own. By authorizing the Free French sortie at St. Pierre and Miquelon, de Gaulle says, "I provoked Washington in order to stir up the bottom of things, as one throws a stone into a pond." The scholar cannot stir up Roosevelt to discover the bottom of things.

"With Roosevelt," according to Black, "the sure guide of his intentions was to detect the trend of his actions." But can that be a sure guide? At the beginning of his 700-page account of FDR's wartime statesmanship, Black gives a capsule reconstruction of FDR's thoughts and plans. He prefaces it by saying that "The reason Roosevelt must have known all this is because there is no other plausible explanation of his conduct as he moved deftly through the world crisis." This assertion indicates both the plausibility and the vulnerability of the method that Black finds himself compelled to adopt, in the face of his statesman-sphinx. Deeds are never univocal; and if that were not enough, FDR encased his own in elaborate equivocations: "As always with Roosevelt, only the general outlines of what he thought can be discerned from the conflicting signals he sent in all directions and only his deeds are a guide to his thoughts—not, as with more direct leaders (such as Truman), the other way round." Ultimately, this is why Black is unlikely to convince doubters that the evidence supports his own assessment. Nevertheless, he has faced the difficulty squarely. His solution is to put forward his best summary of what FDR must have known at the outset, and ask the reader to assess it in the light of the evidence he presents in detail in the rest of his study. Because its subject is "the cunning and violence that prudence needs to have at its command whether in the worst or in the best cause," *Champion of Freedom* is a book for intrepid observers.

Harry V. Jaffa reports that he learned more about Jefferson himself from Merrill Peterson's *The Jeffersonian Image in the American Mind* (1960) than from studying any of the standard Jefferson biographies. He observed that, "from the variety of highly plausible viewpoints about Jefferson, one learns why the study of Jefferson is such a problem." The opposite is true for FDR. One will not learn "why FDR poses such a problem" from the diversity of viewpoints about his image. Instead, an essential conformity of judgment has come to conceal the problem and obstruct serious inquiry. This uniform opinion has even deafened readers to the dissenting assessments of FDR's greatest contemporaries, Churchill and de Gaulle.

Black has come closest to achieving a radical critique of Roosevelt, in the sense of a clear understanding, because he has formulated this problem adequately and has attempted to solve it forthrightly. *Champion of Freedom* makes a frontal assault on several influential "myths" that have formed the established public estimate of Roosevelt's statecraft. Without his searching account of FDR's actions, of course, Black's critique of the prevailing much lower ranking of FDR's capabilities would have no weight. With it, Black has laid the foundation for a comprehensive rethinking, not only of Roosevelt's actions and public image, but also of Roosevelt scholarship and the punditry built upon it.

The great strength of Black's book, then, is his portrait of Roosevelt's distinctive and inimitable abilities, above all, his intellectual mastery of his chosen tasks. This is the source of his book's fecundity and its promise for future scholarship. Yet it comes at a price. Black cherishes certain key myths that cannot go unchallenged. To restore Roosevelt's masterful presence, to recapture his statesmanship in its original energy and radiance, he abstracts Roosevelt from his legislation, and from the routinization of his statecraft in American institutions and customs. Perhaps he thinks this rubble obscures our view of Roosevelt, or might make his actions unintelligible to readers. Black's way of preventing that distortion gives his history a peculiarly utopian cast. He divorces Roosevelt from the army of his imitators, and thus from his legacy in American public life. Black sets out to do justice to "the vast complexity of [Roosevelt's] political designs"—to their character, their execution, and their success in forming the world of concern to us as citizens. But his book does so only for Roosevelt's foreign policy designs. His case for FDR's greatness in foreign affairs is meant to stand up against six decades of subsequent experience. With regard to domestic politics, however, Black is largely silent on what Roosevelt actually wrought, and how his complex schemes were realized in the United States. He has not made a comparable effort to analyze the consequences of Roosevelt's New Deal. This disproportion is reflected in the (relatively) short shrift he devotes to Roosevelt's first two administrations. *Champion of Freedom* is divided into five equal parts, each of 225 pages. The war years occupy three parts, a full three-fifths of the book. The New Deal occupies one part.

In my opinion, Black has left the lion's share of his great subject yet to be surveyed; it will be for future scholars to combine a just estimate of Roosevelt's intelligence and prudence with a realistic account of the fulfillment of his "designs" in the United States. (It seems Black is unaware of the good work that has already been done in this direction by Sidney Milkis, Gary Dean Best, Richard Vedder, and Lowell Gallaway. He has not mastered, and does not mention, Benjamin Anderson's *Economics and the Public Welfare: A Financial and Economic History of the United States, 1914–1946* [1949], which is still fundamental reading and still in print from Liberty Fund). Though Black's command of many episodes in Democratic Party politics is impressive, the central challenge of FDR's first two administrations was the Depression, and that is a subject that *Champion of Freedom* does not illuminate. Young Black was surely right that Roosevelt was a talented shaman. But while FDR was casting spells and exorcising demons, the Great Depression continued for twelve years in the United States. Other countries adopted sound policies and recovered rapidly. Here unemployment never fell below 12% until mid-1941. This high figure of 12% had been reached once before, briefly, in the worst previous crisis, the postwar depression of 1920. But that downturn lasted only a year. Never before, or since, has there been anything like this prolonged paralysis of the American economy. It was an experience of social disintegration and demoralization unparalleled in previous American history; and the long fear it instilled is only now being laid to rest, with the generation who lived through it.

No reader of Black's biography can doubt that Roosevelt was a man of prodigious personal courage and high intelligence. But as Black acknowledges, Roosevelt had not prepared himself to address a crisis of this kind. I would add that Roosevelt never put his powerful mind to work on it, because he was unwilling to shoulder the political risks of meeting it head on. Lincoln learned the art of war after he became president because he was determined to win; Roosevelt did not learn the art of economic recovery because he had other fish to fry. Calvin Coolidge and Herbert Hoover had paved the way for the Depression by pushing a high-price, high-wage economy. Recovery required that it be dismantled. Roosevelt could not liquidate it without riling large numbers of voters. Instead of mustering the public courage to do what economic recovery required, Roosevelt developed a spectacular, circus-like distraction. His programs ameliorated the catastrophe slightly, and very selectively; but they lengthened it indefinitely, so that the United States did not recover until the end of the Second World War.

Moreover, it was the Great Depression from 1930 to 1942 which set in motion the perpetual social revolution through which Americans have been living ever since, and which is now formalized and valorized in our public law as the "living constitution." One of the legacies of Roosevelt's domestic statesmanship has been to "constitutionalize" social experimentation on a national scale, conducted by permanent governmental institutions, and funded by taxation. From the outset these have been deliberately insulated from national, state, and local elections to an extent unprecedented in American public life prior to 1932. In *Champion of Freedom*, Black remains under the spell of his youthful illusion that Roosevelt somehow saved the United States from a European-style social democratic or Communist Left. It is true that the Great Depression was a cornucopia of miseries on which the Left could thrive, so long as it could be perpetuated. But no one on the Left, until Roosevelt, knew how to make the wretchedness of social and economic disintegration a stable platform for partisan power in American public life. Roosevelt should be given credit both for figuring out how that could be accomplished and for institutionalizing that platform in an ever-expanding welfare state. His wonderful contraptions transformed a fringe Left into the most powerful and long-lived social and political establishment in American history. The Machiavellian "effectual truth" of Roosevelt's statesmanship is precisely the creation and perpetuation of this novel regime. It has enjoyed an incumbency in the councils of power for some five decades, an accomplishment rivaled only by the Southern slavocracy before the Civil War.

In Conrad Black's judgment, during most of his lifetime the United States has been "without rivals but uncertain of its purpose." He argues that Roosevelt was responsible for bringing the United States to its present position in the world, and he has written *Champion of Freedom* to fortify American confidence and sense of purpose. He admires Roosevelt because Roosevelt was unshakably sure of his purpose. Black's grand illusion is that the United States can recapture its purpose through Roosevelt's shamanism, by co-opting and suborning the Left.

Roosevelt's legacy in domestic policy is a regime that stands or falls with the authority of its "living constitution," an authority that requires the electorate to submit to social experimentation by governors who can never be held responsible for the consequences of their experiments. To keep this regime going, the elements of the American constitutional order on which the economic, social, and political health of the United States depend, have been progressively neutralized, or weakened beyond recognition. It is clear that this "progress" now requires that judicial appointments be frozen until the presidency and the Congress are again in the hands of "progressives." This has become imperative because the regime of the "living con-

stitution" must expand, or it will die. To prevent that expansion, we must reinvigorate the constitutional forms and reassert the constitutional orders that Roosevelt's
admirers have demeaned, weakened, and corrupted during their long march toward
an American nanny-state. That cannot be done by citizens who fear to take on all
the establishments in the American polity that now depend for their livelihood and
prestige upon continued funding of the social-experimentation regime. Roosevelt
had the intellect for that kind of challenge, and he had sufficient courage. But he
never shared the purpose.

In *Democracy in America*, Alexis de Tocqueville offers us a useful epigraph to
Champion of Freedom. For Black too might well say that,

> [t]he ground I wish to cover is vast. It includes the greater part of the [actions] which
> are responsible for the changed state of the world. Such a subject is certainly beyond my
> strength, and I am far from satisfied with my own achievement. But if I have not suc-
> ceeded in the task I set myself, I hope I shall be credited with conceiving and pursuing
> the undertaking in a spirit which could make me worthy of success.

We should credit Lord Black for the magnanimity with which he has conducted
his undertaking, and welcome the great controversy that his book reopens.

The Endless Party

William Voegeli

(Winter 2004/05)

The epilogue of a presidential election is strangely like the opening chapter. Before the primaries there are several candidates. First this one is in the lead, then that one, and finally the party settles on the nominee. After the general election, the party that lost has to make sense of what went wrong. For a while one explanation gains favor, then another, and finally the party settles on the lesson to draw from defeat.

It's been only two months since John Kerry gave his concession speech, but the process of explaining the loss has already had phases. In the first and angriest one, the Democrats blamed the voters. Within two days of the election, Jane Smiley, Maureen Dowd, and Garry Wills (among others) fingered the electorate's stupidity and bigotry as the decisive factor. Although a candid expression of what lots of Democrats really do think, vilifying the people creates problems for a party that might like to win an election at some point in the future.

If it won't do to blame the voters, maybe the thing to do is blame the candidate. A variety of criticisms have been put forward. But few Democrats can work up the anger against Kerry that they directed at Al Gore after the 2000 election or Michael Dukakis in 1988. It's not that Kerry engendered more affection than his predecessors, or that he ran a much better campaign. Instead, the Democrats realize that it's pointless to keep blaming the candidate for the party's defeats.

Certainly, Kerry was not a perfect candidate. No one suitable for Mount Rushmore, however, was running in the Iowa caucuses. It's hard to see how any of the alternatives to Kerry—Howard Dean? Richard Gephardt? *Wesley Clark?*—would have done better in November. Political parties don't exist to nominate a new Pericles every four years. Their mission at the presidential level is to provide the institutional resources and political rationale that make it possible to win an election with a nominee who, inevitably, has flaws and makes mistakes.

The Democrats certainly did not lose because they (and allied groups, like MoveOn.org and America Coming Together) failed at the nuts-and-bolts level of finding their voters and getting them to polling places. John Kerry received 6 million more votes than Al Gore. The problem, as Matt Bai explained in the *New York Times Magazine*, is that Democrats have believed from the time of FDR right up to the 2000 election that a majority of Americans agreed with them, were *with* them—and thus they could not lose a high-turnout election.

But in 2004 they registered and brought to the polls every prospective voter they might realistically hope to find—and still lost. It is clear, Bai wrote, that "turnout alone is no longer enough to win a national election for Democrats. The next Democrat who wins will be the one who changes enough minds."

FINDING A NARRATIVE

By the process of elimination, then, a clear front-runner has emerged in the race to explain the 2004 election: the Democrats lost because they couldn't change enough minds. But then, they can't change minds if they don't know their own. Even those who argue that the lack of a clear message was the Kerry campaign's chief problem go on to say that it reflected a larger confusion in the Democratic Party and, indeed, in American liberalism.

According to Ryan Lizza in the *New Republic*, "the no-message critique is congealing into conventional wisdom." He argues that "the Kerry campaign had a laundry list of policy proposals, or, in the words of James Carville, a litany rather than a narrative." In his *Washington Post* column, Harold Meyerson wrote, "Cover the Democrats for any length of time and you become expert in campaigns that don't seem to be about anything. They have policies; Democrats are good at policies. But all too often the campaigns lack a message—a sense of what the candidate's about and what he aims to do." Ruy Teixeira, the co-author of 2002's *The Emerging Democratic Majority*, a title that sounds ever more forlorn, said in a post-election interview that, "Democrats have to have large and good ideas that people can recognize—ideas voters can sum up in a couple of sentences."

Many of the Democrats attracted to this explanation appear to have spent time in creative writing workshops. Everyone, suddenly, is talking about the crucial importance of the "narrative." "A narrative is the key to everything," according to Democratic pollster Stan Greenberg. Even Senator Kerry's brother, Cam, said, "There is a very strong John Kerry narrative that is about leadership, character, and trust. But it was never made central to the campaign."

The narrative of Democrats trying to find a narrative might be more promising, or at least more interesting, if it were fresher. The problem is the Democrats have lost five of the last seven presidential elections, not to mention control of Congress in 1994, and have talked about the urgent need to redefine and re-explain themselves after every one of those defeats. It has been *24 years* since that dim, unelectable extremist Ronald Reagan won a landslide against Jimmy Carter. A generation later, can there really be any promising ideas that haven't already been taken down from the shelf?

Here is what the Democrats have to show for two-and-a-half decades of introspection, besides a worsening win-loss record: after Walter Mondale lost 49 states in 1984, the Democratic Leadership Council was brought forth, conceived in panic and dedicated to the proposition that a politically viable party must become less liberal. In reaction, various groups and candidates have asserted that the prescription for Democratic victories is to become *more* liberal, to present the voters a choice, not an echo. It's hard to say who will win this tug-of-war, and twice as hard to see how either approach will reverse the Democrats' losing streak.

The only other nostrum has been that of the neo-liberals (once called "Atari Democrats"). To the extent their advice ever came into focus, it was that more liberalism or less liberalism, bigger or smaller government, was not the issue. Making government smarter—more effective, flexible, and responsive—was. Gary Hart nearly wrested the 1984 Democratic nomination from Walter Mondale by baiting him about being beholden to such interest groups as the AFL-CIO. The hot public affairs book after Bill Clinton's victory in 1992 was called *Reinventing Government*, now available in a remainder bin near you. Vice President Gore went on the David Letterman show with a hammer, a glass ashtray, and safety goggles to demonstrate something-or-other about how the Clinton Administration was making big government safe for democracy.

Most of the footprints left by neo-liberalism have been washed away; the rest are fading. Bill Clinton, in seeking a Third Way, disparaged the false dichotomy between big and limited government. With the passage of time, Clinton's triangulation looks less and less like a political philosophy and more like a personality disorder, the type afflicting a man who thinks *every* dichotomy is false. (As Charles Kesler has pointed out, Clinton apparently believed that there was a Third Way between fidelity and adultery, and between telling the truth and lying.) Good government is, in any case, too small and banal an idea to settle the problem of the proper size and scope of the welfare state, and too slender a thread to tie together a majority coalition for the Democratic Party.

ARCHITECTS, NOT HOUSEKEEPERS

If the Democrats' current attempt to figure out what they stand for is going to be more enlightening than their previous efforts, they will have to grapple with fundamental questions, not peripheral ones. The gravity of the situation calls for architects, not housekeepers. The 2004 campaign, after all, was a single episode in a much longer narrative, the story of American liberalism trying to define and advance itself. What's curious is that although intellectual clarity has never been liberalism's strength, for a very long time this confusion did not cause any political problems. Almost 40 years ago, the political philosopher Joseph Cropsey observed that while its contradictions were "damaging to liberalism as a theory, [they have] not hindered liberalism as a political movement." "It is instructive," he commented, "to note how wide is the gap between theoretical sufficiency and political efficacy."

The "no message" interpretation of the 2004 election claims that this gap has now closed, finally and completely: liberalism cannot become politically strong again until it stops being so theoretically weak. But Democrats need to recognize how far back, and how far down, liberalism's confusion goes. The notion that liberalism is fundamentally indecipherable was voiced frequently during the 1930s, when liberals absolutely dominated American politics. Raymond Moley, an erstwhile advisor to FDR, wrote of the New Deal in his memoirs, "To look upon these programs as the result of a unified plan, was to believe that the accumulation of stuffed snakes, baseball pictures, school flags, old tennis shoes, carpenter's tools, geometry books, and chemistry sets in a boy's bedroom could have been put there by an interior decorator." In 1940 another New Dealer, the economist Alvin Hansen, admitted, "I really do not know what the basic principle of the New Deal is. I know from my experience in the government that there are as many conflicting opinions among the people in Washington as we have in the country at large."

But the complaint that it's impossible to figure liberalism out has, until recently, typically been voiced by exasperated conservatives. For decades they have watched liberals rushing around with wheelbarrows and ladders, busy, busy, busy at building the welfare state. New programs are created, old ones expanded, urgent needs discovered and rediscovered. Conservatives marvel at this vast construction site and ask prosaic questions: What is this thing going to look like when it's done? How big is it going to be? How will we know when it's finished? And just in case there's any doubt that they *are* conservatives, how much is all this going to cost?

The replies have not been illuminating. Their major motif has been soaring humbug. In 1943 Archibald MacLeish expressed liberals' hopes about realizing the "America of the imagination":

> We have, and we know we have, the abundant means to bring our boldest dreams to pass—to create for ourselves whatever world we have the courage to desire. We have the metal and the men to take this country down, if we please to take it down, and to build it again as we please to build it. We have the tools and the skill and the intelligence to take our cities apart and put them together, to lead our roads and rivers where we please to lead them, to build our houses where we want our houses, to brighten the air, clean the wind, to live as men in this Republic, free men, should be living. We have the power and the courage and the resources of good-will and decency and common understanding . . . to create a nation such as men have never seen.

One could discount this as rhetoric, considering that MacLeish was a poet by trade. It is, however, language that working politicians relied on as well. President Lyndon Johnson's speech in 1964 calling for the creation of a Great Society "explained" it in these terms:

> The Great Society rests on abundance and liberty for all. It demands an end to poverty and racial injustice, to which we are totally committed in our time. But this is just the beginning.
> The Great Society is a place where every child can find knowledge to enrich his mind and to enlarge his talents. It is a place where leisure is a welcome chance to build and reflect, not a feared cause of boredom and restlessness. It is a place where the city of man serves not only the needs of the body and the demands of commerce but the desire for beauty and the hunger for community.

IS THERE A MASTER PLAN?

Parsing such blather might seem as pointless as it is cruel. But MacLeish and Johnson do reveal, inadvertently, truths about liberalism's meaning and its problems. First, conservatives' questions about the welfare state's ultimate size and cost are turned aside by rhetoric that emphasizes the processes and attitudes that go into building it. What's important, liberals say, is that the creation of government programs to promote social welfare be pursued in a vigorous, confident, optimistic manner, suffused with concern for the vulnerable and respect for the common man, unconstrained by the stifling precepts of the past. (Looking forward to an activist Kennedy presidency after the somnolent Eisenhower Administration, Arthur M. Schlesinger, Jr., wrote, "The '60s will probably be spirited, articulate, inventive, incoherent, turbulent, with energy shooting off wildly in all directions. Above all, there will be a sense of motion, of leadership, of hope.") Conservatives wonder if all this lofty talk is a smoke screen—they wonder, that is, whether there really are blueprints in a safe back at the central office, detailing the vast, Swedish-style welfare state that is liberalism's ultimate goal for America.

The answer is, probably not. If that answer is correct, it then raises this question: which would be more troubling—the existence or the absence of those blueprints? That is, should conservatives conclude that liberals pose a graver threat to self-government, freedom, and prosperity if they have an ambitious but hidden agenda, or if liberalism has no master plan at all because it is, ultimately and always, an adhocracy?

Liberals have a practical reason why they won't say what they ultimately want, and a theoretical reason why they can't say it. The practical reason is that any usably clear statement of what the welfare state should be would define not only a goal but a limit. Conceding that an outer limit exists, and stipulating a location for it, strengthens the hand of conservatives—with liberals having admitted, finally, that the welfare state can and should do only so much, the argument now, the conservatives will say, is over just how much that is.

Keeping open, permanently, the option for the growth of the welfare state reflects the belief that the roster of human needs and aspirations to which the government should minister is endless. Any attempt to curtail it would be arbitrary and wrong. (In his concession speech after losing to Ronald Reagan in 1984, Walter Mondale listed the groups he had devoted his political career to assisting: "the poor, the unemployed, the elderly, the handicapped, the helpless, and the *sad*" [emphasis added].)

This gets us to the theoretical reason why liberalism cannot incorporate a limiting principle or embrace an ultimate destination. Given humankind's long history of sorrows, most people would consider securing "abundance and liberty for all," ending poverty and achieving racial justice, a pretty good day's work. For LBJ it was, astoundingly, "just the beginning."

Liberal intellectuals who drew up the blueprint for the Great Society regarded peace, prosperity, and justice as achievements that were not merely modest but troubling. They lived with a strange dread—that if Americans' lives became too comfortable the people would decide that the country had been reformed enough, thank you, even though liberals knew there was still—always—work to be done. In 1943 the National Public Resources Board, which FDR hoped would chart the course for a renewed, enlarged post-war New Deal, advocated the recognition of various welfare rights, including the right to "rest, recreation and adventure." In a speech he gave to the Americans for Democratic Action in 1948, the group's first chairman, Wilson Wyatt, rejected "the view that government's only responsibility is to prevent people from starving or freezing to death. We believe it is the function of government to lift the level of human existence. It is the job of government to widen the chance for development of individual personalities."

HOW SHALL WE LIVE?

The fear that liberalism would be thanked for its service and given a gold watch became more acute as the American economy soared after World War II. In 1957, the year before John Kenneth Galbraith published *The Affluent Society*, Arthur Schlesinger tried to redefine liberalism's mission for such a society. He wrote that the New Deal's establishment of the welfare state and Keynesian management of the economy heralded the completion of the work of "quantitative liberalism." Its logical and necessary successor should be "qualitative liberalism," which would "oppose the drift into the homogenized society. It must fight spiritual unemployment as [quantitative liberalism] once fought economic unemployment. It must concern itself with the quality of popular culture and the character of lives to be lived in our abundant society."

To speak of *lifting* the level of human existence suggests that there are higher and lower levels of human existence. Such thoughts imply a certain congruence between modern liberalism and the worldview of classical philosophy and the great monotheistic religions. But, of course, the rejection of those traditions has been crucial to modern liberalism, and to modernism generally. Plato poses, as the central question of philosophy, how shall we live? The liberal response, expressed most directly by John Stuart Mill, is that the question is unanswerable, and the practical imperatives of politics cannot be put on hold forever while philosophers debate it. Therefore, the only realistic answer, one that reflects both the need to find a way to live together and the futility of ascertaining the meaning of the good life, is that we should all live however we want, constrained only by the need to choose a "lifestyle" that does not interfere with anyone else's living the way *he* wants to live.

In *A Theory of Justice* (1971), John Rawls argued that "democracy in judging each other's aims is the foundation of self-respect in a well-ordered society." Rawls goes on to say that the person whose aims consist of counting blades of grass should not be denigrated but supported—that is, both praised and publicly subsidized. "Different strokes for different folks" is a meager philosophy, but also a coherent one. If liberals were content to leave it at that, they would at least have one large idea voters could sum up in a couple of sentences.

But they have never been content to leave it at that. Liberalism has never found a way to regard the "character of lives to be lived in our abundant society" with indifference, in the good sense of being tolerant, for fear of also being indifferent in the bad sense of being callous. The social critic inside every liberal cannot resist berating other people's unsatisfactory lifestyles—some are merely inane, others are actually menacing. Fifty years ago this scorn was directed at suburban split-levels. Today the target is evangelical churches. Meanwhile, the social worker inside every liberal cannot resist treating these unfortunate lifestyle choices as problems to be solved.

How does liberalism square this circle, embracing relativism while declaring that millions of non-liberals are "spiritually unemployed?" (It's hard to imagine anyone being more spiritually unemployed than Rawls's grass-counter.) The moral standpoint from which liberalism passes judgment is one it derives from John Dewey, for whom the highest imperative was "growth." According to political scientist Robert Horwitz, Dewey looked to "the bright promise of an evolutionary understanding of human potentialities, a view which presents boundless possibilities for development." The point of growth is more growth; the only standard by which we judge the direction of past growth is whether it facilitates or stymies future growth. It is in this vein that Johnson spoke of a Great Society where the government will enrich minds, enlarge talents, and concern itself with monitoring our leisure hours to make sure we are constructive and reflective, not bored and restless. It is an agenda for which prosperity, liberty, and justice are "just the beginning," and one which, constantly advancing the constantly evolving goal of personal growth, can have no end.

Bill Clinton was fond of saying that character is "a journey, not a destination." But to leave home without a destination, convinced that the very idea of a destination is arbitrary and false, is to embark on a "journey" that will be no different from just wandering around. How, then, shall we live? The entirety of liberalism's answer is, according to Rawls, that it is better to play chess than checkers: "human beings enjoy the exercise of their realized capacities (their innate or trained abilities), and this enjoyment increases the more the capacity is realized or the greater its complexity." Humans can rescue their lives from meaninglessness by striving, however they pass their days, to employ more rather than fewer of their talents, finding new ones and expanding known ones, to the sole purpose of being able to enlarge them still further, endlessly. We have seen the future, and it's an adult education seminar, where ever-greater latitude is afforded to ever-smaller souls, and where freedom means nothing higher than the care and feeding of personal idiosyncrasies.

As an ethical precept this position is risible. As the basis for social criticism, it is infuriating. *This* is the standard by which liberals judge us to be spiritually unemployed, the basis on which they are going to lift the level of our existence? Many Democrats lament that Republicans have been successful in getting working-class Americans to vote "against their own interests," by stressing social issues like abortion and gay marriage. Thomas Frank wrapped an entire bestseller, *What's the Matter with Kansas?* (2004), around this idea. It's a "false consciousness" diagnosis that betrays rather than describes the Democrats' problem: the smug assumption that *we* know, far better than they do themselves, the "real interests" of people who live in dorky places and went to schools no one has heard of.

WHAT ARE DEMOCRATS AGAINST?

As a political philosophy, the belief that "it is the job of government to widen the chance for development of individual personalities" is not merely lame and insulting, but dangerous. The endless widening and development of our personalities will require and legitimize the endless widening and development of our government. The threat goes beyond taxes, spending, borrowing, and regulating that increase without limit. It culminates in a therapeutic nanny state that corrupts both its wardens and its wards. Convinced that they are intervening, constantly and pervasively, to assist the growth of people who would otherwise stagnate, the enlighteners don't need coercion to enfold the people in a soft totalitarianism. The objects of this therapy, meanwhile, may grow accustomed to it, and ultimately prefer being cared for to being free; or conclude that being free has no value apart from being cared for.

Lyndon Johnson gave one other memorable speech in 1964. At a campaign rally in Providence he climbed onto his car, grabbed a bullhorn, and summed up his political philosophy: "I just want to tell you this—we're in favor of a lot of things and we're against mighty few." The Democrats' problem is not that they, like *Seinfeld*, are a show about nothing. It's that they are a show about everything, or anything. (At one point, the Kerry-for-President website referred to 79 separate federal programs he wanted to create or expand.)

Ruy Teixeira says that after 2004, "The bigger question is: what do the Democrats stand for?" Here's a better and bigger question still: what do the Democrats stand against? Tell us, if indeed it's true, that Democrats don't want to do for America what social democrats have done for France or Sweden. Tell us that the stacking of one government program on top of the other is going to stop, if indeed it will, well short of a public sector that absorbs half the nation's income and extensively regulates what we do with the other half. Explain how the spirit of live-and-let-live applies, if indeed it does, to everyone equally—to people who take family, piety, and patriotism seriously, not merely to people whose lives and outlooks are predicated on regarding them ironically.

Until those questions are answered, until Americans have confidence about the limits liberalism will establish and observe, it's hard to see when the Democratic narrative will again have a happy ending.

Involuntary Associations

Mark Blitz

(Fall 2005)

Michael Walzer's new book, *Politics and Passion: Toward a More Egalitarian Liberalism*, belongs to a vigorous debate among liberal political theorists that has bypassed most conservatives. Even when we discuss similar issues, our orientation, references, and concerns differ. Indeed, the book reminds us, usefully, how a large segment of the liberal-Left now talks.

Walzer's thoughts come from someone whose independence and intelligence make him a force in his own right, however; so his arguments are not merely emblematic but individual. They eschew concocted illustrations and technical analysis to concentrate instead on major themes and what he believes are factual examples. Unlike thousands of younger liberal-Left theorists, moreover, he does not feel obliged to trace his every thought, faithful or transgressive, to father John Rawls, as if he were a maiden honoring the potent Maypole in convoluted dance.

Walzer's book stems from his well-known (in his circles) 1990 paper, "The Communitarian Critique of Liberalism." The book has three main purposes. One is to reassert the importance of groups and group identity, especially of what Walzer calls "involuntary associations" in liberal democracies. We are not born as isolated individuals, but with belongings and attachments. A second is to use this idea to press for the greater equality for which, as a democratic socialist, he always has argued, because inequality attaches not only to isolated individuals, but also to the associations that help to define them. A third is to criticize the excesses of the liberal "deliberative democracy" movement that he correctly identifies as the American domestication of Habermas's abstraction. If we take these elements together, especially the first and third, we find ourselves defending some of what is irrational or passionate about politics, as opposed to cold, individual calculation and deliberation. Hence, *Politics and Passion*.

Involuntary associations are groups into which we are born, such as ethnic or religious groups, not ones we choose. Because we all are born into such groups, the notion that in liberal societies every association is joined voluntarily is for Walzer a myth or, at least, an overstatement. Being born into such groups affects one's equality because some groups face a tougher time than others: "No Irish need apply." It is, therefore, not enough to equalize people's chances as individuals, because they never are seen as themselves alone but also as blacks, Jews, women, and so on. More than this, the liberal picture is problematic or, indeed, unfair for groups that need total or at least significant control to reproduce their way of life, groups that cannot allow their members to act or conceive of themselves as independent individuals. Walzer proposes to give groups greater, but not illiberally stultifying, strength by having government channel cradle-to-grave life cycle services through them, providing more to the poorer groups. He hopes or presumes that this "meat and potatoes multiculturalism" will make us more equal.

Walzer's argument rests on what he thinks of as sociology, that is, general views of how groups work and of liberalism's effect on them. He does not, however, actually examine, say, today's Mormons or Amish, the path taken by immigrant Jews or Italians, or the current developments among different Hispanic, Asian, or South Asian populations in the United States or elsewhere. Moreover, when he mentions the groups that he thinks are poor and stigmatized in today's America—blacks and Native Americans—he does not even begin to try to account for the wide disparities in achievement among blacks, the actual record of ethnic-neighborhood empowerment in Lyndon Johnson's Great Society, the effects on Native American poverty of casino wealth, differences among tribes, or a host of other concrete matters. The absence of facts makes for unconvincing sociology.

Walzer's argument also rests on a rather extreme view of liberalism. As he interprets (or somewhat caricatures even) Rawls's version, liberals believe or hope that each of us someday will be a completely independent individual, the absolute arbiter of his own life-plan, creator of his own self, all of whose associations are voluntary. The Supreme Court's infamous opinion in *Planned Parenthood v. Casey* (1992) expresses a version of this view, as it has migrated from rococo feminist fantasy to vulgar law school cartoon: "At the heart of liberty is the right to define one's own concept of existence, of meaning, of the universe, and of the mystery of human life."

To this radical-feminist, academic-poetic, or vaguely democratic-Nietzschean dream, Walzer opposes the reality of his involuntary groups. The effect is similar to what occurred when liberals opposed an idealized bureaucracy, which they pretended was real, to actual markets in their ugliest forms, in order to show how much better government is than markets. It also is similar to the way that some conservatives oppose an idealized free market, which they pretend is real, to actual government in its greatest stupidities, in order to show how worthless anything is but markets and the motive of wealth. Walzer takes a liberalism more bereft of attachment than anything Locke and the American Founders defended, Tocqueville described, or that one actually sees today and opposes to it an overly airbrushed version of group definition and control. This exposes some of his opponents' blind spots and promotes some of his own strengths, but the overall result is misleading.

In a sense then, much of Walzer's book is a solution—greater equality through government-subsidized meat-and-potatoes multiculturalism—in search of a problem. He does not show why our current regime of individual choice does not produce appropriate loyalty to appropriate groups; dig down to the specific levels where group stigma actually may remain damaging; or make a case why we should be unhappy that life in the tolerant United States is difficult for totalizing communities. Oddly, he therefore never describes just what about inequality, and how much of it, is harmful and, thus, why his solutions are best. Perhaps some combination of school choice and decreased regulation, from the Right, and higher taxes for the very rich, from the Left, would do the trick.

If one does not agree that Walzer makes involuntary groups seem more desirable than they are, one should at least agree that his discussion of them is vague, not just factually but conceptually. What are they exactly, and who speaks for them? Sometimes he has in mind groups as broad as race and gender. Other times he has in mind groups as narrow as the American Amish. Occasionally he has in mind religion in general, orthodox groups in Israel, or a faith such as Catholicism.

This conceptual vagueness often makes it difficult to know what to make of his argument. As Walzer recognizes, some of these groups control their members' lives more than others, and their leaders want to keep it so. Why, however, should an Amish child be a pawn of his elders' wishes, or sacrificed to the small-group, small-town sentimentalities of cosmopolitan academics? If the child's group, with all its power, and with a government such as ours that is not bent on destroying or even very much controlling it, is insufficient to hold his complete loyalty, why should we be responsible for helping the group's leaders or spokesmen maintain their dominance? Walzer would, for the sake of furthering some liberal practices (equal education of men and women, for example) not allow state subsidies to groups that violated these practices. Why should we subsidize them in the first place, or allow them to deviate from effecting equal rights? In his wish to recognize the reality of associations, Walzer sometimes is too forgiving of illiberalism.

If we focus on large groups such as race, gender, and faith broadly defined, the analysis is odd in a different way. It is, as we said, unclear why any of our sympathies should rest with, say, those particular Muslims (for what else could Walzer mean when he says that "the group" wants this or that?) who want more and more control rather than with those who long for liberation. Unclear also is why we should allow the self-proclaimed spokesperson for blacks or women to tell us what the group wants and then encourage members to receive services, or even define themselves, primarily in that way. In these cases, we lack the excuse of the more organic totality of small, particular, churches and neighborhoods. We lack as well any good argument why someone should (or does) think of herself primarily as a woman and not a Catholic, lawyer, Irish American, and so on. Walzer himself notes this, but this does not make his argument more precise. For if we are compounded from many groups, is not the individual who associates voluntarily the primary fact, even when she chooses to dwell within the ties into which she is born?

Although we belong from the start to certain associations (and have certain talents), some of them are easier to shrug off than others. It is easy enough to stop going to church, to move out of town, to choose a better or worse job than one's parents did, and, except if one is an academic, to vote for a Republican or marry one. These free steps may require gumption and luck but not prodigies of spirit or talent. It is, by contrast, not yet possible to become Heifetz or Einstein at will, although not so hard to become better educated. Race and gender are impossible (now) to change completely, but a single race is in any event an increasingly difficult category to apply to any individual, and even gender already can be changed, externally. Should we, then, determine ourselves more by what we cannot change—talents and their best use, as well as original associations—or by what we can? Walzer would like us to be loyal to the groups that (helped) make us what we are, whether we chose them or not. There is something to this fidelity, of course, but he does not succeed in showing when and where our involuntary ties should guide us more than our voluntary ones. A significant discussion of natural limits, not merely historical ones, is struggling to take flight within an argument that, however intelligent, is overly determined by his political commitments and intellectual audience.

The meat-and-potatoes part of Walzer's desire to enhance groups' standing also is vague. He may have in mind targeted welfare (faith-based initiatives directed only at those of one's own faith?), but welfare should be self-overcoming, not perpetual. He surely cannot mean laws that require that one earn one's living in a particular place or be married or buried only by one's original church. The harmful illiberalism of such suggestions vastly outweighs their putative value in dealing with a vaguely stated problem. He may have in mind vouchers or other mechanisms that advance private schooling: he puzzles about what the state's citizenship requirements allow it to demand of schools' curricula. But he does not support state funding of private schools in so many words. In any event, a voucher one can use only for schools appropriate to what the law determines is your child's faith, race, or other group-identity also would be breathtakingly illiberal. The less restrictive "conservative" measures of individually controlled school vouchers, faith-based welfare, and greater federalism within an open economy strike a better balance between advancing liberal freedom and protecting mediating institutions.

One sees in Walzer's book an attempt to complicate the liberal notion of what is right and good by introducing certain elements of "one's own." This is healthy within limits, for he recognizes and seeks to preserve the importance of religious, traditional, and other involuntary attachments. The major difficulty with his discussion, however, is that he does not examine or elaborate the argument for natural rights, or examine with care what makes our individual choices, or the choices of groups to which we belong, worthwhile. Rather than defending natural rights, he makes the state's liberalizing and enlightening interests rest on citizenship. He then uses citizenship requirements to oppose cultural ties he finds offensive. But democratic citizenship is too thin a reed on which to rest our freedoms. The sheer fact of equal voting in a state does not by itself require very much liberalism or enlightenment, especially if more and more choices are made through groups that may not be very democratic. Walzer's approach loses or at least covers up the purpose of democratic citizenship, namely, the expansion and protection of equal rights. My justification for alleviating your moral and intellectual degradation is not limited to the fact that we will be voting together.

Liberal rights and liberal regimes are not merely things that we happen to prefer, to which illiberal groups that operate in their midst must accommodate themselves, and we to them. There are reasons that we choose liberalism and that justify our (we hope responsibly executed) wish to liberalize the illiberal. These reasons are inseparable from individuals who stand apart from every group, not "sociologically" but in their rational freedom and pride. Liberalism attempts to elevate our attachment to our own free self into a rational understanding of the rights that constitute this self, and the character and competition that best develop and satisfy it. However much the individual belongs to associations, he is freely in tension with them, potentially more cosmopolitan and normally more self-interested. The ethnic, religious, and neighborhood groups that help convey our self-interest and develop our intellectual and moral independence are healthiest when they abet, but do not seek to replace, the natural, individual ground of self-interested satisfaction, or the rational ground of cosmopolitan openness.

These points may seem too theoretical, even if one largely agrees with them. They do make a practical difference, however. Liberal democracy will not sustain itself if it does not believe itself to be rationally defensible; attempts to "thicken" it that occlude the clarity of its principles—that depart too far from individual rights—are unnecessarily risky. They incorrectly make it look too arbitrary or too low. Because Walzer concentrates on groups and citizenship, moreover, he pays too little attention to the content of liberal character. (His few remarks do not constitute an argument.) The tolerant, industrious, decent, and responsible individual is a worthy goal, however—not just a liberal necessity. The fact that his attachments are voluntary in principle will square well enough with the loyalty and good sense to which his character will dispose him in practice. This is not to say, however, that the truth of natural rights is sufficient on its own to distinguish in each case genuine happiness from false contentment.

A Left-Handed Salute

Wilfred M. McClay

(Summer 2007)

A short, loosely organized collection of occasional essays, *The Intellecctuals and the Flag* makes for a surprisingly interesting and valuable book, well worth reading and pondering. Sociologist and radical activist Todd Gitlin, who has been a figure in the American Left since his Vietnam-era days in Students for a Democratic Society (SDS), has made a serious effort to reflect on the failures of the American Left since the 1960s. The criticisms he puts forward here, which are inevitably self-criticisms in part, are unsparing and penetrating, made all the more memorable by his unacademic, direct, and often epigrammatic style.

Gitlin's criticism is relentless, and will win him few new friends on the Left, though it will likely energize the many enemies he already has there. He sees a story rich with irony, in which it has been precisely the Left's most triumphant expressions in contemporary American life that led it into the spiritual wasteland in which it now finds itself. And for this lost condition, he believes, the Left has only itself to blame. It embraced the smug disassociation from existing society epitomized in the sweeping call by émigré philosopher and '60s hero Herbert Marcuse for a "Great Refusal" of the confining ideals and crass manipulations of the modern capitalist political economy. But the embrace of Marcuse's influential but ill-defined slogan has amounted in practice to a "great withdrawal," a narcissistic retreat into self-proclaimed "marginality," an obsession with ever more minute forms of identity politics and the infinite "problematizing" of "truth," a reflexive opposition to America and the West, and an immurement in "theories" whose radicalism is so pure that they never quite touch down to earth—follies all underwritten and protected by the perquisites and comforts of academia.

Gitlin argues that the results may have benefited individual leftists, who have feathered their own nests quite nicely by fusing radicalism and academic careerism, but they have been unambiguously disastrous for the Left as a political force outside the academy. "If we had a manual," Gitlin remarks, "it would be called, *What is Not to Be Done*" The Great Refusal turns out to have been little more than "a shout from an ivory tower," an advertisement of futility that was unable to conceal the despair, paralysis, and general contempt, including self-contempt, that lay behind it.

One of the many negative side effects of this Refusal has been a summary rejection of patriotic belief. There is no denying this, and Gitlin, to his credit, does not try. Indeed, this self-imposed restriction and its malign consequences are the deep subject of the book. He provides an honest account of the reasons for his generation's disenchantment with patriotism—an account that helps explain why, even now, the term almost never escapes the lips even of mainstream liberal Democrats without being prefaced by the indignant words "impugning" and "my." For Gitlin's generation, the "generation for whom 'the war' meant Vietnam and perhaps always will," it could be said that the "most powerful public emotion in our lives was *rejecting* patriotism." Patriotism became viewed as, at best, a pretext, and at worst, an abandonment of thought itself. It became of interest only in so far as it entered into calculations of political advantage. Far from being a sentiment that one might feel with genuine warmth and intelligent affection, it was merely a talisman, which, if used at all, served chiefly to neutralize its usefulness as a weapon in the hands of others, by making it into a strictly personal preference that others were forbidden to question: "my" patriotism.

It may be that this state of affairs will continue, at least for a certain segment of Gitlin's generation. One reason the Iraq War has been so galvanizing to that segment is that it offered badly needed reconfirmation of the very premises around which they had built their adult lives. And let it be said that those premises are not completely cockeyed. The claims of the nation-state should never be regarded as absolute and all-encompassing. To do so would violate the nature of the American experiment itself, which understands government as accountable to higher imperatives, which we express in various ways: in the language of natural rights, for example, or of "one nation under God." The possibility of dissent against the nation for the sake of the nation is built into that formulation. The dissenters are right about that.

But by the same token, the claims of critical detachment have their limits, both practically and morally. For one thing, there needs to be a clear and responsible statement of what those higher imperatives are. And even then, the habitual resort to the ideal of dissent "against the nation for the nation" can easily become indistinguishable in practice from yet another manifestation of the Great Refusal, in which the second "nation" is a purely imaginary one to be "achieved"—and the "troops" one "supports" are entirely distinct from the actual causes for which they are risking their lives, and such "support" shows no respect for the series of conscious choices that made them into "troops" rather than civilians. When we make our commitments to one another entirely contingent, then we have made no commitments at all. There will always be reasons to hold back, always sufficient reasons to say No, if the standard against which one judges the nation is an ahistorical and abstract and imaginary one, and the only consideration in view is the purity of one's own individual position.

For the Left, with its traditional emphasis upon *fraternité*, or the cultivation of human solidarity and communal values, such realities are particularly difficult to reconcile with an ethos of limitless criticism. To say that we are a part of one another— or even to acknowledge that man is by nature a "political animal," thinking here of Aristotle and not of James Carville—is not merely to say that we should deliberate together; it is also to say that, at some point, the discussion ceases and we make a commitment to one another to act together. Furthermore, it is to say that we cannot sustain serious, demanding, and long-term commitments to one another if those commitments are regarded as provisional and easily revoked for light and transient causes. We make an agreement and we agree to stand by it. Call it a contract, a covenant, or a constitution, it is the same general kind of commitment, a commitment not merely of the intellect but also of the will.

For any freely organized political undertaking, this vital qualification presents a difficulty. But for the Left, it becomes a profound dilemma. It is no accident, if I may put it this way, that the more attractive elements of the Left also tend to be the most schismatic and ineffectual, while the uglier ones tend to be the most disciplined and unified, in which solidarity becomes a byword for the silent obedience of the herd.

Gitlin's generation accomplished much more than it wanted to by "demystifying" the nation and popularizing the idea that all larger solidarities are merely pseudo-communities invented and imposed by nation-building elites. By doing so, it also made "the nation" into an entity unable to command the public's loyalty and support—and willingness to endure sacrifices—for much of anything at all, including the kind of far-reaching domestic transformations that are the Left's most cherished aspirations. The hermeneutic of suspicion knows no boundaries, so that what is true for war-making is also true for Social Security or national health insurance. The fact is, the Left needs the nation, too, and needs it all the more in an era in which the cause of international socialism is but a faint and discredited memory. The nation is all the Left has left, whether it knows it or not.

Along with a small number of others on the Left, Gitlin now recognizes this fact, and recognizes that it was a grievous error to have abandoned patriotism. His book is an effort to inch his way back toward an embrace of the national idea, without which the Left has nowhere to go, but to do so in ways that carefully avoid the embrace of "conservative" ideas of patriotism.

The abandonment of patriotism, he says, was a sure recipe for political irrelevance: how can one hope to sway an electorate toward which one has all but declared one's comprehensive disdain? Now there is another reason. The events of 9/11 convinced him that the civilized world faces a deadly threat and that the exercise of American power in the world is not always an unmitigated evil—it may even be desirable and necessary. He was one of the many New Yorkers who flew the American flag out his window after 9/11 (though by his own admission he did not keep it up very long). He supported the invasion of Afghanistan, and sees the necessity of a continuing American struggle against the forces of jihadism.

Perhaps, he argues, there can be a "patriotic left" that stands somewhere "between Cheney and Chomsky," here borrowing the words of Michael Tomasky, in much the same way that the anti-Communist liberals of the '40s and '50s stood between, say, McCarthy and Stalin. Such a Left would be critical—it being the Left's business, in his view, to be critical—but critical "from the inside out," always looking for possibilities for genuine improvement rather than lapsing into empty (or dangerous) gestures of condemnation. It would recognize and affirm the fact that one inevitably takes one's stand as an American.

Such a formulation recalls the ideal—put forward some two decades ago by Michael Walzer—of "connected criticism," which would acknowledge that no one has the ability to stand entirely outside his society or context, and that the ideal of the independent intellectual has to be balanced against the idea of intellect working within a cultural context for the common good. Gitlin's version of this is somewhat more robust; he is even inclined to praise patriotism as a kind of "community of mutual aid," as opposed to the sort of "symbolic displays," "catechisms," or "self-congratulation" that pass for patriotism. But the qualifiers are all important. Patriotism is never a blank check, and it is always undertaken with a certain provisionality and pragmatism in mind.

His formulation has many admirable aspects. For example, there is this statement: "We are free to imagine our country any way we like, but we are not free to deny that it *is* our country." Or this: "It is with effort and sacrifice, not pride or praise, that citizens honor the democratic covenant." Or his superb analysis of why what is called "community" is, in practice, often nothing more than a new form of insularity: "The crucial difference here is between a community, consisting of people crucially *un*like ourselves, and a network, or 'lifestyle enclave,' made up of people *like* ourselves. Many 'communities' in the sense commonly overused today . . . are actually networks, a fact that the term disguises." Precisely right.

But there are also troubling aspects to Gitlin's formulations, which make one suspect that his rethinking has stopped well short of its goal. One finds far too many overtones of the past, of a patriotism that can turn on a dime and see itself as "against the nation for the nation," and as such may not have the reliability or resiliency to withstand tribulations and crises, or the power to summon the nation to great enterprises that might be costly, difficult, and lengthy. Gitlin himself places "sacrifice" at the center of "lived patriotism," and asserts that where there is no sacrifice (as, in his view, there has been none in the global war on terrorism as the Bush Administration has prosecuted it), there is no genuine patriotism.

I think he is partly on target here, but only partly, for he reduces the effect to the cause. As Ernest Renan and other theorists of nationalism have insisted, the nation is constituted in large measure by the shared *memories* of sufferings and sacrifices past, sufferings and sacrifices that make the present generation willing to endure sufferings and sacrifices of its own—not only to keep what it has, but to keep faith with those who have come before. The role of memory is crucial; that is to say, the role of history. Abraham Lincoln's First Inaugural Address, with its invocation of the "mystic chords of memory," or the Gettysburg Address, with its gesture toward the "honored dead" as a source of inspiration and a spirit of rededication, are paradigmatic examples of such uses of the memory of suffering. We are willing to sacrifice in part because we see that the sacrifices of those who came before us have been honored, and we too wish to be honored, as they are. But what if those who came before us cease to be honored—what then? Here Gitlin has a problem, because his view of American history is so bleak, with so few bright spots, and his contempt for the shallowness of American patriotism at present is so deep, that there hardly seems to be anything worthy of one's sacrifice to be found in either place.

Moreover, it is not sacrifice itself, but the *willingness* to sacrifice for the sake of the cause of the nation, that is the crucial element in the makeup of patriotism. More than once Gitlin cites his admiration for the passengers of Flight 93 on September 11, 2001, whose airborne rebellion probably saved the White House or the Capitol building from destruction. "They hadn't waited for authorities to define their patriotism for them," Gitlin remarks. "They were not satisfied with symbolic displays. It dawned on me that patriotism was the sum of such acts." Elsewhere Gitlin praises them as "activist passengers" engaging in "mutual aid."

But this is all surely wrong, and a misappropriation of the meaning of their acts. We will never know exactly what thoughts went through their minds, but one rather doubts that the question, "What would be the genuinely patriotic thing to do?" was one of them. They did not "become" patriotic by choosing terms for their death that served the cause of the nation. No, we honor them because they were willing to act on highly imperfect knowledge, in a terrifying situation very like the fog of war, except that it was inflicted suddenly on civilians minding their own business. They behaved in ways that proved their love of country; in their willingness to sacrifice for it, they acted on a patriotism that was already *in* them.

There is much to like and even admire in this book, and the fact of its appearance is encouraging. But Gitlin remains, as he always has been, a man of the Left, and no one should underestimate the depth of his contempt for almost everything and everyone right of center. The book is very much in the tradition of criticism of the Left *from* the Left, à la Christopher Lasch and Russell Jacoby and before them Richard Hofstadter and Reinhold Niebuhr. It is written for readers who are committed to the general positions of the Left—the tacit assumption being that only the Left has ever offered anything worth criticizing, and that the Right is concerned with little more than greed and hypocrisy and the naked exercise of conscienceless power by unaccountable elites.

And yet one is almost willing to set that aside, given the usefulness of the book's principal aim. Almost everyone, even those on the Right, ought to be able to agree with the desirability of Gitlin's stated goal of a "new start for intellectual life on the left." God knows we would all benefit from the emergence of a more mature, more thoughtful, more responsible, and more constructive Left than the one we have now.

But it is harder to set aside Gitlin's unusually poisonous and quite unhinged diatribes against George W. Bush—"this lazy ne'er-do-well, this duty-shirking know-nothing who deceived and hustled his way to power," whose rise showed that "you could drink yourself into one stupor after another, for decades and . . . come out on top" through "a bloodless coup d'etat"—words which are, alas, illustrative of the steep decline of public discourse that he otherwise decries. Gitlin lowers his book by not only lapsing into but luxuriating in such invective. He laments that "rarely does a fair, thorough, intelligible public debate take place on any significant political subject" in contemporary America. Too true. Yet it is hard to see how character assassination of the president contributes to rectifying this. Indeed, we see a growing decay today in the very idea of a loyal opposition—a much better term than "connected critic," by the way, because it contains the concept of loyalty—the maintenance of which is central to the work of a civilized democracy.

The word "loyalty" itself has, like patriotism, been reduced to one of the impermissibles of discourse, conjuring as it does images of "loyalty oaths" and other constraints upon conscience and freedom of thought and expression. But there is no enduring solidarity, large or small, without loyalty, a form of commitment that endures in and out of season, and serves to lift oneself out of oneself, and acknowledges that there are imperatives and duties in life beyond the range of one's own desires and inclinations. No one is talking about blind loyalty, and loyalty, like all virtues, has its limits. But it is an indispensable virtue, and anyone who wants to speak compellingly about patriotism cannot afford to be mute on the subject.

Gitlin has not quite come to terms with the fact—though to his credit, he does not ignore it—that this country he professes to love, or seeks to find an acceptable rationale for loving, has an alarming propensity for electing to high office people of whom he does not approve. Perhaps the first step in fostering a more genuine patriotism is being willing to take such an electorate seriously, and not to dismiss its patriotism as shallow, insubstantial, and manipulable. One might also take seriously the motives behind the soldiers, sailors, and Marines that serve the nation, men and women who most certainly make sacrifices for the common good as they understand it, and deserve at least a word or two in this book.

Still, I do not want to end on a negative note. *The Intellectual and the Flag* offers penetrating, even devastating, criticisms of the intellectual state of the Left, and of the academic world that it dominates. It is a courageous book, and, with all its faults, an honest one. One hopes that it is not this talented author's last word on the subject.

Flights of Fancy

Steven F. Hayward

(Summer 2010)

Peter Beinart has terrible timing. One of the iconoclastic young things the *New Republic* generates with regularity, he ranks among the handful of left-of-center thinkers like Paul Berman and Michael Walzer who engage in self-criticism of liberalism. In the aftermath of John Kerry's loss in the 2004 election, Beinart took to the pages of the *New Republic*, where he was then editor, with a long essay entitled "A Fighting Faith" that connected Kerry's haplessness with liberalism's broader fecklessness about foreign policy. Unfortunately, the Democratic Party was by then in thrall to MoveOn.org and Michael Moore, heirs of Henry Wallace, who minimized—when they did not outright deny—the significance of the jihadist threat to the Western world. Liberals need to wrest the party back, Beinart argued, like the early Cold War liberals had done in the late 1940s:

> Islamist totalitarianism—like Soviet totalitarianism before it—threatens the United States and the aspirations of millions across the world. And, as long as that threat remains, defeating it must be liberalism's north star. Methods for defeating totalitarian Islam are a legitimate topic of internal liberal debate. But the centrality of the effort is not. The recognition that liberals face an external enemy more grave, and more illiberal, than George W. Bush should be the litmus test of a decent left.
>
> Today, the war on terrorism is partially obscured by the war in Iraq, which has made liberals cynical about the purposes of U.S. power. But, even if Iraq is Vietnam, it no more obviates the war on terrorism than Vietnam obviated the battle against communism. Global jihad will be with us long after American troops stop dying in Falluja and Mosul. And thus, liberalism will rise or fall on whether it can become, again, what [Arthur] Schlesinger [Jr.] called "a fighting faith."

The article created a sensation and naturally produced furious argument on the Left along with a book contract for Beinart. Like many in the *New Republic* circle, he supported the Iraq War at the outset, but by the time his book *The Good Fight: Why Liberals—and Only Liberals—Can Win the War on Terror and Make America Great Again* arrived in 2008, Beinart along with a majority of Americans had soured on the Iraq War. Although *The Good Fight* repeated and deepened his critique of the Left's indifference to radical Islam and congenital aversion to the use of American power, his overall argument was necessarily more defensive.

Now a senior fellow with the Council on Foreign Relations and the New America Foundation, Beinart has doubled-down with *The Icarus Syndrome: A History of American Hubris*, tracing the roots of the Iraq mistake to a generation-skipping hubris that has produced an epicycle of disastrous foreign policy overreach. Once again his timing is off. The Iraq War has turned around, and doesn't look as hopeless as it did four years ago. In his new book he notes that the Korean War was very unpopular in its day, but that public opinion reversed itself as the conflict receded into the rearview mirror. The same dynamic may be starting to play out over Iraq, perhaps setting up the vindication of David Brooks's prediction that 25 years from now few will argue that the Iraq War wasn't the right thing to do. Now it is the Afghan War—the one Barack Obama and other liberals said was *necessary*—that is looking doubtful and hopelessly open-ended. Beinart criticizes Iraq's disproportionate, unsustainable cost, but has less to say about Afghanistan—where every year we are spending more than that sorry nation's total GDP.

The Icarus Syndrome begins with the elderly and frail Arthur Schlesinger asking Beinart over lunch, "Why did your generation support this [Iraq] war?" The rest of the book can be read as Beinart's mea culpa. As the title suggests, he applies the classical myth of Icarus to U.S. foreign policy over the past century, arguing that American power and success led us to soar ever higher, but with the same result—burning our wings and crashing back to earth, first in World War I, then Vietnam, and now in Iraq. But the United States doesn't merely overestimate its power and mastery—a common mistake of empires since the beginning of time. According to the author, American hubris stems from a particular post-Enlightenment combination of naïveté about human nature, and overconfidence in pure reason. His book is a gloss on Santayana's cliché about those who forget the past being doomed to repeat it; or, to be more charitable, the volume is a restatement of Paul Kennedy's *The Rise and Fall of Great Powers* (1987) or even Schlesinger's *Cycles of American History* (1986). Therein lies both the strength and weakness of its argument.

Much of *The Icarus Syndrome* is a well-written overview of 20th- and early 21st-century American foreign policy, and especially of "the three moments in the last century when a group of leaders and thinkers found themselves in possession of wings. . . . Politicians and intellectuals took ideas that had proved successful in certain, limited circumstances and expanded them into grand doctrines, applicable always and everywhere." Beinart's mostly conventional narrative is punctuated here and there with a telling detail or pungent judgment. In explaining Franklin Roosevelt's departure from Wilsonianism, for example, Beinart notes FDR's "blood pressure spiked to 240 over 130" while watching the gushing 1944 movie *Wilson* (Roosevelt watched the movie with Winston Churchill—another Wilson critic—at the Quebec conference in 1944. The prime minister's private secretary Jock Colville wrote in his diary that Churchill had watched "a shockingly bad film chosen by the President. The PM walked out halfway through which, on the merits of the film, was understandable, but which seemed bad manners to the President.") Although Beinart's portrait of Woodrow Wilson is suitably lacerating, his perception of the broader phenomenon of Progressivism is crabbed, deferring to recent historiography that sees Progressivism as "a swarm of impulses and interests, often colliding with each other" and summed up as "faith in human reason."

Beinart thinks the Truman Doctrine and the ensuing Korean War came close to being another Icarus-like disaster for America, rescued only by Dwight Eisenhower's calm good sense. Here, in Beinart's praise of Eisenhower and later of Ronald Reagan, we encounter a major difficulty with his overall argument. Beinart is not the first center-left thinker to embrace Eisenhower retrospectively, a process that has been going on at least since Murray Kempton in the late 1960s. Nor does Beinart airbrush the fact that liberals in the 1950s held Eisenhower in contempt. But he doesn't ask why liberal astuteness is good only in hindsight, and not contemporaneously. Won't the next statesmanlike conservative to arrive on the scene enjoy the same kind of liberal contempt that Eisenhower and Reagan did? There's a blind spot here somewhere, and Beinart does not acknowledge, much less investigate it.

A vital clue comes in his treatment of George H.W. Bush, whom he compares to Eisenhower and praises for not expanding the first Gulf War beyond its initial aim of ousting Saddam Hussein from Kuwait: "His signature word—it became a running joke on *Saturday Night Live*—was *prudence*, which Merriam-Webster defines as 'caution or circumspection as to danger or risk.'" This lightweight dictionary definition is all we hear about statesmanly prudence, though Beinart's narrative provides the perfect set-up for serious reflection on the difficulty of matching up a hierarchy of ends to a hierarchy of means.

His criticisms of pure reason and of naïve faith in human nature's goodness and plasticity question, implicitly, modern liberalism's central pillar. The eclipse of prudence by scientific, idealistic politics was a defining feature of Progressive statecraft, and it remains so for modern liberalism today—at least on the domestic scene. In making an elegant call for greater circumspection about government's mastery over all things, Beinart's skepticism stops at the water's edge. Why not apply the lessons of hubris—of overreaching and presuming a greater command of flawed human nature than is realistically possible—to, say, health care reform, or social policy generally?

"The hubris of dominance," Beinart writes, "like the hubris of reason and the hubris of toughness before it, had relied on faith in political authority." But isn't faith in political authority the central premise of domestic liberalism? Beinart doesn't contemplate that the same conceit that leads to foreign debacles is at work in domestic affairs, with similar results. At one point late in the book he offers up the throwaway line, "As our welfare state has withered. . . ." This is a worthy nominee for one of those "sentences-we-didn't-finish" contests, because there is no way the conclusion to this sentence can be sensible. What can Beinart be thinking, even if this was written before Congress passed Obamacare? The U.S. spends more per capita on social programs than honest-to-God Scandinavian welfare states.

Beinart has all the pieces of the story in front of him, but he only assembles half the puzzle. He criticizes the conceit that we could remake Vietnam in our own image because, as Arthur Schlesinger said, "We thought for a moment that the world was plastic and the future unlimited." (Beinart neglects to mention that Schlesinger supported the Vietnam War until the late 1960s, having lost that healthy sense of limits he possessed in the 1940s.) Beinart also raps the utopianism of Walt Rostow, who thought "American society was 'now within sight of solutions to the range of issues which have dominated political life since 1865.'"

But *The Icarus Syndrome* tacitly perpetuates (by omission) the liberal fiction that treats the twin wars of the '60s—the War in Vietnam and the War on Poverty—as separate and mutually exclusive phenomena, when in fact they need to be understood as twin expressions of the same impulse to political mastery, which failed for the same reason. Communism in Vietnam and racial strife and poverty at home were considered problems of social science, to be remedied with similar exertions of American know-how and willpower. The Vietnam War, the planners thought, would be over long before poverty was completely eliminated (Sargent Shriver said the latter would happen by 1976). Vietnam and Great Society policies were designed by many of the same people, rotating their brilliance from one bureau to another. One assistant secretary of defense said that "the new [social science] knowledge can literally solve any problem." Adam Yarmolinsky, another defense official turned anti-poverty planner, thought their efforts would lead the way to "the rebuilding of cities, not only in the United States but throughout the world."

Liberalism was shaken, if not traumatized, by the failure of the Vietnam War; a few liberals had their whole faith shaken to the core. Daniel Patrick Moynihan acknowledged in 1973 that "[m]ost liberals had ended the 1960s rather ashamed of the beliefs they had held at the beginning of the decade." A new generation of what Beinart calls "post-Cold War" liberals, chastened by the Vietnam experience the same way FDR's cohort had been chastened by World War I, arose to pursue limited uses of American power, such as Bill Clinton's humanitarian interventions in the Balkans. But between Clinton's minor excursions and the first Gulf War, the "hubris bubble" swelled again, just as it had after World War II, sweeping along a younger liberal cohort, including Beinart. He admits now that our obligations exceed our power, that foreign policy untethered to a realistic calculation of interests converts promoting American values into an infinite project. This realization, he argues, "should make us pause and pause and pause again before unilaterally invading tyrannical nations on the assumption that their people will thank us for it."

I doubt Beinart has much to worry about on that score, from the Obama Administration or its likely successors. The Iraq War Syndrome may prove more powerful and long-lasting than the Vietnam Syndrome, which cast a shadow of self-doubt over American power for 20 years. But after an engaging history of American overreach, Beinart's ending disappoints: he essentially revives George McGovern's 1972 slogan "Come home, America." President Obama needs to redefine our national faith, advises Beinart, by

> re-directing American can-do-ism inward. . . . In politics, as in life, we should be most ambitious in those spheres where we have the most power. There are limits to the federal government's capacities at home as well, of course; limits of both money and knowledge. But we know better how to rebuild New Orleans than how to rebuild Afghanistan, more about how to regulate the U.S. financial system than how to establish one in Iraq.

Peter Beinart's book does not go deep enough into the modern liberal soul. Though liberals may have put away their wings in foreign affairs, they are ever ready to soar higher at home, and he thinks our foreign policy travails are reason to cheer them on. I'll await his take, several years from now, on the "Mission Accomplished" banner that was implicitly hung at the signing ceremony for health care reform.

II

RENEWING CONSERVATISM

The Conservative Challenge

Charles R. Kesler

(Summer 2009)

In President Barack Obama, conservatives face the most formidable liberal politician in a generation, perhaps since John F. Kennedy and Lyndon Johnson. Mr. Obama led his party to a large electoral victory, winning the presidency with a majority of the popular vote—something a Democrat had not done since Jimmy Carter's squeaker in 1976. In fact, Obama's was the biggest Democratic triumph since LBJ's landslide in 1964. Though he didn't sweep into office as many congressmen and senators as Franklin Roosevelt or LBJ in their big breakthroughs, Obama handily increased the Democrats' control of both houses of Congress, including a Senate that appears filibuster-proof.

Worse still, from the conservative point of view, Obama came into office not as a status quo liberal but as an ambitious reformer. Far from being content with incremental gains, he's gambling on major systemic change in energy policy, health care, taxation, financial regulation, and (soon) education and immigration, one shocking success designed to pave the way for the next, and all understood and pursued as parts of a grand, in his words "transformative," strategy.

Faced with this liberal blitzkrieg, how have Republicans responded? Paralyzed at first by the rapidity and sheer audacity of the Democrats' advance (and by a plummeting stock market), they hunkered down behind a Maginot Line of safe districts, remembered triumphs, and misaimed slogans, hoping that the Democrats soon would outrun their supply lines or, besotted by success, fall to feuding among themselves. Though their spirit and poll numbers have improved in recent weeks, Republicans and conservatives are still profoundly on the defensive. To discover a way forward, we have to begin by understanding our opponents and learning from our own mistakes.

FOLLOW THE LEADER

Barack Obama is in some respects a new political phenomenon. To state the obvious, he is young, gifted, and black, and as Nina Simone sang 40 years ago, "To be young, gifted, and black / Is where it's at"—especially if you're president of the United States. Most Americans feel a certain pride in his achievement. Beyond that, his combination of Ivy League degrees and Chicago street cred, of high-sounding post-partisanship and hard-core self-interest, leaves people guessing. To call this combination or alternation "pragmatic," as he likes to, is simply to accept his invitation not to think about it.

But in the decisive respect, Obama does *not* represent something new under the sun. Instead, he represents a rejuvenated version of something quite old, namely, the impulses that gave birth, a century ago, to modern American liberalism.

Most political movements in American history come into being to press some putative reform, and dissolve when they have succeeded, or failed, definitively: for example, the anti-slavery and women's suffrage movements, which succeeded, and the campaign for the free coinage of silver, the central demand of late 19th-century Populism, which failed. Prohibition is an interesting case of a movement that succeeded and *then* failed. Modern liberalism is something else again.

Liberalism was the first political movement in America without a clearly defined goal of reform, without a *terminus ad quem*: the first to offer an endless future of continual reform. Its intent was to make American government "progressive," which meant to keep it always progressing, to keep it up to date or in tune with the times. No specific reform or set of reforms could satisfy that demand, and no ultimate goal could comprehend all the changes in political forms and policies that might become necessary in the future.

Obama's campaign slogans were marvelous examples of such open-endedness. It takes an effort to remember them, so gauzy were they; but last year they galvanized millions of voters in the primaries and general election. "Hope." "Change." These catchwords lack what are called, in grammar, subjects and objects. Who should change, and in what way? Hope for what, exactly? Obama's slightly more elaborated tag lines didn't solve the mystery but merely restated it—as with the catchy "We are the change we've been waiting for." Or that classic of self-actualization, "Yes, we can!" These slogans were meant to discourage deliberation, to hover childlike and dreamlike over all debate; each required some external agent to define it. Together they said, in effect, we are ready to follow a leader who will tell us what to hope for.

Obama wasn't shy about answering this call, but he disclaimed any personal glory in the matter. He was merely—merely!—the incarnation of the people's own hopes, rallying them to the causes latent in their hearts but not yet conscious to their minds or their imaginations. Liberals live in anticipation of such prophet-leaders, who bring an end to the reign of the wicked and move History (and not incidentally, liberalism) forward to its next stage. In the 20th century America was blessed, according to liberal hagiography, with Woodrow Wilson and the New Freedom, Franklin Roosevelt and the New Deal, LBJ and the Great Society. In the new century, Obama is the one whom History has chosen to reveal to us our hidden selves, and bring America to a new consummation, to a higher state of consciousness. He is the liberals' Twelfth Imam.

Being progressives, however, they fully expect there will be a 13th hidden imam, and 14th, and so on. For though liberalism can't specify what the future will look like, it's confident that it will forever be improving. In its early days, liberalism backed up this confidence with science—the latest in university learning, including an unhealthy dose of Social Darwinism. These days it's rare to hear liberals boast of their scientific command of the future, except perhaps in the climate change debate, which they do not consider a debate because Science has spoken, dammit, through that inspired non-scientist, Al Gore. Nonetheless, the sense of privileged wisdom lives on in the Left's congenital fondness for policy "experts" from the very best schools; the Obama Administration is full of them. These experts teach a less bombastic version of what liberals a century ago regarded as the highest truth of the most scientific kind of political science: that the future demands an increasingly powerful, provident, and paternal State.

THE COOPERATIVE COMMONWEALTH

The future being the future, however, even liberalism at its most self-confident couldn't describe the exact institutions and policies of this new State. These were to be ever evolving, hence impossible to pin down. As William Voegeli has well argued in these pages ("The Endless Party," Winter 2004), ask a liberal how big he wants government to be, how much of GDP he wants it to spend, and you will never get a definite answer. "Bigger" and "more" are the best he can do. In broad terms, however, liberals promised to generate a society more democratic than any that had ever existed, and to administer it with scientific efficiency via a new kind of bureaucratic government dominated by unelected experts.

The "new order of things," to use FDR's term, would feature abundant rights, very different however from the unalienable rights invoked in the Declaration of Independence. These new rights originated not in God or nature, as the Declaration taught, but in the State. The character of the rights differed, too. According to the new social contract, government would grant to the people certain socio-economic rights or benefits, bestowed primarily on groups and on individuals only insofar as they belonged to an officially recognized group (e.g., the poor, the mortgaged-deprived). In return for these rights, the people would cede to government ever greater powers. The individual didn't completely disappear from this vision of democracy but appeared in a very different role, as a kind of long-term government project.

The spirit of the old American democracy was free, honorable, independent. The new promised instead a cooperative commonwealth, in which spirited individualism would be social-worked out of folks and it would be hard to tell where democracy ended and socialism began.

The U.S. Constitution was designed for a people who thought republican government a rare and difficult achievement, one historically prone to degenerate into tyranny, or first into anarchy and then into tyranny. To avert this fate, the founders argued that America would need public virtue and vigilance—expressed in elections and in reverence for the laws and the Constitution—as well as "auxiliary precautions" like federalism, the separation of powers, and the extended nature of our republic. "It will not be denied that power is of an encroaching nature and that it ought to be effactually restrained from passing the limits assigned to it," warned James Madison in *The Federalist*. Despite America's political advantages, he therefore expected it would be difficult to maintain liberty, and that to do so the American people's "jealousy" of governmental power would have to be enlightened and persistent.

Today's liberals assure us, to the contrary, that political tyranny is a virtually extinct threat, save for the occasional throwback like George W. Bush. Why fear Big Government, after all, when the bigger and more powerful it gets, the more rights it can bestow on us?

THE HIGHER LAWLESSNESS

As a theme of political discourse, the Constitution as a bulwark of *limited* government has quite gone out of fashion. Ronald Reagan was its last great champion. As a theme of constitutional law more narrowly considered, it survives, though largely as an exhibit in the museum of discarded doctrines. For more than a hundred years, liberals have contributed to the Constitution's eclipse by criticizing it as a timebound document, ill-suited to our 19th-, 20th-, or 21st-century realities. At least since Woodrow Wilson, liberal anathemas have been aimed particularly at the Constitution's separation of powers, the alleged cause of the deadlock or gridlock of American democracy, which means the inability of progressives to change our politics as neatly and dramatically as they'd like. This complaint underlies President Obama's insistence on tackling all parts of his agenda at once and as hurriedly as possible. Unless the tempo is *allegro molto* (and he ramped it up to *presto* as the August recess approached), "change" will bog down once more in the normal play of American institutions.

Rather than simply pound away at the old Constitution, however, liberals quickly saw the advantage in reinterpreting it in ways that would be more politically palatable. Collectively, these fall under the rubric of the so-called "living constitution," a later term for Wilson's effort to read the Constitution as a Darwinian document, whose meaning must evolve with the times, and under whose precepts the national government must be allowed and encouraged to outgrow its old limits and blend its powers in novel ways. For conflict among the separated powers—a crucial check on tyranny, according to the founders—must give way to *cooperation*, in order to solve modern problems efficiently.

The living constitution is thus an ever-changing constitution, subject to continual fine-tuning by liberal experts to keep pace with new social problems and putative advances in social justice. It assumes that "change" can never, or only very rarely, be the enemy of good government. In this sense, modern liberalism stands for what might be called the higher lawlessness. This is a two-fold term for a two-faced phenomenon. To begin with, liberalism disputes the notion that there are, or ought to be, higher-law restrictions on what government can do, because these would suggest permanent purposes and limits to the State's power. So with few exceptions liberals deny that the Constitution has a more or less authoritative meaning expressed in its text and principles; that the principles themselves reflect a higher or natural law distinct from positive law; and that it is incumbent on judges and politicians to adhere to the Constitution as higher law when interpreting statutes and regulations, however popular or progressive these may be.

At the same time, modern liberals deny that the living constitution represents *mere* lawlessness, an absence of standards or surrender to subjective judgment. What makes their lawlessness *higher* is their faith that it leads upward, that change is almost always something to be hoped for rather than weighed or resisted, that anything really worthy in the Constitution will be preserved or improved by change, and that anything not preserved is, by definition, not worth preserving anyway.

AFTER REAGAN

To an amazing degree, Obama's agenda represents a return to liberalism's roots. Modernized, reenergized, repackaged, to be sure, but recognizable as a new installment of something that Americans have been resisting for a long time. Democrats have been trying to establish a universal entitlement to health care, after all, ever since Franklin Roosevelt in 1944 declared that "the right to adequate medical care and the opportunity to achieve and enjoy good health" was part of what he called "a second Bill of Rights."

Why then were conservatives caught so flat-footed? In a way, it was Ronald Reagan's fault, or rather the fault of those who carried on his legacy. Reagan was confident, as he said in 1977, that "we who are proud to call ourselves 'conservative' are . . . part of the great majority of Americans of both major parties and of most of the independents as well." His point was that when the social conservatives, drawn from "the blue-collar, ethnic, and religious groups traditionally associated with the Democratic Party," were added to the economic conservatives, traditionally at home in the GOP and among independents, the result would be a conservative majority that would support what he christened "the New Republican Party." He was right about that, as the 1980 and subsequent elections proved (and as the 1968 and '72 elections had already suggested).

He emphasized, however, that it would take "a program of action based on political principle" to unite conservatives into "one politically effective whole," which would not be "a temporary, uneasy alliance, but . . . a new, lasting majority."

Reagan came through with that program of action based on political principle. His successors did not. The confidence that a latent conservative majority existed helped inspire Reagan to activate it, to create it. That same confidence led his successors to take that majority for granted, to "turn out the base" on election day and otherwise say as little as possible about the substance and purposes of serious conservatism.

The assumption that Reagan had achieved a revolution in policy and public opinion led easily to the presumption that his "new, lasting majority" could be counted on. Even when it went AWOL, for instance in Bill Clinton's victories in 1992 and 1996, or in 2006 and 2008, commentators tended to adjust the facts to fit the hypothesis. Clinton was a rogue, they said, and ordinary Americans like rogues; 2006 showed that the voters, like good conservatives, were fed up with spendthrift Republicans; last year Obama kept talking about tax cuts for the middle class, thus sounding more conservative than McCain. Though there's an element of truth to each ad hoc explanation, they overlook the obvious: that latent conservatism doesn't translate into reliable political conservatism, much less into voting Republican, without persuasive appeals, "a program of action based on political principle."

Reaganesque appeals were few and far between in the post-Gipper GOP. George H.W. Bush, Bob Dole, George W. Bush, John McCain—every presidential candidate, even those who most identified with Reagan, chafed at his legacy and took pains to distance himself from it. True, the distances weren't great, but they were instructive. Though each candidate was in some sense conservative, none had been *of* the conservative movement as had Reagan; and so they tried to make a virtue of that fact. From Bush 41's "thousand points of light" to McCain's embrace of campaign finance reform and anti-global warming, they sought to soften conservatism's hard edges, to co-opt some issues of the Left, in general to try to pull conservatism towards the center rather than to try to persuade the center to move further right.

The corollary of this strategy was the assumption that even as the Right had gone as far as it could, so had the Left. In the 1990s, conservatives concluded that the Reagan Revolution had domesticated and even neutered liberalism. Clinton's presidency only seemed to confirm this, notwithstanding some doubts on the latter point.

COMPETING CONSERVATISMS

Just what it would have meant after Reagan to try to shift the center rightward is, of course, a major question. After the Soviet Union's collapse, which occurred on Bush the Elder's watch but in fulfillment of Reagan's policies, the definition of conservatism became newly problematic. For anti-Communism and the anxiety over national defense had always been a key third element in Reaganite conservatism and in his New Republican Party. (In his 1977 speech describing the new Republicanism, for example, he spoke at greatest length about foreign policy.) Without the urgent motivation of anti-Communism, conservatism seemed to lose much of its reason for being.

Many observers predicted a crack-up, with the union of social and economic conservatives dissolving in mutual antipathy. That didn't happen, suggesting that the two constituencies had more in common than it seemed. What ensued in the 1990s was a series of attempts to redefine conservatism for the post-Cold War age. The two most interesting efforts were Newt Gingrich's "Third Wave" and George W. Bush's "compassionate conservatism."

Gingrich's was a striking form of progressivist conservatism; it was almost an inverted Marxism. Mixing wildly disparate sources ranging from Alexis de Tocqueville to techno-futurist Alvin Toffler, Gingrich argued that the Right was now on the right side of history. In speeches and best-selling books, he explained that politics is shaped decisively by technology and the prevailing means of production. In the Second Wave, the economics of the industrial revolution and mass production had dictated the one-size-fits-all, big-government policies of the New Deal. But with the advent of the personal computer and the information revolution, politics would be demassified, individuals empowered, and a new era of entrepreneurship would usher in smaller, more agile, and efficient government. The Third Wave, he predicted, would ensure a Republican majority and conservative policies for a long time to come.

It didn't work out that way, not because the economy didn't do its part but because politics always has a mind of its own, and thus a freedom from even the most up-to-date determinisms. In 1994, the GOP, under Gingrich's leadership, captured control of the House of Representatives for the first time in 40 years. He took this as a confirmation of his thesis and set out to rein in the federal budget as though he had been elected prime minister rather than Speaker of the House. Gingrich was surprised at how Clinton outmaneuvered him in the government shutdown of 1995, and surprised again at the president's re-election. All of a sudden the Republicans seemed to have missed the big swell and were left bobbing in place, far from shore. In fact, however, the GOP congressional majority continued to exert a salutary check on the administration. But Gingrich had overplayed his hand (politics is more like poker than it is surfing) by confusing the public's disdain for Big Government with a libertarian contempt for government as such. Recall that one effect of Reagan's successful presidency was to *increase* the public's trust in the federal government.

David Frum observed that Bush's compassionate conservatism combined "the Left's favorite adjective with the Right's favorite noun." Too bad Bush didn't remember the writer's adage that the adjective is the enemy of the noun. The elementary point conveyed by the phrase was that it was no contradiction for conservatives to be compassionate. True enough, and useful to say, but hardly a revelation. More ambitiously, it sought to form a new combination of social and economic conservatives to replace or renew Reagan's New Republican Party.

In a time of unprecedented prosperity (1999–2000), Bush wanted to invoke a sense of national purpose loftier than material well-being, and so he tried to connect the two kinds of conservatives by asking what was prosperity's point. "The purpose of prosperity," he said many times, "is to make sure the American dream touches every willing heart. The purpose of prosperity is to leave no one out . . . to leave no one behind." What he meant was that the American dream consisted both of making a good living and making a good life, and therefore that prosperity should be a means to the ends of good character. Although compassion was not the only quality that he recommended to his fellow "citizens of character," it was the leading element in his ideal. Compassion is a noble calling, he said—not an easy virtue.

On the campaign trail he laid out a domestic policy agenda that combined economic conservatism with what he regarded as compassionate social policy. On the one hand, he promised tax cuts and entitlement reform. On the other, he offered three broad culture-improving proposals: to usher in the "responsibility era," i.e., to challenge the self-indulgent culture of the '60s, a task he admitted churches would be more effective at than government; to "rally the armies of compassion," that is, to encourage charitable giving and channel federal support to faith-based, private-sector welfare initiatives; and to reform education, through what would become the No Child Left Behind Act.

Even as he aspired to make his version of conservatism a middle way between libertarianism and cultural traditionalism, so he hoped that compassionate conservatism would offer a Third Way—to borrow Bill Clinton's favorite slogan—that would take the country beyond the stalemate or deadlock (symbolized by the government shutdown) to which the Left and Right had led it. Bush sought a way out of the "old, tired argument" between "those who want more government, regardless of the cost," and "those who want less government, regardless of the need. We should leave those arguments to the last century, and chart a different course," he told a joint session of Congress in 2001.

That new course would require government to "address some of society's deepest problems one person at a time, by encouraging and empowering the good hearts and good works of the American people." He would use government to strengthen civil society, and civil society to strengthen American character. A little more government now would lead to a caring, self-reliant people who could make do with less government later on. Jonathan Rauch in the *National Journal* put it nicely: "Conservatives have been obsessed with reducing the supply of government when instead they should reduce the demand for it. . . . Republicans will empower people, and the people will empower Republicans."

THE CONSERVATIVE COLLAPSE

Unfortunately, the supply of government generates its own demand. This Say's Law of politics was amply demonstrated in the Bush Administration. For the effectual truth of compassionate conservatism soon proved to be "big-government conservatism." Bush pushed successfully for Medicare Part D, the first new federal entitlement program since the Great Society. This prescription drug benefit has cost less than projected, but still costs billions that the federal treasury doesn't have—it was passed without even a hint of additional revenue to fund it—and delivers a benefit to 100% of seniors that only about 2% of them actually need.

But the worst of it for conservatives was that compassionate conservatism eviscerated the GOP's reform ambitions. By abandoning even the rhetorical case for limited government, Bush's philosophy left the administration, and especially Congress, free to plunge lustily into the Washington spending whirl. When House majority leader Tom Delay—the heartless right-winger Tom Delay!—protested that Congress could not cut another cent from the federal budget because it was already cut to the bone . . . you knew things were bad.

At bottom, the whole notion that compassion was the virtue conservatives lacked or needed to cultivate to be respectable was highly dubious. The best that could be said was that the slogan may have conferred some marginal electoral advantages in 2000. At a deeper level, however, the prominence of compassion was in tension with Bush's avowal of the responsibility era and his pledge to bring dignity back to the presidency. Compassion is not a virtue, after all. As the name suggests, it's a form of passion, of "feeling with" others—feeling their pain, usually; a specialty of the previous administration. Like every passion, it is neither good nor bad in itself; everything depends on what its object is and its fitness to that object. In practice, our compassion often goes out to whoever is moaning the loudest. That's why the classical political virtue is justice, not compassion, for compassion is often indiscriminate and misdirected.

At any rate, compassionate conservatism's indiscipline seemed to wear down some of the tough Texas virtues Bush might have been expected to bring to the presidency. As he said in 2003, "when somebody hurts, government has got to move." That's compassion speaking, not reason and justice, and certainly not the Constitution. In the end, the spirit of misplaced compassion did serious damage to his administration. It wasn't the only reason he failed for more than six years to veto an appropriations bill, for example, but it helped to sap his administration's tone and to leave the Republican Congress, unchecked and uninspired, to its increasingly porcine ways. And the simple, or sentimental, view of human nature implied in the elevation of compassion had something to do, too, with his expectation that from the ashes of Iraqi tyranny a grassroots democracy would spring forth fairly easily.

In his 2001 Inaugural Address, Bush drew attention to what he termed "a new commitment to live out our nation's promise through civility, courage, compassion, and character." To these four c's he didn't trouble to add a fifth, the Constitution, despite the fact that he owed his election to one of its provisions, the Electoral College. Like most Republican leaders since the New Deal, he assumed the Constitution was basically irrelevant to his task of shaping public opinion and policy, with the significant exception of making judicial appointments, when the usual condemnations of judicial activism would be trotted out. In effect, Bush accepted the Left's view of the Constitution as a living, Darwinian document that ought not constrain very much the Congress and executive branch from experimenting with and expanding the federal government—making it more compassionate, say. But the Court should not be allowed the same leeway. On this, he parted company with post-New Deal liberals.

In other words, like most modern Republicans, he saw nothing except the most vestigial connection between the Constitution and the proper size and functions of government. Those sort of arguments, which in the ancient of days had led conservatives to attack the New Deal, not to mention Medicare and Medicaid, as unconstitutional, had no place in compassionate conservatism, or in most other forms of the prevailing conservatism. Too much water under the bridge, it was thought. And besides, as Bill Clinton had been forced to acknowledge in 1996, the era of Big Government was over. Although this didn't mean that Big Government itself was obsolete or doomed—on the contrary, it was here to stay—Clinton's concession did imply that the era of big growth in the federal establishment was now behind us. Which implied that the Right could at last let down its guard. David Brooks, writing in the *New York Times Magazine*, announced "the death of small-government conservatism." He explained: "Just as socialism will no longer be the guiding goal for the left, reducing the size of government cannot be the governing philosophy for the next generation of conservatives, as the Republican Party is only now beginning to understand."

OBAMA'S MOMENT

That was before the market meltdown, the Republican sell-off in 2006 and 2008, and the rise of Obama. Who's shorting liberalism now? Yet to the generation of American conservatives who opposed the New Deal and the Great Society, there would be nothing unfamiliar about this resurgent liberalism. What shocks today's

Republicans is the Lazarus act it seems to have pulled. They thought it was dead, or dying, or at least tamed. They've forgotten what liberalism was like before Reagan.

As with the Great Depression or urban riots in the '60s, the financial crisis of 2008-09 helped to create the moment that the Obama forces are now exploiting. They were aided, to be sure, by the last act of the Bush Administration. When the Troubled Asset Relief Program (TARP) bill was first submitted, it was three pages long—a blank check to the Treasury secretary to save our economy. In its final form it exceeded 200 pages—still a blank check to "take such actions as the Secretary deems necessary" to buy troubled assets, "the purchase of which the Secretary determines promotes financial market stability." In effect, President Bush and the Congress agreed to establish what the ancient Romans would have called a "dictator" of finance, an emergency office empowered to solve a crisis, in this case, to unfreeze credit markets and stop the financial freefall.

The Romans wisely limited the office to a term of no more than six months. In our case, the TARP authority goes on indefinitely, and the spirit of clever lawlessness, already present to some degree in the liberals' constitutional views, radiates ever further into the administration. Neither Hank Paulsen nor Timothy Geithner (so far) ever got around to purchasing those troubled, mortgage-backed assets, but somehow the government now owns 60% of General Motors and a large chunk of Chrysler, not to mention preferred shares in most of the nation's largest banks, and has poured, so far, about $100 billion into Fannie Mae and Freddie Mac, and another $100 billion or so into AIG, and is eager to regulate the compensation packages of businessmen in and out of these ailing companies. To make the auto company deals happen, the Obama Administration had to subvert the existing laws of bankruptcy, but then once you've accepted the theory of the living constitution it's a small matter to swallow a living bankruptcy code, too.

Not content with its acquisitions, the administration now eyes health care, the energy business, and other vast segments of the economy to tax, regulate, and control. Health care is the signal case, revealing most clearly the nature and illusions of unlimited government in the progressive State.

Here, in outline, is the liberal M.O.: Take a very good thing, like quality health care. Turn it into a right, which only centralized government can claim to provide equally and affordably and—the biggest whopper—excellently to all. Refer as little as possible to the plain logic that such a right implies a corresponding duty; that the duty to pay for this new right's provision must fall on someone; and that the rich, always defined as someone with greater income than you, cannot possibly pay for it all by themselves. Ignore even more fervently that this right, held as a social entitlement, implies a duty to accept only as much and as good health care as society (i.e., government) allows or, ideally, as can be given equally to everyone. Having advertised such care as effectively free to every user, because the duty to pay is separated as much as possible from the right to enjoy the benefit, profess amazement that usage soars, thereby multiplying costs and degrading the quality of care. Blame Republicans for insufficient funding and thus for the painful necessity to increase taxes and cut benefits in order to protect the right to universal health care, which is now a program. Run against those hard-hearted Republicans, and win.

That, at least, is the classic script of liberal governance. With a magician's indirection, it mesmerizes the public with new rights that seem almost free and unalienable, and then poof, it explains that these are positive rights pure and simple, which have to be paid for and are subject to diminution or even abolition by ordinary statute law. When FDR spoke of the second Bill of Rights, he made it sound as though they would be added to the Constitution, as the old Bill of Rights was. In fact, the new socio-economic rights were added only to the small-c constitution, i.e., the mutable structures of contemporary governance, and so are subject to change at any time. Thus an evolving constitution, and supposedly permanent new rights, may come into fatal collision. To speak candidly, the essence and appeal of the modern liberal State depend on the artful misdirection of public opinion—on half-truths that are hard to distinguish from lies, nobly told, doubtless, in the liberals' own view.

To overcome the contradictions of Big Government, liberals cheerfully offer Bigger Government. Consider the present case. Medicare and Medicaid are going broke. Doctor Obama prescribes a brand new, expensive health care program, which the Democrats cannot figure out how to fund, to cure the ills of the existing system. A *third* deficit-laden program to save two already verging on bankruptcy? The reality is that massive middle-class tax increases lie just over the horizon, along with draconian cuts in benefits, which will come partly disguised by long waiting lists, rationing of care, and shrinking investment in new drugs and technologies. Obama is betting that the socialist ethic of solidarity, of shared pain, can be made to prevail over democratic outrage at broken promises, shoddy services, and diminished liberty.

THE CONSERVATIVE CHALLENGE

Will conservatives let him get away with it? So far their best arguments have highlighted the enormous cost of his proposals, added to the enormous and still growing costs of the stimulus bill and financial bailouts; the magnitude of the tax increases needed to fund Obama's spending; and the predictable and abysmal drop in the quality, variety, and innovativeness of American health care if the Democrats' plan passes. These are excellent arguments, which may be powerful enough to sink his health care plan and impair the rest of his domestic agenda. Then again they may not, and in either case they aren't sufficient to the larger task of reinvigorating American conservatism as a positive intellectual and political force, as the animating spirit of a New Republican Party.

To rise to this grander challenge we must rise above the conservatism of the past two decades, and in certain respects above that of the past half-century. One of the most interesting aspects of Obama is his determination to contest conservatism's grip on the American political tradition; he wants especially to recruit Abraham Lincoln and the American Founders to his side. He intends to claim the title deeds of American patriotism as Franklin Roosevelt did in the 1930s, preparing the way for a new New Deal coalition to rule our politics for the next generation or two. Conservatives can't allow him to succeed at this cynical revisionism, which means we have to make the case for our own understanding of, and fidelity to, American principles.

Here there is vast room for improvement, and dire need for relearning. A return to the principles of the Declaration of Independence and Constitution requires something like a revolution not only against modern liberalism but also within modern conservatism. Affronted by Obama's ambitions, a few conservatives here and there already have begun to clamor for their state's secession from the Union, a remedy that is about as un-Lincolnian and anti-Republican (not to mention boneheaded) as any imaginable. In the same vein, restive Republicans have started to invoke the 10th Amendment's guarantee of reserved rights to the states. Whatever its merits, the 10th Amendment's misuse in the defense of segregation in the 1950s and '60s has ignoble connotations that are, shall we say, particularly distracting when the amendment is to be applied against the first black president.

These misfires recall the disagreements and dead ends within the conservative movement prior to the Reagan Revolution. A tendency to defend the antebellum South and its radical view of states' rights—a view that made states' rights more fundamental than human or natural rights in the American constitutional order— cropped up on both the traditionalist and libertarian sides of the movement, and still does. Others imagined conservatism to be a defense of agrarianism, or an attempt to resurrect the medieval *republica Christiana*, or the last episode of the French Revolution, in which its opponents would finally expunge all abstract doctrines of equality and revolution from our political life.

American conservatism stands or falls, however, by its allegiance to the American Revolution and founding, even as modern liberalism really began, in the Progressive era, with a condemnation and rejection of America's revolutionary and constitutional principles.

Reagan himself seemed well aware of the innermost character of American conservatism. Despite his talk of fusing economic and social conservatives together into a new synthesis, in his most important speeches he regarded the two as already united by a patriotic attachment to founding principles. He invoked these principles brilliantly in stirring indictments of the Left's worldview. In his 1964 speech "A Time for Choosing" he said presciently:

> [I]t doesn't require expropriation or confiscation of private property or business to impose socialism on a people. What does it mean whether you hold the deed or the title to your business or property if the government holds the power of life or death over that business or property? . . . Every businessman has his own tale of harassment. Somewhere a perversion has taken place. Our natural, inalienable rights are now considered to be a dispensation of government, and freedom has never been so fragile, so close to slipping from our grasp as it is at this moment.

And elsewhere in "The Speech," as it came to be called, he framed a fateful choice: shall we "believe in our capacity for self-government," he asked, or shall we "abandon the American Revolution and confess that a little intellectual elite in a far-distant capitol can plan our lives for us better than we can plan them ourselves"?

BEYOND REAGAN

It is necessary to reground our conservatism in those revolutionary principles, but it will not be sufficient. Although conservatives cannot remedy America's problems without them, our principles need to be explained in a contemporary idiom and applied prudently to our present circumstances. That requires, for want of a more comprehensive word, statesmanship.

For the problems that face us now are the ones that Reagan helped to diagnose but did not come close to solving, particularly the deeply intractable problem of what to do about the liberal State. It has grown up among us for so long and has entwined itself so tightly around the organs of American government that it seems impossible to remove it completely without risking fatal harm to the patient. And in any case the patient's wishes must be conscientiously consulted on the matter, and he seems rather content with his present condition. Yet the spirit of unlimited government and the spirit of limited government cannot permanently endure in the same nation, either.

Bear in mind, of course, that the worst thing about Big Government is the *reasons* given for it, which always point to more and more programs, to government unlimited in its power and designs. Some—not all—of the agencies and departments established under its rubric may be tolerable, and a few even good. That's one reason the conservative task is so challenging. It requires not only discriminating in theory between the proper and improper functions of government, but also examining in practice the good and bad that government programs do, the second-best purposes they fulfill, the political costs and benefits of altering or abolishing them. All of these need to be elements of a long-term conservative strategy—"a program of action based on political principle"—to reform fundamentally the federal government and its programs.

Though unwinding the damage that has already been done to liberty and constitutional government will take time, we have to insist right now that no *further* damage, particularly the egregious sort promised by the Obama Administration, be permitted. The liberal State has always operated at the borders of constitutionality—often crossing them. But the president seeks to conquer and annex whole new provinces of unconstitutionality: to trample underfoot the rights of property, e.g., in the rush to hand control of Chrysler to his union allies; to compass the health care, housing, energy, automobile, and banking industries under close, indefinite, and highly personal political control; to so extend the tentacles of government as to grip more and more Americans in an unhealthy, unsafe, and unrelenting dependence on the federal establishment and its partisan masters.

If we were ever prone to think that after the Reagan Revolution conservatives faced only second- or third-order issues, we should by now be disabused of that comforting illusion. All of conservatism's past victories and defeats have brought us to the threshold of another epic struggle, a battle for America's soul, a battle that will determine whether free government will survive.

The Right Stuff

Michael M. Uhlmann

(Summer 2005)

Can it be that *National Review*, flagship of the modern conservative movement, is turning 50 years old? And can it be that William F. Buckley, eminence of both magazine and movement, will soon celebrate his 80th birthday? To conservatives who came of age along with *National Review*, both facts must seem highly improbable. It was only yesterday, after all, that Chairman Bill gaveled the ragtag national conservative meeting to order and urged it (as *National Review*'s inaugural issue had famously instructed) to "stand athwart history, yelling Stop."

"Stand Athwart History!" was certainly a bracing imperative for a new political movement, but what exactly did it mean? Buckley and his colleagues did not arrive on the scene with a prefabricated platform, but in due course a conservative program of sorts began to emerge in the pages of their magazine. A more vigorous foreign policy came first in the order of battle. The Eisenhower Administration could hardly be accused of being "soft" on Communism, but it exhibited an almost preternatural fear about discussing foreign policy outside the realist vocabulary of the containment doctrine. To the editors of *National Review*, however, containment was a tactic, not a strategy. What was needed was a specifically moral understanding of the protracted struggle with Communism. Without it, a policy of containment would become a recipe for drift and, ultimately, defeat.

Domestic policy was discussed in only slightly less moral terms. While the urgencies of foreign policy took precedence, the preservation of freedom at home was no less important than the defense against Communist aggression abroad. Left to its own devices, liberalism would by gradual degrees lead America to increasing collectivization of its economic and social life. The Eisenhower Administration seemed to think that a pale Republican version of the New Deal was indispensable to electoral success. Here, no less than in foreign policy, Eisenhower Republicanism was hopelessly adrift. To the editors of *National Review* nothing was inevitable about the growth of the administrative state.

A third programmatic goal transcended the immediate importance of any foreign or domestic initiative. Buckley and his colleagues believed that all enduring political revolutions had been mounted on the backs of ideas. The prevailing ethos of the

84

day, repeated endlessly in liberal journals of opinion, held that conservatism had no ideas worthy of serious consideration by the thinking class. From its very first issue, *National Review* undertook to prove why the charge was false; it undertook, in short, to show that conservatism was intellectually respectable.

There was, finally, a point of the utmost practical importance. Spurred by its publisher, William A. Rusher, *National Review* soon thrust itself into the struggle to define the future of the Republican Party. The logic here was simplicity itself: speculation about public policy was interesting and necessary, but unless conservatives acquired the means to translate their ideas into practice, all would be for nought. The strategic imperative: seize control of the Republican Party.

Such were the major goals of the new conservative movement launched by the founding of *National Review*. Its subsequent success, which within 20 years had moved the center of American politics noticeably to the right, tends to obscure the audacious, some might say quixotic, character of the original program. The cultural and political milieu of the 1950s, after all, offered little evidence to sustain the hope that an explicitly conservative movement was necessary, desirable, or even possible. Did anyone besides the Buckleyites seriously believe that socialism would come creeping in on the little cat feet of Eisenhower Republicanism? Undaunted, the new conservatives responded with the cheerful determination of The Little Engine That Could. If the body politic was ignorant of or indifferent to threats deemed palpably dangerous by the editors of *National Review*, it would simply have to be instructed.

PERPETUAL MOTION

Half-a-century on, three parts of the original four-part platform have been substantially accomplished (rolling back the Soviet Union, capturing the Republican Party, making conservative ideas respectable). As to the fourth, despite the revolution in economic thought initiated by the Chicago School and other free-market votaries, restraining the appetite of the administrative state has proved, so far, beyond human ingenuity—even for conservative Republicans. Still, considering the immensity of what was accomplished and the improbability of its occurrence, the success of modern conservatism is nothing short of remarkable. And much of its success would have been unthinkable without the inspiration, verve, and genius of Bill Buckley.

He would be the first to say that he had a lot of help from his friends—not least a long-time *National Review* subscriber by the name of Ronald Reagan, who gave conservatism a sunny face and a record of measurable political accomplishment. True enough, but a case can be made that without Buckley, there would have been no Reagan. Indeed, Buckley would have been a noteworthy figure even if Reagan had never come on the scene. God graced him with an angel's wit, a zest for life, and an extraordinary capacity for hard work. He has deployed these talents—and others as well—over the past half century in ways that would have depleted the energies of the next three prodigies you'd care to name. *National Review* wasn't simply the conservative magazine of record; it was the *omnium gatherum* for a major political movement that Buckley created more or less *ex nihilo* and thereafter guided like a (mostly) benign monarch.

Buckley practically invented a new style of political combat, in which he was both observer and participant, bringing to both roles beguiling elegance. His writing was marked by a distinctive, even daring mannerism quite unlike any before seen. It was at times unduly Latinate and, as Bill taught us all to say, sesquipedalian, but it was unique and uniquely his own. In less competent hands, such a style might have been reduced to mere eccentricity, but in Buckley's, the result was captivating, at once vigorous and playful, always exhibiting a fine ear for the music of language. These distinctive marks have been sustained over five decades in a body of work astonishing no less for its size than for its grace. A 275-page bibliography, covering his works through 2000 (*William F. Buckley, Jr.: A Bibliography*, edited by William F. Meehan, III; 2002), noted 35 volumes of non-fiction (of which about 10 are collections), 15 novels, some 1,500 articles, reviews, and editorials in *National Review* and other magazines, and more than 4,000 newspaper columns. Hillsdale College is assembling Buckley Online, a searchable archive of his publications, at www. hillsdale.edu/buckley. Neither the bibliography nor the website includes Buckley's voluminous correspondence, which will one day prove to be a treasure trove for historians and biographers. Yale's Sterling Library is said to have some 1,000 boxes of Buckleyana already on file.

Until he began to wind it down in the 1990s, the Buckley perpetual motion machine was for the better part of 50 years an object of popular acclaim on the national speakers' circuit. In as many as 70 appearances a year (often in debate) before audiences large and small, young and old, Preacher Buckley spread the conservative gospel across the land. For 34 of those years, he also hosted a weekly television talk show, *Firing Line*, the longest-running (and easily the most thoughtful) example of its genre. He is, in addition, a passable harpsichord recitalist (he has performed nine concerts with symphony orchestras), as well as an intrepid ocean mariner. And did I mention that Buckley also ran for mayor of New York City in 1965, receiving 13% of the vote in what many regard as the most entertaining political campaign of modern times?

Buckley has slowed his pace in recent years and begun to prepare for what his epilogue to *Miles Gone By* (2004) calls a "final passage." In 1990 he surrendered day-to-day supervision of *National Review*'s editorial activities. He has given up the lecture circuit and now makes only occasional public appearances. He has captained his last ocean voyage, cut his syndicated column to twice a week (after 35 years at three times a week), and signed off on his last *Firing Line* broadcast.

Buckley's letting go would for most mortals constitute a rather full, not to say hectic life. Since he began to slack off in 1990, he has published nine novels, edited three anthologies, written a superb account of the last days of the Cold War (*The Fall of the Berlin Wall*, 2004), and offered considered reflections on his religious convictions (*Nearer, My God*, 1997). Among the recent novels are a more or less true-to-life account of his association with Senator Joseph R. McCarthy (*The Redhunter*, 1999), in which Buckley provides his final (and substantially revised) assessment of the man whose name has become an "era"; and the newly published last installment of his Blackford Oakes spy series (*Last Call for Blackford Oakes*, 2005). Of the anthologies, the most interesting by far is *Let Us Talk of Many Things: The Collected Speeches* (2000), which provides a revealing portrait, sketched over a half century, of Buckley at work in the public arena.

Someone desiring to grasp the essence of the Buckley persona might do well to begin with the speeches, which present him as the world has seen him, and proceed from there to *Nearer, My God* and *Miles Gone By* to glimpse those features of his life for which he would perhaps most like to be remembered.

WORDS AND DEEDS

Miles Gone By, subtitled *A Literary Autobiography*, is a collection of 63 pieces written by Buckley during and about different phases of his remarkable career. (As an added inducement, the volume comes with an accompanying CD on which you can savor Buckley reading excerpts from his excerpts. The CD is so good that it is a shame he did not record the whole book.) In contrast to his previous collections, which drew heavily on Buckley's public policy commentaries, the present volume attempts what he describes as "a narrative survey of my life, at work and play." The public persona is present (how could it not be?), but the emphasis here is distinctly personal. There are warm recollections of his remarkable parents and upbringing, his formal education at home, in England, and at Yale; assorted *billets doux* to wine, the glories and complexities of the English language, skiing, and (at some length) sailing; sketches on travel, public speaking, playing Bach on the harpsichord, and going down to see the *Titanic;* reflections on social mores, thoughts on his pilgrimage to Lourdes, and detailed recollections of two interesting political encounters (running for mayor of New York in 1965, debating Governor Ronald Reagan about the Panama Canal in 1978).

Also included are the author's reflections on 20 friends and colleagues. If everything else were excluded from the book, these alone would make it a treasure. No one in our time has written more perceptively, or more affectingly, about friends and friendship, an undertaking that tells you as much about Buckley as it does about his subjects. The pieces vary in length, from shorter portraits that capture in a mere 750-1,000 words some compelling feature of the person being observed, to longer pointillist sketches that reveal facets of character in the manner of a precious stone being turned beneath a jeweler's eye. Some critics have faulted Buckley over the years for being a serial name-dropper of world-class proportions. That he certainly is, but how many people do you suppose can claim simultaneous close acquaintance with David Niven, Ronald Reagan, Henry Kissinger, Clare Boothe Luce, Tom Wolfe, Vladimir Horowitz, Roger Moore, Alistair Cooke, Princess Grace, John Kenneth Galbraith, William Shawn, and Whittaker Chambers (to name only a dozen whose lives are limned in the present volume)?

The writing in *Miles* is as varied as the author's personality—alternately somber and light, sometimes rhapsodic (never more so than when he dilates upon sailing, about which he has written as beautifully as anyone in our or any other time), sometimes sparse, but invariably witty, lively, and engaging. The overall affect is one of warmth and cheerful vivacity, like the man himself. Even for one who has read most of the pieces before, revisiting them is an amiable undertaking, like sitting down with an old friend one has not seen in many years and picking up where the conversation left off.

Inevitably, any collection of this sort is bound to dissatisfy someone. An anthology, after all, is only an anthology. It cannot, no matter how well woven, tell a complete tale, and as "a literary autobiography" made up of previously published pieces, it intentionally eschews sustained personal reflection. To the disappointment of his friends and admirers, Buckley decided some time ago not to try his hand at a straight autobiography. "I do resist introspection," he once wrote, "though I cannot claim to have 'guarded' against it, because even to say that would suppose that the temptation to do so was there, which it isn't."

He is probably the shrewdest judge of himself in this respect. So much of Buckley's life—at least that part he would wish to have on public view—has been lived in the arena and has already been chronicled by him in millions of words. What more, this dashing man of action must have reflected, what more can I say? Autobiography requires not only a certain kind of introspection that, rightly or wrongly, Buckley believes he lacks, but a certain kind of ego that, one suspects, he greatly disdains. Many years ago, when reviewing the memoirs of some self-important figure, Buckley dryly observed that the work fell into a literary category that might be labeled, "Waters I Have Walked On."

Even putting ego to one side, not all great writers possess the special art necessary to the execution of a memorable autobiography. There may be no great loss in that. What might William Shakespeare tell us about himself half so interesting as his plays or poetry? The same question might be asked of Abraham Lincoln, whose speeches tell us, in a sense, most of what we need to know. Thomas Jefferson's *Autobiography* scarcely bears that description, whereas his other writings give a rather full view of the man. In fact, one can count the great presidential autobiographies on one finger (Ulysses S. Grant's, which some say shows the hand of Mark Twain). Even saints fall short of the mark, unless they happen to be Augustine, or perhaps Teresa of Lisieux, whose *Story of a Soul* hardly fits the definition of autobiography at all. The lesson seems to be that saints, like politicians, are better judged by deeds than words. In the case of writers, their words *are* their deeds, and a sizable literary corpus will often reveal more than conscious efforts at self-analysis would. So, however deprived some may feel, Bill Buckley may be forgiven for sparing us detailed introspections of his own life. Beyond what he has already provided us, heavier lifting will have to await the labors of a thoughtful biographer.

A MAGAZINE AND A MOVEMENT

In the meantime, a preliminary assessment of this remarkable man might best begin by returning to those thrilling days of yesteryear, when the conservative cause enjoyed neither the comfort of intellectual respectability nor the experience of political success. In its early years especially (ca. 1955-60), *National Review* performed multiple functions at once: it created a forum in which conservative ideas were treated seriously; it acted as an information clearinghouse for conservative activists; and (not least) it created a magnetic field that gradually drew into its orbit an astonishing array of intellectual diversity. Contrary to the restrictive paradigms established by fashionable academic opinion, modern conservatism tends to defeat neat doctrinal definition. *National Review* understood and acted upon that fact from its inception. Then as now, five different kinds of libertarians warred with five different kinds of traditionalists, debating everything from theology and epistemology to whether Richard Nixon was or wasn't a "true" conservative. However else they differed, they agreed that they were not liberals. Beyond that, two things held the nascent movement together: the compelling persona of Bill Buckley and the exigencies of the anti-Communist cause.

In the early days, when the tribe was small, everyone knew pretty much everyone else. In 1960, Frank Chodorov, the gentle and generous libertarian who helped to start *National Review*, walked into a relatively modest gathering of the clan in New York, looked around, and declared, "My God, if the Commies only knew, they could rub out the entire conservative movement." Even a modestly alert undergraduate who worked *National Review*'s precincts could get to know most of the magazine's writers and editors, who were wonderfully generous with their time. That included the editor-in-chief, who was conscious of having founded a movement no less than a magazine. Indeed, at the beginning cause and leader were inextricably fused. When factional warfare threatened to break out (which was almost always the case) Buckley held things together through frequent applications of his copious charm. He didn't always succeed, but he was without question The Man.

As to the cause itself, *National Review* provided its readers with a continuing stream of evidence, not otherwise easily available, on the aggressive motives and tactics of Soviet foreign policy. Readers also learned that the Cold War could not be properly understood without addressing its moral dimension. The indispensable guide on that point, the *Ur*-text as it were, was *Witness* (1952), the compelling testament of Whittaker Chambers, whom Buckley induced for a time to serve as a contributing editor. By attending carefully to that great book and the controversy that caused it to be written, one could discover the fatal fault lines of the contemporary liberal establishment. Even more, perhaps, than Chambers himself, Buckley drew the lesson in stark relief: An establishment that could not bring itself to acknowledge the moral fault and legal guilt of Alger Hiss was an establishment that could not be counted on to stand up against Soviet imperialism when the crunch came. The permutations of that proposition, which worked themselves out in a hundred implicit and explicit ways in *National Review*'s editorial policy, became the magazine's *raison d'être*. If membership in the conservative cause had been determined by an entrance exam, the leading question would have been where one stood on the Hiss case. On this, as on many other matters, philosophical understanding preceded and defined the order of battle.

When it came to battle, Buckley was conservatism's Henry at Agincourt, instructing and inspiring through noble speech and leading by courageous example. He seemed to be everywhere on the battlefield at once, directing a charge over here, retrieving the wounded over there, always ready to engage in hand-to-hand combat whenever necessary. He was not conservatism's only hero, but he was certainly its most conspicuous warrior, one who seemed equally at home in philosophical disputation and in political infighting. As the case required, his rhetoric might be high-toned, sardonic, combative, or lyrical, but in any of its carefully orchestrated modes it was not only unique but uniquely enticing. For those even slightly oriented toward a conservative disposition, it was utterly intoxicating.

IN THE ARENA

Turn the clock back, if you will, to September 1960. President Eisenhower, nearing the end of his tenure, had invited Nikita Khrushchev to the United States. Why the Russian premier should have been invited for an extended state visit at that particular moment, and precisely how relations between the U.S. and the USSR would be improved thereby, were questions that our government had failed to address to the satisfaction of *National Review*'s editors. Premier Khrushchev began his American trip with a stop at the United Nations in New York City, which accorded him the sort of hospitality normally reserved for benevolent monarchs or elected leaders of allied states. The attendant obsequies dismayed Buckley and his colleagues, confirming their conviction that the regnant suppositions of the foreign policy establishment, Republican and Democratic alike, were fatally flawed. The invitation betrayed weakness—a foolish diplomatic gesture designed by and for State Department bureaucrats, pleasing to the editorial palate of the *New York Times* and other centers of fashionable opinion, but in the end sure to earn only dangerous contempt on the part of the Soviets.

It simply would not do to have the butcher of Budapest honored like benign royalty—not when millions of slaves behind the Iron Curtain looked to the United States for inspiration and succor. Accordingly, from Buckley's command center at *National Review*, the orders went out. These included organizing a massive rally at Carnegie Hall, where eleven speakers inveighed against Khrushchev, the Soviet Union, American pusillanimity, the editorial policy of the *New York Times*, and a variety of related lesser evils all of which were thoroughly familiar to regular readers of *National Review*. The hall was packed to the rafters, the air electrically charged with conservative fervor. The speakers proceeded one by one to ring the changes, building toward what everyone knew would be the evening's crowning glory, the peroration by Chairman Bill.

He did not disappoint. His speech, even after 45 years, retains an extraordinary capacity to move. If you want a window on the soul of the burgeoning conservative movement, and on the soul of its founding father, you cannot do better than to consult it. (It may be found in *Let Us Talk of Many Things*.) Buckley opened by leading the audience through every implausible reason why Khrushchev should be treated like an honored guest. As one lame rationale after another was demolished with devastating logic and acidic humor ("What reason have we to believe that a man who knows Russia and *still* has not rejected Marx will be moved by the sight of Levittown?"), Buckley built to his major point: that Eisenhower's "diplomatic sentimentality . . . can only confirm Khrushchev in the contempt he feels for the dissipated morale of a nation far gone, as the theorists of Marxism have all along contended, in decrepitude."

> That he should achieve orthodox diplomatic recognition not four years after shocking history itself by the brutalities of Budapest; months after the shooting down of an unarmed American plane; only weeks since he last shrieked his intention of demolishing the West; only days since publishing in an American magazine his undiluted resolve to enslave the citizens of free Berlin—that such an introduction should end up constituting his credentials for a visit to America will teach him something about the West that some of us wish he might never have known . . . .

Will he not return to Moscow convinced that behind the modulated hubbub at the White House, in the State Department, in the city halls, in the country clubs, at the economic clubs, at the industrial banquets, he heard—*with his own ears*—the death rattle of the West?

The major foreign policy point having been established, Buckley then turned to humor, finding his target of opportunity in the hapless Robert Wagner, Jr., mayor of New York. Noting that the mayor had warmly greeted Khrushchev that very afternoon, Buckley expressed puzzlement. Only a year before, after all, Mayor Wagner had ostentatiously refused to greet King Ibn Saud, because Ibn Saud discriminated against Jews in Saudi Arabia, and no one, by God, who discriminates against Jews is going shake the hand of Bob Wagner, mayor of New York. There was a little problem with the mayor's formulation, however, as Buckley now proceeded to point out:

> Now, as everybody knows, what Nikita Khrushchev does to Jews is kill them. On the other hand, he does much the same thing to Catholics and Protestants. Could *that* be why Mr. Wagner consented to honor Khrushchev? Khrushchev murders people without regard to race, color, or creed, and therefore whatever he is guilty of, he is not guilty of discrimination?

It was a classic piece of mordant Buckley wit, which he had spent much of the 1950s honing against the complacent shibboleths of liberalism. The audience loved it and hooted its approbation till the rafters shook.

Following this brief excursus into comic relief, Buckley returned to the sobriety of the early part of the speech. Having twisted the dagger into the conventional hypocrisies of poor Bob Wagner, who was after all only a bit player in Bill's larger moral drama, Buckley now turned, well, priestly:

> Ladies and Gentlemen, we deem it the central revelation of Western experience that man cannot ineradicably stain himself, for the wells of regeneration are infinitely deep. No temple has ever been so profaned that it cannot be purified; no man is ever truly lost; no nation is irrevocably dishonored. Khrushchev cannot take permanent advantage of our temporary disadvantage, for it is the West he is fighting. And in the West there lie, however encysted, the ultimate resources, which are moral in nature. Khrushchev is *not* aware that the gates of hell shall not prevail against us. Even out of the depths of despair, we take heart in the knowledge that it cannot matter how deep we fall, for there is always hope. In the end, we will bury him.

If you unstitch the speech, especially its concluding paragraph, and follow the resultant threads to their original premises, you will in due course understand the animating moral fervor of conservative Cold War policy. If you leap ahead 20 years, what you will find is Ronald Reagan talking about the Evil Empire and telling Gorbachev to tear down the Berlin Wall. The speech also shows Buckley at the height of his rhetorical powers. All of the trademark attributes of the inimitable Buckley style are there—the slashing wit, the artful skewering of pretentious liberal propositions, the call to arms, the metaphysical connection of political action to higher purposes, the musical cadence of the sentences, and (if you happened to be there) the perfectly polished delivery. For conservatives, there was no one to match their darlin' Bill.

CONSERVATIVELY SPEAKING

To their dismay, liberals would spend much of the '60s discovering the same thing. Skip ahead five years to 1965, when Buckley entered the New York City mayor's race on the Conservative Party ticket. He had no expectation of winning, but even in losing believed he might demonstrate the incompetence of liberal urban policy and, as well, the relevance of conservative principles. The Democratic nominee was the colorless Abraham Beame, a decent man utterly in thrall to his party's power brokers. The Golden Boy of the race was the congressman from Manhattan's so-called "silk-stocking" district, John Lindsay, who had received the endorsement of the Republicans and the Liberal Party. Lindsay's supporters believed that the genteel Yale-educated lawyer was destined to become the Republican Party's JFK. The idea seemed to be that Lindsay, having made New York City a showcase for liberal social policies, would launch himself onto the national stage and into the race for the Republican presidential nomination.

To conservatives, New York City was already dying from an overdose of liberal pieties. It was time, perhaps, for some truth-telling about what ailed the city. The opportunity proved irresistible to Buckley, who took to the challenge with undisguised glee. In the event, he received 13% of the vote, demonstrating in the process that John Lindsay was, as an *Esquire* magazine profile had put it, "less than meets the eye." The Conservative candidate had a rollicking good time playing Lindsay off against Beame, Beame off against Lindsay, and both off against the hypocrisies of urban politics, which precluded Beame and Lindsay from saying anything serious about the city's real problems. Buckley has left us a wonderful account, at once droll and serious, of that campaign in *The Unmaking of a Mayor* (1966), which may justly take its place among his best books. In a better universe, it would be required reading in a course on the decline of American cities. (A generous excerpt from his account is included in *Miles*.)

Buckley announced his candidacy with a characteristically elegant statement of high conservative principle, which he proceeded to read, with the signature Buckley mannerisms, to a jumble of hard-nosed New York reporters. A stenographer who had been hired to log the event later complained that his writing hand ached for two days: "I never heard anything like it before. The syllabic content was tremendous." The sainted Murray Kempton, the most gifted stylist in American journalism, found (as he so often did) the *mots justes*: watching Buckley, he said, reminded him of nothing so much as "an Edwardian resident commissioner reading the Anglican Articles to a captive assemblage of Zulus." Only Kempton, it may be safely said, could have written that, and only about Buckley. The ensuing Q-and-A featured such gems as the following:

Q: Do you think you have any chance of winning?

A: No.

Q: How many votes do you expect to get, conservatively speaking?

A: Conservatively speaking, one.

Buckley's impishness on that occasion, in the debates, and in other press conferences was irresistible, even to hardened reporters who had grown old listening to the bromides routinely dished up by urban politicians. And it was especially enchanting for young conservatives, who knew that Buckley's good-natured humor was but his entrée to the salient point: that our cities were being governed by mountebanks and fools who indulged in endless cant at the expense of thoughtful policy. Lindsay won, but his victory only served to prove that the emperor wasn't wearing any clothes. With each year of his increasingly ineffectual administration New York sank deeper and deeper into a fiscal and bureaucratic morass that entangles it even now. Lindsay's national ambitions sank along with the city.

The S.S. Buckley sailed merrily on to other ports of call but not without leaving an important legacy. Buckley's candidacy had helped to make the Conservative Party a permanent fixture of state politics, powerful enough, for example, to elect his brother Jim as U.S. senator from New York in 1970. The wise men of the eastern GOP establishment, for their part, continued their search for a liberal Republican JFK. Little did they realize that the party machinery was now already in the hands of conservatives, where it has remained ever since. Even less could they imagine that when the Republican JFK finally appeared, his name would be Ronald Reagan. In no small part, we have Bill Buckley to thank for that too, but that's another story.

Civil Rights and
the Conservative Movement

William Voegeli

(Summer 2008)

On April 4, 2008, mourners gathered at St. Patrick's Cathedral in New York to memorialize William F. Buckley, Jr., who had died five weeks earlier. That same Friday, mourners one thousand miles away gathered at the Lorraine Motel in Memphis to memorialize Martin Luther King, Jr., who had been murdered there exactly 40 years before.

The coincidence resonates. Drawing on exceptional rhetorical talents without ever being elected to public office, each man transformed the terrain where mere politicians clash. Buckley and King, born less than four years apart, both attained national prominence while still in their 20s. Buckley founded *National Review* in 1955; its first issue appeared two weeks before Rosa Parks set in motion the Montgomery bus boycott, which turned Dr. King into the nation's preeminent black leader. Buckley and King went on to forge the conservative and civil rights movements, respectively, each of which reshaped American politics in the second half of the 20th century.

These two political movements were not, as conceived, antagonists. In its formative years the conservative movement was preoccupied with defeating international Communism and reversing the New Deal, while the civil rights movement existed to end Jim Crow. Neither objective required opposing, or even noticing, the other. The elaboration of each movement's premises, however, quickly turned them into adversaries.

On the questions where the movements confronted each other directly the simplest judgment is that King was right and Buckley was wrong. Although Buckley's personal generosity and talent for friendship resulted in warm tributes from writers on the Left, such as John Judis and James Galbraith, the first item always cited to disparage his legacy was Buckley's record during the decade between the Montgomery bus boycott and passage of the Voting Rights Act of 1965. "Buckley was not himself a bigot," Tim Noah wrote in *Slate* the day Buckley died, "but he was at best blind and at worst indifferent to the bigotry all around him, and there can be no question that he stood in the way of racial progress." In 2006 Noah's *Slate* colleague, Daniel Gross, made the same point more heatedly:

At a time when a portion of the U.S. maintained a system of racial apartheid, Buckley and his magazine, time and time again, sided with the white supremacists. And in the decades since, I haven't seen any evidence that he and his many acolytes are sorry, or ashamed—or that they've ever engaged in anything like an honest reckoning with their intellectual complicity in segregation.

These blunt judgments are similar to the one delivered from within conservative ranks by Jonah Goldberg in 2002:

> Conservatives should feel some embarrassment and shame that we are outraged at instances of racism now that it is easy to be. Conservatives . . . were often at best MIA on the issue of civil rights in the 1960s. Liberals were on the right side of history on the issue of race. And conservatives should probably admit that more often.

All of Buckley's writings are now available at Hillsdale College's website (www.hillsdale.edu/buckley). Through them runs the line Goldberg gently suggests, the one separating the ways conservatives *avoided* the campaign to end America's caste system, from the ways they *impeded* that campaign.

GOVERNMENT AND RACE

Viewed from 2008, the movement Buckley led was detached from the civil rights struggle because conservatives, despite frequent and apparently sincere expressions of hope for racial harmony, rarely viewed the fight against pervasive, entrenched, and episodically brutal racial discrimination as a question of great moral urgency. Conservatives were personally opposed to Jim Crow as liberals of a later generation insisted they were personally opposed to abortion. Making the opposition personal was a way to keep the states, in the case of abortion, or the nation, when it came to segregation, from making it governmental.

Buckley did not mention race in his famous publisher's statement in the inaugural issue of *National Review*. The magazine was going to stand athwart history and yell Stop. But it would be yelling at Communists, "jubilant" in the belief they had an "inside track to History," and at liberals "who run this country" and who, having embraced relativism, rejected "fixed postulates . . . clearly enunciated in the enabling documents of our Republic" in favor of "radical social experimentation."

It was within this framework that *National Review* conservatism addressed the issues raised by the civil rights movement. Integration and black progress were welcomed when they were the result of private actions like the boycotts of segregated buses or lunch counters, which Buckley judged "wholly defensible" and "wholly commendable." He also praised a forerunner to the socially responsible mutual fund, an investment venture started in 1965 to raise capital for racially integrated housing developments, calling it "a project divorced from government that is directed at *doing* something about a concrete situation," one that "depends for its success on the spontaneous support of individual people."

The corollary was that conservatism opposed the civil rights agenda when it called for or depended on Big Government. "We frown on any effort of the Negroes

to attain social equality by bending the instrument of the state to their purposes,"
Buckley wrote in 1960.

> But we applaud the efforts to define their rights by the lawful and non-violent use of
> social and economic sanctions which they choose freely to exert, and to which those
> against whom they are exerted are free to respond, or not, depending on what is in bal-
> ance. That way is legitimate, organic progress.

This opposition to Big Government engendered conservative opposition to every
milestone achievement of the civil rights movement. *National Review* denounced
Brown v. Board of Education (1954), calling it "an act of judicial usurpation," one that
ran "patently counter to the intent of the Constitution" and was "shoddy and illegal
in analysis, and invalid as sociology." It opposed the 1964 Civil Rights Act and 1965
Voting Rights Act on similar grounds. A Buckley column dismissed the former as

> a federal law, artificially deduced from the Commerce Clause of the Constitution or
> from the 14th Amendment, whose marginal effect will be to instruct small merchants
> in the Deep South on how they may conduct their business.

Senator Barry Goldwater used similar reasoning to justify voting against the bill
on the eve of his general election contest with Lyndon Johnson. Saying he could
find "no constitutional basis for the exercise of Federal regulatory authority" over
private employment or public accommodations, Goldwater called the law "a grave
threat" to a "constitutional republic in which fifty sovereign states have reserved to
themselves and to the people those powers not specifically granted to the central
or Federal government." Goldwater arrived at this conclusion, according to Rick
Perlstein's book on the 1964 campaign, *Before the Storm: Barry Goldwater and the
Unmaking of the American Consensus* (2001), after receiving advice from two young
legal advisors, William Rehnquist and Robert Bork.

LIBERALS AND CONSERVATIVES

It would be unfair to leave the impression that conservatism was uniquely preoccupied with its own agenda as the civil rights cause was gaining salience. Liberals, too,
had other fish to fry, such as consolidating and expanding the New Deal, prosecut-
ing the containment doctrine against the Soviet Union, and forestalling any second
act to McCarthyism. Adlai Stevenson won two Democratic presidential nominations, and numberless admirers among liberals, despite: selecting an Alabama
segregationist, John Sparkman, to be his running mate in 1952; opposing (more
forcefully than did President Eisenhower) any federal role in integrating Southern
schools in 1956; and denouncing "the reckless assertions that the South is a prison,
in which half the people are prisoners and the other half are wardens."

One difference between Eisenhower-era liberals and conservatives is that the former kept their distance from the civil rights movement for practical reasons while
the latter did so for principled ones. Democrats would imperil their chances for a
majority in the Electoral College and Congress without the Solid South, a reality
that constrained both FDR and JFK. Legend has Lyndon Johnson turning to an aide

after signing the Civil Rights Act and saying that the Democrats had just lost the South for a generation. Johnson was the least politically naïve man in America, of course; he looked forward to an election victory and beyond it to forging a Great Society coalition that would secure Democratic victories without the New Deal co-alition's reliance on the South. Nevertheless, none of this was assured, and liberals have been nearly as reluctant as conservatives to praise the big political risk Johnson took for the sake of a deep moral conviction.

Having embraced the destruction of Jim Crow and the broader cause of pro-moting black progress, liberals' belief in the federal government's plenary power facilitated their support for any measure that would, or might, promote civil rights. Conservatives opposed to racial discrimination, however, had few obvious ways to act on that belief without abandoning their long, twilight struggle to re-confine the federal government within its historically defined riverbanks after the New Deal had demolished all the levees. Perlstein portrays Goldwater, a member of the NAACP who had fought against segregation in the Phoenix public schools while on the city council, as anguished by the choice between a moral and a constitutional impera-tive confronting him in the vote on the civil rights bill.

William Buckley's writings, by contrast, leave the impression that he found the choice between civil rights and the Constitution of limited, enumerated powers re-grettable but not especially difficult. (It's worth noting that Buckley's father, born in 1881, grew up in Texas, while his mother was born in 1895 and raised in New Or-leans. The "cultural coordinates of our household were Southern," Buckley wrote in his mother's obituary.) If the conservative understanding of constitutional govern-ment meant that segregation would persist for decades . . . then segregation would persist. Conservatives "know that some problems are insoluble," Buckley wrote in 1961. "Should we resort to convulsive measures that do violence to the traditions of our system in order to remove the forms of segregation in the South?" he asked. "I say no." Instead, Buckley expressed the hope

> that when Negroes have finally realized their long dream of attaining to the status of the white man, the white man will still be free; and that depends, in part, on the mod-eration of those whose inclination it is to build a superstate that will give them Instant Integration.

Forty years later Buckley and Michael Kinsley shared a series of email exchanges with the readers of *Slate*. The discussion turned to the 1964 Civil Rights Act, about which Kinsley offered the opinion "that using the power of the government to tell people whom they must do business with really is a major imposition on private freedom. . . . There's no question the imposition is justified—and has been hugely successful—in rectifying the historical injustice to African-Americans." Buckley, in a formulation John Kerry would have done well not to borrow, responded: "I'd have voted against the bill, but if it were out there today, I'd vote for it, precisely for the reason you gave."

In other words, convulsive measures to overturn segregation *were* necessary. But then again perhaps not, since Buckley immediately goes on to tell Kinsley, "I'd vote with trepidation, however, for the obvious reason that successful results cannot necessarily legitimize the means by which they were brought about." The desegregation omelet was worth making, but the limited government eggs might or might not have been worth breaking.

Buckley had his reasons, then, for opposing the civil rights movement. Even though he ultimately came to regard that movement's initial and unassailable goal—the end of second-class citizenship in both its petty and vicious aspects—as the more compelling imperative, it was always a close call. Buckley never retracted his limited-government arguments against the civil rights agenda, nor did he relinquish the hope that civil rights could be advanced in ways that impinged only slightly on the conservative project of restoring the founders' republic.

WORSE THAN MISSING IN ACTION

The constitutional principles at the heart of this project were—*are*—ones that liberals find laughable, fantastic, and bizarre. Because they cannot take them seriously they reject the possibility that conservatives do. Thus, liberals dismiss "states' rights" as nothing more than a code word for racism. There is no point in conservatives even asking what the code word for states' rights is, because liberals cannot imagine anyone believes this to be a legitimate political concern.

From this viewpoint, conservatism's "reasons" for opposing civil rights were, in fact and from the beginning, excuses for oppressing blacks. Buckley's least judicious writings make it difficult to wave away that allegation. These are moments in conservatism's history where it was, in Goldberg's sense, worse than merely missing in action in the battle for racial equity.

Exhibit A, quoted triumphantly by Paul Krugman in his new book *The Conscience of a Liberal*, was a 1957 *National Review* editorial Buckley wrote, "Why the South Must Prevail." In it, Buckley said that the "central question" is neither "parliamentary" nor one "that is answered by merely consulting a catalogue of the rights of American citizens, born Equal." Rather, it is "whether the White community in the South is entitled to take such measures as are necessary to prevail, politically and culturally, in areas in which it does not predominate numerically?"

And? "The sobering answer is Yes—the White community is so entitled because, for the time being, it is the advanced race." In other words, the South "perceives important qualitative differences between its culture and the Negroes', and intends to assert its own," an intention Buckley approves:

> If the majority wills what is socially atavistic, then to thwart the majority may be, though undemocratic, enlightened. It is more important for any community, anywhere in the world, to affirm and live by civilized standards, than to bow to the demands of the numerical majority.

Buckley's subsequent treatment of civil rights issues was more circumspect. In 1957 he regarded the whites' civilization as more advanced both subjectively and objectively. The South *perceives* important differences between white and black culture, and the white community *is* the advanced race and what blacks would bring about *is* atavistic.

Later, Buckley emphasized only the subjective element. Abandoning the argument that whites were objectively more civilized, however, sometimes led to expressions of solicitude for Southern whites who were conspicuously *un*civilized. A 1961 editorial beseeches readers to try to understand those whites who responded to the provocation posed by the Northern "Freedom Riders" by beating the crap out of a few of them. "Jim Crow at the bus stations strikes us as unnecessary, and even wrong," Buckley said, but this is "irrelevant" because it "does not strike the average white Southerner as wrong."

> That is what *they* feel, and *they* feel that *their* life is for *them* to structure; that the Negro has grown up under generally benevolent circumstances, considering where he started and how far he had to go; that he is making progress; that the coexistence of that progress and the Southern way of life demand, for the time being, separation.

This was indeed what the South felt, or at least what it said it felt during the early years of the civil rights movement. Buckley's characterization resembles that of the "Southern Manifesto," signed in 1956 by nearly every senator and representative from the South. The Manifesto charged the Supreme Court's *Brown* decision with

> destroying the amicable relations between the white and Negro races that have been created through 90 years of patient effort by the good people of both races. It has planted hatred and suspicion where there has been heretofore friendship and understanding.

It's hard for modern readers to decide whether cynicism, or delusion, explains such an assessment.

The single most disturbing thing about Buckley's reactions to the civil rights controversies was the asymmetry of his sympathies—genuine concern for Southern whites beset by integrationists, but more often than not, perfunctory concern for Southern blacks beset by bigots. This disparity culminated in a position on violence committed by whites against blacks and civil rights activists that was reliably equivocal. Like the liberals of the 1960s who didn't condone riots in Watts and Detroit but always understood them, Buckley regularly coupled the obligatory criticism of Southern whites' violent acts with a longer and more fervent denunciation of the provocations that elicited them. Thus, "the nation cannot get away with feigning surprise" when a mob of white students attacks a black woman admitted to the University of Alabama by federal court order in 1956. "For in defiance of constitutional practice, with a total disregard of custom and tradition, the Supreme Court, a year ago, illegalized a whole set of deeply-rooted folkways and mores; and now we are engaged in attempting to enforce our law." Thus, the Freedom Riders went into the South to "challenge with language of unconditional surrender" the whites' "deeply felt" beliefs, and were "met, inevitably, by a spastic response. By violence."

There is much to be said for the Burkean notion that social change unfolds best when it is the unplanned, incremental result of particular actions and concrete realities, rather than imposed sweepingly, from afar, on the basis of lofty abstractions. There is something to be said for the position that modern Burkeans can demonstrate their attachment to this idea by applying it to the hard cases as well as the easy ones. There is almost nothing to be said in defense of conservatives' profound misjudgment about the civil rights movement. Their response to it was that the only solution to the problem of apartheid in the American South was to wait, for however many decades it required, for blacks' infinite forbearance and whites' latent decency to somehow work things out. To act more assertively, in this view, amounted to intolerable, heavy-handed social engineering, far worse than the problem that needed fixing.

The one thing in conservatives' favor is that people passing judgment many years later on the conduct of historical actors in turbulent and fraught situations should remember that we know how the story turned out and they didn't. The fact that "massive resistance" by irreconcilable Southern whites collapsed fairly quickly, rather than metastasizing into protracted and bloody chaos, doesn't prove the chaos couldn't possibly have happened, or that the conservatives who warned against it were either fools or hypocrites. This lone mitigation does not, however, absolve the conservatives who, confronted with the outrage of sanctioned racial oppression, calibrated how little rather than how much they could do to end it.

FRINGE OR MAINSTREAM

Among conservatives in the 21st century—the ones in politics, journalism, and think tanks—99% would never praise segregation with faint damns, in print or even in thought. Many of them, born after the battle against Jim Crow was fought and settled, don't even realize there *is* another 1%. It's constituted by dogmatists who have extended the logic of libertarianism to blaming Big Government on Abraham Lincoln, then to admiring the Confederacy, and finally to speaking—both matter-of-factly and stridently—about the civilizational and genetic inferiority of blacks. When the mainstream conservatives do become acquainted with the fringe, either in print or in person, they quickly conclude that it's populated by cranks and creeps.

There's no rule, however, that a repellent person can't have a legitimate gripe. The pariahs are entitled to ask whether they missed a memo. The rest of the conservatives quietly abandoned the old complacency about racial discrimination, but never really repudiated it. Though Randians, Birchers, and anti-Semites were expelled from the conservative movement in the 1950s, all were extended the courtesy of eviction notices in *National Review*. A decade later, apologetics for the brutality of Jim Crow disappeared from *NR*'s pages, but without explanation. By 1968 Buckley was telling George Wallace on "Firing Line" that the constitutional rights of the people of Alabama were being trampled—but he was referring to blacks' rights to demonstrate and vote, not to whites' rights to perpetuate segregation. Buckley himself seemed bewildered by this pivot. "Honestly," he said to Wallace, "you're forcing me to sound like a liberal, which has never happened to me before in my entire life."

In December 2002 Trent Lott resigned as the Senate majority leader after it was revealed he had said,

> When [in 1948] Strom Thurmond ran [as a "Dixiecrat"] for president, we [in Mississippi] voted for him. We're proud of it. And if the rest of the country had followed our lead, we wouldn't have had all these problems over all these years, either.

Charles Krauthammer accused Lott of "historical blindness that is utterly disqualifying for national office." William Buckley wrote that, whatever else is to be said about the old South, segregation was an ugly feature of it, and that to think back poignantly about how it was in those golden days requires, if you are a public figure doing the nostalgia, the reiterated expulsion of features of that life.

According to Jonah Goldberg,

> Racism, at least the open and active racism which sustained the 1948 Dixiecrat vision, is simply astoundingly rare on the Right. In fact, prior to Trent Lott's idiocy, most conservatives I know would have assumed it did not exist at all—except among the fever swamps of the so-called paleo-Right.

In rebuttal, one resident of that swamp, Paul Craig Roberts, approvingly cited another:

> It was left to the libertarian Llewellyn Rockwell to point out that, fundamentally, states' rights is about the Tenth Amendment, not segregation. Thurmond's political movement sought a return to the enumerated powers guaranteed by the Constitution to the states.

This was exactly the position taken by Buckley in a 1956 *National Review* editorial:

> [S]upport for the Southern position rests not at all on the question whether Negro and White children should, in fact, study geography side by side; but on whether a central or a local authority should make that decision.

It's a position he reiterated in a 1962 column, which acknowledged at some length "the suspicion that the entire white Southern community is simply seeking, in its war against the Negro, to find a respectable terminology through which to fight that fight." Nonetheless, the South's "*political* cause is admirable," because "It is the cause of home rule, and it is the essence of the American system."

Conservatism won't be undone because an embittered fringe insists that it alone remains true to the faith abandoned by the faint-hearted mainstream. The real danger comes from adversaries who insist the fringe embodies the movement better than the mainstream. The Lott story was driven by liberals, principally the blogger Joshua Micah Marshall, who believe—or avail themselves of the political advantages of professing to believe—that the essence of conservatism is and always has been Dixiecrat-ism. This is not a point of antiquarian interest; the clear implication is that everything that conservatism has accomplished and stood for since 1965— Reagan, the tax revolt, law-and-order, deregulation, the fight against affirmative action, the critique of the welfare state . . . everything—is the poisoned fruit of the poisoned tree.

LINES IN THE SAND

Harsh as it is, this liberal accusation misses an important point: the hardest question the triumph of the civil rights movement raises about conservatism is not whether its stated purpose of restoring the founders' republic was a ruse designed to perpetuate racial inequality. Rather, it is to what extent that sincerely held belief was ever feasible and coherent. The troubling incongruity is not conservatives' initial tolerance of segregation for the sake of limited government, but the later, tacit admission that America did well to expand the purview of the federal government in order to end Jim Crow. Trent Lott had only to suggest lightly that relying on those means to secure that end was still regrettable to set off a stampede of conservatives to denounce him.

The problem is that conservatives' acquiescence, long after the fact, in using Big Government to abolish segregation is the kind of exception that devours the rule rather than proving it. This is so particularly because it is not the lone exception. To take one example, modern conservatives have been more disposed than liberals to say that the exigencies of the wars against Communism and Islamic terrorism require, in George Will's disapproving words, the "silent repeal" of the Constitution's assignment to Congress of important powers over whether to go to war and how to wage it.

By the same token, conservatives have long agreed with liberals that the imperative to maintain and expand prosperity requires a federal government equipped with all the powers it needs to accomplish that goal. This was the burden of an article Walter Lippmann wrote in 1935, "The Permanent New Deal." He deduced the permanency by arguing that the Hoover and Roosevelt administrations had spent the foregoing six years contending with the Depression in ways that were far more similar than different. The bitter arguments of the day, according to Lippmann, masked the fact that Hoover and FDR had much more in common with one another than either did with their immediate yet distant predecessor, Calvin Coolidge. The bipartisan embrace of federal intervention for the sake of prosperity, continuing by such means and until such time as prosperity is restored, meant that the Coolidgean idea that it was better to suffer macroeconomic dislocations than constitutional ones was a dead letter.

Conservatives spent the 20th century drawing lines in the sand, in other words, before stepping back to draw new lines after the old ones were disdainfully trespassed. It's the kind of thing that leads to credibility issues. Conservatives drew a line against the civil rights movement, asserting that the republic would be irreparably harmed if the federal government arrogated to itself the powers necessary to end segregation. They eventually came to regard this line, too, drawn in front of a federal government confined to its limited, enumerated powers and by the need to respect states' rights, as politically and morally indefensible. By 2001 William Buckley, like the overwhelming majority of conservatives, had long since discarded the idea that segregation was one of those insoluble problems we had no choice but to live with. The qualification of his retrospective support for the Civil Rights Act of 1964—the success of which "cannot necessarily legitimize the means" that brought it about—makes sense only if there was at least one alternative way to achieve the same result without augmenting Big Government.

Conservatives *have* offered some trenchant criticisms of the civil rights movement over the past half century. Many commentators, not all of them conservative, have contended that *Brown v. Board of Education* demonstrated that jurists are foolish to base epochal decisions on social science research they have no competence to evaluate, as they did with Kenneth Clark's problematic black and white dolls experiment. The misguided foray into sociology undermined the work the justices *were* qualified and authorized to carry out, the interpretation and application of the law, and the articulation of its principles. Although the Court gave the NAACP a policy victory, it denied the legal victory the plaintiffs sought, the explicit repudiation of *Plessy v. Ferguson*'s doctrine of "separate but equal" (1896) in favor of the principle, articulated by Justice John Marshall Harlan as the lone dissenter in *Plessy*, that "[o]ur Constitution is color-blind, and neither knows nor tolerates classes among citizens." The failure, or refusal, to make that simple point left the door ajar for all the subsequent assaults on logic and republicanism committed in the name of civil rights—affirmative action, set-asides, race-normed employment tests, busing, and tortuously drawn "majority-minority" legislative districts.

THE BEST VS. THE GOOD

It's not clear, however, that such criticisms add up to a road not taken, an alternative assault on sanctioned racial discrimination. And even if they did, would this more conservative and more constitutionally scrupulous civil rights movement have ended Jim Crow as decisively as the historical one? Allowing that counterfactual questions are inherently unanswerable, it's hard to see that segregationists would have been any more receptive to a desegregation campaign waged on these terms, or that they would have had a harder time resisting it.

The other question is whether this hypothetical alternative to the civil rights movement would have elicited a warmer response from conservatives than the actual civil rights movement did. This, too, is doubtful, given Buckley's opposition to *any* black efforts to "attain social equality by bending the instrument of the state to their purposes." It's difficult to imagine, in other words, a solution to the problem of segregation in which the powers asserted by the federal government were both large enough to accomplish the task and small enough to satisfy conservatives wary about the growth of Big Government.

In the statement explaining his vote against the 1964 Civil Rights Act Barry Goldwater said that if the people really want the federal government to undertake the tasks set out in the bill, they should amend the Constitution to give the government those powers. But such statements from conservatives were conversation stoppers rather than conversation starters. The point was not to offer, or convey the urgent need to develop, an alternative to the constitutionally reckless approach of the civil rights movement to ending segregation. It was to suggest that there *was* no alternative to that reckless approach and that, therefore, the least bad thing to do about segregation was to wait and hope for the sensibilities of the segregationists to yield gradually to the imperatives of a humane conscience.

Modern conservatives, those not members of the irreconcilable fringe, count the advances in racial tolerance over the last half century as one of America's proudest accomplishments. The ease with which whites once uttered venomous remarks about blacks and shrugged off racist actions toward them is scarcely believable today. The soundest reading of Buckley's insistence on "organic" progress was that the only safe and legitimate path to those markedly different sentiments was through incremental changes in attitudes in response to social rather than political pressures. There is no way of knowing whether that train, running on those tracks, would have ever come into the station. The pace of its progress prior to 1955 was hardly breathtaking. We do know that the civil rights movement catalyzed a revolution in Americans' minds, one that no mainstream conservative wishes could be undone. Asked by *Time* in 2004 whether he regretted any positions he had taken in the past, Buckley said simply, "Yes. I once believed we could evolve our way up from Jim Crow. I was wrong: federal intervention was necessary."

Any political movement that looks back in relief and gratitude on the battles it lost needs to take inventory. The conservative movement in the first decade after the founding of *National Review* insisted that the only acceptable response to Jim Crow was one that furthered the conservative goal of delegitimizing the New Deal. This was a textbook example of letting the best be the enemy of the good. By holding out for such a solution, conservatives squandered the opportunity to fashion a constitutionally principled argument in favor of either augmenting the federal government's powers so they were equal to the task of ending Jim Crow, or activating latent powers afforded by the Constitution that were not being brought to bear against segregation. To the urgent insistence that ending segregation justified the government in doing whatever it had to do, conservatives responded by calling for the indefinite reliance on other people's patience.

For the want of that nail, much was lost. Conservatives have spent half a century trying to overcome the suspicion that they are indifferent to black Americans' legitimate demands, and indulgent towards people who are blatantly hostile to blacks. As a result, the party of Lincoln has become much whiter as it has become more conservative. Dwight Eisenhower got 40% of the black vote in 1956, the first presidential election after the *Brown* decision and the Montgomery boycott. Barry Goldwater got 6% in 1964, and in the ten subsequent presidential elections the Republican candidate's performance has never been more than a slight improvement on Goldwater's. As Ta-Nehisi Coates recently argued in the *Atlantic Monthly*, a sizeable portion of the black electorate consists of latent conservatives "who favor hard work and moral reform over protests and government intervention." Invariably, however, the black American who feels this way "votes Democratic, not out of any love for abortion rights or progressive taxation, but because he feels—in fact, he knows—that the modern-day GOP draws on the support of people who hate him."

The "honest reckoning with their intellectual complicity with segregation" that Daniel Gross called for is, however, more than a propitiation conservatives owe blacks. It's also a duty they owe their own best ideas. The obtuseness about segregation, the big way in which Buckley and the conservatives were wrong, obscures all the important ways they were right, and prescient.

GETTING IT RIGHT

Conservatives' complicity with segregation made it easy for liberals to dismiss all their arguments against the post-1965 civil rights agenda. Conservatives are not the only ones today who have reason to regret that conservative arguments of an earlier day were ignored. It would be as hard today to find a liberal who thinks busing was a good idea, a well-considered venture we should eagerly try again, as to find a conservative willing to accept the resegregation of restaurants in order to effect the reinvigoration of the Commerce Clause. Conservatives tried to draw the line in an indefensible place, holding out for a solution to segregation that involved no expansion or invigoration of government at all. In doing so, they ceded moral authority to those who insisted there should be no lines whatsoever, who were determined to embrace any expansion of government that might further the nebulously defined goal of racial justice. Liberals came to grief over civil rights because they had no stopping point, while conservatives came to grief because they had no starting point.

As a result, conservatives have had to struggle for 40 years to assert the standing to criticize the civil rights movement's excesses. Conservatives were right, for example, about the extent and implications of Martin Luther King's enterprise. King has been turned into a dashboard saint for the anodyne, apolitical cause of human brotherhood. There's insufficient recollection of the King who in 1967 called for "a radical revolution of values" to "get on the right side of the world revolution" against a society where "profit motives and property rights are considered more important than people."

By 1979 Buckley urged, ungrudgingly, a national holiday in recognition of King's "courage," the "galvanizing quality" of his rhetoric, and his role as "the black American who consummated the civil war Abraham Lincoln undertook, largely animated by his belief in metaphysical equality." Buckley sensed early on, however, that the consummation of the Civil War was not the consummation of King's ambitions, and that a radical leftward shift of America's foreign policy and political economy was.

Buckley understood as well that the civil rights movement was fully prepared to resort to expansive methods to achieve its expansive goals. The point of "nonviolent direct action," according to King's "Letter From a Birmingham Jail," was to "create such a crisis," "foster such a tension," and "so to dramatize the issue that it can no longer be ignored." King's stipulation, "One who breaks an unjust law must do so openly, lovingly, and with a willingness to accept the penalty," was likely to prove a thin membrane restraining the individual conscience free to decide which laws were just or unjust, and therefore deserved to be obeyed or violated.

At the time of his murder, King was planning a Poor People's Campaign that, according to a recent CNN story, intended to "paralyze the nation's capital" if the government refused to enact an "economic bill of rights for poor people," part of, in King's words, the "radical redistribution of economic power" America required. It was in keeping with an agenda King had announced the previous year, and which Buckley had derided:

> Now Dr. Martin Luther King proposes massive "dislocations." Not violent dislocations, understand. Just "massive civil disobedience," like blocking plant gates, highways, government operations, sit-ins in federal buildings, that kind of thing. But not violent, repeat. The man reporting to work at his factory is not expected to press his way through Dr. King's human wall, nor the wife driving her car to pick up her child at school, to trample the toes of the *satyagrahi*. No violence, just a national convulsion.

In 1969 Buckley wrote, "Dr. King's discovery of the transcendent rights of the individual conscience is the kind of thing that killed Jim Crow all right. But it is also the kind of thing that killed Bobby Kennedy." Though King and Malcolm X are usually recalled as opposites, the Franciscan and the militant, Buckley's argument is that the logic of King's position carried him closer and closer to the stance, By Any Means Necessary, associated with Malcolm. That assertion would have gained more traction had it not been for Buckley's earlier expressions of sympathy for those who defended segregation by any means necessary.

THE GIFT OF AFFIRMATIVE ACTION

As it happens, By Any Means Necessary is the name of a group that agitates on behalf of affirmative action. (Among other things. Its full name is the Coalition to Defend Affirmative Action, Integration & Immigrant Rights and Fight for Equality By Any Means Necessary.) Affirmative action has been the civil rights movement's political gift to the conservative movement. Conservatives have been delighted by the chance, finally, to present themselves as the ones articulating a principled egalitarian argument on behalf of innocent people whose prospects in life were diminished when they were judged according to the color of their skin rather than the content of their characters.

Since conservatives strenuously opposed all the major civil rights laws, they can't really be aghast that liberals are not eager to sign off on their interpretation of what the laws demand and proscribe. Barry Goldwater criticized the Civil Rights Act of 1964 not only because its provisions "fly in the face of the Constitution," but because they "require for their effective execution the creation of a police state," which sounds a lot over the top. Though he was wrong about its enforcement, Goldwater had grasped something important about the law, especially the employment discrimination provisions: the new crimes, by and large, were going to be thought-crimes. Employers who were stupid and racist enough to actually announce they didn't hire blacks couldn't possibly be the only ones the law was meant to sanction. There had to be some way to protect blacks who were the victims of covert rather than overt discrimination.

The problem is that one employer's—or bureaucrat's, or judge's—covert discrimination is another's good-faith effort to hire and retain the best available workforce at market wages. Goldwater anticipated that endless disputes over why Jones was *really* promoted over Smith would result in

> the development of an "informer" psychology in great areas of our national life—neighbors spying on neighbors, workers spying on workers, businessmen spying on businessmen, where those who would harass their fellow citizens for selfish and narrow purposes will have ample inducement to do so.

To their credit, the civil rights enforcers declined to turn America into East Germany for the sake of equal opportunity.

To their discredit, the civil rights enforcers decided that since hiring processes were essentially thought processes, and therefore difficult to police, the thing to regulate would be hiring *results*, which were easy to police. The employer whose workforce was a perfect miniature of the local labor market had nothing to worry about. The bigger the demographic disparity between the employee roster and the phonebook, the more explaining the employer would have to do.

One might have expected that businessmen would push back against the bureaucrats leaning on them about which employees to hire, retain, and promote. In fact, the spirit of the shrewd Yankee trader, looking for an edge, triumphed over the spirit of the don't-tread-on-me patriot. Each employer realized that every other firm in his industry faced the same regulatory regime, so there was no competitive disadvantage to complying with it. Firms that become adept at pursuing ordinary business objectives while avoiding exposure to equal opportunity litigation would secure an advantage, particularly against smaller competitors not yet savvy about gaming the system and more dependent on getting just the right workers in the right jobs. As a last resort, while all sorts of ostensibly race-neutral personnel practices have gotten employers into trouble if they had a "disparate impact" on racial minorities, the disparate impact test has never been applied to business decisions about where to locate factories and offices. This is why the civil rights law is sometimes referred to as the Minnesota Full Employment Act.

The conservative argument against affirmative action is that it's a brazen violation of the letter and spirit of the civil rights laws, the most flagrant bait-and-switch operation in American political history. Among the rebuttals, the weakest is "So what?"—the purpose of the law was to help blacks and those enforcing it have set out to do so by, well, any means necessary. The strongest though least admirable is caveat emptor—if you'd read the fine print you would have seen that the potential, the inevitability, of affirmative action was there all along. Conservatives warned that the civil rights movement would create a superstate, and that didn't happen. What did happen is that interest-group liberalism extended its regime of "policy without law," in Theodore Lowi's phrase, to the adjudication of civil rights.

DOING THE RIGHT THING

William Buckley wrote about affirmative action less often, and less angrily, than other conservatives. For someone accused of standing in the way of racial progress, he regularly addressed the issue by expressing hope for a solution that promoted racial reconciliation and black advancement. As early as 1968, writing on the fierce battle between black radicals and white public school teachers in New York City's Ocean Hill-Brownsville neighborhood, Buckley listed himself as one who approved of "discriminatory hiring in favor of blacks"—provided that "the concomitant obligation to protect the whites whose jobs are taken" was discharged. By 1977, as the *Bakke* case was being considered by the Supreme Court, he was retrieving the Burkean perspective he had applied to the South. Blacks' problems, he said,

> are best handled by the myriad decisions reached in a million situations every day. . . .
> The employer who surveys the application forms of a half-dozen candidates for an
> opening and quietly gives the advantage to the black candidate is, in my opinion, doing
> the right thing. But what he did could not stand the test of universalization. You could
> not take that discreet preferment and write legislation about it.

Buckley and the early *National Review* conservatives went too far in hoping that such discreet preferments would suffice to end Jim Crow. Their subsequent acknowledgments that the suffering and national disgrace caused by segregation required stronger measures have not satisfied their opponents. Given the political advantages to liberals of conflating racism and conservatism, it's doubtful there is any degree of contrition they would find acceptable.

Martin Luther King and the civil rights movement went too far in the other direction, overconfident about the large benefits and negligible costs of politicizing all the spaces in which Americans live their lives. The lesson that federal government intervention could extinguish the wickedness of segregation was learned too well, and reinforced the liberal conviction that government could—and therefore must—intervene to eradicate every social ill, no matter how large or amorphous, affecting minority groups. The higher lawlessness of civil disobedience was absorbed by the lower lawlessness of interest-group liberalism. Myriad decisions in a million situations—such as job interviews, college applications, and training programs—need now comply with federal "standards" that are rarely clear or constant, and are always subject to further revisions driven by perpetual interest-group lobbying. Any reckoning of what William Buckley and the conservatives failed to see in the civil rights era must also account for these deformities, which they did see and which everyone else missed.

The Myth of the Racist Republicans

Gerard Alexander

(Spring 2004)

A myth about conservatism is circulating in academia and journalism and has spread to the 2004 presidential campaign. It goes something like this: the Republican Party assembled a national majority by winning over Southern white voters; Southern white voters are racist; therefore, the GOP is racist. Sometimes the conclusion is softened, and Republicans are convicted merely of base opportunism: the GOP is the party that became willing to pander to racists. Either way, today's Republican Party—and by extension the conservative movement at its heart—supposedly has revealed something terrible about itself.

This myth is not the only viewpoint in scholarly debates on the subject. But it is testimony to its growing influence that it is taken aboard by writers like Dan Carter, a prize-winning biographer of George Wallace, and to a lesser extent by the respected students of the South, Earl and Merle Black. It is so pervasive in mass media reporting on racial issues that an NBC news anchor can casually speak of "a new era for the Republican Party, one in which racial intolerance really won't be tolerated." It has become a staple of Democratic politicians like Howard Dean, who accuses Republicans of "dividing Americans against each other, stirring up racial prejudices and bringing out the worst in people" through the use of so-called racist "codewords." All this matters because people use such putative connections to form judgments, and "racist" is as toxic a reputation as one can have in U.S. politics. Certainly the 2000 Bush campaign went to a lot of trouble to combat the GOP's reputation as racially exclusionary. I even know young Republicans who fear that behind their party's victories lies a dirty, not-so-little Southern secret.

Now to be sure, the GOP had a Southern strategy. Willing to work with, rather than against, the grain of Southern opinion, local Republicans ran some segregationist candidates in the 1960s. And from the 1950s on, virtually all national and local GOP candidates tried to craft policies and messages that could compete for the votes of some pretty unsavory characters. This record is incontestable. It is also not much of a story—that a party acted expediently in an often nasty political context.

The new myth is much bolder than this. It insists that these events should decisively shape our understanding of conservatism and the modern Republican Party.

In *From George Wallace to Newt Gingrich: Race in the Conservative Counterrevolution, 1963–1994* (1996), Dan Carter writes that today's conservatism must be traced directly back to the "politics of rage" that George Wallace blended from "racial fear, anticommunism, cultural nostalgia, and traditional right-wing economics." Another scholar, Joseph Aistrup, claims in *The Southern Strategy Revisited: Republican Top-Down Advancement in the South* (1996) that Reagan's 1980 Southern coalition was "the reincarnation of the Wallace movement of 1968." For Earl and Merle Black, the GOP had once been the "party of Abraham Lincoln," but it became the "party of Barry Goldwater," opposed to civil rights and black interests (*The Rise of Southern Republicans*, 2002). It is only a short step to the Democrats' insinuation that the GOP is the latest exploiter of the tragic, race-based thread of U.S. history. In short, the GOP did not merely seek votes expediently; it made a pact with America's devil.

The mythmakers typically draw on two types of evidence. First, they argue that the GOP deliberately crafted its core messages to accommodate Southern racists. Second, they find proof in the electoral pudding: the GOP captured the core of the Southern white backlash vote. But neither type of evidence is very persuasive. It is not at all clear that the GOP's policy positions are sugar-coated racist appeals. And election results show that the GOP became the South's dominant party in the least racist phase of the region's history, and got—and stays—that way as the party of the upwardly mobile, more socially conservative, openly patriotic middle-class, not of white solidarity.

CODE WORDS

Let's start with policies. Like many others, Carter and the Black brothers argue that the GOP appealed to Southern racism not explicitly but through "coded" racial appeals. Carter is representative of many when he says that Wallace's racialism can be seen, varying in style but not substance, in "Goldwater's vote against the Civil Rights Bill of 1964, in Richard Nixon's subtle manipulation of the busing issue, in Ronald Reagan's genial demolition of affirmative action, in George Bush's use of the Willie Horton ads, and in Newt Gingrich's demonization of welfare mothers."

The problem here is that Wallace's segregationism was obviously racist, but these other positions are not obviously racist. This creates an analytic challenge that these authors do not meet. If an illegitimate viewpoint (racism) is hidden inside another viewpoint, that second view—to be a useful hiding place—must be one that can be held for entirely legitimate (non-racist) reasons. Conservative intellectuals might not always linger long enough on the fact that opposition to busing and affirmative action can be disguised racism. On the other hand, these are also positions that principled non-racists can hold. To be persuasive, claims of coding must establish how to tell which is which. Racial coding is often said to occur when voters are highly prone to understanding a non-racist message as a proxy for something else that is racist. This may have happened in 1964, when Goldwater, who neither supported segregation nor called for it, employed the term "states' rights," which to many whites in the Deep South implied the continuation of Jim Crow.

The problem comes when we try to extend this forward. Black and Black try to do this by showing that Nixon and Reagan crafted positions on busing, affirmative action, and welfare reform in a political climate in which many white voters doubted the virtues of preferential hiring, valued individual responsibility, and opposed busing as intrusive. To be condemned as racist "code," the GOP's positions would have to come across as proxies for these views *and* in turn these views would have to be racist. The problem is that these views are not self-evidently racist. Many scholars simply treat them as if they were. Adding insult to injury, usually they don't even pause to identify when views like opposition to affirmative action would *not* be racist.

In effect, these critics want to have it both ways: they acknowledge that these views could in principle be non-racist (otherwise they wouldn't be a "code" for racism) but suggest they *never* are in practice (and so can be reliably treated as proxies for racism). The result is that their claims are non-falsifiable because they are tautological: these views are deemed racist because they are defined as racist. This amounts to saying that opposition to the policies favored by today's civil rights establishment is a valid indicator of racism. One suspects these theorists would, quite correctly, insist that people can disagree with the Israeli government without being in any way anti-Semitic. But they do not extend the same distinction to this issue. This is partisanship posturing as social science.

THE SOUTHERN STRATEGY

This bias is evident also in how differently they treat the long Democratic dominance of the South. Carter and the Black brothers suggest that the accommodation of white racism penetrates to the very soul of modern conservatism. But earlier generations of openly segregationist Southerners voted overwhelmingly for Woodrow Wilson's and Franklin Roosevelt's Democratic Party, which relaxed its civil rights stances accordingly. This coalition passed much of the New Deal legislation that remains the basis of modern liberalism. So what does the segregationist presence imply for the character of liberalism at its electoral and legislative apogee? These scholars sidestep the question by simply not discussing it. This silence implies that racism and liberalism were simply strange political bedfellows, without any common values.

But the commonality, the philosophical link, is swiftly identified once the Democrats leave the stage. In study after study, authors say that "racial and economic conservatism" married white Southerners to the GOP after 1964. So whereas historically accidental events must have led racists to vote for good men like FDR, after 1964 racists voted their conscience. How convenient. And how easy it would be for, say, a libertarian conservative like Walter Williams to generate a counter-narrative that exposes statism as the philosophical link between segregation and liberalism's economic populism.

Yet liberal commentators commit a further, even more obvious, analytic error. They assume that if many former Wallace voters ended up voting Republican in the 1970s and beyond, it had to be because Republicans went to the segregationist mountain, rather than the mountain coming to them. There are two reasons to question this assumption. The first is the logic of electoral competition. Extremist voters usually have little choice but to vote for a major party which they consider at best the lesser of two evils, one that offers them little of what they truly desire. Segregationists were in this position after 1968, when Wallace won less than 9% of the electoral college and Nixon became president anyway, without their votes. Segregationists simply had very limited national bargaining power. In the end, not the Deep South but the GOP was the mountain.

Second, this was borne out in how little the GOP had to "offer," so to speak, segregationists for their support after 1968, even according to the myth's own terms.
Segregationists wanted policies that privileged whites. In the GOP, they had to
settle for relatively race-neutral policies: opposition to forced busing and reluctant
coexistence with affirmative action. The reason these policies aren't plausible codes
for real racism is that they aren't the equivalents of discrimination, much less of
segregation.

Why did segregationists settle for these policies rather than continue to vote
Democratic? The GOP's appeal was mightily aided by none other than the Democratic Party itself, which was lurching leftward in the 1970s, becoming, as the contemporary phrase had it, the party of "acid, amnesty, and abortion." Among other
things, the Democrats absorbed a civil rights movement that was itself expanding,
and thus diluting, its agenda to include economic redistributionism, opposition to
the Vietnam War, and Black Power. The many enthusiasms of the new Democratic
Party drove away suburban middle-class voters almost everywhere in the country,
not least the South.

Given that trend, the GOP did not need to become the party of white solidarity
in order to attract more voters. The fact that many former Wallace supporters ended
up voting Republican says a lot less about the GOP than it does about segregationists' collapsing political alternatives. Kevin Phillips was hardly coy about this in his
well-known book *The Emerging Republican Majority* (1969). He wrote that Nixon did
not "have to bid much ideologically" to get Wallace's electorate, given its limited
power, and that moderation was far more promising for the GOP than anything
even approaching a racialist strategy. While "the Republican Party cannot go to the
Deep South"—meaning the GOP simply would not offer the policies that whites
there seemed to desire most—"the Deep South must soon go to the national GOP,"
regardless.

ELECTORAL PATTERNS

In all these ways, the GOP appears as the national party of the middle-class, not of
white solidarity. And it is this interpretation, and not the myth, that is supported by
the voting results. The myth's proponents highlight, and distort, a few key electoral
facts: Southern white backlash was most heated in the 1960s, especially in the Deep
South. It was then and there that the GOP finally broke through in the South, on
the strength of Goldwater's appeals to states' rights. Democrats never again won the
votes of most Southern whites. So Goldwater is said to have provided the electoral
model for the GOP.

But hidden within these aggregate results are patterns that make no sense if white
solidarity really was the basis for the GOP's advance. These patterns concern which
Southern votes the GOP attracted, and when. How did the GOP's Southern advance actually unfold? We can distinguish between two sub-regions. The Peripheral
South—Florida, Texas, Tennessee, Virginia, North Carolina, and Arkansas—contained many growing, urbanizing "New South" areas and much smaller black populations. Race loomed less large in its politics. In the more rural, and poorer, Deep
South—Alabama, Mississippi, Georgia, South Carolina, and Louisiana—black com-

munities were much larger, and racial conflict was much more acute in the 1950s and '60s. Tellingly, the presidential campaigns of Strom Thurmond, Goldwater, and Wallace all won a majority of white votes in the Deep South but lost the white vote in the Peripheral South.

The myth that links the GOP with racism leads us to expect that the GOP should have advanced first and most strongly where and when the politics of white solidarity were most intense. The GOP should have entrenched itself first among Deep South whites and only later in the Periphery. The GOP should have appealed at least as much, if not more, therefore, to the less educated, working-class whites who were not its natural voters elsewhere in the country but who were George Wallace's base. The GOP should have received more support from native white Southerners raised on the region's traditional racism than from white immigrants to the region from the Midwest and elsewhere. And as the Southern electorate aged over the ensuing decades, older voters should have identified as Republicans at higher rates than younger ones raised in a less racist era.

Each prediction is wrong. The evidence suggests that the GOP advanced in the South because it attracted much the same upwardly mobile (and non-union) economic and religious conservatives that it did elsewhere in the country.

Take presidential voting. Under FDR, the Democrats successfully assembled a daunting, cross-regional coalition of presidential voters. To compete, the GOP had to develop a broader national outreach of its own, which meant adding a Southern strategy to its arsenal. In 1952, Dwight Eisenhower took his campaign as national hero southward. He, like Nixon in 1960, polled badly among Deep South whites. But Ike won four states in the Peripheral South. This marked their lasting realignment in presidential voting. From 1952 to the Clinton years, Virginia reverted to the Democrats only once, Florida and Tennessee twice, and Texas—except when native-son LBJ was on the ballot—only twice, narrowly. Additionally, since 1952, North Carolina has consistently either gone Republican or come within a few percentage points of doing so.

In other words, states representing over half the South's electoral votes at the time have been consistently in play from 1952 on—since before *Brown v. Board of Education*, before Goldwater, before busing, and when the Republicans were the mainstay of civil rights bills. It was this which dramatically changed the GOP's presidential prospects. The GOP's breakthrough came in the least racially polarized part of the South. And its strongest supporters most years were "New South" urban and suburban middle- and upper-income voters. In 1964, as we've seen, Goldwater did the opposite: winning in the Deep South but losing the Peripheral South. But the pre-Goldwater pattern re-emerged soon afterward. When given the option in 1968, Deep South whites strongly preferred Wallace, and Nixon became president by winning most of the Peripheral South instead. From 1972 on, GOP presidential candidates won white voters at roughly even rates in the two sub-regions, sometimes slightly more in the Deep South, sometimes not. But by then, the Deep South had only about one third of the South's total electoral votes; so it has been the Periphery, throughout, that provided the bulk of the GOP's Southern presidential support.

The GOP's congressional gains followed the same pattern. Of course, it was harder for Republicans to win in Deep South states where Democratic-leaning black electorates were larger. But even when we account for that, the GOP became the dominant party of white voters much earlier in the Periphery than it did in the Deep South. Before Goldwater, the GOP's few Southern House seats were almost all in the Periphery (as was its sole senator—John Tower of Texas). Several Deep South House members were elected with Goldwater but proved ephemeral, as Black and Black note: "Republicans lost ground and stalled in the Deep South for the rest of the decade," while in the Periphery they "continued to make incremental gains." In the 1960s and '70s, nearly three quarters of GOP House victories were in the Peripheral rather than the Deep South, with the GOP winning twice as often in urban as rural districts. And six of the eight different Southern Republican senators elected from 1961 to 1980 were from the Peripheral South. GOP candidates tended consistently to draw their strongest support from the more educated, middle- and upper-income white voters in small cities and suburbs. In fact, Goldwater in 1964—at least his Deep South performance, which is all that was controversial in this regard—was an aberration, not a model for the GOP.

Writers who vilify the GOP's Southern strategy might be surprised to find that all of this was evident, at least in broad brush-strokes, to the strategy's early proponents. Kevin Phillips drew the lesson that a strong appeal in the Deep South, on the model of 1964, had already entailed and would entail defeat for the GOP everywhere else, including in what he termed the Outer South. He therefore rejected such an approach. He emphasized that Ike and Nixon did far better in the Peripheral South. He saw huge opportunities in the "youthful middle-class" of Texas, Florida, and other rapidly growing and changing Sun Belt states, where what he called "acutely Negrophobe politics" was weakest, not strongest. He thus endorsed "evolutionary success in the Outer South" as the basis of the GOP's "principal party strategy" for the region, concluding that this would bring the Deep South along in time, but emphatically on the national GOP's terms, not the segregationists'.

The tension between the myth and voting data escalates if we consider change across time. Starting in the 1950s, the South attracted millions of Midwesterners, Northeasterners, and other transplants. These "immigrants" identified themselves as Republicans at *higher* rates than native whites. In the 1980s, up to a quarter of self-declared Republicans in Texas appear to have been such immigrants. Furthermore, research consistently shows that identification with the GOP is stronger among the South's younger rather than older white voters, and that each cohort has also become more Republican with time. Do we really believe immigrants (like George H.W. Bush, who moved with his family to Texas) were more racist than native Southerners, and that younger Southerners identified more with white solidarity than did their elders, and that all cohorts did so more by the 1980s and '90s than they had earlier?

In sum, the GOP's Southern electorate was not rural, nativist, less educated, afraid of change, or concentrated in the most stagnant parts of the Deep South. It was disproportionately suburban, middle-class, educated, younger, non-native Southern, and concentrated in the growth-points that were, so to speak, the least "Southern" parts of the South. This is a very strange way to reincarnate George Wallace's movement.

THE DECLINE OF RACISM

Timing may provide the greatest gap between the myth and the actual unfolding of events. Only in the 1980s did more white Southerners self-identify as Republicans than as Democrats, and only in the mid-1990s did Republicans win most Southern House seats and become competitive in most state legislatures. So if the GOP's strength in the South only recently reached its zenith, and if its appeal were primarily racial in nature, then the white Southern electorate (or at least most of it) would have to be as racist as ever. But surely one of the most important events in Southern political history is the long-term decline of racism among whites. The fact that these (and many other) books suggest otherwise shows that the myth is ultimately based on a demonization not of the GOP but of Southerners, who are indeed assumed to have Confederate flags in their hearts if not on their pickups. This view lends *The Rise of Southern Republicans* a schizophrenic nature: it charts numerous changes in the South, but its organizing categories are predicated on the unsustainable assumption that racial views remain intact.

What's more, the trend away from confident beliefs in white supremacy may have begun earlier than we often think. David Chappell, a historian of religion, argues in *A Stone of Hope: Prophetic Religion and the Death of Jim Crow* (2004) that during the height of the civil rights struggle, segregationists were denied the crucial prop of religious legitimacy. Large numbers of pastors of diverse denominations concluded that there was no Biblical foundation for either segregation or white superiority. Although many pastors remained segregationist anyway, the official shift was startling: "Before the Supreme Court's [*Brown v. Board*] decision of 1954, the southern Presbyterians . . . and, shortly after the decision, the Southern Baptist Convention (SBC) overwhelmingly passed resolutions supporting desegregation and calling on all to comply with it peacefully. . . . By 1958 all SBC seminaries accepted black applicants." With considerable understatement, Chappell notes that "people—even historians—are surprised to hear this." Billy Graham, the most prominent Southern preacher, was openly integrationist.

The point of all this is not to deny that Richard Nixon may have invited some nasty fellows into his political bed. The point is that the GOP finally became the region's dominant party in the least racist phase of the South's entire history, and it got that way by attracting most of its votes from the region's growing and confident communities—not its declining and fearful ones. The myth's shrillest proponents are as reluctant to admit this as they are to concede that most Republicans genuinely believe that a color-blind society lies down the road of individual choice and dynamic change, not down the road of state regulation and unequal treatment before the law. The truly tenacious prejudices here are the mythmakers'.

The Long Detour

William A. Rusher

(Summer 2005)

In 1964 the American conservative movement made its first bid for national political power, by seizing control of the Republican Party and nominating Senator Barry Goldwater as its candidate for president. The attempt failed disastrously: Goldwater carried only six states and won just 38% of the popular vote.

But far from disappearing, the conservative movement actually seemed strengthened by its defeat. It continued to grow, organizing the supporters who had cut their teeth in the Goldwater campaign, developing the issues that would make it more relevant in the years ahead, and grooming candidates and spokesmen who could carry its banner. Just four years later in 1968, it had a new national champion in the governor of the nation's largest state, who had been elected in 1966 by a margin of one million votes over the incumbent Democrat. If ever a new political movement seemed poised to take over the governance of America, it was conservatism in 1968.

Yet at just that moment, history paused in what seemed its inevitable course. The conservative movement would be compelled to spend 16 years, from 1964 to 1980, waiting in the wings for its victory. The Republican Party would win (albeit narrowly) in 1968 to be sure, then overwhelmingly in 1972, only to witness in 1974 the first presidential resignation in American history, and then spend six years in the wilderness licking its wounds. The Democrats, despite the growing unpopularity of liberalism, managed to duck the bullets and continue to control both Houses of Congress and even, from 1976 to 1980, the White House. The whole political history of the United States seemed to hiccup and stall, while the country contended, for 16 precious years, with the phenomenon and consequences of one strange, stubborn, and ambiguous man: Richard Nixon.

Having served as Dwight Eisenhower's vice president for eight years, Nixon had a strong claim on his party's presidential nomination in 1960. Some early Goldwater supporters put their tiger's name before the convention, but the senator wisely withdrew it and urged conservatives to await a better day. New York governor Nelson Rockefeller, on behalf of the fading liberal wing of the party, made the first of what was to become a series of failed bids for the nomination. But the delegates were adamant: 1960 was Nixon's year.

Or would have been, had the American people not preferred John Kennedy by a narrow margin. What then was left for Nixon? He ran for the governorship of California in 1962, but was defeated by Democrat Pat Brown. At that point he seems to have concluded that his political career was over. Snarling to the press that "You won't have Nixon to kick around any more," he abandoned California for New York, accepted a lucrative partnership in a posh Wall Street law firm, and told a friend as they strolled up Park Avenue, "This is where the action is—not back in California with those peasants." (Nixon had always harbored a conviction that the real power in America resided in certain key corporate boardrooms and the locker rooms of the "right" golf clubs—perhaps a vestige of the inferiority he had felt as a minor California political figure when Tom Dewey, Henry Luce, and other New Yorkers ran the Republican show.)

American history would have been spared a great many tragic missteps if Richard Nixon had adhered to his resolve to turn his back on politics and live the good life in New York. It seems likely that Ronald Reagan would have won the 1968 nomination (at the age of 57) and the presidency that fall. With the conservative movement in full and early blossom, there would have been a far different, and far better, outcome in Vietnam. There would have been no Watergate, and no presidential resignation under threat of impeachment. In all likelihood, the elder Bush or someone like him, serving as Reagan's vice president and heir, would have succeeded to the presidency in 1976.

But once the presidential bug has bitten a man, he is infected for life. (Thus John Kerry gazes admiringly in a mirror and dreams of 2008.) Richard Nixon was fascinated by Barry Goldwater's capture of the nomination, and by his subsequent overwhelming defeat. He was sure that he could do better—and he meant to try.

This is the point at which Robert Mason, a lecturer in history at the University of Edinburgh, picks up the story. *Richard Nixon and the Quest for a New Majority* is a detailed and workmanlike study of how Nixon approached the problem of winning the presidency in 1968 and again in 1972. It also spells out the plans he had for subsequent victories by his surrogates (notably John Connally), had not Watergate and its *sequelae* ruined them.

One might suppose that Nixon, surveying the field about 1966, would have realized that the conservative movement, which had lost with Goldwater and not yet attached itself to Reagan, lay ready to hand. One might imagine that the Nixon of 1966 would have heard and thought enough about the conservative movement to recognize, and perhaps even admire and identify himself with, the sheer power of its ideas.

But apparently Goldwater's massive defeat blinded Nixon to the important strengths of the conservative movement. He recognized the attraction it held for many people, but regarded it as a problem for the Republican Party, rather than a solution.

In an early and revealing comment that Mason curiously omits to quote, Nixon told a group of reporters in early October 1965 that "the Buckleyites" were "a threat to the Republican Party even more menacing than the Birchers." That was the report of columnists Evans and Novak in an October 14 column, and it was confirmed a few days later by Scripps-Howard by-liner Bruce Biossat, who stated that Nixon had been "emphatic . . . in chats with newsmen" that Buckleyites were "the worst threat to the Party's difficult rebuilding efforts."

Presumably it was Pat Buchanan (whom Nixon had already hired full-time as his contact with the right wing) who explained to Nixon that his statement had been a blunder. But it took repeated demands for an explanation from various "Buckley-ites" (including myself), and an editorial in *National Review* itself, to elicit almost six months later the following convoluted climb-down from Buchanan to *National Review*: what Nixon had "invariably" asserted was only that, in Buckley's 1965 race for the mayoralty of New York City, "Mr. Buckley, by his repudiation of the [John] Birch Society in his magazine and syndicated column, had thereby made himself a much stronger candidate and a greater threat to the Republican candidate, Representative [John] Lindsay."

The episode seems to have taught Nixon the danger of antagonizing the conservative movement. But it does not seem to have occurred to him to make common cause with it, let alone harness his presidential ambitions to it. Instead, in the run-up to the Republican convention of 1968, Mason describes Nixon as formulating his own recipe for a political realignment that would return the GOP to power: To the "base of traditional Republicans, who emphasized the importance of free enterprise," he would add "sections of the population whose needs and expectations differed superficially from the Republican core of support, such as 'new liberals,' who emphasized participatory democracy; the 'new South,' interested in 'interpreting the old doctrine of states' rights in new ways'; most surprisingly, black militants, rejecting welfarism in favor of self-help; plus the 'silent center.'"

The result was that Nixon came within a whisker of losing the 1968 nomination to Reagan, who having encountered no serious competition from Nixon, emerged as the conservative movement's champion.

Reagan's bid for the 1968 nomination is widely forgotten these days—not least, because like most politicians, Reagan didn't enjoy recalling his defeats and in later years minimized the whole affair. But the fact is that he allowed his agents to test the waters thoroughly as early as the fall of 1967, formally declared his candidacy when his plane landed in Miami for the convention, and worked hard for the nomination. Three British reporters who covered the contest and wrote a book about it afterward (*An American Melodrama: The Presidential Campaign of 1968* [1969]) rightly observed that Nixon's margin over Reagan was "almost insultingly small." Nixon prevailed only because conservatives, who controlled the convention as thoroughly as they had controlled its predecessor in 1964, were split. Many, including some who had prematurely committed themselves to Nixon, were in their hearts for Reagan. But a decisive minority of conservatives, led by Senator Strom Thurmond (who in turn had been heavily influenced by his former colleague Barry Goldwater) argued that Reagan, who had only served two years as governor, was too green politically, and that Nixon was conservative "enough." To this misguided belief were owed 12 years of misery for the conservative movement—and for the nation.

Once elected, Nixon put his dream of fashioning a new political majority in the hands of three close aides: H.R. Haldeman, John Ehrlichman, and Charles Colson. There were other, more conservative advisers—notably speechwriter Pat Buchanan—but these three were dominant, and they shared Nixon's disdain for the burgeoning conservative movement, preferring to put together a coalition that would be anti-liberal, but more ambiguous and (they hoped) more attractive than out-and-out conservatism.

In doing so, they noted but rejected the counsel of Kevin Phillips, a brilliant political analyst who was a special assistant to Attorney General John Mitchell. Phillips's book, *The Emerging Republican Majority*, was published in 1969. Nixon's thoroughly "moderate" speechwriter William Safire warned Ehrlichman that it was "most dangerous." On the contrary, it was the most profound and accurate analysis of American politics to appear in decades, and correctly predicted, and explained, the upsurge in Republican fortunes that began in 1968 and has continued almost uninterruptedly ever since. In subsequent years Phillips has published a series of progressively less perceptive books, denouncing what he considers the direction of the Republican Party and laying special blame at the door of the Bush "dynasty." But in *The Emerging Republican Majority*, he made a major and permanent contribution to the field of political science.

Unfortunately its significance was lost on the Nixon high command. Too many people denounced its message that the Republican Party could and should capture the South and the Southwest, wrongly believing that Phillips favored wooing racists, when in fact he merely recognized the enormous change being brought about by young couples from the North flooding into the growing cities of the Sunbelt. Phillips's book was read (though they denied it) by everybody from Nixon down; but it was treated as just another piece of debatable advice.

Instead, "[a]t the start of 1970, Nixon fully believed," asserts Mason, "in his ability to use the silent majority as the foundation of a new majority coalition." That ambiguous phrase—"a new majority"—was capable of being used, and revised, and re-revised, to represent any cocktail of issues and interests that seemed transiently attractive. Mason diligently reports them all.

In the spring of 1970, for example, a crowd of construction workers marching on Wall Street to protest the antics of anti-war activists signaled to the White House the possibility of winning previously unheard-of support from blue-collar workers. Nixon "soon thereafter invited a group of construction workers to the White House," and toyed with the idea of changing the name of the Republican Party to "the Conservative Party."

By September, with the Congressional elections less than two months away, Nixon was ordering his staff to "emphasize anti-crime, anti-demonstrations, anti-drugs, anti-obscenity." But the 1970 election returns were disappointing. There was a gain of just two Republican senators, whereas Nixon had hoped for "at least several more." In the House, the Republicans suffered a net loss of nine. Worst of all, in 45 states holding gubernatorial elections, Republicans lost control in 11, giving them 21 to the Democrats' 29.

So then it was on to the presidential election of 1972. Even now, Nixon kept his distance from the conservative movement. Mason explains why:

> Despite the birth of a modern movement of conservative thought in the 1950s and its growth in the 1960s, conservative ideas remained relatively marginal to intellectual and wider public debate. Moreover, many members of this conservative movement were not unequivocally pledged to the cause of the new majority. Their approach to politics often emphasized an anticommunist foreign policy and a laissez-faire domestic policy. Nixon shared neither guiding principle, so his relationship with movement conservatives was at best uneasy.

One wonders what the conservatives who preferred Nixon in the late 1960s and early 1970s, reading that passage today, will think of their indulgence toward him.

Certainly some conservatives, even at the time, felt acutely uneasy. In July 1971 Nixon announced his intention to visit Beijing in 1972, a move clearly designed to pave the way to formal diplomatic recognition. And on August 15 he imposed wage and price controls, a policy anathema to every economic conservative. As a result, in the summer of 1971 a group of conservatives that became known as the Manhattan Twelve announced their tentative decision to support a more conservative candidate against Nixon in 1972. This group (of which I was a member) was broadly representative of the major organizations in the conservative movement—*National Review*, *Human Events*, the American Conservative Union, Young Americans for Freedom, and so on—but did not represent a serious political threat to Nixon, in part because their own determination to oppose him was, in several cases, distinctly half-hearted. Nevertheless, most of them endorsed Congressman John Ashbrook of Ohio for the nomination against Nixon, and supported him doggedly through the New Hampshire primary. When Nixon returned from his visit to Beijing in February 1972, Bill Buckley (one of 80 journalists who had accompanied him) wrote bluntly: "We have lost—irretrievably—any sense of moral mission in the world." But it hardly mattered; Nixon won the Republican primaries overwhelmingly.

Meanwhile, he kept adding ingredients to his New Majority cocktail. Sensing broad public sympathy for Lieutenant William Calley, who had been convicted of murder and sentenced to life in prison for his role in the massacre of 300 Vietnamese civilians at My Lai, Nixon identified himself with the cause of reducing the sentence. Ultimately Calley spent less than four years under house arrest before obtaining parole. Union leaders, in particular, were delighted.

Desegregation, too, attracted Nixon's attention and his cautious opposition. He openly declared his opposition to forced busing and "residential desegregation" (building public housing in ethnic neighborhoods). Nor were Catholic voters overlooked: despite the reservations of his staff, Nixon supported public financial aid to private (and therefore to parochial) schools.

Mason is rightly unimpressed with these efforts. "Against a strong opponent, [they] might not even have been enough to win reelection for Nixon." But the Democrats, incredibly, nominated George McGovern, a candidate on the far left of American opinion.

Mason's description of Nixon's campaign is almost chilling. "[Nixon's] strategy depended on the rejection of concern for the Republican Party at large." His vehicle was not the party but the Committee for the Reelection of the President (CRP, forgivably bastardized as CREEP). He calculated that after the election would be the moment to launch, as the vehicle for his New Majority, a new conservative party, with Texas Democrat John Connally at its head.

As the campaign of 1972 began, Nixon spoke of "character," and praised the "moral and spiritual strength" of the American people. They were, he declared, "united in their continued belief in honest hard work, love of country, spiritual faith." Slowly the voters began to develop deep reservations about McGovern. Nor did it hurt that there seemed to be fresh progress in peace negotiations with North Vietnam. The "one overriding issue," Nixon told voters, was "the issue of peace—peace in Vietnam, and peace in the world at large for a generation to come."

When the smoke cleared on election night, Richard Nixon had received the greatest presidential plurality in American history, and carried every state but Massachusetts. The Republican Party had much less to brag about: ticket-splitters had actually caused it to suffer a net loss of two senators and one governor, and a gain of only 13 seats in the House. But to Nixon the victory confirmed his strategy. He claimed in his memoirs that it was "truly a New Majority landslide of the kind I had called for in my acceptance speech in August."

What Richard Nixon might have done with his vaunted New Majority if all had gone well is fodder for endless speculation. Would it have absorbed and superseded the growing conservative movement, or swiftly evanesced? We will never know, because all did not go well. Within three months of Nixon's second inauguration, the Watergate scandal overwhelmed the White House. In August 1974, facing certain impeachment, Nixon became the first and only president to resign from office. Ironically, in the nearly two decades of life that remained to him, he devoted himself to rehabilitating his own image without the slightest reference to, or any further support for, his concept of a New Majority. Instead, he carefully cultivated his reputation as a master of foreign policy among the very liberals he had once so cordially detested.

Meanwhile, what of the conservative movement he had contemptuously disdained? It had supported him for election in 1968, despite the disappointment many conservatives felt at Reagan's narrow defeat for the nomination. It supported him again for reelection in 1972, with a few exceptions and a good many reservations. But the very fact that Nixon so zealously excluded leaders of the conservative movement from major appointments in his administration (Bill Buckley, for example, was named merely a member of the U.S. delegation to the United Nations) meant that they were virtually immune to collateral injury when the administration's collapse finally came.

Instead, the conservative movement spent the Nixon years building its strength quite independently. The names and addresses of the many thousands of people who had made small financial contributions to the Goldwater campaign were painstakingly copied, computerized, and made available to subsequent conservative campaigns. Paul Weyrich established the Committee for the Survival of a Free Congress to facilitate his involvement in congressional primaries and elections in both parties. John T. ("Terry") Dolan created the National Conservative Political Action Committee to raise conservative campaign funds and spend them where they would do the most good. Jay Parker founded the Lincoln Institute for Research and Education to work directly on issues affecting his fellow blacks. Phyllis Schlafly launched her war against the Equal Rights Amendment, winning in 1978 a victory that will always be associated with her name. Consumer affairs were the field of Consumer Alert, the brainchild of a remarkable Vietnam War widow named Barbara Keating. Medical topics were the province of a panel of distinguished medical scientists assembled by Dr. Elizabeth Whelan's American Council on Science and Health. Issues related to defense were the focus of John Fisher's American Security Council, and global strategic concerns were the specialty of Frank Barnett's National Strategy Information Center.

On the college front, the Intercollegiate Studies Institute had been founded in the early 1950s, and Young Americans for Freedom had been on the scene since 1960.

They were now joined by Irving Kristol's Institute for Educational Affairs, which specialized in encouraging conservative college journals. The early 1970s also saw the founding of the American Legislative Exchange Council, which soon boasted a membership of 2,000 state legislators. In the same period a number of "public service legal foundations" were launched, to litigate conservative causes in the nation's courts.

Perhaps most important of all was the founding of the Heritage Foundation in 1973 by Paul Weyrich, Joseph Coors, and Edwin Feulner. This provided the conservative movement with an aggressive and competent "think tank" to furnish conservative political leaders and spokesmen with policy guidance and technical backup facilities. Within 10 years it had an annual budget of $9.5 million.

Thus did the American conservative movement expand and arm itself for battle in the very years when Richard Nixon was concocting his New Majority. As we have seen, he disdained the movement, and gradually those conservatives who had once given him their support came to disdain him. By 1974, when he resigned the presidency, the divorce was complete. Gerald Ford, whom Nixon had appointed vice president when Spiro Agnew resigned, ratified it (if that was necessary) when he assumed the presidency on Nixon's resignation and promptly appointed Nelson Rockefeller as vice president. This move—putting the leader of the rapidly vanishing liberal wing of the Republican Party within a heartbeat of the presidency, thereby mortally affronting the conservatives—is surely in the running for the stupidest blunder ever committed by an American president. There was no way the Republican convention of 1976 could be bludgeoned into nominating Rockefeller for vice president, and Rockefeller himself practically admitted as much when he took himself out of the running.

The conservatives were by now solidly behind Ronald Reagan, and with their support he won the nomination in 1980 and went on to trounce Jimmy Carter that November. Four years later he was reelected, carrying every state but Minnesota.

It would be interesting to know Richard Nixon's inmost thoughts as he watched Reagan assume the leadership of the powerful movement he himself had so cavalierly disregarded, win election and reelection, and become one of the greatest presidents of the 20th century. There had been a time when Nixon himself might have seized the leadership of that movement, and in consonance with its principles contributed to American history the high and honorable legacy we now rightly associate with Ronald Reagan.

But Richard Nixon was at heart a Machiavellian, which is to say that he believed that the fundamental truths of politics were not about principles but about power. His "quest for a New Majority" was simply an attempt to assemble a coalition of interests muscular enough to take over the country. When a concept like freedom crossed his mind, it was only as an ideal that he realized some people prized enough to die for. Of politics as he understood it, he was a master. But he never comprehended the richness of its potential as a vehicle for the principles that can alone conduce to the happiness of mankind.

Why Conservatives Lost the War of Ideas

Thomas B. Silver

(Winter 2001/02)

A century has not diminished the hold of progressive ideas on the American mind. In the years before World War I, known as the Progressive Era, philosophers, academics, and intellectuals like John Dewey, William James, Charles Beard, Walter Lippmann, and Herbert Croly set out to transform America's self understanding. They sapped and shattered—and then rebuilt—America's original foundation, the work of our Founding Fathers. At the beginning of the 21st century, we are ever more firmly in the grip of their powerful ideas, still standing on the new foundation they built. The 20th century, in terms of the American political tradition, was rhythmic, calling to mind the cyclical interpretation set forth by Arthur M. Schlesinger and later carried forward by his son, Arthur M. Schlesinger, Jr. The first 20 years of the 20th century—the decades of Theodore Roosevelt and Woodrow Wilson—constituted the first of three progressive waves that would dominate American politics for 100 years. They were followed by the 1920s, a decade of conservatism under Republican Presidents Warren Harding, Calvin Coolidge, and Herbert Hoover. Then came the second wave of progressivism, 20 years of the New Deal and the Fair Deal, beginning with Franklin D. Roosevelt and ending with Harry Truman. They were followed by the 1950s, another decade of conservatism under President Dwight Eisenhower. A third 20-year wave of progressivism began with John F. Kennedy and the New Frontier, continued through the Great Society with Lyndon Johnson, and finally petered out with Jimmy Carter. Ronald Reagan was the leading political figure of the 1980s, but Reagan, like Coolidge and Eisenhower before him, lived to see the Democratic Party back in the White House. There is an obvious logic to the progressive dynamic. So long as there is no realistic prospect of dismantling the administrative state whose foundations were laid by Wilson and built upon by the New Deal and the Great Society, the movement of history must be in a progressive direction. Every major conservative political victory becomes a victory for the status quo; every major liberal victory becomes another step forward. Progressives are always just one electoral victory away from resuming the forward march of history.

A powerful reason for the current state of affairs is that, at the deepest level, progressivism long ago won the battle of ideas with conservatism. Certainly this was part of FDR's grander purpose in 1936. That election overwhelmingly ratified the New Deal. His objective was not just to win an immediate political victory but to interpret that victory for succeeding generations. The mandate of 1936 remains intact; it has not been overturned by a later critical election. Reagan's counterattack against the New Deal, always fiercer in rhetoric than in its actions, never came close to undoing what Roosevelt set out to do—namely, to enlarge public power, partly as a corrective to private social and economic inequities, partly as means of accomplishing great public purposes. Reagan rode into Washington on a white horse, promising to decapitate government spending, slash taxes, and slay the great dragon bureaucracies. He did not fulfill those promises. The federal tax bite in 1999 was at its highest peacetime level in history: 20.7% of GDP. Taxation by government at all levels—two decades after Reagan's first inauguration—was 35.7 cents for every dollar taxpayers earned, a record high. This is not to say that Reagan accomplished nothing of his agenda; it is to say he failed to break the hegemony of the New Deal. From our vantage point more than 20 years after Reagan took office, it is evident that the man who would overthrow the New Deal rode into Washington as Saint George and rode out as Don Quixote. Still, is there not a body of academic scholarship in place that has refuted progressive thought and that will, over time, have an increasingly large political effect?

A MOTLEY CAMP

Certainly the most successful area of conservative scholarship has been in economics. A generation of free-market economists has added immensely to our understanding of how markets work, and has undermined much of the Keynesian rationale for the fiscal and monetary policies of the New Deal and its successors. But economics is an instrumental discipline; its sphere is the study of means, not of ends. Progressivism was—and is—at its deepest level a teaching about human and political ends. The successes of free-market economics, to the extent that they are broadly convincing, can be assimilated, sometimes easily, into the pragmatic framework of American progressivism or liberalism.

It became clear during the 1970s, for example, that various government regulations were, in fact, harmful to the people they were supposed to check. President Carter and other liberals had no trouble supporting deregulation in certain areas. And if a steady monetary policy, like the one conducted from 1987 to 1997 by a free-market disciple of Ayn Rand, can be shown to produce sound results, it was no violation of his liberalism for President Clinton to embrace it, as he did.

Free-market economists have not overthrown progressivism, finally, because conservatives do not all agree that prosperity is the key issue. Prosperity for what? It is precisely this question that divides the Right and gives it the appearance of being nothing more that an alliance of convenience. Consider those irascible yokefellows, the libertarians and the Christian Right. Many libertarians (not all) are atheists, i.e., they deny the authority of both revelation and of reason in telling people how they should live. On this view, it supposedly follows that (a) human beings should be "free to choose" their own ends and lifestyles, and (b) the government is best that gives its citizens the widest latitude to make such choices; in other words, that government is best that governs least (or, in some extreme versions of libertarianism, not at all).

A softer version of this libertarian argument (but leading to the same practical conclusion) is agnosticism. This is not the flat denial of the authority of God or reason, but the more subtle claim that we simply don't know. As a practical matter, agnosticism collapses into atheism. If there is no objective right or wrong, then who is to tell someone else how to live his life? Everyone should have the absolute right to do as he pleases, so long as he accords everyone else the same right. Thus across a wide expanse of the libertarian Right, the absolute right that we have in our persons and property is regarded as a deduction from the relativism of all values. Obviously, it would not take a rocket scientist to drive a truck through this argument. It would take a truck driver. For the Christian Right, the question of how to live is not open but closed. For this reason, liberals and libertarians both fear that the victory of the Christian Right would usher in something like the reign of Ayatollah Khomeini. And indeed, to the extent that they could identify themselves as the Christian Right, do not religious conservatives point to the Bible as the source of their moral beliefs? Does this mean that their political agenda comes directly from Biblical revelation? If so, how authoritative can it be for citizens in a constitutional democracy, one of whose glories is the separation of church and state? How can the concern for morality or virtue be reconciled with freedom?

Into the motley camp of economic conservatives, libertarians, and religious conservatives come the traditionalists, or "original intent" conservatives. Their view is that on the fundamental issues of today we ought to be guided by the will of the American people—the American people, that is, who lived 200 years ago—as codified in the U.S. Constitution, until such time as the people themselves dictate a change in policy through the proper constitutional channels. But why should we be bound by what some people—people ignorant of our own circumstances—thought two centuries ago? An argument is needed to connect the two.

In traditional societies, the old is identified with the good because the ancestral is divine: the ancestors, or the ancestors of ancestors, were gods. One might place that in a modern context as follows: for Americans our "ancestral" faith is the creed expressed in the Declaration of Independence, whose principles are said to be derived from "the laws of Nature and of Nature's God." The constitutional authority of the people, whether those living two hundred years ago or those living today, is derived from, and limited by, something higher than the mere will of the people. Apparently, however, our "original intent," conservatives would sooner have their tongues cut out than mention the "n"-word—*Nature*—in the same breath with the Constitution.

Thus, their constitutionalism degenerates into conventionalism, and they find themselves in the awkward position of defending the old merely because it is old, which is no more plausible than defending the new merely because it is new.

RETURN TO THE FOUNDERS

We begin to see how the perplexities of conservative thought contribute to the progressive hold on the American mind and why progressivism cannot be dislodged by mere policy studies, however many and however persuasive. Ronald Reagan understood this and unified the Right through a patriotic rhetoric that harkened back to the founders and to the laws of Nature and of Nature's God. Reagan's purpose was to accommodate moral, economic, and national security concerns within a single framework. The question, however, is this: Is it possible to regard such rhetoric as anything more serious than mere rhetoric? Or is it not just a pretty papering over of fundamental difficulties, akin to hiding the fatal structural defects in a house by putting up colonial wallpaper? Reagan's rhetoric is exposed to one massive problem: most serious thinkers today, including many (if not most) on the Right, no longer accept that idea of Nature articulated in the Declaration of Independence. The whole weight of modern science and philosophy has been brought up against the idea of Nature as the universal ground of political obligation, valid for all human beings everywhere and always. Thus, it would appear to be profoundly reactionary to attempt to return in any serious way to the 18th-century thought of the Founding Fathers.

The Conservative Cocoon

Ross Douthat

(Winter 2005/06)

Not that long ago, the liberal media simply *"was* the mass media," writes Brian Anderson, senior editor of *City Journal*, in his *South Park Conservatives: The Revolt Against Liberal Media Bias*. As recently as the Reagan era, a George Will here, a William Safire there, and a few lonely bastions like *National Review* were the only counters to the biases and assumptions pervading every half-hour segment and column inch of the nation's networks, newsmagazines, and high-profile daily newspapers.

How all that changed, how Dan Rather and Bill Moyers gave way to Hugh Hewitt and Brit Hume, is a well-known but worthwhile story, and Anderson offers an engaging account of the rise of the right-wing media, and the sputtering, stupefied reaction from the liberal establishment as conservatives gate-crashed their garden party. The Right has come far enough in the last 20 years that it's useful to remember how it all began—with Brian Lamb founding C-SPAN and Newt Gingrich taking advantage of it; with the repeal of the unfair "Fairness Doctrine" that prohibited one-sided political talk radio and the subsequent debut of Rush Limbaugh's "talent on loan from God"; with Ted Turner promising to squash the fledgling Fox News like a bug and instead watching his network eat Roger Ailes's dust. It's useful, too, now that many reporters have all but acknowledged their political biases, to be reminded of how an illiberal liberal media spent decades insisting that it enjoyed a monopoly on fairness and balance.

What isn't clear from Anderson's look backward, however, is whether conservatives have come quite as far as he thinks they have. *South Park Conservatives*, as its title suggests, isn't just concerned with the rise of right-leaning media—it aspires to cover the entirety of the culture wars, from late-night comedy to the groves of academe. And once Anderson moves beyond talk radio and Fox News, his examples of cultural counterrevolution don't always bear the argumentative weight he ascribes to them. At times, he hedges his bets, remarking sensibly that "it's too soon to tell" if even the modern, media-savvy Right is doing more than merely holding its own. But a tone of breezy triumphalism pervades much of the book, and too often

127

Anderson only skims the surface of things, shying away from the harder questions that loom beneath.

For instance, many of the developments that he insists favor conservatives—from the declining influence of the mainstream media (MSM) to the anti-P.C. inclinations of cable television—have less to do with the Right's advance than with larger, post-1960s trends toward cultural fragmentation. This breakdown has been good for conservatives in certain ways: the genteel and biased liberalism of, say, Walter Cronkite or Arthur Schlesinger, Jr., no longer infuses every nook and cranny of the public sphere. But it's worth wondering whether trading in Cronkite for Paris Hilton—that is, stultifying old-guard liberalism for vulgar libertinism—really represents such a great victory for the Right.

True, the current Republican majority probably wouldn't exist without the alternative media universe that conservatives have created amid the rubble of the old establishment. But *South Park Conservatives* is supposed to be about culture, not Congress, and once you move to the realm of arts and ideas, manners and mores, the impact of Fox News and talk radio is harder to gauge. The new conservative media infrastructure is ideally suited to rapid-response punditry and rallying the base, but it's not really an *alternative* to the major cultural institutions—the big dailies, networks, universities, and Hollywood studios. Talk-show hosts and bloggers criticize the mainstream media's excesses, but rarely do any reporting of their own. Conservative think tanks provide a corrective to Ivy League liberalism, but aren't in the business of actually educating undergraduates and churning out Ph.D.s. *The O'Reilly Factor* can give a right-leaning movie a much-needed boost, but aside from a few outliers like *The Passion of the Christ*, it isn't clear that Hollywood has become any more hospitable to conservative values and themes in the last decade or so.

Anderson tries to make the case that in certain areas, the Right is moving beyond parasitism to parity: he celebrates the emergence of conservative publishing imprints like Crown Forum and Sentinel, and the appearance of right-leaning academic institutes like Princeton's James Madison Program. But the fact that publishers have discovered the money to be made in right-wing books doesn't necessarily tell us anything about whether conservative writers have succeeded in escaping the intellectual ghetto—especially when many of the right-leaning imprints hailed by Anderson seem more interested in turning up the next Ann Coulter than an heir to Allan Bloom or James Q. Wilson.

Similarly, the climate in the American university may be less politically correct, and less politicized in general, than in past decades, but a turn away from P.C. isn't the same as a move toward conservatism. "The Left's iron hold on academe is beginning to loosen," Anderson insists, but the case he makes is long on anecdotes, mostly from conservative students and activists like David Horowitz, and short on compelling evidence. College students today are unquestionably more hawkish (at least prior to the Iraq War, whose aftermath has pushed many doveward) and less stridently socialist than a generation ago (not least because of the size of the salaries they'll be earning after graduation), but their politics are more centrist and Clintonian than they are conservative. The institutional culture at most elite schools is still unremittingly hostile to conservative ideas, and there's little sign that the liberal ice is cracking in faculty lounges and administrative offices. A few conservative professors and campus newspapers do not a counterrevolution make. The '60s Left actually took over academia, remember, whereas the 21st-century Right seems content merely to lob stones through the university's more vulnerable windows.

Then there's the ever-more-libertine pop-culture scene, from the *Maxim*-Britney axis of hedonism at the lowbrow end to the self-satisfied lifestyle liberalism of highbrow novels and Oscar-bait movies. "Many young people" may be turning "to family values (at least in theory) with the enthusiasm of converts," as Anderson says, but you wouldn't know it from the youth-culture trends in movies, music, clothes, and magazines. Even *South Park*, Anderson's prize example of right-leaning pop culture, is more anti-liberal than pro-conservative. The show gleefully mocks liberal pieties, but does so, one suspects, as much from expediency as conviction, for those happen to be the pieties that dominate the lives of Comedy Central's target audience, well-off teens and twenty-somethings. This makes for superb satire, and conservatives shouldn't feel bad about laughing along with it, but the adolescent libertarianism that *South Park* promotes isn't anything like a real conservatism.

Anderson might retort that you don't look for Burkean messages in a scatological television show. But in that case, he needs to provide a few solid, non-*South Park* examples to back up his assertion that "a right-leaning news and culture junkie could flick across the television channel array these days and never feel alone." Sure, there's Fox News and C-SPAN and perhaps the History Channel, but on the creative side of the dial, Anderson quickly finds himself celebrating the lousy and the obscure, claiming preposterously that Dennis Miller's dreadful, since-cancelled CNBC show was "riveting television," or heaping praise on mediocrities like Colin Quinn and deservedly marginal figures like Republican stand-up comic Julia Gorin, just because they have a flair for the politically incorrect. For decades, conservatives have rolled their eyes at liberal critics who confused political correctness with artistic merit, whether it was Toni Morrison winning the Nobel Prize or *American Beauty* taking home Best Picture. Anderson has no business falling into the same trap.

This kind of cheerleading suggests a danger for conservatives that *South Park Conservatives* scarcely addresses, the danger of cocooning. The old liberal media establishment was often described, all-too-accurately, as a left-wing echo chamber, rarely penetrated by the clamor of reality. Now the Right has its own mini-establishment, which likewise runs the risk of becoming less a forum for original ideas than a museum case for stale assumptions.

You can already see this echo-chamber tendency in the right-wing bloggers and pundits who eagerly pounce on every liberal folly, however minor, while passing over conservative blunders in silence, or frantically spinning GOP dross into gold. Confident that the Right has won the war of ideas, too many conservatives don't bother to grapple with liberalism as it actually exists, preferring instead to train their fire on straw men and minor-league extremists. And secure in the knowledge that the hated MSM will always misinterpret the world, conservatives—including, by his own account, the current occupant of the White House—often close their ears to the things that the liberal media gets right, preferring to filter their news through more congenial outlets.

Anderson is no exception to this disquieting trend. Seen through his red-state-colored glasses, the rise of the blogosphere is an "explosive change that is shaking liberal media dominance"—a claim that might have been tempered by at least some mention of how the leftist blog Daily Kos or the Deaniacs easily turned the internet to left-wing ends. He seems to have no enemies to the right: in Anderson's telling, an embarrassment like Michael Savage becomes a "firebrand," while the Swift Boat Veterans' patchwork of largely baseless accusations was an "explosive anti-Kerry book" that treacherous Borders employees tried to squash. And he un-critically celebrates the blogs and pundits who attacked every negative report from Iraq as "relentless pessimism and antiwar spin"—even though, two years on, the pessimistic MSM dispatches hold up better than the glass-half-full assumptions of many right-wingers. Every political party and administration needs its cheerleaders, of course, but Anderson is far too smart to play this kind of knee-jerk role, and it's a shame to see him lapse into it so easily.

None of these failings makes what *South Park Conservatives* has to say, in the main, any less important or any less encouraging. It's a good thing that conservatives are fighting back against the biases of the mainstream media. It's a great thing that an illiberal liberalism no longer dominates the national discourse. It's marvelous news that political correctness seems to be on the run. But having spent a generation complaining about liberalism's less-than-intimate relationship with reality, conser-vatives need to think hard about whether they're in danger of spinning themselves a similar cocoon.

Tailgunner Ann

William F. Buckley, Jr.

(Winter 2003/04)

Arrived in Montreal, I put aside Ann Coulter's book, and descended the gangway. At the baggage claim area I spotted a newsstand. I was drawn to the headline featuring—Ann Coulter.

That day's copy of the *National Post* boasted Coulter at the top of the page in full color, her long blond hair southbound, interrupted only by a news headline. Alongside her picture the text was, "ANN COULTER: *New York Times* publisher is a traitor to U.S., Comment: A10."

Her advertised finding certainly warranted immediate examination. But I did of course wonder, as I turned the pages, whether the lure of textual tabloidization had taken over in the *Post*, the straight Toronto daily founded only five years earlier (and sold in 2001) by the conservative Conrad Black, now Lord Black. And I was curious to know whether Ms. Coulter had sharpened her taxonomic tools since writing the book I was reading.

She wasted no time passing sentence.

> During my recent book tour, I resisted the persistent, illiterate request that I name traitors. With a great deal of charity—and suspension of disbelief—I was willing to concede that many liberals were merely fatuous idiots. But after the *New York Times*'s despicable editorial on the two-year anniversary of the 9/11 terrorist attack, I am prepared—just this once—to name a traitor: Pinch Sulzberger, publisher of the *Times*.

What followed was two *ad hominem* references to Sulzberger (he allegedly hadn't made it into Columbia University) embedded in a boiling-mad 600-word account of the offending *New York Times* editorial. She paraphrased its meaning: "When General Pinochet staged his coup against a Marxist strong man [in 1973], the U.S. did not stop him—as if Latin American generals were incapable of doing coups on their own. And—I quote [the editorial]—'It was September 11.' Parsed to its essentials, the *Times*'s position is: We deserved it."

I dug up the editorial in question. It was titled, "The Other Sept. 11," and undertook the dark comparison without mincing words. "Death came from the skies," it began. "A building—a symbol of the nation—collapsed in flames in an act of terror that would lead to the deaths of 3,000 people. It was September 11."

Get it? Coulter certainly got it. The overthrow of Salvador Allende on 9/11/73 had led to 3,000 deaths—the same death toll as in 9/11/01. Not immediately dead, the Chileans, but dead in the weeks and early years ahead of the military dictatorship.

So here we Americans found ourselves, on September 11, 28 years later, confronting our own tragic loss of life. The *Times* was calling on us to reflect that for all the apparent differences between the two 9/11's, a bloodline ran from Santiago, 1973, to New York, 2001. The preacher's apocalyptic simile had poetical and material weaknesses.

The Chilean building in which Allende died did not, in fact, collapse in flames. The flames were doused. A random act of terror in 2001 is not the same as a *coup d'etat* in 1973. The staging of the Chilean coup did not call for "death from the skies." It was in fact conceived as a bloodless coup.

But all of that is by the way in an inquiry into the Coulter thinking machine, which is my mission. What she wrote was that 1) the publisher of the newspaper that 2) printed an editorial that 3) reiterated the old historical argument that denounced U.S. acquiescence in the removal of Allende, was 4) engaging moral equivalence and therefore, 5) a traitor. We don't need to come up with the weaknesses, or even the depravities, in the *Times*'s reasoning. But even as Ms. Coulter clearly intends to shock, why shouldn't her reader register that shock? By wondering whether she is out of her mind, or has simply lost her grip on language.

What except that prompts her to come up with (or the *Post* to publicize) her syllogism? The man who heads the paper that employs an editorial writer who dangles the proposition that a thought given to moral equivalency is appropriate and humbling on September 11, 2003 is a "traitor"? That end-of-the-road word, bear always in mind, is hers. Coulter is a law school graduate and isn't using the "t"-word loosely. The opening sentences of her article reject any such explanation. She means to charge that Sulzberger is engaged in traitorous activity. That, after all, is what traitors engage in.

The thought-process used here is everywhere in evidence in her best-selling book, *Treason: Liberal Treachery from the Cold War to the War on Terrorism* (2003). The book's central contention is that liberals critically situated on the American scene aren't fatuous asses—that's baby talk. They are enemies of the United States and of American freedom.

As expected, much of the book is devoted to rejecting commonly accepted charges against Senator Joe McCarthy. She gives the reader the names of a dozen indisputably traitorous actors who worked in government while concealing their ties to the Soviet Union. Quite properly, she lists Alger Hiss and Owen Lattimore as prime examples of liberal obstinacy, and she wonders very much out loud whether that obstinacy arose because these liberals were concerned with due process and the presumption of innocence and all that, or whether they were, in heart and mind, on the Soviet side in the Cold War. McCarthy simply made up the charge that Lattimore was the "top agent" of the Soviets in the United States, but that exaggeration did not mean that the evidence against Lattimore, Communist agent, was less than overwhelming.

But as one reads along, one gets used to exaggerations—not McCarthy's, but Coulter's. She is carried away. Yes, the Rosenbergs were justly and correctly executed for treason, but get a load of the language that flows from it, in the hands of Ms. Coulter. She is talking about the famous Army-McCarthy contest and focusing now on the army dentist. The McCarthy committee spotted Major Irving Peress, a Communist, who had been kept on in the army and even promoted. "When were they [the army] to learn? Thanks to the Army's incompetence in dealing with the Rosenbergs, nearly 300 million Americans would spend the second half of the 20th century under threat of nuclear annihilation." That is something of a stretch, for-want-of-a-nail compounded to the 10th power. The Coulter reader, impelled by the momentum of Coulter, Historian, might wonder why, in high pitch of wrath and anger, she let the army off merely with the charge of incompetence. Why not make the army traitorous, too?

She writes with scorn and derision of the critics of McCarthy and of the lengths to which many of them went, and still do. The late Brent Bozell and I spent 18 months attempting to distinguish what McCarthy had said and charged in the years we examined, and where (not often) he was indefensible. Our book was titled *McCarthy and His Enemies* (1954), because we sought to make the point that many enemies of McCarthy had earned a derision and contempt that they nevertheless never had experienced in the cooler, reflective chambers of historical criticism. Coulter's rejoinders to many of McCarthy's critics are well aimed, and the offenders eminently vulnerable. In an introduction to a new edition of *McCarthy and His Enemies*, in 1961, I wrote that "The McCarthy business of course was deadly serious, and if it was not, there surely was no excuse either for his activities or his enemies'." I was under the mistaken impression, in 1961, that the totality of such as Richard Rovere expressed in his book *Senator Joe McCarthy* (1959), would bring a critical reaction: "Can it be, indeed, that we are coming out of it?" That is, out of hysterical anti-McCarthyism? The terminal extremities of the Rovere book, I judged,

> may prove to have been the great disintegrating thunderclap that shattered the storm cradle itself. Perhaps this volume [*McCarthy and His Enemies*] can now be read in the grayish light that augurs the dawn of a national composure on the subject of McCarthyism. There are already those who are embarrassed by the lengths to which McCarthy's enemies went in prosecuting their myth. Lord Bertrand Russell actually said that McCarthy had made it unsafe for Americans to read Thomas Jefferson.

Arthur Herman's *Joseph McCarthy: Reexamining the Life and Legacy of America's Most Hated Senator*, published in 1999, sought to be balanced. Coulter goes in the opposite direction, sounding sometimes like Roy Cohn, whose defenses of McCarthy were in the language of Biblical inerrancy: "If he said it (did it), it was the right thing to say (to do)." But as we have seen, Coulter is much, *much* more extreme in her judgments than McCarthy ever was, though from one particular passage of McCarthy she takes explicit encouragement, ending up on the road to Pinch-as-traitor.

Senator McCarthy, I wrote a few years ago (in my novel *The Redhunter*, 1999), here and there gave evidence of being the prototypical John Bircher—the man who believes that the objective consequences of a man's deeds reflect his subjective designs. Coulter approvingly recalls the sentence from McCarthy's speech against

General George Marshall that makes exactly that point. "If Marshall was merely stupid," McCarthy said, "the laws of probability would dictate that part of his decisions would serve America's interests." That sentence declares, in a word, that George Marshall was in fact a Communist agent. One pauses, if only for a tiny moment. Could Ann Coulter really believe that? Naw. She is just making rhetoric, as in the Pinch-is-a-traitor column.

Yet no mention of Ms. Coulter's work should omit acknowledgment of her adroit wit in treating of political correctness. She has a lovely passage on P.C.'s fatuity:

> In early December 2001, "60 Minutes" host Steve Kroft interviewed [Transportation Secretary Norman] Mineta about his approach to securing the airlines from terrorist attack. Kroft observed that of twenty-two men currently on the FBI's most-wanted list, "all but one of them has complexion listed as olive. They all have dark hair and brown eyes. And more than half of them have the name Mohammed." Thus, he asked Mineta if airport security should give more scrutiny to someone named Mohammed—"just going down a passenger manifest list: Bob, Paul, John, Frank, Steven, Mohammed." The secretary of transportation said, "No." In fact, Mineta was mystified by Kroft's question, asking him, "Why should Mohammed be singled out?" The Federal Aviation Administration had a computer profiling system on passengers, but it actually excluded mention of passengers' race, ethnicity, national origin, or religion. (What does it have?)

There was the dogged *New York Times* defense of the so-called Lackawanna Muslims, brought in by the FBI and interrogated. The *Times* expressed deep sympathy for the detainees, and reported the dismay of their neighbors. "It was just like the *Times*'s man-on-the-street interviews on Bush's tax plan. For the *Times*, an ordinary American is a sociology professor in Oregon whose wife teaches tantric sex at the community college." Coulter accosts the defense of the detained Yemeni-Americans to the effect that they were no more suspicious than the man next door with some of the data the FBI had come up with. "The prosecution's case, at least in part, is that a terrorist can be the kid next door. Yes—if the kid next door trained with al-Qaeda. Mohammed Atta lived next door to somebody, too. Don't all criminals live next door to somebody? What was the *Times*'s point?"

There is a lot of such fun and shrewdness as this in Ann Coulter's book, but there is also mischief, which of course can be fun. Especially mischief about the other guy.

III

THE WAR WE ARE IN

Victory: What It Will Take to Win

Angelo M. Codevilla

(Fall 2001)

It is not that they love peace less, but that they love their kind of peace more.

—Saint Augustine, *The City of God*

In the end, there was no one so small or weak that they could not do them harm.

—Montesquieu, *The Greatness of the Romans and Their Decline*

By their fruits shall ye know them.

—Jesus, the Sermon on the Mount

As Americans mourned on the night of September 11, many in the Middle East celebrated. Their enemies, 280 million people disposing of one third the wealth of the earth, had been bloodied. Better yet, Americans were sadly telling each other that life would never be the same as before—and certainly not better.

The revelers' joy was troubled only by the fear that an angry America might crush them. For a few hours, Palestinian warlords referred to the events as *al-Nachba*—"the disaster"—and from Gaza to Baghdad the order spread that victory parties must be out of sight of cameras and that any inflammatory footage must be seized. But soon, to their relief, the revelers heard the American government announce that it would not hold them responsible. President George W. Bush gratuitously held out the cachet of "allies" in the war on terrorism to nations that the U.S. government had officially designated as the world's chief sponsors of terrorism. Thus Yasser Arafat's, Saddam Hussein's, and Bashar al-Assad's regimes could enjoy, *undisturbed*, the success of the anti-Western cause that alone legitimizes their rule. That peace is their victory, and our lack of peace is our defeat.

Common sense does not mistake the difference between victory and defeat: the losers weep and cower, while the winners strut and rejoice. The losers have to change their ways, the winners feel more secure than ever in theirs. On September 12, retiring Texas Senator Phil Gramm encapsulated this common sense: "I don't want to change the way I live. I want to change the way they live." Common sense

137

says that victory means living without worry that some foreigners might kill us on behalf of their causes, but also without having to bow to domestic bureaucrats and cops, especially useless ones. It means not changing the tradition by which the government of the United States treats citizens as its masters rather than as potential enemies. Victory requires killing our enemies, or making them live in debilitating fear.

The flood of authoritative commentary flowing from the U.S. government and the media soon washed common sense out of America's discourse. The conventional wisdom is foursquare in favor of the "War on Terrorism." But it defines that war in terms of an endless series of ever more sophisticated security measures at home; better intelligence for identifying terrorists; and military as well as economic measures to "bring to justice" the shadowy al-Qaeda network. Notably, this flood averts attention from the fact that sowing terror in order to get America to tie itself in rancorous knots is the principal element of several governments' foreign policy. It also discourages questioning the competence of the U.S. officials under whose guidance, in a single decade, America became the object in much of the world of a fateful combination of hatred and contempt. In short, the conventional wisdom envisages no effort to make mourners out of revelers and vice versa.

There will surely be more attacks, and of increasing seriousness. That is because the success of the September 11 attacks and of their aftermath has mightily encouraged America's enemies, and as we shall see, no security or intelligence measures imaginable stand any chance of diminishing the opportunities for successful terrorist attacks. Why should America's enemies stop doing what has proved safe, successful, and fun?

Let us first examine the attitudes and policies of the U.S. government that guarantee defeat—in fact, are defeat itself. Then we will be able to see more clearly what victory would look like, and how it could be achieved.

ANATOMY OF DEFEAT

The U.S. government's "War on Terrorism" has three parts: "Homeland Security," more intelligence, and bringing al-Qaeda "to justice." The first is impotent, counterproductive, and silly. The second is impossible. The third is misconceived and is a diversion from reality.

Security Is Illusory

The nationally televised statement on October 31 of Tom Ridge, President Bush's head of Homeland Security, that the national "alert" and the new security measures would last "indefinitely," is a conclusive self-indictment. The Homeland Security office's vision of the future for ourselves and our children and our children's children involves identification cards for all, with biometric data and up-to-the-minute records of travel, employment, finances, etc., to be used to authorize access to places that are vulnerable to terrorist attack. This means that never again will the government simply trust citizens to go into a government office, a large building, a stadium, an airplane, or for that matter merely to walk around without what the Germans call *Ausweis*—papers. Checking everyone, however, makes sense only if officials will never be able to tell the difference between the average citizen and the enemy—and if the enemy will never be defeated.

But to assume such things is deadly. Unable to stop terrorists, Homeland Security will spend its time cracking down on those who run afoul of its regulations. In Chicago's O'Hare Airport, for example, a man was taken off an aircraft in handcuffs for having boarded before his row number had been called. Ridge, with the demeanor of every state trooper who has ever pulled you over for exceeding 55 miles per hour, reassured Americans that he has the authority to order the shoot-down of civilian airliners. As Machiavelli points out in his *Discourses on Livy*, security measures that hurt, threaten, or humiliate citizens engender hatred on top of contempt. No civil libertarian, Machiavelli teaches that true security comes from armed citizens to whom the government is bound by mutual trust. America fought Nazi Germany, Imperial Japan, and the Soviet Union without treating the public as potential enemies, and without making officials into a protected class. By governing from behind security screens, America's leaders today make our land less free and prove themselves less than brave.

Impotence worsens contempt. In *The Prince*, Machiavelli points out that no defense is possible against someone who is willing to give up his life to kill another. In our time we have seen suicide gunners and bombers shred Israel's security system, surely the world's most extensive. Studies carried out by the CIA's Counterintelligence Center generalize the lesson: whereas terrorist attacks against undefended targets have a rate of success limited only by the terrorists' incompetence, the rate of success against the most heavily defended targets hovers around 85%. In short, the cleverest, most oppressive defensive measures buy very little safety. In America, the possibilities for terrorist attack are endless, and effective security measures are inconceivable. How many school buses roll every morning? What would it take to toss a Molotov cocktail into 10 of them at precisely the same time? How easy would it be to sneak into a Safeway warehouse and contaminate a case of breakfast cereal? What would it take to set afire a gasoline tanker in a U.S. port?

Security measures actually magnify the effects of terrorism. The hijackings of September 11 have set in motion security measures that shut down airports on receipt of threats or merely on the basis of technical glitches in the security system itself. Similarly, attacks on the food distribution system, the schools, ports, etc., would cripple them by setting in motion attempts to make them secure. Indeed, manipulating the security system in order to cause disruption must rank high on the agenda of any competent terrorist. What's more, any successful attack through, or around, the security systems (remember, such attacks are very likely to succeed) proves that the government cannot protect us.

On top of this, most security measures are ridiculous on their face. Airport security is prototypical. Everyone who flies knows that September 11 ended forever the era of hijacking, and not because of the ensuing security. In fact, hijacking had become possible only because of U.S. policy. Bowing to pressure from the Left in the 1960s, the U.S. government failed to exercise its right to force Castro's Cuba to return hijackers, and instead defined security as disarming passengers. This succeeded in disarming everyone but hijackers. By 1969, Cuba's immunity had encouraged Arab governments to get into the hijacking business. The U.S. government's response to failed policy, however, was not to reverse it, i.e., to attack foreign governments involved with hijacking and to empower passengers to defend themselves. Rather, the government reemphasized its approach. The official instructions to passengers (in force on September 11) read like an invitation to hijackers: "Comply with your captors' directions"; "Relax, breathe deeply"; "If told to maintain a particular body position, talk yourself into relaxing into that position, you may have to stay that way for a long time." Indeed. U.S. security policy *guaranteed* the success of the September 11 hijackings.

But the first plane that hit the World Trade Center forever ended the free ride for hijackers by showing that the federal regulations exposed passengers to death. The passengers on United Airlines flight 93 violated the regulations (for which they technically could have been prosecuted—remember: "you must comply with all federal regulations, posted signs and placards, and crew member instructions") and attacked the hijackers, who unfortunately were already at the controls of the plane. Had they disobeyed minutes before, they would have saved themselves. Since then, a few incidents aboard aircraft have shown that the only function that henceforth a sky marshal might be able to perform would be to save a would-be hijacker from being torn apart by the passengers.

Despite the fact that anti-hijacking measures are now superfluous, the U.S. government now requires three checks of the same identity documents before boarding an airplane, and has banned more items that might be used as weapons. These now superfluous measures would have been futile on September 11. The hijackers would have satisfied any number of document checks, and could have carried out their operation using as weapons things that cannot be excluded from aircraft, such as nylon stockings; or even barehanded, using martial arts. Nor could the gun-toting, camouflage-clad soldiers who nowadays stand out like sore thumbs in America's airports have done anything to prevent September 11.

For passive security to offer any protection against enemies while reducing aggravation of innocents, it must focus very tightly on the smallest possible groups who fit terrorist profiles. In America's current war, terrorists are overwhelmingly likely to be a tiny, mostly visible minority—Arabs. But note that even Israeli security, which carries this sort of profiling to the point of outright racial discrimination, reduces the success of terrorist attempts only marginally.

Intelligence Is Impossible

Are America's intelligence agencies culpable for failing to stop September 11? No. But for the same reasons that they could not have prevented that atrocity, it is futile to suggest that they might help punish those responsible for it and be able to prevent future terrorism. It is impossible to imagine an intelligence system that would deal successfully with any of the three problems of passive anti-terrorism: security clearances for most of the population; the multiplicity of targets that must be defended as well as the multiple ways in which they can be attacked; and an unlimited stream of possible attackers.

Imagine a security investigation in which neither the investigators nor the evaluators can ask or even listen to anything about the subject's ethnic identity or political or philosophical beliefs, never mind sexual proclivities. This is the system in force today for clearing a few people for "Top Secret—Codeword" information, which concerns nuclear weapons, among other things. How could the U.S. government deny access to a job in Homeland Security, or as an airline pilot, to an Arab Muslim opposed to U.S. policy in the Middle East, for example? Consequently, although The Card (the American equivalent of the Soviet Internal Passport) would contain all sorts of data on your personal life, it would do nothing to impede terrorism. The first act of terrorism committed by a properly credentialed person would dispel any illusion. Alas, the routine occurrence of such events in Israel has not shaken official faith in documentation.

To protect against future terror, U.S. intelligence would have to gain foreknowledge of who, precisely, intended to do what, where, when, and how. It cannot do this both because of fundamental shortcomings and because the task is beyond even the best imaginable system.

Roughly, U.S. intelligence brings to bear against terrorism its network of communications intelligence (COMINT) and its network of human collectors. The value of COMINT with regard to terrorism has never been high and has been diminished by the technical trends of recent decades. The exponential growth in *the number of sources* of electronic communication—cell phones, computers, etc.—as well as of *the volume* of such communications has made nonsense of the standard U.S. practice of electronic sorting of grains of wheat in mountains of chaff. Moreover, the advent of near-perfect, cheap encryption has ensured that when the nuggets are found, they will be unreadable. It would have been a fluke had U.S. intelligence had any COMINT data on September 11 prior to the event. It has had none since. If any of the thousands of CIA human intelligence collectors had acquired prior knowledge, the surprise would have been even greater. These collectors simply are not in contact with any of the people who are involved with such things. CIA people work in embassies, pretend to be diplomats, and have contact only with people who normally see diplomats. Human intelligence means human contact. To make contact with terrorists, the CIA would have to operate the way the Drug Enforcement Agency does—becoming part of the drug business. But nobody at CIA knows how to do that, is capable of doing that, or wants to learn. As for the FBI, alas, they are cops who get pay raises not so much for accurate intelligence as for the number of people they put behind bars.

Imagine, however, that U.S. intelligence were excellent in every respect. What could it contribute to passive anti-terrorism? The (new, much improved) official doctrine of the new CIA-FBI Joint Counterintelligence Office states that the intellectual point of departure for counterintelligence and counterterrorism must be identification of the U.S. assets and secrets that enemies are most likely to attack. Then analysts should identify the ways in which enemies might best wage the attacks. Once this is done, they can investigate whether in fact these attacks are being planned, how, and by whom. When analysis of "what" leads to knowledge of "who," the attacks can be frustrated. This approach makes sense as regards counterintelligence, because the targets of the attacks are few and the attacks themselves have to be in the form of slow-developing human contacts or technical deceptions. But it makes no sense with regard to terrorism because the assets that are vulnerable to attack are practically infinite in number and variety, and the modes in which they are liable to be attacked are legion. There cannot be nearly enough investigative resources to explore every possibility.

Hence counterterrorist intelligence has no choice but to begin with the question "who?" Answering this question as regards those who are preparing attacks is difficult in the retail sense, and irrelevant on the wholesale level. Both the difficulty and the irrelevance stem from the fact that those who perpetrate terrorist acts are the equivalent of soldiers in war—there are lots of them, none is remarkable before he shoots, and there are lots where they came from. How would the Drug Enforcement Agency's intelligence operate if it tried to target mere drug couriers or petty salesmen? Its agents would haunt the drug dens, cultivating petty contacts a few of which might be recruited into trafficking. By the same token, today's CIA and FBI (in the unlikely event they could manage the cover) would haunt mosques, Islamic schools, and so forth, in the hope that some of their contacts might be among those recruited for terrorism. Very occasionally all this hard work would be rewarded by a success. But all this would amount to picking off a few drops from a fire hose.

That is why intelligence is useful only in the service of intelligent policy, that is, policy that aims at eliminating the people whose elimination would turn off the hose. But as we shall see, the identity of such people is discoverable not by espionage but by intelligence in the ordinary meaning of the word. It is in this regard that U.S. intelligence is most defective. For example, since September 11, for want of sources of its own, the CIA has been accepting information on terrorism from the intelligence services of Syria and of Yasser Arafat's Palestinian Liberation Organization (PLO)—outfits whose agendas could not be more opposed to America's.

The gullibility of U.S. intelligence is not merely an intellectual fault. The CIA's judgment is corrupted by its longstanding commitment to certain policies. It is only a small exaggeration to say that radical Arab nationalism was invented at the CIA. Secretary of State John Foster Dulles, when speaking to his brother, CIA director Allen Dulles, about the granddaddy of Arab radicalism, Gamal Abdul Nasser, used to call him "your colonel" because his takeover of Egypt had been financed by the CIA. Franz Fanon, the father of the anti-American Left in the Third World, was so close to the CIA that he chose to die under the Agency's medical care. Within the government, the CIA long has championed Arafat's PLO, even as the PLO was killing U.S. ambassadors. Under the Clinton and George W. Bush Administrations, CIA director George Tenet has openly championed the fiction that Arafat's "Security Forces" are something other than an army for the destruction of Israel. Before Iraq's invasion of Kuwait, the CIA's National Intelligence Estimate described Saddam Hussein as no threat to the region and as ready to cooperate with the United States. These are not mere errors.

Intelligence officers are most corrupted by the temptation to tell their superiors what they want to hear. Thus in September, the CIA prevailed upon the intelligence service of the Czech Republic to cast doubts on reports that Mohammed Atta, the leader of the September 11 attacks, had twice met in Prague with Iraqi intelligence as he was preparing for the attacks. The Czech government later formally disavowed its service's denial and affirmed the contacts between Atta and Iraq. But the CIA insists that there is no evidence that these two professional terrorists met to discuss terrorism. Gardening, perhaps?

When weapons-grade anthrax began to appear on Capitol Hill and in U.S. post offices in October, attention naturally turned to Iraq, whose regime had run the world's largest or second-largest program for producing it. But the FBI in November, after failing to discover anything whatever concerning the provenance of the anthrax, officially gave the press a gratuitous profile of the mailer as a domestic lunatic. The domestic focus of the investigation was doubly foolish. Even if Saddam Hussein had not thought of anthrax attacks on America before October 2001, the success of the attacks that did occur, as well as the U.S. government's exoneration of foreigners well-nigh ensured that Saddam would quickly get into the business of spreading the disease among us. Why shouldn't he? Moreover, the further "identification" of the source of the anthrax by an unidentified "intelligence source" as "some right-wing fanatic" aggravated the naturally worst effect of foreign wars: to compound domestic rivalries.

The use of intelligence not to fight the enemy but to erect a bodyguard of misimpressions around incompetent policy is not a sign of brilliance.

Al-Qaeda Is Not the Problem

The third pillar of the Bush strategy, the hunt for Osama bin Laden and military action first and foremost against the Taliban, is equally problematic.

In life as in math, we judge the importance of any part of any problem or structure by factoring it out. Does the equation still work? Does the building or the argument still stand? Imagine if a magic wand were to eliminate from the earth al-Qaeda, Osama bin Laden, and Afghanistan's Taliban regime. With them gone, would Americans be safe from Arab terrorists? No way. Then what good does it do for the U.S. government to make war on them and no one else? Why not make war on those whose elimination would eliminate terrorism?

Talk of bringing bin Laden "to justice" would sound less confident were ordinary rules of evidence to apply. The trial of bin Laden would be a nightmare of embarrassment for U.S. intelligence. Any number of uncorroborated reports from sources both unreliable and with an interest in deflecting U.S. anger away from Arab governments have painted bin Laden and his friends as devils responsible for all evils. This picture is attractive because it tends to validate decades of judgments by U.S. policymakers. The only independent test of these reports' validity came in 1998, when President Clinton launched a cruise missile strike against what "sources" had reported to be al-Qaeda's germ warfare plant in Khartoum. It turned out to be an innocent medicine factory. None of this is to deny that bin Laden and his friends are America's enemies and that their deaths would be good for us. But people like bin Laden are far from the sole practitioners of violence against Americans and the people and conditions that brought forth all these violent anti-Americans would soon spawn others like them.

Moreover, even if bin Laden had ordered September 11, as he boasts in a recruitment video, the fire that it started in America's house has been so attractive to potential arsonists that America will not be able to rest until they are discouraged. Getting bin Laden won't help much.

The Taliban are mostly irrelevant to America. Typically Afghan and unlike the regimes of Syria, Iraq, and the PLO, the Taliban have little role in or concern with affairs beyond their land. They provide shelter to various Arabs who have brought them money and armed help against their internal rivals. But Afghans have not bloodied the world. Arabs have.

The loyalty of the Taliban to their Arab guests is of the tribal kind. The moment that the Taliban are under serious threat, they probably will give the foreigners up. But absent the complicity of someone where bin Laden may be hiding, it is inconceivable that U.S. intelligence would find bin Laden's location and dispatch Special Forces that could swoop in, defeat his entourage, and take him out. It is surprising that no one has yet lured the U.S. into such an operation—and into an ambush. Destroying the Taliban regime in Afghanistan was always the only way of getting bin Laden, for what little that is worth.

From the beginning of U.S. military operations in Afghanistan on October 7, the lack of strategy for ousting the Taliban was evidence of incompetence. Since then, obvious changes in the character of operations belied U.S. spokesmen's claims that the war is "on schedule," and confirmed that those who planned the operation made no intellectual connection between the military moves they were making and the political results they expected. During the first weeks, U.S. actions were limited to bombing "fixed targets," mostly primitive air defenses and mud huts, unrelated to the ongoing civil war in Afghanistan. Only after it became undeniable that the only force that could make a dent in the regime was the Northern Alliance did U.S. bombers begin to support the Alliance's troops—but tentatively and incompetently. All war colleges teach that bombs from aircraft or artillery are useful in ground combat only insofar as they fall on enemy troops so close in time to the arrival of one's own infantry and armor that they render the enemy physically unable to resist. Whether in the two World Wars, in Vietnam, or in Kosovo, whenever significant amounts of time have passed between bombs falling on defenders and the arrival of attackers, the defenders have held. The Afghan civil war is very much a conventional war. Nevertheless, U.S. officials began to take seriously the task of coordinating bombing and preparing the Northern Alliance for serious military operations only after more than a month of embarrassment. In the initial days and weeks, the operation was a show of weakness, not strength.

The U.S. government's misuse of force was due to its desire to see the Taliban regime lose and the Northern Alliance not win—impossible. When the Alliance did win, the tribal nature of Afghanistan guaranteed that the tribes that stood with the losers would switch sides, and that they would sell to the winners whatever strangers were in their midst. This, however, underlined the operation's fundamental flaw: just as in the Persian Gulf War, the objective was so ill-chosen that it could be attained without fixing the problem for which we had gone to war. We could win the battle and lose the war.

Hence the worst thing about the campaign against Afghanistan was its opportunity cost. Paraphrasing Livy, Machiavelli tells us "the Romans made their wars short and big." This is the wisdom of the ages: where war is concerned, the shorter and more decisive, the better, provided of course that the military objective chosen is such that its accomplishment will fix the problem. By contrast, the central message of the Bush Administration concerning the "War on Terrorism" is hardly distinguishable from that of the Johnson Administration during the Vietnam War: this war will last indefinitely, and the public must not expect decisive actions. In sum, the Bush Administration concedes that the objectives of its military operations will not solve the problem, will not bring victory. Whatever its incidental benefits, the operation is diverting U.S. efforts from inconveniencing any of America's major enemies, and it is wasting the American people's anger and commitment.

You Can't "Spin" Defeat

Sensing mounting criticism at home and abroad for ineffectiveness, President Bush addressed the world and the nation on November 8. But he did not address the question that troubled his audiences: Do you have a reasonable plan for victory, for returning the country to the tranquility of September 10? Conscious that economic activity and confidence in America were sinking, he tried to rally the public by invoking the cry of the passenger on Flight 93 who attacked the hijackers: "Let's roll!" But the substance of what he said undercut the spirit. Rather than asking Americans to take security into their own hands, he asked Americans for indefinite tolerance of restrictions on their freedom. Typical of the result was a *New York Times* interview with a young laid-off professional. When he watches the news, he said, "it feels like the world is going to hell, like nothing is going to get better." That is defeat.

What would victory look like?

VICTORY

For Americans, victory would mean living a quiet and peaceable life, if possible even less troubled by the troubles of other parts of the world, even freer from searches and sirens and friction and fear, than on September 10. Hence all of the U.S. government's actions subsequent to September 11 must be judged by how they relate to that end. So what should be the U.S. government's practical objectives? Who is the enemy that stands in the way? How is this obstacle to be removed? In sum, as Thucydides' Archidamus asked the Spartans, "What is to be our war?"

The Tranquility of Order

Our peace, our victory, requires bloody vengeance for the murder of some 5,000 innocent family members and friends—we seek at least as many deaths, at least as gory, not to appease our Furies, nor even because justice requires it. Vengeance is necessary to eliminate actual enemies, and to leave no hope for any person or cause inimical to America. Killing those people, those hopes, and those causes is the *sine qua non* of our peace—and very much within our power.

Fortunately, our peace, our victory, does not require that the peoples of Afghanistan, the Arabian Peninsula, Palestine, or indeed any other part of the world become democratic, free, or decent. They do not require any change in anybody's religion. We have neither the power nor the right to make such changes. Nor, fortunately, does our peace depend on making sure that others will like us. We have no power to make that happen. Neither our nor anyone else's peace has ever depended on creating "New World Orders," "collective security," or "communities of power." International relations are not magic. Our own peace does not depend on any two foreign governments being at peace with each other. It is not in our power or in the power of any third party to force such a peace except by making war on both governments. Much less does our peace depend on a "comprehensive peace" in the Middle East or anywhere else. It is not in our power to make such a peace except by conquering whole regions of the world. Our peace and prosperity do not depend on the existence of friendly regimes in any country whatever, including Saudi Arabia. That is fortunate, because we have no power to determine "who rules" in any other country.

Virtually all America's statesmen until Woodrow Wilson warned that the rest of mankind would not develop ideas and habits like ours or live by our standards. Hence we should not expect any relief from the permanent burdens of international affairs, and of war. Indeed, statesmen from Washington to Lincoln made clear that any attempt to dictate another people's regime or religion would likelier result in resentment abroad and faction at home than in any relief from foreign troubles. We can and must live permanently in a world of alien regimes and religions. The mere difference in religion or mode of government does not mean that others will trouble our peace. Whether or not any foreign rulers make or allow war on America is a matter of their choice alone. We can talk, negotiate, and exercise economic pressure on rulers who trouble our peace. But if they make war on us we have no choice but to make war on them and kill them. Though we cannot determine who will rule, we surely can determine who will neither rule nor live.

What do we want from the Middle East to secure our peace? Neither democracy nor a moderate form of Islam—only that the region's leaders neither make nor allow war on us, lest they die. We have both the right and the capacity to make sure of that. But is it not necessary for our peace that the countries of the region be ruled by regimes friendly to us? No. By all accounts, the Saudi royal family's personal friendship with Americans has not affected their aiding and abetting terror against us. It is necessary only that any rulers, whatever their inclinations might be, know that they and their entourages will be killed, surely and brutally, if any harm to Americans originates from within their borders. Respect beats friendship. Do we not have to make sure that the oil of the Middle East continues to fuel the world economy? Is this not necessary to our peace? Indeed. But this does not burden us with the impossible task of ensuring that Saudi Arabia and the Oil States are ruled by friendly regimes. We need only ensure that whoever rules those hot sands does not interfere with the production of the oil that lies beneath them. That we can do, if we will.

In sum, ending the war that broke out on September 11 with our peace will require a lot of killing—to eliminate those in any way responsible for attacking us, and those who might cause further violence to us or choke the world's economy by troubling the supply of oil. It turns out that these mostly are the same persons. Who then are the enemies whose deaths will bring us peace?

It's the Regime, Stupid

When the suicide pilots of September 11 died, they made nonsense of the notion that terrorism was perpetrated by and on behalf of "senseless" individuals, and that the solution to terrorism lay in "bringing to justice" the bombers and trigger-pullers. If this notion were adhered to, the fact that the terrorists had already gone to justice should have ended the matter, except for some ritual exhortation to states to be a bit more careful about madmen in their populations.

But these terrorists were neither madmen nor on the edges of society. They came from well-established families. They had more than casual contacts with the political movements and intelligence services of their own regime and of neighboring countries. They acted on behalf of international causes that are the main sources of legitimacy for some regimes of the Middle East, and are tolerated by all. These causes include a version of Islam; a version of Arab nationalism; driving Westerners and Western influence from Islamic lands; and ridding the Arab world of more or less pro-Western regimes like that of Egypt, Saudi Arabia, and the Emirates. Moreover, peoples and regimes alike cheered their acts. In short, these acts were not private. Rather, they were much like the old Western practice of "privateering" (enshrined in Article I of our own Constitution, *vide* "letters of Marque and Reprisal"), in which individuals not under formal discipline of governments nevertheless were chartered by governments to make war on their behalf. Since the terrorists of September 11 are dead and we sense that their acts were not merely on their own behalf but rather that they acted as soldiers, the question imposes itself: Whose soldiers? Who is responsible? Whose death will bring us peace?

Islam is not responsible. It has been around longer than the United States, and coexisted with it peacefully for two hundred years. No doubt a version of Islam—Islamism—a cross between the Wahabi sect and secular anti-Westernism, is central to those who want to kill Americans. But it is neither necessary nor sufficient nor possible for Americans to enter into intra-Muslim theological debates. Besides, these debates are not terribly relevant. The relevant fact is that the re-definition of Islam into something harmful to us is the work of certain regimes and could not survive without them. Regimes are forms of government, systems of incentives and disincentives, of honors and taboos and habits. Each kind of regime gives prominence to some kinds of people and practices, while pushing others to the margins of society. Different regimes bring out different possibilities inherent in the same people. Thus the Japanese regime prior to World War II changed the meaning of the national religion of Shinto from quaint rituals to militant emperor-worship. Germany meant vastly different things to the German people and to the world when it was under the regime established by Konrad Adenauer, as opposed to the one established by Adolf Hitler. In short, regimes get to define themselves and the people who live under them. Note that Palestine's Yasser Arafat, Iraq's Saddam Hussein, and Syria's Assad family have made themselves the icons of Islamism despite the fact that they are well known atheists who live un-Muslim lives and have persecuted unto death the Muslim movements in their countries. Nevertheless, they represent the hopes of millions for standing up to Westerners, driving Israel (hated more for its Westernness than its Judaism) out of the Holy Land, and undoing the regimes that stand with the West. These tyrants represent those hopes because they in fact have managed to do impressive anti-Western deeds and have gotten away with it. The Middle East's memory of the Gulf War is that Saddam tried to drive a Western lackey out of Kuwait and then withstood the full might of America, later to spit in its face. The Middle East's view of Palestine is that Arafat and the Assads champion the rights of Islam against the Infidels.

Nor are the Arab peoples or Arab nationalism necessarily our enemies. America co-existed peacefully with Arabs for two centuries. Indeed, the United States is largely responsible for pushing Britain and France to abandon colonial and neo-colonial rule over Arab peoples in the 1950s. U.S. policy has been unfailingly—perhaps blindly—in favor of Arab nationalism. It is true that Egypt's Gamal Abdul Nasser founded Arab nationalism on an anti-American basis in the 1950s. It is true that in 1958 the Arab Socialist Party's (Baath) coup in Iraq and Syria gave Arab nationalism a mighty push in the anti-American direction. It is true that the Soviet Union and radical Arabs created the Palestinian Liberation Organization as an anti-Western movement. But it is also true that Jordan, Saudi Arabia, the Emirates, and, since 1973, Egypt have been just as Arab and just as nationalistic, though generally more pro-Western.

How did the PLO and the Baath regimes of Syria and Iraq gather to themselves the mantle of Arab nationalism? First, the Saudis and the Emirates gave them money, while Americans and Europeans gave them respect and money. Saudis, Americans, and Europeans gave these things in no small part because the radical Arabs employed terrorism from the very first, and Saudi, American, and European politicians, and Israelis as well, hoped to domesticate the radicals, buy them off, or divert them to other targets—including each other. Second and above all, we have given them victories, which they have used as warrants for strengthening their hold on their peoples and for recruiting more terrorists against us.

Today Iraq, Syria, and the PLO are the effective cause of global terrorism. More than half of the world's terrorism since 1969, and nearly all of it since the fall of the Soviet Union, has been conducted on behalf of the policies and against the enemies of those three regimes. By comparison, Libya, Iran, and Sudan have been minor players. Afghanistan is just a place on the map. Factor these three malefactors out of the world's political equation and what reason would any Arab inclined to Islamism or radical nationalism have to believe that such causes would stand a chance of success? Which intelligence service would provide would-be terrorists with the contacts, the money, the training to enter and fight the West or Israel? For whom, in short, would they soldier?

The Iraqi, Syrian, and the PLO regimes are no more true nationalists than they are true Muslims. They are regimes of a party, in the mold of the old Soviet Union. Each is based on a narrow segment of society and rules by physically eliminating its enemies. Iraq is actually not a nation-state but an empire. The ruling Baath party comes from the Mesopotamian Sunni Arabs, the smallest of the empire's three ethnic groups. The ruling faction of the party, Saddam's Tikriti, are a tiny fraction of the ruling party. The Assad family that rules Syria is even more isolated. The faction of the local Baath party that is their instrument of power is made up almost exclusively of Alewites, a neo-Islamic sect widely despised in the region. It must rely exclusively on corrupt, hated security forces. Yasser Arafat rules the PLO through the Fatah faction, which lives by a combination of buying off competitors with money acquired from the West and Israel, and killing them. Each of the regimes consists of some 2,000 people. These include officials of the ruling party, officers in the security forces down to the level of colonel, plus all the general officers of the armed forces. These also include top government officials, officials of the major economic units, the media, and of course the leaders of the party's "social organizations" (labor, youth, women's professional, etc.).

All these regimes are weak. They have radically impoverished and brutalized their peoples. A few members of the ruling party may be prepared to give their lives for the anti-Western causes they represent, but many serve out of fear or greed. The Gulf War and the Arab-Israeli wars proved that their armies and security forces are brittle: tough so long as the inner apparatus of coercion is unchallenged, likely to disintegrate once it is challenged. Killing these regimes would be relatively easy, would be a favor to the peoples living under them, and is the only way to stop terrorism among us.

On Killing Regimes

It follows that killing regimes means killing their members in ways that discredit the kinds of persons they were, the ways they lived, the things and ideas to which they gave prominence, the causes they espoused, and the results of their rule. Thus the Western Allies de-Nazified Germany not by carpet-bombing German cities, which in fact was the only thing that persuaded ordinary Germans that they and the Nazis were in the same boat. The Allies killed the Nazi regime by killing countless Nazis in battle, hanging dozens of survivors, imprisoning hundreds, and disqualifying thousands from social and economic prominence. The Allies promised to do worse to anyone who tried Nazism again, left no doubt in the minds of Germans that their many sorrows had been visited on them by the Nazis, and made Nazism into a dirty word.

Clearly, it is impossible to kill any regime by killing its people indiscriminately. In the Gulf War, U.S. forces killed uncounted tens of thousands of Iraqis whose deaths made no difference to the outcome of the war and the future of the region, while consciously sparing the much smaller number who made up the regime. Hence those who want to "bomb the hell out of the Arabs" or "nuke Baghdad" in response to September 11 are making the same mistake. Killing must be tailored to political effect. This certainly means invading Iraq, and perhaps Syria, with ground troops. It means openly sponsoring Israel's invasion of the PLO territories. But it does not mean close supervision or the kind of political reconstruction we performed in Germany and Japan after World War II.

It is important that U.S. forces invade Iraq with the stated objective of hanging Saddam and whoever we judge to have been too close to him. Once those close to him realize that this is going to happen and cannot be stopped, they will kill one another, each trying to demonstrate that he was farther from the tyrant than anyone else. But America's reputation for bluff and for half measures is so entrenched that the invasion will have to make progress greater than in the Gulf War in order for this to happen. At this point, whether or not Saddam himself falls into U.S. hands alive along with his subordinates, it is essential that all be denounced, tried, and hanged on one charge only: having made war on America, on their own people, and on their neighbors. The list of people executed should follow the party-government's organization chart as much as possible. It is equally essential that everyone who hears of the event be certain that something even more drastic would follow the recrudescence of such a regime. All this should happen as quickly as possible.

After settling America's quarrel, America should leave Iraq to the peoples who live there. These would certainly break the empire into its three ethnic constituents: Kurds in the north, Mesopotamian Sunnis in the center, and Marsh Shiites in the south. How they may govern themselves, deal with one another and with their neighbors, is no business of ours. What happens in Iraq is simply not as important to us as the internal developments of Germany and Japan were. It is enough that the Iraqis know that we would be ready to defend whatever interest of ours they might threaten. Prestige is a reputation for effective action in one's own interest. We would have re-earned our prestige, and hence our right to our peace.

In the meantime, we should apologize to Israel for having pressured her to continue absorbing terrorist attacks. We should urge Israel to act decisively to earn her own peace, which would involve destroying the regime of the PLO in the West Bank and Gaza. Israel could do this more easily than we could destroy Saddam's regime in Iraq. The reason is that the regime of the PLO, the so-called Palestine Liberation Organization, is wholly dependent on Israel itself for most basic services, from money and electricity to telecommunications, water, food, and fuel. Moreover, the PLO's key people are a few minutes' driving distance from Israeli forces. A cutoff of essentials, followed by a military cordon and an invasion, would net all but a few of these terrorists. The U.S. could not dictate how they should be disposed of. But it would make sense for Israel to follow the formula that they deserve death for the harm these criminal gangs have done to everyone with whom they have come in contact, even one another. With the death of the PLO's gangsters, Palestinian politics would be liberated from the culture of assassination that has stunted its healthy growth since the days of Mufti Hussein in the 1920s.

After Iraq and Palestine, it would be Syria's turn. By this time, the seriousness of America and its allies would speak for itself. A declaration of war against the Assad regime by the U.S., Israel, and Turkey would most likely produce a palace coup in Damascus—by one part of the regime eager to save itself by selling out the others—followed by a revolution in the country. At that point, the Allies might produce a list of persons who would have to be handed over to avert an invasion. And of course Syrian troops would have to leave Lebanon. Americans have no interest in Syria strong enough to require close supervision of successors to Assad. But Turkey's interest might require such supervision. The U.S. should make no objection to Turkey's reestablishment of a sphere of influence over parts of its former empire.

Destroying the major anti-Western regimes in the Middle East might come too late to save the moribund government of Saudi Arabia from the anti-Western sentiments that it has shortsightedly fostered within itself. Or the regime might succumb anyway to long-festering quarrels within the royal family. In any case, it is possible that as a consequence of the Saudi regime's natural death, the foreigners who actually extract and ship the oil might be endangered. In that case, we would have to choose among three options: 1) letting the oil become the tool of whoever might win the struggle (and taking the chance that the fields might be sabotaged in the war); 2) trying to build a new Saudi regime to our liking; or 3) taking over protection of the fields. The first amounts to entrusting the world's economy to the vagaries of irresponsible persons. The second option should be rejected because Americans cannot govern Arabs, or indeed any foreigners. Taking over the oil fields alone would amount to colonial conquest—alien to the American tradition. It would not be alien, however, to place them under joint international supervision—something that Russia might well be eager to join.

Our Own Worst Enemies?

What stands in the way of our achieving the peace we so desire? Primarily, the ideas of Western elites. Here are a few.

Violence and killing do not settle anything. In fact they are the *ultima ratio*, the decisive argument, on earth. Mankind's great questions are decided by war. The battle of Salamis decided whether or not there would be Greek civilization. Whether Western Europe would be Christian or Muslim was decided by the battle of Tours. Even as the U.S. Civil War decided the future of slavery and World War II ended Nazism, so this war will decide not just who rules in the Middle East, but the character of life in America as well.

Our primary objective in war as in peace must be to act in accordance with the wishes and standards of the broadest slice of mankind. In fact, the standards of most of mankind are far less worthy than those prevalent in America. America's founders taught this, and forgetting it has caused harm. Alliances must always be means, never ends in themselves, and as such must be made or unmade according to whether or not they help secure our interest. Our interest in war is our kind of peace. That is why it is mistaken to consider an ally anyone who impedes the killing of those who stand in the way of our peace. With allies like Saudi Arabia, America does not need enemies.

When involved in any conflict, we should moderate the pursuit of our objectives so as to propitiate those moderates who stand on the sidelines. Individuals and governments stand on the sidelines of conflict, or lend support to one side, according to their judgment of who will win and with whom they will have to deal. "Extremist" is one of many pejorative synonyms for "loser." The surest way to lose the support of "moderates" is to be ineffective. Might is mistaken for right everywhere, but especially in the Middle East. Hence the easiest way to encourage terrorism is to attempt to deal with "the root causes of resentment against us" by granting some of the demands of our enemies.

Learning to put up with security measures will make us safer, and is a contribution we can all make to victory. On the contrary, security measures will not make us safe, and accustoming ourselves to them is our contribution to defeat. The sign of victory over terrorism will be the removal of security measures.

The Arab regimes that are the matrices of terrorism have nothing going for them except such Western shibboleths. Their peoples hate them. Their armies would melt before ours as they have melted before Western armies since the days of Xenophon's Upcountry March. They produce nothing. Terror is their domestic policy and their foreign policy. The oil from which they get the money that they lavish on themselves and on terrorism comes from revenues that Westerners give them to satisfy Western ideas of what is right. The regimes that are killing us and defeating us are the product of Western judgments in the mid-20th century that colonialism is wrong and that these peoples could govern themselves as good stewards of the world's oil markets. They continue to exist only because Western elites have judged that war is passé. It is these ideas and judgments, above all, that stand in the way of our peace, our victory.

War in the Absence of Strategic Clarity

Mark Helprin

(Fall 2003)

America has approached the war on terrorism as if from two dreamworlds. The liberal, in which an absurd understanding of cause and effect, the habit of capitulation to foreign influence, a mild and perpetual anti-Americanism, reflex allergies to military spending, and a theological aversion to self-defense all lead to policies that are hard to differentiate from surrender. And the conservative, in which everything must be all right as long as a self-declared conservative is in the White House—no matter how badly the war is run; no matter that a Republican administration in electoral fear leans left and breaks its promise to restore the military; and no matter that because the secretary of defense decided that he need not be able to fight two wars at once, an adequate reserve does not exist to deal with, for example, North Korea. And in between these dreamworlds of paralysis and incompetence lies the seam, in French military terminology *la soudure*, through which al-Qaeda, uninterested in our parochialisms, will make its next attack.

IDENTIFYING THE ENEMY

The war is waged as if accidentally, and no wonder. For domestic political reasons and to preserve its marginal relations with the Arab World, the United States has declined to identify the enemy precisely. He is so formless, opportunistic, and shadowy that apparently we cannot conceive of him accurately enough to declare war against him, although he has declared war against us. Attribute this to Karl Rove's sensitivity to the electoral calculus in key states with heavy Arab-American voting, to a contemporary aversion to ethnic generalities, to the desire not to offend the Arab World lest it attack us even more ferociously, to the fear of speaking truth to oil, to apprehension about the taking of hostages and attacks upon embassies, and to a certain muddledness of mind that is the result both of submitting to polite and obsequious blackmail and of having been throughout the course of one's life a stranger to rigorous thought.

Reluctance to identify the enemy makes it rather difficult to assess his weaknesses and strengths. Thus, for want of a minimum of political courage, our soldiers are dispatched to far-flung battlefields to fight an ad hoc, disorganized war, and, just as it did in the Vietnam War, Washington explains its lack of a lucid strategy by referring to the supposed incoherence of its opponent. From the beginning, America has been told that this is a new kind of war that cannot be waged with strategic clarity, that strategy and its attendant metaphysics no longer apply. And because we cannot sufficiently study the nature of an insufficiently defined enemy, our actions are mechanistic, ill-conceived, and a function of conflicting philosophies within our bureaucracies, which proceed as if their war plans were modeled on a to-do list magnetized to some suburban refrigerator.

The enemy must and can be defined. That he is the terrorist himself almost everyone agrees, but in the same way that the United States extended blame beyond the pilots who attacked Pearl Harbor, it must now reach far back into the structures of enablement for the sake of deciding who and what must be fought. And given the enormity of a war against civilians, and the attacks upon our warships, embassies, economy, capital, government, and most populous city, this determination must be liberal and free-flowing rather than cautious and constrained, both by necessity and by right. The enemy has embarked upon a particular form of warfare with the intent of shielding his center of mass from counterattack, but he must not be allowed such a baseless privilege. For as much as he is the terrorist who executes the strategy, he is the intelligence service in aid of it, the nation that harbors his training camps, the country that finances him, the press filled with adulation, the people who dance in the streets when there is a slaughter, and the regime that turns a blind eye.

Not surprisingly, militant Islam arises from and makes its base in the Arab Middle East. The first objective of the war, therefore, must be to offer every state in the area this choice: eradicate all support for terrorism within your borders or forfeit existence as a state. That individual terrorists will subsequently flee to the periphery is certain, but the first step must be to deny them their heartland and their citadels.

Recognizing that the enemy is militant Islam with its center the Arab Middle East, it is possible to devise a coherent strategy. The enemy's strengths should not be underestimated. He has a historical memory far superior to that of the West, which has forgotten its thousand-year war with Islamic civilization. Islamic civilization has not forgotten, however, having been for centuries mainly on the losing side. Its memory is clear, bitter, and a spur to action. And it dovetails with a spiritual sense of time far different from that of the West, where impatience arises in seconds, for the enemy believes that a thousand years, measured against the eternity he is taught to contemplate and accept, is nothing. Closely related to his empowering sense of time are his spiritual sense of mission, which must never be underestimated, and Islam's traditional embrace of martyrdom.

This militant devotion, consciously or otherwise, pays homage to the explosive Arab conquests, which reached almost to Paris, to the gates of Vienna, the marchlands of China, India, and far into Africa. War based on the notion of Islamic destiny is underway at this moment in the Philippines, Indonesia, Sinkiang, Kashmir, Afghanistan, Pakistan, Chechnya, Iraq, Palestine, Macedonia, Algeria, the Sudan, Sub-Saharan Africa, and throughout the world in the form of terrorism without limitation or humanitarian nuance—all in service of a conception far more coherent than the somnolent Western nations seem to comprehend. The object long expressed by Osama bin Laden and others is to flip positions in the thousand-year war. To do this, the Arabs must rekindle what the 10th-century historian Ibn Khaldun called *'asabiya,* an ineffable combination of group solidarity, momentum, *esprit de corps,* and the elation of victory feeding upon victory. This, rather than any of its subsidiary political goals, is the objective of the enemy in the war in which we find ourselves at present. Despite many flickers all around the world, it is a fire far from coming alight, but as long as the West apprehends each flare as a separate case the enemy will be encouraged to drive them toward a point of ignition, and the war will never end.

DEMORALIZING THE ENEMY

The proper strategic objective for the West, therefore, is the suppression of this fire of *'asabiya* in the Arab heartland and citadels of militancy—a task of division, temporary domination, and, above all, demoralization. As unattractive as it may seem, in view of the deadly alternative it is the only choice other than to capitulate.

How might it be accomplished? As much as those who make war against the West find advantage in Arab history and Islamic tradition, they are burdened by its disadvantages. Living in a world of intense subjectivity where argument is perpetually overruled by impulse, they suffer divisions within divisions and schisms within schisms. Though all-consuming fervor may be appropriate to certain aspects of revealed religion, it makes for absolutist politics and governance. A despotic political culture in turn decreases the possibilities of strong alliances and is (often literally) murderous to initiative, whether technical, military, or otherwise. And it is of no little import that the Middle East has developed so as to be unreceptive to technology.

The natural environment of Arabia is so extreme that the idea of mastering it was out of the question, submission and adaptation being the only options, and the Middle East had neither the kind of surplus agriculture that permitted Europe to industrialize, nor the metals and wood upon which the machine culture was built. Technology was viewed not as a system of interdependent principles, but rather as finite at all stages, not an art to be practiced but a product to be bought. Magical machines arrived whole, without a hint of the network of factories, workshops, mines, and schools, and the centuries of struggle and genius it took to build them. Islam provides a successful spiritual equilibrium that the whole of Islamic society strives to protect. The West, by its very nature, stirs and changes everything in "creative destruction." Wanting no part in this, the Middle East, to quote the economic historian Charles Issawi, "believed that the genius of Islam would permit a controlled modernization; from Europe one could borrow things without needing to borrow ideas," which is why, perhaps, in 19th-century Egypt, students were sometimes taught a European language to master a craft, and then told to "forget" the language.

Even more potentially fatal to the Arabs than the fact that they cannot ever win a technological duel with the West is their Manichean tendency to perceive in wholly black or wholly white. In the Middle East the middle ground is hardly ever occupied, and entire populations hold volatile and extremist views. This is traceable perhaps to the austerities of the desert and nomadic life, and is one of the great and magnetic attractions of Islam—severity, certainty, and either decisive action or righteous and contented abstention. In Arab-Islamic culture, things go very strongly one way or they go very strongly the other, and, always, a compassionate haven exists for the defeated, for martyrs, as long as they have not strayed from the code of honor. In the West, success is everything, but in the Arab Middle East honor is everything, and can coexist perfectly well with failure. The Arabs have a noble history of defeat, and are acclimatized to it. Their cultural and religious structures, far less worldly than ours, readily accommodate it. Though wanting victory, they are equally magnetized by defeat, for they understand, as we used to in the West, that the defeated are the closest to God.

The West seems not to know, George W. Bush seems not to know, and Donald Rumsfeld seems not to know, that there can be but one effective strategy in the war against terrorism, and that is to shift Arab-Islamic society into the other of its two states—out of nascent *'asabiya* and into comfortable fatalism and resignation. The British have done this repeatedly, and the United States almost did it during the Gulf War. That the object of such an exercise is not to defeat the Arabs but to dissuade them from making war upon us means it is more likely to succeed now than when it was joined to religious war in the Crusades or to the imperial expansion of Europe. Now we want only to trade with the oil states even at scandalous expense, and not (assuming that "nation-building" is properly allowed to atrophy) to convert, control, or colonize. How, exactly, does one shift Arab-Islamic society into the other of its two states?

If one were to calculate *a fortiori* the scale of military effort involved in the 19th-century division of the Ottoman Empire and the subsequent European domination of the Middle East, one would undoubtedly assume that the Europeans deployed great armadas and large armies. More than 30 years ago, a graduate student asked the late and eminent Oxford historian Albert Hourani what numbers the Europeans did, in fact, deploy. He said he would look into it, and a week later reported that, to his astonishment, the only European military presence within the periphery of the Ottoman Empire that he could discover, from Napoleon until the latter part of the 19th century, were 1,500 British and 500 Austrian troops in 1840, and 6,000 French in 1860. Thus can miniscule expeditions conquer vast empires, Aztec, Inca, or Ottoman.

But not today, or at least that would seem to be a reasonable conclusion. For in the last century the Arabs have organized into separate and self-stabilizing states; they have raised large military establishments, so that now Egypt, Jordan, Syria, Saudi Arabia, and (non-Arab) Iran have 1.5 million regulars under arms; they have bought and sometimes successfully absorbed huge inventories of modern weapons; they have fought wars of independence and revolution, civil wars, against Israel six times, and against the great powers; and from T.E. Lawrence, Mao Zedong, and Ho Chi Minh they have learned at least the rudiments of asymmetrical warfare.

Nevertheless, the fundamental relation has not been altered, and it is still possible to maneuver the Middle East into quiescence vis-à-vis the West. It is a matter mainly of proportion. The unprecedented military and economic potential of even the United States alone, thus far so imperfectly utilized, is the appropriate instrument. Adjusting military spending to the level of the peacetime years of the past half-century would raise outlays from approximately $370 billion to approximately

$650 billion. If the United States had the will, it could, excessively, field 20 million men, build 200 aircraft carriers, or almost instantly turn every Arab capital into molten glass, and the Arabs know this. No matter what the advances in regional power, the position of the Arab Middle East relative to that of the United States is no less disadvantageous than was that of the Arab Middle East to the 19th-century European powers. But, given the changes listed in the previous paragraph, the signal strength necessary to convey an effective message is now far greater.

JUST ENOUGH FORCE

In the Gulf War, the overwhelming forces marshaled by the coalition might have sufficed as such a signal but for the fact that they were halted prematurely and withdrawn precipitously, gratuitously leaving both Saudi Arabia and Iraq an inexplicable freedom of action that probably left them stunned by their good luck.

Before the Iraq War, high officials were seriously considering an invasion force of 500 backed by air power. The numbers climbed steadily: 5,000; 10,000; 20,000; 25,000; 40,000; 50,000; 60,000; and so on, with the supposedly retrograde "heavy army" prevailing finally, and 300,000 troops in the theater. When offered vehement advice to go into Iraq with massive force and many times overkill, a brilliant and responsible senior official responded, almost with incredulity, "Why would we need the force that you recommend, when in the Gulf War we used only 10% of what we had?" In the Gulf War, we did not occupy a country of 23 million.

As of this writing, the army reportedly has 23 combat brigades, 18 of which are deployed in Iraq and Afghanistan, three of which are in refit, one in Kosovo, and two in Korea, leaving nine brigades, or about 45,000 men, to pick up the slack anywhere and everywhere else. Though independent echelons and the Marines increase this figure many fold, they do not have sufficient lift and logistics, and even if they did it would not be enough. This is as much the result of the Bush Administration's failure to increase defense spending appreciably and rebuild the military before (and even after) September 11, as the lack of real shock and awe was the result of the administration's desire to go to war according to a sort of just-in-time-inventory paradigm. Managers rather than strategists, they did not understand the essence of their task, which was not merely to win in Iraq but to stun the Arab World. Although it is possible, with just enough force, to win, it is not possible, with just enough force, to stun. The war in Iraq should have been an expedition originating in the secure base of Saudi Arabia, from the safety of which the United States could with immense, husbanded force easily reach anywhere in the region. The eastern section of the country, far from Mecca and Medina, fronting the sea, with high infrastructure and large spaces for maneuver, basing, and an air-tight defense, is ideal. Had the Saudis not offered this to us, we might have taken it, which probably would have been unnecessary, given that our expressed determination would likely have elicited an invitation. As it was, we were willing to alienate the entire world so as to thrust ourselves into a difficult situation in Iraq, but unwilling to achieve a commanding position in Saudi Arabia for fear of alienating the House of Saud. One might kindly call this, in that it is about as sensible as wearing one's clothes backwards, "strategic hip hop."

It was, in any case, some kind of deliberate minimalism. Sufficiency was the watchword. The secretary of defense wanted to show that his new transformational force could do the job without recourse to mass. The president wanted no more than sufficiency, because he had not advanced and had no plans to advance the military establishment beyond the levels established by his predecessor. With the magic of transformation, he would rebuild it at glacial pace and little cost lest he imperil his own and Republican fortunes by embarking on a Reagan-style restoration after an election decided by as many voters as would fit in a large Starbucks, and that he won by leaning, un-Reagan-like, to the center.

The war in Iraq was a war of sufficiency when what was needed was a war of surplus, for the proper objective should have been not merely to drive to Baghdad but to engage and impress the imagination of the Arab and Islamic worlds on the scale of the thousand-year war that is to them, if not to us, still ongoing. Had the United States delivered a *coup de main* soon after September 11 and, on an appropriate scale, had the president asked Congress on the 12th for a declaration of war and all he needed to wage war, and had this country risen to the occasion as it has done so often, the war on terrorism would now be largely over.

But the country did not rise to the occasion, and our enemies know that we fought them on the cheap. They know that we did not, would not, and will not tolerate the disruption of our normal way of life. They know that they did not seize our full attention. They know that we have hardly stirred. And as long as they have these things to know, they will neither stand down nor shrink back, and, for us, the sorrows that will come will be greater than the sorrows that have been.

Leo Strauss and American Foreign Policy

Thomas G. West

(Summer 2004)

Quite a few of President Bush's critics maintain that since some prominent members of the administration and their defenders are known to be former students of Leo Strauss or of Straussians, one can trace Bush's foreign policy to Strauss's political ideas. Straussians in Washington tend to be neoconservatives, and, in foreign policy, prominent neocons like William Kristol and Robert Kagan advocate a policy of "benevolent hegemony." In their argument, a benign American imperialism is justified for two reasons. First, it provides security against foreign attack; that is, it delivers "strategic benefits." But their real enthusiasm is reserved for its second purpose, which is democratic reform of the rest of the world.

That stance, they argue, not only serves American interest; it is a moral imperative. The policy of benevolent hegemony will "relish the opportunity for national engagement, embrace the possibility of national greatness, and restore a sense of the heroic." Kristol and Kagan also argue that their view is supported by the principles of the American Founding: "For conservatives to preach the importance of upholding the core elements of the Western tradition at home, but to profess indifference to the fate of American principles abroad, is an inconsistency that cannot help but gnaw at the heart of conservatism."

My impression as an outside observer is that Straussian influence in the administration has been grossly exaggerated. But let us assume for discussion's sake that it is strong. Since Strauss has been wildly accused of everything from being an admirer of Hitler to being a devotee of Wilsonian progressivism, I think it high time to clarify his understanding of foreign policy. I shall argue that although there is some common ground, Strauss's overall approach is quite different from that of Kristol, Kagan, and other prominent neoconservatives in and out of the administration.

CLASSICAL FOREIGN POLICY

The confrontation of the West with Communism, Strauss wrote in *The City and Man* (1964), has demonstrated that "no bloody or unbloody change of society can eradicate the evil in man: as long as there will be men, there will be malice, envy and hatred, and hence there cannot be a society which does not have to employ coercive restraint." Strauss implies, among other things, that the extravagant hope for permanent progress in human affairs believed in by Woodrow Wilson and his contemporary admirers is a delusion. In particular, he wrote, the ideal of "a universal state, unitary or federative" (Strauss appears to be speaking of the United Nations) is also a delusion. "If that federation is taken too seriously," wrote Strauss, "as a milestone on man's onward march toward the perfect and hence universal society, one is bound to take great risks supported by nothing but an inherited and perhaps antiquated hope, and thus to endanger the very progress one endeavors to bring about."

To begin with, then, according to Strauss each nation should conduct its own foreign policy, and it should not turn its policy over to international organizations. In current parlance, Strauss was a unilateralist, not a multilateralist.

He concluded the passage quoted above by remarking that the lesson of the Cold War is that "political society remains what it always has been: a partial or particular society whose most urgent and primary task is its self-preservation and whose highest task is its self-improvement."

In his book *What Is Political Philosophy?* (1959) Strauss addressed the grounds of that lesson in the principles of classical political philosophy. For the classics, wrote Strauss, foreign policy is primarily concerned with "the survival and independence of one's political community." For that reason, "the ultimate aim of foreign policy is not essentially controversial. Hence classical political philosophy is not guided by questions concerning the external relations of the political community. It is concerned primarily with the inner structure of the political community . . . ."

For Strauss, then, who closely followed the classics on this subject, foreign policy is ministerial to domestic policy, because "self-improvement" or human excellence is the "highest task" of politics. The purpose of foreign policy is therefore to secure the means, admittedly the "urgent and primary" means, namely, preservation, or national security, to that high end. For that reason, Aristotle singled out Sparta for strong criticism in his *Politics*. Sparta's error was to organize its laws around the belief that the purpose of politics is the domination of other nations by war.

Thus according to Strauss, the purpose of foreign policy is or ought to be survival and independence, or self-preservation, and nothing else.

He comments on this passage as follows:

> the good city is [not] guided in its relations with other cities, Greek or barbarian, by considerations of justice: the size of the territory of the good city is determined by that city's moderate needs and by nothing else; the relation of the city to the other cities belongs to the province of wisdom rather than of justice; the good city is not a part of a community of cities or is not dedicated to the common good of that community or does not serve other cities.

The last part of Strauss's remark implies that the foreign policy of a sensible nation is never devoted to the good of other nations, except to the extent that the good of another nation accidentally happens to promote one's own nation's existence. For the same reason, a sensible nation will not engage in imperial expansion for its own aggrandizement—though it might have to do so for its own survival. In Plato's *Republic*, Socrates advocates a war of imperial expansion in order to acquire the

territory needed to sustain the city's material needs. By the time Socrates has finished purging the city of luxuries, its territorial needs are likely to be quite small.
This expansionist war, then, is not likely to amount to much.

We must face up to this disturbing Socratic endorsement of expansionism or imperialism in case of necessity. For although the size of the conquest may not "amount to
much," it might mean something quite drastic to the neighboring city that happened
to be in the wrong place at the wrong time. It will definitely require the seizure of
property and killing of men who oppose this expansion. Socrates in effect shows that
he knows how problematic his open defense of aggressive warfare is, when he says
that the government must lie to the citizens about the true origin of the city's territory.
The citizens will be told, in a noble lie, that the native land on which they are born
was their mother, not that it was taken by force from a foreign nation.

We may sum up the Socratic approach by saying that although foreign policy is in
principle amoral, because it is dictated by the selfish needs of the political community, it is also moderate, because the needs of the city are limited, given the primacy
of its concern for civic virtue and therefore domestic policy.

Later in the *Republic*, Socrates proposes a striking mitigation of the usual Greek
manner of conducting war: the city that they are founding will no longer kill or
enslave the conquered population, nor destroy its property, if the conquered city
is Greek. The ground of this policy is that Greeks are ethnically akin. If a city is
defeated in war, says Socrates, only those who are responsible for the war will be
punished. It is probable that this Socratic suggestion arises from the humanity of his
philosophic orientation, which transcends loyalty to a particular political regime.
We can perhaps see in this proposal the roots of the much milder rules of conquest
established by John Locke and other early modern thinkers.

THE PERILS OF EMPIRE

Would Aristotle agree with this Strauss-endorsed Platonic approach to foreign
policy? One of Aristotle's arguments against domination of other nations is that
it is "not even lawful" for one city to "rule and exercise mastery over" other cities
"whether they wish it or not." That is, Aristotle, who is always closer to "common
sense" than Plato, speaks as if there is, after all, such a thing as justice and injustice
among nations. Strauss seems to take Plato's view, not Aristotle's, as the genuine
expression of the classical approach. Perhaps that is because Plato's analysis goes
to the root of the matter, while Aristotle deliberately remains on the level of the
perspective of the citizen and statesman (visible in Aristotle's interchangeable use
of "lawful" and "just" in the passage quoted).

The classical thinker who seems to be the most obvious exception to Strauss's account is Thucydides. Unlike Plato or Aristotle, he made foreign policy central to his
account of the political. Nonetheless, Strauss denied that Thucydides disagreed with
Plato about the importance of a good regime at home. Instead, Thucydides showed
that the intransigent urgency of questions of survival, conquest, and war often over-
whelms what would otherwise be, in Strauss's words, "the overriding concern with
domestic politics." As for "the good order within the city," Thucydides "leaves [it]
to the moderate citizens."

Strauss's discussion of Thucydides brings out forcefully the same twofold theme that we noticed in his interpretation of Plato. In Thucydides' opinion, as summarized by Strauss, there is on one side "what one may call the natural right of the stronger" to conquer and expand, but on the other side, this natural right "does not lead in all cases to expansionism. There are limits beyond which expansion is no longer safe." In other words, "to say that under certain conditions empire is possible and necessary is not the same as to be an 'imperialist.'"

The Athenian experiment with indefinite expansionism was doomed (among other reasons) by a simple fact, which the Athenian leaders after Pericles failed to recognize: "it is in the long run impossible to encourage the city's desire for 'having more' at the expense of other cities without encouraging the desire of the individual for 'having more' at the expense of his fellow citizens." The Athenians did not see, as Socrates did see in his recommendation of the "noble lie" in the *Republic*, that a frankly expansionist foreign policy is bound to undermine the political order at home as well as, eventually, the imperialist policy abroad.

It is important to understand why, for Strauss and the classical political philosophers, the purpose of foreign policy should be limited to self-preservation or necessity. Obviously, it is not because life has no higher purpose than mere survival. Rather, it is because all policy, foreign and domestic, should be in the service of one thing: the well being or happiness of society. This means that government's most important task is to help the citizens live the good life by promoting the right ideal of human excellence. That is emphatically a matter of domestic policy, not foreign. For that reason, in principle, foreign policy is easy, and domestic policy is very difficult. No one disputes that preservation is better than death; but all claims about the content of the life of human excellence are inherently controversial.

Someone might object that the classical approach endorsed by Strauss seems to be nothing but a crass "realism" It might seem that any nation, however tyrannical or degraded, is justified in defending its own survival using any means that happen to be effective. This would be a correct assessment of the classical position, if it were not for the point just mentioned: for the classics, the fundamental rightness or wrongness of political action or policy depends on the rightness or wrongness of the political regime which it supports. For the classics, justice, or what Strauss called *natural right*, is to be found in the best political order, called by Strauss the best political regime. "Political activity is then properly directed," he wrote in *Natural Right and History* (1953), "if it is directed toward human perfection or virtue . . . . [Therefore] the end of the city is peaceful activity in accordance with the dignity of man, and not war and conquest."

In sum, the classics' "realist" conception of foreign policy is ultimately justified only insofar as it serves their "idealist" conception of domestic policy.

STRAUSS'S PRINCIPLES TODAY

Today, liberals favor the idea that the nations of the world should turn their foreign policy over to international bodies like the United Nations or the European Union. On this point, the neoconservatives as well as the classics would dissent. No one can be expected to understand the interests of a nation better than its own citizens

and statesmen. For this reason, the classics would have viewed multilateral organizations with suspicion. Strauss did so explicitly, as we saw earlier.

Moreover, the purpose of foreign policy is national security, not humanitarian
benevolence, though this does not imply that all alliances are to be shunned.

For one thing, it is easy to see that the United States, or any nation, is justified in
making alliances with other nations for the sake of its own survival. In a dangerous
world, one needs allies, and alliances may require sending one's own soldiers to die
on behalf of other nations.

In the classical or Straussian approach, alliances are justified even with nations
who oppress their own people. One's own survival, not the well-being of the
peoples of other nations, is the standard. In order to defeat Hitler, America had to
support Stalin, the most murderous tyrant in world history. To defeat Iraq, America
arguably had to ally itself with despotic Saudi Arabia.

But another implication of Strauss's approach is more controversial. It is the
ruthless subordination of the good of other nations to one's own good. The foreign
policy of the classics is essentially selfish, because the main purpose of all good
politics is "self-improvement," the advantage of one's own political community, not
the common good of other political communities. The foreign policy of Strauss and
the classics seeks neither *hegemony* over other nations nor *benevolence* toward other
nations, unless, accidentally, one or the other is a means to survival.

Yet this very selfishness leads to results that are quite moral, if morality is defined
as cultivation of the good life for one's own people, while refraining from injuring
others unless they attempt to injure you. Straussian foreign policy does not seek to
be benevolent, but its inherent moderation makes it in effect benevolent, especially
in contrast with the kind of imperialism practiced by regimes that merely want to
lord it over as many nations as possible.

Let us apply this criterion—improve one's own nation, but leave other nations
alone, except when one's security is at risk—to the war in Iraq that began in 2003.
For Strauss and the classics, the sole justification for the war would have been that
Iraq was a national security threat to the United States, or, what is the same thing,
to the allies of the United States. The most convincing evidence of that threat would
not have been whether or not Iraq possessed "weapons of mass destruction." After
all, many other nations, such as France and Britain, have nuclear weapons, and no
serious American is arguing that this poses some sort of threat to America's security.
For Strauss, the truly important question to consider is whether Iraq (or any other
nation) has been actively planning or supporting the killing of American citizens or
citizens of America's most important allies. As it happens, there is quite a bit of evidence that Iraq was doing just that. Angelo Codevilla's excellent series of articles in
the *Claremont Review of Books* has convincingly shown the connection between Iraq
and terrorists who seek to harm, and who have harmed and do harm to, American
citizens and their allies. But for some reason the Bush Administration was not very
energetic in presenting that case to the public. The administration sometimes does
make this kind of argument in defense of the war, but it seems to prefer to stress
that the war is good because it serves the interest of other nations.

Obviously it is in America's interest that foreign governments stop sponsoring
and aiding murderous acts against America and its allies, especially against Israel,

its most reliable ally in the Middle East. To that end, it was appropriate not only to defeat Iraq militarily, but also to deter future hostility to America by punishing the members of the former Iraqi government who supported these murderously anti-American policies. So far American forces have not done much punishing. Instead, their focus has been on responding to attacks, and "nation-building." But if Strauss is right, it is not America's job to provide its defeated enemies with democratic or just governments, unless there is some real connection with American national security. The question is whether there is such a connection. If there is, and if it is possible to build a democratic Iraqi government, then nation-building makes sense. If the classical-Straussian approach is right, neoconservatives and other defenders of the Bush policy should explain how nation-building (1) is possible, and (2) serves America's security. Whether it happens to be good for the Iraqis should not be the criterion of America's Iraq policy.

From Strauss's point of view, however, the case against nation-building in Iraq is strengthened by the fact that neither Iraq nor any of its major regions has ever in history been governed democratically. It appears that Iraq lacks the elementary preconditions of constitutional democracy. I mean the minimal democratic virtues of personal self-restraint and feisty self-assertion in defense of liberty, along with a widespread belief in the moral and/or religious obligation of everyone to respect the equal rights of others to life, liberty (including the free exercise of religion), and property.

It has been reported that American academics have been giving lectures in Iraq telling their audiences that they need to adopt Thomas Jefferson's view of religious liberty. What these academics seem not to understand is that government protection of the free exercise of religion only works when there are enough people in the regime who actually believe in it. But for most of the world and through most of human history, there has been no separation of religious from political authority. This is true of Iraq, alas. Words on a piece of paper (an Iraqi Constitution, for example) will have zero political effect if there is no strong support for their enforcement, and no understanding of why their enforcement is a good thing.

Strauss would recommend that America stick to doing what serves its security. If that involves doing good to other nations, so be it. If it involves leaving other nations alone, that is fine too. But Americans should not confuse matters by engaging in enthusiastic talk about national greatness and restoring a sense of the heroic by sending their own soldiers to die in battles that perhaps serve the interests of others, but not our own.

Worse, the attempt to build democracy in a place where the minimal preconditions of democracy are not present may well cause more harm than good. How many civilians will the American forces have to kill before it becomes clear that that well-intentioned goal is indefinitely out of reach? The attempt to do good where the good in question is impossible may lead to the unnecessary deaths not only of American soldiers, but also of many Iraqis.

If victory in Iraq is defined as democracy in Iraq, American forces will have to remain there for a long time. During their prime, Rome and Britain were pretty good at governing other nations. With few exceptions, Americans have never had the heart for it.

AMERICAN FOREIGN POLICY

Kristol and Kagan have another argument for benevolent hegemonism. This one is grounded on the specific nature of the American political order. They argue that the principles of the founding imply that America has a moral obligation not only to make the world safe for democracy but to make the world democratic. I believe that the political thought of the founding is opposed to that view. With regard to foreign policy, the principles of the founding lead to the same conclusion as do the principles of Strauss and the classics, though by a different path.

The classical approach is one of ruthless selfishness for an elevated end: the noble and good life of the citizens. The founders rejected that approach in the name of the natural moral law, which denies the legitimacy of expansion and hegemonism except in case of necessity. Yet both approaches lead to a moderate foreign policy in the service of a just political order.

According to America's Declaration of Independence, every nation is entitled to a "separate and equal station" among "the powers of the earth." That is because of "the laws of nature and of nature's God," which tell us that "all men are created equal" and that we are obliged to respect men's equal rights to "life, liberty, and the pursuit of happiness." One way that the right to liberty is exercised is through each nation's collective right to consent to its own government, in a "separate and equal station" independent of the government of other nations. There is therefore no right of one nation to conquer or interfere in the affairs of any other nation, except to the extent required for self-preservation. Locke's strictures against conquest in the *Second Treatise* are based on exactly this understanding of the law of nature.

In *The Federalist*, James Madison explains what the relations will be between the United States under the proposed Constitution of 1787, and any states that may refuse to ratify the Constitution. His answer: "although no political relation can subsist between the assenting and dissenting States, yet the moral relations will remain uncancelled. The claims of justice, both on one side and on the other, will be in force, and must be fulfilled; the rights of humanity must in all cases be duly and mutually respected." As we have seen, this is not the orientation of Plato or Thucydides.

For Madison and the founders, the natural law obligates a nation to respect "the rights of humanity" in other nations. The same natural law, which is also the ground of the social compact, obligates a nation's government to secure the lives, liberties, and estates of its own citizens. It does not authorize government to sacrifice its own citizens for the sake of other nations' citizens.

That is why John Quincy Adams, one of the chief architects of early American foreign policy, declared in a speech delivered on July 4, 1821: America "goes not abroad in search of monsters to destroy. She is the well-wisher to the freedom and independence of all. She is the champion and vindicator only of her own."

Commenting on this famous Adams quotation, Kristol and Kagan write, "But why not [go abroad in search of monsters to destroy]? The alternative is to leave monsters on the loose, ravaging and pillaging to their hearts' content, as Americans stand by and watch."

Strauss and the classics, together with John Quincy Adams, would admit that there always will be many monsters abroad in the world, ravaging and pillaging to their hearts' content. It is not the obligation of one nation to solve other nations' problems, no matter how heartbreaking. For the founders, that would be to violate the fundamental terms of the social compact. For Strauss and the classics, that would be a distraction from the highest purpose of politics, self-improvement through the right domestic policy. The Americans rejected Machiavelli's belligerent republicanism, with its celebration of hegemonism and conquest. Instead, the founders, following thinkers like Locke and Montesquieu, restored to politics a proper restraint on the dangerous human passion to dominate others, both at home and abroad. For this reason, the founders' anti-imperialist conception of foreign policy remains fully comprehensible and defensible in terms of Strauss's account of classical political philosophy.

To avoid misunderstanding, I should emphasize that neither Strauss nor the founders were isolationists. In his Farewell Address, when George Washington warned, "'Tis our true policy to steer clear of permanent alliances, with any portion of the foreign world," he was thinking of America's former ally France, whose quarrel with Britain was not America's quarrel. "Europe has a set of primary interests, which to us have none, or a very remote relation. Hence she must be engaged in frequent controversies, the causes of which are essentially foreign to our concerns." But Washington was far from opposing all alliances. Without the alliance with France a few years earlier, America's war for independence might have failed. He therefore recommended "temporary alliances" so that America would retain freedom of action to "choose peace or war, as our interest guided by justice shall counsel." America's *interest* (national security) was to be limited by *justice* (refraining from violating the rights of other nations).

In light of this summary of the positions of Strauss, the classics, and the American Founders, one must conclude that the neoconservative approach, as articulated by Kristol and Kagan, is only partly compatible with that of Strauss and the American Founders. It appears that the neocons are influenced by the political principles of American Progressivism—of modern liberalism. That is why, I suspect, Kristol and other neocons frequently express their admiration for Theodore Roosevelt, a man who by and large rejected the principles of the founding and the limited foreign policy spawned by those principles. Roosevelt's foreign policy did not seek merely to preserve the nation against foreign enemies. Instead, as T.R. wrote his essay in "Expansion and Peace," the best policy is a frank imperialism all over the world: "every expansion of a great civilized power means a victory for law, order, and righteousness." Thus the American occupation of the Philippines, T.R. believed, will enable "one more fair spot of the world's surface" to be "snatched from the forces of darkness. Fundamentally the cause of expansion is the cause of peace."

Yet there is still a big difference between Kristol and today's liberals who, also, follow the Progressive ideal of Theodore Roosevelt and Woodrow Wilson. Kristol, like Roosevelt, but unlike Wilson, never forgets that "strengthening America's security" must always remain a leading purpose of foreign policy. At the beginning of this article, we noted that the neoconservatives defend benevolent hegemony as being both in America's security interest and in the interest of the nations whom we liberate. As Max Boot has observed, neocons are "hard," not "soft" Wilsonians. Kristol therefore opposes the liberal-Wilsonian preference to turn American foreign policy over to international institutions like the United Nations. He also opposes the

Wilsonian tendency to think that any policy that serves the self-interest of America is morally suspect.

The question that remains, however, is whether the neoconservative devotion to benevolent hegemony really is compatible with a foreign policy that secures the lives and liberties of Americans. A vain attempt to establish democracy in places like Iraq that have lived for millennia under one despotism after another may lead not to a more secure America, but to a needless and immoral waste of American lives.

What then should be done in Iraq? Answer: America should return to the principles of Washington and John Quincy Adams, and focus on two things. First, it should make sure that important Iraqis who supported Saddam Hussein are punished. Second, it should help Iraqis to set up a government which is likely to have at least some stability and decency, and which is unlikely to turn against America in the near future. American military forces should leave as soon as these two goals can be achieved. Events themselves may be moving American policy in precisely this direction. Lest my judgments seem too categorical, I will add this: given the multitude of possible means to these two simple ends, much must be left up to the prudence, the good sense, of the politicians to whom we constitutionally entrust our foreign policy.

None of this is meant to disparage the war in Iraq, or any other American intervention abroad, so long as it truly promotes the preservation of America. Nor are Americans obliged to wait for a foreign threat to become imminent before going to war, as many of President Bush's critics have argued. War is effectually declared, to invoke Locke again, whenever anyone evinces "by word or action, not a passionate and hasty, but a sedate settled design," upon the life of another. Saddam Hussein's decade-long series of attempts to kill Americans, using either his own forces or surrogates, was evidence enough. But we must not forget that in the end, war, like all public policies, must serve what Leo Strauss, the classics, and the founders regarded as the purpose of political life—namely, the cultivation of "peaceful activity in accordance with the dignity of man."

Democracy and the Bush Doctrine

Charles R. Kesler

(Winter 2004/05)

George W. Bush's first presidency, devoted to compassionate conservatism and to establishing his own bona fides, lasted less than eight months. On September 11, 2001, he was reborn as a War President. In the upheaval that followed, compassionate conservatism took a back seat to a new, more urgent formulation of the Bush Administration's purpose.

The Bush Doctrine called for offensive operations, including preemptive war, against terrorists and their abetters—more specifically, against the regimes that had sponsored, encouraged, or merely tolerated any "terrorist group of global reach." Afghanistan, the headquarters of al-Qaeda and its patron the Taliban, was the new doctrine's first beneficiary, although the president soon declared Iraq, Iran, and North Korea (to be precise, "states like these, and their terrorist allies") an "axis of evil" meriting future attention. In his stirring words, the United States would "not permit the world's most dangerous regimes to threaten us with the world's most dangerous weapons."

The administration's preference for offensive operations reflected a long-standing conservative interest in taking the ideological and military fight to our foes. After all, the Reagan Doctrine had not only indicted Soviet Communism as an evil empire but had endeavored to subvert its hold on the satellite countries and, eventually, on its own people. The Bush Administration's focus on the states backing the terrorists implied that "regime change" would be necessary, once again, in order to secure America against its enemies. The policy did not contemplate merely the offending regimes' destruction, however. As in the 1980s, regime *change* implied their replacement by something better, and the Bush Doctrine soon expanded to accommodate the goal of planting freedom and democracy in their stead.

CAPTIVE NATIONS

On this point, the Bush Doctrine parted company with the Reagan Doctrine. Although the Reagan Administration's CIA and other agencies had worked to build civil society and to support democratic opposition groups in Eastern Europe, Central America, and other strategic regions, these efforts were directed mostly to helping "captive nations" escape their captivity. That is, they presupposed a latent opposition against foreign, usually Soviet, oppression, or as in the satellite and would-be satellite countries, against domestic oppressors supported by the Soviets. The Russian people themselves counted as a kind of captive nation enslaved to Marxism's foreign ideology, and Reagan did not flinch from calling for their liberation, too. He always rejected a philosophical détente between democracy and totalitarianism in favor of conducting a vigorous moral and intellectual offensive against Communist principles.

But as a practical matter, the Reagan Doctrine aimed primarily at supporting labor unions, churches, and freedom fighters at the Soviet empire's periphery—e.g., Poland, Czechoslovakia, Afghanistan, Nicaragua, Grenada—rather than at its core. Even in these cases, the administration regarded its chief duty to be helping to liberate the captive nations, that is, expelling the Soviets and defeating their proxies, rather than presiding over a proper democratization of the liberated peoples. Not unreasonably, the Reaganites thought that to those freed from totalitarian oppression, America's example would be shining enough, especially when joined to their visceral, continuing hatred for the Soviet alternative.

In countries where bad or tyrannical regimes were homegrown or unconnected with America's great totalitarian enemy, the administration's efforts in support of democratization were quieter and more limited still. These involved diplomatic pressure, election-monitoring, and occasional gestures of overt support, such as the administration's endorsement of "people power" in the Philippines. Most importantly, Reagan wanted to avoid the Carter Administration's hubris in condemning the imperfect regimes of America's friends, while neglecting the incomparably worse sins of America's foes.

The distinction between authoritarian and totalitarian regimes, classically restated by Jeane Kirkpatrick in her article that caught Reagan's eye, "Dictatorships and Double Standards," provided intellectual support for his administration's policies. Authoritarian regimes, like Iran's shah or Nicaragua's Somoza, though unsavory, were less oppressive than totalitarian ones, Kirkpatrick argued. What's more, countries with homegrown monarchs, dictators, or generalissimos were far more likely to moderate and perhaps even democratize themselves than were societies crushed by totalitarian governments. And it was this potential of non-democratic but also non-totalitarian states to change their regimes for the better, in their own good time, that helped to justify America's benign neglect of or, at most, episodic concern with their domestic politics. Once freed from the totalitarian threat, countries like Nicaragua or Afghanistan could more or less be trusted to their own devices.

The wave of democratization that occurred in the 1980s, especially in Asia and South America, seemed to confirm the wisdom of the administration's approach. Even when America was called to play a role, as it was in the Philippines, our intervention was short and sweet, confined mainly to persuading Ferdinand Marcos to leave office.

By comparison, the Bush Doctrine puts the democratization of once totalitarian, quondam authoritarian, and persistently tribal societies at the center of its objectives. The case of Afghanistan shows, to be sure, that the Reagan Doctrine had its drawbacks. Left to itself, Afghanistan after the Soviets' withdrawal did not resume its former ways, at least not for long, and certainly did not evolve into a democracy. Instead, it succumbed to the Taliban's peculiar Islamic totalitarianism. Nevertheless, the Bush Administration's policy is not merely to expunge the totalitarians there and in Iraq, but to ensure that they never return by reconstructing their societies along democratic lines. Authoritarianism (at least in the Middle East) is no longer acceptable. The U.S. now proposes to liberate these nations from the captivity of their own unhappy traditions.

So far as it goes, that policy, or some version of it, might be justified by the circumstances and stakes of U.S. involvement, even as the American refoundings of Germany and Japan after the Second World War were justified on prudential grounds. Occasionally, the Bush Administration makes this kind of argument. (The analogies are not exact, of course—about which more anon.) But usually this claim is mixed up with a very different one that is more characteristic of the Bush Doctrine as such: America's supposed duty, as the result of our respect for human rights, to help the Iraqis and others realize their democratic entitlement and destiny.

RIGHTS AND REPUBLICANISM

Political scientists James W. Ceaser and Daniel DiSalvo draw attention to this dimension of the Bush Doctrine when they observe, in a recent issue of the *Public Interest*, that "President Bush has identified the Republican party with a distinct foreign policy, which he has justified by recourse to certain fixed and universal principles—namely that, in his words, 'liberty is the design of nature' and that 'freedom is the right and the capacity of all mankind.'"

Bush's appeal, in their words, to "the universality of democracy and human rights" is a watershed moment in the history of American politics, with enormous significance for the Republican Party and the conservative movement. "Not since Lincoln has the putative head of the Republican party so actively sought to ground the party in a politics of natural right."

Bush's revival of natural or human rights as the foundation of political morality is welcome, and should be taken seriously. Like Lincoln, Bush is, in his own way, looking to the American Founding for guidance in charting his course through the dire circumstances that confront him. But there is, in his use of these noble ideas, a certain ambiguity or confusion between the natural *right* to be free and the *capacity* to be free. The two are not quite the same.

The founders affirmed that every human being has, by nature, a right to be free. Unless men were endowed by nature with a certain minimum of faculties, inclinations, and powers, that right would be nugatory. Taken together, those endowments—which include reason, an access to morality (variously traced to reason, conscience, or the moral sense), a spirited love of freedom for its own sake, passions (especially the powerful desire for self-preservation), and physical strength—constitute the capacity or natural *potential* for human freedom. But this potential needs to be made *actual*, needs to be awakened by practice and habit.

James Madison, for example, writes in *The Federalist* of "that honorable determination which animates every votary of freedom to rest all our political experiments on the capacity of mankind for self-government." In the largest sense, those experiments aim to prove whether the latent capacity of mankind for self-government can, at last, after centuries of slumber, be activated, realized, and confirmed by the conduct of the American people—in particular, by their ratification of the newly proposed Constitution. Alexander Hamilton underlines the point in that work's famous opening paragraph: "It has been frequently remarked that it seems to have been reserved to the people of this country, by their conduct and example, to decide the important question, whether societies of men are really capable or not of establishing good government from reflection and choice, or whether they are forever destined to depend for their political constitutions on accident and force."

The human right to be free, in other words, does not guarantee the human capacity to be free. That capacity must be elicited and demonstrated, and its noblest and most persuasive proof is by the establishment of "good government," along with the habits necessary to perpetuate it; the habits of heart and mind that, among other things, allow a people's "choice" to be guided by "reflection."

Notice, too, that the founders are not content with (merely) democratic regimes, i.e., with governments that hold elections and empower majorities to rule. The test of mankind's political capacity is that its self-government should culminate in good government, in regimes that not only have elections but actually achieve the common good and secure the rights of individuals, whether or not they belong to the ruling majority. This blend of constitutionalism and republicanism is extremely difficult to attain. Well acquainted with the history of failed republican regimes, the founders by and large thought it the *most difficult* of all forms of government to establish and preserve. Hence good, republican government is an achievement, not an entitlement.

THE LIMITS OF REGIME CHANGE

Thus even with the improvements in political science celebrated by Madison, Hamilton, and the other founders, most of them never expected republican government to spread easily and universally across the globe. Though fervent believers in universal moral principles, they knew that these had to be approximated differently in different political situations. In this sense, they were students of Montesquieu and Aristotle, who taught that governments have to be suited to a people's character and conditions.

None of this implies, of course, that dramatic political change is not possible. America's founders could not have been *founders* if they did not think regime change possible and, in their own case, desirable. Founding is possible because culture is not destiny; politics can reshape a nation's culture. But they knew also that no founding is completely *de novo*. Every attempt at regime change begins from the existing habits and beliefs of the people for whom you are trying to found a new way of life. Accordingly, the founders would have been cautious, to say the least, about America's ability to transform Iraqis into good democrats.

In the last century, we saw in the cases of Germany and Japan that it is possible to remake even Nazi and imperial Japanese institutions into democratic regimes. But these are really exceptions that prove the rule that it is very difficult to pull off this kind of transformation. Germany and Japan were exceptional, first, because the U.S. and its allies had beaten them into complete submission. Then we occupied them for decades—not merely for months or years, but for the better part of a half-century. And both were civilizations that had the advantage of having enjoyed beforehand a high standard of living, widespread literacy, and considerable political openness. Besides, America was reorganizing them at the beginning of the Cold War, when circumstances compelled them, as it were, to choose between the West, with its democratic institutions, and the East, with its bleak tyranny.

To his credit, President Bush recognizes the difficulty of the task in Iraq. He acknowledged to the National Endowment for Democracy that "the progress of liberty is a powerful trend," but that "liberty, if not defended, can be lost. The success of freedom," he said, "is not determined by some dialectic of history." In his elegant speech at Whitehall Palace, he affirmed that "freedom, by definition, must be chosen and defended by those who choose it." And he warned that "democratic development" will not come swiftly, or smoothly, to the Middle East, any more than it did to America and Europe.

Nonetheless, he finds strong support for the "global expansion of democracy" in human nature itself. "In our conflict with terror and tyranny," he said at Whitehall, "we have an unmatched advantage, a power that cannot be resisted, and that is the appeal of freedom to all mankind." In a speech in Cincinnati, he declared, "People everywhere prefer freedom to slavery; prosperity to squalor; self-government to the rule of terror and torture." Aboard the *U.S.S. Abraham Lincoln*, after announcing that "major combat operations in Iraq have ended," he said, "Men and women in every culture need liberty like they need food and water and air."

DEMOCRATIC FEELINGS

Here he stumbles. It is one thing to affirm, as the American Founders did, that there is in the human soul a love of liberty. It is another thing entirely to assert that this love is the main or, more precisely, the naturally predominant inclination in human nature, that it is "a power that cannot be resisted." In fact, it is often resisted and quite frequently bested, commonly for the sake of the "food and water and air" that human nature craves, too. The president downplays the contests within human nature: conflicts between reason and passion, and within reason and passion, that the human soul's very freedom makes inescapable. True enough, "people everywhere prefer freedom to slavery," that is, to their *own* slavery, but many people everywhere and at all times have been quite happy to enjoy their freedom and all the benefits of someone else's slavery.

In his 2002 State of the Union Address, one of his best speeches, he amplified his point. "All fathers and mothers, in all societies, want their children to be educated and live free from poverty and violence. No people on earth yearn to be oppressed, or aspire to servitude, or eagerly await the midnight knock of the secret police." There is truth in the president's words, but not the whole truth. No one may want to be oppressed, but from this it does not follow that no one yearns to oppress. The love that parents feel for their children does not necessarily transfer to benevolence, much less equal solicitude, for the children of others. This is why "do unto others" is not a moral rule automatically or easily observed. This is why, when Abraham Lincoln distilled his moral teaching to its essence, he did not confine himself to the wrongness of slavery simply. "As I would not be a slave," he wrote, "so I would not be a master. This expresses my idea of democracy. Whatever differs from this, to the extent of the difference, is not democracy."

In other words, that "people everywhere" or "all fathers and mothers" have the same *feelings* for themselves and their own kind does not (at least not yet) make them believers in human equality, human rights, or democracy. President Bush, in effect, plants his account of democracy in common or shared human passions, particularly the tender passions of family love, not in reason's recognition of a rule for the passions. He does not insist, as Lincoln and the founders did, that democracy depends on the mutual recognition of rights and duties, grounded in an objective, natural order that is independent of human will. Bush makes it easy to be a democrat, and thus makes it easier for the whole world to become democratic.

HISTORY AND CULTURE

Yet democracy based on feelings or compassion has obvious limits. What takes the place of the rigorous moral teaching that once lifted compassion to the level of justice? What summons forth the embattled statesmanship and republican striving that sustain democracy, especially in crises? Despite his comments that democratic progress is not inevitable and that "the success of freedom is not determined by some dialectic of history," Bush finds himself appealing again and again to a kind of providential or historical support for democracy. In the same speech in which he uttered the words just quoted, he concluded by saying: "We believe that liberty is the design of nature; we believe that liberty is the direction of history." At Goree Island, Senegal, the slave ships' point of departure from Africa, Bush declared:

> We know that these challenges can be overcome, because history moves in the direction of justice. The evils of slavery were accepted and unchanged for centuries. Yet, eventually, the human heart would not abide them. There is a voice of conscience and hope in every man and woman that will not be silenced—what Martin Luther King called a certain kind of fire that no water could put out . . . . This untamed fire of justice continues to burn in the affairs of man, and it lights the way before us.

In this eloquent address, the president praises the role that John Quincy Adams and Lincoln, among others, played in the fight against slavery, but he salutes their "moral vision" as though that alone had been sufficient to doom the peculiar institution. In his words, "Their moral vision caused Americans to examine our hearts, to correct our Constitution, and to teach our children the dignity and equality of every person of every race." What happened to the Civil War, not to mention Jim Crow? Bush leaves the impression that "history moves in the direction of justice," and that once Americans were awakened to the Truth, they went with the flow. Yet the antislavery cause, at least in Lincoln's mind, did not depend in the slightest on history's support for the triumph of free labor and free men. Rather, it was a very close issue, requiring for its resolution all of Lincoln's genius and the Union's resources, not forgetting a considerable measure of good luck. And the triumph, so dearly won, soon gave way to tragedy and renewed tyranny in the South.

Bush's position recalls the important recent dispute between Francis Fukuyama and Samuel Huntington. Huntington insists that, after the Cold War, international politics will be marked by the inevitable clash of civilizations, e.g., between the Islamic and non-Islamic nations. Fukuyama argues that history is overcoming all such cultural clashes and culminating in liberal democracy, which is destined to spread all over the world. In this dispute, Bush seems to be firmly on Fukuyama's side. At West Point, the president explained, "The 20th century ended with a single surviving model of human progress, based on non-negotiable demands of human dignity, the rule of law, limits on the power of the state, respect for women and private property and free speech and equal justice and religious tolerance . . . . When it comes to the common rights and needs of men and women," he said, "there is no clash of civilizations."

If not dialectical, Bush's account of history certainly seems Darwinian; history has winnowed itself down to a "single surviving model of human progress." He dismisses doubts that the Middle East will grow increasingly democratic as narrow-minded, if not downright prejudiced. From his 2004 State of the Union Address: "[I]t is mistaken, and condescending, to assume that whole cultures and great religions are incompatible with liberty and self-government. I believe that God has planted in every human heart the desire to live in freedom." Yes, but the question is whether some cultures and religions are *less* compatible with freedom and democracy than others, and if so, how in his second term the president ought to adjust our foreign policy. Granted, too, that God has implanted in men a love of freedom, but cultures, rulers, and religions each diffract that love, accentuating, obscuring, or perverting it. Bush calls those who raise such contentions "skeptics of democracy," when in fact they are skeptical mostly of his easy-going account of democracy.

James Q. Wilson, with his usual insight and learning, takes an empirical look in the December *Commentary* at the relation between Islam and freedom. He declines to inspect Islam and democracy, on the grounds that there are too few examples from which to generalize and that, in the long run, personal liberty is more important. From liberty, liberal democracy may spring; democracy without liberty is despotic (Fareed Zakaria's recent book, *The Future of Freedom: Illiberal Democracy at Home and Abroad* [2003] reinforces this point). Wilson proffers Turkey, Indonesia, and Morocco as reasonably liberal Muslim states; of these only one, Morocco, is both Muslim and Arab. What these cases have in common, he suggests, is a "powerful and decisive leader" who can "detach religion from politics"; an army that "has stood decisively for secular rule and opposed efforts to create an Islamist state" (a condition that Morocco does not quite meet); the absence of "a significant ethnic minority" demanding independence; and the lack of major conflicts between Sunni and Shiite Muslims.

Iraq shares *none* of these advantages. Straining to find some cause for optimism, Wilson notes that in one opinion poll more than 75% of Iraqis express support for liberties like free speech and freedom of religion. In the same poll, about 40% endorse a European-style parliamentary democracy.

RETHINKING THE DOCTRINE

In this vein, it is heartening to see elections in Afghanistan, with thousands upon thousands lining up to vote. It is encouraging, too, that elections are about to be held for the new Iraqi national assembly. As the president says, "it is the practice of democracy that makes a nation ready for democracy, and every nation can start on this path." But not every nation will finish it, because democracy is not just a matter of elections. Democracy requires that majorities restrain themselves and practice sometimes disagreeable tasks out of respect for law and for their fellow citizens. These tasks, in turn, require a willingness to trust one's fellow citizens that comes hard to tribal societies, whose members are not used to trusting anyone who is not at least a cousin.

Of course, it is a wonderful thing to hear President Bush reassert the natural-rights basis of just government and, incidentally, of the Republican Party. As against today's shallow culture of liberal relativism, his willingness to point out the plain difference between good and evil is bracing, and recalls Ronald Reagan's denunciation of the Evil Empire. The worry is that in tracing the individual right to be free to ordinary human compassion or fellow-feeling, and then confounding that right with an entitlement to live in a fully democratic regime, Bush promises or demands too much and risks a terrible deflation of the democratic idealism he has encouraged.

As he begins his second term, the president and his advisors must take a hard, second look at the Bush Doctrine. In many respects, it is the export version of compassionate conservatism. Even as the latter presumes that behind the economic problem of poverty is a moral problem, which faith-based initiatives may help to cure one soul at a time, so the Bush Doctrine discovers behind the dysfunctional economies and societies of the Middle East a moral problem, which "the transformational power of liberty" may cure, one democrat and one democracy at a time. "The power of liberty to transform lives and nations," he admonishes, should not be underestimated. But it may be that the administration underestimates the difficulty of converting whole societies in the Middle East into functioning democracies. By raising expectations—by making democracy appear as an easier conversion and way of life than it really is—Bush risks not only the erosion of liberal and pro-democratic support within Iraq, but also at home a loss of public confidence in the whole war effort.

One wonders, for example, whether his version of compassionate democracy is sufficiently alert to the problem of security. In most American wars, the reconstruction did not begin until the fighting had ended, until the enemy was subjugated and peaceful order imposed on the country. Vietnam was an exception, but not a very helpful one. Bush criticizes previous administrations for making short-sighted bargains with Mideast kings and dictators, trading security for liberty in the region. Without liberty, he argues, there is no long-term security. Although he has a point, liberty itself presupposes a certain minimum security for life, liberty, and property that is woefully absent in much of Iraq. Earlier American statesmen, including the founders, would have been keenly aware of this requirement because their argument for republican government put great weight on the passion, and the right, of self-preservation. A government that could not protect the life and liberty of its citizens (better than they could left to themselves) was no government at all.

But in its first term the Bush Administration underestimated the problem of security because it overestimated the sentimental or compassionate grounds of democracy. Expecting the Iraqis quickly and happily to get in touch with their inner democrat, the administration was surprised that so many of them took a cautious, more self-interested view, preferring to reserve their allegiance for whichever side would more reliably protect them from getting killed. In general, the Bush team needs to recall that weak, contemptible, authoritarian regimes are not the only breeding grounds of trouble in the Middle East or elsewhere. Weak, contemptible democracies can be the source of great evil, too, as Weimar Germany attests.

Finally, the Bush Doctrine's all-absorbing focus on bringing democracy to Iraq tends to crowd out concern for the kind of constructive, wide-ranging statesmanship that is needed there and in other Islamic nations. Unfortunately, the administration has never thought very seriously about constitutionalism, either at home or abroad, except for the narrow, though important, issue of elections. As the example of Turkey suggests, it may take many years, if ever, before Iraq is capable of a fully-functioning liberal democracy. In the meantime, the Iraqis need to adopt what arrangements they can to create strong executive powers; security forces able to protect their countrymen's life, liberty, and property; a free, prosperous economy; local experience in managing local affairs; and impartial courts. Better regimes than the Taliban or Saddam Hussein are surely attainable, and are being attained. But these new governments are haunted by dire threats, including the danger of civil war and national disintegration.

Aboard the *U.S.S. Abraham Lincoln*, President Bush promised, "we will stand with the new leaders of Iraq as they establish a government of, by, and for the Iraqi people." But let us not expect that they will reform themselves—much less that we shall transform them—all at once up to the standards of the Gettysburg Address.

Tribes of Terror

Stanley Kurtz

(Winter 2007/08)

Lord Curzon, Britain's viceroy of India and foreign secretary during the initial decades of the 20th century, once declared:

> No patchwork scheme—and all our present recent schemes . . . are mere patchwork—will settle the Waziristan problem. Not until the military steam-roller has passed over the country from end to end, will there be peace. But I do not want to be the person to start that machine.

Nowadays, this region of what is today northwest Pakistan is variously called "Al-Qaedastan," "Talibanistan," or more properly, the "Islamic Emirate of Waziristan." Pakistan gave up South Waziristan to the Taliban in Spring 2006, after taking heavy casualties in a failed four-year campaign to consolidate control of this fierce tribal region. By the fall, Pakistan had effectively abandoned North Waziristan. The nominal truce—actually closer to a surrender—was signed in a soccer stadium, beneath al-Qaeda's black flag.

Having recovered the safe haven once denied them by America's invasion of Afghanistan, al-Qaeda and the Taliban have gathered the diaspora of the worldwide Islamist revolution into Waziristan. Slipping to safety from Tora Bora, Osama bin Laden himself almost certainly escaped across its border. Now Muslim punjabis who fight the Indian army in Kashmir, Chechen opponents of Russia, and many more Islamist terror groups congregate, recuperate, train, and confer in Waziristan. This past fall's terror plotters in Germany and Denmark allegedly trained in Waziristan, as did those who hoped to highjack transatlantic planes leaving from Britain's Heathrow Airport in 2006. The crimson currents flowing across what Samuel Huntington once famously dubbed "Islam's bloody borders" now seem to emanate from Waziristan.

Slowly but surely, the Islamic Emirate's writ is pushing beyond Waziristan itself, to encompass other sections of Pakistan's mountainous tribal regions—thereby fueling the ongoing insurgency across the border in Afghanistan. With a third of Pakistanis in a recent poll expressing favorable views of al-Qaeda, and 49% registering favorable opinions of local jihadi terror groups, the Islamic Emirate of Waziristan may yet conquer Pakistan. Fear of a widening Islamist rebellion in this nuclear-armed state was General Musharraf's stated reason for the recent imposition of a state of emergency. And in fact Osama bin Laden publicly called for the overthrow of Musharraf's government this past September. It is for fear of provoking such a disastrous revolt that we have so far dared not loose the American military steamroller in Waziristan. When Lord Curzon hesitated to start up the British military machine, he was revolving in his mind the costs and consequences of the great 1857 Indian "Mutiny" and of an 1894 jihadist revolt in South Waziristan. Surely, Curzon would have appreciated our dilemma today.

AN INDISPENSABLE GUIDE

Foreign journalists are now banned in Waziristan and most local reporters have fled in fear for their lives. Because scholars have long neglected this famously inhospitable region, Waziristan remains a dark spot, and America remains proportionately ignorant of the forces we confront in the terror war. Yet an extraordinary if neglected window onto the inner workings of life in Waziristan does exist—a modern book, with deep roots in the area's colonial past.

The British solution in Waziristan was to rule indirectly, through sympathetic tribal *maliks* (elders), who received preferred treatment and financial support. By treaty and tradition, the laws of what was then British India governed only 100 yards on either side of Waziristan's main roads. Beyond that, the maliks and tribal custom ruled. Yet Britain did post a representative in Waziristan, a "political agent" or "P.A.," whose headquarters was protected by an elite military force, and who enjoyed extraordinary powers to reward cooperative maliks and to punish offenders. The political agent was authorized to arrest and jail the male kin of miscreants on the run (particularly important given the organization of Waziristan's tribes around male descent groups). And in special cases, the political agent could blockade and even destroy entire settlements. After achieving independence in 1947, Pakistan followed this British scheme, indirectly governing its many tribal "agencies" and posting P.A.s who enjoyed the same extraordinary powers as under the British.

Akbar Ahmed, a British-trained social anthropologist, served as Pakistan's P.A. in South Waziristan from 1978 through 1980. Drawing on his academic background and political experience, he has written a fascinating book about his days as "king" (as the tribesmen used to call the political agent). First published in 1983 under the title *Religion and Politics in Muslim Society*, the book was reissued in 1991, and revised and released again in 2004, each time under the title *Resistance and Control in Pakistan*. Its obscure title and conventional academic introductory chapters explain why it has been neglected. Yet that neglect is a serious mistake. Given Waziristan's new-found status as the haven and headquarters of America's global enemies, Ahmed's book is an indispensable guide to thinking through the past and anticipating the future of the war on terror. In addition to shedding new and unexpected light on the origins of the Taliban, *Resistance and Control in Pakistan* offers what is, in effect, a philosophy of rule in Muslim tribal societies—a conception of government that has direct relevance to our struggle to stabilize Iraq.

Since completing the book, Ahmed, a devout Muslim who holds a chair in Islamic Studies and is a professor of International Relations at American University, has gone on to write several works analyzing the dilemmas of the Islamic world and explaining Muslim perspectives to Westerners. These include *Islam Under Siege: Living Dangerously in a Post-Honor World* (2003), and his recently published *Journey into Islam: The Crisis of Globalization*. For a time, he served as the High Commissioner of Pakistan to Great Britain, and in a note at the end of *Journey Into Islam*, he says that he coined the term "Islamophobia" shortly after taking that post.

Having once been tasked with governing the most notoriously unruly tribes in the Muslim world, Ahmed never entirely embraces the politically fashionable line. More than his academic colleagues in Middle East studies, he acknowledges the contribution of tribalism's violence and traditionalism to the Middle East's contemporary dilemmas. In fact, the story of the "king" of Waziristan's transformation into the man who coined the term "Islamophobia" reveals some extraordinary tensions and tragedies lurking beneath our polarized political debates.

UNDER SIEGE

The first thing that strikes the reader of *Resistance and Control in Pakistan* is the pervasive nature of political violence in South Waziristan. And here, in contrast to his later work, Ahmed himself is at pains to emphasize the point. A popular novelist of the British Raj called Waziristan tribesmen "physically the hardest people on earth." British officers considered them among the finest fighters in the world. During the 1930s Waziristan's troublesome tribesmen forced the British to station more troops in that agency than in the remainder of the Indian subcontinent. In more settled agricultural areas of Pakistan's tribal Northwest Frontier Province, Ahmed says, adults, children, and soldiers mill about comfortably in the open, while women help their men in the fields. No guns are visible. But arid Waziristan is a collection of silent, fortress-like settlements. Women are invisible, men carry guns, and desolation rules the countryside.

Even in ordinary times, from the British era through the present, the political agent's headquarters at Wana in South Waziristan wears the air of a fortress under perpetual siege. Five British political agents died in Waziristan. Ahmed reports that during a visit to Wana by Zulfikar Ali Bhutto in 1976, the entourage of Pakistan's prime minister was kept nervously awake most of the night by machine gun and rifle fire from the surrounding hills. In short, the Wana encampment in South Waziristan seems like nothing so much as a century-old version of Baghdad's Green Zone.

Politics in Waziristan is inseparable from violence. A British official once called firing on government officers the local "equivalent for presenting a petition." Sniping, explosions on government property, and kidnappings are common enough to necessitate continuous military protection for political officials. And the forms of routinized political violence extend well beyond direct attacks on government personnel.

Because government allowances are directed to tribal elders who control violent trouble-makers in their own ranks, ambitious maliks have reason to insure that such outlaws do in fact emerge. Waziristan's many "Robin Hoods," who make careers out of kidnapping even non-government officials and holding them for ransom, are simultaneously encouraged and controlled by local maliks. This double game allows the clans to profit from their own capacity for causing trouble, while also establishing a violence valve, so to speak, through which they can periodically convey displeasure with the administration. "To create a problem, control it, and terminate it is an acknowledged and highly regarded yardstick of political skill," writes Ahmed. For the most part, income in Waziristan is derived from "political activity such as raiding settled districts" and "allowances from the administration for good behavior." Unfortunately, a people who petitions by sniper fire seems poorly suited to democratic citizenship.

In his later work, Ahmed's insight into the subtle choreography of tribal violence dissolves in a haze of cultural apologetics. In *Islam Under Siege*, for example, he argues that Americans misunderstand what they see when Afghan tribesmen fire rifles into the sky, or store ammunition and weapons in caves. Although Americans associate these actions with terrorism, Ahmed calmly explains that firing into the sky is simply a mark of celebration at birth and marriage. Weapons storage, he reassures his readers, is merely "insurance against tribal rivalries." But is there not some connection between the resort to terror tactics, on the one hand, and societies characterized by violent tribal rivalry and demonstrative gunfire, on the other?

TRIBAL SOCIETY

The connection arises from the way Middle Eastern tribes are organized. These tribes are giant lineages, traced from male ancestors, which sub-divide into tribal segments, which in turn divide into clans, sub-clans, and so on, down to families, in which cousins may be pitted against cousins, or brother against brother. Traditionally existing outside the police powers of the state, Middle Eastern tribes keep order through a complex balance of power between these ever fusing and dividing ancestral groups. (Anthropologists call such tribes "segmentary lineages.")

In such tribes, the central institution is the feud. Absent state policing, security depends on the willingness of every adult male in a given family, clan, tribe, etc., to take up arms in its defense. An attack on a lineage-mate must be avenged by the entire group. Likewise, any lineage member is liable to be killed for an offense committed by a relative, just as all lineage members would collectively share in compensation should peace be made (through, say, a tribal council or the mediation of a holy man). Tribal feuding and segmentation allow society to keep a rough (sometimes very rough) peace in the absence of a state. Conversely, societies with strong tribal components tend to have weak states.

A powerful code of honor ties the system together. Among the Pushtun tribes that populate Waziristan and much of Afghanistan, that code is called "Pushtunwali." Avenging lineage honor is only one aspect of Pushtunwali. The code also mandates that hospitality and sanctuary be provided to any stranger requesting them. Thus a means is provided whereby, in the absence of a state, zones of security are established for travelers. Yet the system is based on an ever-shifting balance of terror which turns friends into enemies, and back again into friends, in a heartbeat. And this ethos of honor writes violent revenge and collective guilt deep into the cultural psyche. Although the British political agents who learned to live with Pushtunwali generally lionized it, Winston Churchill condemned it as a "system of ethics, which regards treachery and violence as virtues rather than vices." In any case, the dynamics of the war on terror are easily recognizable as an extension of this tribal system of collective guilt, honor, humiliation, and revenge.

A SYMBOL OF HONOR

The years immediately prior to Ahmed's term as South Waziristan's P.A. saw the rise and seeming collapse of an Islamist rebellion that, in retrospect, clearly stands as a precursor to the Taliban. Led by a mullah named Noor Muhammad, the movement was crushed by Pakistan's army in 1976. Armed with documentary resources, including access to the personal diary of Noor Muhammad, Ahmed takes us through the riveting story of this uprising.

On the one hand, the mullah's rebellion was classically Islamist. He established a traditional *madrassah* (religious school) in South Waziristan, whose students, or *talibs* (whence the word "Taliban"), were among the rebellion's core supporters. He criticized Pakistan's government for failing to adopt Islamic law, forbade the use of "un-Islamic" innovations, like the radio, and had violators of his various prohibitions beaten. Yet these familiar Islamist features were built upon a tribal foundation. The mullah's ascent was due, in part, to his ability to mediate tribal feuds.

South Waziristan is populated by two major tribes, the Wazirs and the Mahsuds. (A century ago the Mahsuds were part of the Wazirs, but have since split off and gained their own identity.) The Mahsuds traditionally outnumbered the Wazirs and were at least relatively more integrated into modern society. After Pakistan gained independence in 1947, a few Mahsuds moved to "settled areas" and entered school. Many of these made their way into government service, thus connecting the Mahsuds to influential bureaucratic networks. Others started businesses, which brought a modern source of wealth to the tribe.

Noor Muhammad's ability to resolve tribal feuds at a time when the Wazirs felt intense humiliation in the face of rising Mahsud power and wealth, turned him into a symbol of Wazir honor. Under the mullah's leadership, the Wazirs effectively declared a jihad against both the government of Pakistan and the Mahsuds, demanding a separate tribal agency for themselves. Properly speaking, of course, a jihad can only be fought against non-Muslims. The mullah solved this problem by declaring the Mahsuds to be infidels—a tribe of toadies to an un-Islamic Pakistani regime—who had sold out their Wazir cousins for government allowances and debased modern ways. Of course, this accusation of infidelity is exactly how al-Qaeda and the Taliban justify their attacks on fellow Muslims today.

Notice, too, that Noor Muhammad's movement developed in the early '70s, well before the Soviet invasion of Afghanistan in 1979. The rise of the Taliban is often ascribed to "blowback" from CIA support of Pakistani Islamists who fought the Soviets in the 1980s. Ahmed's account shows that simplistic "blame America" theories cannot hold. Critics of the blowback argument rightly note that America had no other means of fighting the Soviet invasion than to work through the Pakistani government, which for its own reasons needed to deploy Islamist proxies. (Supporting Pushtun nationalist proxies, the only other option, would have played into the hands of those in Afghanistan and India seeking to dismember Pakistan.) The problem is that this entire debate passes over the deeper social sources of the contemporary Islamist ascendancy.

Ahmed argues that the mullah's insurrection was "generated by Muslim actors as a result of internal tensions in society." And at one level, this proto-Taliban movement was deeply traditional. Mullah-led tribal rebellions have a long history, not only in Waziristan but in Muslim society as a whole. The great 14th-century philosopher-sociologist Ibn Khaldun famously described a cyclical process in which, unified by a righteous mullah, fierce outlying tribes conquer an effete and corrupt state. Over time the new set of ruling tribesmen falls into luxury, disunity, and corruption, and is in turn overthrown by another coalition of the righteous. These rebellions generally fuse an Islamic aspect with some narrower tribal interest, and the Wazirs' jihad against an allegedly "infidel" rival tribe certainly fits the bill.

There may be at least something new under that harsh Waziristan sun, however. Modernity's manifold economic opportunities seem to supercharge traditional tribal resentment at substantial disparities of wealth and status. And paradoxically, modern wealth also subverts such shallow internal tribal hierarchies as once existed, with explosive results.

CULTURAL SELF-DEFENSE

Following the oil boom of the 1970s, Wazirs and Mahsuds alike migrated to the Persian Gulf to work the oil fields and send their remittances back home. Maliks from the most prestigious tribal lineages initially resisted the call of migration. So the oil boom created an opening that "depressed lineages" happily filled. By the time the maliks began to send their sons to the Gulf, intra-tribal disparities of wealth and influence were disappearing.

So while the Mahsuds had outpaced the Wazirs, the power of maliks was waning among the Wazirs themselves. Now the Wazirs could afford to throw off those pliant elders who had taken and distributed British and later the Pakistan government's pelf; and by supporting a radical mullah, the restive tribe could feed its resentment of both the government and the Mahsuds.

As Ahmed notes, and in pointed contrast to the "poverty theory" of Islamism, modern education and wealth seem to have sparked this early Islamist rebellion. Instead of spurring further development, economic opportunities have fed the traditionalist reaction. Waziristan's tribesmen understand full well that their rulers mean to transform their way of life, thereby "taming" them through the seductions of education and modern forms of wealth. While some have accepted the trade, the majority consciously reject it. During the colonial period, education was despised as an infidel plot. In the 1970s conservative tribesmen systematically destroyed electrical poles, which were seen as a threat to Waziristan's isolation and therefore to the survival of traditional Pushtun culture. Economic development might well "tame" these tribesmen, yet poverty is less the cause of their warlike ways than the result of a deliberate decision to preserve their traditional way of life—their Pushtun honor—even at material cost.

The Islamist revolution is a conscious choice—an act of cultural self-defense against the intrusions and seductions of an alien world. Although the social foundations of the traditional Muslim way of life have been shaken, they are far from broken. So long as these social foundations cohere, advancing globalization will provoke more rebellion, not less—whatever America decides to do in Iraq and beyond. The root of the problem is neither domestic poverty nor American foreign policy, but the tension between Muslim social life and globalizing modernity itself.

In a sense, we are the Mahsuds. The Wazirs ached with humiliation at the loss of their dominance. Their grudge against the Mahsuds stemmed far more from Waziri decline than from any specific complaint. Even as the Mahsuds were scapegoated for the Wazirs' diminishment, America and the West have been blamed for worldwide Muslim decline. Addressing Muslim "grievances" won't solve this problem, because the professed grievances didn't start the jihad to begin with.

Ahmed is clearly embarrassed by the Wazirs' intra-Muslim jihad against the Mahsuds. Foreshadowing his later apologetics, he is at pains to distinguish between "authentic" Islam and Noor Muhammad's seemingly bogus claim of Mahsud infidelity—a claim obviously rooted in narrow tribal rivalry and interest. In his recent work, Ahmed puts much of what seems warlike or problematic in traditional Muslim society into the "tribal" basket, segregating out a supposedly pure and peaceful Islam. There is some justification for this procedure. Middle Eastern conceptions of honor, marriage practices, female seclusion, revenge, and much else can fairly be understood as practices with tribal roots, rather than formal Islamic commandments. Reformist Muslims therefore make a point of separating the tribal dross from authentic Islamic teachings.

Yet there is clearly some sort of "elective affinity" between Islam, in the strict sense, and tribal social life. The two levels interact and interpenetrate, leaving the boundaries undefined. Pushtuns who set out to avenge purely personal offences will dress and scent themselves as if embarking on jihad. So a given theologian's "true" Islam is one thing; "actual existing" Islam on the ground is another. Noor Muhammad's jihad against Muslims-he-judged-to-be-infidels turns out to be representative of the new religious wave, and reflects a complex and long-standing Muslim synthesis between theology and tribalism. Nor was the mullah's accusation of Mahsud infidelity without resonance. He accurately identified the modernist thread that united his immediate tribal enemies, the developing state of Pakistan, and ultimately the West itself.

REDISCOVERING CLASSIC STRATEGIES

If Islamist rebellion and narrow tribal interest are difficult to disentangle, the opportunity to separate them is the key to America's sophisticated new counterinsurgency strategy (actually a rediscovery of classic British and Pakistani strategies for dealing with Muslim tribes). Inveterate Wazir-Mahsud rivalry was the single greatest weakness of the tribes throughout the British era in Waziristan. The British ignored tribal feuding when the stakes were small. Yet if one tribe seemed at risk of gaining a permanent upper hand, the Brits intervened to keep opponents more-or-less equally at each other's throats. And since nearly every clan trouble-maker has rival kin, the P.A. cultivated multiple factions, so as to play one off against the other. Under Pakistan, the tribes have sometimes turned this game against the government, playing a sympathetic official (often a fellow Pashtun) against a rival administrator.

America's new counterinsurgency strategy seeks to appeal to tribal interests, as a way of breaking the link between al-Qaeda's global jihad and its erstwhile Sunni allies in Iraq. So far the new strategy has helped to stabilize Anbar and other rebellious tribal regions in Iraq. The danger is that the tribal winds will shift, and our military will likely come under constant pressure to favor one tribal faction or another. If mishandled, this could drive less favored clans back into enemy hands. Tribal politics can be mastered, yet it requires a constant presence. And learning to play the tribal game is very different from establishing a genuine democracy, which would mean transcending the game itself.

Can America or Pakistan adopt this new strategy in Waziristan itself—breaking the link between al-Qaeda and the tribal coalition now united against us in jihad? Theoretically this is possible, yet the outlook is far from ideal. Al-Qaeda has already murdered many of Waziristan's maliks. (Mullah Noor Muhammad rose to power in the '70s on assassination threats and violence against traditional maliks.) Insofar as economic and educational change has penetrated Pakistan's tribal areas, it seems to have undercut the basis for creating a new generation of government-friendly maliks, and fed into a populist Islamist revolt instead. Nevertheless, there are unconfirmed reports that America and Pakistan are even now exploiting latent tensions between al-Qaeda and the Taliban in Waziristan.

In the 1970s, once Noor Muhammad's combination Islamist rebellion/tribal war got out of hand, Pakistan was forced to crush it. The army bulldozed Wana's thriving traditional market, turning the Wazirs' most important trading center into little more than freshly plowed ground. Tipped off, the mullah took to the hills. Employing tactics reminiscent of Britain's original P.A.s, Pakistan seized his followers' property and systematically blew up their homes and encampments. After three months of this, the disheveled mullah and his followers came down from the hills and surrendered. Nowadays, burning a thriving Waziristan marketplace to the ground and blowing up civilian settlements as ways of getting to Osama bin Laden would doubtless elicit global howls of protest. Yet far from the glare of international publicity, Pakistan once freely employed such tactics.

SUNNY CONCLUSIONS

When, a couple of years after the destruction of Wana's market, Ahmed took over as P.A., the defeated Wazirs were looking to restore their lost honor and prove their loyalty to Pakistan. Trained as an anthropologist and convinced he could use the Pushtun's code of honor to good effect, he decided to give the Wazirs their chance. Breaking with established agency precedents, he placed his own life at risk by taking regular evening strolls around Wana without bodyguards. Ahmed could easily have been kidnapped and held in exchange for the imprisoned mullah's release, but the Wazirs left him untouched.

Ahmed then visited the Wazirs' holiest shrine, on the far border with Afghanistan—territory where no P.A. had ever set foot. As a guest of the Wazirs, he once again staked his own life and honor on the Pushtunwali of his Wazir hosts. In this way, he both pacified the Wazirs and extended Pakistan's writ in Waziristan further than it had ever gone. He even managed to coax a number of the region's storied "Robin Hoods" into surrender.

Based on these impressive successes, Ahmed concludes in his book that despite their reputation for violence and double-dealing, tribesmen can be peaceably governed within the terms of their own code of honor, if only they are given the chance. He regards solving tribal problems through military action as a sign of failure. Unfortunately, despite his considerable insight, his optimistic conclusions far outrun the terms of his own account.

Ahmed was the consummate good cop, in the right place at the right time. His ability to use the Pushtunwali code to evoke the best in the Wazirs clearly depended upon the army's violent actions in Wana two years before. Even the cross-border miscreants talked into surrender were balancing the refuge and respect he promised against the substantial dangers of living under the Soviets, who had entered Afghanistan during Ahmed's term. The former P.A. acknowledges some of this in passing, yet his unrelievedly sunny conclusions about tribal governance don't begin to acknowledge the depth of his own dependence on Soviet and Pakistani bad cops for success. His account has much to teach us. The honor code can indeed serve to offset and minimize tribal violence, and that effect can be encouraged by wise rule. But taken alone, Ahmed's analysis and prescriptions are dangerously misleading and incomplete.

The thesis of his next book, *Islam Under Siege*, was an extension of the analysis presented in *Resistance and Control in Pakistan*. The Muslim world as a whole is suffering from a loss of dignity and honor, Ahmed argues. As mass-scale urbanization, uneven economic development, migration, and demographic expansion undercut traditional social forms, the Muslim response has been to resist these changes and interpret them as outrages against collective honor. His solution was for the West to accept, support, and ally with traditional Muslim society, thereby helping the Islamic world to recapture its lost sense of honor.

THE ALIGARH MODEL

Ahmed's latest book, *Journey into Islam*, is riven by tensions between the author's public battle against "Islamophobia" and his reluctant acknowledgment that the Islamist ascendancy might be worth fearing after all. *Journey Into Islam* is based on Ahmed's recent travels across the global Muslim community, and he bills this tour of the Muslim world (with American students in tow) as an "anthropological excursion." Yet constant coverage of his entourage in Middle Eastern media outlets likely gentled his interviewees' responses. Pictures of Ahmed and his smiling American students posing with friendly Muslims get the central message across. Unless one desperately wants to be persuaded that all is well, however, his reassurances fall flat.

The book's Panglossian façade is broken by a single, searingly powerful moment. Ahmed's entourage visited Aligarh University in India, expecting to rediscover an academic beacon of Anglo-liberalism that had long and famously spread democratic values throughout India and Pakistan. Aligarh University shaped Ahmed himself in his youth, allowing him to synthesize his pride in Islam with a genuinely liberal and modern sensibility.

Yet moments after entering the Aligarh University campus, Ahmed and his American companions were surrounded by furious Muslim students praising bin Laden and raging at President George W. Bush. Students came even closer to descending into mob violence here, at India's erstwhile bastion of Muslim liberalism, than they had during Ahmed's visit to Deoband, the acknowledged center of South Asian Islamism. This frightening, unexpected encounter at his beloved alma mater was clearly agonizing for Ahmed, and forced him to acknowledge the collapse of the "Aligarh model" of liberal Islam. "The nation-state and the Aligarh model are not a viable alternative in the Muslim world at present," he concedes sadly.

This is indeed a tragedy. Ahmed himself embodies another side of the Aligarh model's fate in today's world. Modern and liberal though he may be, he is unwilling to concede the need for fundamental reform within Islam. Instead of facing the evident incompatibility with modernity of core aspects of Muslim religious and social life, he reverts to sanitized accounts, accusations of Islamophobia, and complaints about American foreign policy. Although he bitterly resents the influence of Bernard Lewis on American conservatives, Ahmed periodically (and reluctantly) mimics Lewis's claim that Americans are being scapegoated for the Muslim world's own decline. Lewis's conviction that the use of force must be a key aspect of American foreign policy in the Middle East infuriates Ahmed. Yet, rightly understood, his own account in *Resistance and Control in Pakistan* confirms Lewis's insight. Without the destruction of the Wana market and the capture of Noor Muhammad, not to mention the Soviet invasion of Afghanistan, Ahmed's gentle, honor-based rule in Waziristan would not have been possible.

LONG-TERM STRUGGLE

In a sense, global Islam is now Waziristan writ large. Ahmed rightly spots tribal themes of honor and solidarity throughout the Muslim world—even in places where tribal social organization per se has receded. Literally and figuratively, Waziristan now seeks to awaken the tribal jihadist side of the global Muslim soul. This has effectively thrust the leaders of the Western world into the role of British and Pakistani P.A.s (a famously exhausting job, Ahmed reminds us). With technological advance having placed once-distant threats at our doorstep, the West may soon resemble South Waziristan's perpetually besieged encampment at Wana. Perhaps it already does. Yet Waziristan was ruled indirectly, without ordinary law or policing. Preventing terror plots and the development of weapons of mass destruction requires a more active hand.

Muslim society will have to reform far more profoundly than Akbar Ahmed concedes if the worst is to be avoided. Our best option may be to reintroduce somehow the Aligarh University tradition of liberal learning and merit-based employment (independent of kinship ties) to the Muslim world. With our strategy in Iraq now reinforcing tribalism, the obvious front to try this is Europe, where concerted efforts must be made to assimilate Muslims to Western values. Globalization might then work for us, as cultural changes bounce back to the Middle East.

Even in the best case, we face a long-term struggle. Simmering tensions between modernity and Muslim social life are coming to a head. Yet all our present recent schemes are patchwork. And someday, perhaps at the peak of a post-emergency civil war between the army and the Islamists in Pakistan, the military steamroller may be called upon to settle the Waziristan problem once and for all. Who knows if, even then, it will work.

The Home Front: Left, Right, and (Elusive) Center

Christopher Flannery

(Fall 2002)

> *[S]ince 1947 America has been the chief and pioneering perpetrator of "preemptive" state terror . . . .*
>
> *For several decades there has been an unrelenting demonization of the Muslim world in the American media . . . .*
>
> *Once we meditate upon the unremitting violence of the United States against the rest of the world . . . one begins to understand why Osama struck at [America] . . . in the name of 1 billion Muslims.*

Welcome to the world of Gore Vidal. Looking down from his villa, *La Rondinaia*, nestled in 12 lovely acres perched high above Italy's Amalfi coast, Vidal thinks that he sees things unnoticed by lesser mortals—especially those very lesser mortals who have been proudly and defiantly flying the American flag this past year.

In *il mondo* Vidal, "most of today's actual terrorists can be found within [American] governments, federal, state, municipal" (a note for innocents: Vidal does not mean terrorists working *against* our governments). The unremitting terror that America inflicts upon the outer world is amply mirrored by the terror inflicted by the American "police state" upon its own citizens. America's terrorist police state is in the grips of a "Pentagon junta," goaded on by the "neofascist" *Wall Street Journal* and promoted by the "provincial war lovers" at the *New York Times*, whose "mindset" is essentially indistinguishable from the neofascists down the street. And the afflicted citizenry? Sheep. And not just your garden variety, easily bewildered, too easily led but lovable lambs. No, these are sheep worth loathing.

Vidal concedes that Americans today are endangered by an "absolutist religious order," but the danger emanates from the U.S. Justice Department and the Supreme Court, where a Christian conspiracy is afoot that traces its roots back to real fascists. The immediate occasion for Vidal's book is the September 11, 2001, attack on the United States for which Osama bin Laden takes credit, but *Perpetual War for Perpetual Peace: How We Got to Be So Hated* consists mainly of old Vidal essays from *Vanity Fair* and the *Nation* on other subjects. Most of its pages are devoted to Timothy McVeigh and the bombing of the Alfred P. Murrah Federal Building in Oklahoma City on April 19, 1995. "With both bin Laden and McVeigh," writes Vidal, "I thought it useful to describe the various provocations on our side that drove them to such terrible acts" and make them "understandable."

Conspiracy theorists to this day continue to speculate (with Vidal) that McVeigh was connected with international Islamist terror networks—but that is tame stuff. Vidal wants his readers seriously to consider the possibility that the Oklahoma City bombing was a conspiracy by agents of the federal government analogous to the Nazis' burning the Reichstag in 1933—to justify further strengthening of the American terror-police state. And September 11? Well, it never hurts to keep an open mind.

Gore Vidal has always liked to be a naughty boy, but it is hard for him to keep it up at 77. His perverse passions are beyond the wane. He comes across as an aging scold, desperately applying the rouge. To give him his due, he can still pretend to be aroused by a remarkable variety of objects. To get a sense of his range, imagine him sporting with ironic pride a World War II uniform and wandering around his medieval town of Ravello, crying from the heart: "Remember Ruby Ridge and Waco—and stop persecuting the pedophiles!" But although his book manages to be eccentric, intemperate, and paranoid, it is primarily lazy.

He markets his book as a work of intellectual and political daring, too explosively heterodox for even the most left-wing American publication. In truth, although its eccentricities can be inadvertently amusing, the book is the bearer of tired old news. Its central message has been rehearsed and rehashed by and for the intellectual, cultural, and academic establishments of the Western world for decades. The message is—hold on to your hats—that in this troubled and complex world the essential thing to understand is that Americans are not "the good guys."

Vidal is about as shocking as Julia Child. As he himself boasts, his odd little collection of recycled essays was "an instant best-seller" when first published in Italian and was quickly "translated in a dozen other languages." The American edition has been for weeks on the (neofascist!) *New York Times* best-seller list. In his brief American tour to promote the book Vidal was greeted with gleeful applause by (sheepish?) audiences of college students and other well-fed fans who knew as well as Vidal and his publishers that anti-Americanism is as American as apple pie, and sells like hotcakes.

Still, the old news does take on a fresh significance in the world made new by the events of September 11. And it is in opposition to both the old and the new anti-Americanism that William Bennett writes *Why We Fight: Moral Clarity and the War on Terrorism.*

Bennett writes at the end of 2001, not about the military battle but about the "battle of public opinion" that accompanies it, that can decisively affect it, and that promises to continue for a long time to come. Bennett is, of course, engaged in this battle. He writes to defend and sustain what he regards as the encouraging response of America to the attacks of September 11—the unity, patriotism, and, in particular, the righteous anger, that are necessary conditions for a successful prosecution of the war. This patriotic response needs to be defended because of the barrage of arguments that descended upon it immediately from what he calls America's "peace party": America brought the attacks upon itself; the president's rhetoric of "good" and "evil" is more dangerous than the terrorist threat; this is a "mad rush to war"; we must above all beware of "Islamophobia" and overreaction; conflict and confrontation never solve anything; we must seek a multilateral solution, etc.

But the arguments of the "peace party" are merely the latest expression of a deep-rooted intellectual and civic disposition, which Bennett (borrowing the term) calls the "debellicization" of America. His book is intended, so to speak, to *rebellicize* America. He wants to help restore the political conviction in the American mind that seemed to have been lost but came forcefully to life on September 11—namely, that "some things are worth fighting and dying for," and that America and Western civilization are certainly among them.

Bennett's strategic intellectual concern must therefore be the "adversary culture"—the moral relativists, postmodernists, multiculturalists, and assorted Leftists entrenched in American educational and cultural institutions—who have successfully taught a generation of Americans that on the one hand nothing is right or wrong and on the other America and Western civilization are great evils.

Bennett is determined, but he is not optimistic. So deeply rooted are the Left's disabling ideas that it will be a "work of generations" to uproot them and replace them with healthier growths. A "deep revolution in consciousness," a "vast relearning," must take place before America can fully regain the "moral clarity" that is needed. While our armed forces are doing their work—and long after they are done—our politicians and public officials, clergymen, mothers and fathers, and above all "educators, at every level," must undertake this larger work. They must restore to public authority the reasoned ground for distinguishing right from wrong and for defending America and the civilization it represents.

If there is any cause for optimism in this endeavor, it lies in something like the following reflections. Reason—and even, surprisingly, history—is on the side of "the good guys." The case that there is a rational ground for distinguishing good from evil, for example, is just intrinsically stronger than the alternatives that have been fashionable for so many years. And the intellectual exhaustion of these nihilist alternatives produces, with each new terrorist attack, a stronger odor of overripe fruit. The strained attempts by Stanley Fish in recent months to demonstrate the moral seriousness of postmodernism are a case in point: "Stand up and fight for . . . whatever!"

Great ratiocination, to be sure, is still required—will always be required—on behalf of common sense and common decency. But the efforts are interesting, and each small victory adds relish to the work. And as reason regains the ground that has been ceded for so long to the various lunacies of the Left (and Right), a more fair and balanced—a more reasonable—view of history cannot help but follow.

In this reasoned view, Western civilization has nothing to fear from comparisons. Quite the contrary, the rediscovery of its glories (and the increasingly vivid contrasts with the alternatives) has every chance of inspiring a global renaissance. As for America, its detractors and debunkers have made their case for many, many years. The title of Gore Vidal's book, for example, is taken from that pioneering debunker, progressive historian Charles Beard, whose work was exciting 80 years ago, around the time Mr. Vidal was born. The lasting influence of Beard's work does indeed demonstrate that bad (and fully refuted) ideas can last a long time and do a lot of damage. And certainly there are able successors to Beard who continue quite energetically to spread false rumors about America. But as for the future, when the old panjandrums of political correctness have assumed eternal emeritus standing, will American students continue to be taught *ad nauseam* that America is evil to the core? There is a good fighting chance that they will not. If truth is intrinsically stronger than slander—and it is—there is reason to hope that things will change, so long as the champions of truth stick to their guns.

In the (optimist's) future, the ravings of Gore Vidal and the anti-American diatribes of his high-salaried comrades in the "adversary culture" will be gathering dust in the museum of 20th-century intellectual malice. A fair and informed history will teach a coming generation of students, in Bennett's words, that whatever may be America's many faults,

> we have provided more freedom to more people than any nation in the history of mankind; that we have provided a greater degree of equality to more people than any nation in the history of mankind; that we have created more prosperity, and spread it more widely, than any nation in the history of mankind; that we have brought more justice to more people than any nation in the history of mankind; that our open, tolerant, prosperous, peaceable society is the marvel and envy of the ages.

If our "vast relearning" is ultimately to succeed, Bennett argues that it must especially recover "the American idea," the American "vision." But what is that vision? Dinesh D'Souza has some ideas about this, and they are, as usual, engaging and provocative.

If you have a ring in your nose, a tongue stud, loads of tattoos, spiked hair, an overblown estimation of your own authenticity, no particular interest in America, and absolutely no ability to aid in her defense, D'Souza wants to talk with you. Bill Bennett writes deliberately in anger; D'Souza writes in love. As Pericles appealed to ancient Athenians to fall in love with Athens, in *What's So Great About America* D'Souza would show contemporary Americans, and especially America's pierced and tattooed youth, the good in America that should make them love their country. It is urgently necessary to articulate this good in the immediate circumstances, not only because American and Western intellectuals have done so much to obscure it, but because our Islamist enemies are themselves animated by "an intelligent and even profound assault on the very basis of America and the West."

D'Souza, like Bennett, writes to defend American patriotism. He defends it not only against American detractors, but against European, Asian, and in particular Islamic critics of America and the West. An adequate defense, he rightly argues, requires "an examination of first principles." A "genuine patriot loves his country not only because it is his, but . . . because it is good." But D'Souza differs explicitly with Bennett and other "cultural conservatives" because they identify America's goodness with outdated ideas like the principles of the American Founders. They do not take sufficiently into account the "moral revolution" that took place in America in the 1960s and '70s, as a consequence of which "America became a different country." As a result of this revolution, "a new morality is now entrenched and pervasive" in America, and it is not only imprudent but wrong not to try to accommodate it.

The new morality—the new America—is especially to be found among American youths. And D'Souza's book is in part an attempt to reach out to them, which he thinks conservatives like Bennett are incapable of doing. To reach out to them, he accepts what he takes to be their vision—the new morality—at least up to a point.

At the root of this new morality is a new vision of "freedom." The founders understood human freedom to be intelligible only within a moral order that exists and can be understood independently of individual passions and interests and that must be nurtured within an authoritative tradition. The new freedom, inherited mainly from Rousseau, is the freedom of the individual to "determine what is good" unencumbered by any external "moral order" or principles or traditions. It is an "inner freedom," an "authenticity" that can be found only through the genuine expression of the "self." This "ethic of authenticity" has even been endorsed, and perfectly encapsulated, by the Supreme Court, "when it declared [in 1992] that all Americans have a 'right to define one's own concept of existence, of meaning, of the universe, and of the mystery of human life.'" This is now the idea that "America stands for"; this is the vision to which we owe "moral allegiance."

To personify the new American, D'Souza conjures from his experience "the Starbucks guy"—with "the Mohawk hair, the earrings, the nose ring, the studs on his forehead and tongue, the tattoos." The Starbucks guy would dismiss people like Bennett or Robert Bork as "fascists," "enemies of freedom," "un-American," "self-righteous mullah[s]," trying to take away his "inalienable right to determine his own destiny, to make his own choices." And D'Souza thinks the Starbucks guy is largely right. First, because in a democratic society it is impossible to "enforce norms based on a moral order that is no longer shared by the community." The new freedom has become "America's core value." It is fruitless and even un-American to oppose this new American vision. But, in addition, Rousseau's idea of freedom is at least partly true. Conservatives should "embrace it," if somewhat gingerly. They should "acknowledge the legitimacy of the ideal of authenticity." They could then engage the Starbucks guy in conversation, leading him from his mantra "I can choose for myself" to the question "What are you going to choose?" and from his insistence on "the autonomy of choice" to "some substantive understanding of the good life."

"[T]he question of the content of the good life," says D'Souza, is the central question both for Western civilization and for the American Founders. The new morality of the 1960s and 1970s abandoned that question. Celebrating their "radical freedom," the new Americans ceased to ask "what that freedom is for." It is the conservatives' challenge to resurrect that question. "Their mission . . . is to steer the American ethic of authenticity to its highest manifestation and to ennoble freedom by showing it the path to virtue."

D'Souza's rhetorical (and logical) problem is that he has presented the "path to virtue" as the path to a dead past, the path to nowhere. Having buried the old America (alongside Western civilization), he wants to invite the Starbucks guy to join it and, even more difficult, he then wants to summon the corpse to the defense of the new America and the Starbucks guy for which it stands. Praising the heroes of September 11 and the armed forces on which American liberties and civilization itself depend, D'Souza sensibly writes: "Authenticity, thank God, is not the operating principle of the U.S. military. America's enemies should not expect to do battle against the Starbucks guy." Suddenly the America that had died a few pages earlier is revived and sent into battle. It becomes the "older, sturdier culture of courage, nobility, and sacrifice . . . that will protect the liberties of all Americans, including that of the Starbucks guy."

D'Souza is right to want to make America, and virtue, and conservatives more appealing to American youth (though the Starbucks guy is not very promising material). But he underestimates what the principles of the American Founders have to contribute to this. The founders' idea of freedom is more robust than he realizes. As for Rousseau, D'Souza underestimates his potency as well. Rousseau's teaching of unfettered freedom contributes mightily to doctrines of unfettered will. The "noble savage" does not have to travel far to meet the "blond beast." The "ethic of authenticity" is not the ground on which to build if we are to ennoble American freedom.

Roger Rosenblatt joins Bennett and D'Souza in defending the American "way of life." He, too, has written a book about "love of country," *Where We Stand: 30 Reasons for Loving Our Country*. But Rosenblatt accurately presents himself as "the conventional liberal." On the one hand, he departs decisively from the anti-American Left in having affectionate respect for ordinary Americans, in wanting "to make a case for preserving the core values of the country," and in his belief that "the country has . . . done more to benefit the rest of the world than any in history." On the other hand, he despises "purveyors of simple-minded virtue, like William Bennett." It is, therefore, no simple-minded book that he writes.

Rosenblatt has barely finished professing his "love of country" before his liberal conscience compels him to assure the reader that this is no "unalloyed love." It is "complicated." He will, indeed, try to make a case for preserving America's "core values," but at the same time he will be arguing on behalf of "all the oddities and nonsense that make us us." Alas, the core is immediately and hopelessly lost in the complications. The book—and America—fragments into oddities, and especially into nonsense. The 30 "love songs" deliberately meander from one jejune paradox or self-celebratory self-contradiction to the next. What Rosenblatt proudly thinks he finds at America's core is a "clear inner confession of mixed feelings." But this is really a work more of introspection than of observation. What he has discovered is the confusion of his own conventional liberal soul.

Although his age would seem to make this impossible, Rosenblatt writes as if he were a graduate of the self-esteem curriculum that has prevailed in America in recent years. He is "sure that [his] book contains some lulus of errors and porous arguments," but so what! He writes it anyway, because "I felt like writing it, felt like saying anything I chose to say, and knew that I had the freedom to say it." Give him at least a gold star for honesty—he is right about the lulus and the pores. To mention a few: when trying to talk reverently about the founders, he mistakes Hamilton for Madison; he discovers that "the Constitution . . . states that government has no right to prevent free expression"; and he has the odd recollection that "Clinton was not impeached."

As if to complete the liberal stereotype, Rosenblatt gives us a weepy book, in which the author goes misty on us and wants us to share his weepiness, and in which America is lovable in part because it is inclined to be weepy, too. But he is not done.

Rosenblatt is celebrated on his dust jacket as a writer and a teacher of writing at Harvard University. But his explanation of the title of his book shows that he is no prose model for undergraduates and, as a bonus, offers a memorable image of the hapless divagations of American liberalism:

> These are the pillars of the Republic: to protect the weaker, to rescue the endangered, to dignify every individual, but centrally, to continue the search for a more noble expression of existence. However we have blundered in the history of this search, it is *where we stand* [italics added].

Leave aside that these pillars do not seem exactly to be cut from Washingtonian marble. Are they not moving around a bit too much for good pillar work? Especially that central pillar that seems to be on an endless search? And it is on this endlessly searching pillar that "we stand" as Americans. Here the muse of liberalism took hold of Roger Rosenblatt's quill pen and, unbeknownst to him, revealed for all to see the conventional liberal's plight. The ground keeps shifting beneath him. His pillars keep moving. And as a consequence, though he does genuinely want to love his country, he cannot come up with a cogent reason for doing so.

All of which tells us that, in an America that is asking serious questions with an urgency not felt in years, conventional liberalism has nothing serious to say. The battle of public opinion is between the anti-American Left that commands the strategic cultural heights of the Ivory Tower and the Hollywood Hills and the pro-American Right that occupies the American plains. The conventional liberal wants to be pro-American, but he takes his bearings from the Tower and the Hills. And so he wanders weepily on his weary pillars, back and forth across the land. What are the prospects in the battle? If you are a betting American and any kind of an optimist, put your money on the good guys, and hope they can work out that vision thing.

Theater of War

Christopher Hitchens

(Winter 2006/07)

A small but significant sentence occurs in one of the early chapters of *The Greatest Story Ever* Sold: *The Decline and Fall of Truth from 9/11 to Katrina*: "Like the 'lovely war' the British foresaw in the early going of World War I, the illusion of a painless engagement in Iraq was short-lived."

Now, it is true that some British jingoists believed that the combat begun on August 4, 1914, would be "all over by Christmas," and that this early euphoria forms a small part of the tragic sense with which that catastrophe has been imbued ever since. But the concept of a "lovely war" is derived from a musical satire of stage and screen, dating from the 1960s and deftly staged by some English radicals. (*Oh! What a Lovely War* was the title; it was actually based on a book called *The Donkeys* by the Tory historian Alan Clark, son of the Lord Clark who authored the *Civilization* series.) Mr. Frank Rich began his career as a theater critic: Broadway is his milieu. It comes naturally to him, perhaps, to conflate a world-historical calamity with a catchy tune from a subsequent smash-hit, and then to cleverly re-deploy the idea to ridicule "Shock and Awe." The problem is that his book is supposed to be a critique of showbiz values in public life. But, with its Hollywood-echo title, it is instead an example of how universal those very values have now become.

Suppose, for a thought experiment, I picture what Frank Rich might have said about the war led by the first President Bush to recover Kuwait from its annexation by Saddam Hussein. It was never made very clear quite what this war was, as they say, "about." At one point we were told it was to restore the pre-existing territorial borders of Kuwait—a subject which the Bush Administration had previously said could not constitute a *casus belli*. So Secretary of State James Baker, then as now the glass of fashion and the mold of form for all "realists," came out and said that the war was for "jobs"—a shot in the arm for the American economy. The vulgarity of this appearing excessive, it was determined that Saddam Hussein was another Hitler who had gassed "his own" people. But once one has announced that someone is another Hitler, further coexistence with him becomes impossible, and the overthrow of his regime is morally necessitated. However, there was no international or U.N. warrant for the removal of the Saddam Hussein system (which indeed was eventually confirmed in power by General Norman Schwarzkopf). I vividly remember saying to the late Peter Jennings, as we journeyed toward the Gulf on the eve of hostilities, that the measure of success would now be, not the recovery of Kuwait, but the replacement of the Baathist order. And I shall never forget his response, which was, journalist to journalist: "That's only true if we say so."

Once the war was over, the U.N. inspectors discovered something that has been erased from many memories. Saddam Hussein had built an enormous secret nuclear reactor at Tuwaitha, and had acquired most of the elements of a nuclear weapon. Had he waited to develop this, and only then moved to take Kuwait, that small yet incredibly wealthy country would be a part of Iraq to this day, and we would all be living—as, unknowingly, we did then—partly at the pleasure of a psychopathic dictator. Accommodations would soon enough have been made to this reality by many powers, perhaps including our own.

But the weapons had not been part of the justification for the war! So they did not "really" count. Imagine what fun Mr. Rich could have had, gaily pointing out the inconsistencies and hypocrisies of the administration's position. At one point, Colin Powell had gone before the cameras and shown aerial photography of Iraqi troops on the Saudi border, as if poised to take the greatest oil fields of all. This alarmist story turned out to be a canard. At still another stage, trained Kuwaiti witnesses were brought to Capitol Hill and coached to tell a tear-jerking tale about babies torn from incubators in a hospital and left to die on the floor. This, too, was soon exposed as a piece of atrocity propaganda. It was almost too easy to point up the absurdities and exaggerations of the Bush Administration's case. I know this very well, because I used to do it myself and was even somewhat celebrated for doing so, until I took a slightly closer look at Iraq and became mightily impressed by what a menace its despotism had become, to its own subjects, to the region, and to the world beyond. At this point, the contours of an inescapable eventual confrontation with Saddam became more important to me than rating the dubious P.R. skills of a Republican White House.

Rich prefers the latter task and is, in his way, quite an accomplished reviewer. He seems to have watched an absolutely extraordinary amount of television, and to have retained most of what he absorbed. And he's very deft at employing the standards of this medium while pretending simultaneously to decry them. Thus: "As the reigning cliché had it, 2002 was the Seinfeld election—an election about nothing." I don't remember this being the reigning cliché and I have never seen an episode of Seinfeld, but that the show itself was about nothing I do not for a moment doubt. With much else of Rich's TV reviewing I am inclined to agree also: there certainly ought to be more fighting and more bloodshed shown on our screens, and it ought still to be possible to see the scenes of mass incineration from September 11, 2001, as well. Let us by all means not "sanitize" anything, let alone euphemize it. I would change the name of the Defense Department back to the War Department right away, for example, and perhaps Rich would even support me here.

Or perhaps not. If I have it right, the special signature of today's media-savvy writer is his or her capacity for "irony." (This noble and elusive term has now been reduced to a signature wink, or display of the fingertips as if to signal quotation marks, though conceivably that is better than nothing.) However, the supposedly ironic Mr. Rich can be determinedly literal-minded when the exigencies of his political position demand it.

Even the villain at hand, Saddam Hussein, remained a vague figure from stock, since the specific history of his reign of terror got far less airtime than the tacky décor of his palaces. When Torie Clarke said in a Pentagon briefing that Saddam was responsible for "decades and decades and decades of torture and oppression the likes of which I think the world has not ever seen before," few journalists were going to gainsay the Pentagon mouthpiece by bringing up Hitler and Stalin.

See how high his standards are? Unless the Pentagon can find a briefer who in unscripted remarks can put Iraqi Baathism in its exact historical context, the Pentagon's position is as trivial and evanescent as the "airtime" which merely concentrates on palace décor. I personally doubt that there were many members of the Defense Department press corps who could have taken Ms. Clarke up on the point, but then I doubt that Rich could tell us much about the ideological debt of the Baath party to both Nazism and Stalinism, either. So does he mean to say that there is no proper comparison, or that Clarke was wrong to imply one? Of course he would not dare venture so far. Thus the potential "seriousness" of his own point becomes just another part of the media wallpaper: a cheap and easy observation made for no better reason than to pass the time.

Any fool can have great fun with the ineptitudes of departmental spokesmen (and once again, I speak as one who knows). Rich has been thundering on for years now about the supposedly chilling and oppressive effect of Ari Fleischer's admonition, a few days after September 11, 2001, that people should "watch what they say." He alludes to this terrifying moment several times in these pages, putting the most literal construction on the hasty but decent reply of a powerless and meek official, who was attempting to fend off questions about the bigotry of a Republican backwoodsman and the spurious moral equivalences of Bill Maher. I have written about the whole context of this non-episode elsewhere (see *Slate* magazine, September 11, 2006, if you are curious) but for now I will simply say that if you sometimes find the responses of public officials at press conferences to be stupid or inarticulate, you should always make a point of looking up the original journalistic questions. For another instance of Rich's pseudo-forensic style, you might try the following:

> "I don't think we ever said—at least I know I didn't say that there was a direct connection between September the 11th and Saddam Hussein," Bush said in the spring of 2006. That is technically true, but it is really just truthiness: Bush struck 9/11 like a gong in every fear-instilling speech about Iraq he could.

Now, "truthiness" is a laugh-word invented by Steven Colbert who (along with his friend Jon Stewart and the other heroes of Comedy Central) is the beau ideal of what Rich considers to be the ironic. In this book and in his regular column, he gives "truthiness" a workout whenever he can. He clearly wishes he had coined it himself, and he has kept it going for perhaps a touch longer—may I hint?—than even Colbert might wish. Let us examine it in the present case. The administration did not, in point of fact and as Rich concedes, ever make the case that Saddam Hussein had sponsored the assault of 9/11. It did, however, strongly imply that he might have an interest in, or enthusiasm for, this kind of activity. And many Americans when polled were found to suspect him of an even more direct connection. Well, Saddam Hussein had sheltered the Iraqi-American fugitive who mixed the chemicals for the 1993 attack on the World Trade Center. He had allowed the internationally-wanted criminal Abu Nidal to use Baghdad as his headquarters. He had boasted of paying a bounty to the suicide-murderers of Hamas and Islamic Jihad. The man who hijacked the Achille Lauro cruise ship, a certain Abu Abbas, who was responsible for rolling Leon Klinghoffer in his wheelchair off the vessel's deck and into the Mediterranean, had to be released when apprehended because he was traveling on an Iraqi passport. A diplomatic passport.

The Baghdad state-run press had exulted at the revenge taken on America on 9/11. This does not exhaust the "truthiness" of the suggestion that Saddam Hussein might have to be taken seriously as a sponsor of nihilistic violence. Could one even suggest that those who thought so might be intuitively and even objectively wiser than those who thought it crass to mention Saddam Hussein and "terrorism" in the same breath? Not without being jeered at by Rich, who either does not know any of the above facts or who chooses not to include any of them in his proudly truth-centered narrative.

It would be good to have a demotic word for the way in which journalism, commentary, "spin," and official propaganda converge, though I think "truthiness" would be too feeble to cover it. All that the term does is to condense what we already "know," which is that perception trumps reality as often as not. Rich himself gives a fine illustration of the point when he idly says that Michael Moore's entirely mendacious film *Fahrenheit 9/11*, which mobilized Democrats and liberals behind a completely fictitious account of events, was both a "movie eviscerating Bush" and "an instant media sensation." His stale phrasing comprises one very smelly value-judgment—the president was not in fact "eviscerated" by this contemptible movie, which surely cannot be praised even faintly by anyone with the smallest regard for veracity—as well as one statement of near-fact which is almost true by definition. As Peter Jennings might have put it, if the *New York Times* describes something as "an instant media sensation," then an instant media sensation is what it becomes. But who's the "truthy" one here?

As if sensing the need for a change of cultural pace, Rich turns off the TV at the midpoint of his book, and snatches up a work of fiction:

> A month before the election, the country's mood was captured with startling acuity in a recently published Philip Roth novel, *The Plot Against America*. The book's resonance with ongoing events may have been part of the reason why it became Roth's biggest seller in years, joining a bestseller shelf crowded with books about George W. Bush.

Note the easy, near-automatic way in which—like movies these days—books are reviewed according to their initial sales. But Roth's book is about Charles Lindbergh. How does it "join a bestseller shelf crowded with books about George W. Bush"? Well, that's easy. Lindbergh could fly a plane, was a Christian, had a populist manner when it suited him. He is also (and here I switch tenses out of respect for the novel form, because now he's being fictionally portrayed by Roth as a might-have-been president) a fear-monger and an invoker of "national security." That does it. Bush to the life! I cannot be absolutely sure that Rich has even bothered to observe the difference between the actual Bush and the hypothetical Roosevelt who is defeated by the hypothetical Lindbergh. (Nor can I be certain if he really thinks that a national "mood" can be "captured with startling acuity.") But it will always remain the case that Lindbergh and his anti-Semitic "America First" movement accused Franklin Roosevelt of scaring the nation into a war, and of being prepared to promulgate falsehoods in order to do so. Indeed, two of the most prominent figures of today's anti-war movement, Gore Vidal and Patrick J. Buchanan, remain strikingly loyal to the memory of Lindbergh and accuse the president of staging a new Pearl Harbor to stampede us into a war in which Israeli (as they sometimes remember to put it) interests are paramount. If Rich was going to discuss Roth at all, as a writer or as a counterfactual historian, he would have had to notice that the isolationists of today are, as they were yesterday, the foes of regime change. But why trouble to make the effort, when one can scan the reviews of the reviews and call the result cultural criticism?

Frank Rich is an expert on the ways in which a deadline or a news-cycle can make all the difference, and on the advantage that this knowledge can give to those who "spin." He is an adept when it comes to such Washington tricks-of-the-trade as the official passing out of unwelcome news late on Fridays or early on Saturdays (though he never seems to ask himself why the press keeps falling for this obvious and notorious trick). So it is amusing to be able to say that he himself falls a hapless victim to the difference between quotidian journalism and even the most instant type of book-publishing. Readers of these pages will have noticed that, toward the end of summer 2006, the greatest white whale-hunt ever mounted was shamefacedly called off. Nothing has been heard lately of the grand White House plot to unmask and destroy the innocent Valerie Plame and her Galahad, the fearless Joseph Wilson. The story went from *grand peur* to yawn in no time flat. Alas this bathos came too late to rescue the book under review, which went to press while many, many reporters still scented the scandal of a lifetime, or at the very least of a career. It then became widely known that the man who disclosed the identity of Ms. Plame to Robert Novak was Mr. Richard Armitage—a consecrated opponent of the then-policy of "regime change" and democratization in the Middle East, whose role goes unmentioned here. Should you ever wish to recover the atmosphere of hectic conspiracy-mongering that pervaded the press in those days, and overrode even the most basic rules of evidence or analysis, here it all is, as if preserved in amber. Best of all is the knowing way in which Rich talks of matters that are well beyond his ken: "The leaks, in time-honored fashion, went to the reporters the White House judged most reliably sympathetic: Woodward, Miller, Novak, in that order of preference and chronology." Not really: Woodward and Miller never even wrote the story, and Novak (who did) is one of the most dedicated opponents of the Iraq War in print, as well as an admirer of the CIA, a sometime foe of Israel, and a partisan of Joseph Wilson's. From his pen we eventually learned what had long been obvious, or obvious to anyone not intoxicated by hatred of the White House, which is that he had approached the authorities and not the other way around. A goodly chunk of Rich's book, and of the portentous and padded "time-line" section that makes up a great part of it, is rendered entirely nugatory thereby. The remainder can stand as an instance of the weed-like spread of second-order media phenomena such as "truthiness," and as a warning to those who suppose that the profound can be deduced from an intense but myopic scrutiny of the superficial.

Why We Don't Win

Angelo M. Codevilla

(Winter 2009/10)

More than eight years after a gang of Arabs murdered 3,000 Americans, no one argues that the U.S. government has managed to avenge our fellow citizens, much less ensure our peace, safety, and "Enduring Freedom." Nearly a decade after September 11, lower Manhattan's Ground Zero remains a hole—in Bret Stephens's words, "a site of mourning turned into a symbol of defiance turned into a metaphor of American incompetence." Only a third of Americans now tell pollsters that we are winning against the terrorists. Two thirds of respondents are angry with their government; about half of these are "very angry," having lost faith in its capacity to perform even basic functions. Rasmussen reports that although a third of those polled think the country's best days are ahead, a majority believes that America's future will be worse than its past.

For decades, under Democrats and Republicans, liberal internationalists, neoconservatives, and realists, the U.S. government let the terrorist wave build. Then after 9/11 it spent over 5,000 American lives in Afghanistan and Iraq without achieving anything that it had promised, while conducting a self-discrediting diplomacy toward Iran, Russia, North Korea, and China. At home, the Homeland Security department diminished our liberty without increasing our security. In this respect, the differences among Presidents Barack Obama, George W. Bush, Bill Clinton, George H.W. Bush, Jimmy Carter, and Richard Nixon, and among Secretaries of State Hillary Clinton, Condoleezza Rice, Madeleine Albright, Warren Christopher, George Shultz, and Henry Kissinger, are less important than their similarities: the "small war" of terrorist acts that has beset us since the 1960s—infinitesimal as wars go—was enough to expose our bipartisan ruling class's incomprehension and incompetence. America's problem is that this class has set the country on a downward slope in foreign as well as domestic matters, and that it is increasingly difficult to imagine America on any other trajectory with it at the helm.

WHATEVER IT TAKES?

On September 11, 2001, fifteen Saudi Wahabis, plus two from the Emirates and one from Lebanon, led by an Egyptian Muslim Brother, brutally deprived America of peace. They executed a plan devised by the (secular) terrorist network of Khalid Sheik Muhammed—the very people who had first attacked the World Trade Center in 1993, carrying passports from Iraq. But though peace is the natural aim of statecraft, American statesmen never considered how to restore our peace.

Defeat and victory are obvious and undeniable. Winners celebrate a better future; losers mourn a better past. Winners live confidently in peace; losers scurry after ever receding mirages of it. The news of 9/11, the images of burning Americans jumping to their deaths and of iconic buildings in flames, set off victory dances in the Arab street. Crocodile tears from what our political class likes to call "the international community" thinly veiled its satisfaction that, as Barack Obama's mentor Jeremiah Wright would put it, "America's chickens came home to roost." To the many who celebrated the end of the American era, the future looked brighter than the past. Not so to the American people. Combining outrage with mourning, they demanded (as a rescue worker at Ground Zero shouted to President Bush) "whatever it takes" to destroy terrorists and all who had anything to do with them. But America's bipartisan ruling class never intended to turn the mourners into revelers, and vice versa.

Our best and brightest refused to take seriously the possibility of holding Middle Eastern governments responsible for the incitement of these attacks, for both the money and the terrorists that flow from their jurisdictions. Nor did they identify any other source of the problem. Hence, regardless of how the operations they ordered might fare, our experts were not going to solve America's problem. Instead, they promoted the notion that 9/11 would "change everything, forever"—*in America*. They accepted terrorism as a fact of modern life and told Americans to get used to finding public spaces turned into fortresses, to showing documents and being frisked. The slogan "united we stand" did not tell Americans to eliminate our enemies, but to stand still, to commemorate our dead, to believe and obey Washington. There would be no victory, much less peace. Demands for either would be deemed extremism. The terror threat would remain "orange" indefinitely, and the bloodletting would have no end. It's a wonder that Americans' spirits held up as long as they did.

September 11 brought to America the Muslim world's endemic warfare. As a routine matter, Sunni Arab secular regimes violently repress the Muslim Brotherhood while deflecting their zealous anger toward Westerners. Somewhat similarly, Saudi Arabia's regime turns the murderous Wahabi sect with which it is intertwined against impure Muslims and Westerners. All repress the Shia in their midst. Iran's Shia regime fights its Sunni neighbors for elbow room by supporting Shia elements in Iraq, Lebanon, and Palestine, and affirms its Muslim credentials by fighting Westerners. Terrorism is the Muslim world's tool of choice for international as well as domestic affairs.

The diplomacy of Iran, Syria, Saudi Arabia, and Egypt toward the West combines demands—and vague suggestions that satisfying those demands might lead to some lessening of terrorist activity against us—with dark hints of violence if the demands are not met. By contrast, America and Europe now live in fear of attacks on behalf of causes espoused by these states. Western policy is based on the notion that peace for us depends on satisfying them. Hence every president since Richard Nixon has promoted one version or another of "the peace plan," seeking to trade our side's concrete concessions for Arab promises to stop trying to destroy Israel, Western civilization's outpost in the Middle East; to curtail Arab governments' anti-Western incitement; and to stop facilitating terrorists. Every secretary of state from Henry Kissinger to Hillary Clinton has pressed Israel to "take chances for peace."

America's own concessions have resulted in a Muslim world ever less inclined to give us peace. In the 1970s the U.S. government agreed to the Arab world's demands to treat Yasser Arafat's Palestinian Liberation Organization as the Palestinian people's sole legitimate representative, and even started financing it secretly. Similarly, in the 1980s the U.S. helped Syria take over Lebanon, and in 1991 ensured the survival of Saddam Hussein's regime in Iraq. The Bush Administration's reaction to 9/11 was gratuitously to declare Arab governments allies in the war against terrorism. Barack Obama confessed America's sins (not his own) to the Muslim world and proposed mutual understanding. Today, it is inconceivable that any of the Muslim world's governments, which routinely police public expression in their countries with iron fists, would recommend to its subjects even elementary courtesy to Jews, Christians, or mere Westerners.

PROFILES OF DEFEAT

By contrast the U.S. government has officially declared that Islam—all parts of it—is a "religion of peace," and that Muslim countries are pillars of the international community. To discourage the American people's natural reaction to their attackers as well as to search for ways of reaching out to Muslims at home and abroad, the U.S. employs Muslims to craft codes of speech and behavior for its employees and for members of the armed forces, codes that the mainstream media effectively spread through civil society. In 2006, under Hasham Islam, a protégé of then-Deputy Secretary of Defense Gordon England, the Pentagon franchised the American Muslim Council (whose leader was later convicted of plotting a murder) to supply Muslim chaplains for the U.S. armed forces.

When a Muslim murders shouting "Allahu Akhbar," as did U.S. Army Major Nidal Malik Hasan as he shot 51 colleagues at Fort Hood, Texas, the official reaction grimly recalls Groucho Marx's joke about how a man answered his wife when she caught him *in flagrante*: "Who you gonna believe, me or your own eyes?" After the shootings, President Obama warned against "jumping to conclusions," and Army Chief of Staff George Casey added that "it would be a *greater* tragedy if diversity became a casualty here" (emphasis added). Never mind that Hasan identified himself on his business card as "SoA" (a soldier of Allah), that he attended a Wahabi mosque, and that he had lectured colleagues, on the Koran's authority, that infidels should have burning oil poured down their throats and be beheaded. The *New York Times* editorialized that many soldiers returning from deployments exhibit high levels of violence, that Americans had taunted Hasan for being Muslim, and in its letters column that America itself manufactures many Hasans. Chicago's mayor Richard Daley blamed the American public's love of guns. The presidential commission's report on the matter, prepared by former Army Secretary Togo West, blamed "extremist behavior" (of which Americans and Christians are at least as guilty as anyone) and never mentioned Muslims, Arabs, or any reason for avoiding the obvious.

Why do our leaders avoid the obvious? Because, as *Newsweek*'s Evan Thomas pointed out, talking about Muslims committing terrorist acts tends to "get the right wing going," which the ruling class fears more than they fear foreign terrorism. Noting that terrorism comes chiefly from the Muslim world is in bad taste among our rulers because it amounts to "profiling." Yet they profile all the time. The FBI fruitlessly focused its investigation of the 9/11 anthrax attacks tightly on two persons it hounded to death and on another to whom it was forced to pay $5.8 million in damages—because these three fit its profile of the "mad scientist." Attributing anti-American terrorism to the American people's own defects is an even more common profile, part of that polite narrative which Thomas Friedman describes as

> the cocktail of half-truths, propaganda and outright lies about America that have taken hold in the Arab-Muslim world since 9/11. Propagated by jihadist Web sites, mosque preachers, Arab intellectuals, satellite news stations and books—and tacitly endorsed by some Arab regimes—this narrative posits that America has declared war on Islam, as part of a grand "American-Crusader-Zionist conspiracy" to keep Muslims down.

Adopting the narrative of those who would kill you is the surest sign of defeat.

Consistent with this narrative, the FBI also launched operation "Vigilant Eagle" in February 2009, which profiles for surveillance as possible terrorists American "militia/sovereign-citizen extremist groups" and veterans returning from Iraq and Afghanistan. On April 7, a Department of Homeland Security memo made this official U.S. policy. No evidence told our ruling class that these Americans were dangerous. But the profile did. By contrast, though the government had intercepted Major Nidal Hasan's e-mail exchanges with an al-Qaeda cleric in Yemen (who later wrote: "the only way a Muslim could Islamically justify serving as a soldier in the U.S. Army is if his intention is to follow in the footsteps of men like Nidal"), he fit a profile that allowed him to become part of an advisory group to President Obama's 2009 transition task force on security. In short, our governing class's profiles reflect prejudices at odds with reality.

THE LOGIC OF INSECURITY

The logic of our ruling class's burgeoning security apparatus is that any person is neither more nor less likely to be a terrorist than any other, and that focusing on Muslims (especially of a certain age, etc.) is some kind of crime. That logic mandates bothersome but impotent surveillance of the general population. Whenever terrorist incidents spotlight that impotence, this logic prescribes ever-greater doses of the same. On Christmas Day 2009, a young Nigerian whose prominent father had warned the U.S. embassy of his son's Muslim anti-Americanism almost blew up an airliner over Detroit with a bag of high-explosive powder attached to his underwear—having been let on board without even showing his passport. Republicans and Democrats rushed to enhance security by forcing all air travelers through scanners that would show us naked (with faces obscured) to security officers. (Inevitably, these officers' cubicles will be tagged "Peeping Toms' Cabins.") What can be said of a ruling class that pursues security through universal nakedness?

To what next step will our rulers' security paradigm take us? It is no secret that nakedness is insufficient because drug couriers routinely take onto airliners far more stuff hidden in body cavities than the Christmas bomber had in his underwear, and because objects hidden in body cavities can be discovered only by body cavity searches. That is why male and female inmates processed into maximum-security prisons undergo body cavity searches either manually or by ultrasound. Were a jihadist to use a cavity bomb to bring down an airliner, might the notion of treating us all like high-security convicts be ludicrous enough for our rulers to rethink their cultural-political paradigm? What would it take for our experts to admit that security starts with focusing on political and social differences, rather than with the pretense that these are irrelevant?

INGRAINED INEPTITUDE

Our ruling class's persistent denial of the fact that war arbitrates human differences, and its belief that "victory" is a dangerous relic from a less enlightened age, explain why terrorists have confounded it so easily. Consider the record. During the Korean War our best and brightest chose not even to cut the enemy army's supply line from China, and prevented the Chinese Nationalists on Taiwan from opening a second front. On such sophistication they established an academic orthodoxy. Bernard Brodie's canonic book *The Absolute Weapon* (1946) assumed that because the next war would wipe out mankind, all nations now shared a primordial interest in peace. In the 1950s Robert Osgood (*Limited War: The Challenge To American Strategy*, 1957), Henry Kissinger (*Nuclear Weapons And Foreign Policy*, 1957), and Thomas Schelling (*The Strategy of Conflict*, 1960) expanded the orthodoxy, arguing that all peoples want essentially the same things and that all governments maximize their interests by acting within matrices of rational choices.

In that fertile decade, too, our bipartisan ruling class came to see itself as the patron of the world's truly progressive, revolutionary forces, persuading itself that they would be America's pupils and friends. Thus the CIA financed Gamal Abdul Nasser's Free Officers' movement that took over Egypt in 1953, as well as parts of the National Liberation Front that took Algeria from France between 1954 and 1962. Saddam Hussein got his start as a lowly CIA agent in 1959. When Fidel Castro took over Cuba in the same year, he joked: "I got my job through the *New York Times*," the slogan of the want-ad section of the American establishment's newspaper.

Always surprised whenever the "Third World" they helped create turned against them, our experts grew to accept William Appleman Williams's explanation in *The Tragedy of American Diplomacy* (1959): the American people are racist, greedy, and arrogant, and have been on the wrong side of oppressed peoples' struggles for justice and progress. The Vietnam War showed what happens when a country's ruling class believes that foreign enemies are less the problem than its own citizens. Robert McNamara, secretary of defense under Presidents Kennedy and Johnson during most of the Vietnam War, later admitted in *In Retrospect: The Tragedy and Lessons of*

Vietnam (1995) that he had always regarded the American majority's pressures for victory as more dangerous than the North Vietnamese. Henry Kissinger acknowledged in *Diplomacy* (1994) that only a minority of Americans ever favored *reducing* military pressure on the enemy. But, like McNamara, he was part of that ruling bipartisan minority.

When fantasies and proclivities clash with foreign realities, our experts have sought "exit strategies" and accepted what they formerly had deemed unacceptable. In the 1960s they outgrew their commitments to Vietnam. In 1979 they repudiated their commitment to Iran's shah, then bet on ingratiating themselves with the Ayatollah Khomeini's regime, then loudly deemed his Islamic Republic unacceptable, and finally tried to accommodate it in ever more embarrassing ways. When the U.S. government sent Marines in token objection to Syria's takeover of Lebanon in 1983, Secretary of State George Shultz boasted: "the Marines can take care of themselves." But when Syria's agents killed 241 of them with a truck bomb, the U.S. government preferred leading America in mourning to loosing its furies. Hollow boasting followed by impressive mourning is now a U.S. specialty.

Our government's reaction to American leftists' hijacking passenger aircraft to Cuba in the 1960s exhibited the priorities and assumptions that have dictated its reaction to terrorist acts ever since: Do not hold any foreign government responsible for facilitating the acts, or failing to stop them. Take no account of the perpetrators' or sympathizers' political identity. Remember that the American majority's overreaction poses a greater danger to peace and good governance than any terrorist act. And if forced to use the armed forces against foreigners, avoid focusing them on regimes, and instead use them as cops and as shields behind which you can try turning your enemies into friends. But wrap it all in patriotic rhetoric.

EVADING THE QUESTION: AFGHANISTAN

After September 11 the U.S. government tied itself in knots over the question "who's responsible?" But the answer was as self-evident as it had been for just about every terrorist act since the 1960s—namely, the host of governments that espouse violent anti-American causes and that facilitate the individuals who actually do the killing. Our rulers shunned this reality in order to avoid coming to grips with the practical question: "what do we have to do to make those governments crush the very causes they encourage and the people who serve them?" Hence, they fixed on a far less meaningful inquiry: "who had been the hijackers' direct supporters?" Based on evidence never made public, George W. Bush adopted unquestioningly the CIA's answer that Osama bin Laden had masterminded 9/11, and he accepted, too, the Agency's consequent equation of America's terrorist problem with al-Qaeda. Subsequently, the government, followed by the media, defined the "war on terror" as a campaign to destroy al-Qaeda. In practical terms, that meant doing something in Afghanistan, where al-Qaeda was living.

But nothing that Americans might do in Afghanistan could have removed our terrorist problem. Crushing the Taliban for having hosted bin Laden—our enemy, to be sure, regardless of whatever role he had in 9/11—might have been useful as an example of what America would do to any and every regime that abetted our enemies. But even the death of every "Afghan Arab" would hardly have dented a problem that predated 1998—when bin Laden and company came to the U.S. government's notice by bombing U.S. embassies in Africa—and that involved far greater numbers of people, institutions, and anti-American trends. At best, the U.S. military operations in Afghanistan that began in October 2001 might have been incidental to later operations aimed at the problem's heart. No such operations were ever conceived.

Military success in Afghanistan came after the White House decided to support the war that the Northern Alliance of Tajik and Uzbek tribes had been waging against the Pashtun Taliban's regime. With U.S. air support, the Alliance routed the Taliban coalition's tribes, most of which switched sides and sold the "Afghan Arabs" in their midst to the Americans, who shipped these "terrorist detainees" off to Guantanamo Bay. But this success proved how insignificant the Taliban and al-Qaeda were. Though the U.S. captured most of the people who had ever associated with bin Laden—perhaps a fifth of whom had committed crimes or were highly motivated at the time of capture—others who had never heard of al-Qaeda before 9/11 started committing anti-Western acts in its name around the world. No one has reported seeing Osama bin Laden alive since October 2001, though several people have reported attending his funeral. Nevertheless, the U.S. government continued to speak and act as if he and al-Qaeda were the fount of anti-American terrorism. Although capturing him would not have eliminated our terrorist problem, not finding him, and accepting as genuine the tapes issued in his name, actually exacerbated the problem.

Our ruling class was impervious to the fact that artificial national boundaries divide all of Afghanistan's five major ethnic groups from their kin in neighboring states, and that each tribe always welcomes money and guns, but seldom foreigners. Misreading their 2001 success as a victory of moderates over extremists, the Americans set about trying to moderate the whole country. The resulting flow of billions of American dollars through some tribal networks to the disadvantage of others, American lecturing on lifestyles (including birth control), and the killing or maiming of innocents in dragnets for Taliban remnants, roused Afghans to insurrection. The non-Pashtun resented the central government because the Pashtuns dominated it. But many Pashtun resented the government because it represented the forces that had defeated a Pashtun regime, and because the national army now contained 80,000 Tajiks. So when money from wealthy Wahabis in the Gulf began paying the Pashtun tribes on both sides of the Afghanistan-Pakistan border to do what they increasingly felt like doing, and funneled suicide bombers to them, the insurrection grew. Americans might have left Afghanistan in 2001 having strengthened the Tajiks and Uzbeks, shielded the Hazara from pressure from the Pashtun, and made clear to the latter that harboring Afghan Arabs hostile to America is a bad idea. Instead, by 2006 Afghanistan was a problem bigger than ever and Americans were stuck occupying an increasingly hostile country.

EVERYTHING BUT WAR: IRAQ

In 2002, the State Department and CIA were particularly protective of Saddam Hussein's Iraq—State because keeping Iraq under Sunni rule pleased the Arab world, and CIA because it believed that Saddam's Baathist ruling party contained "moderate" kindred souls. Hence both strove to prevent the 2003 U.S. invasion of Iraq. Afterward they pressed for occupying the country to further their own particular visions of it. Meanwhile the Pentagon just wanted to overthrow Saddam. Because straddling these conflicts took priority over critical thinking about ends and means, the U.S. government's official justifications for the 2003 invasion of Iraq gave no strategic guidance; and its decision to occupy and reform the country turned an initial military success into a parody of war deadlier than war itself.

The United States might have decided to invade Iraq because it sponsored terrorism. Saddam's defiance of America had made him, arguably, the Arab world's most prominent person. He used that prominence to whip up hatred against us, and televised his encouragement of all manner of terrorism against both America and Israel. The people who attacked the World Trade Center in 1993 had come from Iraq. There was plenty of evidence of contacts between his intelligence service and al-Qaeda. Had the U.S. government invaded to make the country inhospitable to terrorism, any military planner could have designed operations to inflict on its governing class the kind of terrible end that would discourage its successors and other regimes from risking the same fate. In fact, this is what the Pentagon wanted to do: turn Iraq over to the people who had been fighting its regime, and who would finish it off. Then America's Iraq operation would have ended. But CIA argued that Iraq's past or present support for terrorism was not a legitimate reason for using force against it, because CIA could not (nor did it want to) prove Iraq's "direction and control" of 9/11.

Was the invasion meant to rid Iraq of Weapons of Mass Destruction (WMDs)? The State Department and CIA argued that the only legal justification for military action against Iraq was its defiance of United Nations resolutions requiring it to rid itself of WMDs, and that the only danger Iraq posed to America was that it might pass these weapons on to terrorists at a future time. President Bush invoked WMDs as the principal reason for the invasion. But had the invasion really been a weapons hunt, any military planner could have worked up an operation to scour the country, with high assurance of doing so successfully and then to end. But it was never going to be a mere weapons hunt. What precisely, then, should U.S. forces do in Iraq beyond overthrowing its government? And what would it take to accomplish that ultimate end? Neither the president nor any of those who advocated reforming Iraq had a clear notion.

Precisely because neither the president nor the relevant bureaucracies had settled on coherent ends and means, the invasion was named "Iraqi Freedom." That Saddam's regime was beastly to its own people was obvious, as was the fact that his overthrow would free them from him. But what "Iraqi Freedom" might mean was hotly disputed in Washington and would be argued with blood in Iraq. The concept's inherent imprecision and the disputes arising from it made it impossible for military planners to devise operations with a logical end, in the sense both of a purpose and a termination point. What was the problem that overthrowing Saddam's regime was supposed to fix? The answer should have determined what was to be done there. But the problem was never defined, and America left its operations in Iraq open-ended.

Iraq itself was torn by a multitude of conflicting factions with very long memories: Kurds (about 25% of the population) would fight to separate from all Arabs; Shia Arabs (55%) would fight to do unto Sunnis what the Sunnis had been doing unto them; and the Sunni (15%) would fight to keep as much of their historic privileges as they could. Iraq's neighbors would take sides for their own reasons: Iran sent arms, men, and encouragement to their fellow Shia; the Saudis sent money, Wahabis, and suicide bombers to their fellow Sunni; and Syria provided sanctuary, headquarters, and transit routes as well as arms to their fellow Baath Party members, who were organizing the Sunni insurgency against the Americans and the Shia. In short, Iraq was full of, and surrounded by, people who killed for very particular interests. They knew *their* war. Our political class never figured out its own war.

Imagining that America's interest lay in achieving harmony among Iraqis, the U.S. government tried to effect a "national reconciliation"—in practice, offering concessions to the Sunnis and Baathists to entice them to give up their war. But the majority Shia wanted to shake off their Sunni masters, the Kurds were even less kindly disposed toward them, and the proclaimed goal of democracy posed an insurmountable problem. Iraq's national elections in 2005 confirmed that Iraq comprises not one people but several, whose desires are incompatible. Hence war. Our highly credentialed officials placed American troops in the middle of that war and kept them there in the service of an objective that none of the parties to the war shared. This made our troops everybody's target.

Only one fifth of American casualties came in what one normally thinks of as combat. Some three fifths came from "improvised explosive devices," roadside bombs, or other booby traps. That is, from our troops having to operate in what amounted to a constantly replenished minefield. About one fifth came from rules of engagement that prohibited our troops from defending themselves until after enemies had started trying to kill them. Although living in minefields and among people who are as likely to shoot you as not is contrary to military common sense and fits neither the definition of war nor of occupation, it was essential to a so-called strategy that required Americans to mix with hostile factions on their terrain. The field-grade and general officers who made careers executing this "strategy" made their predecessors in Vietnam look like faithful stewards of their men's lives and forthright advocates of military truths to political power.

EXIT STRATEGY IN IRAQ

As early as 2004 our officials had begun looking for an "exit strategy"—that is, for a way out of Iraq without looking too bad. The insurgency's Baathist leaders in Damascus demanded that the Americans establish a new government in Baghdad much like the Baath regime overthrown in 2003. But forcing such wholesale surrender upon the Shia would have taken an even bigger, more senseless war. So the U.S. government tried surrender at the retail level. In May 2004, it turned Fallujah over to insurgents in exchange for their no longer shooting at Americans. Immediately, Fallujah became the insurgency's fort, which the Marines had to pay with their lives to retake in November. Despite American soldiers' valor and sacrifice, their government's objectives and rules of engagement could not secure such an "exit strategy," much less victory.

Nor did U.S. force determine the war's outcome, because the violence in Iraq after April 2003 had always been (and always would be) about which Iraqi group would get what, at which other group's expense. A "united and democratic" Iraq had always been an exclusively American chimera. Freedom from the Baath regime was always going to mean ethnic-religious separation and cleansing. The practical questions always were: What would be the boundaries between Kurdistan and an Arab world with which it would deal as little as possible? And because Sunni and Shia Arabs could not get away from each other so neatly, what would the relationship be between the Shia in Baghdad and southern Mesopotamia, and the Sunni in the northwest of what had been Iraq?

The resolution of these questions and the end of America's involvement began in February 2006, when Sunni insurgents bombed the Shia Golden Mosque in Samarra. This loosed the Shia's fury. They squeezed the Sunni out of most of Baghdad and into western Iraq, torture-killing thousands, and the question quickly became not how much the Sunni would *gain* by war, but how much more they would *lose*. Only the Americans could stop the Shia.

Hence the Sunni insurgents asked American commanders for a version of the Fallujah deal: they would stop shooting Americans, would withdraw the welcome they had extended to Saudi suicide bombers, and would turn over people whom *they* designated al-Qaeda sympathizers. In return, the Americans would arm and pay the Sunni insurgents, now called "sons of Iraq," and entrust to them their zones' security. The Americans would also move lots of troops into Baghdad and other places where the Shia death squads had been raging. On top of that, the Americans would get the Shia government to promise to take the Sunni units into the Iraqi army, pay them, and continue entrusting security to them. The U.S. government grabbed the deal as a lifeline. The outline of the Sunni-Shia provisional settlement emerged. This was "the Surge."

According to conservative mythology, "surging" an extra 40,000 troops to Iraq crushed the insurgency. But American troops never crushed it. During 2008, the year of the Surge, there was *much less* contact between Americans and hostile forces, and two-thirds *fewer* casualties than any of the previous three years. American troops were used primarily to separate Sunni and Shia populations, especially in the Baghdad area, often by erecting physical barriers. Leaders of groups that had slaughtered Americans and Shia expressed delight that the Americans were leaving them—entrenched, better armed, better paid—in a superior position to press their enduring agenda upon the Shia after the Americans' departure.

In short, by turning Iraq's two main Arab communities over to the persons and groups strongest within them, having already done that in the Kurdish provinces, the U.S. government helped to consummate de facto Iraq's tripartite division. And so Iraq in 2010 looks very much like what would have resulted after the 1991 Gulf War, had our political class stood aside and allowed the Shia and Kurdish revolt to topple Saddam's regime—instead of keeping him in power, and later occupying the country, precisely but futilely to prevent its division. As the *New York Times*'s John Burns reported, "Six and a half years from the moment when American troops captured Baghdad on April 9, 2003, nothing is settled." After America's departure, the locals will do the settling. They never forgot their stakes. Our ruling class never settled what America's stakes were.

ACCEPTING THE UNACCEPTABLE: IRAN

Just as military operations depend on how well strategy employs arms to serve well-chosen ends, so diplomacy depends on how well diplomats' words represent well-calculated actions to achieve such ends. Lucius Annius summed it up in the 4th century, B.C.: "How we act will affect the main issue more than what we say. Once we have set our plans in order, it will be easy to find words to fit our deeds." Diplomacy works only at the service of a competent ends-means calculus. First, set in motion events apt to make your version of peace happen. Then, express in words the coercive situation you are managing to a successful conclusion. Words can serve policy, but never substitute for it. But U.S. diplomacy has squandered the fruits of our military power by placing it at the service of nonsensical policy, and ended up by accepting what its words once had deemed unacceptable. Our dealings with Iran are a prime example.

U.S. diplomacy bears much responsibility for making Iran into an ever-worsening problem for America. From the 1950s through the 1970s, when Iran's royal regime was the fulcrum of American interests in the Middle East, our experts in foreign affairs persuaded its shah that secularizing his country would serve his own interests as well as America's. This helped make the shah a stranger in his country and vulnerable to the anti-American Ayatollah Khomeini. As the ayatollah beat on the palace gates in 1978, the same experts concluded that America's interest lay in getting along with his prospective regime. When that regime seized the American embassy in Tehran along with the diplomats in it, the United States chose to respond to a textbook act of war with a combination of verbal abuse and token actions—what Theodore Roosevelt used to call "peace with insult," the most disastrous of policies. Our ruling class's Iran policy has been bankrupt ever since.

For example, our experts never considered sending a bill for the geopolitical favor that America did Iran by ending Saddam Hussein's rule in Iraq. Without a Sunni-dominated Iraq, Iran is freer to pursue its agenda against the Sunni world, and against America. Our diplomats might have demanded that Iran stop sponsoring Hezbollah lest perhaps the U.S. expeditionary force in Iraq add Iran's Kurdish zones to the new Kurdistan. Conversely, they might have considered asking Iran to support our mission in Iraq in exchange for the U.S. lessening support for the Sunni Arab regimes of the Persian Gulf. Competent diplomacy would have faced the Iranians with the choice between easy gains against ancestral Sunni enemies, and big losses inflicted by Americans who would pursue the Iranians from Iraq back into Iran. But U.S. diplomacy neither coerced Iran nor diverted it. Instead, it declared unacceptable various Iranian-backed militias' attacks on our troops in Iraq, and then accepted them.

Similarly, our ruling class has dealt with Iran's development of nuclear weapons by complaints, and declarations of unacceptability, followed by acquiescence. It forgot that giving in is less contemptible when not preceded by chest-thumping.

To Iran's highly consequential weapons programs, our foreign policy establishment opposes grandiose words and inconsequential means. Under President Obama as under President Bush, public discussion reflects the high-level policy oscillation between bombing Iran's nuclear facilities and negotiating the Iranians into forsaking nuclear weapons, supposedly by threatening economic sanctions while offering the country full membership in "the international community." Both options are evidence of incompetence. Bombs and missiles could destroy some but far from all of Iran's nuclear program. They could start a war, but not finish it. Indeed, no one who advocates such strikes proposes a plan to bring hostilities to a successful conclusion, or to occupy Iran indefinitely, or explains why Iran's post-strike regime would abstain from rebuilding the nukes. On the other hand, those who advocate bargaining fail to see that their sticks and carrots are orders of magnitude too small for the objective they seek.

The economic sanctions our foreign policy establishment considers are unserious because they would not involve banning trade with any country that trades with Iran. Such secondary proscriptions are what make economic warfare serious, because they force every country to take one side or the other of the fight. But this is out of the question precisely because our establishment knows that its ritual statements that "the international community is united" in opposition to Iran's acquisition of nukes are untrue, and because it fears Iran's nukes less than it does displeasing Russia and the European Union.

Is a "grand bargain" to turn Iran's Islamic Republic away from anti-Americanism possible? We will never know, because serious bargains are beyond our establishment's imagination. The Iranian regime's rhetoric aside, most Iranians' immanent foreign policy concern is their millennial confrontation with the Arab Sunni world, wherein Wahabism preaches killing the Shia to Arabs inclined to do it. For a generation, by far the most hurtful thing America has done to Iran has been to take sides against it in that struggle. An American offer to switch sides, henceforth to support Persian and Shia interests as it did in the days of the shah, might or might not move Iran to reset itself on the international scene in ways pleasing to America and reassuring to Israel. Such a reset would also involve rejecting Russia's 30-year role in the Islamic Republic. Were there to be such a bargain, the resulting peace would deprive nuclear weapons of much relevance.

The nuclear issue would also loom much smaller within a peace achieved by a no-nonsense American war. Such a war should leverage opposition to the regime by focusing on the very authorities who have earned their compatriots' hatred by their ever more corrupt and repressive rule. These elites happen to be America's enemies, the very people responsible for kidnapping U.S. diplomats and for making war on U.S. troops in Iraq. We should insist that these individuals be killed or turned over to us, and we should squeeze Iran's economy and food supply until this happens. The regime's overthrow from within would soon follow. Military operations would become necessary if the regime retaliated by trying to close the Straits of Hormuz or by unleashing Hezbollah and other terrorists—all of which America could crush disproportionately, to the regime's discredit. But to direct the war against the nuclear program rather than against the regime would be counterproductive because it would preclude a peace acceptable to Iran's majority, which has an inalienable interest in the Shia world's strength and status *vis-à-vis* the Sunni.

Serious war and serious diplomacy are both beyond our foreign policy establishment. Its fecklessness contributed to making Iran a problem, and condemns us at present to accepting the unacceptable. Iran's people may well resolve that problem by changing their regime by themselves, for their own reasons. The less they listen to Washington's wisdom, the likelier this will be.

AFGHANISTAN: A FOREGONE CONCLUSION?

Reforming problem nations by using force, but not really making war, has been American statecraft's default tool since the 1960s. It failed in Vietnam and, more recently, in Somalia, Bosnia, and Haiti. During the 2000 presidential campaign, George W. Bush's strong criticism of nation-building was part of the longstanding conservative "hard-line" position that America should pursue its own interests, by war if necessary, without meddling in other nations' business. But when the Bush Administration turned the "war on terror" into a nation-building counterinsurgency in Iraq, the Left opposed this as "Bush's war." Because the liberals' "soft line" now occupied the opposite pole from nation-building, partisan logic led many Republicans to regard the latter as the new conservative hard line. Between 2002 and 2009, however, that logic became more convoluted as the Left criticized Bush for not devoting even more troops to nation-build Afghanistan—but only as a way of urging withdrawal from Iraq. The Bush Administration increased troops in Afghanistan from 2,000 to 68,000, plus some 30,000 support personnel, to pursue what seemed to have become Washington's bipartisan modus operandi.

By 2009 nation-building in Afghanistan had turned bloodier and less popular. When Barack Obama's election completed his party's control of Washington, Democrats had to choose between leaving Afghanistan, which most of the party really preferred, and devoting even more resources to a style of foreign affairs in which they no longer had to pretend to believe, but in which many Republicans actually had come to believe. But the Democrats feared that advocating withdrawal would brand them as endangering America by abandoning Afghanistan to the terrorists.

So as 2009 ended, President Obama finessed this dilemma with a pretend strategy: more troops would be sent . . . to immunize Democrats against Republican criticisms. But the president also required more of European allies than they would deliver, and set "performance benchmarks" for the Afghan army that its members' loyalties to their several tribes made it impossible to meet. These unmet requirements would be the putative basis for withdrawal—after the next election cycle. Clever as this strategy might be in domestic politics, it foreclosed seriousness about the serious things happening in Afghanistan.

In November 2009, the *New York Times* reported from northern Afghanistan's Kunduz province that "[t]his year the Taliban arrived 'with lots of cash, new dollars, and guns.'" The Taliban had vanished from Kunduz eight years earlier. Once, they hardly ventured into places like Kunduz, where warlike Tajik tribes dominated. But now the U.S.-led international coalition had displaced the Tajik warlords and entrusted security to the Afghan army, composed largely of Pashtuns (hence easily infiltrated), backed up by the non-shooting Germans. This situation had become typical in areas of mixed population. But wherever Pashtuns are a majority, more and more people now find safety and money, and see a future, in calling themselves Taliban.

What can explain the remarkable fact that U.S. forces, disposing of practically endless money, firepower, and mobility, became enablers of the people they had routed eight years before? What can turn overwhelming power into self-defeating impotence? Only ideas that insulate against reality. Self-evidently, neither of the options that our establishment lets into its digestive system—a long occupation with counterinsurgency forces, along with nation-building in a non-nation; or more remote-controlled pinprick drone strikes based on third-hand intelligence—is relevant to stopping the flow of dollars, guns, Wahabi missionaries, and suicide bombers into both sides of the Afghanistan-Pakistan border.

Officially, our establishment supposes that the insurgents' lavish financing and modern arms come from local opium traders, despite little evidence of eleemosynary links between the Taliban and drug trafficking. Our establishment chooses not to see that dollars arrive in Afghanistan and Pakistan by courier from Saudi Arabia and the Emirates, whence also come guns, Wahabi missionaries, and suicide bombers. In fact while parts of Saudi Arabia's vast royal family and vaster entourage send these things, its government openly sponsors Pakistan's most problematic party, Nawaz Sharif's Muslim League. Yet the notion of tackling international problems at the source is taboo in Washington.

But so is making war, in the old-fashioned meaning of the term. When Pakistan's army launched a no-holds-barred offensive into the western mountains against any and all who had organized against Pakistan, nothing but dysfunctional ideas kept the U.S. government from ordering its forces in Afghanistan to run the same sort of pitiless campaign up the same mountains' eastern slopes to crush an inferior force between two superior ones.

Not that conventional war is the most economical means of dealing with enemies in Afghanistan. Where tribal allegiances are paramount, where outsiders are worth the guns and goods they bring to the tribe minus the trouble they cause and whatever enemies come after them, the calculus of conflict is straightforward: make it deadly for any tribe or clan to entertain your enemies, by empowering *its* enemies to do unto it as they please. This is how it's usually done. This is how the United States defeated the Taliban in 2001: by supporting the Tajiks and Uzbeks but not otherwise interfering with them. This is how the Taliban have retaken much of Afghanistan in recent years: by making offers to clans and families that they dare not refuse—to take good money to fight against people they don't like much anyway, or to be treated as enemies. But because American authorities see the tribes' and warlords' selfish interests as obstacles to nation-building, they dispense money and arms through central institutions for central purposes, asking the recipients to be part of something that includes their enemies and is led by foreigners. Thus do Americans spit against Afghanistan's prevailing winds.

This is because the logic that flows from the heights of American universities through the bureaucracies and the war colleges, which transforms conscientious junior officers into nodding generals, forecloses fruitful options leaving only the choice between the futility of nation-building counterinsurgency and the deadly unseriousness of drone strikes and hit teams. Typical of our ruling class's decisions, President Obama's December 2009 Afghanistan plan committed to both: to nation-building while denying that he was doing so, and to remote strikes while holding out no hope of eliminating enemy strongholds.

On December 30, 2009, a suicide bomber's killing of the CIA officers to whom he had been providing intelligence provided a glimpse into the underlying reason for the strikes' limited effectiveness: the provenance of the information on which the targeting is based. Although our military controls the missile firing drones exquisitely, the CIA's congenital scarcity of information disposes it to look none too closely at what it does receive, or at its purveyors. Hence CIA's notion of who might actually be in the places that it designates as Taliban targets comes disproportionately from Taliban agents such as Hammam al Balali, who bombed our CIA officers *after* he had fooled them. That may explain why, after each strike, the U.S. government claims success against terrorists while Afghans and Pakistanis claim that innocents have died.

More and more of Afghanistan's tribes seem to be realizing how disastrous for them is the Americans' inept wielding of mighty force and endless cash among them. Curbing the Taliban may happen if and when these tribes manage to reestablish traditional balances of power and restraint among themselves.

The men and women who run our government and occupy the commanding heights of our society seldom miss the fact that their ideas have not yielded the results they expected. But their very status and authority blind them to the reason why: the false axioms of their own miseducation. Lacking intellectual diversity and flexibility, they double down on their bets and dig deeper in failure. Akin to coaches who lead good teams to loss after embarrassing loss at the hands of inferior ones, they should be replaced. But firing a ruling class is hard. Replacing it is still harder. Nevertheless, just as sports teams rebuild by bringing in new talent, by reemphasizing blocking and tackling, pitching, fielding, and hitting, so countries intent on renewal must begin by rejecting the fashions—and the fashionable—of the age, by going back to basics, and drawing solutions for new problems from statecraft's perennial principles.

Intermezzo: A Portfolio of Illustrations from the *Claremont Review of Books*

by Elliott Banfield

Illustration for "John Rawls, Historian" from the Fall 2002 issue.

Illustration for "The World of Morals, and its Delinquent Observer, Alan Wolfe" from the cover of the Spring 2002 issue.

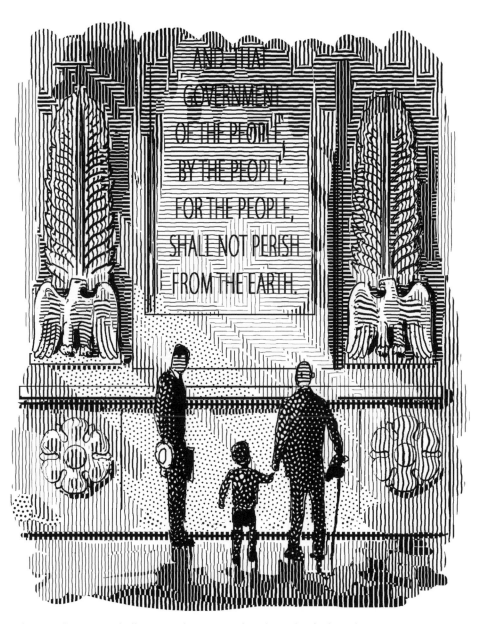

AND THAT
GOVERNMENT
OF THE PEOPLE,
BY THE PEOPLE,
FOR THE PEOPLE,
SHALL NOT PERISH
FROM THE EARTH.

The Lincoln Memorial. Illustration for "Statecraft and Wordcraft" from the Summer 2007 issue.

Illustration for "The Right Stuff" from the Fall 2006 issue.

Illustration for "High Noon: A Symposium on the War" from the cover of the Fall 2002 issue.

Illustration for "Mythic Morals" from the Fall 2004 issue.

Illustration for "Political History for a Political Nation" from the Fall 2008 issue.

Woodrow Wilson, Theodore Roosevelt, and Franklin Delano Roosevelt. Illustration for "Three Men in a Tub; or, The Perils of Progressivism" from the cover of the Winter 2002/03 issue.

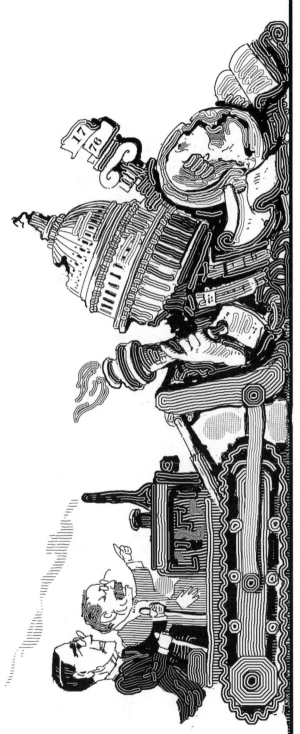

Illustration for "The Liberals' Constitution" from the Summer 2009 issue.

Lyndon Baines Johnson. Illustration for "The Making of LBJ" from the Fall 2002 issue.

Illustration for "Why We Don't Win" from the cover of the Winter 2009/10 issue.

Napoleon Bonaparte. Illustration for "The Little Tyrant" from the Summer 2003 issue.

Illustration for "War in the Absence of Strategic Clarity" from the cover of the Fall 2003 issue.

Illustration for "The World at Work" from the Spring 2005 issue.

Illustration for "Reading Up on the Right" from the Winter 2009/10 issue.

Illustration for "November Surprise" from the Winter 2007/08 issue.

Illustration for "Conservatism's Challenge" from the cover of the Summer 2009 issue.

Paul Ryan. Illustration for "Paul Ryan's Roadmap" from the Summer 2010 issue

Charles Darwin. Illustration for "Darwinian Conservatism" from the Spring 2004 issue.

George W. Bush. Illustration for "Between Idealism and Realism" from the Summer 2005 issue.

Illustration for "The Presidential Nomination Mess" from the Fall 2008 issue.

Illustration for "Man of a Thousand Faces" from the Summer 2008 issue.

Illustration for "Republican Triumphs, Old and New" from the cover of the Summer 2003 issue.

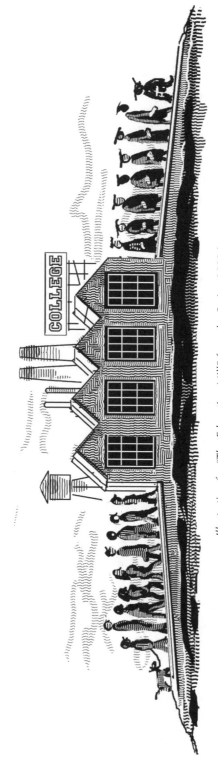

Illustration for "The Education Mill" from the Spring 2009 issue.

Ann Coulter. Illustration for "Tailgunner Ann" from the Winter 2003/04 issue.

Illustration for "Thinking Like a Terrorist" from the Spring 2009 issue.

Illustration for "Continental Drift" from the Fall 2005 issue.

Saddam Hussein. Illustration for "War at Last?" from the Winter 2002/03 issue.

P.G. Wodehouse. Illustration for "The Master" from the Spring 2008 issue.

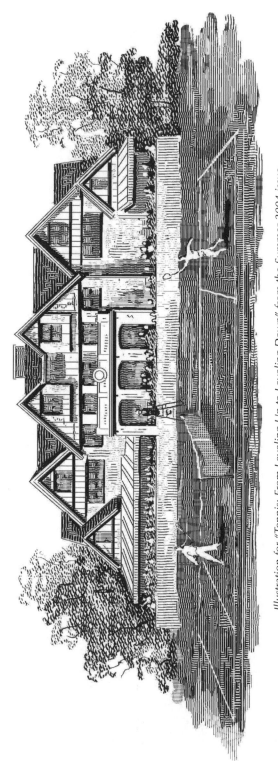

Illustration for "Tennis: From Leveling Up to Leveling Down" from the Summer 2004 issue.

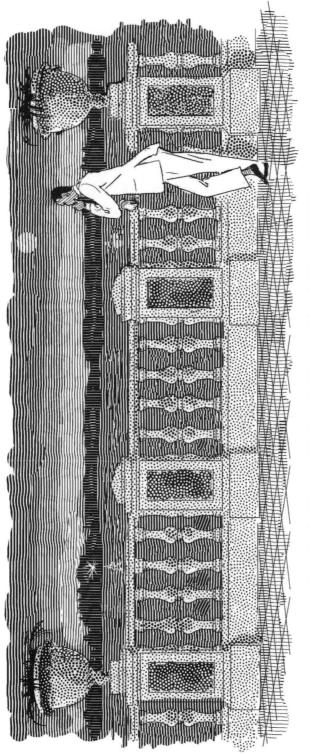

Illustration for "Gatsby and the Pursuit of Happiness" from the Winter 2003/04 issue.

New York City Hall, built 1802-1812, designed by Mangin and McComb

An Illustrations for "Building Democracy" from the Sumer 2007 issue.

Rotunda at the University of Virginia, Charlottesville VA, built 1818-19, designed by Thomas Jefferson

An illustrations for "Building Democracy" from the Summer 2007 issue.

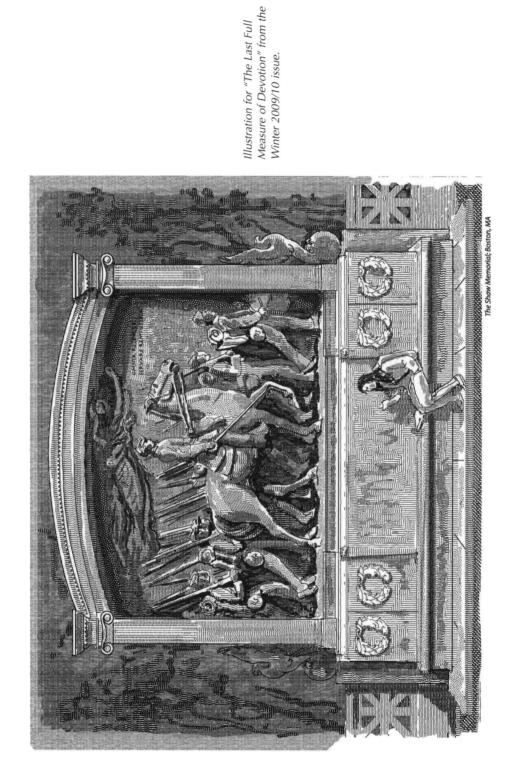

Illustration for "The Last Full Measure of Devotion" from the Winter 2009/10 issue.

Illustration for "Architecture of Liberty" from the Winter 2005/06 issue.

IV

STATESMEN AND DESPOTS

Aristotle and Locke
in the American Founding

Harry V. Jaffa

(Winter 2000/01)

In his review of A *New Birth of Freedom: Abraham Lincoln and the Coming of the Civil War*, in the inaugural issue of the *Claremont Review of Books*, Charles Kesler writes, "Jaffa doesn't draw attention to his revised view of Lincoln or of the American Founding. In fact, he is strangely silent about the whole subject, leaving it to the readers to figure out the relation between the two remarkably different accounts in [*Crisis of the House Divided*, 1959] and *A New Birth*."

I do not think that I have been as silent, or strangely so, as Professor Kesler seems to think. That the founding, which Lincoln inherited, was dominated by an Aristotelian Locke—or a Lockean Aristotle—has been a conspicuous theme of my writing since 1987. It has gone largely unnoticed because it contradicts the conventional wisdom of certain academic establishments. Like the "Purloined Letter," however, it has been in plain view all along.

RIGHTS AND ENDS

After speaking of our unalienable rights, to secure which governments are instituted, the Declaration of Independence goes on to say that "whenever any form of government becomes destructive of these ends, it is the right of the people to alter or abolish it, and to institute new government, laying its foundations on such principles and organizing its powers in such form, as to them shall seem most likely to effect their safety and happiness." Notice that in the second institution, or reinstitution of government, "rights" become "ends." And these ends are now said to be "safety" and "happiness," the alpha and omega of political life in Aristotle's *Politics*.

In one form or another, the metamorphosis of Lockean "rights" into Aristotelian "ends" (or vice versa) recurs in many of the documents of the founding. George Washington in his First Inaugural Address as president, says that "there is no truth more thoroughly established than that there exists in the economy and course of nature an indissoluble union between virtue and happiness." The pursuit of happiness is thus understood as the pursuit of virtue. It is difficult to imagine a more forthright Aristotelianism in Richard Hooker or Thomas Aquinas. Nor do Washington and the founders generally suppose that either virtue or happiness is something private or idiosyncratic. In *Federalist* 43, James Madison speaks of the "transcendent law of nature and of nature's God, which declares that the safety and happiness of society are the objects at which all political institutions aim, and to which all such institutions must be sacrificed." The pursuit of happiness, while that of individuals in the state of nature, is a social or political happiness, within civil society.

Neither Washington nor Madison imagined for a moment that, in speaking of the happiness of society, he was contradicting the idea of all human individuals being equally endowed by their Creator with unalienable rights. In his letter transmitting the Constitution to the Congress of the Confederation, Washington speaks of "Individuals entering into society [having to] give up a share of liberty to preserve the rest." But where—except in the state of nature—can individuals be, before "entering society"? How can they enter society, except by a social contract, or compact, in which each recognizes the equal natural rights of all, in a society dedicated to preserving the equal natural rights of each? It is this mutual recognition which is the foundation, at once, of majority rule and minority rights, of the rule of law.

DICTATE OF PRUDENCE

One might object that the idea of rule of law arising from a social contract is purely Lockean, and has no tincture of Aristotelianism. To think this, however, is to ignore what Aristotle says about all of natural right being changeable. Consider that, according to Aristotle, whatever the law does not command, it forbids. This is perfectly consistent with the idea of law in the Mosaic polity, which is another example of the ancient city. Remember that, according to Aristotle, a city with more than 10,000 citizens would be too large. Law for an ancient city and for a modern state—whether the 4 million inhabitants of the 13 original American states, or the 280 million of the 21st-century America—must of necessity be very different. It must be very different as to the ways and means by which it is formed, yet altogether the same for the human ends that it must serve. The ancient conception of law would, in the modern world, serve only tyranny, while the very purpose of law, according to Aristotle, is to prevent tyranny. The common ground of the ancient and the modern conception of law is shown by Aristotle's dictum that law is reason unaffected by desire.

Locke's state of nature is not a merely hypothetical construct. It is rather a dictate of that very prudence which is, according to Aristotle, the hallmark of all political wisdom. It arises from that fundamental transformation in the human condition from the world described in Fustel de Coulanges's *The Ancient City* (1864)—from a world in which each city had its own god—to one in which there was but one God for the human race. This God however was not the God of any one city, or the author of its laws. The obligation of a citizen of an ancient city to obey its laws followed from the obligation to the god of that city. Under Christian monotheism each individual has a relationship with God that is prior, both logically and ontologically, to his membership in his political community. Each individual is a citizen, actual or potential, of the City of God, before being a citizen of his own particular country.

The meaning of this distinction I have discussed at some length in chapter 2 of *A New Birth* in the context of Shakespeare's discussion between Bates, Williams, and King Henry V (in disguise) around the campfire, before the battle of Agincourt. Their conclusion is that each man has an unconditional duty to the king who is alone responsible for the justice of his cause. But the king is not responsible for the fate of each man's soul. Every man is responsible to God, but not the king, for this. Shakespeare, while displaying unflinchingly the defects of kingly rule, does not in the English histories have on his horizon any alternative to divine right monarchy. The American Founding's Lockean republican political theory provides an answer to the defects of Christian divine right monarchy, the answer that Lincoln inherited. This supplied as well the theoretical foundation for Lincoln's assault on slavery.

According to Saint Peter and Saint Paul, all power was held to come from God. Submission to the power of the emperor was submission to God. This theory underlay the authority of the king, as Bates and Williams saw it in Henry V. In the Declaration of Independence, the origin of political authority is held to reside, not in emperor, king, or church, but in those unalienable rights with which every human individual is equally endowed by his Creator. From the fact of this equal endowment, no one has by nature more authority over another than the other has over him. Hence the state of nature, and hence the social contract that takes men from the state of nature into civil society, a contract which initially is unanimous, and based upon mutual recognition of that equality of right. It is this unanimity which authorizes majority rule, rule which is understood in principle to be in the interests of the indefeasible rights of the minority no less than of the majority. The "just powers of the government" are moreover understood to be only those to which there has been unanimous consent *a priori*. Excluded thereby from all political control are the rights of conscience which make man a citizen of the City of God. From this follows the separation of state and church, from which is derived the distinction between state and society, from which, in turn, are derived those civil rights which are the outstanding feature of all decent modern constitutions. These limitations upon political power have no standing whatever in the constitutions of the ancient city. From all of the foregoing, I concluded long ago that, had Aristotle been called upon, in the latter half of the 17th century, to write a guide book for constitution-makers, he would have written something very closely approximating John Locke's *Second Treatise*. For he would have recognized instantly those differences from his *Politics* that prudential wisdom required, in the world of Christian monotheism, with all its peculiar dangers of tyranny, especially from the union of divine right monarchy and established church.

BREAKING THE SPELL

My critics, friendly and unfriendly, may ask why it took me so long to see the purloined letter on the mantelpiece. The reason is that I took for granted that the account of the Hobbesian Locke in Leo Strauss's *Natural Right and History* (1953) represented the Locke that informed the American Founding. That rights were prior to duties, that duties were derived from rights, that civil society arose from a contract solely for mutual self-preservation, and that the goods of the soul were subordinated in all decisive respects to the goods of the body, were conclusions of Strauss's interpretation. Strauss himself never said this Locke was the founders' Locke, but the spell cast by his book led many of us to apply it to the founders. Many former students of Strauss, to this day, regard it as heresy to think that Strauss's chapters on Hobbes and Locke do not constitute the authoritative account of the philosophic foundations of American constitutionalism. When presented with the evidence of Aristotelianism in the founding, they react like the Scholastics who refused to look into Galileo's telescope: "If it confirms Aristotle it is redundant; if it contradicts him it is false." Strauss himself said that Aristotle would have been the first to look through the telescope.

Strauss was clear, in *Natural Right and History*, that his was an account of Locke's esoteric teaching, but that Locke's exoteric doctrine was far more conventional, and far more consistent with both traditional morality and traditional (albeit more tolerant) Christianity. Strauss also taught us that the authors of the past—and this certainly included political men no less than philosophers—were to be understood as they understood themselves, before the attempt was made to understand them differently or better. It was, and is, an anachronism to assume that the founders read Locke through the eyes of Strauss! One is reminded of Shakespeare's *Troilus and Cressida*. Hector, himself a young man, denounces the elders of Troy, who are so bewitched by Helen's beauty that they are unwilling to return her to her husband, and thus save their city from destruction. "You gloz'd [commented]," he said, "[like] young men whom Aristotle thought unfit to hear moral philosophy." It seemed to me that imputing to the Founding Fathers Leo Strauss's esoteric interpretation of Locke would be not unlike finding the *Nicomachean Ethics* in Hector's library.

Moral Monster

John Zvesper

(Summer 2004)

Napoleon Bonaparte died in May 1821. He had spent the last five-and-a-half years of his life as the involuntary guest of Britain's Royal Navy on St. Helena, a small, wet, and windswept island in the South Atlantic. During this bleak enforced exile he devoted much of his ample spare time to dictating complaints about his treatment, and to constructing elaborate justifications for his eventful political life. His companions collected and published several versions of these "memoirs."

In 1823, Thomas Jefferson read one of these collections. Reviewing it in one of his wonderful exchanges of letters with John Adams, he went back on his earlier assertion that Bonaparte deserved whatever he got ("His sufferings cannot be too great," he had written to Albert Gallatin in 1815), and commiserated to the extent of saying that it was inhumane (of the British and their allies) to have inflicted this lingering death on him. But Jefferson did not at all retract his earlier and decidedly unfavorable judgments of Napoleon's character; nor did he think Napoleon deserved much less punishment than he received. In his letter to Adams, Jefferson concluded that Napoleon had by his own words proved that he was "a moral monster, against whom every hand should have been lifted to slay him."

Steven Englund, an American scholar who teaches French history to university students in Paris, presents a more ambivalent view in his new book, *Napoleon: A Political Life*. He thinks that those who revile Napoleon "fail to explain his hold on contemporaries," not to mention his fascination to later generations. Discussing this fascination, he alludes to Jefferson "seeing Napoleon on St. Helena in a different and more sympathetic light" than previously. We have just seen that this is a misleading summary of Jefferson's view. The continuing fascination with Napoleon is something worth pondering, but there is no reason we cannot do that—indeed, we can probably do it more successfully—if, with Jefferson (who, remember, loved France), we maintain the ability to see the monstrosity of the man and his politics. We would not have to base this ability on a "remorseless wish to cut Napoleon down to size" that Englund sees in many "Anglo-Saxon writers" (as the French often call us). In fact, we could confidently base it only on an effort to see moral and

257

political things as they are, with their vileness, their mediocrity, and their grandeur. To understand healthy politics, we have to understand political diseases.

Englund explains contemporaries' and later generations' fascination with Napoleon by asserting that there is something unique and admirable in Napoleon's life. The unambivalent revilers, he says, fail "to grasp the power of the man's uniqueness, and the good he also did." Yet he is an assiduous and painstaking historian, and his finely crafted and comprehensive biography gives us plenty of evidence of the bad, and little if any evidence of the good, in Napoleon's political life. His book often lets us see fairly precisely what the bad consisted of. So, apart from avoiding uncomfortable scenes when he gives dinner parties to other historians in Paris—he recounts one such scene in his "Bibliographical Comments"—it is not clear why he is so insistently ambivalent. Having collected so much evidence for the case against Napoleon, why does he resist connecting the dots?

Englund quotes Napoleon's often-repeated "imperial sigh" with which he justified his aggressiveness and constant wars: "Five or six families share the thrones of Europe and they take it badly that a Corsican has seated himself at their table. I can only maintain myself there by force; I can only get them used to regarding me as their equal by keeping them in thrall; my empire will be destroyed if I cease being fearsome." Englund spots that this "cunning exercise in self-pity" is also the classic "rationale for an aggressive child"; Napoleon falsely assumes that a constant series of wars was needed "to confer legitimacy on the Emperor, that he was not safely on his throne unless he was mounted in the saddle at the head of the Grande Armée." Later he shows that the European War of 1812—in which a million or more men died for no good reason—clearly resulted from this Napoleonic aggressiveness, coupled with an equally childish dialectic of vanity between Emperor Napoleon and Czar Alexander.

Englund links Napoleon's sense of unique greatness, godlike self-sufficiency, and cool detachment to "Aristotle's portrait of the 'great-souled' man who is indifferent to opinion." This is seriously inaccurate. The "great-souled" man as described by Aristotle is not indifferent to honor by those whose good opinion is worth having, and he is open to friendship that helps confirm his own moral excellence. He is not a tyrannical bully who smothers his insecurity with belligerence, disdains friendship, and craves glory. What Englund is discerning in Napoleon is not megalopsychia. It is megalomania. (Jefferson saw this and its political dimensions very clearly: "After destroying the liberties of his country, he has exhausted all its resources, physical and moral, to indulge his own maniac ambition, his own tyrannical and overbearing spirit.")

In this context Englund draws our attention to Napoleon's last public utterance, the last line of his will: "Nothing to my son, except my name!" Englund may be right to identify this narcissism and megalomania with the "will to power" analyzed by Nietzsche (who, as he notes, claimed Napoleon for one of his own). But this identification is not well calculated to improve Napoleon's reputation as an admirable statesman, except perhaps among "postmoderns" prepared to admire any commitment as long as it is made with enough style and irony.

Napoleon's unhealthy political psyche was complemented by an illiberal modern political philosophy, with which he explained and justified his dictatorial politics. More than previous biographers, Englund focuses on the young Napoleon's reading and writing. In Valence, in his first posting as an artillery officer in 1785–1786, he would skimp on food in order to buy books on history and politics, which he passionately consumed. Jean-Jacques Rousseau was a particular favorite. Englund shows that what Napoleon learned from Rousseau—and maintained throughout his career—was fully compatible with a Hobbesian way of thinking: the natural equality of men consists of their self-interested drive for domination, so the State, although based on a general will (and not on divine right monarchy), must be strong and active, even absorbing religion into itself. (Priests are too ready "to foment rebellion among the people against injustice"!) The purpose of government is not to secure justice and the natural rights to life, liberty, and the pursuit of happiness, but to "permit each person to taste sweet tranquillity, to find himself on the road to happiness." Quiet despotism is the goal, and patriotic glory, foreign wars, and domestic political repression are legitimate means to that goal.

Englund does not raise any alarm about these illiberal, Hobbesian-Rousseauan roots of Napoleon's politics. He is also too uncritical of the Hegelian fruit that grows from these roots: Napoleon's attempt to suppress partisan political conflict in France, in favor of patriotic unity supporting the State. He correctly points out that Napoleon was not the only Frenchman in his day (and there remain many in ours) to whom "Anglo-Saxon" constitutions with limited government and loyal but robust opposition parties are "an invitation to social dissolution in a free-for-all of market forces and factional or corporatist interest." This distrust of politics and its absorption into the State (which Hegel so much admired in Napoleon) may or may not have been necessary in the France of Napoleon's day. But, contrary to Englund's suggestion, this distrust, and the consequent construction of a centralized technocratic State for "a post-political society," is not a "liberal vision."

In Napoleon, the combination of a megalomaniac personality with a radical, illiberal political philosophy was lethal. It destroyed ten million human beings, set back the cause of political liberty in Europe, gave political philosophy a bad name, made conservatism reactionary, and boosted the world's already strong propensity to equate might with right. What is there to set against this enormous debit? Not a lot. Maybe we can agree with Englund that Napoleon was an admirable city planner, with an un-Napoleonic and "profoundly human tendency to hesitate, back down, accept criticism, defer to opinion, tolerate indecision, change his mind, evolve his thinking." So there's a career alternative for you, M. Bonaparte! But there were larger issues. Outside France, as Englund recognizes, the 19th-century European liberal nationalism (which in any case was not dependably liberal) that is often credited to Napoleon owed more to the local resistance to French conquest than to the inspiration of French ideals, which in practice were generally subordinated to French interests. Within France, politicians and citizens are still wrestling with the centralized State that Napoleon bequeathed as a "solution" to political conflict, and that has been justified ever since Napoleon (incorrectly, Jefferson would assert) as a necessity for France's self-defence. In any case, even if centralization has been desirable or necessary for France, it is well known that it was originated not by Napoleon but by the *ancien régime*, so we had better give credit where credit is due, if any is due.

Could it all have been otherwise? Hypothetical history can be annoyingly speculative, but sometimes it can be useful for seeing what did happen more clearly.

First of all, could those massively destructive wars have been avoided? Englund's accounts show how, during Napoleon's years in power, a durable European peace, honorable to France, could have been arranged, if Napoleon had been more peacefully inclined. Englund tries to apologize for Napoleon's bellicosity by drawing our attention to the contemporary climate of opinion, which, unlike ours, celebrated military conquest and glory. But that simply won't do, given the number of contemporary condemnations (in France as well as elsewhere) of Napoleon's egregiousness.

Could the French Revolution itself—the violence of which made Napoleon seem necessary—have unrolled more moderately? It is true that circumstances in 18th-century France made liberal reforms more difficult there than in Britain and America. But many historians—French as well as "Anglo-Saxon"—have shown that the violent Revolution arose not out of historical inevitability, but from the indecisive policies of the king's governments, and, especially, from the histrionic insobriety of the critics of these governments. It was not just extreme social resentments, it was also flawed political philosophy and radical chic that led the Revolution to replace the absolute sovereignty of divine right monarchy with the absolute sovereignty of democratic administrative tyranny. It was unfortunate but not preordained that in their constitutional thinking so many French revolutionaries—like the young artillery officer who would soon join and dominate them—were captivated by bad political ideas and ignored good ones, preferring "Lightning to the Light" (as Gouverneur Morris reported from Paris).

Finally, could Napoleon have been a French George Washington? During his exile on St. Helena, Napoleon explained why he had consciously rejected this possibility:

> If [Washington] had been in France, with domestic disorder and the threat of foreign invasion, I defy him to have been himself. If he had, he would have been a fool and prolonged the unhappiness of the country. As for me, I could only have been a Washington with a crown, amid a congress of conquered kings. Only under such circumstances could I have shown his moderation, wisdom, and disinterestedness. These I could attain only by a universal dictatorship, such as, indeed, I strove for.

Englund does not go as far as Napoleon, but he does share some of Napoleon's doubts. He asks: "would French political circumstances and traditions have sustained" a Washington?

Well, by 1799 (when the 30-year-old Napoleon came to power), maybe not, but if Napoleon was the alternative, then surely a Washingtonian approach would have been worth a try, even then. Napoleon's pre-emptive strike on liberal politics ruled out the experiment. He didn't want to try to be a Washington, and he made sure that no one else could try. Englund lets us see that there were liberal roads that the government could have taken even during Napoleon's rule, if Napoleon had wanted to. And after all, when Napoleon had finally been removed from the French political scene, what happened in France? An experiment in constitutional monarchy—which was what pre-Revolutionary liberals had favored as the first step in France's political reform. This suggests that France's more liberal political life could have begun—and, without having had to go through the Jacobin and Napoleonic experiences, more easily and promisingly begun—at any time before 1802, when Napoleon chose to rule it out and insisted on being made First Consul for Life. France could have set a good example to the rest of Europe, and saved the whole world a great deal of trouble.

The Man Who Made Modern America

Stephen F. Knott

(Fall 2004)

Alexander Hamilton was buried in New York City's Trinity Churchyard, where his monument reads: "The Statesman of consummate Wisdom whose Talents and Virtues will be admired . . . long after this Marble shall have mouldered into Dust." Unfortunately, it has not worked out that way.

Throughout the nation's history, with the exception of the period between the Civil War and the early 20th century, Hamilton was viewed as the founding's villain—the man who sought to foist a crown upon the nation and to subvert Jeffersonian democracy. President Andrew Jackson and his successor, Martin Van Buren, considered their Whig opponents to be the heirs to Hamilton's party of privilege and saw Jackson's war with the Bank of the United States as a continuation of the struggle between the people and the plutocrats, which began with Jefferson and Hamilton. While Ivy League-educated writers such as John Torrey Morse, Henry Cabot Lodge, and Theodore Roosevelt sang Hamilton's praises during the Gilded Age, dubbing him the father of American capitalism and American constitutionalism, by the turn of the century, when both the Constitution and capitalism were increasingly seen as impediments to social progress, his reputation once again began to recede. Hamilton's status was further damaged by the fact that he was a hero to Warren Harding and Calvin Coolidge, two chief executives guaranteed to repulse right-thinking, i.e., left-thinking, historians and political scientists.

It was Franklin D. Roosevelt who elevated Thomas Jefferson into the trinity of American immortals (alongside George Washington and Abraham Lincoln), forcing Hamilton into deep eclipse. The only book review FDR ever wrote was of Claude Bowers's *Jefferson and Hamilton: The Struggle for Democracy in America* (1925), a breathless account of how close the nation came to slipping into despotism, had it not been for the heroic efforts of the Sage of Monticello. FDR loved the book, and later rewarded Bowers with an ambassadorship for his work on behalf of the Democratic Party. Dumas Malone was inspired to publish his monumental biography, *Jefferson and His Time* (1946–1981), as a result of reading Bowers's book, and its simplistic Manichean approach to the Hamilton-Jefferson controversy influenced the work of many 20th-century American historians. Hamilton's few lonely defenders were reduced to arguing during the Second World War that he would in fact have opposed Nazism.

By the century's end Hamilton's reputation had improved, in part due to his record on racial matters, which set him apart from his great rival, one of the largest slaveholders in Virginia. Throughout the nation's history it appeared to be a truism that as one fell the other rose ("opposed in death as in life," Jefferson allegedly told bewildered visitors gazing at Hamilton's bust in the entrance hall at Monticello), and the 21st century may well be Hamilton's moment.

If he is indeed rehabilitated, it will be thanks in large part to Ron Chernow's splendid new biography. The author of the blockbusters *The House of Morgan* (1990) and *Titan* (a biography of John D. Rockefeller, 1998), Chernow unearths new information about Hamilton, but more importantly this beautifully written book recounts the formidable obstacles he surmounted to become, next to George Washington, the indispensable American Founder. Chernow's *Alexander Hamilton* is the best biography of Hamilton ever written, and it is unlikely to be surpassed.

Born illegitimate in the West Indies on a "speck more obscure than Corsica," Hamilton suffered an endless series of personal tragedies that would have broken most mortals. Chernow notes, chillingly, that between 1765 and 1769 Hamilton's father abandoned him (at the age of ten), his mother died, then a cousin in whose care he was entrusted committed suicide, followed in rapid succession by the demise of his aunt, an uncle, and a grandmother. Unlike, say, Bill Clinton, Hamilton did not dwell on these awful events, or milk them as an all-purpose excuse for boorish behavior. In fact, he seldom mentioned his painful early years, and his triumph over these youthful horrors was heroic. Not surprisingly, Hamilton lived every day of his life as if it might be his last.

With the assistance of patrons from St. Croix impressed with his intelligence and ambition, Hamilton came to the United States in 1772 and never looked back. An agitator for revolution at King's College (later Columbia), he distinguished himself as a responsible rebel. This "committed revolutionary," writes Chernow, "had a profound dread that popular sentiment would boil over into dangerous excess. . . . Even amid an insurrection that he supported, he fretted about the damage to constituted authority and worried about mob rule." Moderation was the touchstone of his political philosophy, which set him apart from his famous rival from Virginia, the armchair revolutionary who extolled the virtues of shedding blood to water the tree of liberty and only belatedly, reluctantly, saw anything particularly disturbing about Robespierre and the Terror.

Hamilton served honorably, and at times heroically, as a soldier in the American Revolution, unlike many of his critics who later questioned his loyalty to the new nation and accused him of being a British agent. Chernow vividly recounts the obstacles confronting Washington's army as it faced the world's greatest superpower, and dealt with dithering state governments and a feckless Congress. For most of the war Hamilton served as Washington's ablest staff officer, possessing an innate ability to translate the general's wishes into clear prose. He was at the center of Washington's intelligence operations, and also served as his eyes and ears in dealing with political challenges that erupted in Congress and elsewhere. Over time he bristled, however, at the role of staff officer, yearning instead for a combat command. This, coupled with Washington's sometimes brittle personality, led to a brief falling-out between the two men. Their relationship was marked, Chernow observes, by "more mutual respect than true affection." Hamilton "never openly criticize[d] Washington" and understood that the Virginian "was a great leader of special gifts and the one irreplaceable personage in the early American pageant." Eventually, Washington gave Hamilton the command he wanted, and he led a critical charge at Yorktown that led to the British surrender. The wartime alliance of Washington and Hamilton would shape the course of American history, for both concluded that if the American experiment were to succeed, the nation required "a national army . . . centralized power over the states . . . [and] a strong executive," all for the sake of "national unity."

In the midst of war, Hamilton was able to compose complex essays outlining proposals for a new American government. As a lieutenant colonel in his twenties he developed a mastery of administration and finance and caught the eye of those willing to set aside their bias against youth and foreign birth. Not all were able to do so—and Hamilton did not help matters with his sensitivity to slights, which led him to burn far too many bridges. Nevertheless, at a time when his comrades were preoccupied with war, he was already envisioning a new government for the United States, one that would earn respect from its own citizens and around the globe. In 1780, at the ripe age of 25, he wrote James Duane a 7,000-word letter calling for a revision of the Articles of Confederation. As Chernow notes, "[S]even years before the Constitutional Convention, Alexander Hamilton became the first person to propose such a plenary gathering. Where other minds groped in the fog of war . . . Hamilton seemed to perceive everything in a sudden flash."

Hamilton continued to demonstrate "his unique flair for materializing at every major turning point in the early history of the republic." One such turning point was the Annapolis Convention of 1786, where Hamilton worked closely with James Madison and authored the appeal to the states calling for a convention to amend the Articles of Confederation. The Annapolis communiqué, Chernow writes, "with its conception of the political system as a finely crafted mechanism, composed of subtly interrelated parts, had a distinctly Hamiltonian ring. It reflected his penchant for systemic solutions, his sense of the fine interconnectedness of things." At the Constitutional Convention Hamilton was unusually silent, perhaps due to the political split in the New York delegation, until he rose on June 18, 1787, to deliver a six-hour speech that would, as Chernow puts it, acquire "diabolical status in the rumor mills of the early republic, providing gloating opponents with damning proof of his supposed political apostasy." He proposed a president and Senate that would be elected for life, dependent on good behavior.

It is quite possible, as Forrest McDonald has suggested, that Hamilton was attempting to provide "cover" for the more moderate delegates who wished to enhance the powers of the central government. His more radical proposals suddenly rendered their proposals almost benign. Hamilton sought to push the new government as far in the direction of permanence and stability as republican principles would permit. Still, this was a long way from endorsing a monarchy or the creation of an aristocracy of wealth. In fact, Hamilton's proposed House of Representatives was more democratic than the one ultimately approved by the convention: he proposed a House "chosen directly by universal male suffrage every three years."

It was in this speech that Hamilton uttered a line that is cited, usually out of context, to this day: "Give all power to the many, they will oppress the few. Give all power to the few, they will oppress the many." Many historians and journalists have taken to citing the first sentence while ignoring the second to prove that Hamilton advocated a hereditary aristocracy or a plutocracy. (See Howard Zinn's *A People's History of the United States* [1980] for an example of this.) That is nonsense.

Hamilton's reservations about the new Constitution, Chernow correctly observes, "had less to do with the powers of the new government than with the tenure of the people exercising them." Nevertheless, no one worked harder, with the possible exception of James Madison, to secure the adoption of the Constitution. Hamilton urged the holdout delegates to sign despite their misgivings; fought against powerful forces led by Governor George Clinton in his home state of New York, narrowly winning ratification (30 votes in favor, 27 opposed); and perhaps most importantly, marshaled his formidable pen in the ratification cause by composing some 51 of the 85 essays in *The Federalist*. For this masterpiece alone Hamilton deserves inclusion in the ranks of the American pantheon.

Hamilton pleaded with George Washington to accept the presidency, noting that the whole American experiment would collapse without strong leadership—"it is to little purpose to have *introduced* a system, if the weightiest influence is not given to its firm *establishment* in the outset." Washington wasted little time in selecting Hamilton as his secretary of the treasury, although he apparently first offered the job to Robert Morris. Hamilton was warned by friends that he would be harshly criticized in the job since he would, in essence, become the nation's tax collector. The warnings proved prescient, because every proposal he offered to elevate the nation beyond its lowly status—"a central bank, a funded debt, a mint, a customs service, manufacturing subsidies"—became the subject of various conspiracy theories, and each had the added disability of appearing to be "a slavish imitation of the British model."

It was not long before Jefferson and Madison began to suspect the worst in Hamilton, including personal corruption; thus began the bitter battles of the 1790s that launched the American two-party system. Though Hamilton engaged in his share of mudslinging, he preferred to openly confront Jefferson, while the latter opted to use surrogates, such as the scurrilous James Callender, whom Jefferson described as "a man of genius." Callender and other Jeffersonian operatives portrayed Hamilton as the corrupt agent of Great Britain, an accusation that persists even today. It is no exaggeration to say that Hamilton was one of the first victims of the politics of personal destruction.

Chernow brings a fresh, balanced perspective to this ancient struggle; nonetheless, one reads his account persuaded more than ever that had Jefferson and Madison's positions prevailed in the early republic, American history would have taken a very different and disturbing turn. It was Washington's statesmanship that prevented this from happening; unlike his counterparts from the Old Dominion, Washington was a nationalist to the core, and he generally sided with Hamilton's proposals to consolidate federal power and expand the presidency's role. Washington and Hamilton built the foundation that set the United States on the path to superpower status, and enabled the nation to become the defender of liberty around the globe. It is telling that toward the end of his life Washington maintained steady contact with and expressed warm praise and affection for Hamilton, but refused to have any contact with Jefferson.

As Treasury Secretary, Hamilton was a stunning, though at the time controversial, success. "Bankrupt when Hamilton took office, the United States now enjoyed a credit rating equal to that of any European nation. He had laid the groundwork for both liberal democracy and capitalism," writes Chernow. "If Washington was the father of the country and Madison the father of the Constitution, then Alexander Hamilton was surely the father of the American government." His specific accomplishments included the creation of a national bank, assuming and funding the debt of the states and the Confederation Congress, and creating the Customs Service and the Coast Guard. Additionally, he played a key role in Washington's issuance of the Neutrality Proclamation of 1793, which enhanced presidential control of foreign policy, and in the suppression of the Whiskey Rebellion of 1794.

Although the latter was dismissed then and now as a contrived show of force by a power-mad Hamilton, the rebellion raised, as Hamilton saw it, the question whether law or force would prevail in America; the former being the definition of liberty, the latter the definition of despotism. As he once expressed it, "A sacred respect for the constitutional law is the vital principle, the sustaining energy of a free government." In popular government, the difficulty of instilling in the citizenry the notion that obedience to law is liberty is perennial. A similar situation would confront Abraham Lincoln on a much larger scale in less than four-score years. Hamilton saw the Whiskey Rebellion as posing in unambiguous terms the question, "Shall the majority govern or be governed? . . . [T]hose who preach doctrines, or set examples, which undermine or subvert the authority of the laws, lead us from freedom to slavery."

When Hamilton left the Washington Administration in January 1795, his greatest accomplishments were behind him. He had, at best, an uneasy retirement. He fought valiantly for the Jay Treaty, published a letter detailing his extra-marital affair with Maria Reynolds (*pace* Bill Clinton, again), battled the slightly deranged John Adams throughout his presidency and ultimately undermined Adams's bid for re-election, lost his eldest son in a duel in 1801, and then was himself felled in the famous "interview" at Weehawken in July 1804. Chernow deals with all these events elegantly and comprehensively.

One minor flaw in the book is its overstated account of Hamilton's commitment to abolition. Hamilton detested slavery, as demonstrated by his early and repeated plea to allow slaves to fight for the Revolutionary cause in exchange for their freedom, and his role as a founder of the New York Society for Promoting the Manumission of Slaves, but he never elevated the issue to the forefront of his concerns. As Yale historian Joanne Freeman observes, when Hamilton cared deeply about a problem he focused on it with a peculiar intensity, and never let go. This simply cannot be said about Hamilton and slavery.

In 1960, historian Merrill Peterson published his award-winning book, *The Jefferson Image in the American Mind*. Peterson contrasted the "spacious grandeur" of Jefferson's plantation at Monticello with Hamilton's "shabby" and neglected Harlem home, and saw them as symbols of their respective standing. For decades (not any more, to be sure) Monticello served as a Potemkin Village where evidence of the existence of Jefferson's slaves (his "family") was concealed from visitors—emblematic of the 20th-century's airbrushing of history by pro-Jeffersonian politicians and scholars. The crowded, slighted Harlem "Grange" and the Trinity Church gravesite, in the midst of New York's poverty and great wealth, is the more revealing destination for Americans seeking the truth about their nation's mixed record of triumph and failure. One can only hope that such a journey, accompanied by a reading of Ron Chernow's *Alexander Hamilton*, will prompt Americans to grant Hamilton his long overdue honors.

Three-Fifths Historian

Lance Banning

(Fall 2004)

Thomas Jefferson has taken quite a pounding for a generation, now, as social commentators and historians have come to be transfixed by slavery and race. In popular imagination, Jefferson is still the quintessential spokesman for equality, democracy, and fundamental human rights, but in "enlightened" circles he is not a hero suited to our age. He owned slaves all his life, did not believe that blacks and whites could live together peacefully as equals, declined to dedicate his life to battling the peculiar institution, and is thought by many scholars to have fathered several children by a slave and treated them into adulthood much like any other children of his household servants. Not only is the man to be decried, the legacy, as it has long been thought of, is to be debunked as well. The founding generation's champions of freedom (if, indeed, we still need heroes from that unenlightened age) have recently been sought among his foes or among the foes or troublemakers of the party he created: Alexander Hamilton, John Adams, Federalists in general, or even Aaron Burr.

Garry Wills, who is both commentator and historian, rejects this bashing of a figure he admires and says he plans to write again on Jefferson's more admirable features. *"Negro President": Jefferson and the Slave Power*, however, concentrates exclusively on Jefferson's "role as a protector and extender of the slave system." The author of the Declaration was indeed a "giant," the book contends, "but a giant trammeled in a net," compelled like other Southerners to do whatever he could do "to prevent challenges to the slave system," to support and even strengthen the constitutional protections on which he and his party depended for their political supremacy and even their "political existence." Thus, for all of Wills's disclaimers, *Negro President* contributes little more than another dose of the debunking he condemns. Since slavery was only rarely at the forefront of attention during Jefferson's political career, and since his record on the subject is by no means as deplorable as a deliberately one-sided treatment may suggest, this is a dreadfully tendentious book. It opens with a faulty premise, builds on that to offer what, at points, might be described as a revival of a partisan position the Virginian understandably condemned, and carries the search for an "anti-Jefferson" (one hopes) to its last extreme. A generous spirit might credit Wills for his desire to bring to wider attention recent scholarly insistence that slavery played a larger role in shaping even the earliest years of the new republic than older historiography suggested, but this is not a clear advantage if the effort leaves its readers with a seriously distorted understanding of the ways that Jefferson and slavery helped shape the new republic. (The works on which Wills leans most heavily include Paul Finkelman's *Slavery and the Founders*, 2001; William W. Freehling's *The Road to Disunion*, vol. 1, 1990; Leonard D. Richards's *The Slave Power*, 2000; and Don E. Fehrenbacher's *The Slaveholding Republic*, 2001.)

During his retirement, Jefferson called his party's victory in 1800 "as real a revolution in the principles of our government as that of 1776 was in its form." He meant by this that, in his view, a set of men whose policies endangered the republican revolution was replaced in 1800 by a set who understood the Constitution as the nation understood it when the document was first approved and who would pursue a set of policies intended to preserve and nurture the United States's historical departure from the world of priests, aristocrats, and kings. Historians, of course, might well contest this claim on several different grounds. The ground that Wills selects, however, is the constitutional provision for including three fifths of the slaves among the people counted when apportioning the Congress and allotting votes in the Electoral College. If slaves had not been counted, he maintains, John Adams would have won the election of 1800 by about four electoral votes. There *was* no revolution. Without this clause, in fact, the broader course of early republican history might have been much different. It tilted the sectional balance from the start and gave all Southerners, including Jefferson, a powerful incentive to extend the slave system. As long as it endured, asked Timothy Pickering, how could the New England states "ever rid themselves of Negro Presidents and Negro Congresses, and regain their just weight in the political balance?" As slavery spread into the old Southwest, New England was increasingly submerged in a malapportioned House of Representatives and subjected to the rule of hypocritical Virginians. From the inauguration of the Constitution, Southerners defended slavery, supported its extension to new states, and dominated national politics with the advantage given them by this provision.

Wills calculates that, in a contest that was actually decided by eight electoral votes, 12 votes for Jefferson can be attributed to the counting of three fifths of the slaves. If votes had been apportioned on the basis of free population (and the states had voted as they did), Adams would have won by a margin of 65-61.

But there are many ways to play this game, and this one quite objectionably accepts the whining and apologetics of New England Federalists for whom the three-fifths clause was not, in truth, the most important problem: Northern sectionalists, who had been thoroughly repudiated at the polls, were endangered in their homeland, and, as Jefferson complained, were just as likely to condemn the slave lords in a bid for partisan advantage as because of heartfelt opposition to the institution. Pickering, who gets as much attention in the book as Jefferson himself, is actually a case in point. This narrow-minded Massachusetts senator, a leader in the previous administration of the most vindictive forces in his party, was hardly the consistent anti-slavery champion who will be found in Wills's pages, any more than Jefferson was really a determined advocate of slavery's protection and expansion. Picking Pickering to serve as the Virginian's mirror image may inadvertently suggest how thoroughly misguided are a range of recent efforts to identify the Federalists as anti-slavery heroes.

Without the three-fifths clause, we might observe, there would have been no presidential contest to begin with. As Wills knows very well, the Constitution rested on a sectional accommodation. North and South were both determined to protect their interests. At the Constitutional Convention, the smaller, Northern states demanded and secured an equal representation in the Senate. Some protection for the wealth and interests of the South—*at least* a partial counting of its slaves—became an unavoidable condition of a stronger union. These constitutional provisions were a trade, the one as little democratic as the other. If, in 1800, only free folk should have counted in apportioning electors, the bonus given by an equal Senate to the smaller, Northern states should be discounted too. If this is done, the simplest calculation shows that Jefferson would have defeated Adams by a margin of some 58 to 47. (Counting free population only, I have allotted votes among the states according to the 1790 census and the 1/30,000 ratio used for apportioning seats in the House and have assumed that the states would still have cast or split their votes in the same manner as they did.)

It is a fact that voters had about as indirect a say in 1800 as they've had in any presidential contest. Each party tried as best it could to stack the voting in its favor. In 11 of the 16 states (and all of New England except Rhode Island), the legislatures kept the choice of presidential electors for themselves. Only two (both slave states) cast divided votes as a result of choosing the electors by district. If our modern practice had been universal in 1800—the winner taking the whole of every state's electoral vote—Jefferson would have defeated Adams by an even larger margin, 84-54. (As Wills himself points out, only a stubborn stand by a lame-duck Federalist state senate caused Pennsylvania to divide its vote, and a switch of 14 Pennsylvania votes would have elected Jefferson if he had not had any of the 12 he got for slaves. Under a winner-take-all system, Pennsylvania, which cast 8 votes for Jefferson and 7 for Adams, and North Carolina, which cast 8 for Jefferson and 4 for Adams, would both have cast their whole total for the former. I have not tried to take account of Maryland, which split its votes 5-5 as a result of district voting.)

The people's sentiments were tested much more fairly in the congressional elections of that year than in the choice of the electoral college. In those congressional elections, the Federalists lost 22 seats, nearly a third of their total strength in the House of Representatives, which Republicans would now dominate by a margin of 63-43. By 1804, when Pickering denounced his Negro presidents and Negro Congresses in a letter advocating the secession of New England and New York, Jeffersonian Republicans had nearly captured even Massachusetts, and many of his correspondents knew full well that Jeffersonian ideas and not the three-fifths rule were grinding Federalists into extinction. (A letter to Pickering from George Cabot, quoted by Wills, conceded that "All the evils you describe and many more are to be apprehended; but I greatly fear that a separation would be no remedy, *because the source of them is in the political theories of our country and in ourselves*.")

The three-fifths rule, in any case, was simply not responsible for most of the defeats of champions of slavery's exclusion from the West, nor is it true that Pickering or Federalists in general stood foursquare on the side of freedom. In 1798, before

John Adams fired him as secretary of state, Pickering actually wrote the bill providing that the Mississippi Territory would be governed according to the terms of the Northwest Ordinance of 1787, *except* that Article VI, excluding slavery, would not apply. Maine Federalist George Thatcher tried to change this in the House. Only two representatives, both Northern Republicans, spoke in favor of his move, while Massachusetts Federalist Harrison Gray Otis roundly objected to meddling in the business of the Southern states: "He thought it was not the business of those who had nothing to do with that kind of property to interfere with that right." (This point I owe to John Craig Hammond, whose recent dissertation and published or forthcoming articles contain a wealth of materials relevant to this subject. See his doctoral dissertation, *Slavery and Freedom in the Early American West: From the Northwest Ordinance to the Missouri Controversy, 1787–1821* [University of Kentucky].)

In 1804, New Jersey Republican James Sloan moved in the House to exclude slavery from Louisiana. This *passed* that body 40-36. Exclusion was defeated in the Senate, where the three-fifths rule had no effect. In Senate voting on James Hillhouse's proposals to prohibit the domestic slave trade to Louisiana and to free any slaves taken to that territory, Northern Federalists voted 4-3 in favor, Northern Republicans 6-4. Contrary to Wills, Pickering as well as John Quincy Adams and Jonathan Dayton voted *against* both of these Hillhouse amendments. Similarly, the Tallmadge amendment of 1819, excluding slavery from Missouri, and the Wilmot Proviso of 1846, which would have barred it from the Mexican cession, were both defeated in the Senate, not the House. And, once again, the men who moved these measures were Republicans from Northern states.

Thomas Jefferson, it is quite true, preferred to permit the domestic slave trade to Louisiana, hoping (however foolish this may appear in hindsight) that diffusion of the institution might prepare the way for its gradual extinction. Jefferson's attitude and actions toward the Negro republic of Haiti contrast unfavorably with Pickering's positions. Haiti is, in fact, almost the only case where Pickering is truly "seen at his most credible, and Jefferson at his least." In passage after passage and chapter after chapter, Wills imparts as favorable a spin to Pickering as anyone could manage and stretches just about as far as anyone but Pickering himself could reach to find a defense of slavery at the root of Jefferson's every action. Mississippi is ignored. Louisiana is mistaken. A patently secessionist letter of 1814 from Pickering to Gouverneur Morris should be read as "aiming to change the government, not withdraw from it." On the other side, anything that might conceivably, or by the longest stretch, be seen as supporting slavery or protecting the South becomes the salient feature and motivating force behind the measure. The capital was "purposely embedded in slave territory" in order to strengthen the institution. The embargo "pitted the slave power against the commercial power" in a deliberate attempt to cripple the carrying trade. The purchase of Louisiana and the occupation of West Florida were aimed at adding slave states, with their three-fifths bonus, to the union. Aaron Burr's real crime, in Jefferson's eyes, was that "[h]e tried to endanger the slave power" by separating slave states from the Union.

Pickering, about whom scarcely an admiring word is uttered in the whole of modern scholarship, perhaps deserves some rehabilitation. Although his record was more mixed than Wills suggests, he *can* be credited for steady hostility toward slavery, the South, and the three-fifths clause, which were the flip sides of his unconquerable New England sectionalism and opposition to Jeffersonian ideas. Jefferson, however, certainly does not deserve to be interpreted as Pickering construed him. He did prefer the spread of slavery into Louisiana. Late in life, he saw exclusion of the institution from Missouri as a neo-Federalist attempt to split the Republican coalition and press an unacceptable construction of the Constitution. His private life can be condemned. But this is not the full and balanced story. He penned some hurtful and pernicious lines about the physical and intellectual capacities of blacks. He also penned some of his generation's strongest and most influential passages denouncing slavery for the abomination that it was. In 1784, he moved the resolution leading to exclusion of the institution from the old Northwest. (That Pickering supported an even stronger prohibition in 1785 hardly destroys the traditional claim for Jefferson's influence on the shaping of the Ordinance of 1787.) He threw his weight as president behind the abolition of the international slave trade at the earliest date possible under the Constitution.

These last two measures, numerous historians have said, were probably the most effective ever passed for limiting American slavery and laying the foundations for its ultimate abolition. And this is not to mention the Declaration of Independence or any of the other deeds and writings that did so much to help enshrine equality and liberty among American ideals. Jefferson's was not the record of an advocate of slavery's protection and expansion. For all his faults, an argument can still be made that no one of his generation was a more effective, influential foe of slavery than Jefferson himself, not even Northern Jeffersonians, with Jeffersonian ideals, who led most of the other efforts to confine the institution.

How the Confederates Won

Mackubin Thomas Owens

(Winter 2002/03)

It has become something of a cliché to observe that the Civil War remains the central event in American history, a cataclysm that casts a long shadow over the United States even today. But the meaning of the Civil War depends a great deal upon how it is remembered. Recent debates over such issues as whether Virginia should celebrate April as "Confederate History Month," whether the city of Richmond should include a mural of Robert E. Lee as part of its Canal Walk along the James River, or whether the Confederate battle flag should fly over the South Carolina Capitol or even on its grounds, indicate that there is substantial disagreement over the war's enduring significance.

How we remember the Civil War is the subject of David Blight's excellent *Race and Reunion: The Civil War in American Memory*. In this wide-ranging cultural history of the half-century following the war, Blight examines Reconstruction, the soldiers' reminiscences of battle, the emergence of a romanticized South in the popular literature of the day, competing African-American memories of slavery and the war, and the ritual of Memorial Day.

According to Blight, a professor of history at Yale, the post-war era engendered three competing memories of the conflict. One, arising out of the Emancipation Proclamation and Lincoln's Second Inaugural, remembered the war as a struggle for freedom, a rebirth of the republic that led to the liberation of blacks and their elevation to citizenship and constitutional equality.

A second, the "Blue-Gray reconciliationist" view, developed out of the necessity for both sides to deal with so many battlefields and so many dead. It focused almost exclusively on the sacrifices of the soldiers, avoiding questions of culpability or the right and wrong of the causes. In this view, the war was the nation's test of manhood. There was nobility on both sides. The essence of this view was captured by Lew Wallace, a Union general who wrote *Ben Hur*: "Remembrance! Of what? Not the cause, but the heroism it evoked."

The reminiscences of the soldiers who fought the war lay at the heart of this view. Most symbolic of this memory were the Blue-Gray reunions in which soldiers of both sides gathered for "fraternalism and forgetfulness." The soldiers, writes Blight, sought to "reassemble the chaos and loss inherent to war into an order they could now control. While doing so, they cleaned up the battles and campaigns of the real war, rendered it exciting and normal all at once, and made it difficult to face the extended political meanings of the war."

The third memory was the white supremacist vision arising in part from the Democratic Party's counterrevolution against radical Reconstruction. The South may have lost the war, according to this view, but it triumphed over Reconstruction and the radical Republican legacy of corrupt, carpetbagger government and the anarchy of Negro rule. It restored labor discipline and economic dependency among blacks, thereby saving white civilization.

The white supremacist view was reinforced by the "Lost Cause" account of the Civil War. As Edward A. Pollard wrote in the 1867 book that gave this interpretation its name, "all that is left the South is the war of ideas." The essence of the Lost Cause thesis was (and remains) that the war was not about slavery, but "states' rights." It is neatly summarized in an 1893 speech by a former Confederate officer, Colonel Richard Henry Lee. "As a Confederate soldier and as a Virginian, I deny the charge [that the Confederates were rebels] and denounce it as a calumny. We were not rebels, we did not fight to perpetuate human slavery, but for our rights and privileges under a government established over us by our fathers and in defense of our homes."

The Lost Cause interpretation of the war was the South's response to physical destruction and the psychological trauma of defeat. In this view, the Old South was a racial utopia, an organic society composed of loyal slaves and benevolent masters. The war pitted this "slave democracy" against the "free mobocracy" of the North, and the noble side lost. The matchless bravery of the Confederate soldier succumbed to the "juggernaut of superior numbers and merciless power." As Robert Penn Warren once wrote, "in the moment of its death, the Confederacy entered upon its immortality."

The argument of *Race and Reunion* is that the imperative of regional reconciliation in the name of national unity led to the emancipationist view's eclipse by an alliance of the reconciliationist and white supremacist views, because the South would permit reconciliation only on its own terms. Its own racism led the North to acquiesce in this bargain. In the words of one writer cited by Blight, "Boston . . . and Ohio hold the coat of Georgia and Mississippi, while they slay the common victim of Northern prejudice and Southern hate." Accordingly, while the nation healed its wounds, it did so at the expense of justice.

Race and Reunion begins with the 1915 visit of President Woodrow Wilson to the Blue-Gray encampment at Gettysburg on the anniversary of the great battle. This encampment was the great symbol of the extent to which reconciliation had progressed. Wilson's appearance was particularly important, as he was the first Southern president since before the Civil War. The United States stood on the verge of entering a world war, and it was critically important that the scars of the Civil War not prevent America's emergence as a world power. But reconciliation came at a cost. The divide between white Americans in the North and the South had been bridged at the expense of African-Americans.

In the war's immediate aftermath, the emancipationist view had been ascendant in the North. Northern politicians frequently "waved the bloody shirt" of treason and rebellion, and there was a strong consensus that the South should be punished for starting the conflagration. In the words of Governor Oliver Morton of Indiana, "the rebellion, the offspring of slavery, murdered its unnatural parent, and the perfect reign of liberty is at hand." After the failure of presidential Reconstruction, the radical Republicans in Congress imposed their own version. But the South was defiant and raised Reconstruction's cost, and the North did not possess the will to see it through.

As Southerners embraced the Lost Cause rationale for the war and Northerners tired of Reconstruction, both sides seemed willing to heed Horace Greeley's admonition to "clasp hands across the bloody divide." The danger of this bargain was apparent to Frederick Douglass, who, on the centennial of American independence, wondered "if war among the whites brought peace and liberty to the blacks, what will peace among the whites bring . . . ? In what position will this stupendous reconciliation leave the colored people?"

Douglass's fears were well-founded. The United States had become a society committed to sectional reconciliation, at the cost of forgetting the African-Americans— especially the black soldiers who had swelled the ranks of the Union army—and their claims to citizenship and political equality. The trend was apparent in both popular literature and politics. As reconciliation à la the Lost Cause progressed, blacks were, in the words of one contemporary writer, reduced in popular literature to two roles: "the devoted slave who served and sacrificed for his master and mistress, or the 'poor nigger' to whom liberty brings only misfortune." The actual African-American experience of slavery and war was pushed aside by the romanticized South created by such popular "dialect writers" as Thomas Nelson Page and Joel Chandler Harris, creator of the Uncle Remus tales. In politics, the Supreme Court in 1883 struck down the Civil Rights Act of 1875, paving the way for Jim Crow.

As reconciliation pushed the emancipationist view aside, the result was what Blight calls the "collective victory narrative." According to this, the Civil War was a noble test of national vigor between two adversaries who believed firmly in their respective causes. The war was followed by an interlude of bitterness and wrongheaded policy during Reconstruction. The war was an heroic crisis that the United States survived and a source of pride, proving Americans could solve their own problems and redeem themselves in unity. The Civil War was the original "good war," a necessary sacrifice, a noble mutual experience that in the long run solidified the nation.

This is the view that prevails for the most part among Americans today. It is visible in popular Civil War magazines like *Civil War Times Illustrated* and *Blue and Gray*. It is visible in Civil War art by such artists as Morton Kunstler and Don Troiani. As Blight explains, such popular history and art reflect a longing for some transplanted, heroic place in the 19th century in which the troubling issues of race and slavery are banished from the discussion.

But this vision is a myth. Blight cites Roland Barthes on myth: it strives to "organize a world which is without contradiction, because it is without depth, a world . . . [of] blissful clarity: things appear to mean something by themselves." Today, of course, this comfortable myth of the war is under attack, as illustrated by the debates I mentioned at the outset.

The most sustained attack today comes from the multiculturalists of the Left, who seek to expose what they charge is the systemic racism that lies at the very heart of

America. This accounts in part for the fervent defense of the South by many conservatives. But the leftist charges are slanderous, as more and more Civil War historians are pointing out.

Yet how does one attack the myth without aiding the cause of the multiculturalist critics of America? As readers of the *Claremont Review of Books* know, the most consistent restatement of the emancipationist account has been advanced by Harry V. Jaffa. In his account of Lincoln and the Civil War, Jaffa has sought to reconcile the outcome of the war—"a new birth of freedom"—with the principles of the American Founding. For Jaffa, as for Frederick Douglass, the Civil War must be understood as a moral drama. As Douglass remarked, "there was a right and a wrong side in the late war that no sentiment ought to cause us to forget." This is the most fruitful way to reinvigorate the emancipationist view without giving aid and comfort to the multiculturalists.

Blight shows that the great tragedy of Civil War memory is that the emancipationist account of the war was sacrificed to reconciliation in alliance with white supremacy. The challenge is to link emancipation with reconciliation. Jaffa's *A New Birth of Freedom* (2000) is the antidote for the ills so skillfully diagnosed by David W. Blight in *Race and Reunion*.

The Bicentennial Lincolns

Allen C. Guelzo

(Winter 2009/10)

One of the most perceptive comments ever made about Abraham Lincoln came from Helen Nicolay, in a small book she worked up in 1912 from the notes her father, John G. Nicolay, had amassed from his four years as Lincoln's chief of staff in the White House. "A few characters live in history uncircumscribed by time or place," she wrote; yet we always manage to think of these characters in modern terms, as though they were "as vital and as modern as ourselves."

Just so with Lincoln. Helen Nicolay's generation, shaped by the Progressives (she was writing in the very year of Teddy Roosevelt's Progressive Party), was unable to "think of Lincoln in any environment except our own." But "the country [Lincoln] knew was vastly different" from the Progressives' America. Up till the Civil War, "America had been the land of individual effort, where those who were dissatisfied could go on into the wilderness and work out their doom or their salvation unmolested," and Lincoln's "life was essentially of the old era." He had no lessons to teach about the new era "of great industrial and social processes" condemned in Woodrow Wilson's First Inaugural Address (a year after Nicolay's book was published). "People have sought to make him a prophet for this generation," Nicolay said, but "the truth is that Lincoln was no prophet of a distant day."

> He made his own career by individual effort. His childhood, on the edge of civilization, had on the one side the freedom of the wilderness, and on the other the very few simple things which have been garnered as necessities from the world's useless belongings. His lawyer's earnings, at their highest, were only a pittance, by modern estimate; and a hundred details of his letters and daily life—like his invitation to an audience in the Lincoln-Douglas campaign, to meet him "at candlelight," which was not a figure of speech but an actual condition, showed how completely he was part of that vanished time.

Of course, it was possible to respond to Nicolay's judgment about Lincoln's historical remoteness in three ways. The most obvious, and the most superficial, was to ignore it, and this is the path taken by that endless stream of leadership gurus and historical second-guessers who want to strike Rodinesque poses and ask "WWLD?" as though Lincoln were an animated figure in a wax museum who could be made to mouth any of the current pieties on current issues—the internet, climate change, stimulus packages. Another, more serious response to Nicolay's warning was to embrace it, and go one better. This was the way chosen by Richard Hofstadter in his scorching 1948 essay, "Abraham Lincoln and the Self-Made Myth," and that was to acknowledge that Lincoln and his ideals were, at best, relics of a simpler age which were now hopelessly lost to modern times, and the sooner we realized this, the better. "Had he lived to seventy, he would have seen the generation brought up on self-help come into its own, build oppressive business corporations, and begin to close off those treasured opportunities for the little man."

The third possibility, taken up by Harry V. Jaffa, was to insist it was modern times that were the problem, not Lincoln. Or rather, the problem was that modern times were being stealthily portrayed as so "different" from the past, so much of an evolution from the simplistic world of the founders, that Lincoln could be dismissed as an artifact, speaking the obsolete political language of pre-modernity—of liberty, of natural law, of the spirit of kings arrayed against the spirit of free men. Jaffa believes that the Declaration of Independence is the "transcendental goal" that guided all of Lincoln's politics; as such, "Lincoln's interpretation" of the founders commits him to "a transcendental affirmation of what [civil society] ought to be," regardless of historical time or place.

The first response is popular but insincere; the second and third responses are worth pondering, but they are inherently irreconcilable, mainly because they represent two mutually exclusive notions of what the American "experiment" (to use both Washington and Lincoln's term) has been and should be. Both of them have the virtue of realizing that what we say or think about the politics, the economics, and the ideas of Abraham Lincoln tends to be what we say or think about the viability of that experiment. That takes us into some very risky territory, which may be why so many of the Bicentennial Lincolns have preferred the popularity—and insincerity—of writing what amount to long essays on WWLD.

LINCOLN AS "ONE OF US"

It might have been a good idea if most of those who flew to their keyboards to write Lincoln books for the bicentennial of his birth had been forced, after a mandatory reading of Helen Nicolay's warning against making Lincoln into a ventriloquist's dummy, to click an "I Accept" box before writing a word. It might have saved them and us much subsequent grief. As early as September 2008, the *Boston Globe* had sighted a tsunami of Lincolniana curving toward us, with "at least 50 titles about Lincoln" in the works, including

> three complete biographies; books of essays and photographs; books about Lincoln as a youth, as president-elect, as a military leader, as a writer, and as an inventor; books about Lincoln and his family, about Lincoln as victim of conspiracy, about Lincoln and his connections with others—his secretaries, his admirals, abolitionist Frederick Douglass, scientist Charles Darwin, even the poet Robert Burns, not to mention "at least seven children's books."

And the justification offered for this dam-cracking tide of Lincolns (apart, of course, from simple literary opportunism)? In a few cases, it was to establish (in the spirit of Hofstadter) that Lincoln is beyond our grasp; in some others, that Lincoln demands a renewal of the principles of the founders (in the spirit of Jaffa). But in most, it turned into what we had the greatest reason to dread, a tedious, one-inch-deep effort to re-model Lincoln as "our contemporary." Because, as Harold Holzer put it so nonchalantly, "He is one of us, not like a prince or a king."

The persistence with which Lincoln has been made and re-made into "one of us" has a lengthy history of its own, which has been extremely well-told by Merrill Peterson in *Lincoln in American Memory* (1994) and by Barry Schwartz in *Abraham Lincoln and the Forge of National Memory* (2000) and *Abraham Lincoln in the Post-Heroic Era: History and Memory in Late Twentieth-Century America* (2009). The ease with which Lincoln has been re-configured into a plaster saint for every decade and every cause grows, ironically, out of Lincoln's own intensely private temperament. In an age of intense diary-keeping and memoir-writing, Lincoln left no easily accessed record of his interior life, and that created blank spaces which others cheerfully filled in with manufactures of their own imagination. (T.R. and Woodrow Wilson were especially guilty of this.) But much of the remaking and refashioning was also a tribute to the sheer magnitude of Lincoln's accomplishments, which even today are hard to grasp without blinking—the complete destruction of slavery, the inauguration of a new pro-business economic regime which lasted pretty well intact until 1932, and the assertion of a national American identity over sectional and state special interests. No one except Lost Cause bitter-enders or perverse literary sensation-seekers had bile enough to spit at such a mountain.

The Bicentennial Lincolns, however, seem driven neither by mystery nor by admiration, but rather by a single-minded determination to make Lincoln precisely the modern-day soft Progressive that Helen Nicolay warned us Lincoln could never resemble. The most unashamed bid to transform Lincoln into a usable historical commodity emerges from the pages of Eric Foner's collection of essays, *Our Lincoln: New Perspectives on Lincoln and His World*, in which Foner unblushingly claims that "Lincoln remains in many ways our contemporary." This is, to say the least, a quixotic anthology: of its eleven contributors, only four have ever published anything substantial about Lincoln, and of those four, only two—Harold Holzer and Richard Carwardine—have really built scholarly reputations around the study of Lincoln. At least Holzer and Carwardine have something worth saying. As for the other seven, their chief credential for inclusion in this book seems to be a more than routine case of left-wing holy-rolling. And, sure enough, the less time the authors have spent in serious work on Lincoln, the more shrill the political annexation of his reputation. The most uncloaked example is David Blight, a Yale history professor, who imagines Lincoln as the victim of "Republicans"—he singles out Karl Rove, Ken Mehlman, Lynne Cheney, and George W. Bush—who "try to steal the meaning of American history and ride Lincoln's coattails while hating the government he imagined." Since "the modern GOP possesses a history it hardly wishes to know," its leaders find themselves driven to claim that Lincoln was a . . . Republican. Or perhaps more to the point, Blight thinks the modern Republican Party is so steeped in white racial supremacist ideas that it needs the Halloween disguise of "Lincoln the Great Emancipator" in order to make an appeal to black Americans.

Yet it is hard to say just *why* Blight wants to tear the Emancipator Lincoln from the grasp of "the conservative movement," since Blight himself frankly doubts whether

Lincoln deserves much credit as the Emancipator. "Numerous books and some slave narratives have demonstrated that slaves' volition in this story [of emancipation] is more than worthy of our attention." Blight thus pledges himself to the "self-emancipation thesis," in which slaves themselves used the exigencies of the Civil War as opportunities to free themselves, running away to safety and liberty with the advancing Union army long before Massa Linkum ever got around to picking up his emancipating pen. The great problem with the self-emancipation thesis (which first received public currency not from serious academic research but from the Ken Burns PBS Civil War series) is the simple lack of evidence that any such mass "self-emancipation" took place. The thesis may serve the noble purpose of promoting "black agency" and African-American self-esteem. But neither Blight nor the authors of "numerous books" have ever yet produced a single statistic on the number of slaves who thus freed themselves without benefit of Lincoln, nor has Blight ever dealt with the singular fact that, absent Lincoln's proclamation, not a single fugitive slave would ever be other than a fugitive, rather than a legally free man.

The same determination to reset "the middle ground" of Lincoln interpretation well to the left emerges from the late George Frederickson's *Big Enough to be Inconsistent: Abraham Lincoln Confronts Slavery and Race*, which tips its hand at once in its title, snipped from W.E.B. Du Bois. Frederickson sets the "extremes" of interpretations on the Left with Lerone Bennett (Lincoln hated black people), and on the right with Richard Striner (Lincoln was "a closet racial egalitarian"), thus leaving the center to be occupied with "a third possibility," which is that "Lincoln's attitude toward blacks and his beliefs about race may have changed significantly during the war years." That any evidence for such a conversion experience is notoriously thin on the ground is no problem for Frederickson; the notion conforms nicely to that conceit so dear to Progressive hearts, that of the Arlen Specter Republican who gradually but inexorably is drawn to the Democratic light. Like Blight, Frederickson imagines that Lincoln was "pressured" into issuing the Emancipation Proclamation "by anti-slavery radicals" and "tens of thousands of slaves" who "had in effect freed themselves from bondage"—although like Blight's fugitive slaves, Frederickson offers no explanation of just how much "pressure" the tiny cadre of "anti-slavery radicals" actually exerted, or who, exactly, took the census that arrived at "tens of thousands" as the number who had "freed themselves."

But even if we grant for a moment that Lincoln underwent a change on race during the war years, Frederickson does not want us to become too lost in new-found love for Honest Old Abe. Not all the good-wishing in the world is ever sufficient to move Lincoln to where Frederickson really wanted him: "He simply did not share the Radical belief that the Civil War constituted a political revolution that had fundamentally changed the relationship between the states and the federal government." But if this is so, with what consistency can we talk about a Lincoln who is supposed to have undergone so much "change"?

A POLITE LEFTY

Two biographies from the bicentennial year give us a less dogmatic but still perceptibly Progressive Lincoln, the first from Ronald White, and the other, more oddly, from George McGovern. At first glance, the books could not appear more different. White's *A. Lincoln A Biography* weighs in at 816 pages of text, while McGovern's *Abraham Lincoln* is only 208 pages long. White is a long-time academic, having taught American church history at San Francisco Theological Seminary for most of his career; McGovern earned a Ph.D. from Northwestern University, but his only visible claim to a place in the Lincoln literature is that he was once a presidential candidate, and a darling of the Democratic Left. The message in both books, however, is more or less the same. White, in the 1970s and '80s, was a peace activist who wrote extensively on race and the Social Gospel. Although almost nothing of that quondam activism survives as a distinct impress in this or his other two Lincoln books (*Lincoln's Greatest Speech: The Second Inaugural* in 2002 and *The Eloquent President* in 2005), what does seep through every page of *A. Lincoln: A Biography* is a mellowed-out sense of Bay-area niceness. White's Lincoln "was always comfortable with ambiguity," had an "inclusive spirit" which was turned-off by "sectarian rivalries," practiced law as a "peacemaker," and believed "that each generation must redefine America in relation to the problems of its time." Think of Lincoln in love beads.

White has read much of the relevant literature on Lincoln—to the point where it is pretty easy to guess whose book he is using at any point without having to turn to the endnotes—but what he lacks is the attention to detail that comes from a long immersion in Lincoln sources. It was in the *militia*, not the "military," that "units elect their own officers"; James Metzker (the victim in the famous "Almanac Trial") did *not* die "while attempting to escape on his horse"; Henry Villard was *not* covering the Lincoln-Douglas debates for the *Illinois Staats-Zeitung*; the voting in the Illinois 1858 elections was *not* "125,430 to 121,609" but rather 244,252 to 211,124; there is no evidence that Lincoln "had long admired the Reverend Henry Ward Beecher"; Leonard Volk was not Stephen A. Douglas's brother-in-law (he married a Douglas cousin); there is no evidence that Mary Todd Lincoln was her husband's "chief adviser" in political matters; John C. Frémont was known as the Pathfinder, not the "Pathmarker"; the number of soldiers killed at Antietam was approximately 3,600 (taking Union and Confederate together), not 6,500; James Cook Conkling did *not* read Lincoln's letter to the September 1863 mass Union rally in Springfield, Illinois, much less read it "slowly." This level of naïveté—I am reluctant to call it simple carelessness—is, unhappily, not mitigated by any new discoveries or dramatic interpretative shifts. In fact, there is scarcely anything in White's biography that could not have been just as easily learned from the Lincoln books currently in print. At the end, the best that can be said is that *A. Lincoln: A Biography* is a very nice book, by a very nice man, about a very, very nice president.

No such niceness, however, comes to the rescue of the McGovern biography. McGovern is almost as aggressive as Foner in trying to re-model Lincoln as a Progressive mascot. McGovern scants all mention of Lincoln's Whig economics, and instead casts Lincoln the lawyer as a sort of legal Robin Hood, and Lincoln the president as the founder of a "people's republic." (A *what?*) Nevertheless, the book reveals moments when even Lincoln fails to live up to the peerless, *soi-disant* social democracy of George McGovern—for example, concerning the wartime suspension of habeas corpus. "The only oath an American president takes is to uphold the Constitution," McGovern intones, and because the nation may "need its constitutional protections even more in times of war than in the less turbulent times of peace," we are left to conclude that it would have been better had Lincoln left draft rioters unarrested, smugglers and blockade-runners undetained, and the Confederacy to go its merry way—as though the Constitution really were a suicide pact. What McGovern does find unarguably admirable in Lincoln is his "remarkable military leadership," although even here, Lincoln had to learn to "change," unlike certain other leaders who never learned "that the military methods of World Wars I and II would not work in Vietnam or Iraq."

Detail is even less important to McGovern than to White, since McGovern cannot get right the names of Anson Henry and James Cook Conkling, mistakes the Missouri Compromise for the Compromise of 1850, mistakes the governor of Virginia for the governor of South Carolina, puts Winfield Scott in command of the Army of the Potomac (which had not yet been created when Scott retired), imagines that Lincoln somehow could regulate "telegraph news through the War Department," and describes the 1862 congressional elections as costing the Republicans 45 seats in the House, then 22 seats. He cannot even quote Lincoln accurately: the famous lines Lincoln wrote in 1858—"As I would not be a slave, so I would not be a master. This expresses my idea of democracy. Whatever differs from this, to the extent of the difference, is no democracy"—now become "So I would not be a slave, so I would not be a master."

Much worse than merely misquoting Lincoln is McGovern's penchant for pushing into Lincoln's mouth words he would never have dreamt of uttering. McGovern's Lincoln "believed in . . . the idea that fairness and justice must govern relations between government and citizens," and that "liberty was something that the government helped to provide." It is safe to say that Lincoln never thought that government had any responsibility for fairness whatsoever. "If any continue through life in the condition of the hired laborer," he said in 1859, it was their own fault, and not some defect in the "fairness" of the American system. "It is not the fault of the system, but because of either a dependent nature which prefers it, or improvidence, folly, or singular misfortune." His advice to those who failed in business was almost cheerfully indifferent: "To such, let it be said, 'Lay it not too much to heart.' Let them adopt the maxim, 'Better luck next time;' and then, by renewed exertion, make that better luck for themselves." Nor did he believe that liberty was the gift of government. "Our reliance is in the *love of liberty* which God has planted in our bosoms," Lincoln said in 1858, and the principal responsibility of government was to create a condition of affairs in which people could look out for themselves. "In all that the people can individually do as well for themselves, government ought not to interfere."

WAR PRESIDENT

Nothing connected to Lincoln and the Civil War would appear complete in 2009 without a word or two from James McPherson. The George Henry Davis 1886 Professor Emeritus in American History at Princeton, McPherson had written little about Lincoln until the Bicentennial. But he is widely-known for his basic Civil War textbook, *Battle Cry of Freedom*, which won a Pulitzer Prize in 1989 and confounded all expectations (for a book published by a university press) by topping the *New York Times* bestseller list. And the Year of Lincoln provided him an opportunity to compensate for any previous inattention by publishing two Lincoln titles, one a short biography from Oxford University Press and the other a full-dress study of Lincoln as a war president, *Tried by War: Abraham Lincoln as Commander-in-Chief*.

The short biography—at 96 pages, only half as long as even the McGovern biography—does little more than recite the bare outline of Lincoln's life, but gracefully and without any untoward interpretive interference. Much more expansive is the project of *Tried by War*, which is to show that Lincoln, the only president "in American history whose entire administration was bounded by war," devoted more "time and energy than anything else" to management of war, and apart from the vexing problem of constitutional and civil liberties violations, did it surpassingly well.

Still, war management was an unlikely burden for a man like Lincoln. As a long-time Whig, Lincoln shared the party's bone-bred suspicion of soldiering as the next door to despotism, and it was not by accident that the worst insult the Whigs could hurl at the head of Andrew Jackson was "the Military Chieftain." Lincoln served as a soldier himself for only a few months as a member of the Illinois militia in 1832, and in an age when politicians regularly sought out state militia commissions as patronage rewards, Lincoln never seems to have solicited any. Even as president, Lincoln looked askance at his own generals, not necessarily because they were incompetent (which a number of them were), but because six decades of dominance of the executive branch by various Democratic presidents had turned the professional army into a Democratic political engine. "Antislavery men, being generally much akin to peace," he told John F. Seymour, brother of Horatio Seymour, New York's Democratic governor, in 1863, "had never interested themselves in military matters and in getting up companies, as Democrats had." Nevertheless, the outbreak of the Civil War a bare six weeks after his inauguration forced Lincoln, if not into becoming a professional "military chieftain," then into taking charge of the ones who were.

And they were, as McPherson makes all too plain, a sorry lot, although in many respects this was not their fault. The U.S. Army in 1861 numbered a little over 16,000 officers and men, in 19 regiments (at a time when the newly re-organized Prussian army numbered 470,000 regulars and 130,000 reservists), most of whom had never been deployed in larger formations than a company, and had never faced anything more demanding than occupation duties in the West. The Military Academy at West Point specialized in training engineers, not combat leaders, and there was no staff college—or even a regular general staff—to provide that training in logistics, transportation, map-making, or communications. The one major exception was George B. McClellan, who had made the closest studies of European military methods and devised the first comprehensive strategic plan for the war in August 1861. But McClellan's gifts, which would have made him an ideal chief of staff (on the order of Helmuth von Moltke), did not extend to the management of actual campaign operations; and what was worse, his political loyalties to the Democratic Party inclined him to pull his tactical punches rather than deliver a clear-cut victory for a Republican president.

This left Lincoln little choice but to initiate his own process of self-education in military affairs, which he approached much in the same way he had learned lawyering—by borrowing books from the Library of Congress and studying them. What he learned from this reading, however, is highly debatable. McPherson believes that, over time, Lincoln learned to become a successful and competent master of "all five functions" of a commander-in-chief—"policy, national strategy, military strategy, operations, and tactics"—and the generals who eventually won the war on the battlefield did so because they embraced Lincoln's "mandate" to concentrate on destroying the rebel field armies rather than conquering territory or cities. This is not a particularly surprising conclusion, nor is *Tried by War* a particularly surprising book—it is actually, for the most part, a fairly conventional narrative of the Union view of the Civil War, indistinguishable from the relevant chapters of *Battle Cry of Freedom*.

But what, actually, did Lincoln learn from his autodidactic pursuit of military science? The standard textbooks of the day were written under the spell of Napoleon Bonaparte, and they hewed to the belief that victory in war was the product of single, decisive battles in which one side, in one massive stroke, disabled the opposing army and compelled its political leadership to come to the peace table. This might have served Napoleon's purposes at Jena and Austerlitz. But by the 1850s, field armies had swollen to dimensions which ensured that single-stroke, "decisive" victories would be impossible. What would certainly cripple an enemy army, however, would be to shift the blow to the enemy's logistics—lines of supplies, depots, and manufacturing centers—since these newly-gargantuan armies had stomachs which no mere foraging on the countryside could any longer satisfy. McClellan, curiously, understood this, and so his initial plans for war-making were aimed at the Confederacy's logistical centers, rather than at its field armies. Hence McClellan's grand plan to side-step the rebel army in Virginia, shift his own Army of the Potomac by water to the James River peninsula, and hit the Confederate capital at Richmond through its back door.

But Lincoln, who already had ample reason to resent McClellan's unconcealed contempt for the president he called "the original gorilla," interpreted McClellan's strategy as politics, not warfare—as a desire to avoid a straight-up, knock-down confrontation with the rebels. When Robert E. Lee and the Confederate army turned the tables on McClellan and ripped out McClellan's own logistical wiring during the Seven Days' Battles, McClellan hastily retreated. This looked to Lincoln like cowardice, not prudence, and when Lincoln finally relieved him of command in November 1862, he was adamant that McClellan's successors stop fooling around with plans to take Richmond, and drive up the middle, overland, to slug it out with Robert E. Lee and the Confederate army. "Lee's Army," he told Joseph Hooker, "and not Richmond, is your true objective point."

But was it? Obediently, a succession of generals—Burnside, Hooker, Meade—struggled to follow Lincoln's directive, and ended up with nothing to show for it but indecisive collisions with the rebels. When Lincoln brought Ulysses S. Grant to take control in Virginia in 1864, Grant was handed the same mandate. But Grant enjoyed Lincoln's political confidence like no other of the generals, and after another resultless string of stalemates, from the Wilderness to Cold Harbor, Grant prevailed on Lincoln to let him try the McClellan strategy below the James River. The result was a siege of Richmond and Petersburg which drained the life out of Lee's army, and when Lee finally broke away and tried to make a run for it in April

1865, the rebel army, lacking a logistical base, stumbled and collapsed into Grant's arms. The same pattern held true elsewhere in the war—it was not the defeat of rebel armies at Perryville or Murfreesboro, but the capture of Chattanooga and Atlanta, which wrecked the Confederacy's war-making capacity. In retrospect, Lincoln's directive to make "Lee's army . . . your true objective" was almost the worst advice a commander-in-chief could have given in the 19th century. Which only goes to show that even a great man cannot be wise in everything. But we do not even catch a glimmer of this from *Tried By War*.

REVEALING GLIMPSES

Harold Holzer, who began life as a public-relations man for Bella Abzug and then for Mario Cuomo, and who now serves as senior vice president for external affairs at the Metropolitan Museum of Art, may seem as unlikely a Lincolnite as Lincoln seemed a commander-in-chief. What Holzer lacks in academic standing, however, is more than made-up for by his relentless energy in carving out a niche all to himself in Lincoln studies, first as a specialist in Lincoln iconography and then as the principal remembrancer of Lincoln's connections to Holzer's own New York City. Although he has contributed numerous essays and chapters to a variety of Lincoln-related books, Holzer's contribution to the Bicentennial, *Lincoln, President-Elect: Abraham Lincoln and the Great Secession Winter, 1860–1861*, is actually only his second full-length study of Lincoln (the first being *Lincoln at Cooper Union: The Speech That Made Abraham Lincoln President* in 2004). But like the Cooper Union book, it is a tale rollickingly well-told, studded with curious details that enliven and humanize Lincoln's difficult progress from the day of his election in November 1860, to the moment he takes the presidential oath from Roger Taney on the steps of the Capitol four months later. Indeed, the focus may be a little too unrelentingly on Lincoln. There is comparatively little in Holzer's book about the larger political context of the "secession winter," which Russell McClintock meticulously lays out in *Lincoln and the Decision for War: The Northern Response to Secession*, a sadly unheralded book that appeared the same year as *Lincoln, President-Elect*.

Politics, however, rules the roost in *The Lincoln Anthology: Great Writers on His Life and Legacy from 1860 to Now*, which Holzer edited for the Library of America series. Conceived as a companion volume to LOA's two-volume *Lincoln: Speeches and Writings* (edited by Don E. Fehrenbacher in 1989) the *Anthology* is a collection of writings about Lincoln, from the odd (Artemus Ward, Bram Stoker) to the famous (Walt Whitman, Leo Tolstoy) to the incongruous (*both* Winston Churchills, the American novelist *and* the British prime minister). And for its first 700 pages, the *Anthology* as a whole has a certain Barnumesque celebrity-walk quality, since almost none of this material would be worth reading apart from its associations with Abraham Lincoln. Where this trajectory loses speed and begins to corkscrew is in the last part—in other words, writings on Lincoln from the 1970s onwards, where Holzer's leftward political tilt becomes risible. In rapid succession, the stage is seized from Jacques Barzun and H.L. Mencken, and turned over to W.E.B. Du Bois, H.G. Wells, Robert Sherwood, Allen Ginsberg, Gore Vidal, Mario Cuomo, Garry Wills, Richard Slotkin (using an excerpt from Slotkin's inept shinplaster, *Abe: A Novel of the Young Lincoln*), E.L. Doctorow, and finally . . . Barack Obama.

Apart from William Safire, modern conservative writing on Lincoln is rigorously airbrushed out of existence—nothing from Harry Jaffa, nothing from M.E. Bradford, nothing from Jack Kemp, nothing from Willmore Kendall, nothing from Thomas Sowell, nothing even from Thomas DiLorenzo. (Not that I think them all equally admirable—but it seems an odd anthology of writing about Lincoln which so arbitrarily and triumphantly *excludes* them). Like *Our Lincoln* (to which Holzer contributed), *The Lincoln Anthology* reeks of Left imperialism, trying to lay hold of Lincoln in much the same spirit that a spoiled child lays claim to another child's toy.

FAMILY ALBUM

There are at least two books among the Bicentennial Lincolns which aspire to do little more than harmlessly amuse and interest, and which are worth a quick look. One is *Looking for Lincoln: The Making of an American Icon*, from Philip and Peter Kunhardt, which is probably the closest thing to being a coffee-table book for the Bicentennial. The Kunhardt family has a long history of its own in Lincoln photography, stretching back to Philip and Peter Kunhardts' great-grandfather, Frederick Hill Meserve, who published the first Lincoln photograph collection, *The Photographs of Abraham Lincoln*, in 1911. Meserve's grandson, Philip Kunhardt, Jr., who would rise to become a managing editor of *Life*, published a number of rare Lincoln photographic discoveries in that magazine (including a memorable article on the final reburial of Lincoln's coffin, together with an interview of the last survivor of the reburial to have actually seen Lincoln's face). He also produced, in 1965, a remarkable photographic history of the Lincoln assassination and funeral, *Twenty Days*, and in 1992, a gorgeous picture book, *Lincoln*, which accompanied a PBS television series. *Looking for Lincoln*, coming from the fourth and fifth generations of Kunhardts, easily outdoes its predecessors, both in its sumptuously glossy reproductions and as an extension of the 1992 *Lincoln* into the post-1865 world of Lincoln remembrance. As such, the principal players (and images) of this volume are not Lincoln, but his family, his biographers, his associates, all the way to the death of Robert Todd Lincoln, the last of his immediate family, in 1926. (For those who expected to get more of Lincoln himself, a convenient "Gallery" offers an enumeration and thumbnail reproductions of all of the 114 currently known Lincoln photographs.)

If there is a fault to find with the Kunhardts' long retrospective, it is that it flattens a little too gently the weirdly-undulating landscape of the Lincoln family after the president's death. This accusation, however, can never be aimed at Charles Lachman, whose *The Last Lincolns* joins a rapidly sprouting sub-division of "Lincoln family" books in the past few years, which includes Stephen Berry's *House of Abraham*, Daniel Mark Epstein's *The Lincolns: Portrait of a Marriage* (2008), Catharine Clinton's *Mrs. Lincoln: A Life*, and Jason Emerson's *The Madness of Mary Lincoln*. The story of Mary Todd Lincoln's slow spiraling into insanity after her husband's murder and the death of all but one of her children has been often told and endlessly debated, and Emerson's *Madness* does little more than confirm the reality of that derangement. Berry's *House of Abraham*, however, makes plain how many of Mary's siblings and step-siblings seem to have sunk into la-la land at some point, and Lachman completes the story of this harrowing descent by recreating in agonizing detail just how very close the Lincoln family, between 1865 and the death of the last direct Lincoln descendent in 1985, came to becoming a model for the Addams Family.

The one family member who seemed to have a reasonably solid hold on reality was Lincoln's sole surviving son, Robert Todd Lincoln. Although William Herndon sneered that Robert was more of a Todd than a Lincoln, Robert was actually one of the few Lincolns who could reasonably be described as perfectly normal, and enjoyed an enormously successful career as a lawyer. Robert's older daughter Jessie, however, was a rebellious serial adulterer (she eloped with her first husband, a drifter named Warren Beckwith, in 1897; they divorced in 1907, after which she married Ned Johnson, who divorced her when he found her in bed with Robert Randolph, whom she married in 1926, all the while picking her parents' pockets for money). RTL's younger daughter, Mary (known as "Mamie" to keep all the Marys in the Lincoln clan apart), married Charles Isham, adding yet another lawyer to the family. But Mamie had only one weak, anemic son, and he lived the swank life of the New York speakeasies and never had children of his own. Jessie had produced two children from her first marriage, Peggy and Robert. Peggy turned out to be the oddest ball in the court, living in her father's Vermont mansion, Hildene, like an eccentric beggar. She ultimately willed the place to the Christian Science Church upon her death in 1976. (The Christian Scientists wisely unloaded Hildene to a non-profit group which now operates it as a Lincoln museum.) Her brother, Robert Todd Lincoln Beckwith, also had a roving streak, which resulted in a paternity suit in 1976, which then resulted in divorce, and then in tests which finally proved that RTLB's supposed offspring could not have been his child, since Beckwith was, as it turned out, impotent.

Lachman could have ended matters there, and the whole story would have been rattlingly strange on its own. And perhaps he should have, since he makes the mistake of inserting into the final chapter the absurd speculation that Jack Coffelt, a grifter who was adept at conning poor Beckwith, was the infamous D.B. Cooper, before Cooper made his famous jump into the Pacific Northwest in 1971. As it is, the miserable story of the Lincolns after Lincoln only recalls the weary comment of Charles Dickens, who was saddened to look around his dining table at his children, only to see not a one who had departed from the fecklessness of his own quite feckless father. If anyone wants fuel for arguing that Abraham Lincoln is strictly an artifact of the past, these two books will more than do the job, at least as far as genetics goes.

A TOUCHSTONE BIOGRAPHY

The score, then, on books for the Lincoln Bicentennial has not been an encouraging one. And this is odd, because the last 15 years have seen a renaissance of Lincoln scholarship, which has made them the golden age of Lincoln studies. A number of currents have combined to swell this flood, not the least of which has been the

rebirth of the Abraham Lincoln Association in the 1980s, the stupendous editing ac-
complishments of the Lincoln Legal Papers project (under Cullom Davis and Daniel
W. Stowell) and *Herndon's Informants: Letters, Interviews & Statements about Abraham
Lincoln* (edited by Douglas Wilson and Rod Davis in 1997), plus the creation of the
Abraham Lincoln Presidential Library and Museum, with the wise but hidden hand
of Illinois state historian Thomas Schwartz at the wheel.

No single historian, however, has done more to roll these developments into one
enormous Lincolnian package than Michael Burlingame, who is himself responsible for a small industry of editions of Lincoln-related memoirs and recollections
(including the papers of John G. Nicolay, the diary of John Hay, and the newspaper correspondence of Noah Brooks). As a student of the late David Donald—the
nation's premier Lincolnian until his death last May—Burlingame re-opened what
seemed to have been the sealed tomb of Lincoln writing in 1994 with *The Inner
World of Abraham Lincoln*. Until that moment, the most conventional of conventions about Lincoln books was that, after so many biographies and biographers
over the years, nothing further could possibly be known about Lincoln, and so all
new efforts at writing about him could be little more than wearing the ruts just a
little deeper.

What occurred to Burlingame, however, was one of those basic—almost primitive—insights that make for the shifting of entire paradigms. Every biographer,
he reasoned, works from notes. Most of the notes never manage to get into the
biography for reasons of space, just as most of the 3×5 cards we amass for college
term papers never get into the final submission. In our case, the excess 3×5s wind
up in the waste basket; in the case of famous writers, they wind up in collections of
authors' papers in various archives and libraries, where no one except the most diligent (or the most antiquarian) ever bother to call for them. Surely the same thing
must hold true for biographers of Lincoln. The more famous (like the muckraking
journalist Ida Tarbell), the more likely the unused material has survived; the closer
they were to Lincoln's time (and Tarbell was really the last to interview people who
had personally known Lincoln), the more likely that the unused material contained
gems of direct information which no one had ever thought to look for. Tarbell being
the easiest example, Burlingame tracked down Tarbell's papers to her alma mater,
Allegheny College, and sure enough, what he found was a gold mine of interviews
and correspondence from Tarbell's informants which had not made the final cut
for Tarbell's *The Life of Abraham Lincoln* (1903). This set Burlingame onto the track
of every archive likely to contain similarly unused cast-offs, and the result, in *The
Inner World of Abraham Lincoln*, was a series of essays, escorted by an armada of 200
footnotes each, which unearthed a Lincoln no one had seen in more than a century.
In some cases, each chapter's footnotes were as long as the chapter, and just as interesting to read on their own terms.

That this would lead to the creation of a new, comprehensive biography of
Lincoln, no one doubted. The only questions were, *how big would it be* and *how
long would it take?* The last super-biography of Lincoln had been Carl Sandburg's
curious, multi-volume *Abraham Lincoln: The Prairie Years* and *Abraham Lincoln: The
War Years*, which appeared between 1926 and 1939. But Sandburg's *Lincoln* was as
much a poetic saga, glorifying the folksy Lincoln who "had walked out of a Chinese
or Russian fairy story . . . with a handkerchief full of presents he wanted to divide

among all the children in the world," as it was a biography, and it played to a far different audience. Burlingame's *Abraham Lincoln: A Life* was originally planned for six volumes (fearful publishers brought that down to two, and *sans* all but the most skeletal footnotes) and took a decade-and-a-half to finish. (Even so, Burlingame's *Lincoln* totals nearly 1,600 octavo pages of text, packaged in a slip-case at $125 a set, but they are worth every *centime*.) Unlike Sandburg, Burlingame has no interest whatsoever in fairy tale Lincolns. "Sandburg was a poet, I am a scholar," Burlingame writes in a prefatory note, and *laus deo* for that. And unlike the Pecksniffian chirping of Lincoln's Left-annexationists, Burlingame's Lincoln is self-consciously "a champion of freedom, democracy, and national unity . . . psychological maturity, moral clarity, and unimpeachable integrity." The Emancipation Proclamation is an unambiguous triumph for freedom, and its apparently desolate vocabulary was designed "to make sure that slaves liberated under the proclamation had a sound legal basis to protect their freedom in court, if necessary." And his death at the hands of John Wilkes Booth was a martyrdom for the cause of black civil rights fully as much as was Martin Luther King, Jr.'s assassination by James Earl Ray.

What is breathtaking is the depth of Burlingame's research—newspapers (the *Belleville Weekly Advocate*, not just the *New York Times*), collections of manuscripts ranging from the Beinecke Library at Yale to the "fragment of the manuscript" from Katherine Helm's *Mary, Wife of Lincoln* (1928) which he found in the William H. Townsend Papers at the University of Kentucky, and of course the Ida B. Tarbell Papers (not only at Allegheny, but at Smith College, too). If there is a comment, phrase, observation, reminiscence, or recollection concerning Abraham Lincoln which Burlingame has *not* exhumed, it can probably stay safely buried. This, at last, simplifies the dilemma of the Bicentennial Lincoln books: If you want to read for amusement, read Holzer's *Lincoln, President-Elect* or Lachman's *The Last Lincolns*. If you want to read for comprehension, read Burlingame, because from now and into the foreseeable future, Burlingame's is the touchstone biography everyone who aspires to the study of Lincoln must embrace, cite, read, and occasionally quarrel with.

THE POLITICAL LINCOLN

Yes, quarrel with—because even amid this refreshing Niagara of data, it is clear that the Lincoln who matters most to Burlingame is the psychological Lincoln, the Lincoln who rises up from mental loss and humiliation as a young man, who suffers what we would call "spousal abuse" at the hands of a near-maniac wife, and who bears the sorrows of a bleeding nation through four years of war without losing his balance or his resiliency. What is missing from Burlingame—in fact, what seems to have taken French leave from almost all the Lincoln Bicentennial books—is the political Lincoln. Not the politically-corrected Lincoln of Holzer's *Lincoln Anthology* or of Foner's *Our Lincoln*, but the political Lincoln as he himself knew and understood politics. "Politics were his Heaven," wrote Lincoln's third law partner, William Henry Herndon, and not just the politics of immediate issues and statutes, but the overarching politics of the American experiment itself. He could be "a trimmer" in politics, wrote Leonard Swett, who had known Lincoln since his days on the Illinois circuit and who carried out discreet personal embassies for Lincoln during the war years, "and such a trimmer the world has never seen . . . . Yet Lincoln never trimmed in principles—it was only in his conduct with men."

Those principles, from the beginning of his political career, were the Whigs'. "He was as stiff as a man could be in his Whig doctrines," recalled his second law partner, Stephen T. Logan, and these included the creation of a national banking system, protective tariffs for American manufacturing, government encouragement to business in the form of "internal improvement" projects, and a profound reluctance to meddle otherwise in the affairs of a free market. Shocking as this may sound to the apostles of redistribution, Lincoln frankly said in 1860, "I take it that it is best for all to leave each man free to acquire property as fast as he can . . . . I don't believe in a law to prevent a man from getting rich; it would do more harm than good." Nor was this merely an offhand genuflection to capitalist hegemony. Lincoln had read long and hard in the classical liberal texts of natural law and political economy—"[John Stuart] Mill's political economy, [Matthew] Carey's political economy, social science . . . [John Ramsey] McCullough's political economy, [Francis] Wayland, and some others," according to Herndon—and like the classical liberals of the Manchester School, what Lincoln wanted was to "allow the humblest man an equal chance to get rich with everybody else." Then, he added, "you can better your condition, and so it may go on and on in one ceaseless round so long as man exists on the face of the earth!"

There is certainly plenty of greatness in Lincoln to go around, plenty in fact to allow whole books devoted to the depth of his character, his capacity for managing military affairs, his concepts of race and of emancipation. But at the end of the day, we will still lack the essential core of the man without his politics and the principles which animated them. Hofstadter's contempt for Lincoln was rooted in Hofstadter's distaste for Lincoln's politics; but he at least understood that the man and his ideas were inseparable. Hofstadter hoped that the ideas had become irrelevant, but he had no illusion that he could re-write or erase the politics and still have the man. This, however, is precisely why Hofstadter's Left-Progressive heirs, from Foner through McGovern, so often seem to be dealing in pasteboard Lincolns. If they took Lincoln as seriously as did Hofstadter, or even Helen Nicolay, they would have to be singing paeans to free markets, free speech, and free men, or else renounce him as a capitalist tool.

But at the other end of the spectrum, there are far too many conservatives who imagine that Lincoln's uncomplicated Manchester liberalism can be dropped into place without sufficient consideration of Hofstadter's (and Nicolay's) point that Lincoln "belonged to the age of craftsmanship rather than industrialism." A mid-sized factory in 1860 meant 15 employees and an owner (or partners) in shirtsleeves; a major industrial establishment might employ 85. Corporations accounted for only 7% of all American manufacturing in 1860. By 1900, however, that share had swollen to 69%; between 1897 and 1905 alone, 5,300 small-scale firms were consolidated and reorganized into just 318 corporations, and 26 super-corporations controlled 80% of American industrial output. After the Civil War, "I found that I had got back to another world," said the title character of William Dean Howells's novel, *The Rise of Silas Lapham* (1885). "The day of small things was past, and I don't suppose it will ever come again in this country."

In that light, the greatness of Abraham Lincoln will rest on how much genuine credit (and not just notional assent) we still give his politics as the embodiment of natural laws written onto the hard disk of human nature and transcending the immediate circumstances of his times; or whether we believe that our America has changed so much that Lincoln's ideas are simply no longer applicable to an interdependent, free-floating, immigrant swamped, mass consumption society. Without making that determination, the question will not be whether Lincoln is *our* Lincoln or *their* Lincoln, but whether he is anybody's Lincoln, any more.

Tyranny and Utopia

Charles H. Fairbanks, Jr.

(Spring 2005)

You're an impossible man. It's impossible to live with you!

—Nadya Alliluyeva to her husband, Joseph Stalin

Simon Sebag Montefiore, a British journalist who has spent a quarter of his life wandering among the smoldering ruins of Soviet civilization, sets out to study the Soviet horrors in a new way. "My mission was to go beyond the traditional explanations of Stalin as 'enigma,' 'madman' or 'Satanic genius,' and that of his comrades as 'men without biographies,' dreary mustached sycophants." In *Stalin: The Court of the Red Tsar*, he has written, instead, "a biography of his courtiers . . . a biography of Stalin himself through his relationships with his magnates." Accordingly, the book, which "does not pretend to be a history of [Stalin's] foreign and domestic policies," is dense with personal matters: old friendships, wives and children, the hobbies of the leaders, their quarrels, reconciliations, and adulteries, their food and clothes— the stuff of *People* magazine. Stalin and his Politburo pals, like the Kennedys, loved throwing people into the pool. As the great Hyppolite Taine remarks of Macaulay, Montefiore "never forgets the actual . . . . The petty details which he . . . selects fix the attention, and place the scene before our eyes . . . . These precise details . . . give to history the animation and life of a novel."

As part of a massive research effort, Montefiore has visited most of Stalin's homes, including his five vacation houses in Georgia's seceded and defiant Abkhaz province; he puts before us the settings for each historic conversation or decision. He has used an incredibly wide range of sources—printed, archival, and living—though, like many post-Soviet writers, Montefiore seems largely ignorant of the rich tradition of Kremlinology. In a book chock full of sourced detail, the distance between footnotes often makes the source of a particular assertion difficult to identify, and sometimes assertions in the text seem to go beyond the evidence. One story, sourced to a Politburo child, differs from my own interview with the same subject. But Montefiore's overall angle of attack—his focus on the personal, on "gossip," on Stalin's "courtiers"—is needed and very promising.

In any regime based on personal authority, the personality and idiosyncrasies of the ruler, and also of his lieutenants, must have a great determining voice in political outcomes. Stalin, for example, had the power, and the warrant from Bolshevik doctrine, to censor and edit literature and music. If Stalin's "deeply conservative tastes remained nineteenth century even during the Modernist blossoming of the twenties," this fact played a great role in exacerbating the intellectuals' estrangement from the regime. With Stalin gone, Khrushchev's de-Stalinization gave the intellectuals hope, but his taste doomed the reconciliation when he reacted against the avant-garde Manezh art show. When Gorbachev eventually liberated the intellectuals, by *glasnost,* to criticize the regime, their accumulated resentment was enough to destroy its public legitimacy.

The ruler of a vast country who is the founder of a new regime—and Stalin, not Lenin, was the founder of the Soviet system that foundered in the '80s—can only consummate his titanic labors by the actions of his chieftains, who leave the imprint of their personalities on the institutions of the regime and on history.

Could we understand the United States built by Washington if we knew Hamilton and Jefferson only as anonymous tools? In the Soviet case, the terror would not have extended so far without the neurotic instability of the tiny, bisexual Yezhov, People's Commissar of State Security, who "does not know how to stop." Hitler might have won the war if Stalin had not turned over war industry and domestic affairs to the businesslike bourgeois Giorgi Malenkov and to Lavrenty Beria. Montefiore says less about the colorless Malenkov, but rightly calls Beria a "gifted, intelligent, ruthless and tirelessly competent adventurer." He notes that Beria was "less devoted to Marxism as time went on," but Beria's daughter-in-law is probably more accurate in labeling him "never a real communist." Beria himself mused, shortly before Stalin's death, "The USSR can never succeed until we have private property." When watching his favorite Westerns, Beria "identified with the Mexican bandits," that is, with southern outsiders who can only get ahead by joining or plundering whatever side offers the best pickings. Without these personality traits and views, Beria would not have carried out his 1953 "bid for popularity by de-Bolshevizing the regime."

After World War II, Stalin retreated from public view, making few public statements but continuing to issue detailed secret instructions on important matters of public policy such as the torture of "murderers in white coats," the Jewish doctors. The most prominent pronouncements Stalin did make were oracular works of Marxist "theory," *Marxism and Problems of Linguistics* (1950) and *Economic Problems of Socialism in the U.S.S.R.* (1952). Like Mao before the Cultural Revolution, Stalin sought the status of a theocrat who does not deign to govern in merely tactical matters, but allows his high priests and Levites to argue over the practical application of his sacred laws. Thus one leader and his team of followers could be made the fall guy for failed or superseded policy. Zhdanov and his followers became the scapegoats, in the "Leningrad Case," for the failed attempt to communize Western Europe through the local Communist parties and to make the radical, and independent, Yugoslav Communists a favored partner. Beria was to be the scapegoat, at the end of Stalin's life, for the prominence of Jews and non-Russians in the party from the revolution until the end of World War II. Perhaps Stalin learned from the disastrous friendship with Hitler, ended by the German surprise attack, never to step forward in public as responsible for risky policy.

This pattern of rule had another clever aspect. Stalin normally allowed the ascendant faction to exterminate the leaders of the superseded group, which in turn provided charges on which the ascendant group could be brought low, leaving Stalin in the position of supreme arbiter. *Kompromat* (material for accusation or blackmail) remained enormously important throughout the brief life of the Soviet regime, from Lenin's testament questioning Stalin's fitness to lead to Gorbachev's *glasnost*. Montefiore perceives that "the system encouraged Terror entrepeneurialism," but does not tease out these deeper techniques of Stalin's rule to the extent that Jonathan Brent and Vladimir Naumov did in *Stalin's Last Crime* (2003). In turning the focus away from policy, he fails to note how distinctive were the policy repertoires advocated by different "magnates." But if Montefiore had included more policy in his mix, it would only have strengthened the argument for his new focus on Stalin's "magnates."

Montefiore's approach leads him to question the convention by which most biographers of Stalin, Hitler, and their lieutenants have presented their actions as absurd or stupid, because the men themselves were evil. We like to think that they desolated the center of world civilization without any particular merits or talents. This view seems somehow instinctive. Perhaps it wells up from some primeval feeling of the oneness of what were once called virtues and their rootedness, against thousands of years of moral teachings, in human strength or wholeness. But this instinct blocks inquiry into why the wicked titans of history did specific things, how they could achieve so much, and ultimately into why they were so evil.

As the son of a drunken, improvident shoemaker, without education, connections, or even being a Russian, Stalin eliminated more-favored rivals one by one, until he ended up in the seat of the glittering heirs of the caesars. Before his throne was stable, he embarked on a campaign to tame and regiment most of those he ruled. No sooner had he broken the peasants than he faced the frenzied, annihilating onslaught of the country where the civilization of Europe had come to its modern peak and perfection, Nazi Germany. And, at the head of the society and regime he had personally crafted in 15 years of hectic demolition and reconstruction, he somehow won the unequal contest. The Anglo-Saxons' contribution was modest. For the first time in modern total war, the more backward society prevailed against the more advanced. By valor, by discipline, by inventiveness, by sheer will, Stalin's Soviet Union emerged in unrivalled dominion of the European continent, and immediately challenged the island powers—as advanced in technology, but far wealthier than Germany—for global hegemony, an unequal fight sustained for 45 years. To do these things Stalin must have been a great man.

Montefiore does not say so in so many words, but his portrait represents a substantial reevaluation of Stalin: a reevaluation upwards.

> Far from being the colourless bureaucratic mediocrity disdained by Trotsky, the real Stalin was an energetic and vainglorious melodramatist who was exceptional in every way. . . . The man inside was a super-intelligent and gifted politician for whom his own historic role was paramount, a nervy intellectual who manically read history and literature, and a fidgety hypochondriac . . . . While incapable of true empathy on the one hand, he was a master of friendships on the other . . . . When he set his mind on charming a man, he was irresistible.

Montefiore rightly identifies Stalin's "dry wit." Stalin "was an intellectual, despite being the son of a cobbler and a washerwoman. Indeed, it would be no exaggeration to say that Stalin was the best-read ruler of Russia from Catherine the Great up to Vladimir Putin." In breadth of knowledge, indeed, he compared well with most world leaders of modern times:

> Before he set off for [vacation] he scrawled to Poskrebyshev [his secretary]: "Order all these books. Stalin. *Goethe's Letters, Poetry of the French Revolution*, Pushkin, Konstantin Simonov, Shakespeare, Herzen, *History of the Seven Years War*—and *Battle at Sea 1939-1945* by Peter Scott."

Beach towel reading! In writing, Stalin had "the ability to reduce complex problems to lucid simplicity."

Montefiore's presentation of Stalin differs from earlier ones in two particular ways. First, we do not see an austere, but a sexually indulgent Stalin amid a debauched and drunken Bolshevik elite. Not only Beria, but Kalinin, Kirov, Kuibyshev, Vlasik, Voroshilov, Yagoda, Yenukidze, and Yezhov could be described as tireless womanizers, while Lenin and many others took advantage of their secretaries or other women. Yezhov's wife was a manic seducer of writers, most of whom were doomed by her whimsies. This picture calls into question the contrast between ancient tyranny and modern ideological tyranny that seems otherwise plausible.

Second, in contrast to most writers on Stalin, Montefiore emphasizes his Georgian qualities.

> His personal Russianness has been exaggerated. His lifestyle and mentality remained Georgian. He talked Georgian, ate Georgian, personally ruled Georgia . . . , becoming involved in parochial politics, missed his childhood friends, and spent almost half of his last eight years in his own isolated, fantasy Georgia.

I am more persuaded by Robert Conquest, who argues, in *Stalin: Breaker of Nations* (1991), that "His temperament was, by all usual standards, very unGeorgian," except for the mountaineer's "readiness for revenge." Stalin rarely saw his mother, even when vacationing in Georgia: most un-Georgian. His own children got the impression "he used to be a Georgian." He forbade speaking Georgian in the presence of Russians, and began to replace "proletarian internationalism" by Russian nationalism from the early '30s, as soon as he was dictator. One can see in this a clever adaptation to his role as the ruler of the former Russian empire, but it is probably more the trait called by psychoanalysts "identification with the adversary." Stalin preferred to identify with Russia, powerful and triumphant, than with passive and downtrodden Georgia. Any such impulses must have been powerfully encouraged by Marxism-Leninism's insistence that everything is a matter of power, and by its contempt for weakness and failure. Ultimately, we should see Stalin, like other members of small, dependent peoples, as responding to his sense of marginality by seeking significance in universal ideas, the ideas of Marx and Lenin.

Montefiore's recognition of Stalin's merits certainly does not block his acknowledgment of Stalin's evil character. Suspicion and fear, which Montefiore calls "paranoia," dominated Stalin's life. To some extent, Montefiore argues, his paranoia was understandable in the light of his circumstances.

His paranoia was part of a personal vicious circle that was to prove so deadly for many who knew him, yet it was understandable. His radical policies led to excessive repressions that led to the opposition he most feared . . . .

This argument is quite persuasive. I believe, however, that Montefiore does not see a more modest, but significant, contributing factor: the inevitable fragility of illegitimate personal rule. Nominally Stalin was selected as General Secretary by the Central Committee, elected in turn by the Party Congress elected freely by millions of Communists. Actually, of course, it was precisely the other way around: Stalin chose his Politburo and Central Committee, which in turn chose the delegates to the infrequent Congresses, and so forth. Because the real mode of power contradicted the formal institutions, the power gained was always under threat, and it could only be defended by informal, out-of-sight means. For Stalin, these methods came to include intimidation, blackmail, and murder. Khrushchev discarded these means, and was removed, in 1964, by a conspiracy of the "magnates" below him. Gorbachev suffered something similar.

Because Montefiore is not writing a history of Stalin's foreign and domestic policies, the reader of his fascinating book is not able to trace the operation of power in the Soviet system and Stalin's reactions to it. He cites the politically crucial September 25, 1936, telegram of Stalin to Zhdanov that touched off the terror against the party elite, but omits the critical words, "The GPU [security police] is lagging four years behind in this." Four years earlier brings us back to August 21, 1932, amid the famines of collectivization, when Martemyan Riutin prepared a platform demanding Stalin's removal from office and circulated it within the party. At that time Stalin apparently demanded Riutin's execution, a demand contrary to the existing convention that members of the party elite not be executed, and resisted by the "magnates" around Stalin. As Montefiore often emphasizes, the failure to secure a political proposal was as personally important to Stalin and his magnates as a love affair or a suicide. But in the end, his concentration on the wonderful personal details crowds out the political. A book cannot do everything, but this is the greatest defect of Montefiore's absorbing work. It is a defect that makes it hard to ground properly any interpretation of Stalin's "paranoia" and cruelty.

Still, Montefiore does full justice to Stalin's "heartless cruelty," displayed at every level from the murder of millions to his enjoyment of deftly placing tomatoes on chairs to ruin Mikoyan's beautiful suits at Politburo dinners. Occasionally Stalin would forgive someone, admitting in an ordinary tone, "We tortured you too much." On one level, Montefiore admits that Stalin knew many victims were innocent. His way of understanding this is to argue:

Did Stalin really believe it all? Yes, passionately, because it was politically necessary, which was better than mere truth. "We ourselves will be able to determine," Stalin told Ignatiev [his last security minister], "what is true and what is not."

Here, I believe, Montefiore comes close to understanding the full problem of a regime based on the public sovereignty of the philosophic truth, which "scientific socialism" claimed to be. Any government is forced to make numerous merely tactical decisions. If, *a priori*, that government's decisions flow from its scientific knowledge, every tactical necessity is invested with the apodictic character of Truth.

The regime based on the truth converts itself in practice into one based on the most systematic falsehood.

Another contributing factor was, in my opinion, Stalin's lower-class origin, one step removed from the peasantry. It is no longer fashionable to say it, but people who lead the tough life of the poor tend to be tough and callous toward others. Across many societies, for example, peasants are cruel to animals—except their own. Peasant coarseness may have set Stalin on the road of indifference to the suffering of millions, just as it predisposed him to crude obscenities and contempt for women.

Without any doubt, however, Montefiore is right to see in Bolshevik ideology the major determinant of Stalin's cruelty. Throughout his life, according to Montefiore, Stalin "remained a fanatical Marxist." Marxism was a comprehensive, pseudo-philosophic explanation of the world and offered a religious salvation to mankind. Montefiore rightly notes that most Bolsheviks came from religious backgrounds, a connection true of many 19th-century Russian radicals before them. But the place of religion had been filled, for them, with the icy grandeur of materialist science.

> Stalin lectured Bukharin that the "the personal element . . . is not worth a brass farthing." . . . They cultivated their coldness. "A Bolshevik should love his work more than his wife," said Kirov.

Kirov, accordingly, had not seen his sisters for 20 years when he was killed. With such an attitude toward their nearest and dearest, it was easy to snuff out any compassion toward those defined as opponents. These Bolshevik attitudes were exacerbated by the pitiless, chaotic civil war that inaugurated their rule.

> It was here that Stalin grasped the convenience of death as the simplest and most effective political tool. . . . [D]uring the Civil War the Bolsheviks, clad in leather boots, coats and holsters, embraced a cult of the glamour of violence that Stalin made his own.

That Bolshevik taste for the absolute—for utopia and violence—seems far distant now in the West that gave it birth. But it has reappeared within the Islamic world. The recreation of a universal caliphate, which ceased to rule all Muslim lands about the year 800, has become a widespread demand of radical Islamic groups from Morocco to Central Asia—a demand as abstract and utopian as Communism itself. In pursuit of such aims a cult of death as pitiless as Stalin's has gained widespread ascendancy over radical Muslims. The war against this style of tyranny demands the same energies, and meets with the same Western equivocations, as the war against Stalinism.

Among us, utopian solutions are no longer advocated as part of a comprehensive political program. Ideology has become more elusive, but perhaps therefore more insidious. Is not a demand like homosexual marriage as comprehensive and drastic a reordering of human practices as the elements of the Bolshevik program? Certainly it is pressed with the same sincere conviction of its moral urgency. With equal urgency American science is dazzled by the prospect of improving men as they are, with all their undeserved deformities and heart-rending sufferings, by genetic measures. To make such changes is now within our grasp, but the eventual objective is far from clear. Perhaps it is useful to brood once more upon the rage emptied on the world by Stalin and his magnates. They, too, had the very best of intentions.

Thoughts and Adventures

Larry P. Arnn

(Spring 2008)

The official biography of Winston S. Churchill is said by the *Guinness Book of World Records* to be the longest biography ever written. Commenced in 1962, and orginally published in England by William Heinemann, it is more than 25,000 pages—almost 10 million words—long. Hillsdale College Press has undertaken the republication of the entire biography. Eventually all eight volumes of the narrative will be back in print. In addition, the 16 existing volumes of documents (up to the year 1941) will be republished. The college and Sir Martin Gilbert, the official biographer, have agreed to complete the publication of the documents to the end of Churchill's life in several more volumes.

So far narrative volumes 1 and 2 and document volumes (now called *The Churchill Documents*) 1 through 5 have appeared. These cover the period from Churchill's birth in November 1874 until August 1914, when the First World War began. The first two narrative volumes were written by Churchill's son Randolph, who was given the job by his father, and who served as biographer from 1962 until his death in 1968. Gilbert wrote volumes 3 through 8 and is the editor of the document volumes beginning with August 1914. More must be said about the qualities of Sir Martin and his decisive contribution to the whole work, but this is better said on a later occasion, in a review of the volumes that he wrote.

For now, reflecting on the first two volumes and their five volumes of companion documents, one is already compelled to wonder, not how can one read it all—that seems impossible—but whatever can fill such a life to such a size? The answer is simple enough: it is a book of adventure—supreme and instructive adventure.

THE ARMORED TRAIN

Consider just one story, which happened at a pivotal moment in the years covered by volumes 1 and 2, and tells us much about the man who is the subject of this vast tome. Once upon a time there was a train . . . .

This was an armored train, which left the station in Estcourt in Natal, South Africa to reconnoiter northwards towards Chieveley, and met its fate early on November 15, 1899. The Boer War was raging, and Boer troops were reportedly in the area. Captain J.A.L. Haldane, who knew young Churchill from soldiering in India, was in command of the train. He invited Churchill, at that moment a war correspondent, to come along. The armored train was not the best idea, and this journey would not go well. Or from another point of view, it would go as Providence decreed.

The Boers got between this armored train and its way home, piled some rocks on the track, and opened fire from a position that would drive the train toward the rocks. The locomotive was in the middle of the train. It got up steam to run for it. Three of the cars it was pushing hit the rocks with a terrible crash, were derailed, and blocked the track. To go forward was impossible. Behind were only Boers, who opened fire from about 1,000 yards with artillery and rifles. It was loud and accurate fire, and it would kill four men and wound at least 30 others.

Churchill was 15 days from his 25th birthday. He had been a commissioned officer for four years and 10 months, and he was already familiar with gunfire. He had been, with a few interruptions, a war correspondent for nearly as long as he had been a soldier. The prominence and makeup of his articles in the press had brought criticism upon him, in one case a letter from the Prince of Wales to Churchill, and in another a letter to the *Army and Navy Gazette* from "a General Officer." The heir to the throne and senior commanders in one's service are not minor critics. The "General Officer" said that young Churchill was "careering over the world, elbowing out men frequently much abler and more experienced" than himself. His articles, continued the general, criticize "general officers highly placed in authority," and they influence public opinion in ways that are out of proportion to Churchill's rank.

These are not unfair points. Churchill did a lot of military service in a hurry, and sometimes he would go to the scene of the action even though the commander had forbidden him to be there. He got himself into some dangerous situations by these methods. What's more, his articles were popular, written without editing or prior comment from higher military authorities, and had very much to do with the public impressions of the war. And they made him a lot of money. Little wonder that colleagues got cross.

Undaunted by the criticism, Churchill replied to the General Officer that it is unseemly for a ranking officer to "bandy words with subalterns in the columns of the public press." He concluded:

> I do not wish to further excite the anger of a gallant officer nor to show disrespect to his high military rank, but it is necessary in conclusion, whether it be painful or not, to observe that to make personal attacks on individuals, however insignificant they may be, in the publicity of print, and from out of the darkness of anonymity, is conduct equally unworthy of a brave soldier and an honourable man.

"The darkness of anonymity": not a bad phrase for a young man aged 24 in a situation of such pressure. Moreover, he came near to calling the General Officer a dishonorable coward. The young Churchill, like the later one, was not easy to cow. Also he liked to argue.

Churchill had resigned his commission in March 1899 in order to write his second book, *The River War*, and to run unsuccessfully for Parliament. He was given a most lucrative contract to go to South Africa as a war correspondent to cover the Boer War. Criticism in the past notwithstanding, he considered applying for a commission upon his departure and even drafted the application, just in case a good opportunity for soldiering should come up while he was down there writing articles. Later he decided to look for opportunities once he reached Africa. They would come soon enough.

UNDER HEAVEN: CIRCUMSTANCE AND GENIUS

So there he was, a war correspondent on a trapped armored train under deadly attack in a war zone. Never mind his civilian status; Churchill volunteered in a heartbeat. "Knowing how thoroughly I could rely on him," Haldane said, he put him to work. Amidst heavy fire, with many wounded and several killed in the train, the locomotive itself damaged and threatening to explode, Churchill began to walk about in plain sight, surveying the damage. Others, shielding themselves as they could, gaped in wonder.

He formed a plan to use the engine to push the derailed cars off the track. This was delicate work. He enlisted help. To the wounded engineer of the train, about to abandon his post, he said: "buck up a bit, I will stick to you." Also, he continued, you will be decorated; later Churchill himself would move the decoration as Home Secretary. For more than an hour, he walked, looked, and labored, calm and calculating. The heat and smoke and noise were oppressive. Metal rained down. Men returned fire, bled, and died. Finally part of the train came free.

Brave men on a battlefield are often animated, dashing about with excitement. A few—George Washington, for example—have instead a special kind of deliberateness. Young Churchill proved himself a member of that serene, lethal company on more than one occasion, but especially here beside the armored train.

The engine got away with the wounded and Churchill on it. The rest of the force was left behind to be killed, wounded, or captured. Having made safety, Churchill abandoned the train and went back on foot to help those left behind. Horsemen with rifles rode him down. He reached for a pistol, but he had laid it down while freeing the engine. He surrendered.

By his own report, this made a sore trial for Churchill. He had exposed himself to artillery and rifle fire for an extended period, but now he had to give up at the prospect of a single bullet. Courage has its deficiency, but also its excess. To run away spooked is the deficiency; to throw one's life down for nothing is the excess. To choose which is right in the heat of fire, when there are not even seconds during which to choose, is a feat that requires courage but consists in prudence, the choosing virtue. The careful reader of this biography will discover that Churchill spent time with one of the great translators of the classics. Then and at other times he learned and eventually wrote very much about the classic themes of the relation between courage and prudence, between the moral and the intellectual virtues, between the circumstances that beset us and the ends that beckon us. For example, he would describe the capacity possessed by the greatest military commander:

> Circumstances alone decide whether a correct conventional maneuver is right or wrong
> . . . . And it is the true comprehension at any given moment of the dynamic sum of all

these constantly shifting forces that constitutes military genius . . . . Nothing but genius, the daemon in man, can answer the riddles of war, and genius, though it may be armed, cannot be acquired, either by reading or experience.

On the one hand, "circumstances alone" must decide. On the other hand, the riddles of war must be answered. Are they answered by the "circumstances alone"? In that case, why must a man be a genius to provide the answer? In a beautiful statement years later Churchill would say that Greece could not be abandoned to Hitler, even by a powerless and jeopardized Britain. He explained:

> By solemn guarantee given before the war, Great Britain had promised them her help. They declared they would fight for their native soil even if neither of their neighbors made common cause with them, and even if we left them to their fate. But we could not do that. There are rules against that kind of thing; and to break those rules would be fatal to the honor of the British Empire, without which we could neither hope nor deserve to win this hard war.

Where, one wonders, can one find these "rules" that command you to risk your life and the life of your nation? Apparently, they can be known. Apparently, they are beyond the power of circumstances, and in some cases, at least, they too must decide "alone."

These two quotations make an interesting contrast. In one case, Churchill the historian is writing about events that happened 200 years before his lifetime. In that case, Churchill directs us to the details, to their commanding nature, to the necessity they represent. When we are studying history, or when we are evaluating the actions of others, especially in politics, these details are distant from us. We know our own circumstances very well. We act in accord with them all the time. We forget that others must do the same. For this reason we lose proportion. Great achievements diminish in our eyes; we fall into the easy and satisfying habit of thinking we could do better. We expect utopian solutions.

In the other case, Churchill is acting as a statesman in desperate circumstances. The life of the nation is threatened. Death, wounds, and servitude await the population, man, woman, and child, and they know it. London is in flames. Churchill has called upon them never to surrender. Here circumstances are in the most urgent condition. If these circumstances are to decide "alone," then what can they possibly decide? The British cannot save the Greeks; they will fall anyway. The British forces are needed desperately at home. So why send them? Because, it seems, there are ultimate things beyond any narrow calculation of advantage, plightings of soul that simply must not be violated. These things are more precious than victory; than life itself. Would these things demand that *everything* be sent to the Greeks, not just a force, but the *whole* force? Apparently not. But something must be done to satisfy honor and keep faith, lest the British concede the very principles that render them worthy of victory.

In his speculative writings, then, Churchill points in some cases to the most immediate practical necessities. In pursuing urgent tasks, Churchill points in some cases to the heavens. He does not provide a formula for explaining when to do which. But he does provide his own example of how thought informs action, and how action rises to contemplation.

A CROSS OF THOUGHT AND ACTION

One reason for the length of the official biography is found in Churchill's habit of writing. He writes as much as he acts; he writes about every action. His books number 16, filling 33 volumes. His speeches, written almost exclusively by him, take up more than 8,000 large and crowded pages in a series that only purports to be exhaustive. His articles are almost numberless, and his memos and letters stream out in eloquent profusion. His writings have a dual character. They are like the actions he takes in being themselves acts of ambition, meant to advance himself and his causes as much as any decision he makes or vote he casts, as much as any charge he launches or retreat he endures. At the same time they are explanations and reflections, commentaries on the way of politics, as politics reflects the way of life. He wrote famously, and also wisely, that "a man's Life must be nailed to a cross either of Thought or Action." He made his choice, but the record he leaves in pursuit of action is a fabric woven seamlessly of thought and action together. He invites us both in precept and example to contemplate their relation and to learn the dance of their distinctness and inseparability.

What did the people who saw the action of the armored train think? Haldane: "indomitable perseverance." Captain Wiley: "as brave a man as could be found." Colonel Long: "thinks Mr. [Churchill] and the engine-driver will get the VC [Victoria Cross, the highest military decoration for valor]." Private Walls: "he walked about in it all as coolly as if nothing was going on . . . . His presence and way of going on were as much good as 50 men would have been." General Joubert (Boer commander), urging the Boer government not to release Churchill from captivity: "I urge you that he must be guarded and watched as dangerous for our war; otherwise he can still do us a lot of harm."

What was Churchill thinking? The record tells us four things.

First, Churchill was thinking about danger. Courage requires a sense of danger. On several occasions he exposed himself to harm to gain the notice of others, and that was apparently part of his motive in this action of the armored train. To his mother he wrote, "Bullets . . . are not worth considering. Besides I am so conceited I do not believe the Gods would create so potent a being as myself for so prosaic an ending." Also: "Nothing in life is so exhilarating as to be shot at without result." From the prison to his American friend Bourke Cochran, Churchill wrote, however: "I think more experience of war would make me religious. The powerlessness of the atom is terribly brought home to me, and from the highest human court of appeals we feel a great desire to apply to yet a higher authority. Philosophy cannot convince the bullet." Churchill was afraid. His fear reminded him of something outside the circumstances; something above them. He did what he did despite the fear, in mind of the thing above it.

Second, Churchill was thinking about politics. Speaking with Haldane right after they were both captured, and as they walked wearily over damp ground, Churchill thanked him for giving him the chance. He realized that Haldane would not get so much glory from the episode as would he. Churchill had been able to act "in full view of the Durban Light Infantry and the railway personnel." This would open "the door for him to enter the House of Commons." He would, he committed, thank

Haldane in the newspaper. He took for granted that Haldane had wanted as much as he to get out there in the open and be shot at with people watching.

Churchill the warrior is preparing to be Churchill the statesman, and already he shows signs of understanding the difference between these realms. Much of this understanding was obtained through the observation of battle. The best of his early books, *The River War*, was published while he was in South Africa, nine days before he was taken prisoner. It concerns the invasion of the Sudan by a British force to avenge the death of General Gordon and retake Khartoum. The invasion is led by General Kitchener, a man with whom Churchill had many differences both then and later. Kitchener refused to permit Churchill to join the force, and, of course, Churchill joined anyway. The battle was the occasion of the last British cavalry charge and, of course, Churchill was in the charge.

One would think that Churchill would exult in the victories of the Sudan campaign, especially the climactic Battle of Omdurman. He fought bravely there. The British won an overwhelming victory—as overwhelming as the American victories in the first and second Gulf wars. Churchill's story of it in *The River War* is like most of his writing, meant to make his reputation and advance his political career. The people of Britain, at that time an imperial people, were indignant over the killing of Gordon. Whereas Churchill admired the Boers openly and highly (except for their attitude to the black people of the region), he despised the Mahdi who ruled the Sudan and his regime. Still, his description of the Battle of Omdurman is no mere exercise in glory.

On the plains of Omdurman Churchill noticed the horror of modern war, a theme that he would return to over the course of his life. In coming to understand its profound costs he saw war first as a political more than a military event, a line of thought that would be sharpened by the terrors of the First World War. Here, in describing the breaking of the Dervish charge at Omdurman, he introduces it:

> The "White Flags" were nearly over the crest. In another minute they would become visible to the batteries. Did they realise what would come to meet them? They were in a dense mass, 2,800 yards from the 32nd Field Battery and the gunboats. The ranges were known. It was a matter of machinery. The more distant slaughter passed unnoticed, as the mind was fascinated by the approaching horror. In a few seconds swift destruction would rush on these brave men.

Notice the phrase "it was a matter of machinery." Churchill continues that "it was a terrible sight, for as yet they had not hurt us at all, and it seemed an unfair advantage to strike thus cruelly when they could not reply." Unfair, he says. Then he describes the British:

> The infantry fired steadily and stolidly, without hurry or excitement, for the enemy were far away and the officers careful. Besides, the soldiers were interested in the work and took great pains. But presently the mere physical act became tedious. The tiny figures seen over the slide of the backsight seemed a little larger, but also fewer at each successive volley. The rifles grew hot—so hot that they had to be changed for those of the reserve companies. The Maxim guns exhausted all the water in their jackets, and several had to be refreshed from the water-bottles of the Cameron Highlanders before they could go on with their deadly work. The empty cartridge-cases, tinkling to the ground, formed a small but growing heap beside each man. And all the time out on the plain

on the other side bullets were shearing through flesh, smashing and splintering bone; blood spouted from terrible wounds; valiant men were struggling on through a hell of whistling metal, exploding shells, and spurting dust—suffering, despairing, dying.

This juxtaposition between the mechanized modern army and the valiant but impotent cavalry portends a generation of writing that Churchill will do about the character of modern war, the immense destructiveness it implies, and the moral problem it presents. He did not understand this moral problem then, or in the future, in only the common way in which most of us view it: a very large number of people can die. Churchill hated that aspect of it, but that is not perhaps the worst. Worse than that is the severance of the moral virtues, particularly courage, from the achievement of victory. Now it would be "a matter of machinery." Worse also is the way modern organized societies, when impelled upon each other, could be required to devote their every resource, even the "last dying kick," to war. What then becomes of liberal society, of limited government, of the protection of private rights as the first purpose of politics? It seemed possible to Churchill that liberal society contains within itself the seed of its destruction, that the prosperity it generated would contrive and fund its own annihilation. Having this problem, liberal society is still also the best available. How can it be rescued?

Churchill came to think it the task of generalship, but more than that, of statesmanship, to avoid these evils. Under modern conditions especially the wrong kind of victory would be the same as defeat. He spent much of his life pursuing the right kind. This helps to make sense of the name that Churchill wanted to give to the Second World War: "The Unnecessary War," a name that seems to besmirch the conflict in which he won his greatest glory. The key lessons to be drawn from the war were how, by prescient combination, by strong preparedness, by recognition of the danger of aggressive tyranny, to avoid such a thing in the future. Lest we think this a perfect solution, remember that Churchill tells us that the kind of genius necessary "cannot be acquired, either by reading or experience." He goes on to say that it is "much rarer than the largest and purest diamonds."

This means that someone possessing rare ability in politics could meet, in principle, a need of supreme urgency. Which leads to the third thing on Churchill's mind as he fought his battle, suffered his capture, and planned his escape in South Africa in those fateful days: time. He was in a hurry. Upon capture, he began immediately a series of urgent appeals to the Boer government for his release. He was, he said, a war correspondent. Sweltering "in durance vile," as he put it in a letter to a friend, was not part of his plan. In these letters he artfully downplayed his part in the escape. He compared himself to the railroad employees seeking to retire to safety with all the scary guns around. One of his letters, revealing about many things, complains that he is almost 25 years old and is nearly out of time. He did not seem to think that he would live to 90, which however he did, nor that his greatest deeds would be done past age 65, which however they were.

Finally, Churchill was thinking about victory. He wanted to win. This had two aspects. One was grand and aggressive: by the time he reached his prison in Pretoria, the Boer capital, he had figured out the lay of the city and where the officers and the enlisted men were kept. Upon reaching the prison, he proposed to the British POW command that the officers overcome their guards and march to the nearby stadium. There they could liberate the British enlisted men, take the capital, seize the president, and end the war. The commanders refused despite much insisting, so Churchill confined himself to the more prosaic matter of his own personal escape. This he effected soon enough to become a hero and, as intended, a Member of Parliament. He still regretted missing the chance to win the whole war with a single blow.

A PHOTOGRAPH

They say a picture is worth a thousand words. One of the best photographs of Winston Churchill was taken three days after his capture. It is not published in the biography, a rare instance of a worthy thing not being included there, but the *CRB* has kindly broken precedent and included it here. The photograph does not mean so much without knowing the events surrounding it. Taken together with its circumstances, one can see in it something essential about Churchill.

Notice that most of the men look bedraggled and down, as well they might, having fought a battle, watched their friends wounded and killed, suffered capture, stood and marched in the rain, traveled by train under guard, and arrived in the capital of the enemy three days after the battle to be displayed before the townspeople. Notice around them are gathered the burghers of Pretoria, to gawk at the vanquished who have committed the indignity of surrender.

Two of the party seem different. One stands with his hands on his hips, his chin out. He is defiant. He looks a fighter. Likely the guards will watch him closely.

The other, Churchill, is aloof, off to the right, erect yet relaxed. He looks at the camera, and though we cannot know if he saw it, he did know he was being observed by a throng. He looks unconcerned; not quite contemptuous. He seems at ease and untroubled. But you cannot quite mistake that he seems not only watched, but watching.

It is the contrast between the face and the posture, on the one hand, and the actions he was taking throughout this time, that makes one think. Churchill is embarked at that moment on both the planning and the execution of several contradictory courses of action. He will inspire an attack on the whole capital; he will argue that he is a non-combatant; he will write his friends of the valor of others while he meditates his own election to Parliament as a hero; he will plan his own escape; he will write for the press; he will talk with his captors, befriend them, and find out information. All this is moving in his mind and very soon in his actions, and yet he shows neither distress nor impatience in his demeanor. As on the battlefield before their shells, so in the capital before his captors, he seems—in the one photograph we have of him in that episode of his life—cool, self-contained, almost indifferent.

Half a lifetime later, a certain former German corporal, in the fatal decision of his life, turned his back on this man and attacked to the east. He might have benefited from seeing this photograph and knowing its story. He might have thought longer before he exposed his entire nation to this calm captive, this vigorous author and proud warrior. Churchill's letters and articles from South Africa revealed the seed of an eloquence that would stir a nation to stand and fight. Churchill's negotiations with the Boers portended the skill that would finally outmaneuver the appeasers in 1940. Churchill's self-restraint and self-effacement before his captors, as he plotted their undoing, were stirrings of a capacity to stoop and to woo that would entice Franklin Roosevelt. The man in this photograph was a man who could live amidst the fires of 1940 and sleep well every night, get up every morning ready to fight, and think it, even at the moment, the best time he had ever had.

Here then, with six volumes and Churchill's greatest achievements still to come, we may reach an initial conclusion. The young Churchill is a character of unusual type. He can fight with the pen and the sword alike. He can say just what he means, in light of the circumstances, even when he is in a hurry, and even under duress. He takes risks that astound the bravest among the onlookers. Then, within minutes, he surrenders before a different risk. He writes out carefully his reasons for just about every action he takes.

This is a man of action. He explains that the quality of the actions can only be measured amidst the circumstances in which they take place. In one sense, this behemoth of a biography exists to explain these circumstances. It exists to explain, for example, that photograph, or rather what it means that the man in the photograph looks just the way he does. Perhaps you will think him a charlatan, a show-off, an opportunist. Here is the material with which to prove your case. Together with his great biographer, he has helped to supply it.

Then again you may think him a hero, bold, assertive, yet humble, a genius who saved the world. Perhaps you will see him as one of the "ambassadors of Providence sent to reveal to their fellow men their unknown selves." Here then is a story of how such a life operates. It is beautiful to see. It is an adventure.

The Greatness and Decline
of American Oratory

Diana Schaub

(Summer 2007)

"To keep silent is the most useful service that a mediocre talker can render to the public." So says Alexis de Tocqueville in his chapter in *Democracy in America* "On Parliamentary Eloquence in the United States." Unfortunately, democratic assemblies encourage the mediocre to sound off—often and at length. There are no back-benchers in the American political system. The result of this universal striving for something to say is not *eloquentia perfecta* but bombast. Tocqueville explains that when Americans talk about matters within the small circuit of their daily lives their speech is simple, direct, and dull. When they are forced out of their accustomed range, however, as public figures are, they have nothing to latch onto but glittering generalities. Tocqueville says of democratic man: "He has only very particular and very clear ideas, or very general and very vague notions; the intermediate space is empty."

Anthony Trollope, who like Tocqueville wrote a two-volume account of his visit to the United States, noted the same phenomenon of the bombastic blowhard:

> He was master of that wonderful fluency which is peculiarly the gift of an American. He went on from one sentence to another with rhythmic tones and unerring pronunciation. He never faltered, never repeated his words, never fell into those vile half-muttered hems and haws by which an Englishman in such a position so generally betrays his timidity. But during the whole time of my remaining in the room he did not give expression to a single thought. He went on from one soft platitude to another, and uttered words from which I would defy any one of his audience to carry away with them anything. And yet it seemed to me that his audience was satisfied.

While Trollope is disgusted by this spectacle, Tocqueville regards the tolerance that Americans show toward bad speechifying as a mark of their democratic sophistication. They accept these verbal parades as an evil inseparable from the good of representative government.

Moreover, for Tocqueville, the flip side of the democratic vice of bloviation is genuine oratorical virtue: "I see nothing more admirable or more powerful than a great orator discussing great affairs within a democratic assembly." Tocqueville explains how the democratic proclivity for general notions can enlarge and elevate rhetoric. Such speeches can appeal even beyond national borders: "from the first debates that took place in the little colonial assemblies of America in the period of the Revolution, Europe was moved." Democratic orators, relying on "verities drawn from human nature," speak to all mankind.

American Speeches, a two-volume collection from the Library of America, very successfully winnows out the petty and the dry, and mostly winnows out the pretentious and pompous, leaving a selection of mighty speeches on the twin themes of liberty and equality. Most of the names one would expect are here, along with some lesser known worthies. Those garnering the most selections are Abraham Lincoln and Franklin Delano Roosevelt with eight apiece, Martin Luther King, Jr., with six, and John F. Kennedy and Ronald Reagan with five each. In both volumes there is a mix of elected officials and what might be called outside agitators—individuals who seek to reach public opinion directly through moral suasion rather than indirectly through the medium of law and legislation. In both volumes, the agitators are usually, but not uniformly, women and blacks. Volume I has Frances Wright, Angelina Grimké Weld, Henry Highland Garnet, Elizabeth Cady Stanton, Sojourner Truth, and Frederick Douglass, along with the radical abolitionists Wendell Phillips and John Brown. Volume II has Sojourner Truth, Susan B. Anthony, Elizabeth Cady Stanton, Ida B. Wells, Booker T. Washington, Mary Church Terrell, Carrie Chapman Catt, Betty Friedan, Malcolm X (the only speaker to address "enemies" as well as friends), and Martin Luther King, Jr., along with the radical socialist Eugene V. Debs and free speech activist Mario Savio.

Each volume also has one speech by a Native American. These are painful pieces to read. Although the movements for political inclusion by blacks and women involved suffering and tragedy, they were ultimately successful. By contrast, the Native American struggle was never about inclusion. It was an encounter between incompatible ways of life. In addressing "the Chief Warrior of the United States" (George Washington), the Seneca leader Red Jacket pleads:

We wish to see your words [of peace] verified to our children, and children's children. You enjoy all the blessings of this life; to you, therefore, we look to make provision that the same may be enjoyed by our children. This wish comes from our heart; but we add that our happiness cannot be great if in the introduction of your ways we are put under too much constraint.

Despite the efforts of Washington and other American statesmen to set our relations with the Indians upon a foundation of justice, in less than a century, the Nez Percé leader Chief Joseph speaks these words of surrender:

He who led on the young men is dead. It is cold, and we have no blankets; the little children are freezing to death. My people, some of them, have run away to the hills, and have no blankets, no food. No one knows where they are—perhaps freezing to death. I want to have time to look for my children, and see how many of them I can find. Maybe I shall find them among the dead. Hear me, my chiefs! I am tired; my heart is sick and sad. From where the sun now stands I will fight no more forever.

Since Cain and Abel, farmers and nomads have been at odds. Coexistence is not possible and the land-hungry farmers who build fences almost always conquer or kill the unsettled and uncivilized, be they shepherds or hunters. Tocqueville, who witnessed the spreading destruction, regarded the extinction of the Indian peoples as inevitable and inexpressibly sad.

Despite occupying only seven of 1,682 pages, these two speeches capture something essential about that extra-constitutional, indeed pre-constitutional conflict. The nation's other "irrepressible conflict" (the phrase is William Seward's from an 1858 speech) provoked a constitutional crisis. Because the institution of African slavery raised fundamental questions about the national self-understanding, it looms much larger in the collective conscience and in the pages of these volumes, confirming Frederick Douglass's claim that "the destiny of the nation has the Negro for its pivot, and turns upon the question as to what shall be done with him." The issue of slavery absolutely dominates the first volume; the problem of the color-line is prominent in the second volume, though not quite to the same degree, testimony perhaps to the nation's confirmed trajectory towards equality. Thus, we move from the crisis over slavery to the controversy over civil rights and finally to the platitudes of political correctness. The last speech in this collection is President Clinton's commemoration of the Little Rock Nine on the 40th anniversary of the desegregation of Central High. While the speech is (as a blurb on the inside flap helpfully says) "a heartfelt tribute," it certainly did not require any moral courage to draft and deliver, unlike, say, Lincoln's House Divided speech or King's Montgomery speech. Although Clinton hinted at a particularly insidious version of lingering race prejudice ("We must not replace the tyranny of segregation with the tragedy of low expectations"), he resolutely refused to examine the connection between this characteristically liberal condescension (which fails to recognize itself as bigotry) and paternalistic policies like affirmative action and racial set-asides. The speech is a disappointing close to the two volumes. Pabulum does not sustain progress.

Astonishingly, although these volumes were published in 2006, they take no account of September 11 or the war on terrorism. The first volume is subtitled: *Political Oratory from the Revolution to the Civil War*. It opens with James Otis in 1761 and closes with Lincoln's Second Inaugural in 1865. The second volume is subtitled: *Political Oratory from Abraham Lincoln to Bill Clinton* (not William Jefferson Clinton, mind you, but "Bill"). It opens with Lincoln's speech on Reconstruction given just four days before his death and closes with the Little Rock commemoration in 1997. I suppose one could justify an editorial decision to end the volume there for thematic or even chronological reasons (closing out the millennium), but it can't help seeming blatantly and inexcusably partisan—refusing to acknowledge September 11 so as not to have to include President Bush's remarks at the National Cathedral on September 14th (the National Day of Prayer and Remembrance), or his remarks to Congress on September 20th, or his 2002 State of the Union address (the "axis of evil" speech). If the editor didn't want to entitle the second volume *Political Oratory from Abraham Lincoln to George W. Bush*, alternatives could have been found: *Political Oratory from Reconstruction to the War on Terrorism* or better just *Political Oratory from Reconstruction to September 11* (better because the outcome of the war is in doubt, while the catalyzing event and its significance are not). It comes as no surprise to learn that the editor, Ted Widmer, was a Clinton speechwriter. I can sympathize with the temptation to plump for one's boss and oneself (isn't *Political Oratory from Abraham Lincoln to Bill Clinton* another way of saying *Political Oratory from Abraham*

Lincoln to Ted Widmer?), but the editors of the Library of America should not have allowed such transparent egocentrism and partisanship.

Aside from Bill and Ted's excellent adventure, there are a handful of other questionable choices. There are two powerful anti-Vietnam speeches, both from King, but there is no speech setting forth the rationale for our involvement; the most likely candidate would be Nixon's "silent majority" speech of November 3, 1969. (Incidentally, Nixon does have two entries, his Checkers speech and his remarks to his staff on leaving the White House—both startlingly self-revelatory.) Although there are seven Democratic National Convention speeches, there is only one Republican National Convention speech (Goldwater's in 1964). Even then, the second volume does not include the likeliest Democratic choices, such as Barbara Jordan's 1976 speech. Instead, we are given Jordan's remarks to the House Judiciary Committee during the Nixon impeachment proceedings. But there is no equivalent speech from Clinton's impeachment, say from Henry Hyde. And finally, there is nothing on the culture wars (no reference whatever to the controversy over abortion or the "naked public square"). A good choice would have been Reagan's March 8, 1983 speech to the National Association of Evangelicals.

Juxtaposing the two volumes reveals striking changes in the locus and character of American political rhetoric. The cover art epitomizes the shift. Volume I has a painting of a robed Patrick Henry declaiming before the Virginia House of Burgesses. It is clear he is speaking to a body of distinguished equals, men who will have their own thoughts on the matter at hand, and one suspects, rather high standards for persuasive speech. The second volume has a photo of President Kennedy speaking in front of three microphones to an undepicted, but one assumes mass, audience. In the first volume there are only seven speeches by sitting presidents, including three from Lincoln. In the second volume, there are 34. Even more telling is that from the Revolution through World War I, there are 19 congressional floor speeches, mostly by senators. After Henry Cabot Lodge's speech in opposition to the League of Nations, there is not a single floor speech (though there are two brief statements made in committee). Oratory and Congress have declined in tandem. The erudite Lodge was the last to employ extensive Latin in a speech; there is one simple Latin phrase in Kennedy's "ich bin ein Berliner" speech, but nothing like the full sentences from men steeped in literature and history.

The only compensation for the decline is that as the speeches get worse, they mostly get shorter. When all you have are bullet-points, your ammunition is pretty quickly spent. Modern presidential speeches are composed of dry, detailed lists of promised programs sandwiched between warmed-over boilerplate. It's the very combination that Tocqueville predicted: the boring particulars and the vapid generalizations; "the intermediate space is empty." The richness of earlier rhetoric, particularly in the Senate, is on display in the great triumvirate of Clay, Calhoun, and Webster. Volume I contains the speech each made in the Senate on the Compromise of 1850. Clay's speech alone is 67 pages long and must have taken at least six hours to deliver. This is not filibustering where a senator reads aloud names from the phone book. This is closely reasoned argumentation on the constitutional powers of the federal government with respect to slavery. Seeing the length of these speeches, I intended to skim them but couldn't. They were gripping precisely because they made demands on the listener.

A more concentrated exhilaration is experienced in reading Lincoln's speeches. Lincoln managed to accomplish his aims in dramatically shorter compass while speaking to a broad audience. You know you're in the presence of sustained dialectics because the paragraphs can't be reshuffled without loss of meaning. By contrast, there is no logical sequence in the following all-too-typical passage from Lyndon Johnson:

> I want to be the President who educated young children to the wonders of their world.
> I want to be the President who helped to feed the hungry and to prepare them to be taxpayers instead of taxeaters.
> I want to be the President who helped the poor to find their own way and who protected the right of every citizen to vote in every election.
> I want to be the President who helped to end hatred among his fellow men and who promoted love among the people of all races and all regions and all parties.
> I want to be the President who helped to end war among the brothers of this earth.

You could play pick-up-sticks with that collection of indistinguishable banalities. Ordered thought has a different structure. Listen to just the opening phrases of successive paragraphs from Lincoln's First Inaugural:

> I hold, that in contemplation of universal law, ...
> Again, if the United States be not a government proper, ...
> Descending from these general principles, we find the proposition . . . .
> But if the destruction of the Union, ...
> It follows from these views that no State, ...
> I therefore consider that, ...
> In doing this there needs to be no bloodshed or violence. . . .

Hierarchy may be antithetical to democracy, but it is essential to logic. The replacement of paragraphs with bullet-points indicates the democratization or leveling or atomization of logic. The equality of all sentences destroys the connectedness of thought. This scattershot technique of contemporary speechmaking can bowl you over, if the speaker has sufficient force of personality, but it can't pierce your mind or heart, and it certainly can't do it as written rather than spoken. Like Shakespeare's plays, Lincoln's speeches are as powerful in the study as on the stage.

So it is fitting that Lincoln is the fulcrum of these volumes. The first volume culminates in him; the second volume begins with him and is filled with subsequent references to him by both Democrats and Republicans who, unfortunately, invoke his memory more than they imitate his mode of analysis and presentation. Of the invocations, the most interesting is Oppenheimer's 1945 "Speech to the Association of Los Alamos Scientists" comparing the evil of slavery to the new evil of atomic weapons and suggesting a Lincolnian (rather than abolitionist) strategy to address the problem of nuclear proliferation. Oppenheimer remarks how Lincoln saw "that beyond the issue of slavery was the issue of the community of the people of the country, and the issue of the Union."

The multilayered, comprehensive vision of Lincoln is on display through the juxtaposing of Lincoln's carefully calibrated House Divided speech with Seward's more extreme and simplistic "Irrepressible Conflict" speech and again through the juxtaposing of Lincoln's generous (and even delicately humorous) "Speech on Reconstruction" with Thaddeus Stevens's violently anti-Southern "Speech in Congress on Reconstruction." Lincoln demonstrated what "charity for all" meant when he said:

> We all agree that the seceded States, so called, are out of their proper practical relation with the Union; and that the sole object of the government, civil and military, in regard to those States is to again get them into that proper practical relation. I believe it is not only possible, but in fact, easier, to do this, without deciding, or even considering, whether these states have even been out of the Union, than with it. Finding themselves safely at home, it would be utterly immaterial whether they had ever been abroad. Let us all join in doing the acts necessary to restoring the proper practical relations between these states and the Union; and each forever after, innocently indulge his own opinion whether, in doing the acts, he brought the States from without, into the Union, or only gave them proper assistance, they never having been out of it.

Stevens, by contrast, insists that the former rebel States are either out of the Union, in the same situation as a defeated foreign belligerent, or "dead carcasses lying within the Union" having "no more existence than the revolted cities of Latium, two thirds of whose people were colonized and their property confiscated, and their right of citizenship withdrawn by conquering and avenging Rome." In either case, Stevens recommends rigorous rehabilitation: "As there are no symptoms that the people of these provinces will be prepared to participate in constitutional government for some years, I know of no arrangement so proper for them as territorial governments. There they can learn the principles of freedom and eat the fruit of foul rebellion."

Although invocations of Lincoln are standard, only Frederick Douglass in his 1876 "Oration in Memory of Abraham Lincoln," reaches beyond reverence and acknowledgment to a critical consideration of Lincoln's statesmanship. His address is a deeply insightful and appreciative (but far from fawning) account of Lincoln's relation to African-Americans. Douglass was a radical who understood and respected the intransigent moderation of Lincoln. Douglass sums up the paradoxical combination of restraint and resolve in Lincoln's policy, and the underlying reasons for it:

> Viewed from the genuine abolition ground, Mr. Lincoln seemed tardy, cold, dull, and indifferent; but measuring him by the sentiment of his country, a sentiment he was bound as a statesman to consult, he was swift, zealous, radical, and determined.

In the second volume, the lecture platform addresses, like Douglass's, are in general less commonplace and more refreshingly idiosyncratic than those by elected figures. One of the most interesting is a speech by Elizabeth Cady Stanton, appearing before the Judiciary Committee in 1892 on behalf of the women's suffrage amendment (then slated to be the 16th; when finally approved, the 19th). Rather than rehash her case (after 20 years of such appearances, "all the arguments . . . are familiar to all you gentlemen"), she instead draws out the basic attitude toward life implicit in feminism. Her talk is accurately entitled "The Solitude of Self," and it is unflinchingly grim. The adjectives she attaches to this solitude are "immeasurable," "awful," "bitter," and "solemn." Human beings live in radical isolation from one another:

> We ask no sympathy from others in the anxiety and agony of a broken friendship or shattered love. When death sunders our nearest ties, alone we sit in the shadows of our

affliction. Alike mid the greatest triumphs and darkest tragedies of life we walk alone. On the divine heights of human attainments, eulogized and worshiped as a hero or saint, we stand alone. In ignorance, poverty, and vice, as a pauper or criminal, alone we starve or steal. . . . Seeing then that life must ever be a march and a battle, that each soldier must be equipped for his own protection, it is the height of cruelty to rob the individual of a single natural right.

Women require full opportunities for individual development to enable them to face (or even better to outface) the horrors of existence. There is some truth in her existential Hobbesianism, but not the whole truth. She misses the better half of truth, and no more so than when she speaks of motherhood:

> Whatever the theories may be of woman's dependence on man, in the supreme moments of her life he can not bear her burdens. Alone she goes to the gates of death to give life to every man that is born into the world. No one can share her fears, no one can mitigate her pangs; and if her sorrow is greater than she can bear, alone she passes beyond the gates into the vast unknown.

Whether or not man can bear (or at least lighten) woman's burdens, the fact that *she bears him* is testament to the naturalness of human connection—connection that Stanton denies. She declares the relations of mother, wife, sister, and daughter to be "incidental" and points out that "a large class of women may never assume" some of these relations. She's right that not all women become mothers, wives, or sisters, but each and every woman is a daughter, as each and every man is a son—even if abandoned or orphaned. The generational link is inescapable and constitutive of our humanity. It is strange indeed when mothers, who have nursed mewling and puking infants, speak of human self-sovereignty.

Interestingly, Teddy Roosevelt's famous talk on "The Strenuous Life" overlaps with Stanton in certain fundamentals, especially the emphasis on "those virile qualities necessary to win [or for Stanton, to endure] in the stern strife of actual life." T.R., though, wants female hardiness to be directed towards traditional (i.e., natural) female pursuits. Accordingly, his version of human striving has room for shared struggle and joint action:

> The woman must be the housewife, the helpmeet of the homemaker, the wise and fearless mother of many healthy children. In one of Daudet's powerful and melancholy books he speaks of "the fear of maternity, the haunting terror of the young wife of the present day." When such words can be truthfully written of a nation, the nation is rotten to the heart's core. When men fear work or fear righteous war, when women fear motherhood, they tremble on the brink of doom; and well it is that they should vanish from the earth, where they are fit subjects for the scorn of all men and women who are themselves strong and brave and high-minded.

Whatever one thinks of Stanton and Roosevelt, their words are their own, bodying forth their inner convictions. Two speeches that seem to offer even more unmediated expressions of self are Sojourner Truth's wondrous 1851 "Speech to Woman's Rights Convention" and George S. Patton's vulgarity-laced "Speech to Third Army Troops." About the middle of the 20th century, despite all the trumpeting of individualism, the individuality of speech seems to lessen. One begins to sense the homogenizing effects of writing by committee. Of course, from the nation's beginnings, public figures have had the benefit of apprentices and editors. Washington asked Hamilton to prepare a draft of his Farewell Address (an address which is not included here since it was published rather than delivered—leading one to wonder how complete a national picture can be gained from the spoken word); Lincoln had Seward's assistance on his First Inaugural; and Benjamin Franklin suggested key changes in Jefferson's draft of the Declaration of Independence. Nonetheless, speechwriting was not the group-work guild that it is now. Just as the great floor speeches vanish post-World War I, so too apparently do the Lyceum-type speeches. I suspect, however, that one could discover impressive performances at newer venues, such as think tanks and similar associations. There is still an active—though more ideologically fractured—lecture circuit.

The fracturing of public speech is seen in the increasing distance between the partisans of liberty and the partisans of equality, crystallized particularly in presidential and would-be presidential rhetoric. Barry Goldwater's 1964 "Speech to the Republican National Convention" is a paean to freedom: "And this party, with its every action, every word, every breath and every heart beat, has but a single resolve, and that is freedom." Reagan's speeches follow the path cut by Goldwater, defending freedom against centralization at home and tyranny abroad. Equality finds its spokesmen in Johnson, the Kennedys (Robert and Edward, who are both here, more than John), and Jesse Jackson. Johnson's 1965 "Address at Howard University" is the most forthright in that he actually downplays freedom's part in justice:

> That beginning is freedom; and the barriers to that freedom are tumbling down . . . .
> But freedom is not enough . . . . We seek not just legal equity but human ability, not just equality as a right and a theory but equality as a fact and equality as a result . . . .
> To this end equal opportunity is essential, but not enough, not enough . . . . The Negro, like these others [American minorities], will have to rely mostly upon his own efforts.
> But he just can not do it alone.

Tocqueville worried that democratic man would be inclined to sacrifice liberty in the quest for ever greater equality of condition. For Americans, the danger of democratic despotism is peculiarly aggravated when the subject is racial equality. Where race is involved, we are sorely tempted to jettison our principles. For centuries this country refused to acknowledge and protect the equality of rights. Once the nation determined to make amends, instead of simply ensuring equal rights and non-discrimination, we went searching for more expedient routes by which to expiate our national sins. In 1865, a full century before Johnson's Great Society programs, Frederick Douglass warned against such well-intentioned projects:

> In regard to the colored people there is always more that is benevolent, I perceive, than just, manifested towards us. What I ask for the Negro is not benevolence, not pity, not sympathy, but simply *justice*. The American people have always been anxious to know what they shall do with us . . . . I have had but one answer from the beginning. Do nothing with us! Your doing with us has already played the mischief with us. Do nothing with us! If the apples will not remain on the tree of their own strength, if they are worm-eaten at the core, if they are early ripe and disposed to fall, let them fall! . . . And if the Negro cannot stand on his own legs, let him fall also. All I ask is, give him a chance to stand on his own legs! Let him alone! If you see him on his way to school, let him

alone, don't disturb him! If you see him going to the dinner-table at a hotel, let him go! If you see him going to the ballot-box, let him alone, don't disturb him! If you see him going into a work-shop, just let him alone,—your interference is doing him a positive injury. Gen. Banks' "preparation" is of a piece with this attempt to prop up the Negro. Let him fall if he cannot stand alone!

The task of government is to assure that schools and hotels, ballot-boxes and workshops, are accessible to all Americans. Beyond that, Frederick Douglass had faith—the democratic-republican faith—that all individuals are capable of self-government.

At the close of his Cooper Union Address, Lincoln warns against "invocations to Washington, imploring men to unsay what Washington said, and undo what Washington did." One step toward the improvement of political oratory today—both in substance and style—might be for our candidates for elective office (and their speechwriters) to stop talking long enough to read these volumes of *American Speeches*, especially the first. We need to be reminded of what those we are forever invoking really said. Perhaps someone might raise again the banner of "Liberty and equal rights, one and inseparable!" According to an 1859 speech by Carl Schurz, that pairing is the essence of "True Americanism."

V

CURRENT CONTENTIONS

Business as Usual

Charles R. Kesler

(Summer 2006)

George W. Bush is the first president with an MBA (from Harvard Business School, no less), but it's not clear that being a Master of Business Administration has made him a better chief executive. The disarray in Iraq, the debacle after Hurricane Katrina—these aren't exactly the kind of triumphs that the alumni office likes to boast about. Still, things could be worse. He might have gone to the Kennedy School.

Business schools are a relatively new institution: the MBA was invented in the Progressive Era as a way to abort future generations of robber barons. The idea was to train up a class of business *administrators* (the ethos was anti-entrepreneurial) who would expiate capitalism's sins by managing their corporations in keeping with the higher morality. The higher morality was whatever the spirit of the age revealed to professors and high-toned Protestant ministers. Over decades, the pursuit of ethical uplift waned and the pursuit of efficiency and new methods of reading a balance sheet waxed, paving the way for the increasingly empty trendiness of modern management books.

It's hard to say what President Bush absorbed from his management studies. We can only draw inferences, though eventually historians may know more. Defending Donald Rumsfeld a few weeks ago, Bush said, "I hear the voices, and I read the front page, and I know the speculation. But I'm the decider, and I decide what is best. And what's best is for Don Rumsfeld to remain as the secretary of defense." Being the decider-in-chief suggests one paradigm of modern management: the executive who makes the final decisions, the tough calls. He "hears" and even listens to others before deciding, but the point of a decision (from *decidere*, to cut off) is to be decisive—not to reason your way to a judgment that can be explained to others.

Bush's management style is long on decisions and short on explanations. He's apparently better at listening to others than questioning their views, which might seem to detract from his decisiveness. In other words, he prefers to have around him people whose judgment he trusts implicitly, even as he insists that they trust his implicitly. This isn't simple cronyism or "hackocracy," as the Left charges. But neither is it a model of political wisdom. It leads to a disinclination to deliberate, a reliance on peremptory assertions of subordinates' good character to quiet doubt about their judgments, and a certain habitual speechlessness. On ordinary rhetorical occasions, Bush and his text seem hardly acquainted. On great occasions, he tends to overshoot the mark, calling for impossibilities like an "end to evil." He lacks a rhetorical mean, much less the rhetorical mien that served Ronald Reagan so well.

Democrats usually turn for inspiration to the universities and law schools, Republicans to business and business schools. Republicans love to call for applying the businessman's common sense to government problems, like balancing the budget or rebuilding New Orleans. Rumsfeld, a former Fortune 500 executive, is applying business methods (just-in-time inventories, information networks, strict control of labor costs) to try to transform the Pentagon and, while he's at it, win the war in Iraq. The precedents aren't entirely encouraging. In the 1960s, Secretary of Defense Robert McNamara tried to revolutionize the Pentagon using the systems analysis techniques he'd championed in his former job as president of the Ford Motor Company. He succeeded in discrediting himself, the techniques, and the war he was trying to win.

Pray things work out better this time. In general, however, the analogy between business and politics so beloved by Republicans is a flawed one. At the simplest level, politicians report to a large electorate and have fixed terms of office, and businessmen do not; and although the latter can hire and fire at will, the former cannot, and thus face vast, recalcitrant bureaucracies.

Second, government deals not merely with property, vital as that is, but also with life and liberty. Government thus involves issues of national defense, criminal justice, and other "involuntary transactions" backed up by a monopoly on the legitimate use of force. Third, though both pursuits involve self-interest, economic self-interest is less complicated. By contrast, there are many forms of political self-interest, frequently in conflict: Should you desire security, or glory? Low taxes, or a balanced budget? Much political skill must be devoted to persuading people where, exactly, their interest lies. (This is the rhetorical part, at which Bush doesn't excel.) Finally, and most significantly, politics has to reconcile multiple goals—consent, security, liberty, prosperity, justice, virtue—in the presence of continuing disagreements about both means and ends.

These inherent differences frustrate, eventually, all businesslike schemes of government. Too bad they don't teach that in business school.

The Presidential Nomination Mess

James W. Ceaser

(Fall 2008)

It is a peculiarity of American government that after more than 200 years no fixed system exists for selecting the president of the United States. Almost every nomination contest brings with it a different arrangement for the schedule of primaries, the allocation of delegates, and the regulation of campaign finance. No one can get used to the system before it has changed again.

This year was surely no exception. The start date of the process was moved up to January 3, with the Iowa caucus virtually ushering in the New Year. There was an unprecedented bunching of more than 20 contests, including both California and New York, on February 5, dubbed "Tsunami Tuesday," to distinguish it from "Mega-super Tuesday" (March 2) of 2004, and from merely "Super Tuesday" before that. The nation is running out of superlatives. With so many contests scheduled up front, most of the candidates formally announced their candidacies and began intense fundraising in the spring of 2007, a full year and a half before the final election. A battery of debates followed, saturating the cable networks throughout the summer and fall.

If, as Alexis de Tocqueville once remarked, the presidential election period marks a kind of "national crisis" in which the political elites are distracted from the normal business of governing, then America is courting danger to the point of obsession.

Given this frontloaded schedule, most analysts predicted that the nomination decisions would be resolved by early February. Things didn't work out that way, especially for the Democrats. What was supposed to be a mad dash turned into a grueling marathon. Judgments about the system seemed to shift as time went on. The early chorus of objections that the contests would be settled too quickly, precluding adequate deliberation, gave way by May to plaintive objections that the campaign had gone on too long, risking division to the party and the nation. By June, all seemed to be for reform, though as usual not the same reform nor for the same reasons.

Is this any way to pick the men (and women) who would be president?

RULES OF THE GAME

To invoke the wooden terminology of political science, the presidential nomination system has not achieved full "institutionalization." In an institutionalized process, rules precede the activity to be governed and structure it in patterned ways; and they remain in place long enough to produce reasonably clear effects. In sports, that's known as the "rules of the game." Nothing approaching this salutary authority governs the nominating process. Candidates and their supporters regularly scheme to change state laws and (in the case of the Democrats) party rules to try to benefit their campaigns, though they are frequently burned by their own machinations. Because each year's arrangement is different, the candidates must make new strategic assessments. (Rudy Giuliani, for example, disastrously concluded that the 2008 schedule allowed him to ignore all the contests up to Florida, a decision netting him one delegate for his $59 million investment). Non-institutionalization has become, all on its own, a factor that influences who is nominated, helping candidates who judge better—or perhaps just guess rightly—the effects of the rules on their race. Whether this skill is a sound predictor of presidential performance is another matter.

Imagine what the rest of the world must think at observing this spectacle. As late as November 20, 2007, six weeks before the provisional start of the campaign, the secretary of state of New Hampshire was preparing to move his state's primary date up (to before Christmas!) to preempt a possible move by the state of Michigan. Two of the largest states (Michigan and Florida) went on to hold primary elections that, in the case of the Democrats, were initially not recognized by the national party because they contravened national party rules—which of course did not prevent Hillary Clinton, who had signed off on the rules, from solemnly demanding, as a matter of highest principle, that the people's voice be heard. And it was truly bizarre that Puerto Rico, a U.S. territory with no vote in the presidential election, had been allocated almost twice as many delegates in the Democratic Party as West Virginia, a state potentially critical to the general election. (The excuse was that since actual delegates after a certain point in the process do not matter anyhow, it would be clever to make a symbolic gesture to Hispanic voters.) Finally, there was Rush Limbaugh's "Operation Chaos," which asked his legions of ditto-heads to vote in Democratic races to gum up the results.

Far from being a model, our presidential selection process is unworthy of a banana republic. To add insult to injury, it is unclear where, if anywhere, the effective authority resides to implement any serious reform. Each state can change its own laws, but not the laws of any other state. Each national party—or, in the ideal case, the two of them working together—can influence state laws, but they are loath to take on this assignment; and the states, in any case, are not obliged to listen. As for the federal government, it is disputed to this day whether Congress has the constitutional power to legislate in this domain.

How did we get ourselves into this situation? No one, surely, could have planned it this way. And no one ever did.

THE FOUNDERS' INTENT

If blame must be assigned, a portion of it must go to the founders for instituting a system that never fully succeeded in managing the problem. But it was certainly not for want of trying. The Constitution, contrary to popular impression, created not three but four national institutions: the presidency, the Congress, the Supreme Court, and the presidential selection system (centered on the Electoral College). The question of presidential selection was just that important to the founders, and they created a system that was meant to institutionalize the process from start to finish—from the gathering and winnowing phase up through the final election. The Constitution, in other words, was intended to control "nominating" as well as electing: the electors, meeting in their respective states, would vote for two people for president (at least one of whom had to come from another state), thus nominating and electing at the same time. When the votes were collected and opened on the floor of the House of Representatives, the winner (if he had a majority) would become president, and the runner-up would become vice president.

The nominating plan, as matters turned out, worked as intended only when there was no real need for it. The electors twice nominated the one individual in American history, George Washington, whose choice was never in doubt. By the time Washington stepped down, national political parties, which the founders never expected, had begun to impose their influence on the electors' nominating function, promoting the parties' own candidates for president and vice president and effectively removing this process from constitutional jurisdiction.

Despite this failure, the founders introduced a comprehensive way of looking at the selection process that continued to exercise a broad influence. One of their simplest but most important principles was to consider the presidential selection system a means to an end, not an end in itself. Its purpose was to elevate a meritorious person to the presidency, in a way that promoted the Constitution's design for the office. Their explanation of the system did not celebrate the process as a positive event in its own right, much less as the consummation of American democracy. They focused instead on the need to avoid the many potential problems and dangers attendant on the choice of a chief executive.

The principal objective was to choose a sound statesman, someone "pre-eminent for ability and virtue," in the words of *The Federalist*, by a method that satisfied republican standards of legitimacy. (The system, with electors to be chosen by the state legislatures or the public, was a remarkably democratic arrangement for its day.) How to identify a person of "virtue" was the crux of the issue. The best way would be a judgment based largely on the individual's record of public service, as determined finally by the electors. The founders' intent was above all to prevent having the decision turn on a demonstration of skill in the "popular arts" as displayed in a campaign. They were deeply fearful of leaders deploying popular oratory as the means of winning distinction; this would open the door to demagoguery, which, as the ancients had shown, was the greatest threat to the maintenance of moderate popular government. By demagoguery, the founders did not mean merely the fomenting of class envy, or harsh, angry appeals to regressive forces; they also had in mind the softer, more artful designs of a Pericles or a Caesar, who appealed to hopeful expectations, "those brilliant appearances of genius and patriotism, which, like transient meteors, sometimes mislead as well as dazzle" (*Federalist* 68). The greatest demagogues would be those who escaped the label altogether.

The selection system was also designed to promote the more elusive goal of shaping the tone of the nation's political class. By sending a clear signal of how and how not to be considered for the presidency, the system was intended to structure the careers of the most spirited leaders, discouraging them from cultivating the popular arts and encouraging them to establish strong records of public service. The task was to make virtue the ally of interest, in order to avoid the danger expressed in Alexander Pope's couplet: "The same ambition can destroy or save / And makes a patriot as it makes a knave."

KING CAUCUS

The founders' nomination system could not survive the advent of political parties during Washington's second administration. Since that time, some four or five (depending on how you count them) methods of selecting presidential candidates have been tried: the congressional caucus (1796–1820); a brief interlude of non-partisan self-selection (1824–1828); the national nominating convention under the control of party organizations (1832–1908); a "mixed" system balancing popular choice with the previous convention system (1912–1968); and the modern system of popular choice (since 1972).

When national parties took control of the nominating function in 1796, it was not by design but in fulfillment of the very logic of a party in a democratic system. To win power through election requires a party to concentrate support behind one person. Otherwise, party supporters might divide their votes among several, allowing a candidate from the opposition party to win. Political parties did not seek to subvert the Constitution's aims for the selection system, but in assuming the function of nominating they added a criterion for selection—fidelity to party principles—that was and still is in some tension with the constitutional spirit of the presidency.

But how would the parties decide—or who among them would decide—on the nominees for executive office? At first, the task fell, *faute de mieux*, to a meeting of the delegation of the party's members of Congress. The originators of the congressional caucus, whoever they were, never viewed themselves as founding a new institution, however. Only afterwards, when the caucus was challenged beginning in the mid-1810s, did its defenders begin to think in these terms. They justified it modestly on the practical grounds that the caucus was the only arrangement available at the time. It also served the party's purposes, and gave the choice to a group well suited to judge the candidates' qualities. In this sense, at least, it kept the founders' goal in mind.

The caucus came under criticism for placing too much power in the hands of a small Washington group, in contrast to the more popular plan envisaged in the Constitution, which had left nomination to electors from each state. In a brilliant public relations ploy, someone branded the institution "King Caucus," a label that helped to insure the institution's demise. A further, more trenchant criticism was that the caucus involved members of Congress in the task of selecting the president, which, as John Quincy Adams noted, "places the President in a state of undue subserviency to the members of the legislature." (Adams might well have had in mind the strong signals sent by some Republican members of Congress to President James Madison in 1812 to go to war with Great Britain.)

The greatest problem the caucus confronted, however, stemmed from growing opposition to party nomination of any kind. When the Federalist Party collapsed as James Monroe assumed the presidency in 1817, the nation was left with only one party. Monroe responded not just by declaring victory for the Democratic-Republicans, but by calling for the elimination of all vestiges of partisanship, which he called the "curse of the country." His aim, which won the day among much of the political class in Washington, was the restoration of the founders' original idea of nonpartisanship. This was the meaning of the Era of Good Feelings.

Monroe's position put enormous pressure on the caucus system, which many Americans now wished to jettison outright. Even those who still believed in political parties found themselves on the defensive. If there were only one party, and all presidential aspirants were faithful members, what need was there any longer to subordinate the individual to the party? There was also the undeniable fact that with only a single party, the caucus was not merely nominating a presidential candidate but picking the president as well. The institution found itself with fewer and fewer supporters, and as the 1824 election approached the "King" was well on his way to exile.

PUTTING PARTY OVER PERSON

The 1824 election took place without binding party nominations and featured, as a result, a multiplicity of candidates (Adams, Andrew Jackson, William Crawford, and Henry Clay). With no formal starting point, electoral activity began very early, and with so many contenders no one received an electoral majority. The election had to be decided in the House, where Clay backed Adams (and became secretary of state), earning him Jackson's wrath as the "Judas of the west." One might compare this contest to the early stage of certain modern nomination races, where each candidate, devising his own strategy and platform, vies to carve out enough votes from limited constituencies to finish among the top two or three contenders, enabling him or her to go on. The appeals can be narrow and demagogic.

Most who look back on this election treat it as an aberration. But it only became so because of certain deliberate steps taken afterwards that changed the character of the nomination system. The changes were orchestrated by one of the great institution builders of American history, Martin Van Buren. The inevitable consequence of a nonpartisan system, Van Buren argued, would be a repetition of the general outcome of 1824, with many candidates participating and an electoral majority forming only in the rare circumstance of an extraordinarily popular candidate (as Andrew Jackson proved to be in 1828). Leading a coterie of leaders from the old Jeffersonian party, Van Buren set out to rescue the nation from the system of 1824. His aim was not merely to revive his own party, the Democrats, but to restore two-party competition—indeed, not just to restore it, but to make it into a permanent and respectable part of the political system. Even his partisan goal, which was second to his grander institutional reform, required founding and supporting an opposition party. One party alone would be like a single hand trying to clap. It would not work.

Van Buren criticized the nonpartisan system because it removed all restraints on individual ambition and opened the presidential election to an endless campaign, which would be conducted on the basis of popular leadership and demagoguery. He feared that such an election process would divide and destroy the nation, most likely by fomenting sectional appeals. Van Buren's solution could be summed up in one phrase: put party over person. National parties, established on safe and broad national principles, would be the gateways through which anyone seeking the presidency would have to pass. This system could hardly depart more dramatically from the original constitutional plan, but it was inspired by the founders' aim of managing ambition and controlling popular leadership for the common good.

As an institution builder Van Buren understood that the task of resuscitating parties could not rely on a change in the Constitution. It was an extra-legal task. Van Buren's ingenious and paradoxical stratagem was to try to connect his project to the most powerful, popular—and polarizing—force in the nation, Andrew Jackson, who, to make matters more difficult, favored a politics of personalism and Monroe's related nonpartisan idea. But Van Buren persisted. If the old party could be connected to Jackson, another party in opposition would be quick to follow. Van Buren's plan did not fully "take" in 1828—Jackson won on a personal appeal—but by 1832, with mounting opposition (and with Van Buren having insinuated himself into his good graces), Jackson concluded that he needed the Democratic Party. He became its nominal founder and great champion.

From early on Van Buren concluded that the caucus system was finished and that a new system of nomination was needed. This was the Age of Jackson in which people demanded a greater role in choosing their leaders. The new institution Van Buren proposed was the party convention, a meeting consisting of a large number of delegates chosen from the states. Not only was the convention more democratic than the caucus, it allowed a large number of politicians to meet face to face to work out the arrangements, including the choice of the nominee, that secured party harmony. As time went on, of course, the conventions also occasionally became the forums for revealing and intensifying factional differences.

Parties were self-created associations, not official public bodies. They determined their own procedures and rules. One of the most unusual and fateful innovations was the Democrats' two-thirds rule for nomination, adopted in 1832, which effectively gave a veto to any geographical section. The rule also produced some conventions of notorious duration; the longest, in 1924, selected the otherwise forgettable John W. Davis after 103 ballots. Party conventions, which operated at all levels of government, became the institution that performed the great "public" function of nomination. Yet they had the legal status of fully private entities in which, as the political scientist V.O. Key once colorfully noted, "it was no more illegal to commit fraud . . . [than] in the election of officers of a drinking club." Following sober reassessment, some states began the gradual process of bringing parties under the control of state legislation. But national parties and the national conventions operated beyond the jurisdiction of any state, and no one at the federal level at the time ever conceived that Congress had the authority to regulate them. A national function of the highest importance—nominating presidential candidates—was carried out by an institution that no political authority could regulate.

POPULAR LEADERSHIP

Like the congressional caucus earlier, the party convention eventually came under fire. Once again, the criticism was only partly directed against its intrinsic flaws as a nominating mechanism; the larger objection was that the convention embodied the alleged defects of the parties of the day. American parties, in the eyes of their Progressive critics at the turn of the 20th century, were thoroughly corrupt, more interested in victory than principle, and willing as a result to settle for weak, pliable candidates. Nominations, it was charged, were settled either by emotional swings among convention delegates or by secret deals struck by party bosses and machine leaders in smoke-filled rooms (tobacco in those days).

As a remedy, the Progressives advocated going over the heads of the party organizations to the people. They prescribed two reforms: nomination by primary elections, in which a wholly new kind of party would form around the victorious nominee, and independent personal candidacies of the sort represented by Ross Perot in 1992. The Progressives' oft-proclaimed faith in democracy, including direct democracy, was no doubt genuine, but it came wrapped within a concept of popular leadership. The heart and soul of their theory of governance was the idea of a special relation between the leader and the public. Popular leadership, located in the presidency, would modify the spirit of our antiquated constitutional system, overcoming the separation of powers and breathing new life into a moribund mechanical structure. As Woodrow Wilson put it, "The nation as a whole has chosen him, and is conscious that it has no other political spokesman . . . . Let him once win the admiration and confidence of the country, and no other single force can withstand him."

To win this admiration and confidence, the leader had to be selected on his own merits, without the help or constraint of the traditional, decentralized party organization. All elements of popular leadership should be on display in the nomination process, to be judged by the public. The Progressives sought to reverse Van Buren's principle of placing the party above the leader. Though sincere in their wish to restore something of the founders' notion of statesmanship, they had in mind statesmanship of a different kind, recognized by different means. Progressives sought to raise the selection process to the status of a grand, exalted good, a centerpiece of republican government, celebrated for discovering the leader and educating the public—who would choose among the candidates on the basis of their positions on issues and their appeal as leaders, revealed especially through their rhetorical prowess. It is only natural, wrote Wilson, that "orators should be the leaders of a self-governing people." Hand in hand with oratory came the celebration of openness in all matters, "an utter publicity about everything that concerns government."

And what of the risks the new method entailed? In an enlightened age, with a vigilant press, the reformers were confident that dangerous appeals had little chance of succeeding: "Charlatans cannot long play statesmen successfully when the whole country is sitting as critic," declared Wilson.

By 1912, another important turning point in presidential selection, 14 states had adopted some kind of primary elections, often including various methods to instruct or bind the delegates. By accepting these delegates, even with qualifications, the parties effectively consented to an alteration of the nomination process. This system was immediately put to use on the Republican side by Teddy Roosevelt. Roosevelt forced a reluctant President William H. Taft out of the White House and into an active campaign, most notably in the Ohio primary, where Taft immediately proceeded to label T.R. a "demagogue." Wilson, too, campaigned in some Democratic primaries. In the end, however, the primaries were not decisive in either contest. Taft bested T.R. at the convention, despite T.R.'s greater success in the primaries, and Wilson, with nowhere near the two thirds needed for nomination, had to await his fate at the Democratic convention, where he was chosen by party leaders after four long days of contest and 46 ballots.

But the issue of a new nominating process was now squarely placed on the national agenda. In his acceptance speech at the Progressive convention, Roosevelt proclaimed "the right of the people to rule," going on to declare, "We should provide by national law for presidential primaries." Wilson took the same tack in his first State of the Union address, urging "the prompt enactment of legislation which will provide for primary elections throughout the country at which the voters of the several parties may choose their nominees for the Presidency without the intervention of nominating conventions." He also suggested bringing party functions under a federal legislative regime. Conventions would be held—*after* the nomination, he proposed—consisting not of elected delegates, but of the nominees for Congress, the national committee members and the presidential candidate, so that "platforms may be framed by those responsible to the people for carrying them into effect."

THE PRESENT SYSTEM

Two things occurred to halt the enactment of an all-primary system. The first was opposition in Congress to national legislation, mainly on grounds that the federal government had no authority to regulate the selection of delegates to party conventions. The second was the rapid decline after the war of the Progressive movement as a whole. States lost interest in establishing new primary elections. Later on, liberal leaders in the Democratic Party, most notably Franklin D. Roosevelt, preferred to work with party bosses rather than pursue procedural reforms through state legislation. The national party on its own, however, at FDR's insistence, eliminated the two-thirds rule in 1936.

This loss of enthusiasm in the Progressive impulse resulted in the rise, in an organic fashion, of a new, "mixed" system of presidential selection. It consisted of an uneasy synthesis of the original party convention idea and the new theory of nomination by primaries. Candidates could pursue a limited primary strategy to impress party leaders and claim the mantle of the people's choice, as John F. Kennedy did in 1960, but the ultimate authority to nominate still lay with the convention. Proof of this point occurred in 1968, when Hubert Humphrey won the Democratic nomination without entering any primaries.

But his selection also proved that the Progressive idea, under its new name of "Reform," had won the battle of legitimacy. Many Democrats regarded Humphrey's nomination as tainted. As a result, enough states adopted presidential primaries to make them the main component in the nomination of candidates. King Convention was dethroned. Since 1976, all nominees of both parties have been selected in advance of the party conventions by a choice of the people in primaries and open caucuses. This year, the possibility that the Democratic Convention might play a role in nominating its party's candidate was enough to provoke horror in the minds of most party leaders. The convention today serves a purely public relations function: to showcase the party nominee in a speech that is now the effective platform of the party.

The nation has been trying since 1972 to work out the new principle's logic. As long as the convention made the ultimate decision, when states held their primary or caucus was a relatively minor matter, because all state delegations might have their say at the convention. With the decision now made *before* the convention, states have been trying to preserve their influence by shifting their primaries nearer to the campaign's start, so that their citizens might vote before the race was over. Of course, some states might decide to hang back, betting that if there is a split they may be in a good spot later on to play a major role—like Wisconsin, North Carolina, and Oregon this year.

FRAUGHT WITH UNKNOWNS

Barack Obama's selection as the Democratic nominee fulfills at least one hope—the Progressive longing to pick candidates who during the campaign exhibit all the arts of popular leadership and oratory. Granted, by the very nature of politics, those who have experience and connections will under almost any electoral process possess an advantage. Most of the nominees chosen under this system could just as easily have been chosen under the past two systems. But the present system has certainly opened the door to other possibilities. Candidates like George Wallace, Jesse Jackson, Pat Buchanan, Pat Robertson, and Howard Dean, to name only a few, have competed, sometimes with promising results, as popular leaders. Many had thin records of public service and treated the presidency as largely an entry-level political position.

Any selection system that permits choice—unlike, for example, selection by seniority or primogeniture—by definition does not determine the outcome; it only influences it. This makes it impossible to attribute a particular result to the system's formal properties alone. But two nominees now seem to be clear "products" of the new system: Jimmy Carter and Barack Obama. Neither won on the basis of a substantial record of public service or high previous standing in his party. Their victories were due to their performance as popular leaders. Carter was a Jimmy one-note, repeating a mantra of promising never to tell a lie that resonated perfectly with the electorate's mood in 1976. Obama, more the maestro than fiddler, has composed his work using a more complex register, alternating motifs of change and hope.

Indeed, Obama's campaign has forged what for many Democrats is an almost spiritual bond between the leader and his followers. The strength and depth of this personal appeal became so apparent and so alarming to others that the candidate felt compelled to declare, "It's not about me"—this, in the extraordinary context of a party acceptance speech he delivered in a football stadium before more than 80,000 in attendance. Obama has also made a conspicuous point of rejecting the low "popular arts" in favor of a more high-minded rhetoric, which many critics nevertheless suspect to be a cleverer form of artful popular leadership.

Yet Obama is a candidate whom many Americans feel they hardly "know" or can confidently place. Despite or because of this, he has become for many the object of their dreams and the vessel of their hopes. His nomination affords the opportunity for the observer to gaze squarely into the heart of the new method of leadership selection. Choosing a president is always a process fraught with unknowns, and more so in this case than in almost any other. If Barack Obama is elected president, fondly can we hope, and fervently must we pray, that the country has avoided the greatest potential danger of its fractured electoral system.

Continental Drift

Jeremy Rabkin

(Fall 2005)

Late last spring, voters in France and the Netherlands rejected the proposed constitutional treaty for the European Union. Conservative critics, especially in America, expressed great satisfaction. The news was, depending on the priorities of the commentator, a reaffirmation of the nation-state, or of democracy, or of constitutional government. Such rejoicing is premature. But the referendums do indicate that Europeans are beginning to see through the vapors of political delusion.

The European Union was formally launched in 1991, after four decades of incremental steps toward "integration." Entering this new, more ambitious phase, just after the final collapse of Communism, Euro-governance emerged as the new standard-bearer of "progressive" hopes. The E.U. became the premier sponsor of political fantasy in the post-Cold War world. And political fantasy is inevitably, perhaps inherently, illiberal—that is, contemptuous of the sober premises of liberal or constitutional democracy. The E.U. promised a world of peace and harmony and respect for human rights, in which everyone would be assured of comfort and security without much effort and certainly without much thought, because all the world would soon be brought to share the guiding assumptions of E.U. bureaucrats.

The rival vision of jihadists—a restored caliphate ruling over a united Muslim world, in perpetual conflict with the infidels beyond—is far less improbable. Al-Qaeda, now terrorizing Europe, understands that its vision can only be fulfilled by disciplining its adherents and wielding force against everyone else. The E.U. vision, supposedly the genuine alternative to terrorism, relies on the gentle guidance of supple bureaucrats in Brussels, earnest lawyers at the Hague, and visionary diplomats, with suitable NGO minders, at any place where the U.N. wants to hold its next conference on saving the world.

The referendums in France and the Netherlands—along with polls showing precipitous declines in support for the constitution in other E.U. countries—indicate that Europeans are no longer beguiled by this dream. The favorable vote in July by Luxembourg (the highest per capita recipient of E.U. largesse) cannot revive the E.U. constitution. But the same qualities which got Europeans into this condition in the first place will make it hard for them to get out of it now, without some painful adjustments to reality.

THE CONSTITUTION THAT WASN'T

It is hard to say with any precision what French and Dutch voters meant when they rejected the proposed constitution, because it is hard to say what the constitution itself was supposed to mean. Its advocates insisted that it was largely a matter of codifying or "tidying up" existing arrangements—while warning, at the same time, that its rejection would be a devastating blow to European integration, possibly triggering cataclysmic consequences. In France, the constitution's advocates insisted that it was essential to prevent American domination of Europe, but its opponents insisted that it would ensure the domination of Europe by American (or in de Gaulle's widely invoked racial terminology, "Anglo-Saxon") economic policies.

Voters could hardly gain clarity by reading the constitution. It is impenetrable, and not merely because it is more than 500 pages of bureaucratic prose. On the most basic questions, it settles nothing. More than two centuries ago, in the debate on the American Constitution, the central issues were whether the federal government could maintain its own standing army and impose its own taxes. Will the E.U. have its own armed forces? Its own capacity to impose taxes? A few throw-away lines in the treaty indicate that new "policies" regarding "security" and "revenue" may be adopted with the unanimous consent of the prime ministers of the member states. In other words, the constitution, which already vests supreme power in national executive officials working together, invites them to extend their collective authority—over against their own individual nations—whenever that seems convenient to them.

The constitution is supposed to establish a division of functions between the European and national governments. In fact, it gives the E.U. potential jurisdiction over almost every undertaking, while reserving almost nothing to the national governments exclusively. Yet the document does not supply Brussels with the means or resources it would need for its many tasks.

The constitution proposes to establish an E.U. minister for foreign affairs, with a fixed term, but acknowledges that states may maintain their own ambassadors to outside countries. Even as the Bundestag endorsed the new constitution, Germany campaigned for a permanent seat on the U.N. Security Council. Did Germany simply intend to echo, *auf deutsch*, the "common foreign policy" to which Britain and France (with their own permanent representatives on the Security Council) would already be bound under the new constitution?

To call this a constitution is to misuse the word. Although intended to supplant all previous treaties by which European authority had been established, it is itself a treaty, not obviously more binding or authoritative than any of the others. It is supposed to establish the supremacy of E.U. law—including any future regulations promulgated by European Commission bureaucrats in Brussels—over national law. Yet actually the constitution would only formalize this arrangement, since the European Court of Justice insisted decades ago that regulations from Brussels must take priority over enactments of national legislatures, and even over national constitutions as interpreted by national constitutional courts.

"Europe" has always been about elevating bureaucratic authority over elected parliaments bound by actual constitutions. The so-called European Parliament is largely a ceremonial entity, empowered neither to initiate legislation nor to choose the commissioners who do propose directives and regulations. Nobody was much exercised about this in the past. It is not likely that Europeans will suddenly rally to democratic propriety now.

But they *are* unhappy about existing conditions in their own countries, and are raising new questions about how they are governed. The most basic question is not answered at all in the constitutional treaty: why should the nations of Europe submit their sovereignty to the E.U.?

NEW WORLD UNION

Imagine a new world counterpart to the European Union. A series of treaties bestows lawmaking power to councils of representatives from the United States, Mexico, Canada, Guatemala, Grenada, Belize, Brazil, and a dozen or so other countries. Agriculture and labor regulations are made in secret meetings of the labor and agriculture ministers; environmental and safety regulations by environment and safety ministers; and so on. These laws and regulations—elaborated in suitable detail by a Commission of the Americas in, let us say, Caracas, Venezuela—exceed the reach of the current U.S. Code and take priority over U.S. laws. A court in, say, Belize, charged with giving force to these laws, has the authority to override any constitutional objections from the U.S. Supreme Court. The presidents or prime ministers of all these states then meet periodically to expand the powers of the Union of the Americas, by mutual agreement among themselves.

Of course, anyone who proposed such a scheme would be dismissed out of hand. It would subvert our Constitution's system of accountability, along with its checks and balances. But to state the objection in this way may be too abstract. Most Americans would instinctively recoil from this project on the grounds that it is, well, nuts. Most Americans would prefer to keep their own country.

Is the comparison unfair? Some Europeans have sentimentalized the project of European integration as a way to restore the unity of medieval Europe before it was shattered by the Protestant Reformation, or the French Revolution, or the terrible wars of the 20th century. But the nations of today's E.U. have never been governed in common. Neither ancient Rome nor its ramshackle successor, the Holy Roman Empire, stretched so far to the north or the east or the west. There has never before been a single political unit stretching from Portugal to Estonia, from Ireland to Greece, from Sweden to Cyprus.

True, before the United States, there was no polity covering the middle of North America, from one coast to the other. But the comparison remains instructive. After the original 13 states established a common federal government, the Union embraced more and more new states until, within little more than 60 years, it had expanded to the far shores of the Pacific. California entered the Union only two years after its territory was acquired from Mexico, but it already had a majority of English-speaking residents from the more settled parts of the U.S. Hawaii became an American possession in 1898, but 60 years later there was still intense debate about whether this territory, where most inhabitants were of Asian descent, could be incorporated as a full state of the Union. Puerto Rico, acquired at almost the same time as Hawaii, is still not a state. If the majority on that Spanish-speaking island ever sought full statehood, it is not at all certain that it would be admitted.

You can denounce Americans or past generations of Americans for racism, intolerance, chauvinism, or xenophobia. There is, no doubt, truth to such charges. But they are largely beside the point. The overwhelming majority of Americans are descended from immigrants who did not originate in the British Isles. In other words, the "native" population is now far outnumbered by descendants of "others." Scarcely any Americans notice this fact. A son of Arab immigrants commands American forces in Iraq, but the ancestry of General John Abizaid is not an issue. Nor does anyone notice that for 20 of the past 40 years, the office of U.S. secretary of state has been held by an immigrant or by the child of immigrants.

Our tradition of assimilating newcomers to America is old—so old that it worked even when we brought America to the foreigners. After acquiring the Louisiana Territory, President Jefferson insisted that the existing French-speaking community conduct its political affairs in English. Louisiana has done so ever since, and without protest, despite the persistence of a sizable Cajun-speaking community.

Since the 19th century, immigrants have been required to learn English and demonstrate their knowledge of American history and institutions before becoming citizens. They must swear an oath, pledging to "support the Constitution of the United States against all enemies, foreign and domestic," and promising, if required, to "take up arms" against these enemies. We have extracted this oath from grandmothers and disabled people, along with more suitable military recruits.

At bottom, the U.S. is, at least by the theory of our founders, a mutual defense agreement among citizens. Despite our differences, we stand together against common enemies. We entrust a common government to make what can be, literally, life or death decisions on our behalf. But it is not simply the government that constitutes our political community. The stability of the government, and of the Constitution that constitutes and limits that government, reflects the solidarity among the people. New Yorkers may not be the most beloved people in America, but the attack on the World Trade Center was seen throughout the country—in distant Hawaii as in Alabama or Michigan—as an attack on Americans, requiring a common American response.

Whatever else it is, the European Union certainly is not a counterpart to the U.S. in this respect. But what it actually is, no one can say. The collapse of the E.U. constitution is a reminder that political entities don't retain authority when they have no clear purpose that citizens can respect—or even grasp.

MUTUAL DISTRUST

America is an exceptional country in many ways, which is part of the reason it continues to provoke so much envy, resentment, and hostility from Europeans. But as a nation-state, the United States is not at all unusual. The European Union itself is a confederation—or a collection, anyway—of separate nation-states. It presupposes these states, even more than the U.S. Constitution presupposes the states in our Union.

The American Founders were eager to ensure that the federal government could make decisions on behalf of the whole American people and execute its own laws and policies. State governors play no role in our federal councils and even senators serve for fixed terms, whether state governments pass to a different local majority or not. By contrast, E.U. policies are made by the immediate representatives of the member-state governments. All E.U. policies are then implemented by the member-state governments, because the E.U. has no police, field agents, or inspectors, and no local courts of its own.

The strange structure of the E.U. reflects the irreducible fact that Europeans do not trust each other all that much. The E.U. Parliament has only very limited powers because member states have never been prepared to trust their fates to a European-wide majority. Europe has known multinational schemes of government in the past, but by the 19th century, the multiethnic Ottoman, Romanov, and Hapsburg empires were seen as backward relics of a less enlightened age. Their collapse, at the end of the First World War, was welcomed by the Western allies and by most citizens of the national successor states. National independence became the universal desideratum—which meant possessing, among other trappings of a modern state, a national constitution and parliament. Borders shaped by language and ethnicity naturally meant that some "national" states would turn out smaller than others, but this was thought to offer the compensating advantage of greater cohesion. And national cohesion made possible liberal and parliamentary institutions, under which members of minority groups could consent to be governed by the representatives of the majority in return for assurances that everyone's rights would be protected. Decades earlier, liberal opinion in Britain, France, and other parts of Europe, had favored independence for the Balkan states and Belgium; Italian and German unification; and Poland's restoration as a separate people. Liberals expected these new states to herald a freer and more peaceful and prosperous world.

Of course, things turned out badly in the interwar period and worse thereafter. Faced with determined aggressors, small nations could not always maintain their independence. Even after World War II, when the integration project began, nations felt little warmth, let alone trust, for their immediate neighbors. A grouping of Portugal and Spain? Of Netherlands with Germany and Austria? Britain with Ireland? National states had come into being precisely in opposition to the claims of neighbors. Europe was only able to "unite" by assuring anxious nation-states that their distrusted neighbors would be outvoted by others, by nations sufficiently distant from traditional rivalries or local enmities.

Still, to what end? In the aftermath of the Second World War, with Soviet troops in the middle of Germany, governments in Western Europe recognized that they needed help in defending themselves. The U.S. actually encouraged them to develop a European Defence Community, wielding a multinational force with a shared command structure. It would, as General Eisenhower put it (when serving as NATO commander in the early 1950s), allow for "rearming Germans without rearming Germany." But the French National Assembly rejected the plan in 1954 as a threat to French "sovereignty." Instead, Germany was allowed to rearm on the condition that it joined NATO. Europeans then ceded "leadership" of NATO to the U.S., partly as an assurance that a rearmed Germany would be carefully chaperoned. In the early 1960s, President de Gaulle tried to entice West Germany and the Low Countries to join a French-led defense structure as an alternative to NATO. The idea remained stillborn, doubtless because France's neighbors recognized its limitations as a provider of security. Whatever else it was, "Europe" was not going to be built around a common defense.

After the collapse of the Soviet empire, however, many European leaders nurtured wider ambitions. The Maastricht treaty that launched the E.U. in 1991 provided for a "common foreign and security policy"—though not a common army. There has been little follow-through on proposals for joint forces, largely because Europeans do not want to finance serious military capabilities, but also because they are not equipped to make common decisions on the deployment of such forces. Still, Europe has distanced itself from NATO. European leaders saw no trouble in expanding the E.U. to include in its "common foreign and security policy" three new states (Finland, Austria, Sweden) that were not in NATO and had pledged themselves, as neutrals, never to join NATO.

What policy can be "common" between states that are pledged to a defense alliance and states that are neutral? Only policies that are so abstract or so global in their reach that they can transcend both sides in almost any conflict. Thus the E.U. became a big booster of wildly ambitious treaty projects like the International Criminal Court and the Kyoto Protocol. It also invested in establishing itself as a "broker" or "mediator" in the Middle East, pouring more financial assistance into the Palestinian Authority in the 1990s than into all of Africa. Perhaps Europeans have noticed that this investment did not bring peace to the Middle East.

The outbreak of war in Iraq was traumatic for Europeans because it exposed the pretense of a "common foreign policy." Of course, public opinion was divided over the war. That was so in America, too, but the American government is equipped to make decisions. While France and Germany rushed to position themselves as opponents of American "unilateralism," governments in Britain, Italy, Spain, Portugal, and Denmark, along with most of those in Eastern Europe, thought it more important to align with the U.S.

The countries flying under the E.U. flag simply don't share the same priorities, nor is the E.U. equipped to reconcile their differences. Following the Madrid bombings, as angry Spanish voters blamed the incumbent conservatives, even officials in Paris and Berlin warned Spain's new socialist government not to act precipitously in withdrawing Spanish troops from Iraq. There was widespread concern that an immediate reversal of Spain's policy would encourage terrorists to think that every European state could be bullied by well-timed terror attacks. Believing that withdrawal would buy it immunity from the jihad, however, the new Spanish government promptly pulled its troops from Iraq. Nor did the German and French governments rush to replace the Spanish contingent in Iraq. Each government heeded its own priorities. Whatever else it was, the rejection of the constitution was a sign that European voters don't place much hope in a common foreign policy.

HUMAN RIGHTS AND CITIZENSHIP

If a common foreign policy remains a distant dream, the idea of Europe as a zone of democratic stability possesses much more credibility. The first postwar organization in Europe, the Council of Europe (1949), had precisely the aim of rallying support for democratic government—at least on the western side of the Iron Curtain. The Council's first and still-paramount project is the European Convention on Human Rights (1950), which is supposed to be given effect by a European Court of Human Rights.

The project had no historical precedent. It assumed that rights were better protected by a group of nations and a supranational court than by a nation's own constitution. And thus it presumed that appeals to respect rights need not invoke concerns like national honor, solidarity among fellow citizens, or political stability. Nations with a long respect for civil liberties, like Great Britain, were encouraged therefore to think that the rights of their own citizens would somehow be better protected with monitoring by German and Italian judges (not exactly renowned for their historic respect for liberty). The problem became more acute in the 1990s, when the collapse of the Iron Curtain allowed nations from the east into the Council. In a system in which each state gets to appoint one judge, British justice can now be further improved by judges from Russia, Ukraine, and Albania.

The system works quite imperfectly. Judgments of the Human Rights Court in Strasbourg are not binding in the national law of all member states, nor are judges in the states always quick to take guidance from the Court's exemplary rulings. The Human Rights Court does not seem to make much difference in Russia, for example.

Since the 1970s, however, the European Court of Justice (an entirely distinct E.U. tribunal, based in Luxembourg) has claimed the authority to invoke human rights norms from the European Convention and other sources. As the ECJ saw it, this practice would answer concerns that regulations from Brussels, now placed above national constitutions, would leave Europeans without constitutional protection for their rights. Under the ECJ's guidance, Europeans would still have their rights protected, but by supranational authorities invoking supranational standards, rather than by their own courts or constitutions.

Embedding the European Rights Convention in E.U. law has provided an incentive for candidate nations to take human rights standards more seriously. That may well have worked to enhance respect for rights in Spain, Portugal, and Greece in the 1970s and '80s. Similar claims have been made about the new democracies in Eastern Europe in the 1990s. But severing rights protections from national authority has come at a price.

For one thing, the new scheme seems to have undermined respect for national legal traditions. In recent years, Britain's government has sponsored measures allowing house arrest without trial, relaxing double-jeopardy prohibitions (when new evidence makes it possible to reconsider an acquittal), and criminalizing speech that expresses disrespect for religious minorities (in deference to the sensitivities of British Muslims). A few decades ago in Britain, any one of these measures would have been unthinkable. They are still unthinkable in the U.S., which prizes its own historic Bill of Rights. Britain, home of the legal traditions that inspired our Bill of Rights, relies increasingly, however, on foreign judges to determine the rights of Englishmen.

There is a more general problem. If a national government does not have ultimate responsibility for protecting the rights of its own citizens, then the nation can no longer be conceived as a political community for the mutual protection of rights. The E.U. avidly subsidizes and encourages "regional governance" arrangements—in practice, encouraging separatist feelings among the Scots and the Welsh, the Basques, and an assortment of German-speaking minorities living outside the borders of today's Germany. The E.U. also promotes special protections for non-citizens who are long-time residents of member states, a practice described as "post-national citizenship."

European governments now speak regularly of "autochthonous" and "allochthonous" residents—those rooted in the local soil and those springing from foreign soils. Such formulas are supposed to be a sign of respect for the distinct cultures of the "allochthonous" residents. In practice, they have allowed European governments to shrug off concerns about integrating immigrants. European cities now have large, resentful populations of Muslim immigrants who do not identify themselves as citizens of their host nation. But why should they, when the host nation does not emphasize that it is a political entity, demanding loyalty in exchange for mutual protection? "Europe" is an amorphous grouping of nations. It is already "multicultural." Why should it matter if its member states become bazaars of contending cultures?

Of course, in an era when jihadists recruit from disaffected Muslim communities across Europe, this vision of multicultural harmony looks much less promising. In both France and the Netherlands, popular opposition to the new constitution seems to have reflected, at least in part, a heightened fear of foreigners. And throughout Europe, public opinion is overwhelmingly opposed to bringing Turkey into the E.U. European leaders have spent years demanding reforms to qualify Turkey for ultimate admission to the E.U., beguiling themselves with the prospect of making that country a model of multicultural tolerance for the rest of the Islamic world. Whatever else the rejection of the new constitution means, it is a sign that Europeans are not prepared to pay much of a price to realize this vision.

POLITICAL ECONOMY

Critics of the E.U., even within Europe, sometimes urge it to revert to the free trade zone it started out to be. There is much sense in this as a recommendation for future development. But as history it is quite misleading. If European governments had wanted simply to reduce barriers to trade, they had perfectly adequate vehicles for doing so. The western European states were founding members of the 1947 General Agreement on Tariffs and Trade (GATT), which has since evolved into the World Trade Organization (WTO). If the Europeans wanted to reduce trade barriers more quickly than other participants in GATT were prepared to do, they could have established a parallel agreement among themselves, as the U.S. and its neighbors ultimately did with the North American Free Trade Agreement (NAFTA). This is, in fact, what Britain, Switzerland, and the Scandinavian countries did in the early 1960s, when they organized the European Free Trade Association (EFTA) as an alternative to the Common Market.

But the Common Market was always more ambitious, which is why its six founding members (France, Germany, Italy, and the Benelux countries) resisted the rival European Free Trade Association, ultimately maneuvering most EFTA members into joining the Common Market. The purpose of the Common Market, like the earlier European Coal and Steel Community (organized among the same six countries in 1951), was to lower trade barriers while simultaneously arranging safeguards, exemptions, and special subsidies as a shield against untrammeled free trade. In contrast to all other trade agreements (GATT, WTO, NAFTA, EFTA, etc.), the economic pacts linking the six required not just a treaty but an implementing bureaucracy, empowered to spell out details in subsequent regulations so that trade liberalization would be coupled with offsetting protections.

So trade in agricultural products would be open among the six, but farmers (especially French farmers) would be compensated by an elaborate scheme of subsidies and price supports. As the Common Market embraced new members and expanded liberalization agreements into new areas, the bureaucracy in Brussels, too, developed new regulations—to protect workers, to protect consumers, to protect the environment.

Underlying this was the insistence of the richer states, especially Germany, that the local standards imposed on their own firms also be imposed on firms in less affluent states, lest the latter derive a competitive advantage in their home countries. For decades, German and French prosperity served as an irresistible attraction for others. Even adopting new regulatory standards, and by the mid-1990s, a common currency, was not too high a price for the less affluent states to pay for a share of German and French prosperity.

The most fundamental reason that the E.U. is now in crisis is that the economies of the core states have performed quite poorly for more than a decade. Germany and France have stagnated, with unemployment hovering around 10%. Their average growth rate has been less than half America's, and their unemployment rate more than double that of the U.S.

Still, some states have continued to do well. Britain prospers, which is taken by many Europeans as a vindication of its decision to retain its own currency. But Ireland has experienced even more impressive growth (making it now among the richest states in the E.U.), despite adopting the Euro. Both Britain and Ireland have benefited from holding down taxes and regulations, which has made their industries more efficient and their markets more attractive to investors.

It is the largest E.U. states, apart from Britain—France, Germany, and Italy—that have done worst in the past decade. They have done less to reduce tax burdens and to free up labor markets. They have also been inclined to hope that a new round of E.U. "standards"—standardizing tax burdens as the Germans have suggested, or sharing social insurance burdens among E.U. states, as the Italians have suggested— would help to cushion them from competitive pressures. E.U. regulatory demands, in fact, have not so much dragged down the core-state economies as propped up their hapless leaders, who continually postpone already long-postponed reforms in the hope that a new scheme of "harmonization" will reduce the scale of unavoidable reform.

France, Germany, and Italy may also have hesitated to undertake more painful reforms for fear of unleashing political instability—long a problem for France and Italy, and a nightmare from the past for Germany. Postwar governments in all three countries tried to dampen political demands from the Left by promising a "third way" between socialism and market competition. Rather than cut back social benefits to lighten taxes and boost economic growth, these countries have resisted any major changes. A vague yearning for "community" constrains governments from unleashing individual economic initiative, and simultaneously discourages national policy initiative. Economic initiative thus remains constrained by excessive government, while beleaguered politicians evade their own responsibilities through supranational commitments.

DIVIDED PROSPECTS

Europe faces daunting problems. Low birthrates mean aging populations, leaving fewer and fewer workers to support more and more retirees. Only increased immigration can ease this long-term bind, but Europeans are increasingly fearful of immigrants—for reasons good and bad. Meanwhile, current trends will require disaffected immigrants to pay more and more taxes to support a larger and larger proportion of the "autochthonous" population. This is a recipe for social conflict, even apart from the cultural strains already in evidence.

Some E.U. members have better prospects than others. But it is unlikely that any will be inclined to make significant sacrifices for the others. Britain, which has long been adamant in its opposition to proposals for harmonizing tax burdens across the E.U., has now been shaken by the July terror attacks in London. Pleas by British officials to tighten European security measures received a chilly response from the European Parliament. Effective measures for British security will mostly have to originate in London. Prime Minister Tony Blair has already warned that should new security measures conflict with provisions of the European Rights Convention, he will ask Parliament to curtail or suspend Britain's obligations to the latter. France has meanwhile announced that, for the sake of security, it is suspending some of its own European treaty commitments in order to assert closer control over travel into France from other E.U. states.

At the other extreme are the Dutch. Churchill called them the "trustful Dutch" for their reliance on international law to protect them from German panzers. They have in the past decade invested still more trust in international law, playing proud host to a succession of pompous international tribunals, culminating in the absurd International Criminal Court. Now the Dutch, too, have awakened to discover that they are hated by a large portion of their fellow citizens. The British are quite worried about a Muslim community that is less than 2% of Britain's total population. In the Netherlands, the proportion of Muslims is well over twice what it is in Britain and less evenly spread through the country. Half of the population of Rotterdam is now of foreign origin.

After last November's brutal murder of filmmaker Theo van Gogh by an angry Dutch Muslim, the government's first response was to enact laws against insulting Islam. There is talk about further efforts to integrate Muslims into Dutch culture. That will be difficult for a culture whose most distinctive qualities, as a British journalist observed, seem to be license for homosexuals to marry and for children to kill their aging parents. (The Netherlands is a world pioneer in the practice of medical euthanasia.)

Although governments fear to provoke resentful immigrants, they also fear to provoke their own "autochthonous" populations, who have been led to expect very comfortable cushions against market pressures. Some Muslims envision the official establishment of sharia law in the Netherlands and other European states within a generation or two. Except when worrying about global warming a century from now, "autochthonous" Europeans, who do not have many children, seem to work with shorter time horizons, focusing on their own retirement packages.

In the U.S., religious faith often seems to provide the confidence necessary for economic risk-taking. In much of Europe, a kind of fatalism seems to prevail, on the part of Muslims who focus relentlessly on the world to come, and post-Christian Europeans who believe in little beyond this generation. They may find it increasingly easy to blame their common problems on America—or Israel.

Surveys document high levels of European resentment against America (and pathological levels of hostility toward Israel). The surveys conducted by the Pew Foundation are often cited as evidence of European anger toward the Bush Administration (an interpretation perhaps not altogether unpleasing to Madeleine Albright, a chief consultant and publicist for Pew). One survey question that received scant attention is particularly striking: "Is success in life pretty much determined by forces outside our control?" Two thirds of Americans say no, while most Europeans say yes (by as much as two thirds in fatalist Germany and Italy, while just under half agree in Britain).

The rejection of the European constitution has killed the dream of a European superstate. What remains to be seen is whether—and which—European states will save themselves by recovering their own freedom.

France's Immigrant Problem—and Ours

Victor Davis Hanson

(Spring 2006)

The three weeks of Muslim rage across France during autumn 2005 brought *Schadenfreude* to many Americans. They saw a thin scab of French hypocrisy scraped off—revealing a deep wound of invidious religious and racial separatism festering in Muslim ghettoes. As during the August 2003 heat wave that killed nearly 15,000 French elderly in stifling apartments while their progeny enjoyed their state-subsidized vacation at the beach or mountains, French talk of solidarity and moral superiority proved spectacularly at odds with the facts.

So for much of last October and November, Americans congratulated themselves that French-style rioting could, of course, never happen in the United States. After all, their economy is moribund. Ours is growing at well over 3% per year. French unemployment hovers near 10%; America's is half that. Fifty-seven million jobs were created in the U.S. during the past 30 years; only 4 million in all of Europe. Our minority youth, as a result, are much more likely to be working than idling in the streets. And sure enough, in France, about 25% of youths between 15 and 24, regardless of race or religion, are out of work.

After the unrest in our cities during the 1960s and 1970s, Americans increasingly sought through assimilation, intermarriage, and integration to fulfill the ideal of an interracial society. As emblems of our success, Americans can point to cabinet members like Colin Powell, Condoleezza Rice, or Alberto Gonzalez. By contrast, it is almost unimaginable that anyone of Arab-French ancestry would head a major French ministry. We long ago jettisoned the notion that proper citizens should necessarily look like Europeans. The French apparently still have not. Second- or third-generation spokespersons of the American Hispanic community, for instance, are often successful, affluent, and integrated. By contrast, imams who barely speak French after decades of living there, and who from their 1,500 mosques decry the decadence of French culture, were often the only intermediaries between the French government and youthful rioters.

The accepted view is not just that the American melting pot differs from European separatism, but that the largest bloc of our immigrant residents is itself quite different—Christian Mexicans who trek across a common 2,000-mile unfenced border, eagerly looking for work. France's Muslim immigrants bring with them age-old, clash-of-civilizations baggage dating from Poitiers in the 8th century to the 20th-century French colonial war in Algeria. In contrast, Mexico was colonized by European Christians—and we have had more or less stable relations with the Mexican government for over a century. Moreover, even illegal-alien drug smugglers and gangbangers are not terrorists; we do not fret about their potential sympathy for radical Islam. And the rioters outside of Paris were almost all males, apparently embracing strict gender separation—antithetical to French culture, and utterly foreign to Mexican immigrant men and women, who cross our border indistinguishably.

ALL'S NOT WELL

Yet such contrasts are not the entire story. For despite the many differences, America is not immune from *all* the destructive social and cultural forces now tearing at the seams of French society. Hundreds of thousands of first-generation illegal aliens currently live in Los Angeles and rural California in what are, in effect, segregated communities. In many cases, they are no more integrated—and no less alienated—than those in the French suburbs. Instead, these immigrants comprise an entire underclass without sufficient language skills, education, or familiarity with their host country to integrate successfully into society, much less to pass on capital and expertise to ensure that their children are not condemned to perpetual menial labor.

Spanish has become the de facto language for many communities in the southwest U.S. in the same way that Arabic dominates the French suburbs. Mexico City newspapers air the same sort of historical gripes and peddle the same kind of myths as Arab fundamentalists, who drug their poor, uneducated expatriates with stories of al-Andalus and a restored caliphate that will spread once again from southern Europe to the Euphrates.

In some respects, our situation is worse than France's. The United States has some 8-12 million illegal aliens—a population of unlawful residents larger than that of any other country in the Western world—not France's 4-7 million mostly Arab-French *citizens*. Ten thousand Muslim youths rioted outside Paris; but there are nearly 15,000 illegal-alien felons from Mexico in the California penal system alone, incarcerated at a cost of almost a half billion dollars a year. Portions of the Arizona and California borders have devolved into a Wild West—a no-man's-land of drug smuggling, shoot-outs, environmental desecration, and random death. Mexico responds by publishing comic books with safety tips about crossing the border, so that its departing citizens can more safely violate U.S. immigration laws. Meanwhile, Hispanic groups in America complain that increased border surveillance near San Diego has cruelly diverted human traffic into the desert.

Granted, Americans have proved far more adept at assimilating the Other than have the French; we have not suffered widespread racial or ethnic violence since the 1992 Los Angeles riots. And we do not have a religious or terrorist overtone to our internal tensions. But there are still enough similarities with the French experience to give us pause.

IMMIGRATION AND ITS DISCONTENTS

In the first place, poor Mexicans come to the U.S. for largely the same reasons that Arabs settle in France (and both were initially welcomed by their hosts). Mexicans and Arabs alike flee corrupt Third World societies and grinding poverty. At least in the beginning, they trust that unskilled and often menial employment in the West—under the aegis of a far more liberal welfare state and the rule of law—are better than anything back home. Perhaps at first such jobs are considered an improvement. But by the second generation, the paradox becomes apparent: employers hire migrants and their children expressly on the premise that they will work for lower wages than the natives would accept. If employers were to pay competitive compensation and provide full benefits, there would be little need for immigrants, since in many counties where illegal aliens reside there are enough unemployed non-immigrants to fill such jobs. In America as in France, the society eventually must pay the difference through greater state entitlements to subsidize an (often persistent) underclass.

So the reasons that Mexicans' and Arabs' rates of poverty, alcoholism, incarceration, reliance on entitlements, and high school drop-out are far higher than those of the host population are similar: in a globalized economy, manual labor in the West is now rarely unionized, respected, well-paying, or lasting. Nor are such jobs often looked upon, as they once were, as a sort of entry-level apprenticeship in which character and discipline are inculcated, in which young people gain education and experience before moving up the employment ladder.

Much of the work offered to immigrants remains in the service sector—cooking food, making beds, cutting lawns, cleaning toilets—jobs that become galling for the perennially second-class citizen in constant proximity to his more affluent host, whom he must serve while never quite receiving the compensation or respect he believes is warranted. Such jobs tend to come and go without breeding loyalty on either side. This is why the French-Arab unemployment rate (nearly 20%) is twice the national average, and why nearly one third of California's Mexican immigrant households are on public assistance. In each case, foreigners are welcomed in due to a perceived shortage of labor, but their families eventually end up either unemployed or on public assistance at much higher rates than non-immigrant households.

Many in the second generation lap up their parents' bitterness, but without the consolation that things are still better in the West than back home. This is one reason that nearly four out of every ten Hispanic high school students are not graduating from high school in four years. Of those that do, only 22.9% meet the minimum entry requirements of the California State University system, the less competitive of the state's two systems. Of Latinos of all statuses in California, less than 10% of those over 25 have bachelor's degrees—a legacy of their parents who in many cases came to the state without English, without education, without lawful entry, and without well-paying, secure jobs. In some sense, the anger of the tattooed gang member who ends up in San Quentin is not that different from the rage of the car-burning Muslim in the Paris suburbs. Both are resentful; have sufficient entitlement aid to indulge the appetites but insufficient skills to earn a good living; and are eager to blame society for their frustrations.

In short, the absence of fluency in the host language, little or no education beyond high school, and retention of much of their home country's culture all conspire to keep millions of unassimilated immigrants—in both France and the U.S.—stuck in ethnic enclaves and static jobs that usually don't pay enough to ensure a middle-class existence for larger-than-average families. This is true even without the specter of prevailing racism and undeniable discrimination. And by middle age their physically demanding jobs often leave such workers injured, ill, or disabled.

THE POLITICS OF RESENTMENT

The problem is not that it is impossible for thousands of maids, street sweepers, fruit pickers, and gardeners to move up to become electricians, small contractors, and government officials, in either France or the U.S. But the pool of newly arrived young immigrants who cannot advance quickly is so large—and growing—that our failures in upward mobility overshadow our successes. In postmodern societies, the number of immigrants is a force multiplier, inasmuch as near-instant parity for all is taken to be the only benchmark of success. Therefore the collective failure of millions is far more relevant politically than the individual success of thousands.

If Islam bolsters resistance to assimilation on the part of French immigrants from the Maghreb, illegality alienates Hispanic immigrants whose cars, taxes, and official documentation exist in a netherworld off the books. Hence many Hispanic youths—like the Arab population of France, but unlike the Cuban, Korean, or Sikh populations in the U.S.—embrace varying degrees of ethnic chauvinism to decry de facto inequality.

Consider, for example, the radical agenda of some of the most vocal ethnic separatists. The slogans of MEChA (*El Movimiento Estudiantil Chicano de Aztlan*)— "Everything for the race. Nothing for those outside the race." (*Por La Raza todo. Fuera de La Raza nada.*)—do not differ much from Islamic nationalists' sentiments in Europe.

Those embarrassed by such racist mottos argue that ethnic triumphalists in the U.S. are ossified relics of the 1960s, and have tempered their rhetoric in the 21st century. Yet ponder the following essay from Ernesto Cienfuegos on the website *La Voz de Aztlan* ("The Voice of Aztlan") in the wake of the French rioting:

> Today, here in Los Angeles, we are already seeing ominous signs of an impending social explosion that will make the French rebellion by Muslim and immigrant youths seem "tame" by comparison. All the ingredients are present including a hostile and racist police as in France. In fact, we came close to having major riots on three separate occasions just this year alone . . . . There is a strange feeling here in Los Angeles that something sinister is about to happen but no one knows when. All it will take is for a "bird-brain cop" to do something stupid and all hell will break loose. If another major rebellion breaks out here in L.A. it could rapidly spread throughout the USA as it has spread in France . . . . The social and economic conditions that exist in France that adversely affect its immigrant and Muslim populations also exist here in the USA . . . . The rebellion that is occurring in France can and will most probably happen here.

The largest Hispanic grievance association is still called the National Council of La Raza ("the Race"), a well-meaning organization that nevertheless appeals to racial solidarity and purity and therefore separatism—a clear repudiation of the idea of American multiracialism. Its nomenclature would hardly be tolerated were it not for the enormous size of the growing Hispanic community.

In a 1997 speech before this activist group, former Mexican President Ernesto Zedillo bragged that "the Mexican nation extends beyond the territory enclosed by its borders" and that Mexican migrants were "an important—a very important—part of this." A Zogby poll of Mexican citizens conducted in late May 2002 showed that 58% believed that "the territory of the United States' southwest rightfully belongs to Mexico." The national newspaper of Mexico, *Excelsior*, agreed: "The American Southwest seems to be slowly returning to the jurisdiction of Mexico without firing a single shot." No wonder then that 57% of Mexicans in that same Zogby poll believed that they should have the right to cross the border freely and without U.S. permission.

In a recent Pew poll, 40% of all Mexicans expressed a desire to immigrate to the U.S. That presents an Orwellian dilemma: almost half the population of our southern neighbor wants to leave home and enter our country, while claiming that this promised land ought to be part of the very system that has made their own country uninhabitable. A parallel phenomenon exists in Europe: radical Islamists who dream of Eurabia fail to realize that, without assimilation and adoption of their hosts' culture, they would only recreate the same discontents that prompted their departure from home in the first place.

Even if we accept that some Mexican-American leaders occasionally indulge in rhetorical excesses, their appeals to notions of race and *reconquista* still echo in mainstream politics. Consider the remarks of Richard Alatorre, a former member of the Los Angeles City Council: "They're afraid we're going to take over the governmental institutions and other institutions. They're right. We will take them over." Mario Obledo, former California state secretary of Health, Education, and Welfare under Jerry Brown—and awarded the Presidential Medal of Freedom by Bill Clinton—once infamously remarked, "California is going to be a Hispanic state. Anyone who doesn't like it should leave." Speaking at a Latino gathering in 1995, Art Torres, then chairman of the California Democratic Party, decried the passage of Proposition 187 denying entitlement benefits to those here illegally: "Power is not given to you. You have to take it. Remember, 187 is the last gasp of white America in California."

Such pronouncements tend to be encouraged by contemporary group-rights liberalism. Both the French and American governments embrace multiculturalism, which exacerbates the problem and empowers racial chauvinists. Multiculturalism teaches that there is nothing really choiceworthy about the economic, social, and political core values of Western culture, given its historic sins of racism, class exploitation, and sexism. At its worst, multiculturalism can end up, as in France, allowing de facto polygamy among immigrants from North Africa (perhaps 15,000 such families), or, more mildly in the U.S., extenuating or even embracing Chicano student manifestos like this one from a MEChA website at San Jose State University:

> Chicanismo involves a personal decision to reject assimilation and work towards the preservation of our cultural heritage . . . . By all means necessary, we Chicana/Chicano

estudiantes of Aztlán, dedicate ourselves to taking our educational destiny into our own hands through the process of spreading Chicanismo, in the spirit of carnalismo . . . . As Chicanas and Chicanos of Aztlán, we are a nationalist movement of Indigenous Gente that lay claim to the land that is ours by birthright. As a nationalist movement we seek to free our people from the exploitation of an oppressive society that occupies our land.

Second-generation immigrants often take away from this student activism, multicultural school curriculum, government bureaucracy, and popular culture a mixed but mostly pernicious message: that long-standing prejudice intrinsic to a corrupt system is what keeps newcomers down; and consequently that self-esteem and self-confidence can only be imparted by a therapeutic course of study, airing past grievances and proposing new group compensation. Shunned is the idea that traditional education alone allows immigrants to master the host language, gain familiarity with the host country's traditions and customs, and acquire enough science, math, and liberal arts to compete with long-standing natives.

The result is often psychological chaos. Too many second-generation Hispanics in the U.S., and Arabs in France, romanticize their "mother" country, which often they have never seen and would never return to if they had—while deprecating their parents' adopted society. This schizophrenia is similar to what the polls reveal about the wishes of Mexican citizens themselves. Large numbers believe that the southwest U.S. belongs to them, yet they don't want to stay in their own country. If Mexico were to absorb the American Southwest, would Mexicans still wish to emigrate there?

HARD CHOICES

With millions of illegal aliens already here, borders wide open in a time of war, and the ideal of assimilation under assault, there really are no more painless choices. Mexico is under no compulsion to reform its corrupt system when millions of its disaffected simply head north and send precious dollars south (some $10-15 billion annually in worker remittances). For Mexico to change the present system would be a lose-lose proposition: more social tension at home, less money coming in from the north.

An end to cheap, industrious labor in the U.S. would cause initial hardship to the American economy, raise wages and costs, and redefine the American attitude to physical and even menial labor—positive in the long run, painful and easily demagogued in the short term. Yet because the U.S. has a far better record of assimilation than Europe, it makes no sense for us to continue to emulate European racial separatism, which offers immigrants neither the economic opportunity nor the cultural discipline to succeed.

We should start by letting in far fewer immigrants from Mexico. An allotment of about 100,000 legal entrants—reasonable people could differ on the numbers— would privilege Mexicans (in recognition of our historic ties) but still ensure that those who came would do so legally and in numbers that would mitigate their ghettoization. Rather than predicating entry into the U.S. mostly on family affiliations, we should try to use sensible criteria to assess suitable Mexican immigrants—knowledge of English, education levels, familiarity with American laws and customs—to ensure that they are competitive with other newcomers and do not perpetuate an unassimilated underclass.

Tripartite border enforcement—a permanent and systematic barrier of some sort, increased manpower for apprehension, and employer sanctions—is crucial to ensure that immigrants arrive legally and in numbers manageable for assimilation. On this the public—in a Zogby poll 68% of Americans favor stationing troops along the border to curb unlawful entry—is far ahead of either political party.

Guest workers are a bad idea, as we learned in the 1950s and '60s from our own bitter *bracero* experience ("good enough to work for you, but not good enough to live beside you"). Temporary laborers, as we see in the suburbs of Germany and other parts of Europe, will inevitably create a permanent helot class. Moreover, these workers would continually depress wages for entry-level jobs for legal immigrants and our own poor, who find it hard to compete with young Third World illegals who are in no position to be choosy about work or to complain to authorities about employer treatment. There is nothing in the American or European experience with guest workers to suggest that they would willingly leave when their tenure expired, that their sense of exploitation would not create and perpetuate social tension, and that they would not need welfare assistance in times of health crisis or unemployment. Nor is it clear that millions of immigrants would cease coming to the U.S. illegally when they found that they were not accorded guest worker privileges.

Amnesty is perhaps the most contentious issue in the present immigration debate—in some polls 70% of Americans oppose it. We have had six prior reprieves of various sorts since the notorious blanket amnesty of 1986. These accomplished little other than encouraging more immigrants to come across the border illegally on the logical assumption that in a few years their lawbreaking would be ignored, or rewarded with citizenship. And yet because the problem has mushroomed over four decades, there are now literally millions of Mexicans in their old age who are here illegally, have forgotten life in Mexico, and have lived essentially as Americans. Deporting long-time residents would, if nothing else, be a humanitarian and public relations nightmare.

Yet some sort of one-time amnesty, as opposed to the old rolling and periodic reprieves, could only be discussed in the context of closing the border, precluding guest worker programs, and returning to assimilationist policies, so that the present pool of millions of illegal aliens would vanish rather than being perpetually replenished. Very rapid assimilation might work if the pool of those who come illegally, without English or education, to work largely in low-paying service jobs, would be vastly curtailed. In some sense, guest workers are far more destabilizing than a one-time amnesty. The former constantly enlarges the number of exploited and soon to be disillusioned aliens; the latter ends it. The prohibition of bilingual government documents and services, and of a racially chauvinistic and separatist curriculum in our schools and universities, would also send a powerful message that one should not come north unless he is willing to become a full-fledged American in every linguistic, cultural, and political sense of the word.

And, of course, there must be radical change in our own minds and hearts. When encouraged by Americans to adopt the customs and language of citizens, immigrants are more easily accepted; intermarriage and integration naturally follow. We must not forget that it is far easier for a Mexican or an Arab to become part of American or

French society, than it is for an expatriate African-American or European-American to be accepted as a Mexican citizen, or a Frenchman to be considered a true citizen of Islamic North Africa.

America could easily end up like France without sharing all of French society's pathologies. Alienated populations in both countries have immigrated for similar reasons. And both groups often have passed on their frustrations and disappointments to a subsequent generation who did not fully assimilate or prove competitive with the non-immigrant populace—and were allowed by their hosts to remain separate from society. Nonetheless, contrary to tendentious and inflammatory predictions, the rebellion in France is not likely to happen here. But there is no reason to tempt fate, and every reason to ameliorate our own problems before they worsen.

Free to Use

James Q. Wilson

(Winter 2009/10)

People who disagree about whether certain drugs such as cocaine and heroin should be illegal tend to argue from strong ideological positions. Those who defend a legal ban emphasize the need for society to reinforce weak personal self-control and thereby help preserve the character and dignity of human beings; those who wish the drugs to be legal argue that human freedom must be protected from a government that, despite lacking any power to decide what people read, tries to decide what they shall eat or snort. To reinforce their views, those who support a legal ban say that the costs are worth the reduction in the number of users, while those who object to a ban claim that the costs exceed any possible benefits.

Aware of the two sides in this endless argument, readers may approach Gene Heyman's new book, *Addiction: A Disorder of Choice*, with suspicion. Heyman, a lecturer in psychology at Harvard Medical School, surely will be endorsing one side or another in this debate. But no: Heyman does not disclose his views on the legal issue; instead, he offers a remarkable book about the extent to which people can choose to use or not to use narcotic drugs. He argues that addiction is not a disease, it is a choice.

This is not the conventional view among many, probably most, researchers, managers of drug treatment programs, and the mass media. The National Institute on Drug Abuse has distributed statements saying that addiction is a disease, and the Diagnostic and Statistical Manual (DSM) of the American Psychiatric Association defines "substance dependence" as "compulsive" drug use that leads a user to continue drug use despite significant drug-related problems. Clinicians usually echo these sentiments. Recent findings that drug addiction is influenced by the genetic makeup of some people strengthen the argument; after all, if genes determine our behavior, then there is nothing we can do about it.

Heyman raises some serious questions about this view. For one thing, the percentage of Americans who become dependent on narcotic drugs has changed dramatically over time. Among people born between 1917 and 1936, less than 1% abused drugs, but among those born between 1952 and 1963, nearly 14% did. If baby boomers are 14 times more likely than Depression-era Americans to become addicts during their lives, then something else must be going on. (By comparison, the two generations are quite alike in the chances of becoming schizophrenic or depressed.)

Another analysis supports this view. The percentage of women who test positive for cocaine use is four times greater in poor inner-city neighborhoods than in smaller urban areas, and *that percentage* in turn is four times greater than the percentage in poor rural areas. To most people there is nothing surprising about this fact; many would explain it by saying that "of course" impoverished inner-city women are more at risk for drug use, just as they are more at risk for being the victims of a crime. But when we think this, we are admitting that people have a choice: in some places they create a market for drug use, and in other places they do not. Drug abuse, in short, is not an equal opportunity disorder.

From these facts Heyman draws a conclusion: "drug availability and changes in attitudes, values, and perhaps sanctions or perceived sanctions explain the large differences." But if attitudes and sanctions affect drug use, how can we explain the familiar claims that people in drug treatment programs are rarely if ever cured and that "once an addict, always an addict"? The explanation is easy: these claims are not true.

Heyman draws on three major national surveys to show the falsity of the argument that addiction is a disease. The Epidemiological Catchment Area Study (ECA), done in the early 1980s, surveyed 19,000 people. Among those who had become dependent on drugs by age 24, more than half later reported not a single drug-related symptom. By age 37, roughly 75% reported no drug symptom.

The National Comorbidity Survey (NCS), done in the early 1990s and again in the early 2000s, came to the same conclusion: 74% of the people who had been addicts were now in remission. As with the ECA, the recovery rate was much higher than in the case of psychiatric disorders. The National Epidemiologic Survey on Alcohol and Related Conditions (NESARC), done in the early 2000s with more than 43,000 subjects, came to pretty much the same conclusion.

Why, then, do so many clinicians say that addiction is a disease? Perhaps, Heyman suggests, it is because they only work with addicts in treatment and are not aware of the life history of drug dependence. And some may think that if addiction is shaped by inherited traits (as it is), then nothing can be done about it.

But virtually every aspect of human behavior has a significant genetic component. Heyman notes that although alcoholism and religious beliefs are importantly shaped by genes, people also retain control over the extent to which genes determine behavior. People at risk for alcoholism will usually not become alcoholic if they live in a dry county or have a spouse who insists on sobriety; people who are genetically predisposed to have fundamentalist beliefs may not join a church or go to meetings where those beliefs are expressed. As I have written elsewhere, genes shape about half of our personality dimensions. This means, for example, that people who are more likely to be neurotic have a steeper hill to climb to avoid that ailment than people who are not at risk. Steeper, but not unconquerable.

Though almost all voluntary activities are shaped by genetics, they are also shaped by the consequences of activities themselves. These consequences, Heyman writes, include benefits, costs, and values. A truly involuntary activity, like a true disease, is elicited by a stimulus, e.g., a bacterial invasion or a body blow: benefits and costs make no difference.

If you believe that addiction is a disease and is not influenced by human choice, then surely it would be cruel and unjust to punish addicts. This would be like scolding, fining, or imprisoning persons for always getting lost because they had Alzheimer's. Instead, we should presumably require health insurance companies to provide the same coverage for heroin or cocaine addiction as they now do for cancer or heart disease.

Some people take this view under the mistaken impression that people can no more control their addiction than they can prevent the onset of Alzheimer's. But the data Heyman has gathered shows that most people do overcome addiction. Addiction is not Alzheimer's.

This, of course, leaves open the question of whether drug dealers should be punished. If we punish a person who sells cocaine, would that not be akin to punishing one who sells alcohol or cigarettes? Answering that question depends on how you compare liquor or nicotine addiction with cocaine addiction, and what you think are the benefits and costs of rendering the trade legal or illegal. Heyman does not address these questions. In my opinion, it would be a grave mistake to add to the number of people who have a destructive addiction to alcohol an additional large number of people addicted to coke, heroin, or methamphetamine.

To be clear on this matter we must decide what proportion of the population we should let become self-destructive addicts, how bad that addiction is for the people who suffer from it, and what the costs and benefits are of enforcing a law against drug abuse. I believe that the abuse of narcotics is destructive of human character, that legalizing certain narcotics would significantly increase the number of addicts, and that the costs of their behavior (on themselves, their families, their job prospects, and their education) outweigh the costs of enforcing laws that keep addiction levels at lower rates than they would be if the drugs were legal.

Heyman and the reader may or may not agree with my view, but everyone should acknowledge that drug abusers do in fact respond to incentives. One of the most dramatic incentives is being married. Married people are about as likely as single people to have schizophrenia and are more likely to suffer from depression, anxiety, and various phobias. But married people are less than half as likely as single people to be drug addicts. The data do not permit us to say whether marriage discourages addiction or whether addicts have a hard time getting married, but clearly it makes a difference.

The drug treatment programs that work involve managing consequences. A Vermont program reduced addiction by paying people in vouchers if they stayed clean, and Alcoholics Anonymous (AA) helps those who stay in the program acquire a mentor.

People with strong religious beliefs are less likely than atheists to become drug dependent, and more generally addiction is less common when the values of the culture are hostile to it and more common when those values erode. One of the ways society makes its values clear is by making actions against those values illegal and reserving praise for people who act in accordance with them. Though Heyman does not mention it, judicial programs such as Project HOPE in Honolulu that quickly punish arrested drug users with small penalties sharply reduce drug use and the attendant criminality.

Whatever your views on drug use, Heyman's book is very helpful for understanding the nature of drug addiction.

All the Leaves Are Brown

Steven F. Hayward

(Winter 2008/09)

"On what principle is it," wondered Thomas Babington Macaulay in 1830, "that when we see nothing but improvement behind us, we are to expect nothing but deterioration before us?" Environmentalism didn't exist in its current form in Macaulay's time, or he would easily have discerned its essential pessimism bordering at times on a loathing of humanity. A trip down the environment and earth sciences aisle of any larger bookstore is usually a tour of titles that cover the narrow range from dismay to despair.

On the surface this is not exceptional. Titles predicting decline, decay, and disaster are just as numerous in the real estate, economics, and social science shelves, though, ironically, not so much in the religion book racks, where one would expect to find apocalypticism well represented. This is an important distinction: unlike the eschatology of all major religions, the eco-apocalypse is utterly without hope of redemption for man or nature. The greens turn purple at the suggestion that most environmental conditions in rich nations are actually improving, and they bemoan the lack of "progress" toward the transformation of the human soul that is thought necessary for the planet's salvation. Yet some cracks are starting to appear in their dreary and repetitive story line. Although extreme green ideology won't go away any time soon—the political and legal institutions of the environmental movement are too well established—there are signs that the public and a few next-generation environmentalists are ready to say goodbye to all that. There are even some liberal authors with environmentalist sympathies who are turning against the environmental establishment. But it is necessary to claw our way through the deepening slough of green despondency to see this potential turning point.

More than 30 years ago political scientist Anthony Downs wrote in the *Public Interest* of a five-step "issue-attention cycle" through which public enthusiasm for an issue gradually diminishes as we come to recognize the high cost of drastic action, and that the nature of the problem was exaggerated or misconceived. The environment, he wrote, would have a longer cycle than most issues because of its diffuse nature, but it appears that the public is finally arriving at the late stages of Downs's cycle. Opinion surveys show that the public isn't jumping on the global warming

351

bandwagon despite a multi-million dollar marketing campaign and full-scale media hysteria. More broadly there are signs that "green fatigue" is setting in. Magazine publishers recently reported that their special Earth Day "green" issues generated the lowest newsstand sales of all issues published in 2008. "Suddenly Being Green Is Not Cool Any More," read a London *Times* headline in August.

This has been building for a long time. Three years ago *New York Times* green-leaning columnist Nicholas Kristof lamented that the environmental movement was losing credibility because of its doomsaying monomania, with the result that "environmental alarms have been screeching for so long that, like car alarms, they are now just an irritating background noise." Environmental leaders did not take well to his wandering from the reservation. In response to the popular indifference to green alarms, conventional environmentalists have ratcheted up their level of vitriol against humanity and democratic institutions. One of the most popular books of 2007 among environmentalists was *The World Without Us* by Alan Weisman, which projects a "thought experiment" about what would occur if human beings were suddenly removed entirely from the planet. Answer: nature would reassert herself, and ultimately remove nearly all traces of human civilization within several millennia—a mere blink of an eye in the planetary timescale. Environmentalists cheered Weisman's vivid depiction of the resilience of nature, but what *thrilled* them was the scenario of a humanless earth. Weisman made sure to stroke his audience's self-loathing with plenty of boilerplate about resource exhaustion and overpopulation. The book rocketed up the best-seller list, the latest in a familiar genre stretching back at least to Fairfield Osborn's *Our Plundered Planet* in 1948, arguably the first neo-Malthusian doomsday tract of modern environmentalism. *Time* magazine named *The World Without Us* the number one non-fiction book of 2007.

RETHINKING DEMOCRACY

The same view of environmentalism is on display in the Library of America's *American Earth: Environmental Writing Since Thoreau*. This collection, though worthy in some respects, has to be judged a disappointment compared to many other fine Library of America offerings—a shortcoming entirely attributable to the selection of Bill McKibben as editor. (The easier clue is the Foreword by Al Gore.) McKibben is another in the sad line of environmentalists who became bores by endlessly reprising the one-hit wonders of their youth (in McKibben's case, his mildly interesting 1989 book, *The End of Nature*). He begins and ends with Henry David Thoreau—"a Buddha with a receipt from the hardware store"—because he thinks *environmental* writing is to be distinguished from *nature* writing. Environmental writing, McKibben explains, "takes as its subject the collision between people and the rest of the world."

It was probably too much to expect that McKibben would balance the usual suspects such as Rachel Carson, Lynn White, Paul Ehrlich, and Garrett Hardin with such intelligent dissenters as Julian Simon, Terry Anderson, Frederick Jackson Turner, and R.J. Smith. But McKibben's adherence to environmental correctness is so narrowly conceived that he excludes a number of American authors who offer worthy reflections on man and nature. His tacit premise that man is not part of nature, or is opposed to the rest of nature, necessarily constricts the range of per-spectives that can be brought to bear on the broad idea of "the environment." So though his collection includes Theodore Roosevelt, by representing American environmental writing as beginning with Thoreau it excludes worthy earlier reflections such as Thomas Jefferson's *Notes on the State of Virginia* (or any of Jefferson's other agrarian reflections that can be read as precursors to Wendell Berry, who is included in McKibben's reader), or Tocqueville's prescient observations on American wilderness, our emerging attitudes toward it, and its relation to our democratic character.

McKibben and many other environmental writers affect an indifference toward, or transcendence of, politics in the ordinary sense, but ultimately cannot conceal their rejection of the liberal tradition. Here we observe the irony of modern environmentalism: the concern for the preservation of unchanged nature has grown in tandem with the steady erosion in our belief in unchanging human nature; the concern for the "rights of nature" has come to embrace a rejection of natural rights for humans. McKibben is one of many current voices (Gore is another) who like to express their environmentalism by decrying "individualism" (McKibben calls it "hyperindividualism"). Finding that individualism is "the sole ideology of a continent," he explains:

> Fighting the ideology that was laying waste to so much of the planet demanded going beyond that individualism. Many found the means to do that in the notion of "community"— a word almost as fuzzy and hard to pin down as "wild," but one that has emerged as an even more compelling source of motive energy for the environmental movement.

This is not a new theme for McKibben. Al Gore employed the same "communitarian" trope in his first and most famous environmental book, *Earth in the Balance* (1992), where, in the course of arguing that the environment should be the "central organizing principle" of civilization, he suggested that the problem with individual liberty is that we have too much of it. This preference for soft despotism has become more concrete with the increasing panic over global warming in the past few years. Several environmental authors now argue openly that democracy itself is the obstacle and needs to be abandoned. A year ago a senior fellow emeritus at Britain's Policy Studies Institute, Mayer Hillman, author of *How We Can Save the Planet* (2006), told a reporter, "When the chips are down I think democracy is a less important goal than is the protection of the planet from the death of life, the end of life on it. This [rationing] has got to be imposed on people whether they like it or not." (Hillman openly advocates resource rationing.) Another recent self-explanatory book is *The Climate Change Challenge and the Failure of Democracy* (2007) by Australians David Shearman and Joseph Wayne Smith. Shearman argued recently that

> [l]iberal democracy is sweet and addictive and indeed in the most extreme case, the U.S.A., unbridled individual liberty overwhelms many of the collective needs of the citizens . . . . There must be open minds to look critically at liberal democracy. Reform must involve the adoption of structures to act quickly regardless of some perceived liberties.

Whom does Shearman admire as an example of environmental governance to be emulated? China, precisely *because* of its authoritarian government: "[T]he savvy Chinese rulers may be first out of the blocks to assuage greenhouse emissions and they will succeed by delivering orders . . . . We are going to have to look at how authoritarian decisions based on consensus science can be implemented to contain greenhouse emissions." Separately, Shearman has written:

> To retain an inhabitable earth we may have to compromise the eternal vicissitudes of democracy for an informed leadership that directs. There are countries that fall within this requirement and we should use them to initiate more active mitigation . . . . The People's Republic of China may hold the key to innovative measures that can both arrest the expected surge in emissions from developing countries and provide developed nations with the means to alternative energy. China curbs individual freedom in favour of communal need. The State will implement those measures seen to be in the common good.

Perhaps the film version will be called *An Inconvenient Democracy*.

Academic political theorists who take up what might be called "green constitutionalism" understand that Lockean liberalism has to be overturned and replaced. In *The Green State: Rethinking Democracy and Sovereignty* (2004), Australian political scientist Robyn Eckersley offers up an approach that, despite being swathed in postmodern jargon, is readily transparent. The "ecocentric," transnational "green state" Eckersley envisions is represented as an explicit alternative to "the classical liberal state, the indiscriminate growth-dependent welfare state, and the increasingly ascendant neoliberal competition state." Achieving a post-liberal state requires rethinking the entire Enlightenment project:

> By framing the problem as one of rescuing and reinterpreting the Enlightenment goals of autonomy and critique, it is possible to identify what might be called a mutually informing set of "liberal dogmas" that have for too long been the subject of unthinking faith rather than critical scrutiny by liberals. The most significant of these dogmas are a muscular individualism and an understanding of the self-interested rational actor as natural and eternal; a dualistic conception of humanity and nature that denies human dependency on the biological world and gives rise to the notion of human exceptionalism from, and instrumentalism and chauvinism toward, the natural world; the sanctity of private property rights; the notion that freedom can only be acquired through material plenitude; and overconfidence in the rational mastery of nature through further scientific and technological progress.

Every traditional liberal or "progressive" understanding is up for grabs in this framework. This passage does not require much "parsing" to grasp its practical implications—the establishment of institutions and governing regimes that are not answerable to popular will, or that depend on transforming popular will in a specified direction. Eckersley makes this clear in a passage about the "social learning" function of "deliberative democracy," which she describes as "the requirement that participants be open and flexible in their thinking, that they enter a public dialogue with *a preparedness to have their preferences transformed through reasoned argument*." (Emphasis added.) In practice, of course, Eckersley's "reasoned argument" would resemble nothing so much as the infamous "ideology struggle" sessions of Mao's Cultural Revolution. This outlook gives new meaning to the old cliché about rulers selecting the people, rather than vice versa.

YESTERDAY'S CRISIS MONGERS

Is there any respite from this dreary despotic nonsense? Here and there, a few authors of sufficient independence of mind can be found who have broken with green orthodoxy in significant ways. The first of note is Matthew Connelly of Columbia University, whose brilliant new history of the population control movement, *Fatal Misconception: The Struggle to Control World Population*, is useful not simply on its theme but for the light it sheds on the political corruption that inevitably accompanies these world-saving enthusiasms. The "population bomb" can be seen as a precursor to the global warming crisis of today: as far back as the early decades of the 20th century the population crisis was put forward as the justification for global governance and coercive, non-consensual rule.

Connelly recounts one of the first major international conferences on world population, held in Geneva in 1927, where Albert Thomas, a French trade unionist, asked, "Has the moment yet arrived for considering the possibility of establishing some sort of supreme supranational authority which would regulate the distribution of population on rational and impartial lines, by controlling and directing migration movements and deciding on the opening-up or closing of countries to particular streams of immigration?" Connelly also describes the 1974 World Population Conference, which "witnessed an epic battle between starkly different versions of history and the future: one premised on the preservation of order, *if necessary by radical new forms of global governance*; the other inspired by the pursuit of justice, beginning with unfettered sovereignty for newly independent nations." (Emphasis added.)

The Intergovernmental Panel on Climate Change (IPCC), the U.N.-sponsored body that is the juggernaut of today's climate campaign, finds its precedent in the International Union for the Scientific Investigation of Population Problems (IUSIPP), spawned at the 1927 World Population Conference. A bevy of NGOs, most prominently the International Planned Parenthood Federation (IPPF) and Zero Population Growth (ZPG), later sprang into being, working hand-in-glove with the same private foundations (especially Ford and Rockefeller) and global financial institutions, such as the World Bank, that today are in the forefront of the climate campaign.

As Connelly lays out in painstaking detail, population control programs, aimed chiefly at developing nations, proliferated despite clear human rights abuses and, more importantly, new data and information that called into question many of the fundamental assumptions of the crisis mongers. Connelly recalls computer projections and economic models that offered precise and "scientifically grounded" projections of future global ruin from population growth, all of which were quickly falsified. The mass famines and food riots that were predicted never occurred; fertility rates began to fall everywhere, even in nations that lacked "family planning" programs.

The coercive nature of the population control programs in the field was appalling. India, in particular, became "a vast laboratory for the ultimate population control campaign," the chilling practices of which Connelly recounts:

Sterilizations were performed on 80-year-old men, uncomprehending subjects with mental problems, and others who died from untreated complications. There was no incentive to follow up patients. The Planning Commission found that the quality of postoperative care was "the weakest link." In Maharashtra, 52 percent of men complained of pain, and 16 percent had sepsis or unhealed wounds. Over 40 percent were unable to see a doctor. Almost 58 percent of women surveyed experienced pain after IUD insertion, 24 percent severe pain, and 43 percent had severe and excessive bleeding. Considering that iron deficiency was endemic in India, one can only imagine the toll the IUD program took on the health of Indian women.

These events Connelly describes took place in 1967, but instead of backing off, the Indian government—under constant pressure and lavish financial backing from the international population control organizations—intensified these coercive programs in the 1970s. Among other measures India required that families with three or more children had to be sterilized to be eligible for new housing (which the government, not the private market, controlled). "This war against the poor also swept across the countryside," Connelly notes:

> In one case, the village of Uttawar in Haryana was surrounded by police, hundreds were taken into custody, and every eligible male was sterilized. Hearing what had happened, thousands gathered to defend another village named Pipli. Four were killed when police fired upon the crowd. Protesters gave up only when, according to one report, a senior government official threatened aerial bombardment. The director of family planning in Maharashtra, D.N. Pai, considered it a problem of "people pollution" and defended the government: "If some excesses appear, don't blame me. . . . You must consider it something like a war. There could be a certain amount of misfiring out of enthusiasm. There has been pressure to show results. Whether you like it or not, there will be a few dead people."

In all, over 8 million sterilizations, many of them forced, were conducted in India in 1976—"draconian population control," Connelly writes, "practiced on an unprecedented scale. . . . There is no way to count the number who were being hauled away to sterilization camps against their will." Nearly 2,000 died from botched surgical procedures. The people of India finally put the brakes on this coercive utopianism, at the ballot box: the Congress Party, which had championed the family planning program as one of its main policies, was swept from office in a landslide, losing 141 of 142 contested seats in the areas with the highest rate of sterilizations. At least the people of India had recourse to the ballot box; the new environmental constitutionalism will surely aim to eliminate this remedy.

A SYSTEM WITHOUT A BRAIN

One reason why enthusiasms and programs maintain their forward momentum in the face of changing facts and circumstances is the culture of corruption that inevitably comes to envelope self-selecting leadership groups organized around a crisis. Connelly ably captures this seamy side of the story:

> Divided from within and besieged from without, leaders created a "system without a brain," *setting in motion agencies and processes that could not be stopped.* The idea of a "population crisis" provided the catalyst. But this was a system that ran on money. Ear-

marked appropriations greased the wheels of balky bureaucracies, and lavish funding was the fuel that drove it forward. But so much poured in so fast that spending became an end unto itself. The pressure to scale up and show results transformed organizations ostensibly dedicated to helping people plan their families into tools for social engineering. . . . Rather than accept constraints or accountability, they preferred to let population control go out of control. (Emphasis added.)

Corruption extended on a personal level to the New Class directing these world-saving crusades, what Connelly calls "the new jet set of population experts."

The lifestyle of the leaders of the population control establishment reflected the power of an idea whose time had come as well as the influence of the institutions that were now backing it. . . . Alan Guttmacher was in the habit of beginning letters to the Planned Parenthood membership with comments like "This is written 31,000 feet aloft as I fly from Rio to New York." He insisted on traveling with his wife, first class, with the IPPF picking up the tab. Ford [Foundation] officials flew first class with their spouses as a matter of policy. One wonders why Douglas Ensminger [the Ford Foundation's India officer] ever left his residence in Delhi—he was served by a household staff of nine, including maids, cooks, gardeners, and chauffeurs. He titled this part of his oral history "The 'Little People' of India." Ensminger insisted on the need to pay top dollar and provide a plush lifestyle to attract the best talent, even if the consultants he recruited seemed preoccupied with their perks. One of these strivers ran his two-year old American sedan without oil just so that the Ford Foundation would have to replace it with the latest model. . . .

For population experts this was the beginning of constantly expanding opportunities. The budgets, the staff, the access were all increasing even more quickly than the population growth their programs were meant to stop. There was "something in it for everyone," Population Association of America President John Kantner later recalled: "the activist, the scholar, the foundation officer, the globe-circling consultant, the wait-listed government official. World Conferences, a Population Year, commissions, select committees, new centers for research and training, a growing supply of experts, pronouncements by world leaders, and, most of all, money—lots of it."

Sounds rather like the moveable feast that is the IPCC's annual meetings, often held in hardship locales such as Bali, to press ahead with anti-global warming efforts. The magnitude of the traveling circus of the climate campaign has come to dwarf the population crusade. Prior to the arrival of climate change as a crisis issue, the largest single U.S. government science research project was the acid rain study of the 1980s (the National Acid Precipitation Assessment Project, or NAPAP for short), which cost about $500 million, and concluded that the acid rain problem had been vastly overestimated. (Public opinion polls in the late 1970s rated acid rain the most significant environmental problem of the time.) Today the U.S. government is spending multiple billions each year on climate research—so much through so many different agencies and budget sources that it is impossible to estimate the total reliably.

With so much money at stake, and with so many careers staked to the catastrophic climate scenario, one could predict that the entire apparatus would be resistant to new information and reasonable criticism. This is exactly what happened in the population crusade. When compelling critics of the population bomb thesis arose—people who might be called "skeptics," such as Julian Simon— the population campaign reacted by circling the wagons and demonizing its critics, just as global warming skeptics today are subjected to relentless *ad hominem* attacks. Connelly again:

> Leaders of the population control movement responded . . . by defending their record and fighting back. They lined up heads of state, major corporations, and international organizations behind a global strategy to slow population growth. But they also worked more quietly to insulate their projects from political opposition by co-opting or marginalizing critics, strengthening transnational networks, and establishing more free-standing institutions exempt from normal government oversight.

This is exactly the playbook of the climate campaign today. Nevertheless, it is likely to follow the same trajectory as the population control movement—gradual decline in salience to the point that even the United Nations, in the early 1990s, officially downgraded the priority of the issue. This is likely to happen to climate change *even if dramatic predictions of climate change turn out to be true.*

LIBERAL ENVIRONMENTALISTS

A few environmentalists on the Left understand the profound defects of the radical green approach to politics, along with the conventional green approach to global warming. Ted Nordhaus and Michael Shellenberger, self-described "progressives" and authors of one of the most challenging recent books on the environment, *Break Through: From the Death of Environmentalism to the Politics of Possibility* (2007), recognize and lament the authoritarianism of conventional environmentalism. "Environmental tales of tragedy begin with Nature in harmony and almost always end in quasi-authoritarian politics," Nordhaus and Shellenberger observe. While environmentalists like Eckersley embrace the postmodern language of "privilege" to denigrate traditional individual rights, Nordhaus and Shellenberger point up the obvious irony that it is environmentalism that is making the boldest claim to be given the most privileged position in politics:

> The problem is not simply that it is difficult to answer the question "Who speaks for nature?" but rather that there is something profoundly wrong with the question itself. It rests on the premise that some people are better able to speak for nature, the environment, or a particular place than others. This assumption is profoundly authoritarian.

Above all, they reject the "limits to growth" mentality that has been near the center of environmental thought for two generations:

> Environmentalists . . . have tended to view economic growth as the *cause* but not the *solution* to ecological crisis. Environmentalists like to emphasize the ways in which the economy depends on ecology, but they often miss the ways in which thinking ecologically depends on prospering economically. . . . Few things have hampered environmentalism more than its longstanding position that limits to growth are the remedy for ecological crises.

For this very reason, Nordhaus and Shellenberger insist that constraints on greenhouse gas emissions as contemplated by the Kyoto process will never work and should be abandoned. Instead they advocate massive research (with government paying for the largest share) into post-carbon energy systems. With due caveats about government-funded research, this seems a better approach than Gore's hairshirt agenda. They may underestimate the sheer technical and economic difficulties of energy technology, but *Break Through* is not primarily a policy tome—it is intended to reorient our general thinking about the environment. In the second half of their book it becomes clear that Nordhaus and Shellenberger aren't just trying to save environmentalism; they are trying to save contemporary liberalism, which they regard as nearly as intellectually dead as environmentalism. "[E]nvironmentalism is hobbled by its resentment of human strength and our desire to control nature, and liberalism by its resentment of wealth and power," they write. This part of the book is less successful though no less serious and thoughtful. In arguing that liberals need to be more philosophical (hear, hear!), Nordhaus and Shellenberger deploy a number of philosophical categories that are problematic, at the very least, and embrace the core principles of postmodernism—though, happily, that overused term does not appear in their generally clear, direct prose. The duo are against Platonic essentialism when it comes to conceiving nature (including, it would seem, human nature), and for a revival of Deweyite pragmatism as well as empowering individual "authenticity." The reader gets dizzy at times following the back and forth between Richard Rorty, Thomas Kuhn, Francis Fukuyama, the "metaphysics of becoming," and more down-to-earth wonkish discussions of gas mileage standards for automobiles.

But despite these flaws, *Break Through* is still a refreshing departure from most environmental discourse, and the young authors probably aren't done, either, rethinking fundamental aspects of political life and man's relation to nature. Their rude treatment from fellow "progressives" (the *American Prospect* dismissed the book as containing "a lot of wasted ink") will surely encourage more reflection.

A GREEN REFORMATION?

Even in academia there are a few lonely voices who've noticed that the conventional green outlook is badly defective and in need of revision. Seymour Garte, professor of environmental and occupational health at the University of Pittsburgh's School of Public Health, makes his bid to become the next "skeptical environmentalist" (after Bjorn Lomborg) with his book *Where We Stand: A Surprising Look at the Real State of Our Planet* (2007). Garte recalls his surprise, and the surprise of fellow experts attending a professional conference in Europe, when presented with data from a speaker showing steadily declining air pollution trends along with the claim, "everyone knows that air pollution levels are continually decreasing everywhere." "I looked around the room," Garte writes:

> I was not the only nonexpert there. Most of my other colleagues were also not atmospheric or air pollution scientists. Later I asked one of them, a close friend, if he had known that air pollution levels were constantly decreasing throughout Europe and the

United States on a yearly basis. "I had no idea," he said. It was certainly news to me. Even though I was a professor of environmental health and had been actively involved in many aspects of pollution research for many years, that simple fact had somehow escaped me. . . . I had certainly never seen it published in the media.

Garte goes on to argue that excessive pessimism about the environment undermines good scientific investigation and distorts our understanding of important environmental challenges. He displays the frequent naïveté of a scientist observing the political world: "I have never understood why pessimism has for so long been associated with a liberal or progressive political world view." He criticizes anti-technological biases prevalent among environmentalists, but is also skeptical that market forces alone will suffice to continue our environmental progress in the future. He is guardedly optimistic that the creativity and adaptability of the human species will enable us to confront surprises and new problems. "We should pay attention to our successes as much as to our failures," Garte writes, "because in order to know where to go next, it is just as important to know where (and how) we went right as it is to know where we have gone wrong."

One of the persistent problems with environmentalism is its bait-and-switch character. The essentially political character of the movement cloaks itself with the seemingly objective authority of modern science, as though science were immune from politicization, or led to self-evident political or policy conclusions. Laying aside the value-laden premises of the ways science is used and misused in environmental controversies, it is startling to discover how limited our scientific grasp of many environmental conditions really is. The worst abuse of science comes in the almost daily predictions of future environmental conditions based on sophisticated computer models that often lack a solid empirical grounding for their assumptions and are seldom validated or back-tested with any rigor. Orrin Pilkey of Duke University and his daughter Linda Pilkey-Jarvis, a government geologist, note these failings in *Useless Arithmetic: Why Environmental Scientists Can't Predict the Future* (2006).

The most famous prediction racket these days is climate modeling, but *Useless Arithmetic* mostly avoids the Super Bowl of enviro-modeling in favor of tackling more limited prediction modeling exercises, such as fishery management or forecasting coastal erosion, invasive species, and nuclear waste at Yucca Mountain. Environmental forecasting is a classic case of being hoist by one's own petard. The inherent weakness of most exercises stems precisely from the core principle of modern pop environmentalism—that everything is connected to everything else. As the Pilkeys point out,

> [p]erhaps the single most important reason that quantitative predictive mathematical models of natural processes on earth don't work and can't work has to do with *ordering complexity*. Interactions among the numerous components of a complex system occur in unpredictable and unexpected sequences.

Contrary to the usual process of science in which defects and errors become the platform for refinement and new approaches to the problem, environmental science finds itself caught in the grip of *"politically correct modeling"* (the authors' emphasis) in which there is enormous pressure on scientists, many of whom discover "that modeling results are easier to live with if they follow preconceived or politically correct notions." The models take on a life of their own, and become obstacles to conducting serious field studies that might strengthen our empirical grasp of ecosystem dynamics. "Applied mathematical modeling has become a science that has advanced without the usual broad-based, vigorous debate, criticism, and constant attempts at falsification that characterize good science," the Pilkeys conclude.

Neither Garte nor the Pilkeys are full-blown green skeptics; to the contrary—they are global warming believers who lean slightly left-of-center in their politics. But they represent a gathering backlash among academic scientists against the straightjacket of orthodox environmentalism. There are a number of others like them whose names never appear in the media or before congressional hearings. The prospect that a new generation of environmentalists such as Nordhaus and Shellenberger, along with academic dissenters such as Garte and the Pilkeys, can work a reformation of the movement may not seem very bright. But such voices were virtually unheard of even ten years ago. Stay tuned: a new shade of green might yet emerge.

Is Health Care a Right?

Andrew E. Busch

(Winter 2008/09)

Last October, in the second presidential debate, Barack Obama declared that health care "should be a right for every American." His electoral victory and the expansion of Democratic congressional majorities virtually assure that the debate over health care in America will heat up again. Liberals and conservatives will joust over a variety of arcane concepts—single-payer, play-or-pay, employer mandates, individual mandates, community rating, pre-existing conditions, health savings accounts, tax credits, risk pools. Beneath the minutiae, however, will lurk a philosophical dispute, framed by Obama's assertion in the debate: is health care a "right"? With Americans deeply ambivalent about health care policy options, it is important to come to grips with the first principles that ought to guide policy. This requires us to engage in some serious thinking about rights.

Modern liberalism has staked much on the notion that health care is a right. Franklin D. Roosevelt declared it so in his 1944 State of the Union message, when he included health care on the list of economic provisions that should form a "second bill of rights" parallel to our existing political one. Since then, several presidents have tried to father universal national health insurance, and Lyndon Johnson won enactment of Medicaid and Medicare. Politically astute liberals (including Roosevelt himself) have attempted to link the right to health care, like other positive economic "rights," to the American political tradition: a natural right of some sort, or a civil right necessary to put into effect the natural right to life or the pursuit of happiness.

NATURAL OR CIVIL RIGHT?

Clearly, however, health care is not a natural right as the founders or John Locke would have understood it. In their view, natural rights exist prior to the formation of government. Since there is no government in the pre-political state of nature, there cannot be a right to government-supplied health care in the state of nature. One has the right to speak one's mind, to defend oneself, and to acquire property in the state of nature, but no one has the right to a free checkup at the National Health Service in the state of nature, because there is no National Health Service.

Nonetheless, perhaps health care could be regarded as necessary to effect the natural right to life or the pursuit of happiness, and consequently, it should be treated as a civil right. This formulation, too, is greatly flawed.

The first problem is that even if the right to life led to a positive government obligation to provide health care, that right would logically be restricted to medical actions essential to preserve life, especially emergency measures. Yet medical professionals already provide life-saving emergency care in practice, without a grand declaration of rights; in any event, such a limited guarantee is far from what policy activists have in mind. Likewise, if a civil right to health care derived from the pursuit of happiness, one would have to show that it is positively correlated—perhaps even necessary—to the achievement of happiness. Yet this conclusion is surprisingly difficult to support. There are, as it turns out, a number of surveys that attempt to measure the happiness of people around the world. Residents of the U.S. tend to rank around 15th among the 90 countries typically surveyed. In recent surveys, 85% of Americans say they are personally happy or very happy. Consistently, a number of countries with universal health care (such as Denmark and Norway) rank ahead of the U.S., and a larger number of countries with universal health care (such as Great Britain, France, and Germany) lag considerably behind the U.S. in happiness. On balance, research tends to show that countries reporting the greatest happiness have political freedom, not universal health care, in common.

The founders, for their part, already named—in the Bill of Rights and several other constitutional provisions, such as the guarantee of habeas corpus—the civil rights they thought necessary for the execution of natural rights. There is no evidence that they considered provision of health care necessary for realizing natural rights, though medical care certainly existed in the late 18th century and was valued, as it is today, for its capacity to prolong life. Indeed, there is no evidence that the founders considered governmental provision of food to be a civil right, though its connection to the maintenance of life was, then as now, more direct and more constant than that of health care.

Guaranteed legal counsel is a rare example of a positive government-funded service that has attained the status of a civil right linked to a natural right, but defense against criminal accusation has a uniquely direct connection to natural rights, since the positive action of government prosecution might deprive the accused of life or liberty. Here the citizen is threatened not by the vicissitudes of nature but by government itself, undoubtedly placing a stronger obligation on government to go the extra mile to respect his due process rights.

In other areas, despite attempts by liberals to translate economic "rights" into civil rights like freedom of speech, America has never enshrined this concept into law. If one were to follow liberal thinking on health care to its logical conclusion, the government would also be obliged to buy a newspaper company or television or radio station for anyone wishing to exercise freedom of the press; pay the costs of petition-gatherers for those who wish to exercise their right to petition the government; purchase firearms for those wishing to exercise their right to keep and bear arms; pay for a church, synagogue, or mosque, on behalf of those wishing to exercise their right to worship as they please. Of course, several of these "rights" would collide with the right of citizens not to be forced to pay for the propagation of be-liefs not their own. But the contradiction would be no greater than that between a right to government health care and the natural right of citizens to enjoy the fruits of their own labor.

Even in latter days, this approach has generally not prevailed. In the 1980 case *Harris v. McRae*, the Supreme Court rejected the argument that the right to abortion translated into a positive government obligation to fund abortions for the poor (leaving aside the controversy over the right itself). Despite considerable effort in the 1960s and 1970s, welfare advocates failed to gain wide acceptance of the notion of government welfare payments as a fundamental civil right, and the landmark welfare reform act of 1996 departed still farther from that goal by turning federal welfare from an entitlement program into an annually-appropriated block grant replete with work requirements and time-limited benefits.

RAWLS TO THE RESCUE

Even though it is not possible to establish a right to health care on the basis of the American political tradition, liberals might try shifting the argument to a differ-ent, and vaguer, level. For example, they might argue on the basis of utilitarianism rather than natural right. If universal health care could be proven to produce the greatest good for the greatest number, it could be mandated in good conscience. Leaving aside the difficulty of asserting a "right" on the basis of utilitarian calcu-lation—how can it be a right if the calculation can change?—John Stuart Mill's utilitarianism held that the "greatest good" could be defined by the degree to which the action enhanced freedom and individual development. He also argued that the only reason for government to use coercion on an individual was to pre-vent him from doing harm to another. Socialized medicine clearly does not pass those tests.

Another approach would be consistent with the liberal welfare-statism ex-pounded by philosopher John Rawls (though he was criticized by liberals for not including health care on his list of basic rights). Imagine two people with identi-cal life-threatening medical conditions. One has money, the other does not. Why should one live and the other die? Any reasonable person hidden behind Rawls's "veil of ignorance" would want government to ensure that he was not the one with-out medical care at the critical moment. For some disciples of Rawls, that by itself is enough to establish a kind of moral right.

But here liberals conflate two notions that are superficially complementary but actually distinct from a moral point of view: the duty to help others in mortal dan-ger, recognized by doctors themselves in the ethics of their profession, and the right to forcibly extract help from others. The first is a noble code cultivated in a free society and accepted by free people who voluntarily take responsibility for their fel-lows. The second is a form of conscription in which some individuals forcibly com-mandeer the services and resources of others for what is, after all, fundamentally their own private benefit. In any event, the argument is disingenuous, inasmuch as liberals are not contending for equal access to lifesaving procedures; they are con-tending for guaranteed issue of the whole panoply of health services.

And the Rawlsian approach, virtually context-free, does not fare so well when it makes, as it eventually must, solid contact with mundane realities. Suppose, for instance, that without knowing in advance your station in life, you may choose either (a) a simple 99% probability of obtaining health insurance, or (b) an 85% probability of obtaining health insurance combined with higher quality of care if you receive it, significantly lower taxes, and less intrusive and less centralized government. It is far from clear that reasonable people would be in favor of (a) at all.

UNDEMOCRATIC RIGHTS

The great danger of health-care-as-a-right is that it threatens to supplant the American republic's key political principles. Accepting a positive government obligation to fund social services claimed as a matter of right would lead inexorably to government without limits. How could one fence off claims on government resources or demands for the exercise of government power, if the right to the pursuit of happiness, for example, became a font of positive economic rights? When applied to health care, this principle could easily lead to individual rights, traditionally understood, being eaten up by confiscatory taxation, health regimentation and rationing, and insurance mandates.

Although the right to health care is an article of faith among modern egalitarians, it does not square with equality as the founders understood it: an equality of natural rights, which led to equality under the law, consent of the governed, and the mandate that law be exercised for the common good, not the private benefit of the few. Yet health-care-as-a-right leaves little room for democratic debate or compromise—after all, the point of a right is to remove an issue from the realm of majority rule—and would mandate a wrenching economic and social dislocation in order to promote the private benefit of the 12% of Americans who do not have health insurance at any given time.

Practically speaking, a right to health care denies the nation an important element of flexibility in fashioning a response to health care problems. Sticking to the founders' sound general principles would actually leave policymakers with greater room for policy innovation.

But it is not enough for conservatives to demonstrate that health care is not a right; they should take a much more assertive interest in health care policy, for three reasons.

First, many if not most of the problems with our health care system have been caused by bad government policy. Government has an obligation to fix its own mistakes. Second, conservative skepticism by itself is not politically tenable. Although Americans remain suspicious of a government takeover of health care, conservatives must offer some way to allay their concerns about the current system. Finally, the longer the issue remains unaddressed by sensible conservative policies, the more likely the Left will be to use it as a wedge for advancing socialism more broadly. It's like leaving a loaded pistol in a room of drunken pirates. No one knows when it will be used or who will use it, but it's clear that nothing good will come of it.

So how should conservatives begin constructing an approach to health care? They first ought to recognize that individuals exist in a social web of family, friends, co-workers, churches, and other associations. One of the great conservative insights is that civil society can often contribute to solutions to social problems because its institutions can act compassionately, possess strength beyond the capacity of individuals, and enjoy local knowledge beyond the capacity of big government. Conservatives need to find a role for civil society.

More generally, they need to promote solutions that openly treat the nation's fundamental principles as a resource. This would mean reducing arbitrary distinctions in the tax code, giving individuals more freedom, using market mechanisms to help restrain costs, guaranteeing that states have an important role, and insisting that Congress retain accountability for whatever it enacts rather than delegating its responsibility to executive agencies. And it means, in true conservative fashion, insisting that reform not make the perfect the enemy of the good.

But first, conservatives will have to prevail in the argument with the new president and his followers over whether health care is a right.

VI

HEARTS AND MINDS

Born American, But in the Wrong Place

Peter W. Schramm

(Fall 2006)

On October 23, 1956, students gathered at the foot of Sandor Petofi's statue in Budapest and read his poem "Rise, Magyar!" made famous in the democratic revolution of 1848. Workers, and even soldiers, soon joined the students. The demonstrators took over the state-run radio station and the Communist Party offices and toppled a huge statue of Stalin, dragging it through the streets. Rebellion spread throughout the country. The demonstrators—now Freedom Fighters—held Soviet occupation forces at bay for several days.

On November 1, the Hungarian prime minister announced that Hungary would withdraw from the Warsaw Pact. At dawn, November 4, the Soviets launched a major invasion of Hungary, in an offensive involving tens of thousands of additional troops, air and artillery assaults, and 6,000 tanks. A heroic resistance was crushed in less than a week.

The last free Hungarian radio broadcast spent its final hours repeating the Gettysburg Address in seven languages, followed by an S.O.S. Over 20,000 Hungarians were tried and sentenced for participation in the uprising, hundreds receiving the death sentence. An estimated 200,000 Hungarians—of a population of 9 million—became refugees. Forty-seven thousand came to the United States. Hungary became a member of NATO on March 12, 1999.

* * * *

In October 1956, my parents, my four-year-old sister, and I shared a small apartment with my father's parents and his brother on the plaza near the eastern railroad station in Budapest. I was two months shy of my tenth birthday when the Hungarian Revolution began.

Because the revolutionaries had taken over the railroad station, the Soviets positioned several tanks in our neighborhood, and we could not leave our apartment. There was heavy fighting, and bodies were strewn everywhere; one lay just outside our window for several days. After a week and a half, the action moved elsewhere and we could once again venture outdoors—carefully. Walking around one day, I came upon a Russian personnel carrier that was stacked with skeletons. It seemed that each was covered with about two inches of black velvet. I later learned that these poor souls had been burned alive by a Molotov cocktail.

It soon became clear that though the Soviets had pulled out of our immediate area, they were winning. The Revolution was going to be defeated, and they would be back. Things were going to get more unpleasant than ever, and Hungary had not been a pleasant place for the Schramms for quite a long time.

My father, William, was born in 1922, into a politically tumultuous Hungary produced by the collapse of the Austro-Hungarian Empire at the end of World War I. His father, an active participant in the 1919 Communist revolution, was hounded by the fascists then ruling Hungary. By the time my father reached his teens, the Depression hit, followed by another world war. My father was placed in the air artillery. He liked it there, he said, because they could pretend to shoot down American planes, knowing that the B-17s were flying well out of range. They couldn't hurt the good guys, yet they did their duty. That was as good as life got in those days.

The war's end brought little relief. When the Communists took control of the country in 1949, they "expropriated" my parents' little textile shop (about half the size of my current living room) and everything in it. Under this new tyranny, my parents were considered part of the dangerous "bourgeoisie." In that same year, the Communists sentenced my father's father to ten years hard labor for having a small American flag in his possession (by that time he had been a leader of the social democrats for some years). At his "trial" he was asked why he had the flag. Was he a spy? He replied that it represented freedom better than any other symbol he knew, and that he had a right to have it. My father tried then, for the first time, to persuade my mother, Rose, to leave the country. But ties to family and friends were too strong, and she could not bear to do it. Soon, my father himself was sentenced to a year of prison for "rumor mongering" (someone claimed he had called a Communist a tyrant, which he had). When he got out, he washed windows for a while and made illegal whiskey to make ends meet as best he could.

My grandfather got an early release from the labor camp in 1956 and came back to us looking like a victim of the Holocaust. Still, the first thing he wanted to know was whether we still had the flag. Of course, we did not. It had long ago been confiscated. But my father didn't want to break his father's heart and had somehow managed to secure another one. We took it out of its hiding place and, at that tender age, I learned the very adult lesson of the complexity of telling the truth. Seeing that flag somehow erased much of the pain and torment of my grandfather's years of imprisonment; it seemed to give him hope.

Now, with the revolution failing, everyone expected that the Communist boot was going to come down harder than ever. But before we had more opportunities to experience it, an odd accident set us on the path to a very different future. On one of his trips out to secure some bread, a hand grenade landed next to my father but, miraculously, did not go off. That was the last straw. He came home and announced to my mother that he was going to leave the country whether she would come or not. Mom said, "O.K., William. We will come if Peter agrees. Ask Peter."

"But where are we going?" I asked.
"We are going to America," he said.
"Why America?" I prodded.
"Because, son. We were born Americans, but in the wrong place."

He said that as naturally as if I had asked him what was the color of the sky. It was so obvious to him why we should head for America that he never entertained any other option. Of course, he hadn't studied American history or politics, but he had come to know deep in his heart the meaning of tyranny. He hungered for its opposite and knew where to find it. America represented to my father, as Lincoln put it, "the last, best hope of earth." I would like to be able to say that this made my father a remarkable man for his time and his circumstances. For, in many ways, he truly was a wonder. But this is not one of those ways. Among the Hungarians I knew—aside from those who were true believers in the Communists—this was the common sense of the subject. It was self-evident to them. I would spend much of the next 20 years acquiring this common sense for myself.

JOURNEY TO AMERICA

We could not tell anyone—including my grandparents and uncle—that we were leaving. It was safer for them (and for us) that they not know where we were, so they could answer honestly and convincingly when questioned. We therefore had to leave with essentially nothing. My sister Marta and I each had a doll and a small bag of clothes. My parents had one small bag between them. And my father had $17 in his pocket in single dollar bills, which he had been hoarding for years; good as gold, he always said. The trains were packed with many other people similarly outfitted and with the same destination—the Austrian border. The Russians were stopping the trains and looking for people. We all just kept our heads down and said nothing to anyone.

When we left the train, hundreds of others left, too, all taking different paths, doing their best to ignore one another but inevitably merging into larger groups, since they were all heading in the same direction. We had many miles ahead of us, most of them in the dark, some across fields and farm land. We did our best to avoid haystacks (where Russians were thought to lie in ambush), and I remember a particularly difficult thing we had to do—ignore the nearby sound of a crying child. That was a well-known Russian trick. We did, however, come upon a boy whose father had been shot. He was immediately welcomed into our growing and informal group of which, it seemed, my father had become the leader.

We crossed a little bridge in the dark before morning. Someone heard the sound of German on the other side of the bridge. It was the Austrian border post! As we stepped over a line, the Austrians asked us to show our weapons. I remember being utterly surprised to see that every man in our group immediately began to drop pistols, knives, etc. We had just finished an expedition of the brave. It had led us to the town of Nickelsdorf, Austria. There we were housed in a big barn, and slept soundly, on beds of straw (I remember the oddness of going to sleep when it was still daylight). The next morning we were moved to an Army camp near Innsbruck. For nearly a month, we were fed and housed there. Dad went out and got a job. I occupied myself in the normal pursuits of ten-year-old boys.

Occasionally, officials from the various embassies of different countries would come by and attempt to catalogue where the refugees were planning to go and why. They wanted to know if we had any relatives in any other country. We did not. The man from the German embassy encouraged us to settle in Germany. We would be made citizens immediately because Schramm was a German name. My father told him we were not German. He was sure of what he wanted. But we had no relatives in America. The representative from the American embassy asked my father, "Don't you know anyone in America?"

As fate would have it, we did. Back in 1946, in war-ravaged Hungary before I was born, my father (who was not a mechanic or an engineer, but was resourceful in all things) had somehow managed to build a car out of scrap parts. It was nothing more, really, than an engine with four wheels and a flat-bed in the back. Apart from military vehicles, cars on Hungarian streets were an extreme rarity at that time. He combed the countryside in this contraption for junk to sell or trade so that his family could survive.

On one such excursion, he came upon a man standing next to a broken-down Volkswagen. The man turned out to be a decommissioned U.S. officer who had been born in Hungary and was taking time off to tour the country. My father was able to help him get the car going again, and the man offered to pay for the help in precious dollars. Dad was too proud to take the money, but he accepted the man's business card. It read, "Joseph Moser, DDS, Hermosa Beach, California." "If you ever need anything," the man said, "don't hesitate to call." Dad gave the card to my mother for safekeeping.

Now, in Nickelsdorf, Austria, ten years later, my mother remembered that we did know someone in America. She ran back to the bunks and out of her little satchel pulled an old, rumpled business card. "Yes," my father said, "I know this man." He showed the business card to the American. We had had no contact with Dr. Moser in all those intervening years. But he was still where his card said he was, and he was willing (thank God!) to sponsor us.

Within a week of contacting Dr. Moser, we were shipped off to Munich and then took a plane to New York City. We landed just before midnight on Christmas Eve, one day after my tenth birthday. When the plane stopped for refueling in New-foundland, the crew of the airline (TWA, as I recall) gave Christmas presents to the children on board. My sister got a doll, and I got a toy Army jeep. This was the extent of the presents for that Christmas—except for the freedom we were about to enjoy. On Christmas morning we were taken to Camp Kilmer, New Jersey, for processing.

A few weeks later we took a train to Los Angeles where we were met by Dr. Moser and his family. Sponsorship meant that they had to guarantee that we would not become a burden to the American people. He had to house and feed us for awhile. Mom and Dad both got jobs right away, Dad at the local newspaper lifting heavy things, and Mom cleaning houses. Soon we had a little beach shack to live in, and my parents were able to purchase their first restaurant with their savings and a bank-financed loan. The whole family went to work. We had to tear the place apart before we could open it. After it was opened, my sister and I washed dishes as Mom and Dad cooked and waited on tables.

THE EDUCATION OF AN AMERICAN

When I reached high school age we moved to Studio City and bought a bigger res-taurant—Schramm's Hungarian Restaurant—right across the street from many of the movie studios. I attended Hollywood High because it had an ROTC program, which the neighborhood high school didn't. But I must say that I didn't learn much, either in high school or college, about the great country to which I'd emigrated. Even in the early '60s (before "political correctness" had been heard of), it was already common for teachers and professors to teach that America was an amazingly hypocritical place. All I needed to know about Abraham Lincoln, one teacher said, was that he was a racist.

When I graduated from Hollywood High in 1964, I enrolled at San Fernando Valley State College (now California State University, Northridge), while continuing to work for my parents. By that time, I had become an avid reader and had accumulated a large and growing library of my own (to the chagrin of my father, to whom this seemed very impractical). But there was no particular focus to my reading—I wandered through history, philosophy, literature, language, as one thing or another struck my fancy. When I started college, I just took classes that I found interesting. I had no plan or major in mind, until I discovered I had to pick one. So I picked political science.

Throughout these years, because of my own experience rather than anything I was taught in school, I maintained an interest in American politics. The anti-Communist positions of the Republican Party were a natural draw for my family and me. We didn't think the Democrats fully appreciated the enemy. I became active in GOP politics and campaigned for Barry Goldwater in 1964 and for Ronald Reagan in his successful race two years later to become governor of California. But my politics were not well developed.

While I was active in the Young Republicans, I attended a few seminars sponsored by the Intercollegiate Studies Institute. They provided an opportunity for students from colleges all around the country to meet and study with some of the leading conservative professors. It was in 1965 at one of these summer seminars that I first met Harry V. Jaffa. He had just moved from Ohio to Claremont Men's College and was teaching a class on Shakespeare; Martin Diamond was teaching one on *The Federalist*. At about the same time, I came across the new journal *Intercollegiate Review* and the youthful *National Review*.

As I met and became friends with other students and teachers in Claremont, I discovered a world of study that united all my interests and included an understanding of America that was worthy of the subject. I enrolled in a doctoral program in government at Claremont Graduate School in 1971. I took classes on Plato's *Phaedo*, the American Founding, Lincoln, Shakespeare's politics, and many other topics. It was intoxicating, made even more pleasant because it took place with friends, who were not only smart and hardworking, but partisans of America and the things for which the country stood. It was here that I started understanding what my father had always understood: that in America human beings could prove to the world that they have the capacity to govern themselves. I came to understand what Lincoln meant when he said that the ideas of the Declaration of Independence were the "electric cord" that linked all Americans together, as though we were "blood of the blood, and flesh of the flesh, of the men who wrote that Declaration." This is what it meant to be an American, and it wasn't all that far from what it meant to be a man.

TEACHING AMERICANS

America became home to me, and these days I continue my life as a student of America. The difference is that now a university pays me to study, rather than my paying it for the privilege. Here at a liberal arts college in central Ohio, I'm in the ironic position of teaching native Americans (I mean native-born Americans) how to think about their country. How odd it seems, and yet how perfectly American, that I, a Hungarian immigrant, should teach *them*.

When I teach them about American politics and American history, I start with a simple thing about their country and themselves. I tell them that they are the fortunate of the earth, among the blessed of all times and places. I tell them this as a thing that should be as obvious to them as it was to my father. And their blessing, their great good fortune, lies in the nation into which they were born. I tell them that their country, the United States of America, is not only the most powerful and the most prosperous country on earth, but the most free and the most just. Then I do my best to tell them how and why this is so. And I teach them about the principles from which those blessings of liberty flow. I invite them to consider whether they can have any greater honor than to pass undiminished to their children and grandchildren this great inheritance of freedom.

The Crisis of American National Identity

Charles R. Kesler

(Fall 2005)

About a decade ago, when he was vice president, Al Gore explained that our national motto, *e pluribus unum*, means "from one, many." This was a sad day for knowledge of Latin among our political elite—and after all those expensive private schools that Gore had been packed off to by his paterfamilias. It was the kind of flagrant mistranslation that, had it been committed by a Republican, say George W. Bush or Dan Quayle, would have been a gaffe heard round the world. But the media didn't play up the slip, perhaps because they had seen Gore's Harvard grades and figured he'd suffered enough, perhaps because they admired the remark's impudence. Though literally a mistake, *politically* the comment expressed and honored the multicultural imperative, then so prominent in the minds of American liberals: "from one," or to exaggerate slightly, "instead of one culture, many." As such it was a rather candid example of the literary method known as deconstruction: torture a text until it confesses the exact opposite of what it says in plain English or, in this case, Latin.

After 9/11, we haven't heard much from multiculturalism. In wartime, politics tends to assert its sway over culture. In its most elementary sense, politics implies friends and enemies, us and them. The attackers on 9/11 were not interested in our internal diversity. They didn't murder the innocents in the Twin Towers or the Pentagon or on board the airplanes because they were black, white, Asian-American, or Mexican-American, but because they were American. (Although I bet that for every Jew they expected to kill, the terrorists felt an extra thrill of murderous anticipation.)

In our horror and anguish at those enormities and then in our resolution to avenge them, the American people closed ranks. National pride swelled and national identity—perhaps the simplest marker is the display of the flag—reasserted itself. After 9/11 everyone, presumably even Mr. Gore, understood that *e pluribus unum* means: out of many, *one*. Yet the patriotism of indignation and fear can only go so far. When the threat recedes, when the malefactor has been punished, the sentiment cools. Unless we know what about our national identity ought to command admiration and love, we are left at our enemies' mercy. We pay them the supreme and undeserved compliment of letting *them* define *us*, even if indirectly.

Unsure of our national identity, we are left uncertain of our national interests, too; now even the war brought on by 9/11 seems strangely indefinite. And so Samuel P. Huntington is correct in his recent book to ask *Who Are We?* and to investigate what he calls in the subtitle *The Challenges to America's National Identity*. What shape will our national identity be in when the present war is over—or when it fades from consciousness, as arguably it has already begun to do?

CREED VERSUS CULTURE

In Huntington's view, America is undergoing an identity crisis, in which the long-term trend points squarely towards national disintegration. A University Professor at Harvard (the school's highest academic honor), he has written a dozen or so books including several that are rightly regarded as classics of modern social science. He is a scholar of political culture, especially of the interplay between ideas and institutions; but in this book he calls himself not only a scholar but a patriot (without any ironic quotation marks). That alone marks him as an extraordinary figure in today's academy.

Though not inevitable, the disorder that he discerns is fueled by at least three developments in the culture. The first is multiculturalism, which saps and undermines serious efforts at civic education. The second is "transnationalism," which features self-proclaimed citizens of the world—leftist intellectuals like Martha Nussbaum and Amy Guttman, as well as the Davos set of multinational executives, NGOs, and global bureaucrats—who affect a point of view that is above this nation or any nation. Third is what Huntington terms the "Hispanization of America," due to the dominance among recent immigrants of a single non-English language which threatens to turn America, in his words, into "a bilingual, bicultural society," not unlike Canada. This threat is worsened by the nearness of the lands from which these Spanish-speaking immigrants come, which reinforces their original nationality.

Standing athwart these trends are the historic sources of American national identity, which Huntington describes as race, ethnicity, ideology, and culture. Race and ethnicity have, of course, largely been discarded in the past half-century, a development he welcomes. By ideology he means the principles of the Declaration of Independence, namely, individual rights and government by consent, which he calls the American "creed" (a term popularized by Gunnar Myrdal). These principles are universal in the sense that they are meant to be, in Abraham Lincoln's words, "applicable to all men at all times." Culture is harder to define, but Huntington emphasizes language and religion, along with (a distant third) some inherited English notions of liberty. *Who Are We?* is at bottom a defense of this culture, which he calls Anglo-Protestantism, as the dominant strain of national identity. Although he never eschews the creed, he regards it fundamentally as the offshoot of a particular cultural moment: "The Creed . . . was the product of the distinct Anglo-Protestant culture of the founding settlers of America in the seventeenth and eighteenth centuries."

Twenty-some years ago, he took virtually the opposite position, as James Ceaser noted in a perceptive review in the *Weekly Standard*. In *American Politics: The Promise of Disharmony* (1981), Huntington declared, "The political ideas of the American creed have been the basis of national identity." But the result, even according to his earlier analysis, was a very unstable identity. The inevitable gap between ideals and institutions doomed the country to anguished cycles of moral overheating ("creedal passion periods") and cooling. He wrote the earlier book as a kind of reflection on the politics of the 1960s and 1970s, noting how the excessive moralism of those times had given way to hypocrisy, complacency, and finally cynicism. In a way, then, the two books really are united in their concern about creedal over-reliance or disharmony.

To bring coherence and stability to American national identity apparently requires a creed with two feet planted squarely on the ground of Anglo-Protestant culture. The creed alone is too weak to hold society together. As he argues in the new book, "America with only the creed as a basis for unity would soon evolve into a loose confederation of ethnic, racial, cultural and political groups." It is not excessive individualism he worries about; he fears rather that individuals, steering by the creed alone, would soon be attracted to balkanizing group-identities. Therefore, the creed must be subsumed under the culture, if creed and country both are to survive; indeed, "if they are to be worthy of survival, because much of what is most admirable about America" is in its culture, at its best.

ANGLO-PROTESTANTISM

Huntington's argument provides a convenient starting point for thinking about the problem of American national identity, which touches immigration, bilingual education, religion in the public square, civic education, foreign policy, and many other issues. While agreeing with much of what he says about the culture's importance, I want to speak up for the creed and for a third point of view, distinct from and encompassing both.

Huntington outlines two sources of national identity, a set of universal principles that (he argues) cannot serve to define a particular society; and a culture that can, but that is under withering attack from within and without. His account of culture is peculiar, narrowly focused on the English language and Anglo-Protestant religious traits, among which he counts "Christianity; religious commitment; . . . and dissenting Protestant values of individualism, the work ethic, and the belief that humans have the ability and the duty to try to create heaven on earth, a 'city on a hill.'" Leave aside the fact that John Winthrop hardly thought that he and his fellow Puritans were creating "heaven on earth." Is Huntington calling for the revival of all those regulations that sustained Winthrop's merely earthly city, including the strictures memorably detailed in *The Scarlet Letter*? Obviously not, but when fishing in the murky waters of Anglo-Protestant values, it is hard to tell what antediluvian monsters might emerge. If his object is to revive, or to call for the revival of, this culture, how will he distinguish its worthy from its unworthy parts?

Huntington is on more solid ground when he impresses "English concepts of the rule of law, the responsibility of rulers, and the rights of individuals" into the service of our Anglo-Protestantism. Nonetheless, he is left awkwardly to face the fact that his beloved country began, almost with its first breath, by renouncing and abominating certain salient features of English politics and English Protestantism, including king, lords, commons, parliamentary supremacy, primogeniture and entail, and the established national church. There were, of course, significant cultural continuities: Americans continued to speak English, to drink tea (into which a little whiskey may have been poured), to hold jury trials before robed judges, to read (most of us) the King James Bible, and so forth. But there has to be something wrong with an analysis of our national culture that literally leaves out the word "American." Anglo-Protestantism—what's American about that, after all? The term would seem to embrace many things that our countrymen have tried and given up—or that have never been American at all, much less distinctively so.

Huntington tries to get around this difficulty by admitting that the American creed has modified Anglo-Protestantism. But if that is so, how can the creed be derived from Anglo-Protestantism? When, where, how, and why does that crucial term "American" creep onto the stage and into our souls? He allows that "the sources of the creed include the Enlightenment ideas that became popular among some American elites in the mid-eighteenth century." But he suggests that these ideas did not change the prevailing culture so much as the culture changed them. In general, Huntington tries to reduce reason to an epiphenomenon of culture, whether of the Anglo-Protestant or Enlightenment variety. He doesn't see—or at any rate, he doesn't admit the implications of seeing—that reason has, or can have, an integrity of its own, independent of culture. But Euclid, Shakespeare, or Bach, for example, though each had a cultural setting, was not simply produced by his culture, and the meaning of his works is certainly not dependent on it or limited to it. It is the same with the most thoughtful American Founders and with human equality, liberty, and the other great ideas of the American creed.

THE CULTURAL APPROACH

Huntington's analysis is closer than he might like to admit to the form of traditionalist conservatism that emerged in Europe in opposition to the French Revolution. These conservatives, often inspired by Edmund Burke but going far beyond him, condemned reason or "rationalism" on the grounds that its universal principles destroyed the conditions of political health in particular societies. They held that political health consisted essentially in tending to a society's own traditions and idiosyncrasies, to its peculiar genius or culture. As opposed to the French Revolution's attempt to make or construct new governments as part of a worldwide civilization based on the rights of man, these conservatives argued that government must be a native growth, must emerge from the spontaneous evolution of the nation itself. Government was a part of the *Volksgeist*, "the spirit of the people." Politics, including morality, was in the decisive respect an outgrowth of culture.

But on these premises, how can one distinguish good from bad culture? What began as the rejection of rationalism quickly led to the embrace of irrationalism. Or to put it differently, the romance soon drained out of Romanticism once the nihilistic implications of its rejection of universals became clear. Huntington is right, of course, to criticize multiculturalism as destructive of civic unity. But he is wrong to think that Anglo-Protestant culture is the antidote, or even merely our antidote, to multiculturalism and transnationalism. Multiculturalism likes to assert that all cultures are created equal, and that America and the West have sinned a great sin by establishing white, Anglo-Saxon, Christian, heterosexual, patriarchal, capitalist—what's next, hurricane-summoning?—culture as predominant. The problem with this argument is that it is self-contradictory. For if all cultures are created equal, and if none is superior to any other, why *not* prefer one's own? Thus Huntington's preference for Anglo-Protestantism—he never establishes it as more than a patriot's preference, though as a scholar he tries to show what happens if we neglect it—is to that extent perfectly consistent with the claims of the multiculturalists, the only difference being that he likes the dominant culture, indeed, wants to strengthen it, and they don't.

Of course, despite their protestations, multiculturalists do not actually believe that all cultures are equally valid. With a clear conscience, they condemn and reject anti-multiculturalism, not to mention cultures that treat women, homosexuals, and the environment in ways that Western liberals cannot abide. Unless, perchance, such treatment is handed out by groups hostile to America; for Robert's Rules of Multicultural Order allow peremptory objections against, say, the Catholic Church, that are denied against such as the Taliban. Scratch a multiculturalist, then, and you find a liberal willing to condemn all the usual cultural suspects.

Whether from the Right or the Left, the cultural approach to national identity runs into problems. To know whether a culture is good or bad, healthy or unhealthy, liberating or oppressive, one has to be able to look at it from outside or above the culture. Even to know when and where one culture ends and another begins, and especially to know what is worth conserving and what is not within a particular culture, one must have a viewpoint that is not determined by it. For example, is the culture of slavery, or that of anti-slavery, the truer expression of Americanism? Both are parts of our tradition. One needs some "creed," it turns out, to make sense of culture. I mean creed, not merely in the sense of things believed (sidestepping whether they are true or not), but in the sense of moral principles or genuine moral-political knowledge. If that were impossible, if every point of view were *merely* relative to a culture, then you'd be caught in an infinite regress. No genuine knowledge, independent of cultural conditioning, would be possible—except, of course, for the very claim that there is no knowledge apart from the cultural, which claim has to be true across all cultures and times. But then genuine knowledge would be possible, after all, and culturalism would have refuted itself.

HARD SELL

One of the oddities of Huntington's argument is that the recourse to Anglo-Protestantism makes it, from the academic point of view, less objectionable, and from the political viewpoint, less persuasive. As a scholar, he figures that he cannot endorse the American creed or its principles of enlightened patriotism as true and good, because that would be committing a value judgment. So he embeds them in a culture and attempts to prove (and does prove, so far as social science allows) the culture's usefulness for liberty, prosperity, and national unity, should you happen to value any of those. The Anglo-Protestantism that he celebrates, please note, is not exactly

English Protestantism (he wants to avoid the national church), but dissenting Protestantism, and not all of dissenting Protestantism but those parts, and they were substantial, that embraced religious liberty. In short, those parts most receptive to and shaped by the creed.

As a political matter, Anglo-Protestantism is a hard sell, particularly to Catholics, Jews, Mexican-Americans, and many others who don't exactly see themselves in that picture. Huntington affirms, repeatedly, that his is "an argument for the importance of Anglo-Protestant culture, not for the importance of Anglo-Protestant people." That is a very creedal, one might even say a very American, way of putting his case for culture, turning it into a set of principles and habits that can be adopted by willing immigrants of whatever nation or race. This downplays much of what is usually meant by culture, however, and it is not clear what he gains by it. If that is all there is to it, why not emphasize the creed or, more precisely, approach the culture through the creed?

The answer, I think, is that Huntington regards the creed by itself as too indifferent to the English language and God. But there is no connection between adherence to the principles of the Declaration and a lukewarm embrace of English for all Americans. In fact, a country based on common principles would logically want a common language in which to express them. The multiculturalists, tellingly, attack English and the Declaration at the same time. As for God, there is no reason to accept the ACLU's godless version of the creed as the correct one. The Declaration mentions Him four times, for example, and from the Declaration to the Gettysburg Address to the Pledge of Allegiance (a creedal document if there ever was one), the creed has affirmed God's support for the rational political principles of this nation.

REGIME CHANGE

Yet it is precisely these principles that Huntington downplays, along with their distinctive viewpoint. This viewpoint, which goes beyond culture, is the political viewpoint. It is nobly represented by our own founders and its most impressive theoretical articulation is in Aristotle's *Politics*. For Aristotle, the highest theme of politics and of political science is founding. Founding means to give a country the law, institutions, offices, and precepts that chiefly make the country what it is, that distinguish it as a republic, aristocracy, monarchy, or so on. This authoritative arrangement of offices and institutions is what Aristotle calls "the regime," which establishes who rules the country and for what purposes. We hear much about "regime change" today but perhaps don't reflect enough about what the term implies. The regime is the fundamental fact of political life according to Aristotle. And because the character of the rulers shapes the character of the whole people, the regime largely imparts to the country its very way of life. In its most sweeping sense, regime change thus augurs a fundamental rewiring not only of governmental but of social, economic, and even religious authority in a country. In liberal democracies, to be sure, politics has renounced much of its authority over religion, society, and the economy. But even this renunciation is a political act, a regime decision.

Founding is regime change par excellence, the clearest manifestation of politics' ability to shape or rule culture. But even Aristotle admits that the regime only "chiefly" determines the character of a country, comparing it to a sculptor's ability to form a statue out of a block of marble. Much depends as well on the marble, its size, condition, provenance, and so forth. Although the sculptor wishes to impose a form (say, a bust of George Washington) on the marble, he is limited by the matter he has to work with and may have to adapt his plans accordingly. By the limitations or potentialities of the matter Aristotle implies much of what we mean by culture. That is, every founder must start from something—a site, a set of natural resources, a population that already possesses certain customs, beliefs, family structure, economic skills, and maybe laws. Aristotle chooses to regard this "matter" or what we would call culture as the legacy, at least mostly, of past politics, of previous regimes and laws and customs. By in effect subordinating culture to politics, he emphasizes the capacity of men to shape their own destiny or to govern themselves by choosing (again) in politics. He emphasizes, in other words, that men are free, that they are not enslaved to the past or to their own culture. But he does not confuse this with an unqualified or limitless liberty to make ourselves into anything we want to be. We are just free enough to be able to take responsibility for the things in life we cannot choose—the geographical, economic, cultural, and other factors that condition our freedom but don't abolish it.

Now it is from this viewpoint, the statesman's viewpoint, that we can see how creed and culture may be combined to shape a national identity and a common good. In fact, this can be illustrated from the American Founding itself. In the 1760s and early 1770s American citizens and statesmen tried out different arguments in criticism of the mother country's policies on taxation and land rights. Essentially, they appealed to one part of their political tradition to criticize another, invoking a version of the "ancient constitution" (rendered consistent with Lockean natural rights) to criticize the new one of parliamentary supremacy, in effect appealing not only to Lord Coke against Locke, but to Locke against Locke. In the Declaration of Independence, the Americans appealed both to natural law and rights on the one hand, and to British constitutionalism on the other, but to the latter only insofar as it did not contradict the former. Thus the American creed emerged from within, but also against, the predominant culture. The Revolution justified itself ultimately by an appeal to human nature, not to culture, and in the name of human nature and the American people, the Revolutionaries set out to form an American Union with its own culture.

IMMIGRATION AND EDUCATION

They understood, that is, that the American republic needed a culture to help uphold its creed. The formal political theory of the creed was a version of social contract theory, amended to include a central role for Founding Fathers. In John Locke's *Second Treatise*, the classic statement of the contract theory, there is little role for Founding Fathers, really, inasmuch as they might represent a confusion of political power and paternal power, two things that Locke is at great pains to separate. He wants to make clear that political power, which arises from consent, has nothing to do with the power of fathers over their children. And so, against the arguments of absolutist patriarchal monarchy, he attempted clearly to distinguish paternal power from contractual or political power. But in the American case we have combined these, to an extent, almost from the beginning. The fathers of the republic are our demi-gods, as Thomas Jefferson, of all people, called them. They are our heroes, who establish the sacred space of American politics, and citizens (and those who would be) are expected to share a general reverence for them and their constitutional handiwork.

In fact, the American creed, together with its attendant culture, illuminates at least two issues highly relevant to national identity, namely, immigration and education. On immigration, the founders taught that civil society is based on a contract, a contract presupposing the unanimous consent of the individuals who come together to make a people. When newcomers appear, they may join that society if they and the society concur. In other words, from the nature of the people as arising from a voluntary contract, consent remains a two-way street: an immigrant must consent to come, and the society must consent to receive him. Otherwise, there is a violation of the voluntary basis of civil society. The universal rights of human nature translate via the social compact into a particular society, an "us" distinct from "them," distinct even from any other civil society constituted by a social contract.

Any individual has, in Jefferson's words, the right to emigrate from a society in which chance, not choice, has placed him. But no society has a standing natural duty to receive him or to take him in. Thus it is no violation of human rights to pick and choose immigrants based on what a particular civil society needs. In America's case, the founders disagreed among themselves about whether, say, farmers or manufacturers should be favored as immigrants, but they agreed, as Thomas G. West and Edward J. Erler have shown, that the country needed newcomers who knew English, had a strong work ethic, and possessed republican sentiments and habits.

For its first century or so, the United States had naturalization laws but no immigration laws, so that, technically speaking, we had open borders. Effectively, however, the frontiers were not so open: most immigrants had to cross several thousand miles of perilous ocean to reach us. Nonetheless, American statesmen wanted to influence as much as they could who was coming and why. Benjamin Franklin, for instance, wrote a famous essay in 1784 called "Information to Those Who Would Remove to America," in which he cautioned his European readers that America was the "Land of Labor": if they were planning to emigrate they had better be prepared to work hard. America was not the kind of country, he wrote, where "the Fowls fly about ready roasted, crying, *Come eat me!*"

As for education, from the creedal or contractual point of view, each generation of citizens' children might be considered a new society. But Jefferson's suggestion that therefore all contracts, laws, and constitutions should expire every generation (19 years, he calculated) was never acted on by him, much less by any other founder. Instead of continual interruptions (or perhaps a finale) to national identity, succeeding generations, so the founders concluded, were their "posterity," for whom the blessings of liberty had to be secured and transmitted. Perpetuating the republic thus entailed a duty to educate the rising generation in the proper creed and culture.

If certain qualities of mind and heart were required of American citizens, as everyone agreed, then politics had to help shape, directly and indirectly, a favoring culture. Most of the direct character formation, of course, took place at the level of families, churches, and state and local governments, including private and (in time) public schools. In the decades that followed the founding, the relation between the culture and creed fluctuated in accordance with shifting views about the requirements of American republicanism. Unable to forget the terrors of the French Revolution, Federalists and Whigs tried to stimulate root growth by emphasizing the creed's connection to Pilgrim self-discipline and British legal culture. This was, perhaps, the closest that America ever came to an actual politics of Burkeanism. Although the American Whigs never abandoned the creed's natural-rights morality, they adorned it with the imposing drapery of reverence for cultural tradition and the rule of law. In many respects, in fact, Huntington's project is a recrudescence of Whiggism.

By contrast, Jeffersonian Republicans, soon turned Jacksonian Democrats, preferred to dignify the creed by enmeshing it in a historical and progressive account of culture. They, too, were aware of the problem of Bonapartism, which had seized and destroyed French republicanism in its infancy; and in Andrew Jackson, of course, they had a kind of Bonaparte figure in American politics whom they were happy to exploit. But in their own populist manner they responded to the inherent dangers of Bonapartism by embracing a kind of theory of progress, influenced by Hegel though vastly more democratic than his, which recognized the People as the vehicle of the world-spirit and as the voice of God on earth. (You can find this in the essays and books of George Bancroft, the Jacksonian-era historian and advisor to Democratic presidents, as well as in popular editorials in the *North American Review* and elsewhere.) The people were always primary, in other words. Jackson and even the founders were their servants; every great man the representative of a great people. Here too the creed tended to merge into culture, though in this case into forward-looking popular culture.

In his early life, Abraham Lincoln was a Whig, memorably and subtly warning against the spirit of Caesarism and encouraging reverence for the law as our political religion. But Lincoln's greatness depended upon transcending Whiggism for the sake of a new republicanism, a strategy already visible in his singular handling of the stock Whig themes as a young man. In fact, his new party called itself the Republican Party as a kind of boast that the new republicanism intended to revive the old. Their point was that the former Democratic Republicans, now mere Democrats, had abandoned the republic, which Lincoln and his party vowed to save. Rejecting Whiggish traditionalism as well as Democratic populism and progressivism, Lincoln rehabilitated the American creed, returning to the Declaration and its truths to set the face of American law against secession and slavery, to purge slavery from the national identity, and to reassert republican mores in American life and culture. This last goal entailed the American people's long struggle against Jim Crow and segregated schools, as well as our contemporary struggle against group rights and racial and sexual entitlements.

Lincoln and his party stood for a reshaping of American culture around the American creed—"a new birth of freedom." Because the creed itself dictated a limited government, this rebirth was not an illiberal, top-down politicization of culture of the sort that liberal courts in recent decades have attempted. Disciplined by the ideas of natural rights and the consent of the governed, this revitalization was a persuasive effort that took generations, and included legislative victories like the Civil War Amendments and the subsequent civil rights acts. Government sometimes had to take energetic action to secure rights, to be sure, e.g., to suppress the culture of lynching. Nor should we forget that peaceful reforms presupposed wartime victory. As with the Revolution, it took war to decide what kind of national identity America would possess—if any. But war is meaningless without the statecraft that turns it so far as possible to noble ends, and that prepares the way for the return of truly civil government and civil society.

WE HOLD THESE TRUTHS

Modern liberalism, beginning in the Progressive era, has done its best to strip natural rights and the Constitution out of the American creed. By emptying it of its proper moral content, thinkers and politicians like Woodrow Wilson prepared the creed to be filled by subsequent generations, who could pour their contemporary values into it and thus keep it in tune with the times. The "living constitution," as the new view of things came to be called, transformed the creed, once based on timeless or universal principles, into an evolving doctrine; turned it, in effect, into culture, which could be adjusted and reinterpreted in accordance with history's imperatives. Alternatively, one could say that 20th-century liberals turned their open-ended form of culturalism into a new American creed, the multicultural creed, which they have few scruples now about imposing on republican America, diversity be damned.

To his credit, Huntington abhors this development. Unfortunately, his Anglo-Protestant culturalism, like any merely cultural conservatism, is no match for its liberal opponents. He persists in thinking of liberals as devotees of the old American creed who push its universal principles too far, who rely on reason to the exclusion of a strong national culture. When they abjured individualism and natural rights decades ago, however, liberals broke with that creed, and did so proudly. When they abandoned nature as the ground of right, liberals broke as well with reason, understood as a natural capacity for seeking truth, in favor of reason as a servant of culture, history, fate, power, and finally nothingness. In short, Huntington fails to grasp that latter-day liberals attack American culture *because* they reject the American creed, around which that culture has formed and developed from the very beginning.

In thinking through the crisis of American national identity, we should keep in mind the opening words of the second paragraph of the Declaration of Independence: "We hold these truths . . . ." Usually, and correctly, we emphasize the truths that are to be held, but we must not forget the "We" who holds them. The American creed is the keystone of American national identity; but it requires a culture to sustain it. The republican task is to recognize the creed's primacy, the culture's indispensability, and the challenge, which political wisdom alone can answer, to shape a people that can live up to its principles.

The Debacle at Harvard

Harvey C. Mansfield

(Spring 2006)

It is a debacle at Harvard: a great university getting rid of its most outstanding president since James B. Conant, the only outstanding president at a major university today, and doing this for no stated reason. His unofficial detractors brought up only his abrasive style. In no way could it be said either that he had completed his mission, and thus deserved retirement, or that he had failed in it, and so deserved to be booted. The event is demeaning to all involved, but especially to the three main parties—the Harvard Corporation, the faculty, and Mr. Summers.

These three share the blame in descending order, and speaking as an informed observer, not an insider, I will assess it as I see it now.

LOSS OF CONFIDENCE

The greatest blame goes to the Harvard Corporation, which brought in Larry Summers and then abandoned him. They set him the task of shaking things up and then became queasy and turned him out when he did just that. For Summers did not truly resign; he was undermined and effectually pushed out. The loss of confidence in him by his superiors was obvious. In the first major public incident of Summers's presidency, his interview with Cornel West, the Corporation supported him publicly. In the second, the controversy over his remarks on the capacity of women for science, the Corporation remained silent. In the third, the reaction to the resignation of Faculty of Arts and Sciences Dean William Kirby, the Corporation actively undermined the president by letting it be known that it was consulting with faculty opposed to him.

In all three incidents, Summers was in the right. Cornel West, for all his virtues, was no model scholar; it's true, apparently, that fewer women than men have capacity for science (or mathematics) at the highest level; the dean had produced very little from the curriculum review that was his main assignment. Summers was trying to hold Harvard to a higher standard of excellence than it was becoming used to—exemplary scholarship from all faculty, hiring only the best without the pressure to

385

meet a quota based on sex, and a challenging curriculum that gets the best out of students as well as faculty.

Since first entering office Summers had many times set forth "greatness" as his goal. He was aware, and he wanted to make the rest of Harvard aware, that there is a difference between a wealthy, famous, and prestigious university and a great one. The prestigious university, complacent and self-satisfied, will in time lose its repute; the great one will keep its luster and gain more renown effortlessly, just by being itself and aiming high. To get Harvard back on the right track, however, takes the effort in which Summers was engaged.

Summers proposed a curriculum review that would result in solid courses aimed to answer students' needs, replacing stylish courses designed to appeal to their whims. Such courses would require professors to teach in their fields but out of their specialties; no longer would they assume that the specialized course they want to teach is just the course that students need. Summers also began a move to rein in grade inflation; he dispelled some of Harvard's political correctness by inviting conservative speakers and looking for conservative professors to hire; he transformed the policy of affirmative action by reducing the pressure to hire more blacks and women as such; he opposed Harvard's hostile attitude toward the U.S. military. Besides these measures, he sought to put or keep Harvard first in science, an intent made possible by a considerable expansion of the university across the Charles River to Allston. This is the substance of Summers's ambitious presidency.

Thanks to the Harvard Corporation, all this effort is suspended—who knows for how long. In forcing Summers out, the Corporation surrendered to the "diehard Left" (Alan Dershowitz's expression) which had opposed him from the start and is now celebrating in triumph and glee. The Corporation gave a veto to Summers's sworn enemies, thus conferring a power that will be difficult to restrain, much less reclaim. I do not know, but I suppose this was done out of sympathy and fear combined, probably out of fear of not showing sympathy. The Corporation is composed of liberals and leftists, and was reportedly led in this action by the feminist Nannerl Keohane, former president of Duke University, and by liberal Democrat Robert Reischauer, president of the Urban Institute.

But the Corporation was also afraid of showing too much sympathy with the Left. It could not summon the manly confidence to avow that Summers was being ousted because his agenda of renewal clashed with the diversity agenda of the feminist Left and its sympathizers. In its letter on Summers's resignation, the Corporation did not criticize him or his policies in any way, not even by hint or allusion. With this failure it let stand the pretensions of the diversity crowd and ducked responsibility for its own action, attempting to palliate imprudence with insincerity.

ENEMIES AND CRITICS

For this sorry misdeed done to Harvard and to other universities around the world that watch Harvard, the Corporation deserves first prize in responsibility for the debacle. But the Harvard faculty comes a close second.

The faculty opposed to Summers were divided into enemies and critics. His enemies planned or intended his demise as soon as he began to show that he had doubts about the diversity agenda. They led the clamor against him in several faculty meetings in 2004. They were joined by critics, not necessarily of the Left, who had been wounded in encounters with Summers. To get more out of the faculty, he had to ask challenging questions, and those who could not make convincing replies sometimes felt they were being bullied, when in fact they had merely lost the argument. Mr. Summers did not pay attention to Machiavelli's advice that "men should either be caressed or eliminated." Yet in the confrontations in faculty meetings he himself was made to endure reproach and rancor beyond anything seen in the last 50 years at Harvard, including the troubles of the late 1960s.

It's no use trying to persuade the diversity Left; they cannot be moved. But something might have been done to conciliate Summers's critics. They did not mean to bring him down, even though they helped to do that. They were irresponsible in bringing small charges that, combined with the hostility of the Left, had a lethal effect. Unfortunately, Summers with various abject apologies and huge gifts—$50 million for the cause of bringing more diversity feminists to Harvard—tried to conciliate his enemies rather than his critics. He encouraged his enemies by showing how weak he was and failed to persuade those who might have been persuaded if he had defended himself and attacked his enemies.

ONE-MAN SHOW

This brings us to Mr. Summers, surely more sinned against than sinner. He gave a noble try to the reform of Harvard, and he failed. During his ordeal of relentless, humorless criticism and especially in his letter of resignation he was gracious to all who were doing him wrong. He was not a bully but his enemies were. They, not he, deserved to be humiliated. He overmatched them one-on-one, but together these ungenerous weaklings brought him down.

Summers did not defend himself but instead demoralized his defenders with his apologies, leaving them with nothing to defend. We do not know whether he was under constraint from the Corporation, but he did not organize his defenders. He believed it would be divisive to admit that there were "sides" in the dispute. He worried about returning to the partisanship within the faculty of the late 1960s. But of course the other side had organized early on in his administration. He and Dean Kirby allowed the election in 2004 of a Faculty Council (the faculty representative body) composed of his worst enemies, which plotted against him throughout. It would have been easy to expose them, for they tended to overreach. Instead, they succeeded in a goal they never thought they could attain.

Summers's administration was a one-man show. He did not build a group of supporters to carry out his plans. He relied on himself alone. It was as if his individual superiority would bring victory in a series of single combats without his having to build an army with soldiers, marshals, and a *Garde Impériale*. His audience would applaud his victories and the common good would be served. Yet this picture is not quite right. Far from imitating Napoleon, Mr. Summers believed in reason and in self-interest as the object of reason. He thought he could prevail without winning and apologize without losing. Nor would he have to out-argue his intellectual inferiors. He would merely question their opinions and show them their indubitable self-interest. He was in a deep sense impolitic, an economic man who knows nothing of war and hence nothing of politics. He lost his own opportunity and in doing so may have spoiled it for others.

The Education Mill

Richard Vedder

(Spring 2009)

The academic establishment has been effusive in its praise of Claudia Goldin and Lawrence Katz's new book, *The Race between Education and Technology*. Larry Summers, Harvard guru and chief economic advisor to President Barack Obama, says "this is empirical economic scholarship at its finest." Princeton's Alan Krueger adds, "this book represents the best of what economics has to offer," sentiments echoed by the University of Chicago's Steven Levitt and University of Rochester's Stan Engerman. Let me be a bit of a skunk at the love fest by offering an alternative view.

Goldin and Katz, professors of economics at Harvard, argue that American higher education contributed, during the 19th and most of the 20th century, both to America's long-term economic growth and the achievement of its egalitarian ideals. In the past three decades, however, a dramatic slowdown in the growth in educational attainment has contributed to something of a reduction in American economic growth and, most importantly to the authors, a sharp rise in economic inequality.

More specifically, Goldin and Katz argue that education enhances productivity, and the recent slowdown in the growth of skills has reduced productivity and income growth. Because technological advances are continuing as fast as ever, and since these tend to favor higher skill attainment, the demand for educated Americans is rising rapidly, which, other things being equal, increases their relative wages. Until about 1975, this rise in demand was counteracted by an equally or even more impressive growth in the supply of highly educated workers, so relative wages did not accelerate, and wage-induced inequality did not rise—indeed, it even fell at times. The slow growth in educational attainment since 1970 or 1975, however, has slowed the supply increase, so relative wages of the educated are rising relatively rapidly, increasing income inequality, which "many commentators" believe "can contribute to social and political discord." What should we do? The authors recommend that we promote better educational performance at the K-12 level through smaller class sizes and higher teacher salaries. We should increase spending for early childhood education. And we should deal with rising college costs by "more generous college financial aid for low-income youth." To deal with rising inequality, they also favor increasing income tax progressivity and judiciously using labor market "institutional interventions" like the minimum wage. In short, increase government spending and regulation, and make taxation more progressive—more or less the prescriptions adopted by the Obama Administration in its stimulus bill and proposed federal budget.

The authors are industrious and detailed in making their arguments, mining neglected historical documents such as the Iowa State Census of 1915. There is even a four-page discussion, complete with regression results, of the role that electricity played in promoting high school graduation in the early 20th century. The authors spent literally years doing the research on educational attainment and economic inequality that gives the book something of an authoritative aura.

Yet I think they make a number of implicit assumptions that are debatable and call into question the accuracy of the story they tell, not to mention the proposed remedies for the alleged problem. Let me outline six: educational attainment lowers inequality; lower inequality is needed and desirable; higher educational attainment promotes economic growth; more public spending will promote higher attainment; therefore, more public education spending will mean more economic growth; and finally, differences between human beings in cognitive skills and other personal attributes are relatively unimportant.

The notion that enhanced educational attainment will raise income equality rests on the assumption that an increase in the proportion of educated workers relative to less educated ones will lower wages of the former group relative to the latter. This is what probably happened around 1970 when college enrollments were soaring. It might well happen that way, but statistical work that Daniel Bennett and I have been conducting suggests that the relation between educational attainment and income equality is not so clear-cut. Some preliminary results even suggest the opposite: higher educational attainment is associated with *more inequality*. But even if Goldin and Katz are right, there are other reasons why conventional policy responses may have little effect. To cite one problem, my associates and I at the Center for College Affordability and Productivity have observed that the statistical relationship between state higher education appropriations and the proportion of adults with college degrees is not positive, even after allowing for various lags for graduation rates to catch up with the higher spending.

Goldin and Katz clearly believe greater income equality is good for America. They grudgingly admit that "some degree of economic inequality *may* [emphasis added] be desirable to spur incentives." But there is no discussion of the equality-efficiency trade-off. Why is the income distribution of 1970 "good" and that of 2008 "bad"? How do we know? Inequality's alleged threat to social order is not documented, and some polling results suggest interpersonal variations in income are less controversial than the authors suggest, Obama's election notwithstanding. Moreover, the inequality in the distribution of lifetime income, or of consumption spending, is far less substantial than suggested by income figures for any single year.

It is true that areas with relatively high levels of educational attainment have typically grown more than areas with less educated populations. But the question is: will the resources devoted to increasing the proportion of well-educated people generate a return, in terms of incremental income, that justifies the expenditure? In reality, human beings differ, and those with the greatest motivation to acquire higher skills have largely done so. Is it necessarily true that increasing the proportion of students attending college will promote higher incomes? Attending college is not costless, and those costs rise and the benefits decline as we reach further down into the pool of talent. The authors approvingly talk of surging educational attainment in Europe—but fail to note that economic growth rates there have fallen, averaging levels lower than in the U.S. in recent decades. Surging European educational attainment has been associated with falling, not rising, growth rates.

Goldin and Katz assume that higher spending on higher education will increase attainment rates. States spending more on higher education do indeed get higher college attendance, but only modestly so. Most such increases do not go to hold tuition charges down or increase financial aid to the poor, and therefore it isn't surprising that we do not find a positive relationship between state spending in higher education and the proportion of adults with college degrees. The call for more public spending on education implies it will enhance economic growth rates, and the authors even state that "the short-run fiscal burdens of increased spending on education are likely to be more than offset in the long run with increased tax revenues from a more productive workforce and lower public spending to combat social problems." Yet when we run numerous regressions using statewide data on the relationship between higher education spending and economic growth, we typically get a negative relationship: higher spending, *lower* growth. Money taken from the market-disciplined competitive sector to finance less efficient universities partially isolated from market forces by third-party payments seems to have a negative growth effect.

Goldin and Katz implicitly assume that education *causes* the difference in incomes and productivity between high school and college graduates. Underlying their argument is an unwritten assumption that all people are created equal in terms of cognitive endowments, motivation, discipline, etc. It is extremely difficult to correct econometrically for all the human variations in characteristics, and I believe at least some of the wage differentials that the authors associate with education relate to the fact that typically college graduates are brighter, harder working, and more dependable, than those who leave school after getting a high school diploma. Had they not even gone on to college, these young strivers would have earned more than the existing pool of high school graduates.

College is a screening device—a point ignored by the authors. Employers hire workers with college degrees because the diploma raises the probability that the graduate will be talented and diligent, because the colleges themselves have screened their entrants, admitting those with some prospects for success, and then not graduating close to half of them (another point ignored by Goldin and Katz), many for being deficient academically. Although their book has a bibliography of well over 500 entries that covers 28 pages, there is not a single reference to *The Bell Curve* (1994), the well-known work of Richard Herrnstein and Charles Murray on the importance of cognitive endowments to educational attainment and vocational success.

Nowhere in this book do you learn that for every 100 students entering high school, only about 20 have four-year college degrees 10 years later. The problem often is not access but attrition. Nor do we learn that in 1970 only three out of every 100 mail carriers had college degrees, compared with 12 today. Do college-educated mail carriers promote economic growth? I doubt it. Maybe Richard Freeman's *The*

Overeducated American (1976) is still relevant. Do we need more than 15,000 Americans with *advanced* degrees fixing people's hair? One study says that, five years after graduation, only 61% of college graduates are in jobs requiring a college degree.

In addition, the rising differential between high school and college earnings beginning in the late 1970s corresponds nicely with the beginning of enforcement of *Duke v. Griggs Power* (1971), a decision making it nearly impossible for employers to test prospective workers, forcing them to rely more on colleges to screen applicants for competency. (Goldin and Katz ignore, by the way, the stagnation in the high school/college earnings differential for females in the past 15 or 20 years.) The authors also accept soaring education costs as a given, not criticizing significantly the perverse effects of unionization and rapidly rising salaries for professors with light teaching loads. Perhaps higher education access would be better enhanced by making professors teach more, and reducing administrative and recreational expenses that contribute to the college cost explosion. Perhaps we should do cost-benefit analysis on more academic research. The authors' implicit faith that the ways of the academy are fixed and invulnerable to change, even as technology forces changes on everyone else, is one this writer cannot embrace.

In short, Goldin and Katz's errors of omission rival their errors of commission. *The Race between Education and Technology* is an interesting book with some good data and historical analysis, but it fails to persuade because its authors seem blinded by a desire to increase resources for the business that feeds them.

Wimps and Barbarians

Terrence O. Moore

(Winter 2003/04)

More than a decade ago the nation was in a stir over the birth of a fictional boy. The boy was Avery, son of Murphy Brown. Television's Murphy Brown, played by Candice Bergen, was a successful news commentator who, after an unsuccessful relationship with a man that left her alone and pregnant, bore a son out of wedlock. The event, popular enough in its own right, became the center of political controversy when then Vice President Dan Quayle in a speech to the Commonwealth Club of California lamented that the show was "mocking the importance of a father." Suddenly the nation polarized over this question of "family values." But the controversy over Murphy Brown's childbearing soon died down. The characters on the show became more interested in Murphy's hairstyle than her baby, as did perhaps Murphy, who eventually found a suitable nanny in her painter so she could pursue her career without abatement. The show was off the air before Murphy's son would have been seven. Vice President Quayle was not reelected. Eleven years later, it is worth pondering what might have happened to Avery had this story not been just a television show. More to the point, what is happening today to our boys and young men who come from "families" not unlike Murphy's and who find the nation as divided now as it was then over the "values" by which we ought to raise them?

For more than a decade I have been in a position to see young men in the making. As a Marine, college professor, and now principal of a K-12 charter school, I have deliberately tried to figure out whether the nation through its most important institutions of moral instruction—its families and schools—is turning boys into responsible young men. Young women, always the natural judges of the male character, say emphatically "No." In my experience, many young women are upset, but not about an elusive Prince Charming or even the shortage of "cute guys" around. Rather, they have very specific complaints against how they have been treated in shopping malls or on college campuses by immature and uncouth males, and even more pointed complaints against their boyfriends or other male acquaintances who fail to protect them. At times, they appear desperately hopeless. They say matter-of-factly that the males around them do not know how to act like either men or gentlemen. It appears to them that, except for a few lucky members of their sex, most women today must choose between males who are whiny, incapable of making decisions, and in general of "acting like men," or those who treat women roughly and are unreliable, unmannerly, and usually stupid.

The young men, for their part, are not a little embarrassed when they hear these charges but can't wholly deny them. Indeed, when asked the simple question, "When have you ever been taught what it means to be a man?" they are typically speechless and somewhat ashamed.

The question for teachers, professors, and others in positions of moral influence is what to do about young women's growing dissatisfaction and young men's increasing confusion and embarrassment. Teachers cannot become their students' parents, but they can give direction to those who have ears to hear. Two lessons are essential. First, a clear challenge must be issued to young males urging them to become the men their grandfathers and great-grandfathers were. This challenge must be clear, uncompromising, engaging, somewhat humorous, and inspiring. It cannot seem like a tired, fusty, chicken-little lament on the part of the old and boring, but must be seen as the truly revolutionary and cutting-edge effort to recover authentic manliness. Second, a new generation of scholars must tell the tale of how men used to become men and act manfully, and how we as a nation have lost our sense of true manliness. The spirit of this inquiry cannot be that of an autopsy but rather that of the Renaissance humanists, who sought to recover and to borrow the wisdom of the past in order to ennoble their own lives.

Historians and political theorists and professors of literature must realize that the topic of gender is not the monopoly of those who would try to eradicate gender but the natural possession of the great thinkers and actors and even the common folk of the Western tradition. Aristotle had a great deal to say about gender and manhood, as did Washington and Burke and Jane Austen. These two enterprises, the one rhetorical and the other philosophical, are and must be related. One comes from and appeals to the heart. The other comes from and appeals to the mind. Young men today have both hearts and minds that are in chronic need of cultivation. Specifically, they need to realize what true manhood is, what it is not, and why it has become so difficult in the modern world to achieve the status and stature of the true man.

CHARACTER COUNTS

Manhood is not simply a matter of being male and reaching a certain age. These are acts of nature; manhood is a sustained act of character. It is no easier to become a man than it is to become virtuous. In fact, the two are the same. The root of our old-fashioned word "virtue" is the Latin word *virtus*, a derivative of *vir*, or man. To be virtuous is to be "manly." As Aristotle understood it, virtue is a "golden mean" between the extremes of excess and deficiency. Too often among today's young males, the extremes seem to predominate. One extreme suffers from an excess of manliness, or from misdirected and unrefined manly energies. The other suffers from a lack of manliness, a total want of manly spirit. Call them barbarians and wimps. So prevalent are these two errant types that the prescription for what ails our young males might be reduced to two simple injunctions: Don't be a barbarian. Don't be a wimp. What is left, *ceteris paribus*, will be a man.

Today's barbarians are not hard to find. Like the barbarians of old, the new ones wander about in great packs. You can recognize them by their dress, their speech, their amusements, their manners, and their treatment of women. You will know them right away by their distinctive headgear. They wear baseball caps everywhere they go and in every situation: in class, at the table, indoors, outdoors, while taking a test, while watching a movie, while on a date. They wear these caps frontward, backward, and sideways. They will wear them in church and with suits, if ever a barbarian puts on a suit. Part security blanket, part good-luck charm, these distinctive head coverings unite each barbarian with the rest of the vast barbaric horde.

Recognizing other barbarians by their ball caps, one barbarian can enter into a verbal exchange with another anywhere: in a men's room, at an airport, in a movie theater. This exchange, which never quite reaches the level of conversation, might begin with, "Hey, what up?" A traditional response: "Dude!" The enlightening colloquy can go on for hours at increasingly high volumes. "You know, you know!" "What I'm sayin'!" "No way, man!" "What the f---!" "You da man!" "Cool!" "Phat!" "Awesome!" And so on. Barbarians do not use words to express thoughts, convey information, paint pictures in the imagination, or come to a rational understanding. Such speech as they employ serves mainly to elicit in others audible reactions to a few sensual events: football, sex, hard rock, the latest barbarian movie. In the barbarian universe, Buckleyesque vocabularies are not required.

Among the most popular barbarian activities are playing sports and lifting weights. There is, of course, nothing wrong with sports or physical training. Playing sports can encourage young males to cultivate several important manly virtues: courage, competitiveness, camaraderie, stamina, a sense of fairness. For this reason, superior cultures have invariably used sports as a proving ground for manly endeavor. As the Duke of Wellington said, "The battle of Waterloo was won on the playing fields of Eton." The problem is that many young males of today receive no manly education apart from sports. When the British boys who later defeated Napoleon were not competing in the sporting contests conducted in elite public schools, they were learning how to become gentlemen. They spoke the King's English, carried themselves with an air of dignity, treated women with respect, and studied assiduously.

Today's barbarians act as though they never leave the playing field or the gym. They wear the same clothes, speak the same language (just as loudly), spit and scratch themselves just as much, whether on the field or off. More properly, nothing off the field matters to them, except perhaps sex, which they also treat as a game, and alcohol. As a result, they live almost a divided life. On the field, they can be serious, competitive, eager, and disciplined. Off the field, they are lazy, careless, disorganized, and disaffected. Such a divided life is the hallmark of barbarism. In his classic account of the ancient Germanic tribes, the Roman historian Tacitus contrasted the energy and purpose of the German men on the field of battle with their listlessness in the camp.

> Whenever they are not fighting, they pass much of their time in the chase, and still more in idleness, giving themselves up to sleep and to feasting, the bravest and the most warlike doing nothing, and surrendering the management of the household, of the home, and of the land, to the women, the old men, and all the weakest members of the family. They themselves lie buried in sloth, a strange combination in their nature that the same men should be so fond of idleness, so averse to peace.

The ancient barbarians did little except fight and hunt. The modern barbarians do little besides play sports and pursue women. To be sure, they have other amusements. But these activities do not as a rule require sensibility or thought. Indeed, typical barbarian pastimes, like drinking mightily and watching WWF wrestling, seem expressly contrived to stupefy the senses and nullify the intellect.

Barbarians, not surprisingly, listen to barbaric music. Allan Bloom famously identified rock-and-roll as the music of sexual intercourse. It was no accident that the progenitor of the rock-and-roll revolution was nicknamed "the Pelvis." Equally basic, but fundamentally different, are the passions enlisted by modern rock without the roll, that is, heavy metal. It is certainly not the music of intercourse, at least not of the consensual variety, since girls and women generally hate it. And with good reason: it is impossible to dance to. You can, of course, thrust your fist over and over into the air. Heavy metal lacks all rhythmic quality, sounding more like jet engines taking off while a growling male voice shouts repeated threats, epithets, and obscenities. Heavy metal lacks all subtlety, reflection, harmony, refinement—in a word, civilization. For good reason did Plato combine music with gymnastic instruction in the education of the guardian class of his Republic. A certain kind of music would soften the souls of young men. Heavy metal softens nothing. It is the music of pure rage.

Barbarians, strictly speaking, have no manners. They shout out to each other in public as though the world were a playing field or a rock concert. To complement the shouting, there is a recognizable barbarian posture, carriage, and comportment. They slouch in their seats. They belch and proudly pass loud gas in public places. They spit practically everywhere they go. A particularly annoying barbarian habit is not looking you in the eye. He will look this way and that, shrug his shoulders, move his body in different directions, but rarely just stand in one place, look you in the eye, and say something intelligible. Speaking to adults used to be one of the first lessons a child learned. Proper speech and posture and other signs of respect helped to bring him into the community of civilized human beings. No longer.

Young males, of course, have always been rough around the edges. But in the past, their edges were smoothed, in part, by being introduced into female company. Boys learned to behave properly first from their mothers and later around other women and girls. They held open doors, pulled out chairs, stood up when a woman entered a room, stood up in public places to offer their seats, took off their hats in the presence of women, and carefully guarded their language so as not to offend the fair sex. All that is gone. In no other aspect of their conduct is barbarism more apparent among a large number of young men these days than in their treatment of women.

Not only do they not show women any special regard. They go out of their way to bother them. A woman does not like to be yelled at by men in passing cars or from dormitory rooms. She does not like to walk by a group of imposing, leering young men only to hear them cutting up after she passes. She does not like to be the subject of jests and sexual innuendo. But this sort of thing goes on all the time. Young women who appear in public, whether in a dance club, at a pub, or in a shopping mall, are constantly accosted by packs of young males on the prowl who consider it their inalienable right to make crude, suggestive advances. These days young males curse with abandon in front of women, often in reference to sex. Nighttime finds barbarians reveling in the pick-up/hook-up culture of the bar scene. In short, the company of women no longer brings out the best in young men. Around the opposite sex, the adolescent and post-adolescent males of today are at their worst.

The problem of the modern barbarian is no academic or fastidious concern. Plato was right to regard the education and civilization of spirited males as the *sine qua non* of a decent political order. They are the natural watchdogs of society. When they are not properly trained, they become at best nuisances and at worst something much more dangerous.

MEN WITHOUT CHESTS

At the other extreme from true manliness is the wimp. Wimps are in many ways the opposite of barbarians. We would be mistaken, however, to classify wimps as simply young men without muscle. Often enough they are the stereotypical 98-pound weaklings who get sand kicked in their faces at the beach. But slightness of build and want of talent in sports do not make one a wimp. The diminutive and sickly James Madison was a man, just as was the towering and vigorous George Washington.

If barbarians suffer from a misdirected manliness, wimps suffer from a want of manly spirit altogether. They lack what the ancient Greeks called *thumos*, the part of the soul that contains the assertive passions: pugnacity, enterprise, ambition, anger. *Thumos* compels a man to defend proximate goods: himself, his honor, his lady, his country; as well as universal goods: truth, beauty, goodness, justice. Without thumotic men to combat the cruel, the malevolent, and the unjust, goodness and honor hardly have a chance in our precarious world. But two conditions must be present for *thumos* to fulfill its mission. First, the soul must be properly ordered. Besides *thumos*, symbolized by the chest, the soul is composed of reason and appetites, symbolized by the head on the one hand and the stomach and loins on the other. Reason has the capacity to discern right from wrong, but it lacks the strength to act. Appetites, while necessary to keep the body healthy, pull the individual toward pleasures of a lower order. In the well-ordered soul, as C.S. Lewis put it, "the head rules the belly through the chest." In the souls of today's barbarians, clearly *thumos* has allied itself with the unbridled appetites, and reason has been thrown out the window.

The second condition that must be present is a sufficient level of *thumos* to enable the man to rise to the defense of honor or goodness when required. Modern education and culture, however, have conspired to turn modern males into what C.S. Lewis called "men without chests," that is, wimps. The chest of the wimp has atrophied from want of early training. The wimp is therefore unable to live up to his duties as a man:

> We make men without chests and expect of them virtue and enterprise. We laugh at honour and are shocked to find traitors in our midst. We castrate and bid the geldings be fruitful.

Wimps make worthless watchdogs. But their failure as watchdogs or guardians has nothing to do with size or physique. My father used to tell me when I was growing up, "It is not the size of the dog in the fight, but the size of the fight in the dog" that matters. Many of today's young men seem to have no fight in them at all. Not for them to rescue damsels in distress from the barbarians. Furthermore, wimps vote. As Aristotle pointed out, to the cowardly, bravery will seem more like rashness and foolhardiness than what it really is. Hence political and social issues that require bravery for their solution elicit only hand-wringing and half-measures from the wimps. Wimps are always looking for the easy way out.

Like the barbarian, the wimp is easily recognized by his personality and preoccupations. His main passion is music. Music does not serve him as it does the Platonic guardian, to balance his soul. Nor is he usually a performer or student of music. He has no affinity for classical symphony or opera. Rather, he finds that certain types of music evoke a mood of listless self-infatuation. He may at times listen to music with friends. And he will probably try to express his interest in a girl by quoting a song lyric. Nonetheless, his absorption with music is essentially a private refuge from the challenges of the world.

In addition to music, the wimp may take an interest in the opposite sex. But his approach to dating and relationships is different from the barbarian. The barbarian has simple appetites. His ideal is the *Playboy* playmate or the winner of a hot legs contest at Daytona Beach, and his ultimate aim in any relationship or encounter, whatever he may say, is sex. As an athlete, the barbarian is a hero of sorts. He walks with an unmistakable air of confidence. The wimp, on the other hand, has more complex reasons for wanting women. Although sex is certainly one of his desires, more than sex he needs affirmation. He desperately needs a girlfriend to boost his self-confidence. Having someone else notice him will somehow show the world that he is not a total loser. The wimp also needs someone to hear his laments, to commiserate with him when he is feeling down, to discover his secret self. Since he has few qualities or achievements to recommend him, he seeks to appear "interesting" or mysterious. Initially, the wimp might seem amusing to an unsuspecting young lady and very different from the insensitive jocks and rowdies she has known. Ultimately, however, the wimp seeks to draw her into his web of melancholy and self-pity. The story always ends unhappily since romance cannot be based upon pity or the thin façade of personality. He might mope and whine his way into a woman's bed but will find excuses to avoid "commitment." The wimp will begin the relationship by saying, "You're the only one who understands me" and end it by saying, "You don't understand me at all." The truth is that there is not much to understand.

The wimp is unmanly in other ways, especially when compared to young men in the past. Throughout history men have come of age by preparing for war, going to sea, felling forests, or even mastering Latin and Greek. Besides listening to music, however, how does the average wimp spend the most formative years of his life? Shopping. Andy Warhol was, in this respect, a paragon of wimpiness. Whenever he felt down and was tired of painting soup cans, he would go shopping to cheer himself up. After his death, bags upon bags of unused products were found in his New York apartment. The wimp is a perfect consumer. In the largest sense, he consumes the liberties and public treasures his forefathers have passed on to him through their "blood, toil, tears, and sweat," without himself adding anything back to the common stock.

Needless to say, these sketches are not exhaustive. Barbarians and wimps come in many forms in a society that celebrates Diversity as we do. But all of them remind us that Plato's quandary was a timeless one and is our quandary no less than his. Our civilization cannot be sustained by barbarians or wimps; it needs true men.

BRAVE NEW WORLD

The world has always had its share of wimps and barbarians. Throughout history and literature they have appeared under the names of rogues, scoundrels, boors, ne'er-do-wells, namby-pambies, fops, and macaroni men, to name a few. What needs explaining is why these two obviously defective character types have become so common, at times seeming like the norm.

A close look at the culture in which boys are raised reveals not only that they are no longer encouraged to become vigorous and responsible men, but also that practically every factor affecting their development is profoundly hostile to the ideals and practices of traditional manhood and the painstaking steps necessary to attain it. The demanding regime of physical and moral instruction that used to turn boys into men and the larger cultural forces that supported that instruction have been systematically dismantled by a culture that ostensibly enables all individuals but in reality disables men. "It's too easy!" complained John the Savage of the overly efficient, overly sexual, overly youthful, overly fun Brave New World. That dehumanizing tyranny of pleasure, described by Aldous Huxley, resembles the world of easy effort and easy virtue that entices adolescent males today to indulge in their appetites at the expense of their nobler longings and passions.

Above all, there is easy sex. The sexual revolution released the sexual urge from its domestic harness. A male need no longer be a man, in character or physique, to have sex. He may be a boy of fourteen. Unchaperoned girls are not hard to find. They can be lured over to one's house under the pretense of listening to some new CDs. Avoiding dual-career parents' supervision is as easy as walking home from school. Indeed, the school will provide the illusion of safe sex in its required sex education classes, and chances are the school nurse will supply the condoms. What more could a boy want? Not only is sex no longer subordinated to marriage, which was predicated on male responsibility, but the most sly and unsavory characters are now the most rewarded with sex. "Boys will be boys," but they have little incentive to be responsible men.

Coupled with easy sex, easy divorce has also had devastating moral and psychological effects on boys. Half of American boys growing up do not live with their natural fathers. The sons of single mothers lack strong men to usher them into the world of responsible, adult manhood. Divorce, whether in reality or in the acrimonious rhetoric of the mother, impresses upon the boy an image of the father, and therefore of all men, as being irresponsible, deceitful, immature, and often hateful or abusive towards women. For sons, the divided loyalties occasioned by divorce actually create profound doubts about their own masculinity. As the boy approaches manhood, he is plagued by subconscious questions which have no immediate resolution: "Will I be like Dad?" "Do I want to be like Dad?" "What is a man supposed to do?"

Even when boys live with fathers, or when divorced mothers remarry, the erst-while "man of the house" has diminished considerably in stature. The traditional father was the sole breadwinner, the chief disciplinarian, and the figure who sat at the head of the table and spoke with authority on matters of politics, economics, and religion. Loving his children, he did not spare the rod. A new breed of parent (fathers are hardly to be distinguished from mothers) has arrived on the scene. The new parent has invented a new way of disciplining sons, adhering firmly to the principles of "self-esteem." The boy is never wrong, is never spanked, and is never made to feel ashamed. Postmodern parents believe, at least until it is too late, that raising children must be easy since the nature of children is basically good. I had no idea how entrenched these post-Spockian ideas were until I became a school principal and began hearing how parents talk about correcting their children. The word "punishment" no longer exists in the parental lexicon; it has been replaced by "consequences." Boys are not made to feel ashamed for bad behavior; they must reconsider their "poor choices." Least of all will parents spank their sons; if you sug-gest that they should, they look at you in horror, for after all, "violence only breeds violence." Of course, this softer form of discipline does not really work. When "time-outs" and restricted use of the internet prove unavailing, then it is time for counseling and Ritalin.

The old form of discipline was quick, direct, clear-cut, and effective. The new non-punitive discipline is time-consuming, indirect, muddled, and ineffective. Ev-ery breaking of the rules requires a long discussion in which the boy gets to express his "feelings" and therefore make his case. This new form of easy discipline actu-ally compromises the boy's moral growth in several ways. First, he receives no real punishment for wrongdoing and is not made to feel shame. The absence of these traditional external and internal sanctions inhibits his development of self-control. Second, rather than truly learning to be responsible and to accept the real conse-quences of his actions, he learns to be litigious and whiny. Worst of all, to the extent his father is involved in all this nonsense, he sees the man who should be his master and mentor not as an authoritative figure who imposes order and dispenses justice but as a craven coddler who shudders to injure an errant boy's self-esteem. On the surface, the boy is glad to skim by without getting into too much trouble. Deep down, he knows that his father is no man and so looks abroad for more energetic examples of thumotic manhood.

SCHOOLS FOR SISSIES

No less than at home, at school the boy encounters a world that thwarts any natural drive to become a true man. As Christina Hoff Sommers has shown, some schools are actively trying to remove any vestiges of traditional culture that work to the benefit and inspiration of boys: older forms of academic competition such as math and spelling bees, the preponderance of male heroes who can no longer outnumber female heroines, even school playgrounds and games like dodge ball. Even when schools are not deliberately trying to emasculate young boys, the world of education can appear feminized and overly pampering to young males. In elementary school, over 90% of the teachers are women. Having no decent curriculum to guide them, as is the case in most schools, these female teachers will quite innocently and un-imaginatively choose books and assignments that do not appeal to boys in the least. The boy student will have to suffer through *Charlotte's Web* three or four times but never hear of *Captains Courageous* or *Treasure Island* or Sherlock Holmes.

When he gets into middle and high school he may begin to have male teachers. But these are the tired, ineffective, jaded clock-watchers and pension-seekers of Theodore Sizer's *Horace's Compromise*. Horace lets the half of the class he cannot control talk for the whole period while he passes out worksheets to the half of the class who still care about grades. Horace is a wimp. If the boy sees any energy on the part of men at the school it is among the coaching staff. Coaches know how to appeal to the thumotic element in boys in order to train them to win, and they actually work hard on the field. They appear far less energetic and in command, however, when they must teach a history class, for there are only so many health and P.E. courses a school can offer.

Beyond these decayed institutions, the broader cultural landscape inhibits the transformation of boys into good men. Radical feminism, to name one feature of this landscape, has in some ways undermined the relations between the sexes. Radical feminists have not directly changed the character of traditional men. There are still a number of gentlemen who will open doors for ladies at the risk of be-ing told off by the occasional woman out to prove her equality and independence. What feminism has done, in conjunction with political correctness, is deprive overly non-offensive, modern parents of the language traditionally used to bring up young boys: "Be a man." "Stick up for your sister." "Quit throwing the ball like a sissy." "Quit crying like a girl." Instead, we have a lot of lukewarm, androgynous talk about "being a good person" and "showing respect to people." A naturally rambunctious and irascible boy, though, is not too interested in being a good person. For if he achieves that status, what will distinguish him from his prim and proper sister? The parents have no language to answer their son's deepest and most natural needs.

RITES OF PASSAGE

Finally, today's boys mill about their adolescent and post-adolescent years lacking any formal, approved rite of passage that would turn them into men. The American frontier disappeared in 1890. The call of the sea did not survive much longer. All-male colleges, where young men used to compete against each other in the lecture halls and on the playing field, can now be counted on the fingers of one hand. President Eliot of Harvard told his student body on taking office in 1869, "The best way to put boyishness to shame is to foster scholarship and manliness." Could a college president say that today to a student body in which males are the distinct minority? While the opening up of commerce and industry to women has increased their economic freedom and equality, men have lost one more arena in which to prove themselves, as George Gilder has elegantly shown. Moreover, most of the jobs offered in the new economy hardly appeal to the spiritedness in man. Certainly, the military still beckons many spirited boys coming out of high school, but the entire armed services constitute less than 1% of the American population and must make room for a fair number of women in their ranks. In short, modern America lacks what virtually every society in the past has established and governed with great effort and concern: a proving ground for male youth seeking some legitimate expression of their erratic and as yet undisciplined spiritedness.

The sum effect is an environment that demands virtually nothing special of boys as they grow into men. Many aspects of modern culture are debilitating for girls as well as boys, but the lack of dramatic challenge is not one of them. The recent statistics comparing girls' to boys' academic achievements worldwide demonstrate what any teacher in the country knows: that girls are achieving as never before and are outdistancing boys. Perhaps the kinder, gentler, nurturing, egalitarian, consultative, non-competitive approach to education and family has been a boon for girls. Yet what is good for the goose is not necessarily good for the gander. As Fr. Walter Ong expressed it, the male nature, in order to prove itself, in order to distinguish itself from the potentially emasculating feminine world into which the boy is born, longs for some "againstness" in the natural or moral world which the boy can overcome. But in our culture everything is too easy. Boys are not compelled, indeed not allowed, to fight anymore. They cannot fight on the playground. Nor can they fight for grades, for a girl, for God, or for country (though September 11 has altered this last). Even the saints of old would find the 21st century an inhospitable place, for how could they "fight the good fight" against their own fallen nature in a world supposedly without sin?

LITTLE AVERY

So how is Murphy Brown's little Avery doing? He is 11 now. He has grown up under an overbearing mother who has occasionally brought men home, though none has stayed. While Murphy has pursued her successful career, Avery has been showered with material possessions to give him something to do during the long stretches of the day when he finds himself at home alone or left to an indifferent nanny, finished with his half hour of easy homework, which his mother will check over and often redo for him after they have eaten the pizza or take-out Chinese she picked up on the way home from work. Every time Avery has a problem at school or in the neighborhood, Murphy solves it for him with the same decisiveness she demonstrates at the network, thus proving to her son and to herself that she is a good mother.

Avery has posters on his wall of Eminem, Kobe Bryant, and Fred Durst of Limp Bizkit. He is becoming interested in girls but is still too shy to say much to them. Still, he has learned a lot about women on the internet, and his favorite rap songs tell him precisely how to relate to women and what women want. His mother, for her part, has told him a lot about the value of "respecting people." Avery has never been hunting or fishing. True, Avery and his mother used to have fun times at the park and on trips when she could get away from work, but now he is beginning to pull away from her when she rubs his head in an affectionate way. They are not as close as they used to be.

The next few, crucial years of Avery's life will determine what kind of man he will be. Will he rest in wretched contentment with the ease and luxury provided by his oft-absent, deep-voiced mother, or will he rebel with other boys his own age, raised much like him, by finding his own rites of passage in drugs and sex and acts of petty delinquency, or worse? Will he become a wimp or a barbarian?

Against the Virtual Life

Joseph Epstein

(Summer 2009)

Mark Helprin's *Digital Barbarism: A Writer's Manifesto* is ostensibly a book about copyright: the need for preserving it and indeed extending its span, the distinctions between it and other forms and kinds of property, the political implications behind recent attempts to eliminate it. As a copyright holder myself, who has not thought lengthily on the subject, but only gratefully collects his peasantries (as I refer to my rather meager royalties) and moves on, Mr. Helprin's argument strikes me as sound, persuasive, even penetrating. But the book is about much more than copyright. *Digital Barbarism* is, in fact, a diatribe, harangue, lecture, attack, onslaught, denunciation, polemic, broadside, fulmination, condemnation, no-holds barred, kick-butt censure of the current, let us call it the digital, age. Reviewers have criticized Helprin for the almost unrelenting note of rant in his book, claiming, as one did, that it "corrodes [his] credibility." Poor benighted fellows, they have missed the best part of this unusual book.

Mark Helprin is a brilliant writer, of great descriptive power and independent mind, whose views are often unpredictable and always lively. He was an advisor on defense and foreign relations for Bob Dole when he ran for the presidency in 1996, which, in the lost-cause department, strikes me as a job akin to having the bagel concession in Hitler's bunker. I mention this odd biographical fact—he brings up many others in the course of his book—to show that Mr. Helprin does not run with the gang, any gang. He doesn't, that is, find much to choose from between Ann Coulter and Al Franken.

Digital Barbarism had its origins in an op-ed in the *New York Times* that Helprin wrote in 2007 in defense of copyright. Such was the reaction against this piece, some 750,000 uniformly ticked-off outbursts on the internet, that Helprin came to realize that forces greater than the matter of the validity of copyright were at issue. He determined, in fact, that a great cultural disruption had occurred, and that the attack on the age-old institution of copyright is merely the tip of the iceberg toward which we, jolly passengers on a cultural Titanic of our own devising, are all blithely sailing.

As for copyright, those who would eliminate it, placing all works in the public domain—a condition to which much recorded music has not aspired but appears to have attained—feel it is little more than selfishness legalized. Art, like ideas, they hold, ought to be common property, enjoyed by all, with future profit for none. Helprin clubs adherents of this view down, showing that copyright is nothing like the monopoly they claim, nor is it the same as holding a patent, which they ignorantly aver. He convincingly makes the case that copyright is a form of property—intellectual property—and that sustaining it is important for stimulating individuality, originality, and creativity of a kind without which life will quickly lapse into a bland collectivity that will make us all much the poorer—and not merely in the economic realm.

"Copyright is important," Helprin writes, "because it is one of the guarantors of the rights of authorship, and the rights of authorship are important because without them the individual voice would be subsumed in an indistinguishable and instantly malleable mass." A mass, one might add, of the kind that ganged up against Helprin in reaction to his *New York Times* op-ed. "The substance [of the reaction to his op-ed] was disturbing if only for its implicit comment on the state of contemporary education," he writes. "The form, however, was most distressing, in that it was so thoughtless, imitative, lacking in custom and civility, and stimulated—as if in a feedback loop or feeding frenzy—by the power it brought to bear not by means of any quality but only as a variant of mass and speed."

Without gainsaying the rich new possibilities that digital technology has made available, Helprin makes the case that this same technology inculcates a frenetic habit of mind, quick on the trigger yet slow to appreciate subtlety and dazzlingly blind to beauty. "The character of the machine is that of speed, power, compression, instantaneousness, immense capacity, indifference, and automaticity," he writes. The other side of this debased coin is that the machine does not understand tradition, appreciate stability, enjoy quality, but instead "[hungers] for denser floods of data" and fosters a mentality in which "images have gradually displaced words."

Early in *Digital Barbarism*, Helprin posits two characters, one a high-flying executive in 2028 of a company that "supplies algorithms for the detection of damage in and the restoration of molecular memories in organic computation," the other a British diplomat in 1908 on holiday at Lake Como. The first is living virtually the virtual life, so to speak, which means that he is hostage to the machinery of communication and information, flooded by e-mail, cell phone calls, screen imagery, in a life lived very much from without. The second, reachable only by slow international post, lives his life with ample room for reflection, cultivation of the intellect, acquiring musical and literary culture directly and at leisure. Helprin naturally prefers the life of the latter, and if you don't grasp the reasons why, you are a digital barbarian in the making, if not already made.

Helprin tells us that "I look at a computer screen as little as possible"; and, later, that his satellite television system "was destroyed by a discerning lightning bolt." Yet he is no Luddite, or even against technology per se. He recognizes, as he puts it, that to deplore "the factual trajectory of things makes one reactionary, a dinosaur, rigid, unimaginative, impotent, a fascist, and a chipmunk." (A nice touch, that chipmunk at the end of the list.) But, boats against the current, Helprin beats on, claiming that "one need not be a Nazi brontosaurus to question the trajectories of one's time if indeed one's time produces people who think their grandchildren are their ancestors."

The real enemy, the digital barbarism of Helprin's title, is the kind of mind that is likely to oppose copyright—a mind propelled by a strong sense of entitlement, inane utopian visions, and less than no regard for those distinctions and discriminations that make a complex culture hum. *Digital Barbarism* is meant to be a torpedo aimed not across but directly into their bow. The anti-copyright movement, he holds, "is against property, competition, and the free market"; and its adherents are those who "favor a world that is planned, controlled, decided, entirely cooperative, and conducive of predetermined outcomes," even though history has long ago taught that those outcomes have a way of working almost precisely against the utopian dreams of the planners.

Nudniks, the Yiddish word for aggressive pests, is only one of the vituperations Helprin casts upon people possessed by minds organized in the movement against copyright. "Unlike the troublesome and annoying classical nudniks of the past," he writes,

> the electronic nudnik is sheltered by anonymity, his acts amplified by an almost inconceivable multiplication and instantaneousness of transmission. This new nudnik is therefore tempted to exchange his previous protective innocence (think Alfred E. Neuman) for a certain sinister, angry, off-the-rails quality (think the Unabomber), which is perhaps to be expected from the kind of person who has spent forty thousand hours reflexively committing video-game mass murder and then encounters an argument with which he finds himself in disagreement.

Helprin believes that he, in his op-ed, offended "a subcult amid those modern people who dress like circus clowns or adorn themselves like cannibals," presenting a spectacle akin to Queequeg having been "dropped on Santa Monica." He also avers that they have "a brain the size of a Gummy Bear" and, elsewhere, "of cocktail onions."

"At risk of straying too far," Mr. Helprin writes well into his slender book, to which one's response is, Not at all, old sport, stray quite as far as you like, plunge on, for the rest of this sentence reads: "I must relate the story of how a long time ago a great friend and I, alighting from a freight train in northern Virginia, proceeded to Crystal City, where we insolently skated in our shoes across an empty ice rink while a Zamboni machine was grooming it, leading to our detention by a security guard with the physique of a whale."

Much of the pleasure in this book is in its digressions, for which the main argument, one sometimes thinks, is merely the excuse. Copyright, in other words, is the trampoline upon which Helprin jumps, the better to pounce on that new cultural type, the digital barbarian, he despises. *Digital Barbarism*, in much briefer compass, gives some of the same oblique pleasure as *Tristram Shandy* and *The Anatomy of Melancholy*, two works that, without their digressions, could scarcely be said to exist.

An "essay-memoir" is the way Helprin describes his book, but it is also something of an advertisement for himself. Normally, this would not be a good thing, but here it is, somehow, amusing, like those television commercials that are superior to the show they are sponsoring. In his preface, for example, he informs us that he would "sometimes write speeches for politicians . . . always from deep anonymity and always without any compensation." He has an interest in physics, he tells us, "half-theoretical, half-empirical, and entirely amateur." He recounts that he went to Harvard, where his classmate was "that spritely lummox, Al Gore," and thence to Oxford, and that he was in the Israeli Air Force. His father, we learn, was in the movie industry, his mother an actress, but he is no more specific than that. (Was his father successful? Is his mother, who goes unnamed, famous, or was she famous in her day?) He claims—no reason to doubt him—to have taken a cross-country bicycle trip at the age of 14. He makes himself out to have been fairly well off, yet lets us know he worked two jobs after Harvard. He taught at the University of Iowa 30 years ago, where he was befriended by the now alas forgotten novelist Vance Bourjaily. He rows, about which he wrote a fine short story called "Palais de Justice," and used to be a climber (mountains, one presumes), and currently fly fishes. Greek sponge-fishing holidays, he instructs us, are "vastly overrated." Had he told us that he had flown three kamikaze missions (insufficient death wish?) or used to play gin rummy with Osama bin Laden's mother, we should, after all these autobiographical tidbits, have taken these, too, in easy stride.

Along with building up this persona, Helprin shoots off lots of lovely zingers. At these prices, he must have concluded, why accept repression? On his bicycle trip, he tells, to illustrate a point about private property, that a farmer caught him eating an ear of corn from his field, and came off as "irate as Al Sharpton," even though the farmer, "perhaps like Van Gogh, would not have missed a single ear." He remarks that the *New York Times Book Review* is our equivalent to the French Academy, deciding "the relative values and appropriate rewards for literary endeavors," but "at least it's not in the Constitution." He cites the "*Chronicle of* [supposedly] *Higher Education*," which "exhibits less intelligence than a Kleenex." He takes time out to attack Levenger's, which sells pseudo-elegant writing equipment, as part of a general tirade against the modern tendency to be over-equipped for all activities. He bangs the idiot professoriat, and bings the contemporary novel, a stellar example of which he feels might be titled

Rimbaud's Macaque, a Novel of the Hypothetical Romance of Isadora Duncan and Nikolai Tesla, or, the Birds of Werbezerk, which, to quote from the publisher's copy, is "the dark and unforgiving account of a Santa Monica professor of Jewish studies who discovers that her parents were Bavarian Nazis and practicing cannibals."

What makes Mark Helprin a gifted polemicist is his ability to combine the humorous with the tiradical. "A man blowing a trumpet successfully is a rousing spectacle," the Welsh writer Rhys Davies noted. Something no less rousing about a man standing up and blowing off, full steam ahead, as Mark Helprin does about, for only one example, the self-importance of BlackBerry-bearing human beings:

[T]he text-messaging approach [to making a dinner date] would take at least four messages, each typed in even more time than required by the entire voice transaction, over a period of hours or days, "from my BlackBerry." Excuse me? From your BlackBerry? I don't think the purpose of this declaration is to explain the brevity of your message, as you could probably type *War and Peace* with one thumb tied behind your BMW. I think its purpose is an ad from BlackBerry to let me know that you have a BlackBerry. May your BlackBerry rot in hell.

Many fine blasts of this kind are to be found in *Digital Barbarism*, some cutting an admirably wide swath. Here is Helprin on the hopeless attempts to fight the relentless debasement through vulgarization of contemporary culture:

> No one has control of what is happening. It is the result of the hundred million decisions that taken together mark the decline of a culture—the teacher, lacking anything to say about his subject, who promotes an ideology instead; the publisher who cannot resist the payout from sensationalism and whips it into a dollar-frosted frenzy; the intellectually lazy reader who buys a prurient thriller, knowing that its effect is equivalent to a diet of gas-station junk food, "just for the plane ride"; the drug-addled Hollywood solons who have blurred the line between general films and pornography, and have created a new nonsexual pornography of hypnotic, purely sensational images, substituting stimulation and tropism for just about everything else (except popcorn); narrow intellectuals who mock the ethical precepts, religions, and long-held beliefs of civilizations that have evolved over thousands of years, in favor of theories of more or less everything that they have designed over an entire semester; writers who write according to neither their consciences nor their hearts, but to sell.

O.K., everyone breathe out. Mark Helprin is a man of belligerent integrity. He recounts turning down an enormous fee from *Time* for a cover story because he attacked the egotism of Lee Iacocca. He has lost lucrative film deals because he refused to yield his copyright to film studios. He does not suffer slovenly editing, and once instructed an editor who inserted the word "pricey" in his copy to bugger off, though he does use the word "seminal," which has always seemed to me greatly to underestimate the power of semen. Although dependent on publishers, as are all we scribblers, he doesn't in the least mind mocking them. The only authority he submits to is that of sound intelligence allied to the mission of saving what is best in Western culture.

Great fun though it is to read, one has to ask, how high is the truth quotient of *Digital Barbarism* in the picture it presents of the general degradation of modern life? When one allows for Helprin's hyperbole, his ripping tirades, his penchant for amusing over-statement, and allows further for the possibility that he believes he is guilty of none of the foregoing, the truth quotient, it strikes me, remains damnably high. Now in his early sixties, Mark Helprin is old enough to recall another time, with different beliefs, and higher standards, and over a long career he has earned the right to be cranky about its fading away. His fate is not so different than that of the Goncourt brothers, who in 1860 wrote in their journal: "It is silly to come into the world in a time of change; the soul feels as uncomfortable as a man who moves into a new house before the plaster is dry." The question facing Mark Helprin, and us with him, is what the place is going to look like once the plaster has dried.

A Dance to the (Disco) Music of Time

John Derbyshire

(Spring 2004)

We are, as everyone knows, living in the, or a, "gay moment." One of the consequences is that we have to put up with a great deal of homosexualist propaganda.
(I favor the usage "homosexualist" for people who are activist about their sexual
orientation, versus "homosexual" for people who are merely, and privately, homosexual. I admit, though, that my attempts to promote this—it seems to me, useful
and non-insulting—usage have fallen mostly on stony ground.) Among homo-
sexualists there are many whose devotion to what Christopher Isherwood famously
called "my kind" is as intense as anything that can be shown by the followers of any
religion or political ideology.

One aspect of this devotion is the urge to recruit long-dead historical names to the
Cause—to comb through history seeking out gayness. Since history is, much more
often than not, a very ambiguous affair, an explorer of this inclination can return
with many trophies, which he will then display triumphantly to us dull-witted, unimaginative breeders, revealing to us that the human race is, contrary to our narrow
brutish prejudices, a very ocean of gayness. Julius Caesar? Gay! Jesus of Nazareth?
Gay! Leonardo? Gay! Frederick the Great? Gay! All of them—gay, gay, gay! I do not
recall having seen it argued that George Washington was gay, but I have not the
slightest doubt that the argument has been made by somebody, somewhere.

Louis Crompton's *Homosexuality and Civilization* belongs to this genre of homo-
prop. It has, I should say here up front, many virtues. Crompton has done prodigies
of literary and historical research across a wide range. His sources are for the most
part secondary, but they could hardly be otherwise in a book of this scope. Nobody
has real expertise on *both* ancient Greece *and* feudal Japan. He writes well for an academic (Crompton is emeritus professor of English at the University of Nebraska),
and the book is beautifully produced, with a high standard of copy editing and
many fine plates to please the eye.

Certainly Crompton has a bill of goods to sell, but there we come to matters of
personal taste in reading. You either like didactic history, or you don't. I myself like
it very much, to the degree that I even like it when an author writes contrary to my
own prejudices. We—the readers of this fine periodical, I mean—are not gaping

rubes, to be lured from the straight and narrow by a silver-tongued swindler. We have powers of judgment, which we can apply to an author's reasoning, and we have knowledge, which we can compare with the facts he presents. Crompton left me unconvinced on his main point, but he proved thoughtful, and entertained me along the way. As propaganda goes, this is a superior specimen.

His topic is, of course, homosexuality, and this raises a number of problems right away. What *is* homosexuality? The term is currently used in reference to those who find erotic fulfillment only with coevals of their own sex. A great deal of Crompton's book, however, deals with different matters. Much of it is about ephebophilia, or boy-love, a phenomenon whose connection to homosexuality is unclear. Indeed, many present-day homosexualist propagandists insist hotly that there is no connection at all.

And the matter of *what people are doing* contains all kinds of knotty sub-problems of language and interpretation. When George Russell tells us that "My intercourse with Jowett was not intimate," or when Dr. Johnson says: "I love Robertson, and I won't talk of his book," a person who had learned English as a second language might suppose—wrongly, of course—that these men are speaking about sexual enjoyment of the other party. How much more difficult to interpret recorded utterances from 2,500 years ago, in languages obscure, dead, or both.

Similarly, researcher Michael J. Bailey, in his recent book about effeminate men (*The Man Who Would Be Queen: The Science of Gender-Bending and Transexualism*), notes the great difficulty of finding out about the sex lives of Americans today, even with our ability to conduct ambitious surveys costing millions of dollars and involving thousands of subjects. What proportion of the current U.S. population is homosexual? We do not know, even to an order of magnitude. (Bailey's own estimate is from "less than 1 percent to more than 4 percent.") What, then, can we hope to understand about the sex lives of the Byzantine emperors—let alone of their subjects? As Sir Kenneth Dover says of Athenian slanders on the Spartans:

> If Spartans in the fourth century B.C. unanimously and firmly denied that their *erastai* and *eromenoi* [i.e., senior and junior partners in an ephebophilic bond] ever had any bodily contact beyond a clasping of right hands, it was not easy for an outsider even at the time to produce evidence to the contrary, and for us it is impossible.

So on the things we really want to know, we have not much of a clue. What did members of the Theban Band actually do with each other in their leisure hours? Human nature being what it is, it would be surprising if nothing at all went on, but beyond that there is little we can say.

Reading Professor Crompton's book, I found that the most useful way of thinking about his topic was as a sort of dance—a "dance to the music of time," as it were. (Apologies to the late Anthony Powell.) The participants in this dance are not individual human beings but invariant components of the human personality, found in all times and places. Principal among those components I would list the following:

- *Homosexual orientation.* Some small proportion of people find erotic fulfillment only with members of their own sex.

- *Ephebophilia.* Some much larger proportion of adult men can be sexually aroused by contemplating the bodies of well-formed adolescent boys. Overt expression of this attraction has been approved in some societies (or among some social strata in some societies—this seems to be controversial), where it has led to open romantic bonding between adult men and boys. Some similar, but much less historically significant, phenomenon is found among women.

- *Faute de mieux homosexuality.* In societies, or institutions in societies—monasteries, prisons, etc.—where social custom or institutional imperative severely constrains access to the opposite sex, some large proportion of adults, perhaps a majority, will find erotic satisfaction, or at least release, with members of their own sex, when there are not strong institutional prejudices against this (as there are, for instance, in elite combat units of the U.S. military).

- *Homophobia.* (Note: this ugly and etymologically stupid word has entered general currency, so I use it here for convenience, though under protest.) The contemplation of homosexuality induces negative emotions—disgust and contempt, mostly, but also sometimes indignation, anger, and hatred—in many people.

The story told in *Homosexuality and Civilization* is in large part the story of a long dance among these four partners, with sometimes this one, sometimes that one taking the lead. The well-known proclivities of the ancient Greeks, for example, arose mainly from the union of the second and third of the factors I have listed.

Louis Crompton's position on some of these core topics is, I do not think it is unfair to say, controversial. On homosexual orientation, for example, consider the numbers again. So far as we understand the science of male homosexuality—which is further than most people realize, though nothing like far enough to make conclusive pronouncements—the orientation is congenital, with events in the mother's womb as causative factors, together probably with some slight effects from genetic predisposition (a perplexing thing in itself, considering the consequences for inheritance) and life events in infancy. On Bailey's estimate, from 1% to 4% of men are affected. Has this proportion been constant across other times and places? It is impossible to know. The science suggests, as a null hypothesis, that it has been. I am not aware of any evidence contradicting this.

Crompton's narrative contradicts that null hypothesis mightily, though. He has, for example, three of the six Stuart monarchs of England as homosexual in orientation. The probability of this on a 4% basis is one in 855. On a 1% basis, it is one in 51,142. Even if you allow the possibility of that slight genetic factor, this is far out of range. Similarly with his catalogs of Chinese storytellers, Arab poets, and Elizabethan dramatists. Literary gents are not, to be sure, representative of the general population in their sexual preferences, but is Crompton quite sure he has made all due allowance for flattery, stylistic fads, flights of fancy, and plain mischief? I once listened in on an e-list discussion among some Shakespeare experts, debating the question: Is there any character in the plays that can reasonably be taken as "gay" in the modern sense? The consensus was that there is not one. Considering the number of characters involved, this seems difficult to square with Crompton's speculations on the *Sonnets* and their author.

On homophobia, Crompton is emphatic: it is all the fault of "the Hebrew scriptures"—especially, of course, Leviticus. Those proscriptions infected Christianity via Saint Paul and then to a lesser degree tainted Islam. I should make it clear here that

I see no signs of any anti-Semitic intent in Crompton's book, though I do think it is quite unpleasantly anti-Christian.

Is homophobia really all the fault of Leviticus and Saint Paul, though? I have said above that "many people" are repelled by homosexuality. How many? In present-day America, I would guess the answer to be: A modest majority of men, a minority of women, though the numbers cut differently according to age, religion, education, and social class. The situation in other times and places is even less clear. However, there seems to have been, at a minimum, a widespread general repugnance, in all times and places, toward the passive partner in male-male buggery—"the man who plays the part of a woman." This repugnance may be sufficiently widespread to belong on anthropologist Donald E. Brown's list of "human universals," along with ethnocentrism, incest avoidance, jokes, and so on. It is not difficult to think of an explanation for it in terms of evolutionary biology, but so far as I am aware, the actual psychological status of homophobia is not known. It might be biologically "hard-wired." Contrariwise, it might be socially conditioned—though if it is, there seems to have been no society that did not condition it to some degree.

In short, there is much more to homophobia than blind prejudice ignited by Hebrew scriptures. One of the most violently homophobic societies that ever existed was Mao Tse-tung's China. Bao Ruo-wang's *Prisoner of Mao* (1973), for instance, includes a grisly eye-witness account of the execution of a labor-camp inmate suspected of having made homosexual advances. Yet practically nobody in that society had heard of Leviticus or Saint Paul. How does Crompton explain this? He doesn't; though he says that the turn toward homophobia in Meiji Japan was a result of "Western influence." Perhaps it was; perhaps Professor Crompton has misconstrued the openness of pre-Meiji times; perhaps the process of modernization *anywhere* excites homophobia for some reason; perhaps half a dozen other perhapses.

Crompton's explanations sometimes fall below the unconvincing down to the preposterous. "Abuse of sodomites [in the mid-18th century] became a way for Englishmen to affirm their manhood and allay any suspicions about their own sexuality." This is only a more highfalutin version of the sneering retort often given by homosexuals to anyone who criticizes their activities: "What's *your* problem?" It has its roots in pop-Freudianism, which is to say, in a trivialized version of an exploded theory. Why did Englishmen at that particular time need to "affirm their manhood" in that particular way, rather than by, say, chasing women, fighting duels, or going to war?

Crompton's book also has odd omissions. Russia, for example, is left out altogether. Does he think that country not sufficiently civilized? Or just not sufficiently "gay"? (If the latter, he may be mistaken. One memoirist observed of the reign of Nicholas I that: "at that time buggery was widespread in high society.") The narrative ends rather abruptly, and early—the latest figure discussed at length is Jeremy Bentham. "Our story concludes here," says the author, "at the moment when executions finally cease in Europe." Why? It did not begin when executions *started*. Perhaps Crompton just got tired. One could not blame him, for the amount of sheer hard work he has put into his book is plain to see. The results, for this reader, were not altogether as intended, but I am glad to have read *Homosexuality and Civilization* anyway, and recommend it to anyone who likes this sort of thing.

The Three Rings

Jaroslav Pelikan

(Fall 2004)

There was once, so the story goes, a magic ring—no, not J.R.R. Tolkien's ring, nor even Richard Wagner's, but Gotthold Ephraim Lessing's (and Boccaccio's before him). As the wise Jew Nathan tells the story to the Muslim Sultan Saladin in Lessing's *Nathan the Wise* (and not far out of the hearing of a Christian crusader), the ring possessed the wondrous power of conferring many blessings on the one who owned it. In each generation the owner would pass it on to the one among his sons who most excelled in wisdom and virtue. Then in one generation there were three sons, each of them with outstanding qualities, so that the father could not decide which one should receive the ring. To resolve his dilemma he summoned a master artisan who created two more rings, so identical to the original that neither the father himself nor anyone else could ever tell the difference, and gave one ring to each son. After his death each of the three sons claimed that he had the true ring. When they brought the dispute before a judge, he advised that each one should behave as though his ring were the one, but in the awareness that there were in fact two others:

> They search, dispute, lament,
> In vain; the proper ring could not
> Be found; 'twas hid as well almost
> As—*the true faith from us today,*
> Nathan explains.

The parable of the three rings is poignant, almost irresistibly charming—and devastatingly relativistic, just as Lessing intended it to be. Without citing the tale in *The Monotheists: Jews, Christians, and Muslims in Conflict and Competition*, F.E. Peters in effect sets forth an alternative to it, a modern way of coping with the "conflict and competition" between the three monotheistic "peoples of the Book" all claiming descent of one kind or another from Father Abraham. A professor of Middle Eastern Studies, Hebrew and Judaic Studies, and History at New York University, Peters opts for "the instruments of the historian." Using those instruments, he has undertaken "not to make peace or stir up war, or even ill feelings, among the three

411

religious communities, but simply to lay out their common roots, their evolution over time, and what I see as their striking resemblances and their equally striking differences." Instead of narrating the history of each community from beginning to end on the basis of a common template *à la* Plutarch, or of giving an account of their interactions in each historical period or region (for example, the Middle Ages in Spain), Peters has taken the bold step of choosing a thematic approach, almost a taxonomic one. Volume I bears the subtitle *The Peoples of God*, Volume II *The Words and the Will of God*. Under each category, the individual chapters are more or less comparative—for example, "Orthodoxy and Heresy" in the first, or "Scripture and Tradition" in the second—with subsections of one or two pages as well as sidebars that concentrate on one or another of the three. There are no footnotes or endnotes, and no bibliography (it would, of course, have to be immense). But there are generous citations, with chapter and verse, from the three scriptures and from many other classic texts of the three traditions, often with the technical terms in one or another of the root languages (Hebrew, Aramaic, Greek, Latin, Arabic).

Anyone who has attempted to concentrate on the history of only one of these three faiths must admire both the imagination of the enterprise and the elegance of the results. In 800 pages of very readable exposition, Peters demonstrates a command of highly complex materials, a sensitivity to the nuances of religious beliefs and practices in each tradition, and what Max Weber called "musicality," the opposite of the historical tone-deafness that so often marks the outsider's interpretation of other and alien faiths. Inevitably, so ambitious a journey will run into a detour or a roadblock or at least a pothole here and there. Just as Christians will often speak about "Reform*ed* Judaism" when it should be "Reform Judaism," so here the Calvinist churches of Protestantism, which (especially in German) refer to themselves as "Reformed [*nach Gottes Wort reformiert*]," come out as "Reform Protestantism." More seriously, the customary Christian attachment of the misnomer "Nicene Creed" (from the Council of Nicaea in 325) to the amplified creed that was adopted only at the First Council of Constantinople in 381 seems to have led here to the impression that the historic marks of the Church as "one, holy, catholic, and apostolic" were legislated already by the former council rather than only in the later confession of faith.

And still more seriously: Peters announces near the beginning his intention to restrict the title "Bible" to the Jewish Bible (although "scripture" is used for the sacred canons of all three faiths). But "Bible" is not Hebrew but Greek, a neuter plural *Biblia* (little books), which in Latin and then in its daughter languages was parsed as though it were a feminine singular—all of this happening in early and especially medieval *Christian* usage. Having just completed a book entitled *Whose Bible Is It?*, which narrates the history of the Jewish and Christian Scriptures and of their interaction through the centuries, I am keenly aware of the ambiguities of terminology especially in speaking about Holy Writ. When Peters observes at one place that "in religious communities disputes about the calendar are *always* [italics his] about something other than counting," that is true *a fortiori* about nomenclature. But it does seem draconian—and, to use his word in another context, "reductive"—to resolve the issue this way. (I finally settled for "Bible" and "Scripture" or "the Scriptures" as the titles in both communities, with "Tanakh" for the Jewish Scripture as such, even in the Greek translation of the Septuagint, and "Old Testament" only for its place in the Christian Bible.)

There is another, more structural difficulty with this use of a synchronic rather than a diachronic method. What Peters observes about "overlaps and repetitions" in the distribution of the Law across the entire Pentateuch applies to his two volumes even more than it does to Moses' five volumes: the notorious "satanic verses" of the Koran, now permanently associated with the name of Salman Rushdie, are explained twice, once in each volume; the distinctive tenets of the Pharisees and their view of the relation between Scripture and tradition appear over and over again; and the political theology of Marsilius of Padua and William of Ockham receives an exposition at two places in the narrative.

As a consequence of this structure, the reader is forced to flip around, with the aid of the numerous cross-references and a fine index, to get anything approaching a comprehensive interpretation of some of the most important figures in the history of each of the monotheistic faiths. Al-Ghazali's *Revivification of the Sciences of Religion* is "arguably the most influential book written by a Muslim," but it takes two pages here and another page or two there to begin to understand why. The same happens to Augustine, for whom there is a one-page discussion of religious coercion, a three-page exposition of nature and grace, a page-and-a-half summary of *The City of God*, and more. Moses Maimonides, "the Rambam," is one of the heroes of the piece, as indeed he deserves to be (Peters does not quote the rabbinical kudos, "From Moses to Moses there was none like Moses," but he does document it very well); but there is a fragmentary, almost tantalizing, quality to his many notices across the entire two volumes.

Corresponding to this is a surprising neglect of certain topics that would appear to be indispensable. The "interconfessional passage of believers from one faith community into another" or individual conversion (as distinct from "social conversion" or "coerced conversion") is almost declared out of bounds as inaccessible to the historian's probings. There is virtually nothing about hymns, spirituals, and chorales. And it is quite astonishing to read that "private and individual prayers and private rituals . . . are generally not the subject of discourse in the three monotheistic religious communities," a judgment that an all-but-apostolic succession from Tertullian and Origen in the 2nd and 3rd centuries to William James and Friedrich Heiler in the 20th (not to mention the almost endless stream of other commentators on the Lord's Prayer and the Ave Maria) would find puzzling.

Compensating for these difficulties are the often striking, and sometimes brilliant, parallels and comparisons. Peters rightly dismisses the overly facile parallelism of some modern Western visitors to the Middle East who "thought they could best understand the Sunnis and Shiites as, respectively, a version of Catholics and Protestants," when in fact, "functionally speaking, the opposite seems closer to the truth." As a result of comparisons, "it is by now almost an article of Jewish faith—a dogma, no less—that there are no dogmas in Judaism." Although Muhammad and Jesus "are both recognized as in some sense the founders of the two religious communities that claim more adherents than any others," closer comparison shows that "they have little in common" and that "the two lives show remarkable differences."

Another comparison between the Christian and the Muslim tradition proves to be more telling: "Far from separating church and state, [John Calvin] described their union in his *Institutes* in language that would be as at home in Tehran in the late 20th century as he convinced the Genevans it should be in the 16th, though

Calvin gave civil officials far more latitude to decide church matters than the Iranian Constitution granted their secular counterparts." Again, in an almost epigrammatic comparison involving all three traditions: "Since the lawyers of Islam were essentially rabbis and not bishops speaking comfortably *ex cathedra*, they had early begun to employ various forms of legal reasoning that have been the staples of lawyers always and everywhere." Or this: "The least bishop in Christendom could pronounce more loudly and consequentially on the faith than either this Jewish rabbi [Maimonides] or this Muslim historian [Ibn Khaldun]."

Such epigrams and one-liners dot the pages throughout and would, even by themselves, be worth the price of admission. Inquiring how monotheists could have a demonology without lapsing into metaphysical dualism, Peters explains that "Satan is no prince; he is the dean of a college." He describes the conflicts between (and within) the three communities over the Western Wall in Jerusalem as "a not untypical example of how a Jerusalem holy place began with the presence of God and ended up in the hands of lawyers." The inhabitants of Mecca who opposed Muhammad may have "thought monotheism would lessen Mecca's appeal as a pilgrimage center (surely one of the gravest miscalculations in the history of commerce)." The translation of Aristotle, Ptolemy, and Galen from Greek into Arabic, at least partly at the hands of Christian scholars (followed some centuries later by the retranslation of Aristotle from Arabic into Latin) was "technology transfer on a massive scale, this passage of the intellectual goods of one culture into the quite different idiom of another."

Always lurking as a subtext, and repeatedly breaking into the exposition (as it repeatedly breaks into the headlines of our newspapers), is the story of how the sibling rivalries in this "fractious family" have erupted into persecution and open war, to which we are indebted for "crusade," "jihad," "pogrom," "auto-da-fé," and many other terms that have so enriched our vocabulary. "Monotheists," Peters explains, "are bred-in-the-bone fanatics, an attitude they learned at the (allegorical) knee of the Creator, who was, as he himself noted, 'a jealous God'"; "whatever the monotheists lack in tolerance," therefore, "they make up in conviction." Christians and Muslims have been guilty of intolerance and persecution far more often than Jews, at least partly because they had more of an opportunity; but excluding a Jewish convert to Roman Catholicism from *aliya*, the Law of Return in the modern State of Israel, did prove to be a test case. More often than not, "forbearance" rather than "tolerance" has been the characteristic stance; and even when it has existed, it was usually limited to other monotheists and did not extend to polytheists or atheists. The great laboratory was medieval Spain, where "the three communities by no means loved one another, but there was a degree of respect and, more obviously, an effective degree of *convivencia*, or coexistence." The same has been true, though much less often, in the Balkans and in Sicily. Peters does not allow himself to speculate about the prospects for any *convivencia* in today's Middle East, nor does he mention Samuel Huntington's thesis of the clash of civilizations. But he clearly does hope, as a historian, that the kind of sympathetic understanding he manifests for all three traditions may become contagious while we still have time. One can only agree—and, yes, pray to the One True God—that we do still have time.

VII

ARTS, LITERATURE, AND LEISURE

Building Democracy

Hadley Arkes

(Summer 2007)

"Why aren't you giving a course on the American Founding?" The question came from Allan Greenberg, the architect, at lunch one day in Washington more than a dozen years ago. The question, sprung in part from curiosity, had the edge also of a reproach: why wasn't I tending to this urgent business? It was the kind of question, with the note of gravity, that comes from émigrés who have fallen in deep love with this country and become rather intense on the question of why others have not become as absorbed as they have in studying the writings and the achievements of the American Founders. Greenberg had come from South Africa with his wife and small children in the summer of 1964, and he records in his new book the impressions that struck at once:

> Standing in the main concourse of the International Terminal at John F. Kennedy Airport in New York, I was aware of being surrounded by voices speaking English with more accents than I had ever imagined existed. An electric energy seemed to pulsate through the ground on which I was standing. At that moment I fell in love with America. It felt as if I had come home.

That love has not abated but deepened over 40 years, and it deepened as he immersed himself in the study of the American Founding in all of its aspects—the writings and letters of the leading figures, the Federalist and Anti-Federalist papers—and all of it amplified by the study of Abraham Lincoln. It was all comparably intense, and all done with that attentiveness to detail that marks the eye of the accomplished architect. Settled in America, Greenberg would become a leading figure in the revival of classical architecture, and he would come to teach a new appreciation of the distinctive American forms of that classicism in the 18th century. He would be recruited by George Shultz to redesign the Treaty Room at the State Department. As his name became known, he would design the flagship store for Bergdorf Goodman in New York, for Tommy Hilfiger in Los Angeles, and he would accumulate a portfolio of the most elegant buildings, private and public (including several pictured in this new book, *Architecture of Democracy: American Architecture and the Legacy of the Revolution*). He settled in New Haven as he began to design for a discerning clientele in Connecticut and New York, and before long he would add an office in Washington, which he makes now his base. Along the way he would teach at Yale, not only in the school of architecture, but in the school of law. With that assignment, he would take his students for overnight stays in prison, partly to study the architecture of those buildings, bound up of course with their purposes and with the understanding of the nature of those beings, those fallen moral agents, that the buildings were designed to house.

Greenberg found his natural, and perfect, ally in the academy in Carroll William Westfall. The professor had fled from Amherst and settled for a long while in Charlottesville, at the University of Virginia. The two would celebrate the achievement of Thomas Jefferson, not only as an architect, but as the designer of a city. What Westfall would add, in the style of Jefferson, was the placing of architecture in a setting with a moral structure—the *polis*, the polity. Or more precisely, architecture would take its bearings, and find its references, in the character of the regime. The grammar of architecture would mark off the difference between a public building, directed to a larger civic or religious purpose, and the lesser buildings, devoted to things more prosaic, which subserved a higher purpose. As Daniel Robinson once remarked, the Man from Mars, landing in Athens and looking at the Parthenon, would know at once that it wasn't a hamburger stand. The Italian cities of the Renaissance, studied by Westfall, revealed that grammar and design, with the churches standing with the highest peaks, pointing to the highest ends of human life. Other buildings would follow in scale, with the awareness marked in stone and board, of the things that were higher and lower.

Westfall and Greenberg formed a powerful combination in that teaching, and what came along with the restoration of a classical perspective in architecture was a confrontation with the doctrines of relativism. For those doctrines, stylishly dressed now with the pretensions of art, were woven in, inseparably, with the radical claims of modernity in architecture. The question would arise, "Why can't we build any longer those beautiful buildings built by McKim, Mead, and White at the turn of the last century?" And the answer emanating from the architectural establishment was, "Those were the buildings of *their time*. We can build only the buildings of our own time." As Westfall recognized, this was simply the vice of "historicism" as absorbed by architects, who had never heard the term; the students of architecture had simply imbibed the notion that understandings of the "good," in morality or anything else, would always be relative to the historical epoch in which those understandings were held. As far as I know, Westfall is the only teacher of architecture and urban form who has incorporated Leo Strauss in his teaching, as a way of breaking out to students those facile assumptions of historicism, which they have witlessly made their own. Greenberg, backed by Westfall, would restore the notion that there is indeed a "good" that is enduring, a good that holds across the historical epochs, both in architecture and politics.

With that sense of architecture and the regime, Greenberg and Westfall would team up for lectures with slides, and in the early 1990s Professor Robert George and I invited Greenberg to do a lecture in that vein for a seminar of federal judges held in Princeton. With his usual polish, Greenberg offered the judges assembled a lesson on the connection between the doctrines of "natural right" held by the founders and the architecture of the period. The judges were utterly riveted, for they had evidently never seen or heard anything like it. And what Greenberg accomplished for the judges he has begun to make available to a larger audience in this new book. Along the way, he wrote a book on George Washington as an architect, in the design of Mount Vernon and its surroundings. But with this new book, Greenberg returns to that deep connection between architecture and the regime.

It has been said often that visitors or newcomers from abroad may see in America things that readily escape the notice of people who were born and raised here. That line has been used most notably in regard to Tocqueville and his account of *Democracy in America*. But my own reading is that Greenberg's *Architecture of Democracy*, in this respect, surpasses Tocqueville. In the same way that he rather astonished the federal judges, he delivers a gentle but telling jolt to ordinary folk by alerting them to the things all around them—to those buildings, those structures of cities, so familiar to them that they no longer notice them. Or, wanting comparison with similar buildings and structures abroad, they no longer see what is so distinctively and movingly American about them. Classical architecture took its bearings from nature and the human body, and American architecture took its bearings from the human person, beginning with the things nearest at hand. What, after all, is the nearest, simplest concern of architecture for the person? The house. Throughout the landscape in Europe one would find the *Palais de Justice*: the buildings would take their character from the palace of the monarch, and they were meant to impress and overawe with the majesty of the law, drawn from the majesty of the monarch. But in America, there was the *house*: the *courthouse*, for the trying of cases; the *statehouse*, where people came to deliberate about the laws they would make together; or even the *jailhouse*, which began in some cases as an annex to the home of the jailor. In Northampton, Massachusetts, the old Meeting House became known as "our town's house." As Greenberg observes, the "American house-based model . . . strove to create a new civic architecture, in which a citizen is at ease and feels a sense of ownership." It often goes unnoticed that the dome of the Capitol in Washington—that striking monument to a government by the people—does not cover the legislative chambers. It covers the vast hall in which ordinary citizens may meet as they come to press their concerns upon their representatives or to visit the scene where laws are made.

Greenberg, as the designer of courthouses and jailhouses, makes a special point of noting the principles that are woven into the design of American courtrooms. In England, the defendant may be placed alone in "dock," raised above the rest of the courtroom and facing the judge. In America, the prosecution and the defense sit at similar tables, set out symmetrically, facing the judge. There is a parity of dignity, because the law presumes the innocence of the accused, and the arrangements in the court are not meant to tilt the judgment. The judge is placed in the center, as the detached observer, judging without bias the two contending parties. Greenberg notes, in a passage that Tocqueville would have appreciated, that "the public, at the rear of the courtroom, faces the judge and observes the law in action." It is the trial as a moment of civic teaching:

> The jurors, who determine guilt or innocence, are placed on one side of the courtroom. They are unbiased observers, removed from the axis of the judge, counsel, defendant, and public. Because defendants are entitled to confront their accusers, the witnesses face the counsel tables but are placed adjacent to, and under the protection of, the judge.

In *Chisholm v. Georgia* (1793), the first case to elicit a set of opinions in the new Supreme Court, James Wilson remarked that the law in America would stand on a different foundation from that of the law in England. The latter began with a sovereign issuing commands. But in America, said Wilson, "the sovereign, when traced to its source, must be found in the *man*." It must be found, that is, in a natural person, tendering his consent to the terms on which he is governed. It did not diminish the dignity of governance that the buildings were scaled to the human person, the subject and object of the laws. On the other hand, even the ordinary home was lifted in its dignity, because it was the abode of that person whose natural rights supplied both the ground and the purpose of the political order. As Wilson remarked, the purpose of this new government was not to invent new rights, but to secure and enlarge the rights we already possessed by nature. The home of that person or citizen, suitably modest, would be suitably elevated in turn. Greenberg offers as an illustration the Hammond-Harwood House (1774-84) in Annapolis, a simple brick house with a pediment, Ionic columns, and an archway framing the door. As he points out, the pediment, in ancient Greece and Rome, marked a temple, or the dwelling of a god. The symbols, carrying over from another time, suggest that "here, in the United States, this new democratic republic, the rights and prerogatives that were once reserved for the gods of the ancient world and the kings of Europe now belong to every citizen."

The pediment could be found, of course, on the Parthenon in Athens, the home of Athena. The pediments were supported by Doric columns, which in turn took their model from the human figure, with the capital for the head, and with the feet proportioned to the body. The building, with its clear, anthropomorphic images, conveyed the sense of the citizens of Athens supporting the home of its goddess and protector. That essential sense of things would be carried over, without strain, to symbolize a democracy under law: a polity that would find its base and its purpose in the standing, and the moral condition, of the human persons who composed it.

That same sense of things scaled to the human body may be the reason we can still find something connected to us—and something strikingly beautiful—in those grand skyscrapers put up in the Age of Art Deco, and even earlier in the last century. Cass Gilbert's Woolworth Building in New York (1913), the tallest building of its time, offers a base of only about three floors, quite graspable. As Greenberg notes, the "articulation of its façade . . . assists an observer's eye and mind to measure it progressively, in parts, each of which is scaled to relate to a human being." The same effect was accomplished in another artful way in the Empire State Building (1931), which succeeded the Woolworth Building and held its place for a longer time as the world's tallest building. The building does not soar until it is set back after the fifth floor. At the level of the sidewalk, in the things that catch our eye, the building does not look gargantuan or out of harmony with the things around it. "In a brilliant move," says Greenberg, "the shaft of the tower is set back from the busy Fifth Avenue sidewalk so that its great height does not loom over the pedestrians and make them feel insignificant."

Something truly different, something reeking of a different modernity, came in after the Second World War. That new state of things could be seen in the skyline that now marks New York, Chicago, and other cities: towering rectangles or ice-cube trays in assembly with one another, without even the articulation, or the embellishments, noble or whimsical, that made the towers of the old buildings say something distinctive in the cities of their day. Edward Durrell Stone's Legislative Building in Raleigh, North Carolina (1963) looks like a ranch house with posts lining the perimeter on all sides. The posts may be a faint gesture toward the columns of old, but with the old understanding faded, the place where the legislature meets is hardly distinguishable from an office building. It might be the headquarters of an investment company, or converted tomorrow into offices for Wal-Mart. In one of his notable slips into understatement, Greenberg describes these kinds of buildings as "self-referential." But it is not merely that they slip into a version of solipsism, where a building is making a statement about itself or offering an expression of the mind that designed it. It is rather that the buildings form a jumble, with no discernible moral structure of the whole. There is no sense that any one of these buildings, with their rich variety of businesses, retail and wholesale, with their array of corporate enterprises—that the purpose of any of these buildings is higher or lower than anything else. It's not like the design we can grasp at once in the Italian cities, where we see no civic building rising above the churches, or no commercial buildings proclaiming their supremacy over civic buildings dedicated to the civic life of the whole. It is not like Washington, D.C., even today, where no buildings eclipse the Capitol or the Washington Monument.

And it is not even like the design, so simple and dramatic, that Mr. Jefferson imparted to his "academical village" in Charlottesville, Virginia. Everything in that arrangement points to the domed Library as the capital or the head, marking the higher purpose of a university. The pavilions, with their classrooms and residences, for masters and students, take their bearings from that central purpose of the campus and lead to the Library. The serpentine walls, the lawns, the furnishings inside the buildings show the hand of the artist, who adds his art guided by the overall design. But that overall design reflects, again, an aesthetic that is informed by a moral understanding, of the purposes or ends that are higher and lower. Greenberg takes the treatment of Jefferson and Charlottesville as the culmination of his book, with Jefferson placed now by Greenberg as the preeminent architect in America. Jefferson might have been, as an architect, self-taught, but his creation, says Greenberg, is unlike any other complex of buildings:

> Its design sophistication rivals the Acropolis, another group of many buildings harmoniously related to each other and the surrounding landscape. Jefferson's academical village creates a coherent community; it is the apogee of architectural endeavor in the United States.

But as artful as Jefferson was, in the designs of furnishings as well as structures, it is hard finally to detach his art from the political understanding that governed the whole. It might be said of him, as an architect, what Lincoln said of him as a founder: that he had the wit to take a moment of practical judgment and articulate "an abstract truth, applicable to all men and all times."

Harry Jaffa remarked to Martin Gilbert, in regard to one of the thickest volumes in his biography of Churchill, that his only complaint was that the book was too short. The comparable complaint here is that Greenberg's book is too beautiful. The book is published by Rizzoli, the premier publisher of books on fine arts. Allan Greenberg, an accomplished artist himself, naturally seeks the most accomplished publisher in this field, and the reproductions are indeed exquisite. But the print itself does not suggest a book meant mainly for reading. The exposition in the book seems to support the striking photographs, with their vivid examples of buildings. But this is a book that should be the natural companion to Tocqueville, for the professors who are trying to explain America to the Americans. It should not be a book splendid for coffee tables or the shelf containing the masterpieces of Rizzoli. It should be a book of graspable size, finding its place in the backpack of every undergraduate in the country.

And yet, the book may be only a beginning. In its text and its presentation, it is geared to a series made for television. I'll offer my own wish that the project makes it to television and the broader public. But in the next phase, we should have the book distilled as a book, to be spread widely in the land, and then followed perhaps by the further lessons Greenberg has to teach as he unfolds his fuller argument and completes his mission. He has before him now, in his grasp, the means of driving a stake through the relativism that has debased our architecture and demeaned our cities. And after that, the rest is in sight: he continues, in his vocation, to design the buildings that show us how to restore a classic architecture, and to confirm again the lessons that the public at large already seems to grasp—that there is, indeed, in politics and in architecture, an enduring good.

Pith and Pen

Joseph Tartakovsky

(Summer 2007)

The anecdote is generally lighter than a parable and weightier than a joke, less misleading than rumor and more entertaining than testimony. It is a story whose subject cannot be ghosts, fish, or cock-and-bull, but only people, preferably famous ones. Finally, it must be neat, pointed, and self-contained. The appeal of the *literary* anecdote, John Gross tells us in his *New Oxford Book* of them, is that "if the writer is someone whom we have read, or whose legend has touched our imagination, we are likely to bring a whole complex of feelings to bear on the story." Here, for instance, as recounted by a biographer, is Matthew Arnold, supreme critic of the Victorian Age, quizzing children in his job as school inspector:

> "Well, my little man . . . and how do you spell dog?" "Please sir, d-o-g." "Capital, very good indeed. I couldn't do it better myself. And now let us go a little further, and see if we can spell cat." (Chorus excitedly,) "C-A-T." "Now, this is really excellent."

It is not easy to have a supreme critic in a literary age as fragmented and anti-heroic as ours, but John Gross perhaps comes as close as one can. He is the distinguished author of *The Rise and Fall of the Man of Letters* (1969) and *A Double Thread* (his charming memoir, 2001), the former editor of the *Times Literary Supplement*, and editor of *After Shakespeare* (an inexhaustible mine of great writers commenting on the poet, 2002), *The Oxford Book of Aphorisms* (1983), *The New Oxford Book of English Prose* (1998), and *The Oxford Book of Essays* (2002). Now, in *The New Oxford Book of Literary Anecdotes*, he arranges over 800 anecdotes about 338 writers into 353 delightful pages.

The subjects of Gross's anecdotes are largely canonic authors writing in English. They span more than six centuries, from Geoffrey Chaucer, fined two shillings by a London court for striking a friar, to J.K. Rowling, granted an injunction by a London court against thieves of an unreleased Harry Potter novel. We see authors as precocious striplings (a four-year-old Thomas Macaulay reassures a lady who spilled coffee on him that "the agony is abated"), and dying geniuses (Jonathan Swift, his mind almost gone, mumbles in a final glimmer of self-knowledge, "I am a fool").

They do everything from stirring pots in their kitchens (Emily Dickinson) to killing their wives (William Burroughs).

With Gross amiably at our elbow, we drift into a London club as Anthony Trollope scribbles away, and slip into Thomas Hobbes's chamber as he sings in bed each night to fortify his health. Reclining under a plum tree on a spring morning, John Keats writes a few lines to a nightingale and tosses them aside; only a friend's reverence saves them to become the classic ode. Henry David Thoreau overhears an aunt complain about his ignoring a book she gave him: "Think of it! He stood half an hour today to hear the frogs croak, and he wouldn't read the life of Chalmers."

Jane Austen's loyal readers will enjoy her reply to a retainer of the House of Saxe Cobourg who had presumed to suggest a theme in return for possible patronage:

> You are very kind in your hints as to the sort of composition which might recommend me at present, and I am fully sensible that an historical romance, founded on the House of Saxe Cobourg, might be much more to the purpose of profit or popularity than such pictures of domestic life in country villages as I deal in. But I could no more write a romance than an epic poem. I could not sit seriously down to write a serious romance under any other motive than to save my life; and if it were indispensable for me to keep it up and never relax into laughing at myself or at other people, I am sure I should be hung before I had finished the first chapter. No, I must keep to my own style and go on in my own way; and though I may never succeed again in that [she had just published *Emma*], I am convinced that I should totally fail in any other.

We love P.G. Wodehouse—and rush out to buy twelve more of his books—when he parries, in his inimitable way, a correspondent pen-named "Indignant" who considers him overrated:

> I do not wish to labour this point, but I must draw Indignant's attention to a letter in *The Times* from Mr Verrier Elwin, who lives at Patangarth, Mandla District, India. Mr Elwin speaks of a cow which came into his bungalow one day and ate his copy of *Carry On, Jeeves*, "selecting it from a shelf which contained, among other works, books by Galsworthy, Jane Austen and T.S. Eliot." Surely a rather striking tribute.

We expect our writers to have lively imaginations, bordering at times on lunacy, and they do not disappoint. Ben Jonson once "consumed a whole night in lying looking to his great toe, about which he hath seen Tartars and Turks, Romans and Carthaginians, fight in his imagination." William Blake, in the stillness of his garden one evening, spied "a procession of creatures of the size and colour of green and gray grasshoppers, bearing a body laid out on a rose leaf, which they buried with songs, and then disappeared." A fairy funeral, he explained to a woman in his company.

This volume lets us eavesdrop as writers of the first rank judge their fellows. Wordsworth thought Byron "somewhat cracked." J.S. Mill choked with emotion when he read aloud Percy Bysshe Shelley's "Ode to Liberty." The great European novelist of the sea was not overwhelmed by his American counterpart:

> [Joseph Conrad and I] talked of books and, expecting him to be interested in Melville's *Moby Dick*, I mentioned it, and Conrad burst into a furious denunciation of it. "He knows nothing of the sea. Fantastic, ridiculous," he said. When I mentioned that the work was symbolical and mystical: "Mystical my eye! My old boots are mystical."

Gross allows us to glimpse not only literary men and women themselves, but the manners, hierarchies, and sensibilities of the vanished worlds in which they moved. A poet named James Hogg drank too much one night and "fairly convulsed" a dinner party by addressing Sir Walter Scott's wife by her first name. Samuel Pepys, his coach robbed at gunpoint, asked the bandits to "be civil to the ladies and not to frighten them." Closer to our liberated times, Mrs. D.H. Lawrence recalls her husband saying, "'Frieda, if people really knew what you were like, they would strangle you.' 'Did he say that angrily,' someone asked. 'No—very quietly, after several minutes deep thought.'"

Should the number of anecdotes allotted to a writer be proportionate to his greatness? Shakespeare gets only four, as few as Samuel Beckett. On the other hand, if proportion held, half the volume would be Shakespeare's. The writers in this book quote him with the reverence clergymen reserve for Scripture. And yet I can't recall an expression of bardolatry that rivals this one, from Frank Harris (1856–1931), a journalist who wrote *The Man Shakespeare*:

> [D]uring a lull in conversation at one of his luncheon parties, the conversation shifted to homosexuality. A great hush descended upon the room at the mention of a subject that, in those days, was taboo. Harris, however, thundered on in his powerful basso: "Homosexuality? No, I know nothing of the joys of homosexuality. My friend Oscar can no doubt tell you all about that." Further silence, even more profound. Harris continued: "But I must say that if *Shakespeare* asked me, I would have to submit."

None but the most intrepid literary explorers will have encountered more than a few of Gross's anecdotes. His sources are often obscure or out-of-print biographies, miscellanies, diaries, letters, and volumes with titles like *I Can Remember Robert Louis Stevenson*. Half of the anecdotes, which average about a paragraph in length, seem to come from dinner parties, if not in London then in New York. Many are embellished or expanded (though not by the editor); so much the better. They range from poignant to quaint to heart-breaking, but most are humorous. One of the book's delights is the language; the sources are full of curious old usages and beauties of diction and phrasing.

This book could not be the work of a typical assistant professor of literary theory, specializing in semiotics. It could only be produced by a man of letters of the old school, who cherishes decorum and decency in literature as in life. In choosing so many anecdotes that capture writers' characters in a glance, Gross shows his biographer's skill, but also his seasoned taste and judgment as a critic. Ezra Pound and Harold Pinter and their ilk come off poorly in this book. The likes of Henry James and Samuel Johnson command our admiration. As Lionel Trilling said of that famous Victorian school inspector, "[T]o analyze the good from the bad, foster the good, diminish the bad—this will be Arnold's program of criticism." It seems also to be Mr. Gross's program of anthology.

Man of Letters

James G. Basker

(Summer 2006)

Despite shifting tastes and trends, Samuel Johnson still looms large in our literary history. And with good reason. He so dominated his own era that his contemporaries nicknamed him the "Colossus of Literature" and the "Literary Dictator," his century came to be called "The Age of Johnson" (not even Shakespeare achieved that kind of accolade), and he pioneered or perfected many of the literary genres that continue to inform our cultural life today. Johnson helped invent the modern magazine, contributing for 16 years to the success of the *Gentleman's Magazine*, ancestor of *Time, Newsweek*, and the like, and he fostered the birth of modern book review criticism with his articles there, in his own *Literary Magazine*, and in several other periodicals over the years. He wrote two of the most important poems of the 18th century, "London" and "The Vanity of Human Wishes." His *Rambler* essays (two a week, 104 weeks straight, 1750-52) were a must-read in his day and remained so for at least 150 years afterwards. Johnson became the first syndicated columnist, from 1758 to 1760, with his weekly *Idler* essays. His novel *Rasselas* (1759) was a bestseller (three editions its first year), has never been out of print in the 245 years since, and has become a classic of world literature, translated into Arabic, Bengali, Japanese, and scores of other languages. His edition of *The Works of Shakespeare* (1765) added momentum to Shakespeare's emergence as the national bard and broke the chokehold that rules-bound criticism (i.e., the "three unities") had long held on literature. Johnson virtually invented literary biography in his *Lives of the Poets* (1779-81), where he also practiced his cranky brand of reader-centered criticism and elevated the "common reader" (with Virginia Woolf's later approval) as the final judge of literary merit. And, had he written nothing, he would still figure in our history as the colorful subject of what is widely regarded as the first modern biography, Boswell's *Life of Johnson*.

None of this, however, makes Johnson fashionable in academic circles, where many write him off not just as a dead white male, but as a high-church, moralistic, Tory, conservative, monarchist misogynist (take your pick). While it is true that Samuel Johnson continues to find favor with various Johnsonian clubs whose members tend to be cultural conservatives, the real Johnson is much more complex than this narrow pigeon-holing would allow. The high Anglican had Methodist, Presbyterian, Quaker, and other low-church friends, admitted to a lifetime of agonizing doubt about his faith, and was known to kneel in prayer at night with the servants. The ardent Tory was also a lifelong opponent of slavery who fiercely criticized the European conquest of Africa and America, and denounced cruelty to indigenous peoples everywhere. He hated capital punishment. His charity to the poor, the sick, and the miserable was so profound that it sometimes shocked his society friends. The supposed misogynist ("A woman's preaching is like a dog's walking on his hinder legs. It is not done well; but you are surprized to find it done at all") was actually a major critic of the exploitation of women, a leading advocate of women's education, and a supportive friend to dozens of women striving for writing careers in an era of male domination. (Mary Wollstonecraft, who met and liked him, put five of Johnson's works in her feminist anthology, *The Female Reader*, in 1789.) As Henry Hitchings acknowledges about midway through his superb book, Johnson was in many ways "a progressive liberal."

Towering over all his other achievements was Johnson's *Dictionary of the English Language* (1755), which Hitchings, in *Defining the World: The Extraordinary Story of Dr. Johnson's Dictionary*, justifiably calls "the most important British cultural monument of the eighteenth century." In this, his first book, Hitchings has accomplished what might seem impossible: an erudite but lively and engaging account of the writing of a dictionary. He has wisely set the story of the *Dictionary* in the context of Johnson's life, deftly interweaving his narrative with factual and anecdotal gems drawn from history, literature, lexicography, and popular culture, and cleverly presenting the whole in 35 short, reader-friendly chapters averaging seven pages each. The chapters are each entitled with a dictionary word, ordered alphabetically from "Adventurous" to "Zootomy," and each ingeniously (for the most part) tied to the chapter's content, so that both the overt orderliness and the latent playfulness of Johnson's *Dictionary* are evoked throughout. The result is a book that will appeal to anyone interested in Johnson, the 18th century, the history of language and lexicography, or just an absorbing bedside read. It is a triumph, and an example of what can happen when wide-ranging scholarship, a fresh approach, and a good storyteller come together in one book.

Much of the life story will be familiar to those who have read Boswell's *Johnson* or modern biographies by W.J. Bate, James Clifford, or Robert DeMaria: the sickly and bookish childhood in Lichfield, the brief and disappointing Oxford career, the failure to make it as a teacher, the struggles as a young writer in London, the protracted eight-year ordeal to produce the *Dictionary*, the psychological woes of his wife's death and his recurrent depressions, the menagerie of odd characters and dependents he cared for in his household, the financial relief and celebrity that eventually came with a government pension and honorary degrees, his emergence—in precisely the years Boswell knew him, 1763 to his death in 1784—as the preeminent literary authority and character of his time.

But Hitchings has a gift for the telling detail or striking statistic that flashes new light on familiar material. He notes, for example, that in the late 1740s as Johnson labored on the *Dictionary* and other writing projects, about 25% of his annual income was going to medical expenses arising from his wife Tetty's illnesses. Hitchings assembles a sampling of 18th-century street names—Cutthroat Lane, Labour in

Vain Yard, Little Sodom, Melancholy Walk—to suggest the "vicious and despairing character" of Johnson's London. He notes that during the course of 47 years living in London, Johnson moved house at least 18 times. One of those moves, in 1759, was from the large house in Gough Square, with the upper gallery he and his clerks had used as a lexicographical workshop, to more modest digs, revealing how close to the edge financially Johnson was still living four years after publishing his greatest work.

When focusing on the dictionary itself, Hitchings maintains the same balance between big picture and striking detail. Drawing on the best scholarship (by James Sledd, Gwin Kolb, Allen Reddick, Robert DeMaria, Anne McDermott, among others), Hitchings gives us an overview, in manageable installments, of Johnson's departure from prior models, the evolution of his lexicographical method, the timetable, the problems and false starts, the progress, the reception, the adaptations and applications it underwent, the influence then and over the centuries since. We get a sense of the *Dictionary*'s sheer mass: 42,773 entries supported by 110,000 illustrative quotations, its two huge folio volumes weighing some 20 pounds, its price of £4 10s as large as a working person's annual income and daunting to all but the most affluent individuals and institutions. We hear Hitchings lament that Boswell is unreliable (as he could also be on such topics as Johnson on women and slavery) in his account of how Johnson compiled the *Dictionary*. Hitchings wonders whether "Boswell was too callow, or maybe too lazy, to probe its real history." More importantly, Hitchings gives an impressive account of the *Dictionary*'s historic importance: how it eclipsed all predecessors in scope and quality, how Johnson's use of illustrative quotations transformed dictionaries forever, how his *Dictionary* held sway for more than 100 years in learned circles and in popular culture, how it was imitated and adapted by Noah Webster even as he criticized it, and how Johnson's influence pervaded even the "definitive" *Oxford English Dictionary*, which, first proposed in 1860, took 68 years and hundreds of contributors to finish. At intervals, Hitchings also gives us other angles of vision on the *Dictionary* as a whole, in terms of the different kinds of book it embodies: a history of English, a grammar guide, a literary anthology, an encyclopedia, a dictionary of quotations, a common-place book, and in places, a book of devotions, a scientific reference book, even a jestbook.

But what finally makes Hitchings's volume fun to read are the clever examples he provides in every chapter. To demonstrate Johnson's improvements over prior dictionaries, Hitchings lists essential words such as "god," "health," "good," and "soul" as typical of the kinds one predecessor didn't include at all, and contrasts another's vague definition of "flowers" ("the offspring of plants") with Johnson's careful presentation of six distinct senses of the same word. To help us see the patterns in Johnson's selection of quotations, Hitchings notes both the 4,617 quotations from the Bible (two thirds of them from the Old Testament) and the fact that, although he drew on more than 500 authors, Johnson refused to include even a single quotation from Thomas Hobbes, "because," as Johnson told a friend, "I did not like his principles." Hitchings gives us a glimpse of Johnson's underlying psychology by reporting that "More than 1 per cent of the *Dictionary*'s illustrative quotations refer explicitly to death, around 300 mention disease, and 'melancholy' and its cognates appear more than 150 times." We learn about interesting readers and their responses. George Eliot probably named Casaubon, the dry pedant in

Middlemarch, after an undistinguished etymologist she found buried in Johnson's *Dictionary*. Thomas Jefferson, who couldn't have liked Johnson for his political views on American independence, habitually rummaged in the *Dictionary* for good passages of literature. Many famous writers read the *Dictionary* and referred to it in their creative works, from Sterne and Austen to Melville and Dickens, though few ever read it cover to cover as Robert Browning did. Most surprisingly, modern American lawyers and judges still turn on occasion to Johnson's *Dictionary*: two of the cases cited by Hitchings are as recent as the year 2000.

The story isn't all hero worship. We get a chapter listing Johnson's mistakes, aptly entitled "Pastern" (for one of his most egregious errors, famously acknowledged with "Ignorance, Madam, sheer ignorance") in which we hear how he botched words such as "shoe," "soup," "lunch," and "reptile," and managed to omit altogether others such as "ultimatum," "blond," "virus," and "anus." In the chapter headed "Nicety," the naughty and obscene words are discussed, both those terms that Johnson censored out ("buggery," "vagina," "shit," "penis") and those he allowed in ("bum," "arse," "fart," "piss"). Hitchings includes a hilarious anecdote about Johnson's mistaken account of the position in which elephants copulate and the eccentric "expert" who provided him that tidbit. We also get a listing of the various usage labels with which Johnson stigmatized words he didn't entirely approve—"cant," "low word," "barbarism," "colloquial," "inelegant," "corrupt," "bad," "unworthy of use"—as he, like so many before him and since, attempted to patrol the boundaries of "correct" English and "proper" usage.

Perhaps inevitably, given the political preoccupations of cultural criticism today, Hitchings mentions at several points the imperialistic implications of Johnson's *Dictionary*, referring to it in the opening pages as "an instrument of cultural imperialism." There is undoubtedly truth in this line of analysis. Even a mother forcing her toddler to use the correct words to refer to "cup" or "apple" is in a sense coercing a subordinate, relatively powerless person into a language system not of his or her own choosing, inescapably enrolling the child in an ideology and world view that (it always turns out) not everyone likes. But he might also have included some discussion of the ways that a dictionary such as Johnson's, which could extend standard usage across a geographically and socio-economically diverse population, might be inclusive and empowering to those who in one sense or another lived on the margins, or outside altogether. Mastering the "King's English," much as one might flinch at the term today, could mean gaining access to the political, economic, and social strata from which one was previously barred. We must remember why slaveholding societies passed laws that made it illegal to teach slaves and free blacks to read, and why Malcolm X, during his transformative years in prison, devoted much of his time to improving his English by studying a dictionary.

But this is a small quibble beside Hitchings's marvelous book, which even specialists will find rewarding and the vast majority of "common readers" will enjoy on every page.

Larry McMurtry and the American West

Douglas A. Jeffrey

(Spring 2007)

Entering his eighth decade, Larry McMurtry has under his belt 29 novels, five collections of essays, several screenplays, and, recently, a few short histories, not to mention his vast journalistic output. Raised up in a ranching family near Archer City, Texas, he has become one of his generation's more prolific men of letters. A bibliophile at his core and a rare book dealer on the side, his knowledge, interests, and the topics and settings of his books range widely. But from the beginning of his career, the American West has been the theme and the place to which he has most often repaired. And he is of two minds about it.

In *Walter Benjamin at the Dairy Queen: Reflections at Sixty and Beyond* (1999), McMurtry lamented that his Pulitzer Prize-winning novel, *Lonesome Dove* (1985), a saga of two legendary retired Texas Rangers, had failed in its purpose. He had intended the book to "demythicize" the West. "[I]nstead," he complained, it "became a kind of American Arthuriad." In later (and lesser) novels, McMurtry tells us, he "tried to subvert the Western myth with irony and parody with no better results." He persists in this quest down to his latest novel, *Telegraph Days* (2006) and his latest history, *Oh What a Slaughter: Massacres in the American West, 1846–1890* (2005). Yet somehow his writings on the West nearly always subvert his subversive intentions.

Telegraph Days is the story of a bright and sassy woman with the Dickensian name of Nellie Courtright (she finds herself courted by, among others, George Armstrong Custer, Wild Bill Hickok, Buffalo Bill Cody, and Virgil Earp), narrated in the first person. It opens in the Oklahoma territory, in and around a desolate town called Rita Blanca, and ends on a Hollywood movie set that perfectly reproduces the town (though appearing now more charming than desolate) from old photographs. The disjunction between town and movie set, and between Nellie's life and the plot of the film—in which she will be played by Lillian Gish—is the novel's theme, and this disjunction between the reality of the past and how it is remembered, artistically and popularly, is the theme of most of McMurtry's recent books.

Telegraph Days—like McMurtry's earlier *The Colonel and Little Missie: Buffalo Bill, Annie Oakley and the Beginnings of Superstardom in America* (2005)—depicts William Cody as the capitalist inventor of this lucrative deception. Nellie writes:

Lots of people live in the past, but Bill Cody seemed to be one of the rare few who lived in the future . . . . The Rita Blanca I was standing in, getting grit in my teeth, wasn't the Old West to me—it was the only west available. But Bill Cody was sincere, and calm as a banker. He was looking ahead to a day when our ordinary day-to-day lives on the prairie would be—what's the word?—picturesque, like the knights and ladies in King Arthur, or the novels of Walter Scott.

"As soon as something's ended," Cody tells her, "people will start flocking to get at least a glimpse of what it was like before it was over . . . . It's human nature." Nellie replies: "I'm a human, and it's not my nature." Then she adds: "Even as I said it I knew that my remark was partly a lie. Why read Walter Scott if not to catch a glimpse of what life was like in older times—times that were surely gone forever?"

Here in a nutshell are the two main questions of fact raised in McMurtry's books on the American West: What was it really like? And what of it remains, if any?

FAILURE OR TRIUMPH

Oh What a Slaughter deals primarily with six incidents, from the little-known Sacramento River Massacre in 1846 to the better-known Wounded Knee Massacre in 1890. Five were perpetrated by whites on Indians, one—the Mountain Meadow Massacre of 1857—by whites (with a few enlisted Indians) on whites. Secondarily, the book considers two military engagements in which Indians slaughtered white soldiers—the Fetterman Battle in 1866 and the Battle of Little Big Horn a decade later. These too qualify as massacres by McMurtry's graphic definition:

The vocabulary of atrocity has always been rather limited . . . . You can burn a body, hack it up, decapitate it, cut off—or out—its genitalia, smash its skull, tear fetuses out of pregnant women, shoot arrows or bullets into it, maybe rip out its heart or other organs; and, really, that is more or less the whole menu.

Although whites were pikers compared to Indians when it came to the art of reducing a human community to a "meat shop," each of these incidents was—in Kit Carson's description of the Sacramento River Massacre—"a perfect butchery." But McMurtry doesn't wallow. He is at pains to point out that the American West's chapter in the age-old history of massacres is relatively minor, given the relatively small numbers involved. And more than the horror of massacres, he is interested in what he calls their context. Wounded Knee, for example, was likely impulsive, triggered by an accidental gunshot; in the most chronicled of the six—at Sand Creek in Colorado in 1864—whites were bedeviled by a confusion between hostile and peace Indians (poignantly, Chief Black Kettle frantically waved an American flag as his camp was attacked). Both here and in his short biography *Crazy Horse* (1999), McMurtry points out that whites vastly overestimated the extent to which Indians were organized politically—and thus the extent to which the chiefs with whom they negotiated controlled their younger warriors. Indians, for their part (with exceptions like Red Cloud, a chief who visited Washington, D.C., and immediately began counseling peace), vastly underestimated the number and power of the whites. But the main contextual element in the West, according to McMurtry, was apprehension:

[D]eep, constant *apprehension*, which neither the pioneers nor the Indians escaped, has, it seems to me, been too seldom factored in by historians of the settlement era, though certainly it saturates the diary literature of the pioneers, particularly the diary literature produced by frontier women, who were, of course, the likeliest candidates for rapine and kidnapping.

It is common sense that context is essential to understanding history. But common sense is generally lacking in the modern historical school and virtually nonexistent in recent scholarship on the West. For making sensible observations—e.g., that although "it is plain to us now, reflecting in tranquility, that the Indians had no chance, that was a fact scarcely evident to the first white settlers who faced them, many of whom were obliterated before they could erect even a first crude cabin"— McMurtry has sometimes found himself at odds with his professional brethren.

In a 1990 article in the *New Republic*, McMurtry characterized Western revisionism as "Failure Studies," in which "[o]ld, brutal, masculine American confidence" is replaced by "new, open, feminine American self-doubt." Revisionists, he wrote, portray America's western expansion as "an irresponsible white male's adventure, hugely destructive of the land itself, of the native peoples, and even of the white male's own women and children." There are two problems with this view, he argued. First, the revisionists are not, as they suppose, the first to notice "how violent, how terrible, and how hard winning the West actually was." His own reading of Western history, McMurtry wrote,

> as well as my boyhood among the old-timers, leads me to exactly the opposite conclusion: everyone noticed how hard it was. Even the young males, of several races, who were the ones most disposed to see it all as a grand adventure and a perpetual frolic, have copiously noted how quickly and how completely the fun could drain out of it.

Thus *Telegraph Days* begins with Nellie's father hanging himself in a barn, an event which she and her last remaining brother had learned by then to take pretty matter-of-factly.

> My younger brother, Jackson, was just seventeen. Here we were, the two surviving Courtrights, having already, in the course of our westering progress, buried two little brothers, three little sisters, an older sister, three darkies, our mother, and now look! Father's tongue was black as a boot.

McMurtry's second point cut deeper: in attempting to tear down the "Triumphalist myths" about the West that have become ingrained in the American fiber, revisionists hurt their own case by "so rarely do[ing] justice to the quality of imagination that constitutes part of the truth." Precisely because the West was so hard on its pioneers, McMurtry pointed out, some amount of embellishment was necessary for survival and, ultimately, for success: "The Triumphalists write about a West where people had callings and were sustained by them. The Revisionists see a West where people had only jobs, and crappy, environmentally destructive jobs at that."

Underlying his sense of callings and moral sustenance are family memories. "My own grandparents were vulnerable pioneers," he writes in *Oh What a Slaughter*, "which is perhaps one reason I began this inquiry." They had settled in a part of Texas still considered Comanche country in the 1870s. Having known them, Mc-

Murtry wrote in *Walter Benjamin*, distinguishes him as "one of the few writers who can still claim to have had prolonged and intimate contact with first-generation American pioneers, men and women who came to a nearly absolute emptiness and began the filling of it themselves." Of working on *Lonesome Dove* he has written, "I didn't feel that I was writing about the Old West, in capital letters—I was merely writing about my grandfather's time, and my uncles', none of whom seemed like men of another time to me."

This may partly explain the persistent failure of McMurtry's intentions in his Western writings: he aims to "demythicize" America's western expansion, yet feels duty-bound to combat its demonization by West revisionists. On the one hand, as he wrote in his first collection of essays—*In a Narrow Grave: Essays on Texas* (1968)—American pioneers (like his grandparents) were "people whom one could not but love." On the other hand, in that book and subsequently, he celebrates the fact that the pioneers' time—and all it entailed (or so he hopes, but this is less certain)—is dead and gone.

THINGS WILL HOPPEN

McMurtry's disillusion with the life of his forebears surfaced early on. Contrasting himself and his father, he recounts that his father at the age of 12 had driven a herd of steers 40 miles alone, sold them, bought new ones, and driven them home, whereas he at that age had read *Don Quixote* and become alienated from his book-less surroundings. In *Roads: Driving America's Great Highways* (2000), McMurtry writes that Marcel Proust provided for him what "the grasslands were to my father, a great subtle text which would repay endless study." Following his university training in Denton, Houston, and Stanford, McMurtry made a splash in Texas literary circles in the mid-1960s by attacking the "Big Three" of Texas letters at the time—J. Frank Dobie, Walter Prescott Webb, and Roy Bedichek—for their idea that rural life could hold a candle to the life of the intellect. That his alienation was reciprocated is evidenced in a letter he received while at Rice University from his Uncle Jeff, a former Texas Ranger and cowboy who had known Geronimo and Quanah Parker:

> What does PhD stand for? To me its post-hole digger, guess that would be about what it would stand for with all the other old Texas cowpokes . . . . I never could understand why a man wanted to spend all his life going to school, I'd get to thinking about the Rancho Grandy, and get rambling on my mind . . . . [G]oing to school was always like being in jail to me, life is too short, sweet and uncertain to spend it in jail . . . .

Uncle Jeff was responding to condolences on the death of his wife of 40 years in a car wreck. Not until the letter's end, between noting the onset of pink eye and questioning the sanity of Jehovah's Witnesses, did he finally refer to the accident: "Yes it was an awful tragidy to have Mint crushed in the smashup, my car was a total loss too. Things like that will just hoppen though." McMurtry comments dryly: "I doubt that Seneca himself could have balanced the car and the wife that simply, and this one week after she was gone." Along the same lines, he recalls (in *Walter Benjamin*) an incident in his youth when a neighboring German dairy farmer woke up one morning and milked his cows, then shot himself. The cowboys at his father's ranch at the time seemed unaffected by the suicide itself, but debated endlessly whether it had been conscientious or foolish for the farmer to have bothered milking beforehand. "Where emotion was concerned," McMurtry has written, "the cowboy's ethic was Roman." Of Charles Goodnight—a legendary Texas cattle baron known as the Old Man of the Plains (and one of the models for *Lonesome Dove*'s Woodrow Call)—he notes that "Kipling would have approved of [such men], for they looked on triumph and disaster with the same stoic, unwavering, unsentimental eye." Typically, McMurtry describes this character with equal parts disapproval and nostalgia.

One of McMurtry's teachers at Stanford, novelist Wallace Stegner, once wrote that "even while the cowboy myth romanticizes and falsifies western life, it says something true about western, and American, character." McMurtry's work is infused with this paradox, though he resists it. In *The Colonel and Little Missie*, he suggests that the idea of the West exported to the eastern U.S. and Europe by Buffalo Bill's Wild West Show, under the manly theme "Advance of Civilization," was somehow akin to Madonna's artificial self-promotion in the 1980s. Yet he cites against this view, among others, no less an authority than Mark Twain, who wrote (prior to Cody's European tours) that the Wild West Show

> brought back to me the breezy, wild life of the Rocky Mountains and stirred me like a war song. Down to its smallest detail the show is genuine . . . . [I]t is often said on the other side of the water that none of the exhibitions which we send to England are purely and distinctively American. If you will take the Wild West show over there you can remove that reproach.

In the same book, McMurtry comments:

> The director John Ford is said to have decreed that if you have to choose between the truth and the legend, print the legend. From my experience I'd say that there's really no choice: for most readers and viewers it's the legend or nothing.

This is triply misleading. First, with regard to the quote's provenance: Ford did not say it; a newspaperman in Ford's *The Man Who Shot Liberty Valance* did. Second, the quote is wrong. What the newspaperman says is, "*When the legend becomes fact,* print the legend." These two errors may be excused by the fact, as related by director Peter Bogdanovich, that McMurtry—although he has worked extensively in Hollywood and has reaped a fortune from film adaptations of his novels—dislikes films and knows little about them. But the third error reflects a kind of willful blindness: McMurtry's own writings, at their best, show that legend and fact intertwine.

STRONG LIVES

A recurring McMurtry theme is how brief a historical moment the Old West spanned: from the Lewis and Clark expedition to Wounded Knee, he points out, was the length of one long lifetime. The debate over how to understand America's western expansion has already far eclipsed it in length, and McMurtry is an ambivalent but valuable figure in that debate. In his introduction to *Winning the Wild West: The*

Epic Saga of the American Frontier (2002), by Page Stegner, the son of his old teacher, McMurtry writes in an elegiac tone:

> My grandparents came to Texas as pioneers in the 1870s. In time they produced twelve children . . . eventually producing nearly fifty children of their own. I have a wonderful photograph taken at the first McMurtry family reunion near Clarendon, Texas, in 1918. . . . Eighty years later . . . I made a speech at the opening of a new library in Pampa, just a few miles from where the picture was taken. Only two people in the large audience had ever heard of the McMurtrys, although the uncle I was named for had fallen to his death from a grain elevator just three blocks from where I spoke. We came as pioneers, we worked extremely hard, for a time we prospered; then the old folks died and their children died; little by little the hard-acquired land got sold and vanished, making it a close question as to what exactly we won. Strong lives, I suppose.

Yet three years later he collected an Academy Award for helping adapt for the screen Annie Proulx's *Brokeback Mountain*, a pathetic short story about gay cowboys (actually, western sheepherders). This calls to mind McMurtry's long- and oft-expressed idea that the cowboy had a "concept of life that simply takes little account of women"—although in the past his point was that cowboys preferred the company of *horses*. It also recalls an essay he wrote in 1968 about *Hud*, the movie version of his novel *Horseman, Pass By* (1961), in which he judged the posture and gait of its star, Paul Newman, to be true to the cowboys on his father's ranch, but not Newman's eyes: "His look was introspected and self-occupied . . . he simply looked more curious about himself than most young ranchers look." Surely, in this respect, *Brokeback* stars Jake Gyllenhaal and Heath Ledger broke the mold even more.

One suspects that *Lonesome Dove* (rather than *Brokeback Mountain*) became such a popular phenomenon—and yes, "a kind of American Arthuriad"—because there is more of the Western character still alive and well in our country today than McMurtry thinks, or perhaps wishes. The question whether we remain capable of strong lives—or whether the postmodern forces of "feminine American self-doubt" will prove overpowering—is the most interesting moral question raised by his books on the West. In the final analysis, if we do prove so capable, we will owe McMurtry at least a parcel of our thanks. Or, as he might have it, blame.

The Genius of Old New York

Cheryl Miller

(Fall 2007)

Edith Wharton, the massive new biography by Oxford English professor Hermione Lee, is the story of success: how Lee's formidable heroine survived a painful child-hood, a disastrous marriage, an only slightly less disastrous love affair, repeated bouts of depression and illness, and the German occupation. Through it all, Wharton remained unflappable. Just two months before her death, she paid a visit to a friend and collaborator, the architect Ogden Codman, to discuss a new edition of their *The Decoration of Houses* (one of Wharton's 48 books). "Everyone was on jump all the time," Codman complained of his frail but nevertheless commanding guest. Only a few days after she arrived, Wharton suffered a heart attack. As she was carried into the ambulance, she admonished her host: "This will teach you not to ask decrepit old ladies to stay."

Wharton's life was a constant flurry of activity. Between 1897 and 1937, she published at least one book a year, including novels, volumes of short stories, memoirs, travel writing, and guides to gardening and interior decoration. She renovated three houses and the accompanying grounds; and she built one from the ground up: The Mount, her stately residence in Lenox, Massachusetts (which was recently restored and opened to the public). She traveled all about the Continent and North Africa. When World War I broke out, she became a tireless war-worker on behalf of her adopted country, France, lobbying for the U.S. to enter the war, writing propaganda, and opening hospitals and shelters for refugees. "I'm afraid I'm an incorrigible life-lover, life-wonderer, and adventurer," she observed. Henry James, half in awe and half in terror of his unsinkable friend, dubbed her the "Angel of Devastation" and "Firebird." "A lady who consumes worlds as you & I (*don't* even) consume apples," he described her. "She uses up everything and everyone."

Wharton's self-assurance and *joie de vivre* were hard-won treasures. One friend joked that both Wharton and Teddy Roosevelt (whom she much admired) were "self-made men." Born Edith Newbold Jones in 1862, Wharton called herself a "morbid, self-scrutinizing and unhappy" child with red hair and big hands and feet. The Joneses were a "patrician clan" and part of "Old New York," the close-knit, con-formist society Wharton would later satirize and celebrate in her 1920 masterpiece,

The Age of Innocence. Although a prosperous household—it was her family that gave rise to the phrase "keeping up with the Joneses"—it was not a happy one. Her mother, Lucretia, bullied Wharton's gentle father and disapproved of her peculiar daughter.

Despite her mother's fastidiousness about written and spoken English, Wharton never received a formal education. (She would always be somewhat self-conscious of her lack of schooling.) Yet "undereducated" as she was, she achieved fluency in French, Italian, and German and was always a voracious reader. Lucretia forbade her to read novels until she was married; so the obedient "Puss" devoured everything else she could find in her father's "gentleman's library"—classics, poetry, history, and philosophy. Browning was her favorite poet, but she loved Whitman too. He proved more of a challenge to procure: in the houses of her childhood, she recalled, "*Leaves of Grass* was kept under lock and key, and brought out, like tobacco, only in the absence of 'the ladies.'"

Besides reading, the young Edith loved telling stories or, as she called it, "making up." In her teens, she wrote a novel, *Fast & Loose*, as well as a collection of poems. But her literary interests were soon set aside, and her new ambition—after her fashionable mother—was "to be the best dressed woman in New York." At 23, Edith was married off to an eligible suitor, Edward ("Teddy") Wharton, and set up housekeeping in Newport.

But she did not settle down to conventional married life. Instead, she began writing, dashing off poems, short stories, and a manual on interior design. A "preponderance of intellectuality on the part of the intended bride" had put an end to Wharton's first engagement, and it would also cause a rift early in her marriage to Teddy, an agreeable man but one whose interests did not extend far beyond hunting and drink. In her diary, Wharton recalled the crucial moment when their incompatibility became clear. She was reading James George Frazer's *The Golden Bough* and pointed out a passage to Teddy for his opinion. He replied: "Does that sort of thing really amuse you?" "I heard the key turn in my prison lock," she wrote. "Oh, gods of derision! And you've given me over twenty years of it!"

She escaped by spending most of her time in France while Teddy remained in Massachusetts to manage affairs at The Mount, their new home. At 43, Wharton published her first major novel, *The House of Mirth* (1905). It was a bestseller, establishing her as one of the country's foremost novelists. Her family did not welcome the news. In their milieu, novelists were as *déclassé* as tradesmen; her parents never read or even implied any awareness of her work. Teddy was slightly more supportive: "Look at that small waist," he bragged. "You'd never think she wrote a line of poetry."

In Europe, Wharton found a more appreciative (and mostly male) circle of friends, including Henry James, the art historian Bernard Berenson, the lawyer and diplomat Walter Berry, and the novelist Paul Bourget. She also met Morton Fullerton, a "bounder" who was as attractive as he was untrustworthy, and they began a doomed three-year love affair. Fullerton had a long line of famous conquests, both male and female; at the time he met Wharton, he was engaged to his adopted sister.

Meanwhile, Wharton kept writing at a frenetic pace, publishing *Ethan Frome* (1911), *The Reef* (1912), and *The Custom of the Country* (1913), among other books. Her relationship with Teddy deteriorated further as he plunged into alcoholism and began exhibiting signs of bipolar disorder. Things came to a head when Teddy confessed to keeping a mistress—and occasionally a bevy of chorus-girls—in a Boston apartment, which he maintained with money from Edith's trust fund. The Whartons divorced in 1913, and Edith settled permanently in France, where she would die in 1937.

Lee treats these ordeals with intelligence and sympathy. (It was good preparation, no doubt, for her to write a biography of another complicated female writer, Virginia Woolf, ten years ago.) Avoiding the excesses of "pathography," she declines to dwell on Wharton's various depressions and breakdowns, instead emphasizing her energy and playful spirit—a choice much more in keeping with the woman who, during the unhappiest days of her marriage, assured a friend: "You mustn't think there haven't been bits of blue sky all the same . . . . I can hardly ever wholly stop having a good time!"

Lee avoids irresponsible speculation in the face of an incomplete or ambiguous historical record. (Before she died, Wharton recovered and burned most of her letters.) And the biographer deals sensibly with one of her more startling revelations: the discovery of an unfinished novella, "Beatrice Palmato," a frankly pornographic fragment detailing the incestuous affair of a father and daughter. Unlike the Freudian and feminist interpreters of Wharton's life, Lee realizes that an author can write about such a thing without necessarily having lived it. She chalks it up to a literary experiment—a variation, perhaps, on Wharton's ecstatic love poetry about Fullerton.

Edith Wharton, writes the author, is "the story of an American citizen in France"—a precise formulation. Although Wharton spent most of her life in France and was often critical of her native U.S., she always remained an American. Unlike James, she never changed her citizenship, and was deeply angry when he did. "A mistake . . . rather puerile, and altogether unlike him," she wrote of his decision. As a friend said of Wharton, "She loved Europe, England, Italy, better than any native—yet remained an American of the old fashion."

Indeed, it's curious how little France figures in Wharton's novels. Henry James was always urging her to "DO New York," but she never really "DID" anything else. Her novels focus always on Americans, and Europe serves chiefly as a foil to America, as in *The Age of Innocence*, where Paris is alternately a symbol of culture (embodied by Ellen Olenska's French secretary, who lives for "good conversation") contrasted to New York's philistinism, and a symbol of decadence contrasted to New York's decency (Ellen's brutish husband).

More often, Wharton's foreign settings provide just another glamorous backdrop for her characters' schemes and machinations, as in her proto-jet-set novels, *The House of Mirth* and the later "Jazz Age" books. These are the Americans who, Wharton complains, regard Europe "simply as affording exceptional opportunities for bathing and adultery." There are hints of the France-versus-America theme in *The Reef* and *The Custom of the Country*, but only hints. *The Reef* takes place at (the American) Anna Leath's chateau in southern France, but the setting serves chiefly as a symbol of her American characters' emotional displacement, of their alienation from one another. (James, in a letter to Wharton, wondered why all "these non-French people" had "to have their story out there.") The only other character to spend any time in France is Undine Spragg, the social-climbing divorceé of *The Custom of the*

Country. With respect to that book, James (giving exasperatingly inconsistent advice) complained that the French section was too short, and wished Wharton had focused more on the comedy of manners between her binational couple. But, as Lee rightly notes, the novel's foremost concern is America: Undine's destruction of her first husband, Ralph, and with him the culture of Old New York.

New York—and thus America—was always Wharton's true subject. Lee calls her "a social anthropologist of her tribe" and a "novelist-ethnographer." She was an avid reader of sociology and science. Her library featured works by Darwin, Weber, T.H. Huxley, Herbert Spencer, and Thorstein Veblen—and she used insights from their researches to understand American society. As a kind of outsider, she felt she could see more deeply into the American soul—claiming as her "symbolic watchword" Rudyard Kipling's famous line, "And what should they know of England who only England know?"

Wharton knew the truth of those words first-hand: only after she left Old New York could she see its value. As a young woman, she had chafed against her society's prejudices and conventions, its narrow-mindedness, its insistence on ignoring all things "unpleasant." But as the world of her youth faded away, she began to question the society that had formed in its wake. Writing to James, she lamented:

> Everything that used to form the fabric of our daily life has been torn in shreds, trampled on, destroyed; and hundreds of little incidents, habits, traditions, which, when I began to record my past, seemed too insignificant to set down, have acquired the historical importance of fragments of dress and furniture dug up in a Babylonian tomb.

Wharton was not religious, but she shared with the other writers she admired, like Hawthorne and James, what she called a "New England conscience," the awareness of something like original sin. This tragic sense of life gave her a profoundly conservative respect for the past. What Wharton wrote of George Eliot applies equally to herself: "She felt no call to found a new school of morals. A deep reverence for family ties, for the sanctities of tradition, the claims of slowly acquired convictions, and slowly formed precedents, is revealed in every page of her books." Wharton was distrustful of modernity with its abstractions and "theoretical visions of liberty." "Life is not a matter of abstract principles," she wrote, "but a succession of pitiful compromises with fate, of concessions to old tradition, old beliefs, old charities and frailties."

In her books, utopian schemes invariably lead to ruin. For Wharton, Lee writes, "there is no other world, no escape, no exit point to the Happy Isles." In *The House of Mirth*, Lily Bart seals all her letters with a stamp of a boat setting sail, with the word "Beyond!" below. But the "Beyond!" Lily seeks—wealth and a place in society, or freedom—always escapes her. Undine Spragg, the grasping embodiment of American capitalism (notice the initials), is always searching for something "more luxurious, more exciting, more worthy of her!" but no matter what she attains, she remains perpetually unsatisfied: "She had everything she wanted, but she still felt, at times, that there were other things she might want if she knew about them."

Nowhere is Wharton's tragic sense more evident than in *The Age of Innocence*, what she called her "simple and grave story" about "two people trying to live up to something that was still 'felt in the blood.'" It is the novel that most recalls James— in its allusions (its protagonist's name, Newland Archer, is a combination of Isabel

Archer's in *The Portrait of a Lady* and Christopher Newman's in *The American*) and in its theme. When the story begins, Newland Archer is a young man in his twenties and is about to marry into one of the best families of Old New York. Then the Countess Ellen Olenska—cousin to Archer's betrothed, May Welland—returns from a disastrous marriage in Europe. The two fall deeply in love, but Ellen, unwilling to hurt her cousin, refuses to run away with Archer. Archer and May marry as planned, and Ellen returns to Paris to live alone.

Around this simple storyline Wharton fashions a complicated portrayal of Old New York. Ellen Olenska, like Wharton herself, had fled the stuffiness of Old New York for the freedom of Europe. She is New York's most perceptive critic because she can see it as Archer cannot, as an outsider. Archer tells her she has "opened his eyes," but America has opened her eyes as well. It is Ellen, not Archer, who becomes the defender of Old New York. When Archer tries to persuade Ellen to run away with him, she asks if he means her to be his mistress, since she cannot be his wife. He protests: he is "beyond" all that; he wants to find a place where they can be "simply two human beings who love each other." Ellen laughs:

> Oh, my dear—where is that country? . . . I know so many who've tried to find it; and believe me, they all got out by mistake at wayside stations . . . and it wasn't at all different from the old world they'd left, but only rather smaller and dingier and more promiscuous.

Ellen, the realist, refuses to engage in fantasies. Archer claims to be "beyond" the moral categories of Old New York, but there is no place "beyond" to go. Having lived in Europe, Ellen knows the price of freedom from social convention: "happiness bought by disloyalty and cruelty and indifference." Europe is cultured and enlightened, but it is also "promiscuous" and "dingy." This new appreciation of America makes the things that were most "precious" to Ellen in her former life seem "cheap in comparison." "I can't go back to that other way of thinking," she explains, "I can't love you unless I give you up."

Ellen has been Americanized. As the French secretary explains, for "an American . . . of your kind" (that is, an Old New Yorker), "things that are accepted in certain other societies, or at least put up with as part of a general convenient give-and-take—become unthinkable, simply unthinkable."

Such things would not remain unthinkable for long. Indeed, polite society would soon come to regard it as tragic that Ellen Olenska and Newland Archer did *not* run away together. How could they defer to social mores in a world where, as one of Wharton's characters observes, "the new adultery was unfaithfulness to self"?

Given her skepticism of modernity, it's not surprising that Wharton always avoided her neighbor in France, the poet Paul Eluard, who hosted at his country home a procession of *avant-garde* artists and writers, including Tristan Tzara, Man Ray, and Marcel Duchamp. She detested modernist art, which she considered over-theorized and sensationalistic. She condemned James Joyce's *Ulysses* as "a turgid welter of schoolboy pornography," Virginia Woolf's *Orlando* as a work of pure "exhibitionism." When her novel, *The Mother's Recompense* (1925), was compared unfavorably to *Mrs. Dalloway*, Wharton tartly observed, "My heroine belongs to a day when scruples existed."

Wharton also disliked the new "proletarian" or democratic novel for its utopianism and its denigration of the past. Why should art focus on "persons so limited in education and opportunity that they live off from all the varied sources of culture which used to be considered the common heritage of English-speaking people?" After Upton Sinclair published *Oil!*, a call for proletarian revolution, Wharton chastised him: "I believe that a wider experience would have shown you that the evils you rightly satirize will be replaced by others more harmful to any sort of civilized living when your hero and his friends have had their way." To another friend, she expressed her doubts that all that was required for the "regeneration of the world" was "exterminating the Vanderbilts."

"There is nothing like a Revolution for making people conservative," Wharton remarked in *French Ways and Their Meaning* (1919), and that epigram would serve as the theme of her Jazz Age novels, *The Glimpses of the Moon* (1922), *Twilight Sleep* (1927), and *The Children* (1928). In all three works, Wharton follows a set of emancipated moderns who find themselves "continually tripped up by obsolete sensibilities & discarded ideals."

Old New York might shy away from anything "unpleasant," but the new society is more childish and self-deceiving, believing as it does that we can "refuse ourselves to pain," that human nature can be remade to serve our purposes. The title *Twilight Sleep* refers to the drug-induced state into which women went to avoid the pains of childbirth. It serves too as a metaphor for its heroine, Pauline Manford, for whom the "avoidance of pain" is the "ultimate end." Pauline believes that to deny evil is to "prevent its coming into being," and she works endlessly to improve herself, partaking in all the latest 1920s fads: New Age spiritualism, free love, exercise regimes, psychoanalysis, self-help books, consumer science ("[s]he wanted to de-microbe life"), drugs, and eugenics (Aldous Huxley's *A Brave New World* was inspired in part by *Twilight Sleep*).

But beneath this welter of activity, Pauline remains dissatisfied. She is vaguely aware that something is lacking but doesn't know what. She experiences what Huxley described as the "contemporary tendency for superstition to be magical rather than religious—to aim at specific acts of power, such as hip-slimming, rather than at a theory of the cosmos." Romance is dead, for example; intimacy, for Pauline, "meant the tireless discussion of facts." The consummate consumer, Pauline acquires more and more, but cannot identify the end for which she strives. "They all had these colossal plans for acquiring power," Wharton writes, "and then, when it was acquired, what came of it but bigger houses, more food, more motors . . . and more self-righteous philanthropy?"

Her characters consciously break with the past, believing themselves beyond their forebears' anachronistic social conventions. But they also cast off the understanding of human nature latent in those conventions. As a consequence, Wharton's characters face all the problems and conflicts that human beings have always experienced, but they do so blindly, ignorantly.

In *The Glimpses of the Moon*—a comedic version of *The House of Mirth*—a penniless young couple, Nick and Susy Lansing, agree to a "trial marriage" that can be broken off if one gets a "better chance" with a wealthy suitor. The experiment is a failure—jealousy, Susy's maternal longings, and Nick's sense of honor all undo what seems, to them both, a sensible and logical arrangement. Neither Susy nor

Nick can explain what went wrong. Their moral vocabulary of self-actualization and personal freedom is too impoverished to explain the "deep-seated instinctive need" that actually guides their behavior. "That was the way of the world they lived in," the narrator explains. "Nobody questioned, nobody wondered anymore—because nobody had time to remember."

Wharton had planned a sequel to *The Age of Innocence* to be called either *The Age of Wisdom* or *Homo Sapiens*. The story was to focus on Newland's thoroughly modern son, Dallas, who married "his Ellen," Fanny Beaufort, at the end of *The Age of Innocence*. As with Wharton's Jazz novels, Dallas and Fanny believe themselves to have "settled in advance all social, religious and moral problems," yet still come "to grief over the same old human difficulties."

It was a theme already latent in the last pages of *The Age of Innocence*. In the novel's last chapter, Newland Archer, now widowed, prepares for a last trip to Paris with Dallas, who will soon be married. Dallas wants to know about Ellen Olenska, who is now living in Paris; he knows that Archer was once in love with her, and he wants to know why they separated. He then gives an astonishing source for this intelligence: on her deathbed, May had told Dallas that she knew he would always be safe with his father because when she had asked he had "given up the thing [he] most wanted."

It is the "innocent" May, the symbol of the old order, who alone understands the extent of her husband's sacrifice. By contrast, the "wise" Dallas is wholly uncomprehending; to him, the thwarted romance is "prehistoric," "a pathetic instance of vain frustration, of wasted forces." The depth of feeling possible to Archer and Ellen is alien to him; like Pauline, he and his generation are too busy with their "fads and fetishes":

> The boy was not insensitive, he knew; but he had the facility and self-confidence that came of looking at fate not as a master but as an equal. "That's it: they feel equal to things—they know their way about," he mused, thinking of his son as the spokesman of the new generation which had swept away all the old landmarks, and with them the sign-posts and the danger-signal.

Dallas, of course, is mistaken in his facility and self-confidence. We can no more be equal to fate than we can cast off the "old human difficulties." Thus the wise son Dallas is the true innocent.

The wise are really innocent; the innocent are wise—it's a reversal that keeps occurring in Wharton's novels. In *The Children* (which Lee rightly calls underrated), a band of children, led by their 15-year-old sister and surrogate mother, Judith, try to make a home together while their frivolous, pleasure-seeking parents marry, divorce, and remarry on a whim. Who are the real children, the novel asks: the youngsters who try to fulfill the duties of family, or the supposed adults who understand no obligation beyond self-fulfillment?

Wharton's tragic sense, so evident in her fiction, never caused her to despair. Despite her epicurean appetites, she retained a stoic acceptance of hardship. Her commonplace book abounds with quotations from Epictetus, Marcus Aurelius, and Seneca. Her favorite was from Epictetus: "On the occasion of every accident that befalls you, remember to turn to yourself and inquire what power you have for turning it to use."

Wharton took a life of adversity—an unhappy childhood, a loveless marriage, an unfaithful lover—and turned it into a life rich in all her "Ruling Passions": travel, good conversation, architecture, and books. She found sanctuary first in her father's library, then in France and her many friends there, and finally in her writing. A stranger in both America and France, she made a "Country of [Her] Own" in the "Land of Letters."

"We're all imprisoned, of course—all of us middling people, who don't carry our freedom in our brains," a character explains in the short story "Autres Temps." Imprisonment was the fate of many of Wharton's characters, but not of Wharton. She carried her freedom in her brains, and that was the secret of her success.

Aryan Sister

Algis Valiunas

(Fall 2007)

Leni Riefenstahl, the Third Reich's great documentary filmmaker, had what a high school coach of mine used to call, when the poetic fit came upon him, testicular fortitude. She combined this virile will and boldness with outrageous feminine wiles to make a dazzling career in one of the most exclusive men's clubs ever. By her own account in the voluminous 1987 *Memoir*, at her first meeting with Hitler she dressed him down for his anti-Semitism, whereupon he made a clumsy pass at her, which she expertly deflected; she had him in her pocket thereafter. Understanding the value of deftly contrived misapprehension, she also put a host of subordinate Nazis in her pocket by creating the impression that she just might be the Führer's bunkmate. Another party chieftain took a shine to her, and a shot at her, as well. Again according to her telling, Joseph Goebbels, the scaly and sexually promiscuous Minister of National Enlightenment and Propaganda, literally groveled at her feet with lust, while she barely restrained herself from trampling his reptilian person in the dirt. Although she spurned these supreme eminences of the Nazi regime, she was not exactly discriminating about the men she did sleep with. On a movie set early in her acting career, she pretty much serviced the troops, and in descending order of cinematic importance, moving blithely from director to co-stars to cameraman to ski instructor. And yet this Amazon, who lived as freely as any whoring sailor, could weep and tear her hair on cue, instantly turning on the waterworks at the mere hint of manly interference with her artistic integrity. Beauty was her holy grail, she would always insist; politics really did not concern her. She remained a true artist, a perfect innocent, all her life long. Again by her own account.

Two recent biographies put her own account to the test and find it wanting in the extreme. Jürgen Trimborn, a professor of film, theater, and art history at the University of Cologne, the author of *Leni Riefenstahl: A Life*, and Steven Bach, a former United Artists producer and biographer of Marlene Dietrich, the author of *Leni: The Life and Work of Leni Riefenstahl*, are in agreement on the essential facts: that in telling her own story Leni Riefenstahl paid no heed to the essential facts, which implicated her as a Hitler devotee and an anti-Semite well aware of the monstrosities of the Reich. Yet ideological purity was not her driving force. She turned out propaganda without compunction because serving the Nazi regime was her main chance. Fame, money, and power enticed her into accepting the devil's bargain; there was nothing in her scantly furnished soul to make her resist.

Leni Riefenstahl was born in a working class district of Berlin in 1902. Her father, Alfred, was a plumbing salesman and a household despot with an imaginary spiked helmet. Her mother, Bertha, prayed while pregnant for a beautiful daughter who would become a famous actress. Leni was one of those uncanny creatures made for stage and screen. At 16 she auditioned for a part as a bare-breasted hoochie-coochie girl in a piece of movie trash called *Opium* (1925); her failure only spurred her longings. Dancing would be her chosen route to glory, though she had to take lessons behind her father's back; when Alfred found out she was dancing in public, he shipped her off to boarding school. "How I wish I were a man," Leni confided in a letter to a friend, "it would be so much easier to carry out all my plans."

Her plans for independence, featuring dancing and men, proceeded nicely when she returned to Berlin. Beginning a storied career as *femme fatale*, she turned a malleable Jewish youth into what Bach calls "something of a love slave," demeaning him until he slashed his wrists, at which point she forced the bleeding boy to crawl under the sofa so her father wouldn't see him. He did time in a mental hospital, emigrated to America, and went blind. Informed years later of his misfortunes, Leni seized upon the salient detail: "he never forgot me as long as he lived."

Sadly, one cannot choose which loves to remember and which to forget: Leni's deflowering at 21, by a caddish tennis star pushing 40, was calculated on her part and brutal on his; afterward, he flung an American $20 bill her way, in case she needed an abortion. She responded to the humiliation by getting engaged to him, though she had the sense not to marry him in the end. This obsessive bondage to an unworthy man warned her off love and taught her to use men for what she could get. These were not perhaps the wisest lessons she could have drawn from the experience.

A subsequent lover and a decent man, the hotshot Jewish banker Harry Sokal, wanted to marry her, but she preferred that he bankroll and promote her solo dance debut. Her career took off in a hurry, abetted by his management behind the scenes, which Leni resented as the meddling of a casual sexual partner she'd had enough of. She later claimed to have loved dancing more than anything else she ever did, but a knee injury cut her career short after only eight months of performing.

Her resourcefulness and ambition never wavered. She got a part in the film *Ways to Strength and Beauty* (1925), which promised "regeneration of the human race" through athletic excellence; Leni appeared stripped to the waist, after the Weimar skin-flick conception of a Greek or Roman (they weren't particular) serving-woman. In the subway one day, she saw a poster for the movie *Mountain of Destiny* (1924), the latest offering in the peculiarly German genre of Alpine films, which showed mountaineers and skiers exhibiting their prowess and refining their Teutonic souls on the snowy heights. Leni knew this was for her, and she sought out the film's director, Dr. Arnold Fanck. He pronounced her "the most beautiful woman in Europe" and declared he would make her "the most famous woman in Germany." Innovative surgery restored her knee to working order, and Fanck wrote a screenplay in three days and presented it to her in the hospital. *The Holy Mountain* (1926) fatured Leni as the dancer Diotima, with whom two climbers and best friends fall tragically in love. "What do *you* seek up here—in nature?" one of the doomed lovers asks Diotima. "Beauty!" she enthuses. The right-wing press shared the enthusiasm for Teutonic men and women in high places, and great politics was clearly a prime ingredient in the witches' brew. As one critic wrote, "THIS WAY, GERMAN FILM, TO THE HOLY MOUNTAIN OF YOUR REBIRTH AND THAT OF THE GERMAN PEOPLE!" Before his first meeting with Leni, Hitler would say, "The most beautiful thing I have ever seen in a film was Riefenstahl's dance on the sea in *The Holy Mountain.*"

Success built on success, and Leni became an established star of the Alpine films, making several more with Fanck before venturing on her own as screenwriter, director, and leading lady in *The Blue Light* (1932). The film tells the story of the beauteous peasant Junta, who brings back lovely, preternaturally glowing crystals from a mountain cavern, while the young men of her village who seek the crystals fall to their deaths. The crystals astonish all who see them, but only Junta can get them until an expert mountaineer, an outsider, reaches the cavern and turns Junta's wondrous treasure into a commercial concern for the village; her world is denuded of magic, and with the light from the cavern no longer there to guide her, Junta falls and is killed. As an actress, Leni is one of the most physically daring women ever to appear on screen, climbing sheer rock faces without a rope. As a director, the novice displays an instinctive sense of alpine romanticism: the mountaintops in the moonlight ravishingly evoke a woman's gleaming breasts. But the critics of the liberal Berlin newspapers rightly found the movie so much hokum, and Leni reacted after the manner of her place and time: she blamed the Jews—overlooking the fact that her co-producer and co-writer were both Jewish. In November 1932 the Jewish psychologist and aesthetician Rudolf Arnheim interviewed her on the radio, and she told him, "As long as the Jews are film critics, I'll never have a success. But watch out, when Hitler takes the rudder everything will change."

She had met Hitler earlier that year. A mass rally at the Berlin Sportpalast, where Hitler had spoken, electrified her:

> I had an almost apocalyptic vision that I was never able to forget. It seemed as if the earth's surface were spreading out in front of me, like a hemisphere that suddenly splits apart in the middle, spewing out an enormous jet of water, so powerful that it touched the sky and shook the earth. I felt quite paralysed.

This psychic orgasm moved her to write Hitler a fan letter, and he responded by inviting her to drop by. It turned out Hitler was a fan of *hers*, and as they promenaded on a North Sea beach the talk turned to her movies, all of which he had seen. "Once we come to power, you must make my films," he insisted. She demurred, protesting her need to follow her own inspiration and exercise complete creative control; moreover, if we are to believe her version of events, she deplored his "racial prejudices" and said she could not "work for someone who makes such distinctions among people." Then came the abortive romantic clinch, followed by Hitler's hangdog reclamation of his dignity: "How can I love a woman until I have completed my task?"

Despite Leni's professed recoil from the Hitlerian touch, other observers later in their relationship, such as Putzi Hanfstaengl, the Führer's pianist and confidant, say Leni all but offered herself on a platter for Hitler's taking, and it was he who refused the sweets. (Hanfstaengl thought his master impotent and perhaps homosexual.)

Leni made the most of her friendship with Hitler by leading people to believe they were sexually intimate: the cachet this gave her got her whatever she wanted for her films.

And her artistic independence and putative revulsion at Nazi anti-Semitism did not hold out for long against Hitler's enticements to make his films. She did turn down his offer to make a biopic about Horst Wessel, in Bach's description "the Nazi pimp whose murder in a drunken brawl had been mythologized as political martyrdom," but in short order she signed on to direct a film of the 1933 Nazi Party Congress at Nuremberg. *Victory of Faith* (1933) soon found its audience. A Jewish *Gymnasium* student in Heilbronn recalled having to attend a screening with his schoolmates: the good Germans stood and sang patriotic songs while the Jews were required to stay seated; then they beat the Jews and urinated on them while their professors watched. Yet even such smashing successes could not disguise the film's shortcomings, in Leni's own eyes as well as others'. "*Victory of Faith* is technically unsure," writes Bach, "and exposes the rally as a messy, amateurish affair rather than the demonstration of precision and efficiency it was meant to be."

Precision and efficiency would come with practice. *Triumph of the Will* (1935), Leni's film of the monumental 1934 Nazi rally at Nuremberg, has rightly been called by just about any critic who matters the greatest propaganda film ever made. Its potency stems from its command of tones that range from Wagnerian grandeur to homely innocence to breathless rapture to flaming demonolatry. The film conjures up a German *Volk* that is as ordinary and peaceable as any other people and that is exalted to martial sublimity by the touch of a spellbinding master. As Hitler's motorcade makes its way through the streets of Nuremberg, there is no raving exultation from the multitudes lining the route; these are the unexceptionable joyous faces of regular folks on a holiday outing or at a sporting event; a cat watching from a windowsill provides the decisive homespun touch. Similarly, when the camera turns to the soldiers preparing for the rally, the pride of the Reich tends to be made up of unremarkable human specimens, running toward the wan and spindly; anything but fearsome in physique or demeanor, they engage in slaphappy horseplay, like the boys they are. At the rally, still younger boys strain on tiptoe to see over the crowd; there is nothing more cinematically wholesome and winning than pubescent Hitler youth. The Führer himself appears only too human at times, sympathetic, approachable. During Rudolf Hess's introductory speech, Hitler gives a hurried perfunctory salute, as though embarrassed by the attention. When the cavalry and armored cars speed on in tight formation, he obviously enjoys the whirring spectacle, like a NASCAR buff at the racetrack.

Of course, malevolence seethes just below the placid surface, and erupts under oratorical pressure. The voices of speechmakers are pitched toward frenzy, in the now familiar manner of totalitarian hypnotism. The high priests scream "Sieg Heil!" as a release into madness; the choral response is feral baying. Hitler himself is as stagy in his rants and rages as a B-movie potentate. Trimborn notes that when Charlie Chaplin saw an abbreviated version of *Triumph of the Will*, he fell about laughing, and found his inspiration for *The Great Dictator*.

It is hard to imagine a civilized people watching Leni's film with a thrill, or indeed without contempt. As the camera cuts from Hitler speaking to attentive schoolboys listening, one cannot but think him as corrupting as a child molester, and more destructive: he is readying the 14-year-olds to die for him on the Russian front, and one does not need hindsight to see it. Most of the Nazi grandees preaching heroic virility are fat-marbled slabs of prime beef, and those who are not blatantly bovine tend to the porcine or rodential or even amphibian. And as the goose-stepping millipede of SA and SS and Wehrmacht marches on and on and on, one suffers the totalitarian tedium unto death. Any irony on Leni's part is unthinkable, however. She believed the whole thing, and helped make her countrymen believe. No one can deny her that distinction.

Hitler was so pleased with the result that he wanted more and more. "Who else but you could make a film of the Olympics?" he entreated her, about the 1936 Games to be held in Berlin, a prospective showpiece for Aryan strength and beauty. Goebbels's propaganda ministry financed Leni's undertaking and set up a dummy corporation, Olympia-Film GmbH, "because the Reich does not wish to be seen openly as the maker of the film," in the words of an internal memo. Leni would later protest that she understood nothing of the financial arrangements, and would eternally uphold the aesthetic purity of her film, which like *Triumph of the Will* was art and not propaganda. It is true enough that *Olympia* (1938) does not celebrate the flagrantly sinister, unlike *Triumph of the Will*, and that it does celebrate strength and beauty even when they come in ideologically impure form, such as the person of the black American track star Jesse Owens. Yet one sees some of the tricks Leni picked up in making the earlier film at work here as well. German innocence undergirds German superiority. German sports fans are not political fanatics, but cheer for German victors—and German athletes dominate the Games—just like fans anywhere; after all, one also hears Finns in the stands chanting "Suomi" for their triumphant distance runners, and sees straw boaters flying in the air when Americans win. Hitler is just a big kid having the time of his life, by turns hopeful, anxious, ardent, revved-up; when the anchorwoman for the German 4x100 relay drops the baton with a big lead, he is crestfallen, totally caught up in the moment. Yet flashes of militant darkness remind us where we really are. German modern pentathletes ride horses and fire pistols in Wehrmacht officers' uniforms. Mass calisthenics outside the stadium, with thousands bending and flexing in unison, suggest less peaceable rites. The political message is subtler in *Olympia* than in *Triumph of the Will* but nevertheless unmistakable: Nazi Germany is a force, and will teach the world more about strength than about beauty. Leni, characteristically, grabbed what she could of both, enjoying the most torrid affair of her life with the American decathlon champion, Glenn Morris, who in the throes of victory tore off her blouse and kissed her breasts in front of the packed stadium.

The Nazi regime feted Leni as a national heroine, but good democrats were finding her less charming. Her trip to America in 1938 came at an inopportune time: *Kristallnacht*, which occurred shortly after her arrival, shocked the American people, and Leni unthinkingly—perhaps madly—denounced the reports of the pogrom as "slander" against Germany and "the greatest man who ever lived." The Non-Sectarian Anti-Nazi League and the Hollywood Anti-Nazi League for the Defense of American Democracy saw to it that *Olympia* would not be distributed in the United States.

Other nations were more generous. Mussolini called Leni to Rome, and unsuccessfully tried to persuade her to make a film about Fascist heroes draining the swamps. When German Foreign Minister Joachim von Ribbentrop returned from signing the Nazi-Soviet Pact in Moscow in August 1939, he delivered a handwritten appreciation of *Olympia* from Stalin.

War brought fresh opportunities, which would contribute to Leni's postwar trials. On September 11, 1939, the Special Riefenstahl Film Unit arrived in the largely Jewish town of Konskie, Poland. The next day Polish partisans killed and mutilated five German soldiers there, and the Nazis forced a group of Jews to dig a grave for them; at some point, the Nazis started shooting, massacred 30 or 40 Polish civilians, and set the synagogue on fire. A photograph of Leni on the spot, her face contorted with weeping, appeared after the war as evidence that, in Bach's words, "she had witnessed murders of unarmed civilians prefiguring murders that would number in the millions." Maintaining to the end of her life that "In Poland, I never saw a corpse, not of a soldier, not of a civilian," she would file the first of many suits for libel that asserted her ignorance of Nazi atrocities.

Unwelcome controversy had a way of seeking her out. From 1940 through 1943, during the shooting of her ambitious but failed feature film *Tiefland* (1954), which called for a Spanish touch, Leni requisitioned Gypsies from the transit camps of Maxglan and Marzahn to serve as extras in the movie—unpaid forced labor, by people whose next stop would be Auschwitz. "We saw nearly all of [the Gypsies] after the war," Leni would declare, though in fact most of them had been exterminated.

After the war, everyone expected contrition and atonement from her, but she persistently eschewed remorse or even regret for anything she had done. "I would have committed suicide had I felt that I shared the responsibility for these crimes," she said, but she was free of any misgivings on that score. At the same time, she was given to muttering about "the Jewish element" as the source of her troubles, which were many. A rash marriage to a man more promiscuous than herself collapsed, and she wound up in a mental hospital for several months. Denazification hearings cleared her of criminality, but the press and public were less forgiving. Breakneck litigiousness became her defense against the numerous attacks on her reputation.

Somehow she rode out the storm. In 1962 she joined an expedition to the Sudan that changed her life; she would return several times, and the photographs she took of the primitive Nuba tribesmen over the next 15 years had people talking of her excellence once again. In 1968 she took up with a man 42 years younger than she, and they remained together the rest of her life. She became the oldest certified scuba diver in the world, practicing the sport well into her nineties, and a brilliant underwater photographer. When she died in 2003 at the age of 101, the public's response equivocated between praise for her genius and condemnation of her Nazi past. But anyone who reads Trimborn's and Bach's fascinating biographies (Bach's is the one to read if you're reading only one) and watches *Triumph of the Will* can have no doubt: Leni Riefenstahl was the cut-rate female version of Doctor Faustus come to life: pliable, malignant, and foolish, who gave evil a beautiful face and claimed innocent beauty was all she lived for.

Is There Intelligent Life on Television?

Paul A. Cantor

(Fall 2008)

If you can tear yourself away from your favorite television shows long enough to wander down to your local bookstore, you will be amazed at all the books you'll find these days—about your favorite television shows. The medium that was supposed to be the archenemy of the book is now giving an unexpected—and welcome—boost to the publishing industry. It is well known that for the genre of literary criticism, publishers are extremely reluctant to bring out what are called monographs—books devoted to a single author or a single work (unless that single author is Shakespeare or the single work is *Hamlet*). Those works of literary criticism that are published often come out in print runs that number in the hundreds. By contrast, a book devoted to a single television show, *The Simpsons and Philosophy: The D'oh! of Homer* (2001), published by Open Court and edited by William Irwin, Mark T. Conard, and Aeon J. Skoble, has reached its 22nd printing and its sales number in the hundreds of thousands.

Partly inspired by the success of *The Simpsons* volume, three serious publishing houses—Open Court, Blackwell, and University Press of Kentucky—currently have series on philosophy and popular culture, with volumes devoted to such TV shows as *Seinfeld*, *The X-Files*, *The Sopranos*, *South Park*, *Battlestar Galactica*, *Family Guy*, and *24*. These volumes use moments in the shows to illustrate complicated issues in ethics, metaphysics, and epistemology. Books from other serious publishers analyze the shows themselves, often using sophisticated critical methodologies originally developed in literary theory.

TV GROWS UP

This publishing phenomenon has been little noted; what are we to make of the surprising synergy that has been developing between television and the book? The answer is that the proliferation of serious books about television is a clear sign that the medium has grown up and its fans have grown up with it. Many of the publications in question are guidebooks to individual shows, containing episode-by-episode plot summaries, cast lists, critical commentaries, and other scholarly apparatus, including explanations of recondite cultural references and allusions in the programs. No one ever needed a guidebook to *I Love Lucy*. If you couldn't tell Fred Mertz from Ricky Ricardo, you probably couldn't read in the first place. But with contemporary shows such as *Lost*, even devoted fans find themselves bewildered by Byzantine plot twists, abrupt character reversals, and dark thematic developments. Accordingly, they welcome whole books that try to sort out what is happening in their favorite shows and to explain what it all means. The fact that we now need books to explain our favorite TV shows suggests that the best products of the medium have developed the aesthetic virtues we traditionally associate with books—complex and large-scale narratives, depth of characterization, seriousness of themes, and richness of language.

I am not insisting that the general artistic level of television has risen; only that, like any mature medium, it has reached the point where it can serve as the vehicle for some true artists to express themselves. Even so, for those who have not been watching television lately and may be understandably skeptical of my claim, I need to explain what has changed in the medium to make it more sophisticated than it used to be, at least in its best cases. A lot of the change has been driven by technological developments. Whereas in its initial decades television programming was largely controlled by the Big Three networks—CBS, NBC, and ABC—the development of cable and satellite transmission has made hundreds of channels available, and vastly increased the chances of innovative and experimental programming reaching an audience. To be sure, the hundreds of channels now spew out a greater amount of mindless entertainment than ever before, and often end up recycling the garbage of earlier seasons. But the move from broadcasting to narrowcasting—the targeting of ever more specific audience segments—has allowed TV producers to aim an increasing number of programs at an educated, intelligent, and discriminating audience, with predictably positive results in terms of artistic quality.

During the same period, the development of VCRs and then DVRs, as well as videocassette and DVD rentals and sales, has freed television producers from earlier limits on the complexity of their programs. In roughly the first three decades of television history, if viewers missed a show in its initial broadcast slot, they had little chance of seeing it again; at best they had to wait months for a summer rerun. As a result, producers tended to make every episode of an ongoing series as self-contained and as easily digestible as possible. But the proliferation of forms of video recording has made what is known as "time-shifting" possible. Viewers can now watch a show whenever they want and can easily catch up with any episodes they have missed (a survey in *TV Guide* revealed that 22% of *Lost* viewers now watch the show on DVR within seven days of its original air date). Some viewers have chosen to skip television broadcasting entirely and to watch shows only when they come out on DVD, a procedure that facilitates a much more concentrated experience of the unfolding of plot and character. Thus producers are now much freer to introduce elements of complexity into their shows, including elaborate plot arcs that may span an entire season—with confidence that viewers can handle such complications. With the advent of DVDs, television shows can now be "read" and "re-read" just like books—one reason why academic writing about television has suddenly flourished. What cheap paperbacks once were to literary scholarship, the DVD now is to television scholarship.

A WRITER'S MEDIUM

The various changes in the way people watch television have made the medium much more attractive to creative talent. At the same time, Hollywood executives have discovered that what makes a TV series succeed from season to season is above all good scripts. As a result, in Hollywood circles, television is now known as a writer's medium. In movies, the director generally calls the shots, largely determining what finally appears on screen. That is why we know the names of individual motion picture directors, but are seldom aware of the screenwriters, even at Oscar time. The situation is just the reverse in television, where almost nobody knows who directs individual episodes of a series, but the writer-creators become famous—such as Chris Carter (*The X-Files*), Joss Whedon (*Buffy the Vampire Slayer*), and David Chase (*The Sopranos*). This situation is admittedly complicated by the fact that some television writers occasionally direct episodes of their shows themselves. Nevertheless, in television the way to have a lasting and creative impact is fundamentally as a writer, and Hollywood has come to value good TV writers accordingly. In an interview in the *Los Angeles Times* last April, Sue Naegle, the new chief of HBO Entertainment, said: "Development by committee or by patching together multiple people's ideas isn't the way to get great television. I think it starts with the writer. Somebody who's very passionate and has a clear idea about what they'd like to do and the kind of show they'd like to produce."

A writer who creates a show often becomes what is called in Hollywood a "showrunner"—the one who puts together all the elements needed to bring the vision of a series to the screen. (For accounts of the role of showrunners, two useful books are Steven Priggé's *Created By: Inside the Minds of TV's Top Show Creators*, 2005, and David Wild's *The Showrunners*, 1999.) A good showrunner becomes responsible for the artistic integrity of his work in a way that no motion picture screenwriter can ever hope for. The TV showrunner has become the true *auteur* in the entertainment business, to use the favorite term of fancy French film theory.

As a result, creative writers are increasingly migrating to television, and it is attracting a higher level of talent than ever before. Today's TV writers are routinely college-educated and often have higher degrees in television writing from schools like USC and UCLA. The writing staff of *The Simpsons* has a high concentration of Harvard graduates, as witness all the jokes in the series at the expense of Yale. An excellent example of the new level of academic credentials of showrunners is David Milch, who served as writer-producer on *Hill Street Blues* and *NYPD Blue* and created a genuine television masterpiece in *Deadwood*. Milch graduated *summa cum laude* from Yale as an undergraduate, went on to get an MFA from Iowa, became a creative writing instructor at Yale, and even worked with Robert Penn Warren revising a literary anthology. In his book *Deadwood: Stories of the Black Hills* (2006), Milch cites an impressive literary pedigree for his Western series:

> The number of characters in *Deadwood* does not frighten me. The serial form of the nineteenth century novel is close to what I'm doing. The writers who are alive to me, whom I consider my contemporaries, are writers who lived in another time—Dickens and Tolstoy and Dostoevsky and Twain.

If academics are now finding material worth studying in television shows, one reason is that writers like Milch are putting it there.

GERMANY VS. HOLLYWOOD

The growing sophistication of television illustrates a general principle of media development. Every medium has a history, no medium has ever emerged full-blown at its origin, all media develop over time, and they only gradually realize their potential. For some of the traditional media, their origins are mercifully shrouded in the mists of time. The earliest Greek tragedies we have are by Aeschylus, and they are magnificent works of art indeed. But they by no means represent the primitive stages in the growth of the form. If we did have the very first tentative steps toward Greek tragedy, we might be appalled at their crudeness and finally understand why this genre we respect so much bears a name that means in Greek nothing more than "goat song." By contrast, television had the great historical misfortune of being born and growing up right before our eyes, and many intellectuals have never forgiven the medium its birth pangs.

Television's problem with its reputation was compounded by the fact that it was the new kid on the media block at just the moment when Cultural Studies in its modern sense was hitting its stride and gearing up to criticize the American entertainment industry. It found its perfect whipping boy in television. I am talking about the Frankfurt School and its chief representative in America: Theodor Adorno. In 1947, he published, along with his colleague Max Horkheimer, *Dialectic of Enlightenment*, which contains a chapter called "The Culture Industry"—perhaps the single most influential essay in Cultural Studies of the 20th century. It epitomized, established, and helped promulgate the tradition of studying pop culture as a debased and debasing mass medium. In this chapter, Horkheimer and Adorno write primarily about the motion picture industry, which they, as German émigrés living in the Los Angeles area during World War II, had a chance to observe firsthand. In terms that have become familiar and that reflect their left-wing biases, they present Hollywood as a dream factory, serving up images of desire that provide substitute gratifications for Americans exploited by the capitalist system, and thereby working to reconcile them to their sorry lot.

In 1954, Adorno published on his own an essay entitled: "How to Look at Television" in *The Quarterly of Film, Radio, and Television*, which extends the Frankfurt School analysis of the culture industry to the new medium. Adorno may well be the first major intellectual figure to have written about television and to this day I know of no one of comparable stature who has dealt with the medium. His essay set the standard and the tone for much of subsequent analysis of television and remains influential.

As always with Adorno, his television essay is in many respects intelligent and perceptive. He does an especially good job of analyzing the ideological work accomplished by various television shows in getting Americans to accept the dull routine of their daily lives. But Adorno shows little awareness that he is dealing with a medium in its earliest stages, that it might develop into something more sophisticated and genuinely artistic in the future. Admittedly, at the end he speaks of the "far-reaching potentialities" of television, but he expects it to improve only because of critics like him, not because of any developmental logic internal to the medium. He hopes that through his essay "the public at large may be sensitized to the nefarious effect" of television, presumably so that government regulation can do something about it. He would not dream that the commercial pressures on an entertainment medium could by themselves improve its quality.

When Adorno was writing in 1954, broadcast television was less than a decade old as a commercial enterprise and still groping toward a distinct identity. As with any new medium, it remained in thrall to its predecessors, following what turned out in many ways to be inappropriate models. In particular, early television modeled itself on radio, structuring itself into national broadcasting networks (in several cases derived directly from existing radio networks) and reproducing radio formats and genres—the game show, the quiz show, the soap opera, the talk show, the variety program, the mystery, and so on. Some of the most successful of the early television shows, such as *Gunsmoke*, were simply adapted from radio precursors.

THE CULTURAL PYRAMID

Thus at several points in the essay Adorno stigmatizes television for features that turn out to have merely reflected its growing pains. For example, he condemns television for creating programs of only 15 or 30 minutes duration, which he correctly views as inadequate for proper dramatic development but incorrectly views as somehow an inherent limitation of the medium. He had no idea that television was soon to move on to one- and even two-hour dramatic formats, and that it eventually was to develop shows like *The X-Files* or *Lost* with a full season arc of episodes—some of the largest scale artistic productions ever created in any medium, comparable to Victorian novels in scope.

Elsewhere Adorno dogmatically proclaims: "Every spectator of a television mystery knows with absolute certainty how it is going to end." This may have been true when Adorno was writing (personally I doubt it), but try telling it to fans of the aptly named *Lost* today. They are not just mystified about how the series is going to end way off in the future; they are not even sure what is going on in the present. Or consider the recent furor over the final episode of the final season of *The Sopranos*. For weeks media pundits speculated about how the series was going to end, but they all proved wrong, and everybody was shocked by a kind of abrupt conclusion that was unprecedented in television history. This surprising turn in *The Sopranos* is exactly what one would expect at a later stage of a medium, when producers, for both artistic and commercial reasons, deliberately thwart their audience's expectations in order to generate interest. Amazingly, for a sophisticated Marxist, Adorno does not appear to grasp that media have histories.

Insisting that television is inferior to earlier examples of popular culture, Adorno contrasts 18th-century English novels favorably with the TV shows he was watching in the early 1950s. But his examples of the popular novel are all drawn from the work of Defoe, Richardson, and Fielding—the three greatest English novelists of the 18th century. And Adorno compares them to the most mindless sitcoms and game shows he can find in the earliest days of American TV. Too many intellectuals like

Adorno score points against television by comparing the apex of achievement in earlier media with the nadir of quality in television. Television is a voracious medium. It now requires filling up hundreds of channels 24 hours a day, seven days a week. The result is that television does show a lot of junk. But inconsistency in quality has always been the bane of any popular medium. For every one of Shakespeare's masterpieces, the Elizabethan theater turned out dozens of potboilers that share all the faults of the worst television fare (gratuitous sex and violence, stereotyped characters, clichés of plot and dialogue). For every one of Dickens's great works, the Victorian Age produced hundreds of penny dreadfuls, trash novels that have been justly condemned to the dustbin of history. A living culture always resembles a pyramid, with a narrow pinnacle of aesthetic mastery resting on a broad base of artistic mediocrity.

Adorno's contempt for American television leads him to treat it in an unscholarly manner. He does not even bother to name the particular shows he is discussing because evidently they all pretty much looked the same to him. One of his examples must be a sitcom I remember called *Our Miss Brooks*. Here is Adorno's capsule description: "the heroine of an extremely light comedy of pranks is a young schoolteacher who is not only underpaid but is incessantly fined by the caricature of a pompous and authoritarian school principal." I have trouble recognizing the show I remember with some fondness in Adorno's characterization: "The supposedly funny situations consist mostly of her trying to hustle a meal from various acquaintances, but regularly without success." One begins to suspect that Adorno's readings of American television are telling us as much about him as they do about television. I hate to think that the great anti-fascist intellectual had an authoritarian personality himself, but he seems to be suspiciously unnerved by the typically American negative attitude toward authority figures, especially when he sees it displayed by women. Could it be that when Adorno looked at Principal Osgood Conklin of *Our Miss Brooks*, he was having flashbacks to Professor Immanuel Rath of *The Blue Angel* (1930), and couldn't bear the image of academic authority humiliated by underlings and students? After all, Germans have always respected their teachers much more than Americans do. One shudders to think what Adorno would have made of Bart Simpson's treatment of Principal Seymour Skinner.

STRANGE CUSTOMS OF AN ALIEN TRIBE

As one reads Adorno on American television, one gradually begins to realize that he is writing about the subject as a foreigner. Indeed, he resembles an anthropologist trying to describe what are for him the strange customs of an alien tribe. All the symptoms of cultural displacement are there—he doesn't find the local jokes funny, differing cultural products look alike to him, he claims to understand the artifacts better than do the people who create and use them, and so on. Standing far above the cultural phenomena he is analyzing, he is quite eager to criticize them and unwilling to appreciate them in their own terms. He does not think of television programs as the product of individual creators and thus has no interest in their distinct identities. In rejecting what would normally be congenial to him—a Freudian analysis of television—Adorno writes: "To study television shows in terms of the psychology of the authors would almost be tantamount to studying Ford cars in terms of the psychoanalysis of the late Mr. Ford." With his conception of the culture industry, Adorno regards television shows as mass-produced and thus completely without any individuality or distinct identity—in short, without a name.

Adorno ignores the promising developments that would have been evident to any sympathetic observer in his day. Sid Caesar, along with writers of the caliber of Mel Brooks and Neil Simon, was already creating some of the most inventive comedy ever to appear on television. And waiting in the wings in the 1950s was the first authentic genius of the medium, Ernie Kovacs. He pioneered many of the camera techniques that have become standard on television, and later was the first person to realize the potential of videotape for special effects, particularly in comedy. One of Kovacs's greatest television achievements was to create what would today be called a video to the music of Bela Bartok's *Concerto for Orchestra*. With Adorno's love of modernist music, here was a television moment he might have appreciated, although I'm afraid he would have dismissed it as just another cheap popularization of classical music, like the American performances of the Budapest String Quartet, which he scorned as too slickly commercial. Adorno condemned even as great a conductor as Arturo Toscanini because he worked for the National Broadcasting Corporation.

I don't mean to berate Adorno for what he missed in the early days of television. He was after all a German émigré, whose command of English was no doubt shaky, particularly of the kind of colloquial idiom necessary to understand comedy in any medium. (I have noticed that Adorno never finds anything funny in American pop culture, not even Donald Duck.) Adorno was doing his best under difficult circumstances to understand phenomena that were profoundly alien to him. But the problem is that the work of this German émigré on American pop culture became the prototype of academic studies of television for decades, and we are still struggling to get out from under his influence. The idea that television is limited to stereotypes, that it is in its very nature as a medium artistically inauthentic, that it serves only the interests of a ruling elite, that it is ideologically reactionary—all these ideas are the intellectual legacy of Adorno, and they are still repeated by many critics of television today.

TAKING THE FAN'S PERSPECTIVE

Adorno's television essay is unfortunately typical of the way intellectuals have dealt with new media over the centuries. When a new medium comes along, intellectuals, trapped in modes of thinking conditioned by the old media, tend to dwell obsessively on the novelty of the medium itself, focusing on the ways in which it fails to measure up to the standards of the old media. Early talking films often seemed like badly staged plays, and early television shows often looked like anemic movies. Fortunately, as a medium matures, it seems to breed a new generation of critics who are able to appreciate and articulate its distinctive and novel contributions. That is what is happening in television criticism today.

As a turning point, I would cite particularly the work of MIT Professor Henry Jenkins in such books as *Textual Poachers: Television Fans and Participatory Culture*

(1992) and *Fans, Bloggers, and Gamers: Exploring Participatory Culture* (2006). Jenkins shows that it is not just the producers in television who can be creative, but the fans as well. Jenkins demolishes the great myth of the Frankfurt School—the myth of the passive consumer. For Adorno, television viewers sit captive in front of the screen, mesmerized by its images, allowing themselves to be shaped in their desires and their ideas by its overt and covert messages. He repeatedly compares American television to totalitarian propaganda. Unlike Adorno—who merely posits what the television viewer is like—Jenkins has studied and chronicled in detail how real people actually react to the television shows they watch. And what he has found is active, rather than passive consumers—fans of shows who take possession of them—his "textual poachers." They quarrel with producers over new story lines, come up with variations of a show's plots in their own self-published magazines, and develop the characters in directions their creators could never imagine. Jenkins persuasively argues in favor of taking the fan's perspective in analyzing television— and this is the cornerstone of the new turn in Cultural Studies. Academics are now writing about television shows because they admire them, not because they hate the medium. They write out of genuine knowledge of and sympathy for a particular show—they even call it by name.

One of the best books I know on participatory culture is Jennifer Hayward's *Consuming Pleasures: Active Audiences and Serial Fictions from Dickens to Soap Opera* (1997). As her title indicates, in discussing the serial form as basic to modern culture, Hayward finds continuities between the serial publication of Victorian novels and the serial broadcasting of TV soap operas. She thus cuts across the conventional divide between high culture and popular culture that so many critics of television labor mightily to maintain. With painstaking scholarship and archival research, she demonstrates how serial forms make possible productive feedback loops between creators and their audience, thus driving a continual process of refinement and improvement in modern media.

There are of course potential pitfalls in adopting the fan's perspective in academic criticism—a loss of objectivity and the ever present danger of taking a show too seriously, and treating a passing fad as of lasting significance. But as we have seen, the Olympian stance of an Adorno has its problems too—he is so far removed from the phenomena he is analyzing that he ends up out of touch with them, unable to separate the wheat from the chaff. We never object when literary critics write about Shakespeare's plays as "fans." In fact we assume that a Shakespeare scholar admires the plays, and expect to broaden and deepen our own appreciation of them by reading Shakespeare criticism. In many ways, the new writers about television are performing a traditional critical function. They are trying to separate the outstanding from the ordinary, the creative from the banal.

As a result, some of the best "literary criticism" today is paradoxically being written about television. Many literary critics seem to have become bored with their traditional role as the interpreters of great literature, and now are as interested in tearing authors' reputations down as they once were in building them up. In the era of literary deconstruction, it can be refreshing to turn to television books and see critics who are still interested in reconstructing the meaning of the works they discuss. The readers of the new books on television will accept no less, since their reason for turning to these books is to help them better understand their favorite programs. At a time when literary critics often seem to be talking only to each other, the lively market for television books tells us something. The reading public is still interested in thoughtful intellectual conversation about what has always made for good narratives in any medium—complex plot lines, interesting characters, serious and even philosophical issues, and insights into the human condition.

Music, Philosophy, and Generation Y

Martha Bayles

(Fall 2000)

"Is there such thing as an evil sound?"

That question, one of the most interesting I've been asked, was posed by a young musician named Kevin Max Smith at a lecture I gave in Nashville to a group of rock musicians who were also evangelical Christians. Smith was with a band called dc Talk, which started out as a rap group then switched to a mixture of styles. But many genres were represented in the room, including heavy metal, which is usually not associated with Christianity.

Smith's question cut to the heart of the ancient view of music, older than Christianity, that I call didactic. The ancients ranked musical sounds in a hierarchy understood to be causally related to the hierarchy of human virtues and vices, in the soul and in the polity. Says Socrates in Plato's *Republic*, "Never are the ways of music moved without the greatest political laws being moved." Confucius, incidentally, said something similar: "If you would know whether a people are well governed, and if its laws are good or bad, examine the music it practices."

I respect this didactic view because it represents the powers of music. These powers range wildly. At one end of the spectrum, music has the power to soothe, to calm, and to "sing the savageness out of a bear," in Shakespeare's words. At the other end, music can also drum the savageness back into the bear. Flaubert had this in mind when he wrote sarcastically, "Music makes a people's disposition more gentle: for example 'The Marseillaise.'"

This is why the ancients sought to control the effects of music. Allan Bloom summarizes Socrates' teaching with his customary eloquence. "The taming or domestication of the soul's raw passions," he writes, must not mean "suppressing or excising them, which would deprive the soul of its energy," but rather "forming and informing them." The trouble comes when we try to apply this wise abstraction to actual music. To do so is to shoot at a moving target, because Western music has long been violating Plato's specific prescriptions.

For example, Plato taught that too much music confuses the mind and distracts from *logos*. The Hebrew prophets took the same view, which is why early Christians spurned the rich instrumental homophony of pagan music in favor of a spare vocal monophony—a single melodic line sung without accompaniment. But during the late Middle Ages, the monks in Notre Dame began to interpolate new sections of chant containing more than one melodic line. The switch to polyphony, or harmonic counterpoint, gave birth to the glories of Western music.

To put my point in a nutshell: we may believe that Bach and Mozart are good for the soul and good for the polity, but we should also keep in mind that they violate quite promiscuously the specific rules set down by Plato.

Where does that leave us? Disinclined, probably, to issue any specific decrees about musical sounds. To the question posed above, "Is there such a thing as an evil sound?", my initial response is "no." No sound by itself is evil. Sounds that are harsh, ugly, or disturbing can be used in aesthetically and morally admirable ways. And the sweetest, most pleasing sounds can be put to evil uses. So it's a matter of how the sound is employed.

If we look at contemporary music in Socratic terms, and ask how well it is forming and informing the raw passions of individual souls and of the polity, what do we see? To judge by the opinion of many experts, we see a stratified musical landscape in which some people listen to "serious" music, others to "popular."

For some critics of our democratic culture (Allan Bloom again), the mere existence of vulgar music exerts a fatal and irreversible downward pressure on the soul, the culture, and the polity. It's a persuasive argument, if all we look at is Mozart on the one hand, and the grossest and most offensive popular music on the other.

Which is pretty much what Bloom did in his famous chapter on music in *The Closing of the American Mind* (1987). He focused on the stuff that Tipper Gore went after in those famous Senate hearings of the mid-'80s: rapaciously violent heavy metal, hardcore, and punk bands out to shock what was left of the bourgeoisie; Madonna in her underwear phase; Prince at his most priapic.

I, too, have criticized this vulgarity. But I also contend that the vilest strain of popular music—and of popular music in general—arises less from ordinary vulgarity than from cultivated perversity.

THE ARTISTIC ELITE

American popular music has not always been vile. On the contrary, certain strands of it, notably popular song and jazz, have achieved worldwide distinction in a century when so-called serious music embraced rationalism, mathematics, noise, and games of chance to the point of cutting itself off from the educated as well as the popular audience.

If you look closely, you see that the most troubling impulses in popular music came from the artistic elite. The process began in the late 1960s, when the counterculture went sour, and rock and roll began to attract the sort of people who were less interested in music than in using such a popular medium for their own culturally radical purposes.

Prior to that, rock and roll was vulgar, but not culturally radical. It was inferior in some ways to the musical culture that had produced Louis Armstrong, Benny Goodman, and Frank Sinatra. But rock also shared many positive traits with the older musical culture, such as a stance of old-fashioned courtesy toward the audience. That persisted into the mid-1960s in soul music, Motown, and the early Beatles.

Then came the transformation. Concerning Mick Jagger, Bloom's instincts are right on target. Jagger's stage persona does express a kind of pop-Nietzchean erotic liberationism. The Rolling Stones relished the blues, especially the rough-edged Chicago blues. But coming from the hothouse atmosphere of British art colleges, they also turned the blues into a vehicle for shocking the bourgeoisie.

More drastic was the transformation wrought by groups marginal at the time but since lionized. Inspired by cutting-edge visual artists and avant-garde theater, Frank Zappa, Iggy Pop, Alice Cooper, and the New York Dolls put on stage shows that resembled "happenings" more than concerts. In turn, they helped to inspire punk, the 1970s phenomenon that was, and is, a form of performance art, not music. The pure legacy of punk, which pervades gangsta rap as well as much of alternative rock, is a cult in-your-face attitude and (in punk, at least) musical incompetence.

Does this stuff have an unhealthy effect on our souls and our polity? It's hard to argue otherwise. There may be no such thing as an evil sound, but we live in a culture very skilled at using all sorts of sounds to create evil effects.

The film soundtrack is a great example. Consider how directors like Quentin Tarantino combine cheerful upbeat music with grisly violence. In *Pulp Fiction* (1994) he used Al Green, Kool & the Gang, surf music, Dusty Springfield, and the Statler Brothers to accompany the happy hit men's splattering of blood and guts over everything—a gimmick that creates instant irony, a feeling of detachment from mayhem that is ever so 20th-century.

Quite different is the soundtrack for *Natural Born Killers* (1994). For that film about two young slackers who go around blowing people's heads off, director Oliver Stone asked the industrial rock band Nine Inch Nails to create an accompaniment that, in my judgment, comes close to being evil. Younger readers will recognize it as neck-breaking mosh pit noise. Older readers will imagine a Stealth bomber forcing its attentions on a threshing machine.

But even so, I can think of good uses for this sound. Scenes of black despair and chaotic passion have their place in great art. Remember Oedipus gouging out his eyes? Or Medea butchering her children? Nine Inch Nails could handle those moments.

DEMOCRATIC VICES

Thus I am not issuing any decrees. I do not wish to live in a didactic culture, one that believes and acts on the notion of a one-to-one correspondence between auditory stimuli and characterological effects. That has been tried, and somehow the guys in charge are never philosopher kings.

The worst stuff is still out there, attracting the vulnerable and being defended by pundits and academics who ought to know better. But for people coming of age today—Generation Y, if you will—there is also incredible ferment, as technology brings all kinds of music to all kinds of ears.

The situation of having every variety of music at our fingertips is part of what is meant by postmodernism. The received wisdom, on the Right as well as the Left, is that this puts everything on the same debased level. I disagree. I think it gives the audience a chance to compare the good with the better, the bad with the worse.

To say this is, I realize, to express far more optimism about democratic culture than the ancients might regard as wise. But consider the positive aspects of the case. Taking the long view of American culture, music included, what do we see?

We see a systematic rejection of snobbery, because snobbery says that to be knowledgeable and cultivated you must be to the manner born, and most of us are not. But at the same time we see a lot of people who acquire knowledge and cultivation by hook or by crook—and then play it down—because they know that the best way to learn about others is to surprise them by not fulfilling their expectations.

We see the widespread belief, against expert opinion, that there do exist fairly objective standards of excellence in the arts: a stubborn tendency to stand in awe of Rembrandt, and to tell the kids that if they don't practice, they won't be able to play like Itzhak Perlman or Artie Shaw.

Finally, we see the conviction that there is such a thing as morality and decency in the arts, and that to be shocked and offended by their blatant violation doesn't make someone a prude or a philistine.

Every kind of audience has its vices. Personally, I find the vices of the democratic audience preferable to those of the elite. Tocqueville, who wrote about the arts in America but sadly failed to mention music, observed that "[i]n democracies, the springs of poetry are fine but few." I'm inclined to turn that around and say that while the springs of great music in America have been few, they have also been very fine.

Macbeth and the Moral Universe

Harry V. Jaffa

(Winter 2007/08)

Macbeth is a moral play par excellence. In this, it stands in stark contrast to two more recent well-known tales of murder, Dostoevsky's *Crime and Punishment* and Camus's *The Stranger*. In *Macbeth* Shakespeare presented the moral phenomena in such a way that those who respond to his art must, in some way or another, become better human beings. In Dostoevsky's and Camus's heroic criminals we see the corruption of moral consciousness characteristic of modern literature.

By the art of Camus we are led to admire his hero, Meursault; young people especially tend to identify with him. What kind of hero is Meursault? He is utterly indifferent to morality and cannot understand what others mean when they say they love other human beings. In the story, he kills a man and is sentenced to be executed, in part because he did not weep at his mother's funeral. Meursault becomes passionate in the end: but the only passion he ever experiences is the passionate revulsion against the idea of human attachment. He thinks no one had a right to expect him to weep at his mother's funeral, or for anyone else to weep at her funeral. By Camus's hero we are taught to be repelled by those who (he believes) falsely teach us that there is any foundation for human attachments, or that there is anything in the universe that is lovable. The benign indifference to the universe is the only form of the benign, of goodness itself, in the universe. To imitate the indifference of the universe to good and evil is to live life at its highest level.

In Dostoevsky's Raskolnikov we find a profound articulation of the psychology of the modern revolutionary. Raskolnikov is a more persuasive embodiment of the revolutionary hero than can be found in Proudhon, or in Marx or Lenin. The hero of *Crime and Punishment* is admired for his heroic suffering, and there is something stupendously powerful in Raskolnikov's suffering. We are taught to sympathize and suffer with him. We undergo (in a milder form) the torture that he undergoes as a result both of contemplating and of committing the murder. The reason his suffering is heroic is that he suffers for the sake of a suffering humanity. He becomes a kind of Christ figure. Unlike Camus's hero, Dostoevsky's hero loves passionately. What is it that he loves? Again, unlike Camus's hero, what he loves above everything is his mother. And of course he is for this reason a much more sympathetic figure, even though he commits a far more brutal crime. But his love for his mother and his sister, and his unwillingness that they suffer the degradation that he thinks circumstances are inflicting upon them, makes him a rebel against the moral order. This drives him to murder a rich pawnbroker, a hateful old woman who is a symbol not merely of a money-grubbing social order but of the Gordian knot which upholds that order. That obstacle—the prohibition of murder—stands between him and a solution of what he sees as at once his personal problem and the problem of all humanity.

The moral order that Raskolnikov violates is represented to us merely and simply as a by-product of Christianity. The ultimate sanction for the prohibition against murder would seem to be incorporated in the ministry of Jesus, which finds its most powerful expression in the story of the raising of Lazarus. The scene in *Crime and Punishment* in which the harlot is compelled by the murderer to read the story is one of the high points in the world's literature. In the scene, Raskolnikov rather scornfully acknowledges the ground of the morality he has violated, but to which he is in some way still committed. Of course, it is clear that he does not believe that Jesus raised Lazarus from the dead.

At the end of the novel, when he is in the process of gaining some kind of redemption, he wonders whether he might some day accept the harlot Sonia's simple faith in the Gospels. The moral order is, as we said, represented to him by Christianity. And he himself is a kind of Christian hero because he shares the compassion for humanity which is presumably the motive of Jesus himself in accepting the sacrifice on the cross. Raskolnikov too suffers on a kind of cross in the tremendous catharsis he undergoes as a result of the murder. This catharsis takes the form of a series of terrible fevers. Yet he recovers. His crime is not beyond redemption. In fact, it is the necessary cause of his redemption, which would not have been possible before the murder.

Raskolnikov's guilt is uncovered by an examining magistrate who is a kind of detective. This man discovers Raskolnikov's guilt by reading Raskolnikov's essay, which is really a profession of revolutionary faith, and of the right of the hero to destroy a corrupt old order in order to build a better new one. The striking thing about this detective is not so much his cleverness in finding Raskolnikov out and bringing him within the purview of the law. What is striking is that he becomes in a way Raskolnikov's partner. Porfiry is not a minister of vindictive justice. He shows the criminal a way to escape any real penalty for his crime. His ultimate sentence is eight years of penal servitude, under conditions which hardly remind us of the Gulag. He seems to be in some kind of minimum security prison, with Sonia nearby to alleviate whatever of hardship there may be. Porfiry remits all real punishment and shows Raskolnikov the way to a new life, in which his legal punishment is as nothing compared to the suffering he already has undergone in the wake of the murder.

Raskolnikov shares with Meursault the fact that his crime leads in the end, not to a fall, but to an ascent to a higher form of consciousness, to a salvation which would not have been possible had the crime not been committed. There is moreover nothing in Raskolnikov's punishment to discourage anyone—e.g., a Lenin—who may look upon him as the prototype of the revolutionary hero. In *Crime and Punishment*, we see a moral consciousness resembling in decisive respects a messianic Christianity. Such reform of society as may be envisioned has nothing to do with politics, and in fact subsists upon the conviction that salvation consists in direct action—such as murdering an old woman, or a royal family. Napoleon's action in destroying the *ancien régime*, and replacing it with the regime of reason, executing whoever stood in the way, is the tacit model.

MORALITY AND POLITICS

When we turn to *Macbeth* we turn to a world so different that it is hard to identify what it has in common with the worlds of Camus and Dostoevsky. Certainly Christianity is present in *Macbeth* as in *Crime and Punishment,* but it is a Christianity so different that one wonders what it shares except the name. Meursault is perfectly amoral. Whether he is a beast or a god, he is "beyond good and evil," and cannot either love or hate. The priest who tries to console Meursault as he awaits execution he regards as the ultimate alien and the ultimate enemy. Raskolnikov, on the other hand, overflows with passion, and is as intensely alive to moral distinctions as Meursault is dead to them. But Raskolnikov thinks it may be necessary to violate the moral law, perhaps even by committing murder, in order to come into possession of the human good, including the moral good.

Macbeth on the other hand is a man who feels the power of morality to the fullest extent. He does so, I suggest, because he is a political man. By a political man, I understand someone who is a vital part of a political community. For Camus's hero the political community does not exist. For Dostoevsky's hero, it exists only marginally. Raskolnikov is the model for a revolutionary, whose cause is that of all humanity. His is a polity—like the City of God—that has no borders. Patriotism is not possible however in a world polity ("world polity" is an oxymoron). Patriotism is possible only if there is a connection between one's father and the political order. (In the City of God, God the Father is the father of that city.) In Macbeth's case, patriotism has a literal meaning, as he belongs to the royal family. He murders the king, forcing the king's sons—one of whom is the confirmed heir—to flee. He becomes king—after the murder—by a process of election, but one which is limited to the royal family. When we speak of patriotism we presume a people descended from a common ancestor. The children of Israel are those descended from Abraham, Isaac, and Jacob. They are the original fathers, the founding fathers. In the most patriotic speech in American history, Abraham Lincoln began by saying, "Four score and seven years ago our fathers brought forth on this continent a new nation . . ." Now the United States, like other modern nation-states, is not a polity in the original sense of the political: the law of the Constitution makes fellow citizens of those of different ethnicities. The unity of the human race, as proclaimed in the Declaration of Independence, in Lincoln's poetic evocation, replaces the particular ancestors of ancient polities with the nature which is the universal ancestor of all human beings.

Lincoln reminds us of the original meaning of citizenship, and invests in our citizenship something of the intensity of that original citizenship. Macbeth as he comes into sight is above all a citizen. As such, he shares responsibility for the commonwealth and, as a citizen-soldier, labors in its service. He feels keenly the honor that accompanies his heroic deeds. In serving the country by serving the king, he is keenly aware of the greatness of the honor that accompanies the person of the king. His ambition is therefore, in its origin, a by-product of his virtue. Aristotle in the *Nicomachean Ethics* characterizes two of the moral virtues as embodying all the others. One of these encompassing virtues is magnanimity, and the other is legal justice. Legal justice is justice in its most comprehensive form. It is justice as seen from the perspective of the law of the ancient city. Aristotle, reflecting that perspective, says "whatever the law does not command, it forbids." In this he is in full agreement with the Mosaic law.

We today would say that "whatever the law does not forbid, it permits." One might think that the difference lies in the permissiveness of our culture. That there is such a difference is undeniable, but its sources go deeper than to our contemporary moral corruptions; and in fact, little, if any, of the difference is due to a changed or lowered conception of human well-being. Aristotle and Moses were agreed in regarding the law as emanating from God or the gods. Their polities were expanded tribal societies, insignificant in size compared to any modern nation-state. In today's polities, any attempt at such comprehensive moral tutelage as we find in the idea of law in the ancient city would result in something like Nazi or Communist tyranny. Yet the moral commands—embodied in the idea of law in the books of Moses and of Aristotle, constitute the negation of tyranny. But what Aristotle calls legal justice, not as a feature of positive law but of moral law, reminds us that we are under an obligation (even if it is no longer legally enforceable) to practice all the virtues.

Whose actions have the widest consequences and are most in need of virtue to direct them? The rulers'. Hence morality in all its dimensions can be best seen in the lives of rulers. Private men or women cannot be moral in the highest degree because they are limited in the scope of their actions. Aristotle quotes the Greek proverb, "Rule shows the man." No one ever knows with certainty how virtuous—or vicious—a man might be until he holds office and has power. Only those in power reveal their real natures. For this reason all Shakespeare's great plays are about rulers: kings and princes and dukes and military commanders. In the Roman plays, these rulers are not kings and princes but great aristocratic warriors like Coriolanus, or great heroes like Julius Caesar, or great soldiers like Mark Antony, who compete among themselves for the rule of the world. Shakespeare's preoccupation is not that of a poet living in an aristocratic age; it is the preoccupation of a moralist who would display human actions on that scale on which alone they can be said to be fully intelligible. Only in a political context can the nature of morality be thoroughly considered. One reason why the works of both Camus and Dostoevsky are deficient in their understanding of morality is their deficiency in understanding politics. Only in a political work in which political actions of the gravest kind are involved can one see the moral phenomena in their fullness.

THIS BANK AND SHOAL OF TIME

Macbeth, at the beginning, is a good man. He is a loyal subject, and much more than a loyal subject. He is one who has displayed courage and fidelity in the service of his king and country in a higher degree than anyone else. He is the most honored man, and the most justly honored man in the kingdom. The tragedy of Macbeth is the tragedy of his fall from that high estate. Macbeth reminds us of Milton's Satan, the most glorious of the angels of heaven, who becomes a fallen angel. We cannot understand the meaning of a fall from virtue if the fall is from a very low position, like that of Meursault. Or even that of Raskolnikov. Although he is lower middle class, Raskolnikov is very proud and thinks himself worthy of great things, but there is nothing to confirm the judgment that he is worthy of the pride he feels. In Macbeth's case we have a man who is certainly proud, but who has demonstrated on the field of battle, in the face of temptation and treachery, that his great pride is justified by his great virtue. And it is his fall that we witness. More than that, we witness the inextricable intertwining of crime and punishment. There is no tincture of salvation resulting from Macbeth's crime—only damnation.

The crime, and the punishment, of Macbeth are inseparable from that of Lady Macbeth. Her fate is not tragic in the sense that his is, because hers is not a fall from grace. She is pure evil at the outset. There is, in her mind, no reason for them not to kill the king. Her invocation of the powers of darkness, when the murder is still in contemplation, is that of a soul already lost to evil. Her punishment, in the end, is different from his, and we must consider in what way it is appropriate to their differences.

Macbeth's soliloquy in Act 1, scene 7, is a dialogue with himself on the question of whether to murder the king. All the arguments are against, but one. And that one is so weak as not to merit serious consideration. Yet it will prove to be the one that will prevail, under Lady Macbeth's tutelage.

> If it were done when 'tis done, then 'twere well
> It were done quickly. If th' assassination
> Could trammel up the consequence, and catch
> With his surcease success, that but this blow
> Might be the be-all and the end-all here,
> But here upon this bank and shoal of time,
> We'd jump the life to come. But in these cases
> We still have judgment here, that we but teach
> Bloody instructions, which, being taught, return
> To plague th' inventor. This evenhanded justice
> Commends th' ingredients of our poisoned chalice
> To our own lips. He's here in double trust:
> First, as I am his kinsman and his subject,
> Strong both against the deed; then, as his host,
> Who should against his murderer shut the door,
> Not bear the knife myself. Besides, this Duncan
> Hath borne his faculties, so hath been
> So clear in his great office, that his virtues
> Will plead like angels, trumpet-tongued against
> The deep damnation of his taking-off;
> And pity, like a naked newborn babe
> Striding the blast, or heaven's cherubim horsed
> Upon the sightless couriers of the air,
> Shall blow the horrid deed in every eye
> That tears shall drown the wind. I have no spur
> To prick the sides of my intent, but only
> Vaulting ambition, which o'erleaps itself
> And falls on the other—

ENTER LADY MACBETH

This soliloquy consists entirely of reasons why Macbeth ought not to murder the king. Macbeth reasons truly to a true conclusion. In so doing, he reaches the peak of his moral stature, the point at which the greatest temptation is met and overcome. It provides us, at one and the same time, the height from which the hero falls, and the mystery of why he falls, after such a clear vision of the impossibility of success and the certainty of retribution.

There are three sets of reasons given, in ascending form. The first is that the murder cannot succeed, because "evenhanded justice" will instruct others to murder the murderer. Those who take up arms against a tyrant will not, like Macbeth, be driven by naked ambition, but by the moral and political necessity to rid themselves of the incubus of tyranny.

Second is the obligation imposed by the moral order, which tells us that it is our duty to protect a kinsman, king, and guest. Implicit is the idea that Macbeth is part of a moral order, to violate which is in some sense to violate himself. Macbeth here understands himself to be, in Aristotle's sense, a social and political animal. His eventual punishment will consist, in part, in his consciousness of his separation from those who have been dear to him, and whose welfare has been intertwined with his own.

Third is the drama, illuminated by Macbeth's powerful imagination, of the moral order personified. Duncan is not only king, he has been a good king, "so clear in his great office, that his virtues will plead like angels, trumpet-tongued against the deep damnation of his taking-off." The lines which follow are perhaps the most moving in all Shakespeare, in rendering the moral order as a self-subsisting palpable reality, with infinite resources for rewarding friends and punishing enemies. They are followed by the conclusion that he has no motive to commit the murder, only his ambition, "vaulting ambition which o'erleaps itself . . . ." That is to say, it is a passion which has no justification beyond itself, a passion at war with reason—certain to be self-defeating.

The soliloquy begins by Macbeth wishing the assassination "could trammel up the consequence." By this he means that if the deed could have no further effects, he would "jump the life to come," that is, ignore the consequences after death. Macbeth believes in heaven, hell, the immortality of the soul, and future rewards and future punishment. Later in the play, when he learns that Fleance has escaped the murderers he has hired, and that Banquo's issue, not his, will occupy the throne of Scotland, he complains bitterly that he has given his "eternal jewel" to the "common enemy of man," and is getting nothing in return. He seems to have expected Satan to keep what Macbeth regarded as Satan's part of the bargain. One might say, Macbeth had to learn the hard way that Satan is not a gentleman. Macbeth does not however actually name Satan (although he does have a servant named Seyton). Nor does he name God. His punishment, as we shall see, is not in his alienation from God, but from beloved human beings.

How can such an overwhelming decision have been so quickly reversed, as it was, by the entrance of Lady Macbeth? Here we must turn to a character as extraordinary as her husband. The meaning of the play must be sought in the comparative analysis of their divergent and convergent courses. In Act 1, scene 5, Lady Macbeth is reading aloud the letter from her husband, in which he tells her of the witches' prophecies, and how, as he "stood, rapt in the wonder," missives came from the king, hailing him Thane of Cawdor. That put him—and her—instantly in mind of the greater hail, of "king that shalt be." Lady Macbeth's soliloquy, which follows, assumes without question that the promised greatness can only be brought to pass by evil means. She does not consider—as we might think she ought—whether the ascent to the throne might not happen by a natural evolution of the political process. This thought must have passed through Macbeth's mind. When he hears Duncan name Malcolm as his successor, he says to himself, "that is a step on which I must fall down or else o'erleap." He must have thought there was some legitimate path to the throne—however remote the possibility—before Malcolm was named Prince of Cumberland. The witches' prophecy did not exclude such possibility and at one point Macbeth says, "If chance will have me king, why chance may crown me without my stir." If Macbeth did not "stir" to become Thane of Cawdor, why might he not await the same dispensation to become king? Why did he not consider that the witches' prophecy was a kind of assurance that, absent other causes, chance would be obliged to make him king? Lady Macbeth will speak of him being crowned by "fate and metaphysical aid." Why do they both assume that this is a sanction for murder, and not the same sufficient cause that made him Thane of Cawdor?

Lady Macbeth drives out of mind any alternative to murder. Here is her thought—after reading the letter—on the task before her:

> Glamis thou art, and Cawdor, and shalt be
> What thou art promised. Yet do I fear thy nature.
> It is too full o' the milk of human kindness
> To catch the nearest way. Thou wouldst be great,
> Art not without ambition, but without
> The illness should attend it. What thou wouldst highly,
> That wouldst thou holily; wouldst not play false,
> And yet wouldst wrongly win. Thou'dst have, great Glamis,
> That which cries "Thus thou must do if thou have it;
> And that which rather thou dost fear to do
> Than wishest should be undone." Hie thee hither,
> That I may pour my spirits in thine ear
> And chastise with the valor of my tongue
> All that impedes thee from the golden round
> Which fate and metaphysical aid doth seem
> To have thee crowned withal.

We see that Lady Macbeth anticipates her husband's reluctance and recalcitrance. She fears his nature, which is too full of the milk of human kindness. There is a great deal about both his nature and her nature in the development of the play. She will call on the spirits of darkness to "unsex" her and to come to her woman's breasts and take her milk for gall. Milk is on the side of nature, or is nature, inasmuch as it is—for her—something that must be overcome. In perhaps the most astounding of her rejections of nature, she says

> I have given suck, and know
> How tender 'tis to love the babe that milks me:
> I would, while it was smiling in my face,
> Have plucked my nipple from his boneless gums
> And dashed the brains out, had I so sworn as you
> Have done to this.

There is, however, no evidence of such an oath by Macbeth, as she asserts him to have sworn. She repeatedly attributes to him a previous commitment to the murder, which he never made. One wonders why he does not correct her. The soliloquy above in which Macbeth debates the question of the murder in his own mind, coming firmly to a conclusion against it, would make no sense if he had taken such an oath. To whom or to what would he have sworn? A proper oath usually ends, whether explicitly or implicitly, "so help me God." But Macbeth could hardly call on God to help him commit murder. Macbeth later implies that he has *given* his soul to the "common enemy of man." Satan, he thought, would help him because Satan would by the murder gain possession of Macbeth's soul. But what kind of oath can Lady Macbeth have had in mind when she speaks of swearing as he has done? What could she desire that would justify her in her own mind in murdering the smiling infant at her breast? This question is all the more relevant when we bear in mind that Macbeth wished above all to found a dynasty, and Lady Macbeth would have been an indispensable means to this end. At the moment they have no living children. The thought of murdering the child she once had—which was, incidentally, male—as a means of gaining the crown, is intrinsically inconsistent with his ambition to found a dynasty.

THE MORAL UNIVERSE

Lady Macbeth says that Macbeth is not without ambition, but lacks the "illness should attend it." This is the only occurrence in Shakespeare of "illness" to mean "capacity for doing evil." That a capacity for evil is an evil capacity is not what Lady Macbeth intends to convey, but Shakespeare conveys it to us nonetheless. That ambition "should" be attended by release from moral restraint is a thesis much older than Machiavelli. It is explored in the greatest depth in both Plato's *Republic* and *Gorgias*, wherein Socrates maintains that the worst fate to befall a human being is not to become the victim of a tyrant—terrible as that may be—but to become a tyrant. The soul of the tyrant makes him the enemy of everyone, and the friend of none. Without friends, the life of the tyrant is barren of every good thing that might have tempted him to become a tyrant. But the actions that made him tyrant make it impossible for him safely to relinquish or abandon his tyranny. As Macbeth discovers, once he crosses the threshold of murder, he almost cannot help being driven to commit ever multiplying murders. Every step of his way, after the first murder, drives him further down that path. But he cannot turn back; he has lost the moral freedom which accompanied his first soliloquy, and he is in the grip of a remorseless and relentless necessity. His career of crime can end only in damnation both in this world and the next. The lesson of the play is the inexorable and inescapable vindictive power of the moral universe.

Callicles in the *Gorgias* presents the anti-Socratic thesis that underlies Lady Macbeth's commitment to tyranny and murder. This thesis looks upon morality not as natural but as against nature, as a conspiracy of the weak against the strong, a conspiracy to deprive the strong of the goods that naturally belong to them. This conspiracy begins in early life, when we are taught that sharing (i.e., justice) is good, and that seizing and possessing whatever is within our power to seize and possess is wrong. We are thus led to accept an illusory good, i.e., a reputation for justice, instead of demanding the natural good of dominance and possession. From this perspective, tyranny is the best regime according to nature. It is this understanding of natural right that informs Lady Macbeth's case for the murder. *Macbeth*, in which Macbeth's reasons for rejecting the murder are utterly and completely vindicated, and in which Lady Macbeth's reasons for contradicting them are utterly and completely defeated, is the very perfection of the Socratic case against the Calliclean.

Lady Macbeth says that what Macbeth "wouldst highly" he wouldst also "holily," implying that he renounces the tyrannical role praised by Callicles. She says that he would not play false, and yet would wrongly win. What does this mean? If someone will not play false, how can he wrongly win? The contradiction, as she sees it, is that he does not abandon the end, even as he recoils from the means. Her task, therefore, is to fire his passion for the end so as to overcome his repugnance for the means. She says that he fears to do what must be done, even though he would not wish it undone, if it were done. She will "chastise" with the "valor" of her tongue this weakness, this essential indecision, that impedes him from "the golden round." The idea of chastisement implies punishment for wrongdoing, and her "valor" a power for good. The moral order appears, in this speech, as an obstruction to Calliclean virtue.

ALL THAT MAY BECOME A MAN

The action of the tragedy originates from the struggle at the outset between Macbeth and Lady Macbeth. The murder takes place only because she is victorious in that struggle. Let us consider how she succeeds. He has concluded the soliloquy presented above. She enters, and he tells her

> We will proceed no further in this business.
> He hath honored me of late, and I have bought
> Golden opinions from all sorts of people,
> Which would be worn now in their newest gloss
> Not cast aside so soon.

She replies:

> Was the hope drunk
> Wherein you dressed yourself? Hath it slept since?
> And wakes it now to look so green and pale
> At what it did so freely? From this time
> Such I account thy love. Art thou afeard
> To be the same in thine own act and valor
> As thou art in desire? Wouldst thou have that
> Which thou esteems't the ornament of life,
> And live a coward in thine own esteem,
> Letting "I dare not" wait upon "I would,"
> Like the poor cat i' th' adage?

Lady Macbeth does not even answer Macbeth's expressed desire to live in the glow of the golden opinions that are deserved tributes for heroic services to king and country. Those opinions, for which Lady Macbeth has nothing but contempt, would have been sufficient for Macbeth to live a happy life. The time will come, after he has lost them forever, when he will realize how sweet they were, and how hollow by comparison is the "mouth-honor" extorted by the tyrant. For Lady Macbeth the just rewards of virtue do not count in comparison to the "ornament of life." Macbeth replies,

> Prithee peace.
> I dare do all that may become a man;
> Who dares do more is none.

Lady Macbeth:

> What beast was't then
> That made you break this enterprise to me?
> When you durst do it, then you were a man;
> And to be more than what you were, you would
> Be so much more the man.

Macbeth says that he dares do all that may become a man, and who dares do more is none. Clearly, they have different and opposing conceptions of what constitutes a man. It was manly of him, she says, to "break this enterprise to me," once again attributing to him an initiative that is really hers. Then, she says, he was a real man, and to go forward with what he had proposed would make him even more a man. To think otherwise is to think that it was not manly, but beastly, to have considered the murder. She invokes, and rejects, the traditional moral distinction between beast, man, and God, which we find in Aristotle's *Politics* as well as in Locke's *Second Treatise* and in the Declaration of Independence.

Macbeth asks, "If we should fail?" Her reply:

> We fail?
> But screw your courage to the sticking place
> And we'll not fail.

She then gives her plan to get the two chamberlains who guard the king drunk, and when

> . . . in swinish sleep
> Their drenched natures lie as in a death,
> What cannot you and I perform upon
> Th' unguarded Duncan? What not put upon
> His spongy officers, who shall bear the guilt
> Of our great quell?

Macbeth now forgets all his own reasoning, abandons all restraint and o'erleaps himself.

> Bring forth men-children only!
> For thy undaunted mettle should compose
> Nothing but males. Will it not be received
> When we have marked with blood those sleepy two
> Of his own chamber and used their very daggers,
> That they have done it?

There is irony in his call for males, when it is the "valor" of her female tongue that has "chastised" his male nature, a nature that she herself has pronounced too full of the milk of human kindness! It is notable that she refers to the murder of the king as a joint enterprise, "What cannot you and I perform," and "our great quell." Macbeth's "Bring forth men-children only" seems certainly misplaced, since the man child here could accomplish nothing by himself. We are, however, put in mind of his overwhelming desire to found a dynasty, something that neither he nor any man can do by himself. She has already made his fidelity to the plot to kill the king fidelity to herself: "From this time, such I account thy love . . . ." Later, when the evil consequences have begun to unfold, and he acts to shield her from what she herself has brought on, he calls her "dearest chuck." It is from within their conjugal relationship that the action of the tragedy emanates. It is his passion for his wife that overcomes the reason he otherwise so amply displays. Rejecting the murder would have alienated her; going forward with the murder meant confirming their partnership. Their bond of matrimony would prove the most powerful of the human attachments in the drama.

What are the merits of her arguments against the possibility of failure? These arguments prove in the end to be those very "bloody instructions" which Macbeth had predicted would turn back upon themselves. Her plan is to get the chamberlains who guard the king drunk, so that they cannot protect him. Their drunkenness will then be alleged as an explanation of the murder. How could anyone believe that they could commit murder when in sleep so "swinish" that their "drenched natures" would lie "as in a death"?

She concludes,

> Who dares receive it other,
> As we shall make our griefs and clamor roar
> Upon his death?

In the event, they fool no one. Macbeth, sensing this, returns to the scene of the crime and murders both the grooms. The killings of these poor innocents is decisive in turning opinion against him. Lady Macbeth did not, however, expect that their "griefs and clamor" would really succeed. She expected rather that no one would "dare" to openly express disbelief. Lady Macbeth tacitly assumes that when the reins of power are in their hands they can either kill or silence those who would question them. It never occurs to her that the value of the "ornament of life" depends upon how it is gained. To be a king, as distinct from a tyrant, the obedience of the subject must in some sense be voluntary, and not rest upon fear alone.

TOMORROW, AND TOMORROW, AND TOMORROW

We have sketched the causes that propelled the tragedy. At the beginning, Macbeth's strength, such as it is, lies in the clarity with which he views the moral order and understands his place within it. But his will is not equal to his reason, and her will, aided and abetted by her conjugal power, sweeps away the reason that is in him. The consequence of her victory and of the murder that follows is a transformation in the characters of both of them. As the drama proceeds, he loses the doubt and hesitation he possessed before, and becomes ever more resolute in acting out the multiplying demands of tyranny. Yet even as he loses all restraint, and all conscience, he is punished by his awareness of the goodness of the life he has forsworn. The crown is not, as Lady Macbeth had supposed, an avenue to felicity but to damnation, in this world no less than in the next. There is in the possession of the "golden round" no such consummation as Lady Macbeth assumed there would be when she urged the murder on her reluctant husband. Even as he hardens to the life of crime, she disintegrates. The change from "infirm of purpose, give me the daggers" in Act 2, to "Out damned spot! Out, I say!" in Act 5, represents, to the best of my knowledge, an unrivalled portrayal of a soul in torment. She had called on the powers of darkness to "unsex her," and had denied nature in its purest form, in envisioning herself as murdering the child at her breast. She had seen the image of her father in the murdered king. We see nature reclaiming its own in the suffering she is compelled to undergo. Her fate contrasts with that of her husband, who goes down fighting, still the warrior.

In the end, his passion for her and for the crown are doomed together. Her death is his ultimate defeat, since it was his partnership with her that was the ultimate cause of his rejecting his own better judgment, and risking everything rather than be rejected by her.

> *Seyton*: The Queen, my lord, is dead.
>
> *Macbeth*: She should have died hereafter,
> There would have been a time for such a word.
> Tomorrow, and tomorrow, and tomorrow
> Creeps in this petty pace from day to day,
> To the last syllable of recorded time,
> And all our yesterdays have lighted fools
> The way to dusty death. Out, out, brief candle!

Life's but a walking shadow, a poor player
That struts and frets his hour upon the stage
And then is heard no more. It is a tale
Told by an idiot, full of sound and fury,
Signifying nothing.

It is paradoxical that this, perhaps the most memorable—and beautiful—passage in the entire drama, is a celebration of despair, of the meaninglessness of life. It is a testament to everything that Macbeth has lost, everything associated with his partnership with Lady Macbeth. Yet at the same time the magic of Shakespeare's celebration is itself a triumph over the very despair it celebrates. It is, in a sense, a vindication of Macbeth himself, a reaffirmation of the greatness of his character before the fall. His fidelity to his wife, although the cause of his fall, nonetheless reminds us of his virtue. There is a non-tyrannical element in his tyranny.

We are reminded, incidentally, that Macbeth's final soliloquy resonates with the many passages in Shakespeare depreciating, and even ridiculing, the acting profession, which was also Shakespeare's. We are also reminded that the actor is the creature of the playwright. Shakespeare was both creator and creature. The images in the souls of the audience are thrice removed from reality. Shakespeare's theater and Plato's cave are closely related. The thesis of *Macbeth* is also the Socratic thesis, set forth especially in the *Republic* and the *Gorgias,* that the worst fate that can befall a human soul, far worse than becoming the victim of a tyrant, is to become a tyrant.

Our analysis has come full circle. Macbeth, like Meursault, ends with "nothing." In the case of the latter, his discovery of the nothingness of the universe and of the idiocy of morality are one and the same. Meursault's discovery is his triumph. Death has no terror for someone for whom life has no meaning, who is not attached to anything in life. The murder—or homicide—he had committed proves in the end to be the fortunate means of the only salvation possible in a dead universe. Macbeth's nothing, by way of contrast, represents the emptying of meaning from a life and world that had been filled to the uttermost with purpose and passion. Lady Macbeth had been the force driving her husband's ambition. It was she who turned his decision not to commit the murder into a decision to commit it. It was she who by the valor of her tongue chastised him into reversing himself. She did so, in part, by declaring that she would take his decision as a measure of his love. The entire tragedy is an emanation of the dynamics of their conjugal relationship. There is no greater irony than that Macbeth has to commit the murder to prove his fidelity. Yet to play her role as murderess, she calls on the spirits of darkness to "unsex" her. She calls upon the spirits, that is to say, to detach her from the nature from which she derives her conjugal power over her husband. In the end, it is that nature which revenges itself upon her, and condemns her to eternal damnation.

The message—I am tempted to call it the moral—of Macbeth, is the inexorability of the moral order. Macbeth's soliloquy in Act 1 tells us with perfect clarity why the murder must fail. The action that follows bears out the truth of that soliloquy. Not only does the plot fail, but neither Macbeth nor Lady Macbeth is allowed one moment of enjoyment of the fruit of their crime. Their punishment begins almost immediately with the murder. The crime is therefore in every sense self-defeating. The moral order, accordingly, is more powerful than the evil spirits that Lady Macbeth called upon. The moral order, according to *The Stranger* or *Crime and Punishment*, lacks any such power. Both of these works record the declining power of morality in Western civilization, and in this sense they record the decline of the West. Yet Abraham Lincoln's Second Inaugural Address reaffirms the same power of morality as *Macbeth*. Perhaps that is why Lincoln said that "nothing equals *Macbeth*."

Index

List of Contributors

Gerard Alexander is an associate professor of political science at the University of Virginia and a visiting scholar at the American Enterprise Institute.

Hadley Arkes is the Edward Ney Professor of Jurisprudence and American Institutions at Amherst College and the director of the Claremont Institute's Center for Natural Law Jurisprudence.

Larry P. Arnn is the president of Hillsdale College, a former president of the Claremont Institute, and the vice chairman of the Board of Directors of the Claremont Institute.

Lance Banning (1942–2006) was a professor of history at the University of Kentucky.

James G. Basker is the Richard Gilder Professor of Literary History at Barnard College, Columbia University, and president of the Gilder Lehrman Institute of American History.

Martha Bayles, who teaches humanities in the Arts & Sciences Honors Program at Boston College, is the columnist on television and film for the *Claremont Review of Books*.

Mark Blitz is the Fletcher Jones Professor of Political Philosophy and director of the Salvatori Center for the Study of Individual Freedom in the Modern World at Claremont McKenna College.

William F. Buckley, Jr. (1925–2008) was the founder of *National Review*, host of *Firing Line*, and a nationally syndicated columnist.

Andrew E. Busch is the Crown Professor of Government and George R. Roberts Fellow at Claremont McKenna College.

Paul A. Cantor is the Clifton Waller Barrett Professor of English at the University of Virginia.

James W. Ceaser is the Harry F. Byrd Professor of Politics at the University of Virginia and director of the Program for Constitutionalism and Democracy.

Angelo M. Codevilla is a professor emeritus of international relations at Boston University.

John Derbyshire is a writer living in New York.

Ross Douthat is an op-ed columnist for the *New York Times.*

Robert Eden is a professor of political science at Hillsdale College.

Joseph Epstein is an essayist, short story-writer, and contributing editor for the *Weekly Standard.*

Charles H. Fairbanks, Jr., a senior fellow at the Hudson Institute, is a former deputy assistant secretary of state and director of the Central Asia-Caucasus Institute at Johns Hopkins University.

Christopher Flannery is a senior editor of the *Claremont Review of Books*, senior fellow of the Claremont Institute, and professor of political science at Azusa Pacific University.

Allen C. Guelzo is the Henry R. Luce Professor of the Civil War Era at Gettysburg College.

Victor Davis Hanson is the Martin and Illie Anderson Senior Fellow in Residence in Classics and Military History at the Hoover Institution, a professor emeritus of classics at California State University, Fresno, and a nationally syndicated columnist.

Steven F. Hayward is the F.K. Weyerhaeuser Fellow at the American Enterprise Institute and a senior fellow at the Pacific Research Institute.

Mark Helprin, whose novels include *Winter's Tale*, *A Soldier of the Great War*, and *Freddy and Fredericka*, is a senior fellow of the Claremont Institute, and writes the regular "Parthian Shot" column for the *Claremont Review of Books.*

Christopher Hitchens (1949–2011) was a contributing editor and columnist for *Vanity Fair*, and a media fellow at the Hoover Institution.

Harry V. Jaffa is a distinguished fellow of the Claremont Institute, and a professor emeritus of government at Claremont McKenna College and Claremont Graduate University.

Douglas A. Jeffrey is vice president for external affairs at Hillsdale College.

Charles R. Kesler is the editor of the *Claremont Review of Books*, a senior fellow of the Claremont Institute, and the Dengler-Dykema Distinguished Professor of Government at Claremont McKenna College.

Stephen F. Knott is an assistant professor and research fellow at the Miller Center of Public Affairs at the University of Virginia.

Stanley Kurtz is a senior fellow at the Ethics and Public Policy Center.

Harvey C. Mansfield is the William R. Kenan Jr. Professor of Government at Harvard University and the Carol G. Simon Senior Fellow at the Hoover Institution.

Wilfred M. McClay is a professor of history and the SunTrust Bank Chair of Excellence in Humanities at the University of Tennessee at Chattanooga.

Sidney M. Milkis is White Burkett Miller Professor of Politics and assistant director of academic programs at the Miller Center of Public Affairs at the University of Virginia.

Cheryl Miller is a writer living in Washington, D.C., and manages the American Enterprise Institute's Program on American Citizenship.

Terrence O. Moore is a professor of history at Hillsdale College, and the former principal of Ridgeview Classical Schools in Fort Collins, Colorado.

Mackubin Thomas Owens, a senior fellow at the Program on National Security of the Foreign Policy Research Institute and the editor of *Orbis*, is the associate dean of academics for electives and directed research and professor of strategy and force planning at the U.S. Naval War College.

Jaroslav Pelikan (1923–2006) was the Sterling Professor Emeritus of History at Yale University.

Ronald J. Pestritto holds the Charles and Lucia Shipley Chair in the American Constitution at Hillsdale College and is a senior fellow of the college's Allan P. Kirby, Jr., Center for Constitutional Studies and Citizenship.

Jeremy Rabkin is a professor at the George Mason University School of Law.

William A. Rusher (1923–2011) was a distinguished fellow of the Claremont Institute, and the publisher of *National Review* from 1957 to 1988.

Diana Schaub is a professor of political science at Loyola University Maryland and a member of the Hoover Institution's Jill and Boyd Smith Task Force on the Virtues of a Free Society.

Peter W. Schramm, a senior fellow and former president of the Claremont Institute, is the executive director of the John M. Ashbrook Center for Public Affairs and a professor of political science at Ashland University.

Thomas B. Silver (1947–2001) was a founder and president of the Claremont Institute.

Joseph Tartakovsky is a contributing editor of the *Claremont Review of Books* and a fellow of the Claremont Institute.

Michael M. Uhlmann teaches politics and law at Claremont Graduate University.

Algis Valiunas is a fellow at the Ethics and Public Policy Center and a contributing editor to the *New Atlantis*.

Richard Vedder is an adjunct scholar at the American Enterprise Institute and distinguished professor of economics at Ohio University.

William Voegeli is a senior editor of the *Claremont Review of Books* and a visiting scholar at Claremont McKenna College's Henry Salvatori Center for the Study of Individual Freedom in the Modern World.

Thomas G. West is a professor of politics at Hillsdale College.

James Q. Wilson is a professor in the School of Public Policy at Pepperdine University.

John Zvesper is a fellow of the Claremont Institute.

List of Books Reviewed and Discussed *

"The Home Front," by Christopher Flannery (Fall 2002)

Perpetual War for Perpetual Peace: How We Got to Be So Hated, by Gore Vidal. Nation Books, 2002

What's So Great About America, by Dinesh D'Souza. Regnery Publishing, 2002

Where We Stand: 30 Reasons for Loving Our Country, by Roger Rosenblatt. Houghton Mifflin, 2002

Why We Fight: Moral Clarity and the War on Terrorism, by William J. Bennett. Doubleday, 2002

"How the Confederates Won," by Mackubin Thomas Owens (Winter 2002/2003)

Race and Reunion: The Civil War in American Memory, by David W. Blight. The Belknap Press, 2001

"Tailgunner Ann," by William F. Buckley, Jr. (Winter 2003/2004)

Treason: Liberal Treachery from the Cold War to the War on Terrorism, by Ann Coulter. Crown Forum, 2003

"The Myth of the Racist Republicans," by Gerard Alexander (Spring 2004)

The Emerging Republican Majority, by Kevin Phillips. Arlington House, 1969

From George Wallace to Newt Gingrich: Race in the Conservative Counterrevolution, 1963-1994, by Dan T. Carter. Louisiana State University Press, 1996

The Southern Strategy Revisited: Republican Top-Down Advancement in the South, by Joseph A. Aistrup. The University Press of Kentucky, 1996

The Rise of Southern Republicans, by Earl Black and Merle Black. The Belknap Press, 2002

---

*Listed by *CRB* issue in which the article first appeared.

A Stone of Hope: Prophetic Religion and the Death of Jim Crow, by David L. Chappell. The University of North Carolina Press, 2004

"A Dance to the (Disco) Music of Time," by John Derbyshire (Spring 2004)

Homosexuality and Civilization, by Louis Crompton. The Belknap Press, 2003

"Moral Monster," by John Zvesper (Summer 2004)

Napoleon: A Political Life, by Steven Englund. Scribner, 2003

"FDR as Statesman," by Robert Eden (Fall 2004)

Franklin Delano Roosevelt: Champion of Freedom, by Conrad Black. PublicAffairs, 2003

"The Man Who Made Modern America," by Stephen F. Knott (Fall 2004)

Alexander Hamilton, by Ron Chernow. The Penguin Press, 2004

"Three-Fifths Historian," by Lance Banning (Fall 2004)

"Negro President": Jefferson and the Slave Power, by Garry Wills. Houghton Mifflin, 2003

"The Three Rings," by Jaroslav Pelikan (Fall 2004)

The Monotheists: Jews, Christians, and Muslims in Conflict and Competition, by F.E. Peters. Princeton University Press, 2 vols., 2003

"Tyranny and Utopia," by Charles H. Fairbanks, Jr. (Spring 2005)

Stalin: The Court of the Red Tsar, by Simon Sebag Montefiore. Alfred A. Knopf, 2004

"The Right Stuff," by Michael M. Uhlmann (Summer 2005)

The Unmaking of a Mayor, by William F. Buckley, Jr. Viking Press, 1966

Nearer, My God: An Autobiography of Faith, by William F. Buckley, Jr. Doubleday, 1997

The Redhunter: A Novel Based on the Life of Senator Joe McCarthy, by William F. Buckley, Jr. Little, Brown, and Company, 1999

Let Us Talk of Many Things: The Collected Speeches, by William F. Buckley, Jr. Prima, 2000

William F. Buckley, Jr.: A Bibliography, edited by William F. Meehan, III. ISI Books, 2002

The Fall of the Berlin Wall, by William F. Buckley, Jr. John Wiley & Sons, 2004

Miles Gone By: A Literary Autobiography, by William F. Buckley, Jr. Regnery Publishing, 2004

Last Call for Blackford Oakes, by William F. Buckley, Jr. Harcourt, 2005

"The Long Detour," by William A. Rusher (Summer 2005)

Richard Nixon and the Quest for a New Majority, by Robert Mason. The University of North Carolina Press, 2003

"The Crisis of American National Identity," by Charles R. Kesler (Fall 2005)

American Politics: The Promise of Disharmony, by Samuel P. Huntington. The Belknap Press, 1981

Who Are We?: The Challenges to America's National Identity, by Samuel P. Huntington. Simon & Schuster, 2005

"Involuntary Associations," by Mark Blitz (Fall 2005)

Politics and Passion: Toward a More Egalitarian Liberalism, by Michael Walzer. Yale University Press, 2005

"The Conservative Cocoon," by Ross Douthat (Winter 2005/2006)

South Park Conservatives: The Revolt Against Liberal Media Bias, by Brian C. Anderson. Regnery Publishing, 2005

"Man of Letters," by James G. Basker (Summer 2006)

Defining the World: The Extraordinary Story of Dr Johnson's Dictionary, by Henry Hitchings. Farrar, Straus & Giroux, 2005

"Theater of War," by Christopher Hitchens (Winter 2006/2007)

The Greatest Story Ever Sold: The Decline and Fall of Truth from 9/11 to Katrina, by Frank Rich. The Penguin Press, 2006

"Larry McMurtry and the American West," by Douglas A. Jeffrey (Spring 2007)

Horseman, Pass By, by Larry McMurtry. Texas A&M University Press, 1961

In a Narrow Grave: Essays on Texas, by Larry McMurtry. Encino Press, 1968

Lonesome Dove, by Larry McMurtry. Simon & Schuster, 1985

Crazy Horse, by Larry McMurtry. Viking Press, 1999

Walter Benjamin at the Dairy Queen: Reflections at Sixty and Beyond, by Larry Murtry. Simon & Schuster, 1999

Roads: Driving America's Great Highways, by Larry McMurtry. Simon & Schuster, 2000

Winning the Wild West: The Epic Saga of the American Frontier, 1800-1899, by Page Stegner. Free Press, 2002

The Colonel and Little Missie: Buffalo Bill, Annie Oakley and the Beginnings of Superstardom in America, by Larry McMurtry. Simon & Schuster, 2005

Oh What a Slaughter: Massacres in the American West, 1846-1890, by Larry McMurtry. Simon & Schuster, 2005

Telegraph Days, by Larry McMurtry. Simon & Schuster, 2006

"A Left-Handed Salute," by Wilfred M. McClay (Summer 2007)

> *The Intellectuals and the Flag,* by Todd Gitlin. Columbia University Press, 2005

"The Greatness and Decline of American Oratory," by Diana Schaub (Summer 2007)

> *American Speeches,* edited by Ted Widmer. The Library of America, 2 vols., 2006

"Building Democracy," by Hadley Arkes (Summer 2007)

> *Architecture of Democracy: American Architecture and the Legacy of the Revolution,* by Allan Greenberg. Rizzoli, 2006

"Pith and Pen," by Joseph Tartakovsky (Summer 2007)

> *The New Oxford Book of Literary Anecdotes,* edited by John Gross. Oxford University Press, 2006

"The Genius of Old New York," by Cheryl Miller (Fall 2007)

> *Edith Wharton,* by Hermione Lee. Alfred A. Knopf, 2007

"Aryan Sister," by Algis Valiunas (Fall 2007)

> *Leni Riefenstahl: A Life,* by Jürgen Trimborn, translated by Edna McCown. Faber & Faber, 2007

> *Leni: The Life and Work of Leni Riefenstahl,* by Steven Bach. Alfred A. Knopf, 2007

"Tribes of Terror," by Stanley Kurtz (Winter 2007/08)

> *Islam Under Siege: Living Dangerously in a Post-Honor World,* by Akbar S. Ahmed. Blackwell Publishers, 2003

> *Resistance and Control in Pakistan: Revised Edition,* by Akbar S. Ahmed. Routledge, 2004

> *Journey into Islam: The Crisis of Globalization,* by Akbar S. Ahmed. Brookings Institution Press, 2007

"A Nicer Form of Tyranny," by Ronald J. Pestritto (Spring 2008)

> *Liberal Fascism: The Secret History of the American Left, From Mussolini to the Politics of Meaning,* by Jonah Goldberg. Doubleday, 2008

"Thoughts and Adventures," by Larry P. Arnn (Spring 2008)

> *Winston S. Churchill, Volume 1: Youth, 1874-1900,* by Randolph S. Churchill. Hillsdale College Press, 608 pages, 2006

> *The Churchill Documents, Volume 1: Youth, 1874-1896,* edited by Randolph S. Churchill. Hillsdale College Press, 2006

> *The Churchill Documents, Volume 2: Young Soldier, 1896-1901,* edited by Randolph S. Churchill. Hillsdale College Press, 2006

> *Winston S. Churchill, Volume 2: Young Statesman, 1901-1914,* by Randolph S. Churchill. Hillsdale College Press, 2007

The Churchill Documents, Volume 3: Early Years in Politics, 1901-1907, edited by Randolph S. Churchill. Hillsdale College Press, 2007

The Churchill Documents, Volume 4: Minister of the Crown, 1907-1911, edited by Randolph S. Churchill. Hillsdale College Press, 695 pages, 2007

The Churchill Documents, Volume 5: At the Admiralty, 1911-1914, edited by Randolph S. Churchill. Hillsdale College Press, 2007

"Is There Intelligent Life on Television?" by Paul A. Cantor (Fall 2008)

Textual Poachers: Television Fans and Participatory Culture, by Henry Jenkins. Routledge, 1992

Consuming Pleasures: Active Audiences and Serial Fictions from Dickens to Soap Opera, by Jennifer Hayward. The University Press of Kentucky, 1997

The Showrunners: A Season Inside the Billion-Dollar, Death-Defying, Madcap World of Television's Real Stars, by David Wild. HarperCollins, 1999

The Culture Industry: Selected Essays on Mass Culture, by Theodor Adorno, edited by J.M. Bernstein. Routledge, 2001

The Simpsons and Philosophy: The D'oh! of Homer, edited by William Irwin, Mark T. Conrad, and Aeon J. Skoble. Open Court, 2001

Dialectic of Enlightenment, by Max Horkheimer and Theodor Adorno, translated by Edmund Jephcott. Stanford University Press, 2002

Created By: Inside the Minds of TV's Top Show Creators, by Steven Priggé. Silman-James Press, 2005

Fans, Bloggers, and Gamers: Exploring Participatory Culture, by Henry Jenkins. New York University Press, 2006

"All the Leaves Are Brown," by Steven F. Hayward (Winter 2008/09)

The Green State: Rethinking Democracy and Sovereignty, by Robyn Eckersley. MIT Press, 2004

Break Through: From the Death of Environmentalism to the Politics of Possibility, by Michael Shellenberger and Ted Nordhaus. Houghton Mifflin, 2007

The Climate Change Challenge and the Failure of Democracy, by David Sherman and Joseph Wayne Smith. Praeger Publishers, 2007

Useless Arithmetic: Why Environmental Scientists Can't Predict the Future, by Orrin H. Pilkey and Linda Pilkey-Jarvis. Columbia University Press, 2007

Where We Stand: A Surprising Look at the Real State of Our Planet, by Seymour Garte. AMACOM, 2007

The World Without Us, by Alan Weisman. Thomas Dunne Books, 2007

American Earth: Environmental Writing Since Thoreau, edited by Bill McKibben, foreword by Al Gore. The Library of America, 2008

Fatal Misconception: The Struggle to Control World Population, by Matthew Connelly. The Belknap Press, 2008

How We Can Save the Planet: Preventing Global Climate Catastrophe, by Mayer Hillman with Tina Fawcett and Sudhir Chella Rajan. St. Martin's Press, 2008

"The Education Mill," by Richard Vedder (Spring 2009)

The Race between Education and Technology, by Claudia Goldin and Lawrence F. Katz. The Belknap Press, 2008

"Against the Virtual Life," by Joseph Epstein (Summer 2009)

Digital Barbarism: A Writer's Manifesto, by Mark Helprin. Harper, 2009

"The Bicentennial Lincolns," by Allen C. Guelzo (Winter 2009/2010)

The Inner World of Abraham Lincoln, by Michael Burlingame. University of Illinois Press, 1994

Lincoln in American Memory, by Merrill D. Peterson. Oxford University Press, 1994

Herndon's Informants: Letters, Interviews, and Statements about Abraham Lincoln, edited by Douglas L. Wilson and Rodney O. Davis, with the assistance of Terry Wilson. University of Illinois Press, 1997

Abraham Lincoln and the Forge of National Memory, by Barry Schwartz. The University of Chicago Press, 2000

Lincoln's Greatest Speech: The Second Inaugural, by Ronald C. White, Jr. Simon & Schuster, 2002

Lincoln at Cooper Union: The Speech That Made Abraham Lincoln President, by Harold Holzer. Simon & Schuster, 2004

The Eloquent President: A Portrait of Lincoln Through His Words, by Ronald C. White, Jr. Random House, 2005

House of Abraham: Lincoln and the Todds, A Family Divided by War, by Stephen Berry. Houghton Mifflin Harcourt, 2007

The Madness of Mary Lincoln, by Jason Emerson. Southern Illinois University Press, 2007

Abraham Lincoln, by George S. McGovern. Times Books, 2008

Abraham Lincoln: A Life, by Michael Burlingame. The Johns Hopkins University Press, 2 vols., 2008

Big Enough to Be Inconsistent: Abraham Lincoln Confronts Slavery and Race, by George M. Fredrickson. Harvard University Press, 2008

The Last Lincolns: The Rise & Fall of a Great American Family, by Charles Lachman. Union Square Press, 2008

Lincoln and the Decision for War: The Northern Response to Secession, by Russell McClintock. The University of North Carolina Press, 2008

The Lincoln Anthology: Great Writers on His Life and Legacy from 1860 to Now, edited by Harold Holzer. The Library of America, 2008

Lincoln President-Elect: Abraham Lincoln and the Great Secession Winter 1860-1861, by Harold Holzer. Simon & Schuster, 2008

The Lincolns: Portrait of a Marriage, by Daniel Mark Epstein. Ballantine Books, 2008

Looking for Lincoln: The Making of an American Icon, by Philip B. Kunhardt, III, Peter W. Kunhardt and Peter W. Kunhardt, Jr. Alfred A. Knopf, 2008

Our Lincoln: New Perspectives on Lincoln and His World, by Eric Foner. W.W. Norton & Company, 2008

Tried by War: Abraham Lincoln as Commander in Chief, by James M. McPherson. The Penguin Press, 2008

A. Lincoln: A Biography, by Ronald C. White, Jr. Random House, 816 pages, 2009

Abraham Lincoln, by James M. McPherson. Oxford University Press, 2009

Abraham Lincoln in the Post-Heroic Era: History and Memory in Late Twentieth-Century America, by Barry Schwartz. The University of Chicago Press, 2009

Mrs. Lincoln: A Life, by Catherine Clinton. Harper, 2009

"Free to Use," by James Q. Wilson (Winter 2009/2010)

Addiction: A Disorder of Choice, by Gene M. Heyman. Harvard University Press, 2009

"Flights of Fancy," Steven F. Hayward (Summer 2010)

The Icarus Syndrome: A History of American Hubris, by Peter Beinart. Harper, 2010